Unifying Systems

Aarne Mämmelä

Unifying Systems

Information, Feedback, and Self-Organization

Springer

Aarne Mämmelä
VTT Technical Research Centre of Finland,
Ltd.
Oulu, Finland

University of Oulu
Oulu, Finland

ISBN 978-3-031-85014-1 ISBN 978-3-031-85012-7 (eBook)
https://doi.org/10.1007/978-3-031-85012-7

This Springer imprint is published by the registered company Springer Nature Switzerland AG
The registered company address is: Gewerbestrasse 11, 6330 Cham, Switzerland

To my wonderful family and friends

Foreword

I have had the pleasure of corresponding with Aarne Mämmelä for many years. Over that time I have learned a great deal from him about systems thinking and have drawn on his ideas at some length in textbooks I have published in both future studies and interdisciplinary studies. I am thus very pleased to see that he is publishing a book in the field. I know that he has been thinking about, researching, and teaching systems analysis for many years while he has worked as a researcher at the University of Oulu and as a research professor at the VTT Technical Research Centre of Finland.

As a scholar of the theory and practice of interdisciplinarity, I am particularly impressed by the breadth of his knowledge. Systems thinking has been applied in dozens of fields. Mämmelä should be applauded first of all for drawing on all of these diverse literatures—the book has over a thousand references—and then secondly for expertly detailing the similarities and differences in how systems thinking has been applied in different fields. Readers who may have already employed systems thinking can thus gain a valuable appreciation of how their particular flavor of systems thinking fits within the broader whole.

For scholars or students that are new to systems thinking, Mämmelä provides an introduction that is detailed yet accessible. Mämmelä is one of those rare individuals who is simultaneously capable of applying in his research mathematically complex approaches to systems thinking and yet in his writing and teaching to explain the basics of systems thinking clearly. This combination requires a very deep understanding of the field.

I wholeheartedly concur with Mämmelä that the scholarly enterprise needs to devote far more attention to systems analysis. Specialized researchers within disciplines do invaluable work in enhancing our understandings of particular phenomena and processes. Yet we collectively devote far too little attention to trying to tie these isolated bits of analysis into a wider understanding of how the world works.

I am also a big believer in diagrams and maps. Mämmelä has put a lot of effort into illustrating his ideas visually. Many of his ideas are best communicated by a simple diagram.

Mämmelä also provides numerous examples of how various elements of systems thinking have been important historically. Mendeleyev's development of the periodic table of the elements was an example of a certain type of systems thinking. Helen Keller was only able to learn how to communicate due to the application of systems thinking. These examples are each interesting in their own right but serve to illustrate important ideas that Mämmelä is seeking to communicate.

The book also provides much useful advice on how to perform research. Mämmelä is able to draw here not only on his own research experience but his teaching in the area and his supervision of Ph.D. students.

In sum, this book addresses a hugely important topic. It is written by someone who has been reading across diverse relevant literatures for many years, and applying systems thinking carefully in his own research. It is full of useful examples and visual aids. It is simultaneously an impressive feat of scholarship and a good read.

Rick Szostak
University of Alberta
Edmonton, Canada

Preface

We must measure our success by the good we have brought to our society, not by the good our society has given us.

Interdisciplinary systems thinking means seeing our environment as a composite of interrelated systems. We purposely cross the borders of disciplines to make a researcher's work more creative and effective ("to do right things"), whereas conventional and still valuable disciplinary work is efficient ("to do the things right").

There are three undeniable reasons to apply systems thinking in addition to the conventional disciplinary analytical thinking: (1) the final goal of science is a unified understanding of the world needing interdisciplinarity, (2) complex problems cannot be solved using the knowledge in one discipline only, and (3) we can use system theories and generic system models called system archetypes for solving the problems. There are only a limited number of them. The greatest problem of our time is sustainable development. Because of the practical and concrete aims, engineering sciences can significantly contribute to systems thinking.

Systems are everywhere, not only in our homes, such as our cooling and heating systems, computers, cars, and other machines, but also in our whole sociotechnical system. They are based on simple principles that this book describes. Some principles using in the natural ecosystem are unknown to us showing finiteness of our knowledge. My book is about *systems thinking*, which is more concrete than the philosophy of science but more abstract than systems engineering. Systems thinking supports *systems architecting*, which according to Eberhardt Rechtin is the art and science building complex systems between a client and engineering. Architecting aims for client satisfaction in ill-structured problems often using heuristics, whereas engineering aims at technical optimization using definite requirements. In systems thinking, a goal is to improve researcher's *general knowledge*[1] by ignoring the arbitrary boundaries between scientific disciplines that are functional for learning but do not directly help us reach sustainable development. We can see a conceptual hierarchy of systems engineering, systems architecting, systems thinking, and philosophy of science, from concrete to abstract.

[1] *Bildung* in German.

Systems thinking is a complement rather than a replacement of conventional *analytical thinking* that starts from an idea and research problem. The discovery phase proceeds from simple to complex towards the formation of theories and concepts that are finally verified and validated in the real world. I use the most critical results from formal, natural, and social sciences and humanities, including history and philosophy. In complex hierarchical systems, there is a phenomenon called *emergence*, which means that some behavior at higher hierarchy levels is not predictable from those at lower levels. An obvious example is life for which no good theories exist. Our world is often seen as *linear*, which means it follows the superposition theorem and is thus *homogeneous* and *additive*, but this is only an approximation. For example, systems cannot handle high signal amplitudes linearly, i.e., the systems are limited in amplitude and there is some kind of saturation. Emergence is assumed to be a result of nonlinearity and feedback. Emergent phenomena are mathematically *intractable*, by definition. If emergence did not exist, we could combine all the disciplines into a single science, and no systems thinking would be needed. It is possible to understand the systems view by first understanding the analytical view. Paradoxically, in the literature, we divide *systems thinking* into several subdisciplines that often do not know about each other.

A simple common thread in the book explains the title *Unifying Systems: Information, Feedback, and Self-Organization.* Our society consists of humans. In social sciences, they are called actors; in artificial intelligence, they are called human agents that are assumed to be intelligent and rational. If there are many agents, we have a multiagent system or, equivalently, a complex adaptive system, i.e., an abstraction of society. We exchange information to make self-organization possible in a model with interacting agents. Each agent is a feedback loop consisting of sensing, deciding, and acting operations. We make decisions based on our senses and act accordingly. The agents may have conflicting goals and can collaborate or compete, and we punish them if they do not follow the agreements, such as laws and often unwritten ethical rules that are more generally called *constraints*, limiting our freedom. The agents may form hierarchies to rationalize collaboration and use competition towards common goals for building our society. There are game theories that describe at least approximately how the society works. The theories are often evolutionary since the agents may learn from their environment, and our fellow agents also learn. This model is simple but versatile and unifies systems thinking leading to dynamic instead of static system models. My book follows the cybernetics thread whose spin-offs are artificial intelligence, system dynamics, and complexity theory, which are all based on the information, feedback, and self-organization concepts although the cybernetic roots have, for some reason, often been ignored.

Criticism on systems thinking The debate between analytical and systems thinking is a rather recent study in the philosophy of science and engineering. Analytical thinking started about 400 years ago when Galileo made his first experiments and later published the first modern scientific textbook in 1638. Systems thinking has existed for 75 years since about 1950 when Ludwig von Bertalanffy published his first papers in English. Many researchers think that nobody should write books with such a broad scope, or many authors should write them as monographs in edited books. However, according to Bertrand Russell, it is good to synthesize the whole in one person's mind to generate some coherence. After that, some other authors can improve the synthesis.

There are many doubtful claims regarding systems thinking. I briefly summarize those claims and my responses to the criticism:

- **This book is not valuable since it describes my area only cursorily.** The book's value is not in the detailed theories but in the similarities and connections between the different theories. It is difficult to see the book's value if we only focus on our area. We then look at the world from a narrow perspective without seeing the whole, which is, in fact, a network of theories rather than a set of isolated theories. This encourages cooperation necessary to solve complex problems.
- **We need more focus to get results.** Systems thinkers are generalists. *Generalists* and *specialists* can help each other; the approaches are complementary. Based on their knowledge of history, systems thinkers can offer visions and define relevant open problems that the specialists can solve together if they can communicate. With the help of generalists, the specialists can select problems in their focus area that are significant also in a broader context. A result from generalists is a unifying, valuable worldview that specialists can use in their work. Not all people can be generalists, but we need some generalists. Specialists have been behind the success of our culture since the 1600s, but generalists have also produced some of the most important results in the history of science. We need more than specialization to avoid disconnected, sometimes contradictory, or even dangerous actions.
- **I am interested only in the newest knowledge since it has accumulated all our knowledge.** Knowing history is necessary to understand the state of the art and provide visions for the future. There is a danger that we use ideas that researchers have thoroughly studied many times before. Some old ideas become helpful when the time is right, for example, when the technology has a certain maturity level. There are Sleeping Beauties, whose value is realized only after several decades. Ludwig Von Bertalanffy noticed that disciplines are converging to similar solutions without knowing about each other. Several ideas have been invented many times over a long period. Repeating everything would be inefficient and a waste of time. Literature is growing exponentially; thus, good books and review papers covering history are valuable for discovering history.
- **Systems thinking does not help solve any real problem.** We often solve new problems by using analogies from already solved problems. Systems thinking is a systematic approach to finding those analogies. The goal is to find generic system structures called system archetypes that have survived the test of time and are helpful in many places. We can solve the most significant problems of our time only using interdisciplinary systems thinking. Independent disciplines can only offer separate and often incompatible solutions. People often think that systems thinking implies centralized decisions and bureaucracy. In fact, systems thinking encourages us to use distributed decisions as a form of wisdom of the crowds because of each individual's bounded rationality. Only enlightened

people can produce wise, distributed decisions. Creativity is among people, not in administration.

- **Systems thinkers use jargon that I need help understanding.** Russell L. Ackoff has noticed that some systems thinkers have developed complicated technical terminology called jargon that they use with their colleagues and do not discuss with potential users of systems thinking. We need a common vocabulary that we can use in our everyday lives. Our goal is to find applicable general terms already available in some disciplines. We want to remove the excuses for rejecting systems thinking by showing its usefulness and doing it with easily understandable terms.

Materials and energy have been our basic resources for centuries. *Information* is the third basic resource that we use when designing systems. My book gives a unified and broad historical and hierarchical review of systems thinking using the information concept developed by Claude E. Shannon and Norbert Wiener (1948) and their predecessors. The book contributes to interdisciplinary work, the unity of science, and our worldview. I focus on the time after about 1950 since it is difficult to find information from the most recent events, and existing books cover the older history well. I briefly summarize history from ancient times to give a stand-alone overview, including ancient Babylon, Greece, the Middle Ages, the scientific revolution that started in the 1600s, and during modern science, since about 1850, one by one, the disciplines separated from philosophy and natural philosophy. Now, professors divide their disciplines into even smaller compartments for their students. If there are relationships to the environment outside our compartment, we cannot see them and do not get the big picture to offer a synthesis.

The author's background My professional career of 38 years was a long journey. A summary of my experiences is now in this book. My background is in wireless communications, especially adaptive systems, which gave me a proper understanding of feedback control, which is the basis of all rational agents. The secret to writing this book was reading, making notes about what I read, and writing myself. Eventually, the notes were longer than the final book. I have learned how to make the complex simple. We can call this process systems thinking.

When I prepared my master's thesis in 1982–1983, I realized how difficult it was to find relevant information using abstract journals and their author and subject indices. I started to develop some systematic methods for this. I collected a bibliography of books and review papers, which are still helpful. I began to study adaptive methods soon after I received my master's degree. I understood that the basis for adaptation is in the feedback concept I learned in a control engineering course. I became interested in hierarchies as a systematic method to manage complexity and describe relationships between systems. I understood the importance of energy in system design and started to think about other basic resources. At that time, Moore's law was going strong, and few researchers were interested in energy. Earlier, we believed that electronics do not consume much energy, but after the complexity increased, the energy became a bottleneck since an integrated circuit can consume a limited amount of energy because of cooling problems. Now everybody knows that the energy is a limited resource.

I started to think about whether any summaries on systems thinking are available. There are, but they were not easy to find since, paradoxically, systems thinkers often did not refer to the work of others. Each started from their ideas, and they did not develop rapidly: there was much overlapping work, and people ignored essential earlier results. The situation has improved since we now have scientific search tools available to everyone. Still, even now, it is almost impossible to get funding for interdisciplinary research often mentioned in speeches. One colleague of mine said to me a few years ago that interdisciplinarity is good but not for him.

I have realized that many good hints on research methods are in some subordinate clauses in different books that do not systematically present analytical and systems thinking. My book is a book that I would have liked to read first as a young researcher. My personal need is to serve our Western culture, which has produced the most creative environment in its representative liberal democracy. These were the reasons why I had to write this book.

The book is based on my work at the University of Oulu from 1982 to 1993 and at VTT Technical Research Centre of Finland from 1993 to 2024. I became an Emeritus Professor of the University of Oulu in 2022. The book also uses my lecturing experiences on research methods at the University of Oulu since 2000. At the beginning of my postgraduate studies, my professor of mathematics encouraged me to select my own approach, using the words of Aaro Hellaakoski, a Finnish poet: "You are a prisoner of the road you follow; only a pathless snowdrift is free."[2] In hindsight, I feel that I have done exactly this without realizing it.

What is needed from the reader When reading the book, a university degree in any discipline is useful. You also need some research experience to appreciate the complexities of the research process. Many ideas are rather abstract, but I have tried to make them more concrete using examples from everyday life. Knowledge about linear system theory, probability, and random processes is beneficial for understanding the references, but I explain each concept from the first principles. The book is about intelligent and rational systems using information and communication technology, which I call information technology, for brevity, despite its narrow definition in the past. The fundamental idea in learning and research is feedback that provides us with tools for self-organization. Each chapter includes a summary, recommended reading, and some discussion questions to support reflective thinking. One chapter also includes some simulation exercises. I have written the text as "timeless" without referring to rapidly changing information, proprietary terms, and disappearing web pages. Thus, I avoid short-lived hot topics.

Contents of the book I must limit the scope, and thus, I focus on the information and feedback concepts leading finally to self-organization. Dependability and security are certainly important but out of the scope of this book. After the introduction in Chap. 1, the book presents in Chap. 2 an overview of the research process. It focuses more on the beginning and end of any research, namely information retrieval and writing a paper. Information retrieval is challenging since the amount of information is exponentially growing, especially when we must cover interdisciplinary

[2] Tietä käyden tien on vanki, vapaa on vain umpihanki. A. Hellaakoski, Huojuvat keulat (1946).

topics where we have not unified the terminology and need unique methods. We must also use secondary sources such as books and review papers in addition to original primary sources. Writing a paper is also a demanding task since the reviewers must be convinced about the importance of broad topics when they are not used to them. Reviewers might only be interested in the simulation results and do not see the difference between a review and original paper. The terminology must be unified and understandable to all readers by avoiding overly theoretical jargon. I also describe, in general terms, what is required from a researcher to work efficiently. Next, in Chap. 3, I emphasize conventional research based on analytical thinking, also called analytical approach or analytical view. Here, analysis and synthesis follow each other. Synthesis is much more complex than analysis; in the past, we have put much effort into analysis. Research starts with the reduction or division of the problem into subproblems. It continues by solving those problems and generalizing them inductively toward a hypothesis we eventually verify by deductive analysis.

We must understand thoroughly the analytical thinking, but it has severe limitations since it cannot easily manage nonlinear relationships having many feedback loops. We need a more general approach called the systems thinking, systems approach, or systems view, presented in Chaps. 4 and 5. The systems thinking also uses analysis, but since not all problems are mathematically tractable, we study them by simulations and practical experiments that replace the analysis. To find hypotheses for such situations, we can use system archetypes, i.e., system models we have tested in many disciplines. For the formation of hypotheses, we use abstractions and analogies. The analytical thinking is a particular case of the systems thinking when the problem is mathematically tractable implying usually linearity, and we reduce systems thinking to deduction. In general, we proceed from analytical thinking to systems thinking. Chapter 6 presents a broad history of the relevant system-level topics described in earlier chapters. Some more detailed history is included also in Chaps. 4 and 5. Chapter 7 is a detailed summary of the most important findings of the whole book.

I have many appendices in the front and back matter of the book. I have a list of abbreviations and a chronology in the front matter. The chronology summarizes the history, and the main emphasis is on the period since about 1950, since the invention of the information concept. I have a glossary, bibliography, and index in the back matter. The glossary includes the most important terms and their definitions. Many definitions are hierarchical. I had to unify the terms since different disciplines use different terms. The unification needed some subjective decisions. Rather than dictionary definitions, I have focused on stipulative definitions by agreement in my disciplines of interest. I have a list of valuable books I ordered according to the subjects in the bibliography. Almost all references at the end of each chapter are in English. Only in some cases, no English translation is available. The readers can use the bibliography to find more information in English.

Novelty of the book The authors of books on the philosophy of science are often philosophers. Their books are handy but primarily descriptive rather than prescriptive. For example, the famous *Oxford Companion to Philosophy* does not include any article on *systems*, which the engineering sciences have developed well. Still, there is an article on *things* that is a much more abstract concept. Many valuable ideas are only as sidenotes in books that cover only some parts of the philosophy of science. I summarize the novelty of this book as follows:

- I have bravely crossed the arbitrary borders between disciplines. I have summarized the philosophy of science using the terminology of engineering sciences, which makes the ideas very concrete, just avoiding any jargon. I have included both analytical and systems thinking, whereas in many cases, they are included in separate books, not knowing about each other. I have described the basic ideas of core disciplines. I have looked for similarities where initially no similarity seemed to exist.
- I have included an extensive bibliography beyond that in any earlier similar book. Earlier authors did not always know about other authors. Everything changed in 2004 when Google Scholar became free for everybody to use.
- I have collected a glossary of systems thinking terms with clear definitions and alternative synonymous terms from other disciplines. These are the *words* of systems thinking.
- I have collected system theories and generic system models called system archetypes useful in information technology whereas earlier archetypes are useful in system dynamics describing social relationships. System theories are presented in other books, but I have shown their similarities. The system theories and archetypes form the *grammar* of systems thinking. For example, I have presented a hierarchy of natural and technical systems, thus showing the relationships between different systems and concepts.
- I have discussed the finiteness of human knowledge to broaden our general knowledge and to evaluate what problems we can solve in a reasonable time. If a problem is hundreds of years old, it is usually best to start with something easier.

Acknowledgments I am grateful to my superiors at the University of Oulu and VTT Technical Research Centre of Finland for all the help. Emeritus Professors Juhani Oksman and Pentti Leppänen of the University of Oulu guided me in the right direction at the beginning of my career. Juhani Oksman was the first tenure professor of the Department of Electrical Engineering since 1967 and changed the education and research of the department towards electronics and information technology. The education included control, computer, and communications engineering, as well as electronics. Pentti Leppänen introduced me to the literature of digital communications, digital signal processing, and digital electronics and suggested adaptive receivers as a research topic for my doctoral studies, leading to my interest in the feedback concept and eventually to self-organizing systems. My superiors, Jyrki Huusko and Jukka Mäkelä at VTT, offered me access to library services through my part-time contracts after retirement. I am grateful to my former superior, Hannu Heusala, with whom I have often discussed recent developments in digital electronics. Dean Jukka Riekki of the University of Oulu became an enthusiastic supporter of systems thinking. I wrote several review papers with him, and he made my emeritus professorship possible after my retirement. I thank my superior, Susanna Pirttikangas of the University of Oulu, for all the support with whom I started our new post-graduate course on interdisciplinary systems thinking.

I want to acknowledge my friends for their support during my career. My two visits abroad, hosted by Prof. Paul Walter Baier in Kaiserslautern, Germany, and Prof. Desmond P. Taylor in Christchurch, New Zealand, are highly appreciated. I want to thank my former doctoral students and my coauthors of papers. I have learned from all of them and used that knowledge in my book. My former doctoral student Adrian Kotelba commented on the whole book and gave several hints for improvement. The following persons commented parts of the book in their fields of expertise: Hannu Heusala, Antti Hiltunen, Jouni-Matti Kuukkanen, Matti Leiviskä, Tiina Myllyniemi, Ilkka Norros, Markku Ojanen, Seija Rajaniemi, Outi Rusanen, Rick Szostak, Tuomo Suntola, and Petri Uusikylä. Mika Aaltonen started a symposium series on complex adaptive systems. Tarja Luukko forced me to improve my communication in this book and elsewhere. During my career, I have also received valuable help and encouragement from many other colleagues and friends, including Antti Anttonen, Barbara Gastel, Marko Höyhtyä, Enso Ikonen, Päivi Jussila, Pertti Järvensivu, Mirjami Jutila, Pekka Kaasila, Kari Leppälä, Petri Mähönen, Erkki Oja, Jussi Paakkari, Susanna Pantsar, Timo Rahkonen, Olli Silven, and Kalle Timperi. The production process of the book was supported by Dieter Merkle, Ashok Arumairaj, and Martina Wiese at Springer Nature.

Last but not least, I would like to thank my family: my parents, who made my studies possible and taught me love, humility, honesty, perseverance, and appreciation of hard work on a small farm in Ilveskorpi, Vihanti (now within Raahe); my uncle who encouraged me in my philosophical studies and helped me to understand my family's history; my seven siblings, who taught me social abilities; my darling wife Seija, who is also a mother and grandmother and who has supported me for over 45 years; our two children, their spouses, and our five grandchildren, who all are the apples of my eye and whose success is always my priority. My gorgeous wife, children, and grandchildren deserve this book. Words cannot express all the never-ending love from and for them.

I might know something; after all, I was there, too.[3]

Oulu, Finland Aarne Mämmelä

[3] Jotakin ehkä tietäisin, olinhan siellä minäkin. J. L. Runeberg, The Tales of Ensign Stål (1860).

Competing Interests The author has no competing interests to declare that are relevant to the content of this manuscript.

Chronology

This chronology summarizes the most important changes in the human culture especially in analytical and systems thinking. The timing of the early events is only approximate.

Year	Discoverer	Discovery
13.8 Ga BP	Big bang	Universe
4.57 Ga	Universe	Sun
4.54 Ga	Universe	Earth
3.77–4.28 Ga	Earth	Life
300000	Earth	Homo sapiens
12000 BCE	Homo sapiens	Agriculture
3400	Sumerians	Cuneiform writing
3400	Sumerians	Numeral system
3300	Near East	Bronze Age
3000	Many discoverers	Urban revolution
1900	Canaanites	Consonant writing
1800	Sumerians	Mathematics and astronomy
1300	Near East	Iron Age
800	Greece	Alphabet
800	India	Concept of infinity
585	Thales	Scientific inquiry, deduction
546	Anaximander	Universal laws, evolutionary theory
530	Many discoverers	Irrational numbers
520	Pythagoras	Spherical Earth
510	Greece	Democracy
500	Rome	Latin alphabet
450	Leucippus	Causality

(continued)

(continued)

Year	Discoverer	Discovery
430	Leucippus and Democritos	Atom theory
400	Thucydides	Scientific history
400	Socrates	Dialectic method
387	Plato	Academy
350	Plato	Political structures
350	Aristotle	Spherical Earth
350	Aristotle	Study of logic
350	Aristotle	Subsidiarity
300	India	Zero
300	Euclid	Axiomatic system
270	Ktesibios	Feedback in a water clock
260	Aristarchos	Heliocentric world view
260	Archimedes	Statics
250	Zhuangzi	Spontaneous order (concept)
50 BCE	India	Indian numerals
50 CE	Hero	Steam power
77	Pliny the Elder	Scientific encyclopedia
105	Tsai Lun	Paper
140	Ptolemy	Geocentric universe using epicycles
628	Brahmagupta	Negative numbers
700	Arabia	Indian numerals to Arabia
1100s	Europe	Scholasticism
1021	Alhazen	Analytical and experimental method
1088	University of Bologna	First modern university
1170	University of Oxford	University of mathematics and science
1202	Fibonacci	Arabic numerals to Europe
1247	R. Bacon	Observation and experiments
1300	Many discoverers	Term university
1320	Europe	Paper from China to Europe
1327	William of Ockham	Ockham's razor
1400s	Florence	Renaissance
1421	Florence	First patent
1454	J. Gutenberg	Printing press
1543	N. Copernicus	Heliocentric world view
1545	G. Cardan	Modern mathematics
1572	R. Bombelli	Complex numbers
1589	Galileo	Law of falling bodies

(continued)

(continued)

Year	Discoverer	Discovery
1600s	Many discoverers	Scientific revolution
1609	J. Kepler	Celestial mechanics
1610	Many discoverers	Hierarchy (term)
1614	S. Santorio	Metabolism
1614	Many discoverers	Abstract journal
1615	Many discoverers	Term physics
1620	F. Bacon	Experimental-inductive method
1624	C. Drebbel	Feedback in thermostat
1624	England	Lasting patent law
1628	W. Harvey	Blood-vascular system
1629	A. Girard	Number line
1632	Galileo	Principle of relativity
1637	R. Descartes	Axiomatization and reductionism
1638	Galileo	Scientific textbook
1651	T. Hobbes	Social contract (concept)
1654	B. Pascal and P. de Fermat	Probability
1660	Royal Society	Scientific society
1665	Royal Society	Scientific journal
1665	R. Hooke	Cells
1665	C. Huygens	Resonance
1669	I. Newton	Calculus
1684	G. W. Leibniz	Calculus
1685	J. Wallis	Complex plane
1687	I. Newton	Newtonian dynamics
1687	I. Newton	Conservation of momentum and angular momentum
1690	C. Huygens	Hypothetico-deductive method
1700s	Many discoverers	Enlightenment
1700	G. W. Leibniz	Binary system
1700	Many discoverers	Abstract in scientific papers
1712	T. Newcomen	Steam engine
1714	C. G. Hoffman	Abstract journal
1735	C. von Linne	Taxonomies in biology
1738	D. Bernoulli	Kinetic theory of gases
1739	D. Hume	Problem of induction
1740s	G.-L. Leclerc de Buffon	Theory of evolution
1751	D. Diderot	Modern encyclopedia

(continued)

(continued)

Year	Discoverer	Discovery
1752	Royal Society	Peer review
1760	England	Industrial revolution
1762	J.-J. Rousseau	Social contract (term), theory of democracy
1765	J. Watt	Modern steam engine
1768	C. Macfarquhar et al.	Encyclopedia Britannica
1769	J. Watt	Governor in a steam engine
1769	A.-L. Lavoisier	Conservation of mass
1776	A. Smith	Free-market economics, supply and demand
1782	Budapest	University of technology
1785	Royal Society	Conference proceedings
1786	P. S. Laplace	Perturbation theory
1788	Linnean Society	Specialist society
1789	J. Bentham	Utilitarism
1789	A. Lavoisier	Conservation of mass
1790	USA	Copyright
1790	J.-B. Delambre and P. F. A. Mechain	Metric system
1792	W. von Hulboldt	*Bildung* system
1798	T. R. Malthus	Exponential law of growth
1798	C. Wessel	Complex plane
1803	J. Dalton	Atomic theory
1806	T. Young	Term energy for work store
1812	P.-S. Laplace	Laplace transform
1814	P.-S. Laplace	Conservation of information, causal determinism
1822	GDNÄ	Nationwide umbrella society
1822	J. J. Berzelius	Review journal
1822	J. Fourier	Fourier series
1824	L. von Rankin	History as a science
1828	N. Webster, Jr.	An American Dictionary of the English Language
1830	A. Comte	Positivism, sociology, hierarchy of sciences
1833	Many discoverers	Word scientist
1833	W. F. Lloyd	Tragedy of the commons
1838	M. J. Schleiden and T. Schwann	Cell theory
1843	J. P. Joule	Energy conservation law
1843	M. Faraday	Conservation of charge

(continued)

(continued)

Year	Discoverer	Discovery
1843	J. S. Mill	Emergence (concept)
1845	G. R. Kirchhoff	Superposition theorem
1847	H. Helmholtz	First law of thermodynamics
1848	G. Boole	Boolean algebra
1848	W. Thompson (Lord Kelvin)	Third law of thermodynamics and absolute temperature scale
1850	R. J. E. Clausius	Entropy law, concept of environment
1850	J. J. Silvester	Matrix algebra
1858	J. H. Newman	Liberal education
1859	J. C. Maxwell	Kinetic theory of gases
1859	C. Darwin	Theory of evolution
1860	F. A. Kekule	International conference
1860	H. J. Labatt	Citation index
1863	H. Spencer	Cultural evolution
1863	Many discoverers	Morphogenesis (term)
1865	ITU	International standardization organization
1865	R. J. E. Clausius	Entropy (term)
1865	G. Mendel	Genetics
1865	J. C. Maxwell	Electromagnetic waves
1865	W. S. Jevons	Jevons paradox
1866	J. C. Maxwell	Statistical mechanics
1866	C. L. and E. de Cyon	Biological regulator
1866	J. M. Gray	Servomechanism
1868	J. Farcot	Servomechanism
1869	M. Mendeleev	Periodic table of elements
1870	Many discoverers	Science as a profession
1873	K. E. Abbe	Diffraction limit
1875	G. H. Lewes	Emergence
1876	W. Gibbs	Thermodynamics
1876	G. Bell and E. Gray	Telephone
1876	L. Pasteur	Methods section
1876	T. A. Edison	Industrial research laboratory
1877	L. E. Boltzmann	Statistical mechanics, heat, and temperature
1878	C. Bernard	Homeostasis and equilibrium
1878	C. S. Peirce	Abduction
1883	Many countries	Paris Convention for the Protection of Industrial Property
1884	Oxford University Press	The Oxford English Dictionary

(continued)

(continued)

Year	Discoverer	Discovery
1884	J. B. Johnson	Engineering Index
1884	W. Gibbs	Statistical mechanics
1888	H. Hertz	Radio waves
1890	H. Poincare	Deterministic chaos, unpredictable systems
1892	A. M. Lyapunov	Lyapunov stability
1893	N. Tesla	Radio
1893	C. P. Steinmetz	Phasors
1896	G. Marconi	Radio
1897	T. C. Chamberlin	Many hypotheses
1898	IEE and Physical Society of London	Science Abstracts (Inspec)
1904	H. Poincare	Speed of light as a fundamental limit
1905	A. Einstein	Noise explained
1905	D. Hilbert	Hilbert transform
1905	A. Einstein	Special theory of relativity
1905	A. Einstein	Conservation of mass-energy
1906	V. Pareto	Multiobjective optimization
1906	IEC	International standardization organization
1907	G. Galton	Wisdom of the crowds
1908	H. Minkowski	Space-time concept
1910	J. Dewey	Reflective thinking and action
1911	F. Taylor	Scientific management
1913	IRE	Proceedings of the IRE
1913	E. H. Armstrong and C. S. Franklin	Positive feedback amplifier
1915	A. Einstein	General theory of relativity
1917	D. W. Thompson	Physics of morphogenesis
1920s	Many discoverers	Circuit theory
1920s	Many discoverers	Network theory
1920	Many discoverers	Inductive feedback
1922	N. Minorsky	PID control
1924	E. Hubble	Big bang theory
1925	A. J. Lotka	Open systems
1925	J. B. Thomson and H. Nyquist	Thermal noise
1925	W. Heisenberg et al.	Quantum mechanics
1925	N. D. Kondratiev	Kondratiev waves
1926	J. Smuts	Holism

(continued)

(continued)

Year	Discoverer	Discovery
1927	H. S. Black	Negative feedback amplifier
1927	W. Heisenberg	Uncertainty principle
1928	J. von Neumann	Minimax theorem
1928	H. Nyquist	Maximum symbol rate
1928	R. V. L. Hartley	Maximum speed of transmission with noise
1929	Vienna Circle	Logical empiricism
1929	L. Szilard	Minimum switching energy
1931	International Council of Scientific Unions (ICSU)	International umbrella organization
1931	Pius IX	Subsidiarity
1931	K. Gödel	Incompleteness theorems
1932	W. B. Cannon	Homeostasis
1932	L. von Bertalanffy	Open systems in biology
1932	H. Nyquist	Stability of feedback
1933	A. Kolmogorov	Modern probability theory
1934	H. L. Hazen	Theory of servomechanism
1934	K. Popper	Falsification
1934	H. F. von Stackelberg	Stackelberg game
1936	A. F. Bemis	Modularity
1936	A. Church and A. Turing	Church-Turing thesis
1936	A. Turing	Computing theory, Turing machine
1936	J. M. Keynes	Macroeconomics
1938	B. F. Skinner	Reinforcement learning
1938	C. E. Shannon	Boolean algebra in switching circuits
1938	C. W. Morris	Semiotics
1938	H. H. Jennings and J. Moreno	Random graph
1938	IEC	International Electrotechnical Vocabulary
1939	L. Pauling	Bond theory
1939	W. A. Shewhart	Specification-production-inspection
1940s	Many discoverers	Systems engineering
1940s	Many discoverers	Operations research
1940	H. E. Kallman	Tapped delay line
1940	H. Bode	Bode plot
1940	W. R. Ashby	Positive and negative feedback
1941	M. Polanyi	Spontaneous order (term)
1943	D. O. North	Matched filter
1943	A. Rosenblueth et al.	Purposeful behavior

(continued)

(continued)

Year	Discoverer	Discovery
1943	W. McCullogh and W. Pitts	Neural network
1944	J. von Neumann and O. Morgenstern	Game theory
1945	H. Cramer and C. R. Rao	Minimum variance of estimators
1945	J. von Neumann	Computer architecture
1945	R. Carnap et al.	Analytical philosophy of science
1946	D. Gabor	Uncertainty principle
1946	D. Gabor	Complex envelope
1946	J. W. Mauchly and J. P. Eckart, Jr.	Programmable computer and computer simulation
1946	K. Lewin	Action research
1946	D. S. Harder	Term automation
1947	W. R. Ashby	Adaptive and self-organizing systems
1947	ISO	International standardization organization
1948	W. B. Schockley et al.	Bipolar transistor
1948	C. E. Shannon	Information theory, channel capacity
1948	N. Wiener	Cybernetics
1948	J. von Neumann	Cellular automaton (concept)
1948	W. R. Ashby	Homeostat, first adaptive system
1948	W. G. Walter	Mobile autonomous robot
1949	M. J. E. Golay	Shannon limit
1949	C. E. Shannon	Sampling theorem
1949	Many discoverers	Modularity in electronics
1949	Many discoverers	Semiconductor logic gate
1950s	Many discoverers	Linear system theory
1950s	Many discoverers	Optimization and decision theory
1950s	Many discoverers	Detection and estimation theory
1950s	Many discoverers	Evolutionary computation
1950s	Many discoverers	Pattern recognition
1950	L. von Bertalanffy	General theory of systems
1950	Many discoverers	Double blind experiment
1950	A. Turing	Turing test
1950	J. Nash	Nash equilibrium
1950	J. Nash	Nash bargaining solution
1951	W. E. Deming	Plan-do-check-act (PDCA)
1952	A. Turing	Chemistry of morphogenesis
1952	R. Bellman	Dynamic programming

(continued)

(continued)

Year	Discoverer	Discovery
1952	W. R. Ashby	Double feedback and ultrastability
1953	F. H. C. Crick and J. D. Watson	DNA structure
1954	H. Simon	Feedback in a human agent
1954	H. Simon	Bounded rationality
1954	N. Barricelli	Artificial life
1954	G. C. Devol, Jr.	Robots
1954	W. W. Peterson and D. Gabor	Orthogonality
1954	M. Minsky	Reinforcement learning
1955	I. Prigogine	Nonequilibrium thermodynamics
1956	K. E. Boulding	Hierarchy of systems
1956	Many discoverers	Society for General Theory of Systems (later ISSS)
1956	H. Simon	Satisficing principle
1956	J. McCarthy et al.	Artificial intelligence
1956	R. Price	Separation theorem in communications (estimator-correlator)
1956	S. S. L. Chang	Decision and information feedback
1957	Many discoverers	Modularity in computers
1957	R. Bellman	Curse of dimensionality
1957	R. Dicke	Anthropic principle
1958	F. Rosenblatt	Perceptron
1958	R. Rosen	(M, R) systems
1958	J. Forrester	System dynamics
1958	W. M. Elsasser	Biotonic laws
1959	R. Noyce	Monolithic integrated circuit
1959	A. Samuel	Machine learning
1959	P.-P. Grasse	Stigmergy
1959	B. Belousov and A. Zhabotinsky	BZ reaction
1959	P. Erdos and A. Renyi	Random graph theory
1959	C. C. Hempel	Deductive-nomological and inductive-statistical explanations
1960	D. Dantzig and P. Wolfe	Distributed optimization
1960	H. von Foerster	Order from noise
1960	P. Eykhoff	Measurement-learning-decision-adjustment
1961	M. W. Nirenberg	Genetic code
1961	L. Kleinrock	Packet switching

(continued)

(continued)

Year	Discoverer	Discovery
1961	P. D. Joseph and J. T. Tou	Separation theorem in control
1961	E. M. Glaser	Decision-directed receiver
1961	J. McCarthy	Cloud computing (concept)
1961	J. R. Lucas	Nonalgorithmic mind
1962	H. Simon	Hierarchy theory
1962	T. Kuhn	Paradigms and scientific revolutions
1962	J. C. Emery	Modular programming
1962	M. Heilig	Virtual reality
1963	M. Maruyama	Positive feedback
1963	AIEE and IRE	IEEE
1964	P. Baran	Degrees of centralization
1964	E. Garfield	Science Citation Index (Web of Science)
1965	R. D. Milne	Weak coupling in control
1965	D. de Solla Price	Scale-free networks (concept)
1965	L. A. Zadeh	Fuzzy sets
1965	E. W. Dijkstra	Concurrent computing
1967	G. M. Amdahl	Fixed-size speedup in computing
1967	S. Milgram	Small-world networks
1968	E. W. Dijkstra	Hierarchical programming
1968	W. F. Buckley	Complex adaptive systems in social sciences
1969	E. W. Dijkstra	Structured programming
1969	Many discoverers	Arpanet
1969	USA	Human to the Moon
1969	J. McCarthy and P. J. Hayes	Frame problem
1969	N. J. Nilsson	Robot architecture
1970s	Many discoverers	Optimization decomposition
1970s	Many discoverers	Pattern formation
1970s	Many discoverers	Message passing
1970	M. D. Mesarovic	Hierarchical control
1970	D. Silverman and S. Schutz	Actors approach
1971	S. Cook and L. Levin	Computational complexity theory, intractable problems
1971	N. Georgescu-Roegen	Thermodynamics in economics
1971	H. Haken	Synergetics
1971	M. Eigen	Hypercycle
1971	T. Ganti	Chemoton
1971	M. S. Hart	Digital library of books

(continued)

(continued)

Year	Discoverer	Discovery
1972	R. Thom	Catastrophe theory
1972	T. C. Chen	Loosely coupled multiprocessor
1972	D. L. Parnas	Hierarchical and modular software design
1972	IEEE	IEEE Standard Dictionary of Electrical and Electronics Terms
1972	R. E. Kahn et al.	Packet radios
1972	M. B. Rosenberg	Nonviolent communication
1973	IEEE	Index to IEEE Publications
1973	H. Simon	Horizontal and vertical loose coupling
1973	J. Maynard Smith and G. Price	Evolutionary game theory
1973	L. A. Zadeh	Fuzzy logic
1973	H. R. Maturana and F. J. Varela	Autopoiesis
1974	E. W. Dijsktra	Self-stabilization
1974	E. W. Dijkstra	Separation of concerns
1974	W. P. Stevens et al.	Loose coupling in software design
1974	H. von Förster	Second-order cybernetics
1975	J. Holland	Genetic algorithms
1976	J. Boyd	OODA loop
1977	Many discoverers	Chaos theory
1977	C. Hewitt	Distributed artificial intelligence (multiagent systems)
1978	J. G. Miller	Hierarchy of living and social systems
1978	C. Argyris and D. A. Schön	Double-loop learning
1979	ANSI	IMRAD structure standardized
1979	C. R. Cutler and B. C. Ramaker	Model-predictive control
1980	M. Minsky	Telepresence
1980	R. M. Dawes	Social dilemma
1981	D. J. Baker and A. Ephremides	Distributed self-organizing network
1982	F. Dyson	Autocatalytic sets
1983	Many discoverers	Arpanet changed to Internet
1984	George Cowan et al.	Santa Fe Institute
1984	Many discoverers	Complexity theory
1984	ISO	OSI model
1984	ISO	International Vocabulary of Metrology (VIM)
1984	D. Kolb	Experiential learning

(continued)

(continued)

Year	Discoverer	Discovery
1985	P. T. Lewis	Internet of Things
1986	R. A. Brooks	Reactive subsumption robot architecture
1986	R. C. Arkin	Autonomous behavior-based robot architecture
1986	B. J. Zimmermann	Self-regulated learning
1986	D. E. Rumelhart et al.	Backpropagation algorithm
1987	M. R. Genesereth and N. J. Nilsson	AI as a theory of intelligent agents
1988	J. L. Gustafson	Fixed-time speedup in computing
1989	C. H. Bennett and R. H. Bassard	Quantum computer
1989	J. Han	Active disturbance rejection control
1989	R. J. Firby	Modern proactive robot architectures
1989	Many discoverers	Multirobot systems
1990	P. Senge	System archetypes
1990	T. Berners-Lee	World Wide Web
1991	M. Weiser	Ubiquitous computing (concept)
1991	D. Christian	Big history
1991	NASA	V-model
1992	J. Holland	Complex adaptive system in complexity theory
1992	M. Mataric	Social robots
1993	X.-H. Sun and L. Ni	Memory-bounded speedup in computing
1993	G. Beni and J. Wang	Swarm intelligence
1993	IEEE	Ad hoc network
1994	Many discoverers	Message passing interface
1995	L. R. Medsker	Hybrid intelligent systems
1995	Elsevier	Engineering Village
1995	W. G. Bowen	Journal Storage (JSTOR)
1996	IEEE and IEE	IEEE/IEE Electronic Library (IEEE Xplore)
1996	B. Kahle	Internet Archive
1997	ACM	ACM Digital Library
1997	R. K. Chellappa	Cloud computing (term)
1998	J. Mashey et al.	Big data
1998	M. K. Molloy	Acronym Finder
1999	J. Mitola, III	Cognition cycle
1999	Akamai Technologies	Edge computing (content delivery)
2000s	Many discoverers	Systems biology
2000	P. Gupta and P. R. Kumar	Transport capacity
2001	D. R. Harper	Online Etymology Dictionary

(continued)

(continued)

Year	Discoverer	Discovery
2001	J. Wales and L. Sanger	Wikipedia
2003	J. O. Kephart and D. M. Chess	MAPE-K loop
2004	Elsevier	Scopus
2004	Google	Google Scholar
2004	Google	Google Books
2006	A. Swartz	Open Library
2006	E. M. Izhikevich	Scholarpedia
2007	A. Avila et al.	Limit for cooling
2008	D. H. Woo and H.-H. Lee	Energy-efficient speedup
2008	N. McKeown et al.	OpenFlow Application Programming Interface
2008	3GPP	Hybrid self-organizing network (concept)
2008	Many discoverers	Guided self-organization
2009	Many discoverers	Discovery tools
2010	Google	Google Books Ngram Viewer
2010	ISO/IEC/IEEE	Software and Systems Engineering Vocabulary
2010	W. B. Arthur	Complexity economics
2011	Many discoverers	Microservices
2012	A. Krizhevsky et al.	Deep learning breakthrough
2017	H. B. McMahan et al.	Federated learning
2017	A. Vaswani et al.	Transformers
2018	ETSI	Generic Autonomic Networking Architecture (GANA)
2020	T. Suntola	Dynamic universe
2024	Scopus	Scopus AI

Contents

1 Introduction 1
1.1 Managing Complexity in an Innovative and Sustainable World 1
1.2 Chapter Summary and Recommended Reading 16
References 18

2 Scientific Research from an Idea to Publication 23
2.1 Introduction 23
2.2 Research Process as a Whole 24
2.3 Beginning of Research: Managing Exponentially Growing Literature 31
2.3.1 Introduction 31
2.3.2 Publications and Publishers 33
2.3.3 Tools and Databases for Information Retrieval 40
2.3.4 Practical Hints for Searching Literature 42
2.3.5 Outlining a Literature Review 46
2.4 Final Result: Writing with Quality to Distribute Knowledge 47
2.4.1 Introduction 47
2.4.2 IMRDC Structure of a Paper 49
2.4.3 Writing the Text 58
2.4.4 Selection of Conference and Journal 63
2.4.5 Peer Review Process 66
2.5 Chapter Summary and Recommended Reading 72
References 74

3 Analytical Thinking 81
3.1 Introduction 81
3.2 Research Is a Demanding Learning Process from the Bottom Up and from Inside Out 86
3.2.1 Learning 86
3.2.2 Research, Development, and Innovations 89
3.2.3 How to Succeed as a Researcher 92

3.2.4 Creativity ... 94
3.2.5 Ethical Rules ... 101
3.3 Conceptual Analysis Starts Any Research: Know What You Are Talking About ... 102
3.4 Formation of Theories to Manage the World ... 104
3.4.1 Types of Reasoning ... 104
3.4.2 Formation of Theories ... 106
3.4.3 Causality and Forms and Reduction ... 113
3.4.4 Methods of Discovery ... 119
3.4.5 Methods of Verification and Falsification ... 121
3.5 Chapter Summary and Recommended Reading ... 124
Appendix ... 125
References ... 128

4 Systems Thinking: Basics ... 137
4.1 Introduction ... 137
4.2 Basics of Systems Thinking ... 142
4.2.1 Definitions of a System ... 142
4.2.2 Isolated, Closed, and Open Systems ... 147
4.2.3 Reductionism and Emergence ... 149
4.2.4 Formation of Visions ... 151
4.3 Hierarchy of Sciences and Technology ... 154
4.3.1 Formal Sciences ... 157
4.3.2 Natural Sciences ... 158
4.3.3 Social Sciences ... 172
4.3.4 Humanities ... 202
4.3.5 Information Technology ... 205
4.4 Chapter Summary and Recommended Reading ... 212
References ... 213

5 Systems Thinking: How Systems Work ... 227
5.1 Introduction ... 227
5.2 General Requirements of Sustainable Systems ... 228
5.2.1 Sustainable Development ... 228
5.2.2 Basic Resources ... 230
5.2.3 Finiteness of Human Knowledge ... 246
5.2.4 Needs and System Requirements ... 257
5.2.5 System Verification and Validation ... 258
5.3 Forming a General Hierarchy of Systems ... 259
5.3.1 Properties of Systems ... 259
5.3.2 Description Levels of Systems ... 265
5.3.3 Principles of Hierarchical Systems ... 267
5.3.4 Hierarchy of Everything ... 270
5.3.5 Hierarchy of Natural and Technical Systems ... 271

5.4 System Theories and Archetypes ... 280
5.4.1 System Theories ... 280
5.4.2 System Archetypes ... 311
5.5 Chapter Summary and Recommended Reading ... 320
References ... 321

6 History for Understanding the Present ... 341
6.1 Introduction ... 341
6.2 Beginning and End of the Research Process ... 342
6.2.1 Information Retrieval ... 342
6.2.2 Publishing of New Knowledge ... 349
6.3 Analytical Thinking ... 353
6.3.1 Development of Scientific Thought ... 353
6.3.2 Science in the Antiquity and Middle Ages ... 354
6.3.3 Scientific Method Since the Scientific Revolution ... 357
6.3.4 Development of Researcher Education ... 361
6.4 Systems Thinking ... 363
6.4.1 Beginning of Systems Thinking ... 363
6.4.2 History of Information Technology ... 364
6.4.3 History of Sustainability ... 372
6.4.4 Principles of Systems and System Theories ... 373
6.4.5 Vision of the Future ... 408
6.5 Chapter Summary and Recommended Reading ... 411
References ... 413

7 Summary ... 429

Glossary ... 439

Bibliography ... 455

Index ... 465

About the Author

Aarne Mämmelä is a professor Emeritus of the University of Oulu and a former research professor of the VTT Technical Research Centre of Finland Ltd. He received the M.Sc. (Tech.) degree with honors in 1983 and the D.Sc. (Tech.) degree with honors in 1996, both from the University of Oulu. He was with the University of Oulu from 1982 to 1993. In 1993, he joined the VTT. For over 25 years, from 1996 to 2021, he was a research professor of wireless communications. After his retirement, from the beginning of 2022 until the end of 2024, he had a part-time contract with VTT. He visited the University of Kaiserslautern, Germany, from 1990 to 1991 and the University of Canterbury, New Zealand, from 1996 to 1997. Since 2004, he has been a Docent (equivalent to an adjunct professor) and, since 2022, a professor emeritus with the University of Oulu. He has lectured on research methodology, including the systems thinking, for about twenty-five years at the University of Oulu. He has also been an advisor to ten doctoral students. From 2016 to 2018, he was a member of the Scientific Council for Natural Sciences and Engineering at the Research Council of Finland, formerly known as the Academy of Finland. From 2014 to 2018, he was an editor of the *IEEE Wireless Communications*. He has published over 45 journal articles, 15 book chapters, and over 100 conference papers.

Abbreviations

3D	Three-dimensional
3GPP	3rd Generation Partnership Project
AAAI	Association for the Advancement of Artificial Intelligence
AAAS	American Association for the Advancement of Science
AC	Alternating current
ACM	Association for Computing Machinery
ADC	Analog-to-digital converter
ADRC	Active disturbance rejection control
AGI	Artificial general intelligence
AHP	Analytic hierarchy process
AI	Artificial intelligence
AIEE	American Institute of Electrical Engineers
AIS	Association for Interdisciplinary Studies
AM	Amplitude modulation
AMC	Adaptive modulation and coding
AMS	American Mathematical Society
ANSI	American National Standards Institute
API	Application programming interface
ARQ	Automatic repeat request
ASD	Agile software development
ASIC	Application-specific integrated circuit
ASSP	Application-specific standard product
BCE	Before common era
BIBO	Bounded input, bounded output
BIPM	International Bureau of Weights and Measures
BP	Before present
BQP	Bounded quantum polynomial
BZ	Belousov-Zhabotinsky
CAES	Complex adaptive and evolutionary system
CAN	Control area network
CAS	Complex adaptive system

CC	Creative commons
CDMA	Code-division multiple access
CD-ROM	Compact disk—read only memory
CE	Common era
CEN	European Committee for Standardization
CENELEC	European Committee for Electrotechnical Standardization
CI	Computational intelligence
CMOS	Complementary metal-oxide-semiconductor
CNT	Carbon nanotube
Compendex	Computerized engineering index
C-SON	Centralized self-organizing network
CSS	Complex systems society
DAC	Digital-to-analog converter
DAI	Distributed artificial intelligence
DARPA	Defense Advanced Research Projects Agency
DC	Direct current
DIKW	Data, information, knowledge, and wisdom
DMAIC	Define-measure-analyze-improve-control
DNA	Deoxyribonucleic acid
DOAJ	Directory of Open Access Journals
D-SON	Distributed self-organizing network
DSP	Digital signal processor
DSST	Digit-symbol substitution test
DU	Dynamic universe
EAI	European Alliance for Innovation
EDS	Elton B. Stephens Company Discovery Service
EIU	Economist Intelligence Unit
ENIAC	Electronic Numerical Integrator and Computer
EPC	European Patent Convention
EPO	European Patent Office
ETSI	European Telecommunications Standards Institute
EU	European Union
EURASIP	European Association for Signal Processing
FBS	Functional, behavioral, and structural
FCC	Federal Communications Commission
FEC	Forward error correction
FM	Frequency modulation
Ga	Billions of years
GANA	Generic Autonomic Networking Architecture
GDNÄ	Gesellschaft Deutsches Naturforscher und Ärzte
GDP	Gross domestic product
GEP	Gross ecosystem product
H-ARQ	Hybrid automatic repeat request
HIPERLAN	High Performance Local Area Network
HMS	Holonic manufacturing system

H-SON	Hybrid self-organizing network
IAAF	International Association of Athletics Federations
IAPR	International Association for Pattern Recognition
IBHA	International Big History Association
ICC	International Criminal Court
ICJ	International Court of Justice
ICSU	International Council of Scientific Unions
ICT	Information and communication technologies
IEC	International Electrotechnical Commission
IEE	Institution of Electrical Engineers
IEEE	Institute of Electrical and Electronics Engineers
IEL	IEEE/IEE Electronic Library
IERE	Institution of Electronic and Radio Engineers
IET	Institution of Engineering and Technology
IEV	International Electrotechnical Vocabulary
IFSR	International Federation for Systems Research
IMEKO	International Measurement Confederation
IMRAD	Introduction, materials and methods, results, and discussion
IMRDC	Introduction, materials and methods, results, discussion, and conclusion
INCOSE	International Council on Systems Engineering
Inspec	Information Service for Physics, Electronics, and Computing
IoT	Internet of Things
IP	Intellectual property
IP	Internet Protocol
IPA	International Phonetic Alphabet
IPC	International Patent Classification
IPS	Instructions per second
IQ	Intelligence quotient
IRDS	International Roadmap for Devices and Systems
IRE	Institute of Radio Engineers
IS	Information Science
ISA	International Society of Automation
ISC	International Science Council
ISO	International Organization for Standardization
ISQ	International System of Quantities
ISSC	International Social Science Council
ISSS	International Society for the Systems Sciences
IT	Information technology
ITD Alliance	Global Alliance for Inter- and Transdisciplinarity
ITRS	International Technology Roadmap for Semiconductors
ITU	International Telecommunications Union
ITU-R	International Telecommunication Union—Radiocommunication Sector
JCGM	Joint Committee for Guides in Metrology

JCR	Journal Citation Reports
JIF	Journal impact factor
JPI	Journal performance indicator
JSTOR	Journal Storage
KPI	Key performance indicator
LDPC	Low-density parity-check
LIO	Liberal International Order
LLM	Large language model
LMS	Least-mean square
LQ	Linear quadratic
LS	Least squares
LTI	Linear time-invariant
M, R	Metabolism-repair
MAP	Maximum a posteriori probability
MAPE-K	Monitor, analyze, plan, execute, and knowledge
MAS	Multiagent system
MCDM	Multiple criteria decision making
MIMO	Multiple-input multiple-output
MKS	Meter, kilogram, and second
MKSA	Meter, kilogram, second, and ampere
ML	Maximum likelihood
MMSE	Minimum mean-square error
MOO	Multiobjective optimization
MOS	Metal-oxide-semiconductor
MPC	Model-predictive control
MSE	Mean-square error
NASA	National Aeronautics and Space Administration
NBS	Nash bargaining solution
NCS	Networked control system
NFV	Network function virtualization
NIH	Not invented here
NLP	Natural language processing
NoC	Network on chip
NP	Nondeterministic polynomial
NSO	Network service orchestration
NTIS	National Technical Information Service
NUM	Network utility maximization
OA	Open access
OECD	Organisation for Economic Co-operation and Development
OED	Oxford English Dictionary
OFDM	Orthogonal frequency-division multiplexing
OODA	Observe, orient, decide, and act
OP	Operation
OPS	Operations per second
OR	Operations research

ORCID	Open Researcher and Contributor Identification
OSI	Open Systems Interconnection
P	Polynomial
PCM	Pulse-code modulation
PCT	Patent Cooperation Treaty
PDCA	Plan-do-check-act
pdf	Portable document format
PDSA	Plan-do-study-act
PDU	Protocol data unit
Ph.D.	Philosophiæ doctor
PID	Proportional-integral-derive
PSK	Phase-shift keying
QAM	Quadrature amplitude modulation
RAD	Rapid application development
RCS	Real-time control system
RFID	Radio frequency identification
RL	Reinforcement learning
RLS	Recursive least squares
SaaS	Software as a service
SDG	Sustainable development goal
SDLC	Software development life cycle
SDN	Software-defined network
SDPS	Society for Design and Process Science
SE VOCAB	Software and Systems Engineering Vocabulary
SEP	Standard essential patent
SERC	Systems Engineering Research Center
SI	International System of Units
SINR	Signal-to-noise and interference ratio
SIR	Signal-to-interference ratio
SJR	SCImago Journal Rank
SMS	Short message service
SNR	Signal-to-noise ratio
SOA	Service-oriented architecture
SoC	System on chip
SON	Self-organizing network
SPEC	Standard Performance Evaluation Corporation
STS	Science and technology studies
SWOT	Strengths, weaknesses, opportunities, and threats
TCM	Trellis-coded modulation
TCP	Transmission control protocol
TDM	Time-division multiplexing
TDMA	Time-division multiple access
TPC	Technical program committee
TRIPS	Trade-Related Aspects of Intellectual Property Rights
TRIZ	Theory of inventive problem solving

TTL	Transistor-transistor logic
UP	Unitary Patent
UPC	Unified Patent Court
URSI	International Union of Radio Science
VDE	Verband der Elektrotechnik, Elektronik und Informationstechnik
VHDL	Very High-Speed Integrated Circuit Hardware Description Language
VIM	International Vocabulary of Metrology
VLSI	Very large-scale integration
WIPO	World Intellectual Property Organization
WoS	Web of Science
WTO	World Trade Organization

List of Figures

Fig. 1.1 Research involving many disciplines 3
Fig. 1.2 **a** General definition of a system. **b** Definition of the dimension, state, variables, and parameters of a system 9
Fig. 1.3 Open system and its environment 10
Fig. 1.4 **a** General negative feedback system. The system is often called an agent. **b** System identification problem as a feedback loop. The switch is closed after the first experiment has been done and the preliminary model has been identified 11
Fig. 1.5 Kolb's experiential learning cycle. This is how we learn. Reduction or orientation is expressed with a magnifier 13
Fig. 1.6 Analytical research method. This is how we discover new knowledge 14
Fig. 1.7 Simplified research process as a combination analysis and synthesis using a V-model 15
Fig. 1.8 Research process as a combination of reduction, experimental-abductive method, and hypothetico-deductive method 15
Fig. 2.1 From criteria of science and papers to structure of publications 24
Fig. 2.2 Structure of science 25
Fig. 2.3 Structure of science, an alternative version 26
Fig. 2.4 General overview of research 27
Fig. 2.5 Research process 29
Fig. 2.6 Structure of a research project 30
Fig. 2.7 Hierarchy of publications 34
Fig. 2.8 Tools and databases for information retrieval 41
Fig. 2.9 Iterative use of references and citations presented as a simple citation graph 43

Fig. 2.10 Conceptual threads, breaks, and intersections. Independent threads are numbered ... 44
Fig. 2.11 Usage frequency of the term "multi-agent systems" in books from 1980 to 2019 showing a typical "hype cycle" (Google Books Ngram Viewer from the corpus English 2019 with smoothing of 3). The unit on the y-axis is 0.0000001%. For example, 20,000 means 0.002% ... 45
Fig. 2.12 Outlining a literature review ... 47
Fig. 2.13 Hourglass model of a paper ... 48
Fig. 2.14 General structure of a paper ... 50
Fig. 2.15 Definition of uncertainty, coverage interval, and coverage probability ... 53
Fig. 2.16 Comparison of trueness, precision, and accuracy with respect to a reference value in the center ... 54
Fig. 2.17 Relationship of two journal papers (left) and a conference and journal paper (right). The percentages refer to overlapping material and additional material, respectively ... 59
Fig. 2.18 A conference calendar for five conferences (C1–C5) ... 63
Fig. 2.19 The form of a typical citation histogram versus citation age in years ... 64
Fig. 3.1 Methodological approaches and research methods ... 82
Fig. 3.2 Comparison of analytical and systems thinking. Dashed arrows refer to weak or linear relationships. Solid arrows refer to nonlinear relationships ... 83
Fig. 3.3 Conflict between professors and students ... 87
Fig. 3.4 We must do vertical integrative learning (within a discipline) and horizontal integrative learning (phenomena between disciplines) in this order since there is nothing to integrate otherwise ... 88
Fig. 3.5 The complementary roles of organization and researcher ... 91
Fig. 3.6 Semiotic triangle ... 103
Fig. 3.7 Types of inference. Induction and abduction correspond to synthesis, and deduction corresponds to analysis ... 105
Fig. 3.8 Relationship of premises and conclusions in induction, abduction, and deduction ... 105
Fig. 3.9 Theoretical and experimental results (l and T are two parameters in the system) ... 105
Fig. 3.10 Strong inference simulates abduction ... 106
Fig. 3.11 Comparison of axiomatic systems and model-based theories ... 109
Fig. 3.12 Hilbertian axiomatic system and hypothetico-deductive system ... 109
Fig. 3.13 Relationship of the IMRDC structure and a model-based theory ... 111
Fig. 3.14 Classification of theories and models ... 111
Fig. 3.15 A concrete whole with its parts and properties ... 113

Fig. 3.16 Forms of causality. Modern science accepts only forward causality based on the efficient cause. Forward causality may also proceed upward or downward 113
Fig. 3.17 Observations and theories in epistemological reduction 116
Fig. 3.18 An example of epistemological reduction 117
Fig. 3.19 From problem to solution or hypothesis 119
Fig. 3.20 Iterative improvement in research 120
Fig. 3.21 Verification by hypothetico-deductive method. In science, the prototype is an object in the reality 121
Fig. 3.22 A system with one dependent variable and several independent variables 122
Fig. 3.23 **a** System identification problem. Difference of verification in **b** science and **c** engineering. In validation, requirements are replaced by user needs in the real world. The figure shows the use of feedback in the hypothetico-deductive method 124
Fig. 3.24 Complex exponential as an example of complex signals 127
Fig. 4.1 Limitations of analysis 138
Fig. 4.2 Different approaches to scientific work 140
Fig. 4.3 V-model for system design 147
Fig. 4.4 Isolated, closed, and open systems 148
Fig. 4.5 Classification of open systems according to the main flow 149
Fig. 4.6 Ecosystem and sociotechnical system and the related sciences and technologies 155
Fig. 4.7 Tripartite structure of the human mind 174
Fig. 4.8 Hierarchy of needs 180
Fig. 4.9 Social dilemma in nature. Fitness does not lead to maximal energy efficiency 188
Fig. 4.10 Double dichotomy in Zeeman's geometrical model of ideologies 195
Fig. 5.1 Basic resources 230
Fig. 5.2 Basic resources in an open system 231
Fig. 5.3 Information and energy flows through a system 235
Fig. 5.4 Difference of latency, transmission delay, and transfer delay in one-way transmission 239
Fig. 5.5 Basic system archetypes 260
Fig. 5.6 **a** Closed loop feedback control. **b** Model of the environment 261
Fig. 5.7 Delay in a feedback loop 262
Fig. 5.8 Different forms of control and adaptation 262
Fig. 5.9 Different forms of hierarchies 263
Fig. 5.10 Pareto optimality and satisficing principle 290
Fig. 5.11 A Venn diagram of computing problems that are solvable in principle. NP problems include P, NP-intermediate, and NP-complete problems 307

Fig. 5.12 Relationship of the sense-decide-act loop and the observe-model-verify learning and research process that produces a model of the environment 313
Fig. 5.13 Feedback amplifier 315
Fig. 5.14 Degrees of centralization 318
Fig. 6.1 Double feedback leading to self-organization and ultrastability 384

List of Tables

Table 2.1	Locations of publications	35
Table 2.2	Scientific societies related to interdisciplinary systems view	38
Table 2.3	Scientific societies and organizations related to the information concept	39
Table 2.4	Commercial publishers in engineering	40
Table 2.5	General IMRDC structure of a paper	49
Table 2.6	Coverage probabilities of normal distribution	53
Table 2.7	Valuable tools for research	59
Table 3.1	Summary of societal and scientific values	102
Table 4.1	Hierarchy of models	144
Table 4.2	Hierarchy of some natural and social sciences and humanities	156
Table 4.3	Information, feedback, and self-organization in natural and social sciences	157
Table 4.4	Some great theories in natural sciences	160
Table 4.5	Ethical values and norms to provide overall satisfaction and happiness in our society	181
Table 4.6	Stages of moral development	183
Table 4.7	Some great theories in economics	189
Table 4.8	Layers and their tasks in the OSI model	211
Table 5.1	Levels of information	236
Table 5.2	Measurement scales	244
Table 5.3	Fundamental limits	246
Table 5.4	Practical limits	247
Table 5.5	Fundamental principles	247
Table 5.6	Paradoxes described in this book	254
Table 5.7	Other major paradoxes of interest	255
Table 5.8	Performance metrics for different basic resources	258
Table 5.9	Description levels of a system	265

Table 5.10	Gajski's hierarchy for the physical level in a simplified form	266
Table 5.11	Different types of systems and their changes	267
Table 5.12	Properties of hierarchical systems	268
Table 5.13	Hierarchical control in robotics and communications	269
Table 5.14	Hierarchy of everything	271
Table 5.15	Boulding's hierarchy of complexity	272
Table 5.16	Hierarchies of natural and technical systems	272
Table 5.17	Alternative terminology for technical systems	273
Table 5.18	Hierarchy of technical systems	274
Table 5.19	Principles of self-organizing systems	277
Table 5.20	Some great theories in systems thinking	281
Table 5.21	Three forms of the second law of thermodynamics	285
Table 5.22	Traditional optimization methods	292
Table 5.23	Different optimization criteria	294
Table 5.24	Classification of problems based on their difficulty	307
Table 5.25	System archetypes	312
Table 5.26	Degrees of centralization	319
Table 6.1	History of scientific societies and publishing	342
Table 6.2	History of major sources for information retrieval	343
Table 6.3	Science in the antiquity and Middle Ages	355
Table 6.4	Science leading to the scientific revolution	358
Table 6.5	Development of systems thinking	380
Table 6.6	Feedback concept in the history of science and technology	398
Table 6.7	Self-organization in the history of science and technology	407

Chapter 1
Introduction

Learn to walk before you can run. Proverb
I am the wisest man alive, for I know one thing, and that is that I know nothing. Socrates (c. 470–399 BCE)
New frameworks are like climbing a mountain – the larger view encompasses rather than rejects the more restricted view. Albert Einstein (1879–1955)
For the best is only bought at the cost of great pain. Colleen McCullough (1937–2015)
Your work is going to fill a large part of your life, and the only way to be truly satisfied is to do what you believe is great work. And the only way to do great work is to love what you do. Steve Jobs (1955–2011)

Abstract Systems thinking is complementary to conventional analytical thinking. In systems thinking, we see the world as a set of interacting systems. Often, a system is complex and includes emergent properties for which we do not have theories. Emergence is a joint result of nonlinearity and feedback. The goal of all science is the unity of knowledge, which we can approach using interdisciplinary research. In the systems thinking, we must use well-tested system models, called system archetypes, that are useful in many disciplines. Most systems are open systems, not isolated. One crucial system archetype is feedback, which we use in learning and research. The feedback loop needs a goal to be stable. In learning and research that goal is the real world with a limited scope. Education and research aim to form an accurate picture of the world through a theory or a model.

1.1 Managing Complexity in an Innovative and Sustainable World

In the book (Strathern 2002), the author describes vividly the moment when Dmitri Mendeleev (also spelled as Mendeleyev) discovered the periodic table of elements in 1869:

A. Mämmelä, *Unifying Systems*, https://doi.org/10.1007/978-3-031-85012-7_1

"Mendeleyev returned to his desk and began searching amongst the drawers. Eventually he pulled out a pile of white cards.... One by one Mendeleyev began writing on the blank white surfaces of the cards. First, he printed the chemical symbol of an element, then its atomic weight and finally a short list of its characteristic properties. When he had filled sixty-three cards, he spread them out face upwards over the desk. As Mendeleyev's eyes ran once more along the line of ascending atomic weights, he suddenly noticed something that quickened his pulse. Certain similar properties seemed to repeat in the elements, at what appeared to be regular numerical intervals.... Mendeleyev soon became convinced that he was on the brink of a major breakthrough. There was a definite pattern there somewhere, but he just couldn't grasp it... Momentarily overcome by exhaustion, Mendeleyev leaned forward, resting his haggy head on his arms. Almost immediately he fell asleep.... In Mendeleyev's own words: 'In saw in a dream a table, where all the elements fell into place as required. Awakening, I immediately wrote it down on a piece of paper.' In his dream, Mendeleyev had realized that when the elements were listed in order of their atomic weights, their properties repeated in a series of periodic intervals. For this reason, he named his discovery the periodic table of the elements."

Mendeleev published the result two weeks later in his historic paper "A suggested system of the elements." He was thus essentially doing a jigsaw puzzle, and after he found the solution, he saw the big picture and could even predict what pieces (i.e., cards) were missing and what the properties of the missing elements were. For example, he predicted the existence and properties of gallium (Ga), which is between aluminum (Al) and indium (In). He also predicted germanium (Ge), which is between silicon (Si) and tin (Sn). Researchers found gallium and germanium in 1875 and 1886, respectively, and they verified Mendeleev's discovery. Modern chemistry was born with an integrating concept.

Mendeleev's discovery includes the idea of systems thinking: to piece together the jigsaw. The pieces are the existing results of the discipline or many disciplines. First, we must study the pieces before collecting them to form the whole picture. Thus, conventional analytical and more recent systems views complement each other: we must first have the pieces, after which we can do the jigsaw puzzle.

Independent discoveries often happen: the idea is in the air since the necessary information is available for many for the first time. In 1870, Julius Lothar von Meyer independently discovered the same table, but he could not explain its irregularities. Neither Mendeleev nor Meyer were the first to propose a periodic law (Rothman 2003). In 1866, John Newlands was the first one, but his table had some things that needed fixing since he left no room for new elements. Mendeleev admitted that he had seen Newlands' work.

Researchers added noble gases to the table in 1900 (Hudson 1992). Finally, in 1913, Henry Mosley noticed that the order of the elements should be determined by the atomic number (number of protons), not by the atomic weight. For example, cobalt (Co) and nickel (Ni) do not follow the order of atomic weights in the final version of the table. The example shows how research is often a staggering process. The table inspired Murray Gell-Mann, who discovered the classification of elementary particles. Mendeleev's result was thus fruitful.

Systems thinking is philosophical thinking that is a product mainly of the last century (Kline 1995; Ramage and Shipp 2020). Depending on the goal, we must focus systems thinking on solving complex problems or finding the unity of all science. Our goal is to fight against the fragmentation of science, which is a natural result of the need to have a narrow focus on deep research since, otherwise, the amount of literature to be managed would be overwhelming. The literature has increased exponentially since 1665 after the first scientific journal was established (Fernandez-Cano et al. 2004; Bloom et al. 2020). We expect saturation because the number of researchers is finite and must be well below the world population expected to saturate during the latter half of this century. After this, new knowledge will probably increase linearly since each researcher can produce only a finite number of papers each year.

Disciplinary and interdisciplinary work The terminology involving many disciplines has been discussed recently in social sciences, but there are different opinions about the definitions (Nicolescu 2002; Hirsch Hadorn et al. 2008). In 1970, the OECD organized a seminar on interdisciplinarity in Nice, France (Klein 1990, p. 43). Since then, some uninformed people have regarded interdisciplinarity as "Nice nonsense." We initially use the terms disciplinarity and interdisciplinarity, which are opposites; see Fig. 1.1. Later in Chap. 4, we explain the different interpretations of the terms multi-, inter-, and transdisciplinarity. We need disciplinary work since the efficiency of our society is based on the division of work by specialization because our problems are complex. In each discipline, the amount of literature is enormous and exponentially increasing, and it is essential to have some focus. Thus, there is a need to work strictly within one's discipline, which is why we call it disciplinary work.

Research groups should be relatively static and organized according to the disciplines such as electronics and control, computer, and communications engineering. Often, we need a more detailed subdivision. In this way, the group continuously develops its expertise, and the researchers get the necessary support from their superiors and colleagues in the same group. Such a group can sometimes continue as an organizational unit for many years. Hot topics come and go, but the group continues its

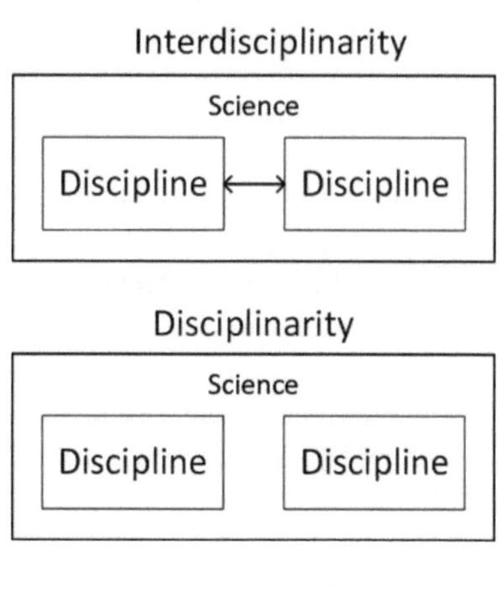

Fig. 1.1 Research involving many disciplines

work and considers the environmental changes regarding topics. Hot topics are relevant focus areas that are useful for getting motivation for the researchers' work, especially for young researchers. Focusing on hot topics is also mandatory since funding organizations appreciate hot topics. We do interdisciplinary work most naturally in project teams, which we form from many groups for each project.

In disciplinary work, disciplines work mainly separately without much interaction. Disciplinary projects are *problem-oriented* (Klein 1990). If many disciplines are involved in a project, the product can be, for example, an edited book or encyclopedia, which often lack a common thread and unified terminology and symbols.

Creativity needs a dynamic situation, which we obtain through interdisciplinary projects whose length is typically only 1–4 years. Interdisciplinary projects are *mission-oriented* although also problem-oriented research is included. Interdisciplinary work can have two different goals. The first goal is to solve a complex problem using experts from many disciplines (Repko and Szostak 2021) and produce a unified solution, for example, in an authored report or book. Interdisciplinary work is more demanding than the disciplinary work for an edited book. Another goal for interdisciplinarity is to produce a unified view of science (Nicolescu 2002). Unification is the fundamental goal of all science, and its best results form our standard general education, which makes our research work more efficient and effective. An important part is the unified terminology we need for communications between disciplines. We can use systems thinking in both forms of interdisciplinarity. Systems thinking, in its most concrete form, produces system theories and generic structures, sometimes called system archetypes (Senge 2006; Meadows and Wright 2008).

In 1930, the author of Ortega y Gasset (1932) warned about overspecialization: we divide science into many disciplines that form compartments without knowing about each other. Encyclopedists interested in comprehensive information disappeared during the 1800s, and overspecialized people replaced them. The latter have called encyclopedists dilettantes. The author of Ortega y Gasset (1932) mentions that if we are not careful, knowledge of natural sciences such as physics may disappear in one generation, resulting in a recession.

One strength of educated people is the ability to conceptual analysis. Leonardo da Vinci has been a model of a Renaissance man. Gottfried Wilhelm Leibniz (1646–1716) is sometimes regarded as "the last scholar to achieve universal knowledge" (Boyer and Merzbach 1991). A recent example is Herbert Simon (1916–2001), who represented multidisciplinary creativity (Dasgupta 2003). He contributed to axiomatic foundations of physics, cognitive psychology, sociology, administrative theory, economics, econometrics, logic of scientific discovery, and artificial intelligence, and received a Nobel Prize in 1978 "for his pioneering research into the decision-making process within economic organizations."

In physics, prominent researchers were interested in philosophy until the times of Max Planck, Niels Bohr, Erwin Schrödinger, Werner Heisenberg, and Albert Einstein (Kragh 1999). After World War II, the interest in philosophy reduced. We have seen similar development in biology, where many accomplished scientists are narrow-minded, and many wise scholars are considered weak (Wilson 1998). Derek J. de Solla Price regarded exponential growth as a "disease of science" that retards the growth of stable science and produces narrow and less flexible specialists that have overdeveloped self-confidence so that they feel competent to comment on topics that they are not familiar with (Ortega y Gasset 1932; Fernandez-Cano et al. 2004).

Unity of science The fundamental goal of all science is unity of knowledge, but without specialists who analyze, there is nothing from which to form a synthesis and unify. Like Albert Einstein, one of the greatest physicists in history, we must be free to look into new directions by philosophical thinking and develop something completely new (Ortega y Gasset 1932). In our opinion, specialists (Nichols 2017) and generalists (Epstein 2019) can build our society, but there is some tension between them. Generalists are modern counterparts of "Renaissance men" (Klein 1990, p. 23) although according to Repko and Szostak (2021, p. 224), there are some generalists who believe that integration of knowledge between disciplines is not really possible.

To understand the world, we must know how researchers produced our knowledge about the world. Scientific knowledge differs from general information: it must fulfill specific criteria, and the research method must ideally combine experiments and analysis.

We briefly discuss the epistemology and cognitive psychology. Epistemology is a theory of knowledge that tells how we should think (Baron 2000), and cognitive psychology tells us how we actually think (Koslowski 1996).

Some valuable topics from epistemology include the following (Baron 2000): (1) how to gather and assess evidence, (2) how to make valid inferences, (3) how to use different forms of logic, (4) what it means to have justified beliefs, (5) differences between formal and informal reasoning, (6) common fallacies in informal reasoning, (7) meaning and ambiguity of natural language, and (8) how to make good decisions. Some of the topics in cognitive psychology include (Koslowski 1996): (1) reliability of our senses and memory, (2) where beliefs come from, (3) how beliefs affect our behavior, (4) biases and shortcuts in making decisions, (5) how we learn and share what we know, (6) how we think about complex things, (7) how we recognize patterns, (8) how we sort ideas and things into categories, and (9) how to notice differences between things. Some of these topics are helpful in learning and knowledge sharing, and thinking or reasoning about complex things.

According to Plato, knowledge is "justified true belief," but this definition also has been criticized. Justification is synonymous with confirmation and verification. Scientific knowledge is explicit (not implicit), public (open to everyone), reliable (stands the test of time), and objective (independent of the observer). The knowledge must be coherent and correspond to reality, but its truth value is unknown. It can be verified but not proved because of its generalizing or sweeping nature. This book includes a detailed description of each of the phases of the research process, including idea, problem definition, definition of the scope, gathering relevant data, especially from the literature, conceptual analysis, formulation of a tentative solution or hypothesis from the data, empirical testing of the hypothesis to guarantee reproducibility of the results, and finally writing a publication.

The reproducibility of results is a cornerstone of the scientific method. The philosophy of the scientific method is called *methodology* (von Wright 1971, p. 3) or method with rationale (Love 1972). The research process is highly iterative. Systems thinking is only possible with the knowledge of all the phases of analytical research. The exponentially growing knowledge in the literature is managed hierarchically by using books, review papers, vocabularies, chronologies, and annotated bibliographies. Writing is an essential part of promoting the systems view. Each chapter includes material for beginners and more advanced readers, but they should have some research experience since the material may look rather abstract. The systems view uses knowledge from philosophy and history. The systems thinking leads to shared goals and vision and thus enables cooperation and improves effectiveness.

In former times, people produced different dialects when they were isolated from each other because of geographical distances and lack of communication and transportation methods. For example, Italian, French, and Spanish are initially dialects of Latin. Later, people developed a standard language and grammar for each new language since they divided into more minor dialects. Knowledge of grammar is essential for learning a language properly. We can formulate understandable sentences if we know the grammar and the words. Science is not unified, but it has produced "dialects" used in similarly isolated disciplines because of the vast amount of knowledge.

The purpose of systems thinking is to make a common grammar and a standard language for all disciplines so that researchers can communicate and understand each other and use the best available knowledge developed during hundreds of years so that we do not need to reinvent everything, and the effectiveness and in fact also efficiency of our work is improved. We may call system theories and archetypes the grammar for systems thinkers. We can, therefore, successfully design complicated systems required in our age of limited natural resources, an age that can be called the *age of sustainability* (Swilling 2020). The fundamental reason for the limited resources is the exponential growth of the population, which we call population explosion, resulting in environmental pollution and climate change caused by the use fossil energy sources especially in developed countries. In the past, the climate also changed for natural reasons (Christian 2004, p. 132). A continuous problem is democracy crisis (Crozier et al. 1975; Stasavage 2020). If we do nothing, the result is a war on resources, mass migration of people from developing countries to developed countries with a cooler climate, and a natural disaster after which the Earth cannot offer living possibilities. We must see the Earth as a total system.

We need a hierarchical approach to manage all the information. The hierarchy consists of secondary sources such as books and review papers and primary sources such as original journal and conference papers whose best results move later upwards in the hierarchy. At the top of that hierarchy are books on interdisciplinary research and systems thinking. When we move upwards in the hierarchy, we pay for generality by sacrificing content (Boulding 1956). When we move downwards in the hierarchy, we pay for content by sacrificing meaning. Thus, we must find the optimal degree of generality for our purposes. The situation is better than it might look since although different disciplines work independently, they tend to converge to similar problems and concepts (von Bertalanffy 1950), although by using different terminology. By applying analogies and abstraction (Epstein 2019), we can use solutions from many disciplines as system archetypes (Senge 2006; Meadows and Wright 2008). There is a limited number of archetypes. For example, in social sciences, one solution to management in human organizations is subsidiarity (Evans and Zimmermann 2014), which is essentially the same as near decomposability in biology (Simon 1962) and a loosely or weakly coupled system in engineering (Pautasso and Wilde 2009; Mämmelä et al. 2023).

Presently, thousands of scientific papers are published every day. We need a compromise: university education should include mandatory courses on systems thinking (Riekki and Mämmelä 2021). Afterward, the researchers can focus on their discipline and better see other disciplines' results to avoid overlapping research. We need interdisciplinary systems thinking because of the following reasons (Klein 1990; ISSS 2022):

- We solve complex problems and address broad questions beyond a single discipline, especially for sustainable development.
- We apply the similarity of concepts, theories, and models to more than one discipline. We develop adequate theoretical models in areas that need them and eliminate the duplication of theoretical efforts in different disciplines. Often the theories are simplified using the systems thinking.
- We improve our creativity using metaphors, analogies, and abstractions and we understand the finiteness of human knowledge.
- We improve our visions by using system models, research problems, and hypotheses to facilitate cooperation toward shared goals.
- We promote the unity of science by improving communication among specialists, using unified terminology, and offering an ever-developing worldview.

Science aims to create a unified picture of the world. Systems thinking will grow in importance since it corresponds the final goal of science, and only interdisciplinarity can solve complex problems. Furthermore, we can support problem solution using system theories and system archetypes. Engineering can act as an integrating factor because of its concrete aims. Still, we need all disciplines to be successful.

Information technology To limit the scope of my book, it focuses on disciplines closely related to the information concept, usually called information and communication technologies (ICT). For brevity, we use the term information technology (IT) (Chandler and Munday 2011, p. 211), which implies the need for communication, computing, and control, especially in distributed systems. Electronics is also needed for implementation. We are in the tradition that followed Nyquist's control engineering (1932), Norbert Wiener's cybernetics (1948), John McCarthy's artificial intelligence (1956), Jay Forrester's (1958) system dynamics, and John Holland's complexity theory (1992).[1]

---

[1] To shorten the list of references, we have sometimes given only the author's name and the year of publication. You can often find the original reference from the reference provided.

Mechanical engineering has long traditions regarding dynamic systems using materials and energy (Hubka and Eder 1988; Pahl et al. 2007). We need materials and energy for information processing and transfer, but they are only among our secondary interests (Wiener 1961). Since the Institute of Electrical and Electronics Engineering (IEEE) is the largest society in information engineering, many examples especially regarding writing instructions are from that society.

In information technology, the information concept has become a central concept. A crucial related theory is decision theory. Wiener (1948) already combined communications and control (Wiener 1961). George N. Saridis defined the discipline of intelligent control as a combination of artificial intelligence (AI) (a form of computing), operations research (a form of decision theory), and control (Saridis 2001). Still, he neglected communication since his interest was in robotics, where he used centralized control. Now in robotics, we are also interested in distributed systems such as social robots. Autonomous control replaces the old term intelligent control (Fu 1971) as in Antsaklis et al. (1989).

Boulding defined several hierarchical levels of systems in the world, and at the top of them, he defined communication and evaluative systems (Boulding 1985), the latter of which we call decision-making systems. We conclude that decision theory is essential for us (Russell and Norvig 2022). All these often separate and fragmented theories (computing, communications, control, and decision theories) give ingredients to a general theory of systems, as we noticed (Mämmelä et al. 2018). They are all combined in modern robotics (Bekey 2005; Hegel et al. 2009).

Charles Francois argued that the commonly used term "general system theory" is a misnomer (Francois 2006), as it is used, for example, in the title of the book (von Bertalanffy 1971). It is a translation from the German *Allgemeine Systemlehre*, which should be translated as a general theory of systems since there is no "general system." We use the correct translation in this book.

This book is about something else than practical tools for system designers since the tools will soon become outdated. Instead, the book is about theoretical systems tools, and the books in each discipline present the deep theory. Our book acts as a glue between those books, making it easier to approach them after having some general orientation and motivation.

Definition of a system A simple example of a system is our solar system with the Sun, planets, and moons. The bodies have certain dynamically changing positions, and they are attracted to each other through gravity. The positions and the gravity define the relationships of the bodies that are the parts or subsystems of the system.

Ludwig von Bertalanffy, Arthur D. Hall, and Robert E. Fagen created early definitions of a system, initially in 1956 (Sillitto et al. 2018). James G. Miller slightly modified Bertalanffy's definition: "A system is a set of interacting units with relationships among them" (Miller 1973). A unique form of *relationship* is an *interaction* or *coupling* (Glassman 1973) where specific outputs of a subsystem are inputs to another subsystem (Hubka and Eder 1988). The connection can be in series or parallel between two systems, or it may use feedback from the output to the input of the same system. Coupling may be in the form of data or control information. More generally, exchanging materials, energy, or information causes the coupling.

The system's *boundary* divides the universe into two parts: in the first one is the system itself inside the boundary, and the second one is outside the system (Fig. 1.2a). The observer defines the boundary. The space around the system outside the boundary is called the *environment* and it can be another system or process that is controlled (Ogata 2010). The number of the parts in a system is called the *dimension* (Boulton et al. 2015, pp. 76–77; Bagnoli 2020). Each part has a state defined by the corresponding *variable* and each interaction between two parts is defined by the corresponding *parameter* (Fig. 1.2b). The system state is a combination of the states of all the parts, but if also the parameters change, they are also included in the state. The set of possible states are included in a multidimensional *state space*, and the consecutive states form a *trajectory* in the state space. Systems thinking starts from the idea of an open system, which interacts with its environment by exchanging matter, energy, and information (Hall 1962; Chestnut 1965); see Fig. 1.3.

The basic system principles or system archetypes include feedback control, optimization and decision-making, hierarchy and modularity, and degree of centralization (Mämmelä et al. 2018). Systems thinking is no rocket science, and feedback is perhaps the most challenging concept to understand since it is usually included only in engineering curricula. However, good books are available for researchers with various backgrounds (Richardson 1991; Meadows and Wright 2008; Ogata 2010; Dorf and Bishop 2017).

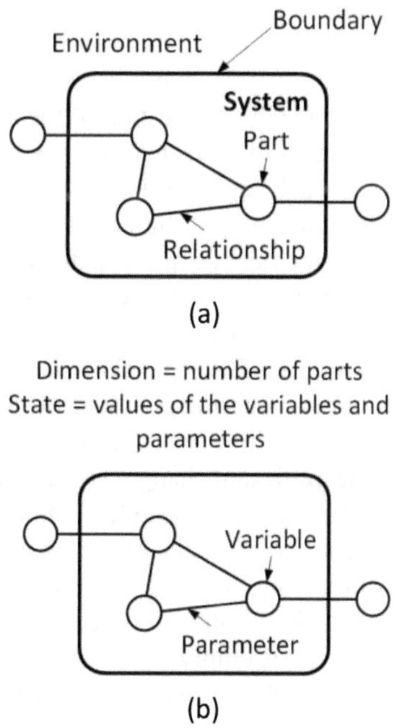

Fig. 1.2 **a** General definition of a system. **b** Definition of the dimension, state, variables, and parameters of a system

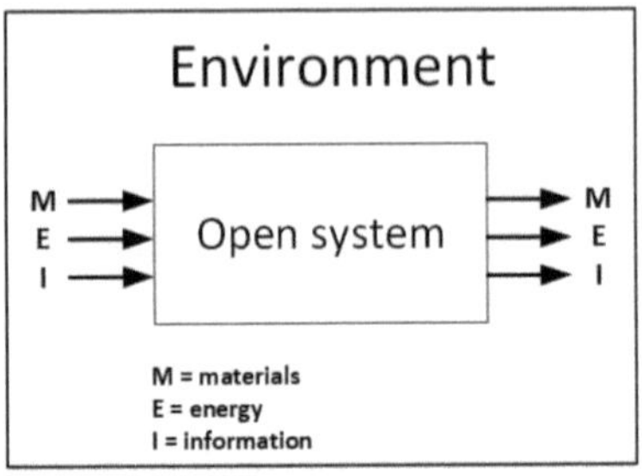

Fig. 1.3 Open system and its environment

Feedback control Intelligent and rational systems use the feedback concept (Stonier 1992, p. 97; 1997, p. 38). A simple example of feedback control is a thermostat controlling a heater (Mämmelä and Riekki 2022). A human defines the goal for the environment's targeted temperature. It is an externally given *set-point value*, more generally called the *reference input* or *reference signal* or simply the *goal* (Ogata 2010; Dorf and Bishop 2017). In metrology (JCGM 2012), the *error* is defined to be the difference between the sensed temperature and the set-point value. In practice, in feedback systems, we do the sign reversal in the adder, and the error is defined to be the difference between the set-point value and the sensed temperature; see examples in Fig. 1.4a and in Ogata (2010), Dorf and Bishop (2017), Widrow and Stearns (1985), and Haykin (2014).

The decision block is within the thermostat in this case. If the error is positive (the temperature of the environment it too low), the thermostat turns the heater on; otherwise, it turns the heater off. We call the method balancing, correcting, goal-directed, or negative feedback since the thermostat tries to reduce the error (Richardson 1991; Sterman 2000; Meadows and Wright 2008). More generally, in negative feedback, the sign of the sensed signal in the feedback is reversed, and the error is multiplied with a small gain so that the changes are slow (Gao 2014). We call the feedback negative since it reduces the error. Otherwise, there is nothing harmful in the concept, just the opposite. Similarly, in a car's cruise control, the set-point value is the desired speed defined by the driver. Negative feedback is known to be stable unless it does not act too fast especially when there are long delays in the loop.

Another slightly more complicated example of the use of feedback is driving a car (Dorf and Bishop 2017). We observe the environment mainly with our senses of sight and hearing and control the car with our hands and legs using the steering wheel, gear shift, brake, accelerator, and clutch in older cars. We observe the road and the traffic and change our behavior accordingly. For example, if the vehicle drifts from the middle of the lane to the edge of the lane, we make a correction: we turn the car back to the middle of the lane using the steering wheel. The middle of the lane acts as a string of goals called a *reference trajectory* (Albus and Meystel 2001). We can also change the reference trajectory to the middle of a nearby lane and continue driving if it is empty.

In general, in *negative feedback*, we form an *error signal* so that we subtract the feedback signal (i.e., sensor output signal) from the reference input as in Fig. 1.4a,

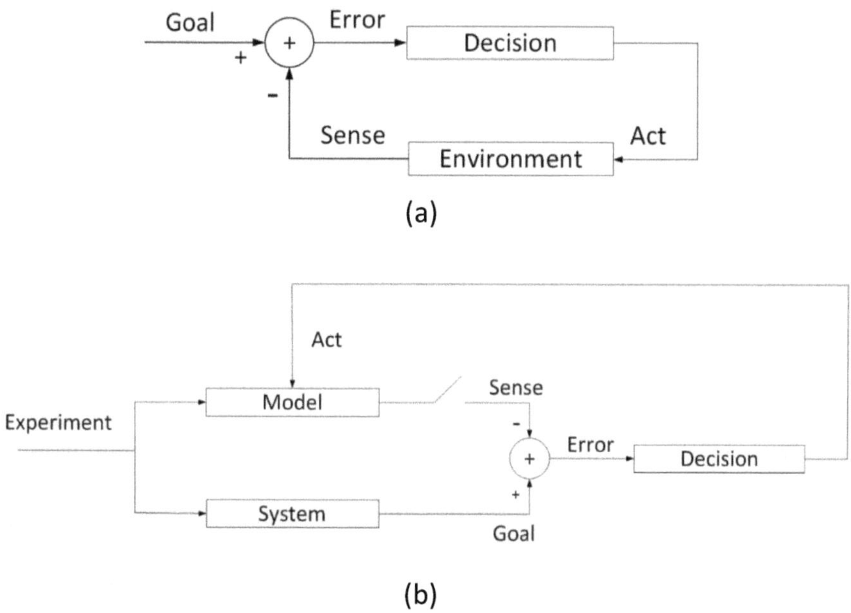

Fig. 1.4 **a** General negative feedback system. The system is often called an agent. **b** System identification problem as a feedback loop. The switch is closed after the first experiment has been done and the preliminary model has been identified

and in *positive feedback* we add the feedback signal to the reference input (Dorf and Bishop 2017). Alternatively, if we change the sign of the error signal in Fig. 1.4a, the negative feedback system would become a positive feedback system. The terms negative and positive feedback form a simplified classification, and in many cases, the classification cannot be used. In general, negative feedback is stable since the error signal is minimized, and positive feedback may be unstable since the feedback signal is amplified. A feedback loop is stable if it has a bounded output to a bounded input. The stability condition is called BIBO stability. Some systems containing positive feedback are stable and thus useful. Stability is more important than the type of the feedback (positive or negative).

The negative feedback minimizes deviations from a reference input or goal. Such feedback is a *goal-directed system* that generates actions to reduce the difference between the desired and actual states or maximize performance. In a time-invariant environment in its simplest form, it moves towards a steady state using exponential decay if the loop is stable (McFarland and Bösser 1993; Checkland 1999; Albus and Meystel 2001; Meadows and Wright 2008). Another form of feedback is positive or reinforcing feedback, which enhances or amplifies the direction of any change, thus potentially causing instability in the form of exponential growth (Meadows and Wright 2008). The positive feedback loop is helpful in some self-organizing systems, especially when used with a stabilizing negative feedback loop (Arbnor and Bjerke 1997).

The definition of a system in Miller (1973) is very general, and in practice, we must define the parts and relationships. Artificial intelligence and complexity theory gives a more specific definition based on agents (Holland 1995; Benbya and McKelvey 2006; Russell and Norvig 2022). Complex adaptive systems, also called multiagent systems, are made up of many interacting active elements that are called agents. *Agents* are systems that act (Online Etymology Dictionary 2024). They are in general *sense-decide-act feedback loops* having an externally given goal, as in Fig. 1.4a (Kline 1995, p. 188; Albus and Meystel 2001, pp. 6–7; Mämmelä et al. 2018; Russell and Norvig 2022). The minimum requirement for the feedback is that it has "the ability to sense the environment, to make decisions, and to control action" (Albus and Meystel 2001, pp. 6–7). A thermostat is a simple agent. We call such loops *closed-loop control loops* (Ogata 2010). The feedback control has two benefits: it is accurate and slow environmental changes can be tracked, but it can also become unstable.

We can also use *open-loop control loops* that do not include any sense block, by definition. Open-loop control loops are also agents although not so advanced as the closed-loop control loops. A minimum requirement is that an agent has the decision and act blocks, but not necessarily a sense block.

In the decision phase, we must be aware of what is happening in the environment so that the decisions are reliable enough (Endsley 1995). If the decisions in the feedback loop are made by humans, we use the term "human in the loop" (Nunes 2015). A purpose of *situation awareness* is to illustrate to humans what the situation in the complex environment is. In systems thinking, we are interested in the situation worldwide, and we do this using a system model that describes the regularities at least in some part of the world.

In control engineering, the goal is a set-point value or reference signal, the decision-making device is a *controller*, and the environment is a *plant* or *process* to be controlled (Ogata 2010). For example, human agents have organs for their five senses (eyes for sight, ears for hearing, skin for touch, nose for smell, and tongue for taste) to observe the environment and some actuators (hands, legs, and vocal tract) to control the environment (Russell and Norvig 2022). An agent senses the environment with its sensors, decides on its following action, and implements it with its actuators. The actions aim to guide the environment to a desirable or better state with an improved performance, which may be satisfactory or optimal.

Learning and research are essentially system modeling problems that are also called *system identification* (Eykhoff 1960; Widrow and Stearns 1985), see Fig. 1.4b. We have in our brain a model of the world (Albus and Meystel 2001). Science can be seen a systematic way to improve the model of the world. Now the goal is to identify the model of the environment that we call an unknown system. The model corresponds to our theory of the system. We make an experiment by sending a test signal through the real system and then we decide what the model could be. Next, we make another experiment with the switch closed, and we improve the model so that the error is minimized. The goal is the output of the system, and the sensing signal is the output of the model. In its general form, the decision-making is a very demanding, highly nonlinear process, but it is much simplified if the system is linear. In that case the identification simplifies to parameter estimation of the parameters of the model that we can find with a simple algorithm essentially based on averaging since the measurements always include some noise, i.e., randomness (Makhoul 1975). It would be too demanding to make a model of the whole world and we need some focus. We identify only a small part of the world, but the fundamental aim is to identify the whole world. So far, we have only partial models, sometimes even mutually incompatible.

Research as a learning process As mentioned in the preface, we can use the complementary analytical and systems view of the world. Research is an advanced learning process. We present David Kolb's (1984) experiential learning in Fig. 1.5. We have drawn Kolb's original cycle (Miettinen 2000) upside down to make the terms top-down and bottom-up reasonable and to show more clearly the similarity of learning and research. Experiments are at the bottom, and generalizations are at the top. Learning has five stages (Ramage and Shipp 2020). At first, we need *reduction* (Stage 1), which we have added externally to the loop and implies focusing on the exciting part of reality since we cannot grasp the whole world simultaneously. A magnifier refers to reduction that limits our scope. In some learning loops, reduction is called *orientation* as in the observe, orient, decide, and act (OODA) loop (Osinga 2005). After concrete experiments and observations (Stage 2), we use *reflective thinking* (Stage 3), which is "careful thought about something, sometimes over a long period of time" (Oxford Learner's Dictionaries 2024). Next, we form abstract concepts and generalizations (Stage 4) and test the implications of concepts in new situations (Stage 5).

Analytical and systems thinking We present a general diagram of the analytical research method in Fig. 1.6, where the reality is at the bottom, and the theory is at the top. Reality is also called the real world, the opposite of the theoretical world. The theory is initially unknown, and a tentative theory is called a hypothesis. The descriptions and figures in Honderich (2005), Felder and Silverman (1988) and Matheson (2015) inspired us. In Matheson (2015), the figure is upside down in a simplified form, whereas our figure is hierarchical so that the abstract concepts are at the top and concrete things are at the bottom (Honderich 2005, p. 668). Figure 1.6 resembles Kolb's experiential learning in Fig. 1.5 (Ramage and Shipp 2020, p. 262) and includes

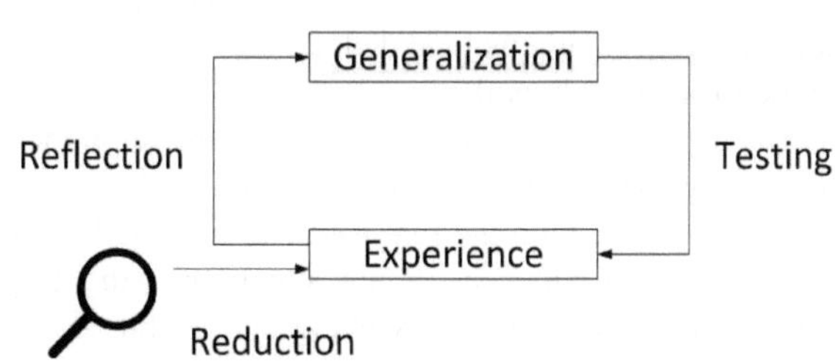

Fig. 1.5 Kolb's experiential learning cycle. This is how we learn. Reduction or orientation is expressed with a magnifier

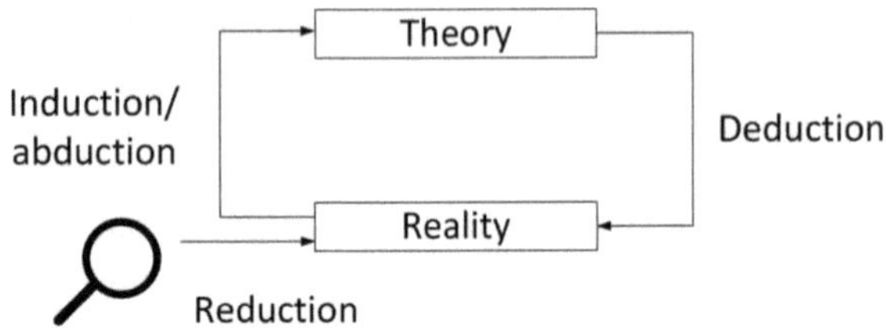

Fig. 1.6 Analytical research method. This is how we discover new knowledge

the idea of feedback in Fig. 1.4b since we improve the theory after comparing it with reality. In learning and research, the goal is to model reality, and no other goal is needed just as in system modeling where our goal is to model of the unknown system (Widrow and Stearns 1985, p. 10).

An example of a theory is a map that is a model of a geographical area. The reality is better known to us; therefore, it is our starting point. A theory such as the map is only an approximation of reality, as explained, for example, in Slepian (1976). We use various forms of inference. Just like learning, research has five stages. We cannot start by studying all the world's phenomena, and therefore, we first must divide the problem by reduction into a manageable set of more minor problems (Stage 1). Stage 1 is the first analytical step we have, limiting the scope.

In *induction*, we infer one possible hypothesis that explains the experiments. The hypothesis may be the best possible but usually not. *Abduction* is "inference to the best explanation" (Honderich 2005). The *deduction* is an inference that preserves the truth. Abduction and deduction are opposites. We move upwards by induction and abduction, corresponding synthesis, and downwards by deduction, corresponding to analysis. We generalize by induction or abduction after doing experiments and observations (Stage 2). We call the generalization the *experimental-abductive method* (Stage 3), usually called the *experimental-inductive method*, since we carry out experiments first and induction next. We also use abduction as a generalized form of induction. A *case study* is an example of the experimental-abductive method in social sciences. It is a natural approach to learning and research since we proceed from simple to more complex.

The process of induction and abduction, which is the process of forming hypotheses, can use reflection as in the learning cycle (Paavola 2015). More generally, it is the *method of the hypothesis* since there may also be other methods for hypothesis formation. The forming of the hypotheses corresponds to the decision regarding a suitable model in Fig. 1.4b after experiments. Engineering inventions do not come from mathematical deductions (Gao 2014) simply because inductions and abductions create hypotheses.

The hypothesis is a tentative theory or model of the part of the world in consideration (Stage 4). The hypothesis is verified by deriving deductively some new results that we compare with the real world (Stage 5). The only way to test a theory is to examine its consequences in new situations using a hypothetico-deductive method (Nola and Sankey 2007; Rosenberg and McIntyre 2020). This corresponds to the decision after the tentative model in Fig. 1.4b exists.

If the system has emergent properties, this conventional analytical view does not work since we do not have proper deductive tools to derive results from our hypothesis. Similarly, the inductive step may be misleading since there may be better hypotheses than we can imagine. The problem of finding the best possible hypothesis using induction is known to be the *problem of induction*, which is why science is always dependent on faith since we cannot prove the hypothesis, only verify it (Rosenberg and McIntyre 2020). Human reason cannot uncover everything we need to know, mainly because of the emergence. In *strong inference* (Platt 1964), to simulate abduction, we use many competing hypotheses found by intuition (Honderich 2005; Larson 2021), i.e., using our earlier experience in the form of analogies and instinct (Raami 2015). A minimum is that the explanation is the most plausible for the time being. Since we cannot, in practice, know the best explanation, research is evolutionary by its very nature, using Karl Popper's *falsifications*. Falsification or refutation means we cannot verify a theory; we can only falsify it (Deutsch 1997; Rosenberg and McIntyre 2020).

In summary, the research proceeds from analysis to synthesis and again to analysis (Fig. 1.7). Analysis and synthesis should follow each other. In practice, we start from reduction and then use induction or abduction, and finally deduction and compare the results with the experimental results and perhaps improve the hypothesis by abduction (Fig. 1.8). Thus, we combine an experimental-abductive method to form hypotheses and a hypothetico-deductive method to verify the hypothesis. In systems engineering, the model is called the V-model because of its shape (Calvez 1993; Ruparelia 2010). We first divide the problem in the real world into smaller pieces by reduction to have some focus; next, we form a hypothesis, theory, or model by induction or abduction; and finally, we generate some results deductively to compare them with the real world.

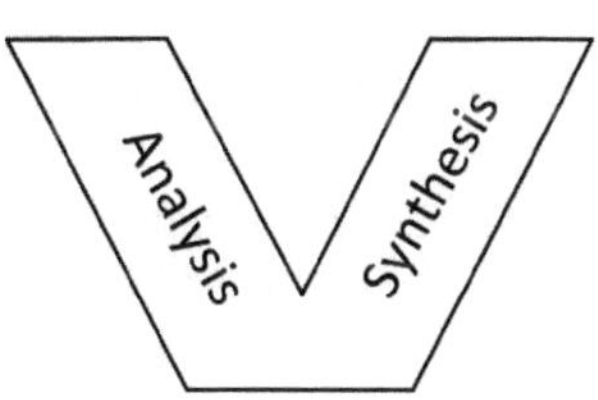

Fig. 1.7 Simplified research process as a combination analysis and synthesis using a V-model

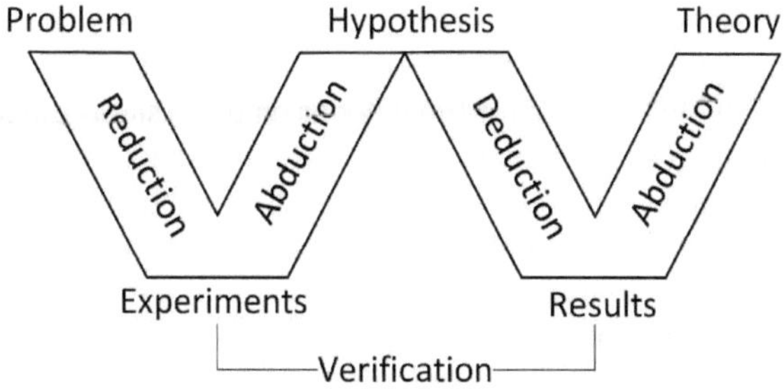

Fig. 1.8 Research process as a combination of reduction, experimental-abductive method, and hypothetico-deductive method

In the philosophy of science, the hypothetico-deductive method describes the whole research process, leaving the formation of hypotheses open. This method is the standard view of scientific reasoning. The results are derived deductively from the hypothesis and compared with experimental results. The crucial verification part is not explicitly mentioned in the method's name, but it is assumed to be included in the method.

1.2 Chapter Summary and Recommended Reading

In this chapter, we presented some motivation to use systems thinking to complement analytical thinking. Analytical thinking is disciplinary thinking, and systems thinking is interdisciplinary thinking. To limit our scope, our focus is on information technology. The systems view is thinking of wholes, which is necessary if the system is complex and, therefore, includes emergent properties for which we do not have theories. Emergence is a joint result of nonlinearity and feedback. Nonlinearity means that the system is neither homogeneous nor additive. In the systems thinking, we must use well-tested system theories and system models, called system archetypes, that are useful in many disciplines. The goal of all science is the unity of knowledge, which we can approach by using interdisciplinary research working towards unified solutions. We presented a general definition of a system. More specifically, we defined a complex adaptive system that consists of interacting agents. For that, we later find some deeper structure. Most systems are open systems that exchange materials, energy, and information with the environment.

One crucial system archetype is feedback, which we use in learning and research. The feedback loop needs a goal that may be a set-point value or reference signal, or reference trajectory. In negative feedback, we change the environment to minimize the error signal. For example, a thermostat changes the environment's temperature so that we approach the set-point value. In learning and research, the goal is to form an accurate picture of the environment through a theory or a model. Thus, the goal is the real world with which we compare our model or theory. First we must focus on something in that world using reduction. The research method combines the experimental-abductive method to create a hypothesis and a hypothetico-deductive method to verify the hypothesis and thus form a theory, usually as a model.

Many books on research methods are writing instructions, but research is much more than that. Most books on research methods present only the analytical thinking, but there are some essential books on the systems thinking. We can divide the books on the analytical thinking into those focusing on the philosophy of science and those focusing on actual research methods. Our book is somewhere between these books: it is more concrete than the philosophical books and more profound than the books on research methods. Furthermore, the books on research methods do not usually discuss the systems thinking.

Philosophy of science is also called theory of science. It studies the fundamentals of science, not only the research methods. A general and practical book is (Rosenberg and McIntyre 2020). It uses the thematic rather than the historical approach, but essential historical notes are also included. Regarding history, general books include (Losee 2001; Nola and Sankey 2007). Robert Nola and Howard Sankey focused on recent theories and emphasized that there really is a scientific method that scientists can benefit from. Imre Lakatos says, "most scientists tend to understand little more about science than fish about hydrodynamics."

We can find many accurate definitions of philosophical terms in the encyclopedia (Honderich 2005). An excellent introduction to research methods in engineering for undergraduate students is (Thiel 2014). More comprehensive books for post-graduate students are (Morawski 2019; Bock 2020). Regarding reliable terminology and definitions, readers would benefit from the views of philosophers of science (Honderich 2005; Rosenberg and McIntyre 2020). Since research is an advanced learning process, we recommend the paper (Felder and Silverman 1988) since it describes inductive and deductive learning. Usually, students learn inductively, but professors teach their theory deductively since they have forgotten how difficult learning is, creating an intellectual conflict between the students and professors.

There are many earlier books on systems thinking, but all have limitations and do not usually refer to each other. That is why it is so difficult to get an overview. We now present some of the most essential earlier books we found useful and reliable.

The broadest book so far is (Ramage and Shipp 2020), which classifies system theories and presents biographies of thirty systems thinkers with text samples. The book is an excellent overview covering information, feedback, and self-organization but the relationships of the actual system theories are not described. The authors write that most significant systems thinkers have either passed away or are very old. The subdisciplines include general theory of systems, cybernetics, system dynamics, soft and critical systems (including management science that we can generalize to social dynamics), complexity theory, and learning systems. The book only includes a limited amount of material about artificial intelligence, evolutionary methods, and systems engineering. We must combine the subdisciplines into a coherent unity.

If you want to gain motivation for systems thinking, we recommend the books (Wilson 1998; Epstein 2019). The authors claim that in the future, complex world, we need generalists or "synthesizers" (i.e., systems thinkers) who can manage the world that tends to be fragmented. Edward O. Wilson says: "We are drowning in information, while starving for wisdom. The world henceforth will be run by synthesizers, people able to put together the right information at the right time, think critically about it, and make important choices wisely" (Wilson 1998, p. 294). David Epstein says that generalists triumph in a specialized world. Using their broad understanding of history, generalists can see the future more clearly than specialists. The essential tool to see behind the borders of disciplines is to move upwards in abstraction and to use analogies since they form transferable knowledge. Learning is always slow, especially if you want to have complex skills. With narrow specialization, you can solve kind problems, but we must solve wicked problems by the breath of expertise, i.e., by interdisciplinary work. A modern detailed description of interdisciplinary thinking in social sciences is in the book (Repko and Szostak 2021). It focuses on social sciences, including suggestions on how to do interdisciplinary work and information retrieval in many disciplines. Books on interdisciplinary and systems thinking using the information concept include (Hall 1962; Kline 1995). More references are at the end of other chapters and in the bibliography at the end of the book.

Discussion Questions

1. What are the complementary benefits of analytical and systems thinking?
2. What are the alternative definitions of a system? How do we define a linear and an open system? What does emergence mean, and from where does it come?
3. Explain how a feedback system works. What is the purpose of the goal?
4. Explain the similarities and differences between learning and research.
5. Define reduction, induction, abduction, and deduction. How are the methods used in research?

References

Albus JS, Meystel AM (2001) Engineering of mind: an introduction to the science of intelligent systems. Wiley, New York

Antsaklis PJ et al (1989) Towards intelligent autonomous control systems: architecture and fundamental issues. J Intell Rob Syst 1(4):315–342

Arbnor I, Bjerke B (1997) Methodology for creating business knowledge, 2nd edn. Sage, London

Bagnoli F (2020) Interaction-based computing in physics. In: Sotomayor M et al (eds) Complex social and behavioral systems: game theory and agent-based models. Springer Science + Business Media, New York, pp 767–789

Baron J (2000) Thinking and deciding, 3rd edn. Cambridge University Press, Cambridge, UK

Bekey GA (2005) Autonomous robots: from biological inspiration to implementation and control. MIT Press, Cambridge, MA

Benbya H, McKelvey B (2006) Toward a complexity theory of information systems development. Inf Technol People 19(1):12–34

Bloom N et al (2020) Are ideas getting harder to find? Am Econ Rev 110(4):1104–1144

Bock P (2020) Getting it right: R&D methods for science and engineering, 2nd edn. Academic Press, San Diego, CA

Boulding KE (1956) General systems theory. Manage Sci 2(3):197–208

Boulding KE (1985) The world as a total system. Sage, Beverly Hills, CA

Boulton JG et al (2015) Embracing complexity: strategic perspectives for an age of turbulence. Oxford University Press, Oxford, UK

Boyer CB, Merzbach UC (1991) A history of mathematics, 2nd rev. Wiley, New York

Calvez JP (1993) Embedded real-time systems: a specification and design methodology. Wiley, Chichester, UK

Chandler D, Munday R (2011) A dictionary of media and communication. Oxford University Press, Oxford, UK

Checkland P (1999) Systems thinking, systems practice: includes a 30-year retrospective, rev. Wiley, Chichester, UK

Chestnut H (1965) Systems engineering tools. Wiley, New York

Christian D (2004) Maps of time: an introduction to big history. University of California Press, Berkeley, CA

Crozier M et al (1975) The crisis of democracy. New York University Press, New York

Dasgupta S (2003) Multidisciplinary creativity: the case of Herbert A. Simon. Cogn Sci 27(5):683–707
Deutsch D (1997) The fabric of reality. Penguin Books, London
Dorf RC, Bishop RH (2017) Modern control systems, 13th edn. Pearson, New York
Endsley MR (1995) Towards a theory of situation awareness in dynamic systems. Hum Factors 37(1):32–64
Epstein D (2019) Range: why generalists triumph in a specialized world. Riverhead Books, New York
Evans M, Zimmermann A (eds) (2014) Global perspectives on subsidiarity. Springer, Dordrecht, The Netherlands
Eykhoff P (1960) Adaptive and optimalizing control systems. IEEE Trans Autom Control 5(2):148–151
Felder RM, Silverman LK (1988) Learning and teaching styles in engineering education. Eng Educ 78(7):674–681
Fernandez-Cano A et al (2004) Reconsidering Price's model of scientific growth: an overview. Scientometrics 61(3):301–321
Francois C (2006) Transdisciplinary unified theory. Systems Research and Behavioral Science 23(5): 617-624
Fu K (1971) Learning control systems and intelligent control systems: an intersection of artificial intelligence and automatic control. IEEE Trans Autom Control AC 16(1):70–72
Gao Z (2014) Engineering cybernetics: 60 years in the making. Control Theory Technol 12(2):97–109
Glassman RB (1973) Persistence and loose coupling in living systems. Behav Sci 18(2):83–98
Hall AD (1962) A methodology for systems engineering. D. Van Nostrand Company, Princeton, NJ
Haykin S (2014) Adaptive filter theory, 5th edn. Prentice Hall, Upper Saddle River, NJ
Hegel F et al (2009) Understanding social robots. In: Proceedings of the 2009 second international conference on advances in computer-human interactions, Cancun, Mexico, pp 169–174
Hirsch Hadorn G et al (eds) (2008) Handbook of transdisciplinary research. Springer Science + Business Media, Dordrecht, The Netherlands
Holland JH (1995) Hidden order: how adaptation builds complexity. Perseus Books, Reading, MA
Honderich T (ed) (2005) Oxford companion to philosophy, 2nd edn. Oxford University Press, Oxford, UK
Hubka V, Eder WE (1988) Theory of technical systems: a total concept theory for engineering design. Springer-Verlag, Berlin
Hudson J (1992) The history of chemistry. Chapman & Hall, New York
ISSS (2022) About ISSS. International Society for the Systems Sciences. https://www.isss.org. Accessed 20 Jan 2022
JCGM (2012) International vocabulary of metrology—basic and general concepts and associated terms (VIM), 3rd edn. Joint Committee for Guides in Metrology (JCGM)
Klein JT (1990) Interdisciplinarity: history, theory, and practice. Wayne State University Press, Detroit, MI
Kline SJ (1995) Conceptual foundations of multidisciplinary thinking. Stanford University Press, Stanford, CA
Koslowski B (1996) Theory and evidence: the development of scientific reasoning. MIT Press, Cambridge, MA
Kragh H (1999) Quantum generations: a history of physics in the twentieth century. Princeton University Press, Princeton, NJ
Larson EJ (2021) The myth of artificial intelligence: why computers can't think the way we do. Belknap Press, Cambridge, MA
Losee J (2001) A historical introduction to the philosophy of science, 4th edn. Oxford University Press, Oxford, UK

Love SF (1972) A new methodology for the hierarchical grouping of related elements of a problem. IEEE Trans Syst Man Cybern SMC 2(1):23–29

Makhoul J (1975) Linear prediction: A tutorial review. Proceedings of the IEEE 63(4): 561-580

Mämmelä A, Riekki J (2022) Systems view in engineering research. In: Rezaei N (ed) Transdisciplinarity. Springer Nature Switzerland, Cham, Switzerland, pp 105–130

Mämmelä A et al (2018) Multidisciplinary and historical perspectives for developing intelligent and resource-efficient systems. IEEE Access 6:17464–17499

Mämmelä A et al. (2023) Loose coupling: An invisible thread in the history of technology. IEEE Access 11: 59456- 59482

Matheson D (ed) (2015) An introduction to the study of education, 4th edn. Routledge, New York

McFarland D, Bösser T (1993) Intelligent behavior in animals and robots. MIT Press, Cambridge, MA

Meadows DH, Wright D (eds) (2008) Thinking in systems: a primer. Chelsea Green Publishing, White River Junction, VT

Miettinen R (2000) The concept of experiential learning and John Dewey's theory of reflective thought and action. Int J Lifelong Educ 19(1):54–72

Miller JG (1973) Living systems. Q Rev Biol 48(2):63–91

Morawski RZ (2019) Technoscientific research: methodological and ethical aspects. Walter de Gruyter, Berlin

Nichols T (2017) The death of expertise: the campaign against established knowledge and why it matters. Oxford University Press, New York

Nicolescu B (2002) Manifesto of transdisciplinarity. State University of New York Press, Albany, NY

Nola R, Sankey H (2007) Theories of scientific method. Acumen, Stocksfield, UK

Nunes DS (2015) A survey on human-in-the-loop applications towards an internet of all. IEEE Commun Surv Tutor 17(2):944–965

Ogata K (2010) Modern control engineering, 5th edn. Prentice Hall, Boston, MA

Online Etymology Dictionary (2024) https://www.etymonline.com. Accessed 5 Nov 2024

Ortega y Gasset J (1932) The revolt of the masses. W. W. Norton & Company, New York

Osinga F (2005) Science, strategy and war: the strategic theory of John Boyd. Eburon Academic Publishers, Delft, The Netherlands

Paavola S (2015) Deweyan approaches to abduction. In: Zackariasson U (ed) Action, belief and inquiry: pragmatist perspectives on science, society and religion. Nordic Pragmatism Network, Helsinki, Finland

Pahl G et al. (2007) Engineering design: a systematic approach, 3rd edn. Springer-Verlag, London

Pautasso C, Wilde E (2009) Why is the web loosely coupled? A multi-faceted metric for service design. In: Proceedings of the 18th international conference on world wide web (WWW'09), Madrid, pp 911–920

Platt JR (1964) Strong inference: certain systematic methods of scientific thinking may produce much more rapid progress than others. Science 146(3642):347–353

Raami A (2015) Intuition unleashed: on the application and development of intuition in the creative process. Ph.D. dissertation, Aalto University, Espoo, Finland

Ramage M, Shipp K (2020) Systems thinkers, 2nd edn. Springer, London

Repko AF, Szostak R (2021) Interdisciplinary research: process and theory, 4th edn. Sage, Thousand Oaks, CA

Richardson GP (1991) Feedback thought in social science and system theory. University of Pennsylvania Press, Philadelphia, PA

Riekki J, Mämmelä A (2021) Research and education towards smart and sustainable world. IEEE Access 9:53156–53177

Rosenberg A, McIntyre L (2020) Philosophy of science: a contemporary introduction, 4th edn. Routledge, New York

Rothman T (2003) Everything's relative and other fables from science and technology. Wiley, Hoboken, NJ

Ruparelia NB (2010) Software development lifecycle models. ACM SIGSOFT Softw Eng Notes 35(3):8–13
Russell S, Norvig P (2022) Artificial intelligence: a modern approach, 3rd edn. Pearson Education, Harlow, UK
Saridis GN (2001) Hierarchically intelligent machines. World Scientific Publishing, Singapore
Senge P (2006) The fifth discipline: the art and practice of the learning organization, rev. Doubleday, New York
Sillitto H et al (2018) What do we mean by "system"?—System beliefs and worldviews in the INCOSE community. INCOSE Int Symp 28(1):1190–1206
Simon HA (1962) The architecture of complexity. Proc Am Philos Soc 106(6):467–482
Slepian D (1976) On bandwidth. Proc IEEE 64(3):292–300
Stasavage D (2020) The decline and rise of democracy: a global history from antiquity to today. Princeton University Press, Princeton, NJ
Sterman JD (2000) Business dynamics: systems thinking and modeling for a complex world. McGraw-Hill, Boston, MA
Stonier T (1992) Beyond information: the natural history of intelligence. Springer, Berlin
Stonier T (1997) Information and meaning: an evolutionary perspective. Springer, Berlin
Strathern P (2002) Mendeleyev's dream: the quest for the elements. Berkley Publishing, New York
Swilling M (2020) The age of sustainability: just transitions in a complex world. Routledge, New York
Thiel DV (2014) Research methods for engineers. Cambridge University Press, Cambridge, UK
von Bertalanffy L (1950) An outline of general system theory. Br J Philos Sci 1(2):134–165
von Bertalanffy L (1971), General system theory: Foundations, development, applications, rev. edn. George Braziller, New York
von Wright GH (1971) Explanation and understanding. Cornell University Press, Ithaca, NY
Widrow B, Stearns AD (1985) Adaptive signal processing. Prentice Hall, Englewood Cliffs, MA
Wiener N (1961) Cybernetics: or control and communication in the animal and the machine, 2nd edn. MIT Press, Cambridge, MA
Wilson EO (1998) Consilience: the unity of knowledge. Vintage Books, New York

Chapter 2
Scientific Research from an Idea to Publication

All truth passes through three stages. First, it is ridiculed. Second, it is violently opposed. Third, it is accepted as being self-evident. Arthur Schopenhauer (1788–1860)
In the field of observation, chance favors only the prepared mind. Louis Pasteur (1822–1895)
Genius is one percent inspiration and ninety-nine percent perspiration. Thomas Edison (1847–1931)
I have always imagined that Paradise will be a kind of library. Jorge Luis Borges (1899–1986)
We are the only species on the planet, so far as we know, to have invented a communal memory stored neither in our genes nor in our brains. The warehouse of that memory is called the library. Carl Sagan (1934–1996)

Abstract We present the research process and then focus on the beginning and end of the process, i.e., information retrieval and writing a scientific paper. We summarize the practical methods to find existing knowledge. We show the strength of using bibliographies, references, and citations in literature reviews to find landmark books and papers. It is essential to know the terminology and the area's history thoroughly. We must classify the material using taxonomies and show the hierarchical relationships. We describe a paper's introduction, materials and methods, results and discussion, and conclusion structure. We also discuss the various moves that describe the contents of each section of a paper. We emphasize the details of the materials and methods section, which standard writing instructions often overlook, especially regarding the system concept.

2.1 Introduction

Science is "organized knowledge of the physical or material world gained through observation and experimentation" (Random House Webster's College Dictionary 1999). Another definition is "a conscious and collective way of simplifying through generalizations" (Poundstone 1988, p. 20). Science is an extension and refinement of our shared knowledge. In a way, science is also an extension of our common sense. For

A. Mämmelä, *Unifying Systems*, https://doi.org/10.1007/978-3-031-85012-7_2

example, nothing in our experience suggests introducing complex numbers (Wigner 1960). A branch of knowledge within science is often called a *discipline*, and a specialization within a discipline is called a *field* or an *area*. In addition to a concrete goal ("ends"), we need to know the methods ("means") to attain that goal. The methods only do not guarantee objectivity, but research results are also dependent on a researcher's ethical behavior.

2.2 Research Process as a Whole

We present the criteria for scientific work and papers and the structure of publications in Fig. 2.1. The requirements for scientific theories include simplicity, coherence, correspondence with reality, generality, and fertility (Barbour 1974, 1997; Wilson 1998). *Simplicity* is parsimony or economy and symmetry of theories with a minimum number of assumptions. Sometimes, such theories are called beautiful. According to Occam's razor principle, the simplest theories that predict all the phenomena are the most elegant. *Coherence* includes external and internal coherence, which implies unity or consistency of theories, usually uses causal and deductive relationships, and avoids contradictions that cannot exist in the real world. *Correspondence* is the most important criterion in modern experimental science. It means agreement with reality. We cannot directly compare reality with our theories but use the hypothetico-deductive method. Correspondence implies that the results can be verified experimentally or by observations. We compare the results of the theory with those produced by the reality. Verification is needed since we make inductive generalizations, and experimental data always underdetermine the theories. We cannot prove a theory is correct; we can only falsify it (Rosenberg and McIntyre 2020). The results must be repeatable in the same laboratory and reproducible in an independent laboratory, after which we find a consensus. Reproducibility and falsifiability make the difference between science and pseudoscience.

Generality means that the theories are helpful in many places. They comprehensively describe general regularities using causal relations and unify previously

Criteria for science	Criteria for papers	Structure of a paper
Simplicity	Originality	Abstract
Coherence	Significance	Intoduction
Correspondence	Correctness	Materials and methods
Generality	Readability	Results and discussion
Fertility	Suitability	Conclusion

Fig. 2.1 From criteria of science and papers to structure of publications

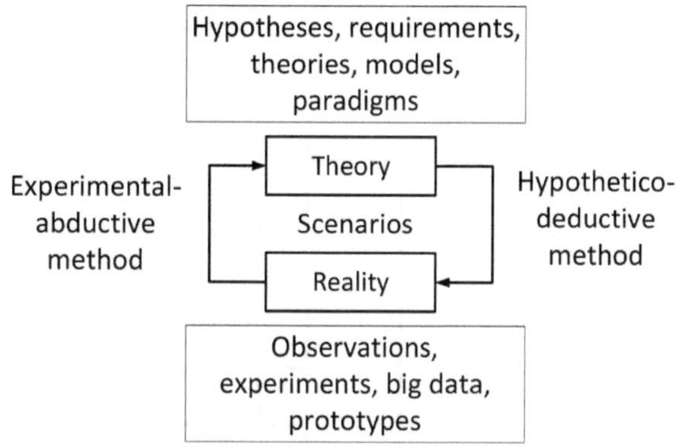

Fig. 2.2 Structure of science

separate theories. *Fertility* implies that a good theory predicts novel phenomena we did not previously anticipate, providing impressive support for a theory and leading to additional discoveries and inventions. We should separate discovery in pure science from invention in engineering. In *discovery*, we find something that already exists but was earlier hidden from us. In *invention*, we produce something that did not exist.

We show two versions of the structure of science in Figs. 2.2 and 2.3 (Barbour 1997, p. 107). Learning and research are carried out bottom up. We divide research into discovery and verification (Honderich 2005). An essential discovery method is the experimental-abductive method or, more generally, hypothesis formation. Abduction means inference to the best explanation, whereas induction means inference to some explanation that may sometimes be wrong or at least inaccurate. Consecutive falsifications lead to the continuous evolution of explanations. According to Boulton et al. (2015), induction is "a research method which starts with data, looks for patterns in those data, and derives a theory from explaining the patterns." A primary verification method is the hypothetico-deductive method. Deduction is a method of inference that preserves the truth.

Science, in general, is a complicated interaction between reality and theory. The reality is the physical or empirical world, and the theory represents the ideal or theoretical world. The reality is conceptually at the bottom, and the theory is conceptually at the top (Arbnor and Bjerke 1997, p. 92; Ransome 2010, p. 417; Riekki and Mämmelä 2021). We separate *theory* that is general and *practice* that is specific (Gao 2014). A theory makes the practice more scientific, rigorous, and systematic. A theory is a generalization from data generated by observations and experiments (Wilson 2013). Research is an advanced learning process that most naturally proceeds from the bottom up through inductive generalizations, although the results are verified and presented deductively from the top down. We use theories to intelligently manage the real world, as discussed by Francis Bacon (Pyenson and Sheets-Pyenson 1999).

A famous example of the need for theories is the Wasa ship, which sunk in 1628 during its maiden trip (West 2017). Scaling rules were nonlinear and unknown: to guarantee stability, the form of the ship had to be changed when the ship became

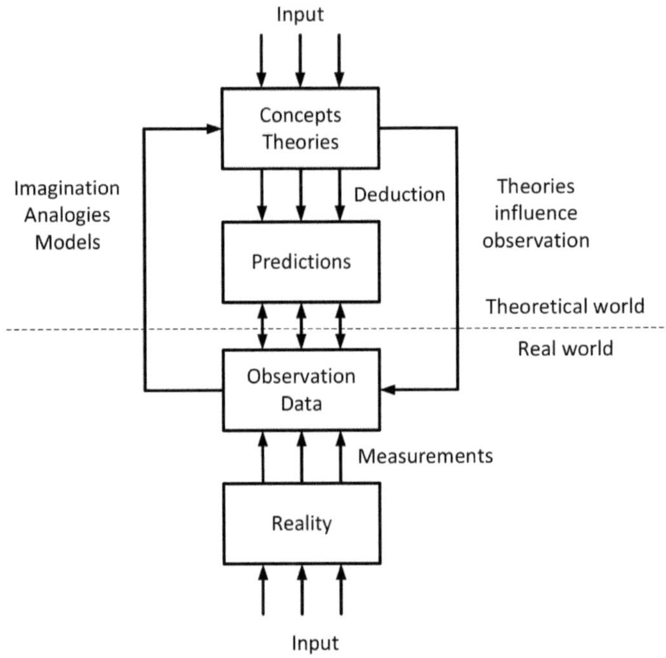

Fig. 2.3 Structure of science, an alternative version

larger. At that time, people used trial and error in shipbuilding, and the ship could be enlarged incrementally in 5% steps, but the king demanded that the Wasa ship be 30% longer than the previous ships, resulting in a failure. William Froude developed the nonlinear scaling theory for ships in 1861, over 230 years later.

In engineering, we need requirements for artifacts. Between reality and theory, we have *scenarios* whose purpose is to facilitate the specification of requirements in the theory (Jarke et al. 1998; Amyot and Eberlein 2003). In the real world, big data represents observations and experiments. Some people have treated the existence of big data as the end of science (West 2017). However, this will not happen. For example, people found the Higgs particle using big data in 2012. They used only a tiny part (0.00001%) of the data based on theory. The search was only possible with a theory guiding us where to look. Without a hypothesis, we cannot obtain theories or models using big data (Larson 2021).

The general goal of *research* is to discover new scientific knowledge (Jain and Triandis 1997). We do observations and experiments in the real world. The theory includes unverified hypotheses and models. Engineering differs from sciences in that in engineering we have functional and nonfunctional requirements describing human needs. We describe nonfunctional requirements with numerical values of specific performance metrics. In sciences, evolution that produced the organisms in nature has progressed to find the best fit for the environment. The survivability can be seen as a requirement in nature.

Fig. 2.4 General overview of research

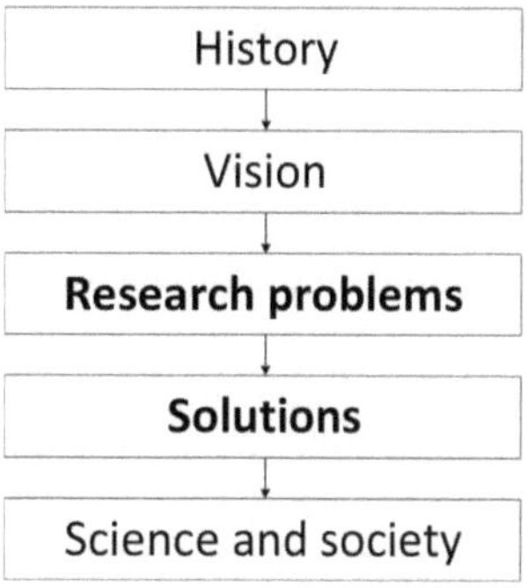

We conduct research to achieve scientific and societal impact, so publications are essential (Fig. 2.4). Research proceeds from a research problem to solutions. According to Larry Laudan (1977), science is a problem-solving activity (Losee 2001, p. 206). We divide problems into empirical and conceptual problems. We can find research problems using visions based on systems thinking. We need historical information for visions. In general, visions in science and engineering over more than a decade are inaccurate (Albus and Meystel 2001, p. 353). For example, in 1932, Albert Einstein thought there was no indication that nuclear energy would be attainable. However, the same year, James Chadwick discovered that neutrons are essential in atomic fission (Asimov 1994; Kragh 1999). In 1939, two chemists, Otto Hahn and Fritz Strassmann, and two physicists, Lise Meitner and Robert Frisch, discovered nuclear fission, but the Nobel Prize was given only to Hahn.

We must know more than ten years of history. Paul J. H. Schoemaker estimated that to make a scenario for the next ten years with a 90% confidence range, we must know the most significant events during the last 30 years (Schoemaker 2020). Stephen Hawking claimed that the time scale of the accumulation of scientific knowledge is 50 years (Hawking 2018). We recommend that visions be made for ten years and updated annually based on the newest information.

Research is essential because we can impact science and society by writing a scientific publication. The best results will finally move to textbooks and encyclopedias. Motivation is improved when researchers develop themselves for example through doctoral studies, and they can offer something to society, thus improving its well-being. In addition, there are many objective and subjective reasons for research:

- We discover new knowledge, technology uses science, and proprietary discoveries are possible (Hicks 1999).
- We gain prestige for ourselves and our employers through scientific papers, patents, research prototypes, and design documents. We join the techno-scientific community. Recruiting is made more accessible, and new customers are attracted.
- We learn the state of the art and can teach it to our colleagues and customers. We see the big picture (i.e., wood for the trees), which is only possible by researching since new concepts and paradigms may be challenging to understand and appreciate otherwise.

- We know the history, see the trends, and keep on the level of our competitors.

Research is exciting because of many reasons (Feynman 1999; Hicks 1999; Jain and Triandis 1997). One is intellectual pleasure: we learn to know something very deeply. The second is the thrill: we work like a detective to seek existing knowledge. The third is new knowledge: we discover something unknown earlier. We will become a doctor and an internationally known expert. The spirit of the scientific community is extraordinary: we have a research culture with the freedom to think, challenge, and criticize authorities, we can judge discoveries impersonally, and integrity or honesty is appreciated. The communication network is unique: we meet some of the most talented people in the world in our discipline.

There are also some not-so-exciting aspects of a researcher's work. The rewards are somewhat different in research to those available in industry since financial rewards are usually modest. Jobs exist only in certain places, and they may be temporary. The work responsibilities include the raising of funds. The quality of work is not straightforward to measure. For example, citations have many weak points. Research topics are sometimes relatively narrow. Guidance may be challenging to find. Not all people understand the value of criticism, which they may reject, although the goal is to improve the quality of the work.

We show a diagram of the research process in Fig. 2.5. Everything starts from an idea based on earlier experience that we define as a question. We form this research problem in engineering as a set of *objectives*. The task is to find an answer or solution to the question. We must also limit the scope so that the literature review is manageable. Next, the relevant data, also called materials, are collected. We present part of them in a literature review. We also do some experiments. Based on the data, we suggest a tentative solution to the problem. A tentative solution is also called a *hypothesis* in science and a *goal* in engineering. In mathematics, a hypothesis regarding a theorem is called a *conjecture*. Initially, the hypothesis is only a guess or hunch for a solution that needs to be verified.

Verification is the essence of any research in empirical or experimental sciences. There is no deductive method from the problem to the hypothesis. The hypothesis is verified through analysis, simulations, and experiments, often using a system model or prototype. The results are then generalized. Research is not finalized before we publish it in a scientific paper, either at a conference or in a journal. The research process is highly iterative. Therefore, one must move back to the original problem and refine all the process phases every now and then.

Rene Descartes summarized the four essential steps of the research process (Checkland 1999):

1. Avoid haste and bias and accept only clear ideas [conceptual analysis].
2. Divide all the problems into as many parts as possible and necessary to solve them best [reduction].
3. Progress from the simple to the complex [induction].
4. Use complete analysis without omitting anything [deduction].

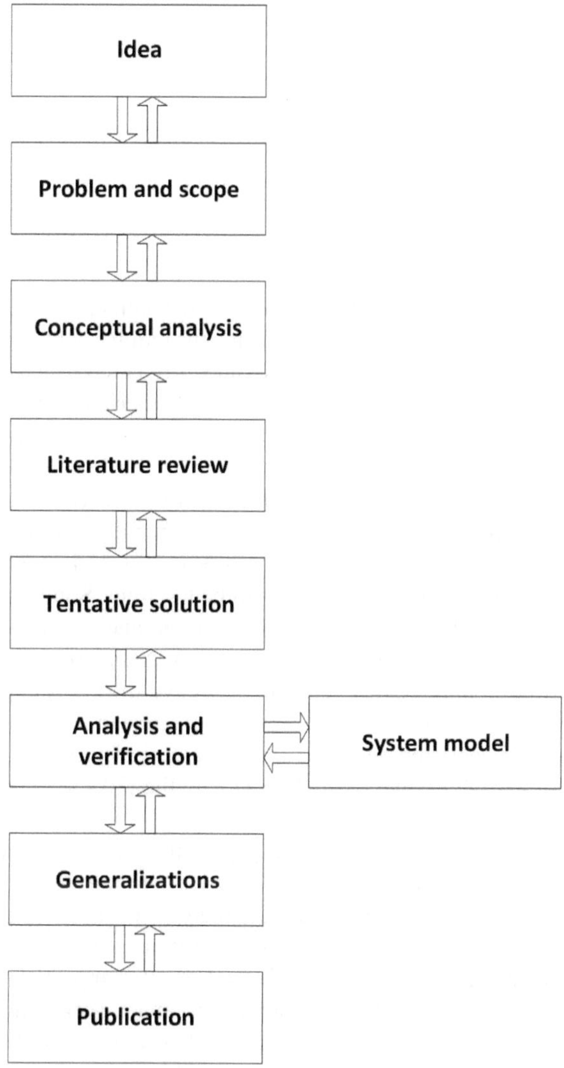

Fig. 2.5 Research process

This description clearly shows that the research should start with conceptual analysis and proceed toward reduction, induction, and deduction. Abduction was invented only in the 1800s. Descartes was a mathematician and did not include empirical verification by experiments and observations in his method. Rule 2 explains the success of the Western culture (Wilson 1998; Checkland 1999).

We present the general structure of a research project in Fig. 2.6. This forms the basis for a research plan, also called research proposal, which should include an overall although tentative solution to the problem, previous related work, research questions and hypotheses, expected research results, work plan, and scientific and

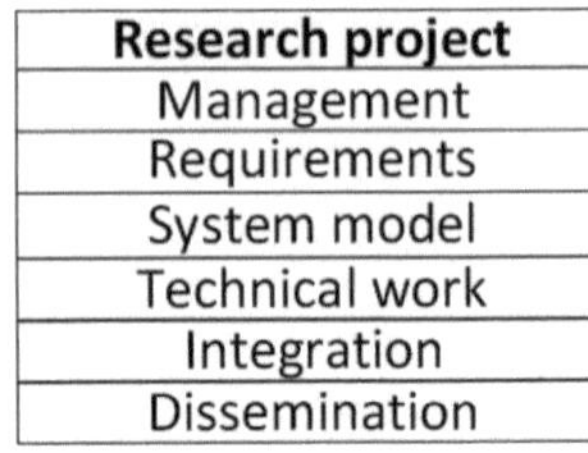

Fig. 2.6 Structure of a research project

societal impact. In addition to the core technical work, we must manage the project. We do technical management using the requirements and specifications of the system model. Defining some scenarios and use cases is usually easier approaches to requirements (Jarke et al. 1998; Amyot and Eberlein 2003). We integrate the results of the work using a demonstration. Usually, with a limited budget, it is impossible to demonstrate the whole system model, but the demonstration must be focused, perhaps divided into several demonstrations. Finally, we must disseminate the results with publications and standardization. Dissemination to the general public is also essential.

A typical length of a research project is 1–4 years, where one year tends to be too short and four years tends to be too long. Some flagship projects may continue for up to 10 years. Usually, there are annual or biannual reviews to check that the project is moving in the right direction. A drawback in the project system is that the proposal must be detailed, but in creative work it is impossible to predict how things evolve (de Bono 2014). A good research team consists of persons generating ideas and persons implementing them. Administrators rarely generate new ideas and are not willing to take risks. That is why the risks are taken by the persons generating ideas.

The criteria for scientific papers include originality, significance, correctness, readability, and suitability (Fig. 2.1). All the results to be published must be *original* or novel since, otherwise, there is no need to publish them again. It is not enough that the results are original; they must also be *significant* or relevant, i.e., they must have some scientific and societal impact. The result must be *correct*, i.e., correspond to reality, but since we cannot verify theories, plausibility is also an important criterion. *Readability* is also appreciated. Otherwise, the readers neglect the results. Although the paper would be scientifically perfect, the editor may only accept it if the manuscript is *suitable* for the journal's readership. Scientific papers follow the general structure, including introduction, materials and methods, results and discussion, and conclusion (IMRDC) (Li 1999; Lin and Evans 2012; Gastel and Day 2016). With this modular structure, we present the results using the top-down approach, which is easy for a reader to follow.

A paper is not a description of the research process but that of the results (Meadows 1985). We do not describe our actual research process, but in the paper we start with requirements or hypotheses and proceed to verification as if we did not take a wrong path at any time.

2.3 Beginning of Research: Managing Exponentially Growing Literature

2.3.1 Introduction

In general, the best way to discover existing knowledge is to study history, and this study should be included in a researcher's toolbox. If we have not done this, we must change our attitude toward history entirely and definitely. Ideas are simple and more straightforward to understand at the beginning of a new concept.

One challenge in information gathering is that terms change according to fashion in the same field, and we often use utterly different terminology in different fields. Thus, similar topics are often studied independently, and the researchers do not know about each other. For example, subsidiarity and loose coupling are similar concepts but seldom appear in the same text. Literature must be approached hierarchically from books to review papers and finally to original papers. We must prioritize the actual reading according to subjective views on readability, reliability, significance, and novelty of knowledge.

Scientific knowledge is freely available in publications, commonly through libraries and often using online tools. The actual publications may be in commercial databases. The most important sources of scientific information are books and journal and conference papers published by prominent publishers. A document without novelty claims based on at least a brief literature review and anonymous peer review is not scientific. A *literature review* is a written, well-organized summary of the state of the art with a clearly defined scope. We need a brief review in every original paper in its introduction. We write the review to experts in the field, and it may include historical notes. The reliability of the literature depends on the peer review process and the publisher's reputation.

In the beginning, we must carefully limit the *scope* of our work. Otherwise, we must read everything, which is an impossibility. In 2009, the total number of science papers published since 1665 passed 50 million (Jinha 2010), and now approximately 3 million new scientific papers are published each year, meaning 8000 documents per day (2018) (Johnson et al. 2018). The growth is exponential. The doubling time for all scientific work is about ten years, and the doubling time for "very high quality" work is about 20 years (Fernandez-Cano et al. 2004). Exponential growth has the property that the doubling time of literature per year is the same as that of all literature. The present rate of growth is thus about 7% per year. In any normal, growing field of science, the doubling time T_d is about ten to fifteen years.

Based on the doubling times of 10–20 years, we can roughly say that the time scale of the accumulation of scientific knowledge is 50–100 years, depending on whether we focus on all scientific work or very high-quality work, the latter of which would improve our understanding. We must study literature for 50–100 years to make reliable visions for the next ten years, see also (Hawking 2018).

The estimate is made more concrete by using the exponential function $N(t) = N \exp(t/\tau)$ where $N(t)$ is the number of papers at time t, N is the number of papers at time $t = 0$, $\exp(x) = e^x$ is the exponential function, $e \approx 2.71828$ is Napier's constant, and τ is the time constant. If the doubling time is $T = 20$ years, the time constant is $\tau = T/\ln 2$, about 30 years. Within four time constants or 120 years, we have 98% of all earlier publications. If the doubling time is ten years, the four time constants is 60 years. The observation gives a rough estimate of the last 50–100 years for most of the existing knowledge. Our work is made more accessible by using good books and reviewing history papers that often cover history from ancient times. Thus, if there is a recent history book or review paper, we must determine the progress made during, say, the last ten years.

Usually, we first focus on some critical original papers, but later, we will find it useful to collect also general information and landmark papers in our specific area or field. An efficient way is to use bibliographies, lists of references, and citations. If a publication refers to an older publication, this is called a *citation*, which we can later use to find new publications. There are many reasons why one paper might cite another: to point out information that may be useful to the reader, to give credit for prior work, to indicate influences on current work, or to disagree with the content of an earlier paper (Newman 2010).

It is essential to find landmark books and papers and the most recent state-of-the-art papers. It is advisable to trace back the history to find the origin of each relevant idea. Understanding historical evolution is very useful, but we may discover history disconnected since there are independent discoveries. We often invent similar concepts, and parallel independent "schools" are formed using different terminology, and the literature becomes easily fragmented, not unified as it should be. We often must make some iterations since not all authors know the most recent papers. Initially, people did not unify the terminology, although they discussed similar concepts. For example, until about 1990, the term "radio communications" was commonly used, but we replaced it with "wireless communications." Initially "wireless" was a term used for a radio receiving set.

We should first summarize the literature in an *annotated bibliography* of our own. In each annotation, we note why the paper or book was helpful. Terminology can be collected in a vocabulary or glossary, and history to a chronology, as in this book. In the vocabulary, it is beneficial to define the translations into our native language, which helps us understand the concepts. All this forms the basis for the literature review in our paper.

There are many reasons for making literature reviews based on information retrieval (Sternberg 1981; Michaelson 1990; Beer and McMurrey 2014). We may wonder why we search for references when we already have many. The point is to find the most relevant references, not just a random set. Sometimes, we get ideas for our research if we see gaps in the existing knowledge. However, most ideas come through discussions and dialogues (Jain and Triandis 1997). We may be overwhelmed by the number of papers and conclude that everything is already studied. We may lose our creativity by concentrating only on past knowledge. Exposing ourselves to literature first perhaps using encyclopedias and monographs is best so we do not need to reinvent the wheel. We must think differently from the way others do. Searching for literature is like the work of a detective, using slight hints to discover an exciting paper. Sometimes, our colleague gives the best reference we have been looking for although we have tried hard.

When using the literature, we can get a big picture, show the originality and significance of our work, and write the literature review and a list of references for our publication. We know when and how somebody originally invented things. We understand the topic better when we study it in its simplest form. We become highly self-confident experts in our discipline. We can also avoid overlapping research. Without any knowledge of history, it is not easy to understand the current technology, commonly called the *state of the art*. Occasionally, new topics appear when they may be tens of years old ideas just using new terms since the old terms wear out. We know the limitations of the present knowledge and see the current trends. We can provide a vision and roadmap to the future. Essential system-level knowledge changes slowly. We can select original and relevant problems for our research based on our broad knowledge. Finally, history is fascinating to read. Information on the origins makes the knowledge interesting. In this way, we also respect the work of earlier generations. Only an arrogant person ignores the history.

When we find an interesting paper, we approach it hierarchically to save time. We read the title, list of authors, and abstract first. If the paper is still interesting, we read the introduction and the conclusions. We try to see the paper in a historical context. We treat the paper initially as a black box without going into the details of the analysis. We study the paper's organization, usually explained at the end of the introduction. We read the headings and definitions of new general terms and look at figures and tables. We read the assumptions, system model, and numerical results. Finally, we study the details: detailed terminology, definitions, and proofs. We implement our models, try to improve the results, and write our paper. It is helpful to underline the most important ideas in existing papers so that we can find them easily. Based on the underlines, we can write an annotation to our bibliography.

2.3.2 Publications and Publishers

After gaining basic knowledge, a researcher should proceed from the top down when looking for existing knowledge. We must narrow the scope of the research at each level since the available literature significantly increases when moving downwards. To publish our results, we must proceed from the bottom up and soon try to achieve conference and journal papers, the most important forums for original research.

Publications can be classified into a hierarchy shown in Fig. 2.7. With some notable exceptions, the most reliable and general publications are at the top, and the newest publications are at the bottom. Journal and conference papers are core *primary sources*, and the publications above them are *secondary sources* needed to learn new things and to locate the primary sources. We should always check when and where the publication was originally published. *Reliability* depends on the review process, causing unavoidable delays in guaranteeing high quality. Thus, there are significant differences in reliability and quality even at the same hierarchy level. We

Fig. 2.7 Hierarchy of publications

Books
Encyclopedias and handbooks
Monographs
Textbooks
Trade books
Reviews
Review and survey papers
Tutorial papers
Bibliographies
Original journal papers
Full papers
Letters
Conference papers
Conferences and symposia
Workshops
Reports
Standards
Patents
Doctoral theses
Unpublished reports

must infer the quality from the reputation of the authors and the publisher. There is false *disinformation* and intentionally misleading *misinformation* available on the Internet. We can use Internet search engines to check whether somebody already published the knowledge in a scientific and reliable book or journal. We describe the locations of publications in Table 2.1. We present them here briefly.

Books Books include encyclopedias, dictionaries, atlases, handbooks, monographs, textbooks, and trade books. The most reliable of them are called reference works. Encyclopedias and handbooks are handy starting points when we move to a new area. Conventionally, they have been in printed form, but now they often have online versions. Encyclopedias are usually edited because of their broad scope. The largest and most prominent commercial encyclopedia in 32 volumes is *Encyclopedia Britannica*. The last printed version was published in 2010. After this, only the online version has been updated. A popular general encyclopedia is *Wikipedia* based on open collaboration or crowdsourcing but does not use peer review. Anybody can correct found mistakes. An alternative is *Scholarpedia*, which is peer-reviewed.

The International Council on Systems Engineering (INCOSE), the Systems Engineering Research Center (SERC), and the IEEE Computer Society are governing the *Guide to the Systems Engineering Body of Knowledge* (SEBoK). A similar report is *Guide to the Software Engineering Body of Knowledge (SWEBOK)*. Interesting

Table 2.1 Locations of publications

Publications	Location
Books	Library databases, online bookstores, online book services, book publishers, databases, see document type: book or book chapter
Review papers	Review journals, special issues of journals, literature reviews in doctoral theses, databases, see keywords: review, survey, overview, tutorial, history; document type: review
Bibliographies	Encyclopedias, monographs, and textbooks, tutorial and review papers, anthologies, introductions of original papers, web pages produced by some experts in the field, keyword or document type "bibliography" in databases
Original papers	Discovery tools, digital libraries, abstract and citation databases
Standards	Standardization organizations
Patents	Patent databases
Doctoral theses	University web pages

encyclopedias for us include the *Oxford Companion to Philosophy* (Honderich 2005), *Stanford Encyclopedia of Philosophy*, *Internet Encyclopedia of Philosophy*, and *International Encyclopedia of Systems and Cybernetics*.

Monographs and textbooks are written for experts and students, respectively. A *monograph* is an extended version of a review or survey paper, and a *textbook* is an extended version of a tutorial paper. A monograph is a book or report that deals with a single topic. *Trade books* are intended for a general readership (Merriam-Webster 2024). Books are either edited or authored books. In edited books, the chapters have different authors, and the editors are responsible for the general contents. Edited books are common in new fields where each theme needs expert authors. An edited book often looks like a set of reviews or original papers with profound knowledge. Sometimes, the problem is that editors must struggle to unify the text and its notation. Such books are not easy to use as textbooks, but they are helpful in new areas, and the different chapters in such a book contain deep knowledge produced by an expert. Thus, edited books are valuable if the reader has some experience. Authored books have a small number of authors (usually a maximum of three) and tend to be more unified. Most textbooks are authored books. Some publishers are open-access (OA) publishers.

Best books and reviews are such that they include both thematic and historical views. The books are often organized using the thematic view, and each chapter includes historical and bibliographical notes. There are also separate history books and even chronologies presenting the progress year by year (Asimov 1994; Carlisle 2004). Ordinary monographs often include at least 600–800 references. Distinctive features of textbooks are the tutorial writing style and the discussion questions or problems at the end of each chapter.

Review papers Journal papers are divided into review, survey, and tutorial papers, and original full papers and letters, all published in scientific archival journals with a rigorous and anonymous peer review. The IEEE has three types of scientific periodicals: journals, transactions, and magazines. The term "journal" is also a collective term for all scientific periodicals. There is not much difference between journals and transactions, but journals nowadays often publish special issues on some hot topics; therefore, the papers are highly cited. Usually, the journals include both full papers and letters or brief correspondence, but some journals publish only letters.

Review, survey, and tutorial papers include integrated information as in books. For brevity, we usually call all of them "review papers." Often, there is no difference between review and survey papers. *Review papers* "critically examine a technology, tracing its progress from its inception to the present and into the future" (Proceedings of the IEEE 2024). *Survey papers* "comprehensively view a technology: its applications, issues, ramifications, and potential." Thus, review papers have a broad scope, presenting the historical development, state of the art, and visions into the future. Surveys are more practical, focusing on the state of the art. Review and survey papers include block diagrams, equations, and a long list of references, often at least 50–100 or even more. Some review and survey papers are invited from top experts in the field. *Tutorial papers* "explain a technology and may give practical information for implementing it" (Proceedings of the IEEE 2024). These papers are written "for the purpose of informing nonspecialist engineers about a particular technology." Especially in magazines, they are often relatively short, including only a few simple equations and a brief list of references. Tutorial papers are written using simple language. Review, survey, and tutorial papers are seldom published in conference proceedings mainly because the space and presentation time are strictly limited. Especially in tutorial papers, numerical simulation results may be helpful as an illustration since they make everything concrete and demonstrate that the ideas work, thus improving plausibility and convincing readers who do not understand all the details.

Experts have collected the best publications in bibliographies that they often arrange according to the subject. They have neglected publications whose quality is not high enough. The choices are always subjective since there is no objective measure to define the value of a publication. The number of citations is only one possibility. We can use an annotated bibliography as the first step towards a review paper. In some magazines, we can include brief annotations in the list of references.

Original journal papers Original journal papers have a thorough peer review before publication. They are at the core of original scientific results. An original *full paper* or a regular paper is for significant technical contributions of archival value. It is a well-rounded treatment of a problem area. A *letter* or correspondence is a short original journal paper that includes "comments on published papers, corrections, and open problems, as well as new high-quality technical contributions primarily representing enhancements of a previous paper" and is published quickly (IEEE Transactions on Communications 2007).

Conference proceedings Conference proceedings are conference paper records, usually with a peer review process before the conference. The authors prepare a camera-ready version of their paper. In some disciplines, large international conferences are called congresses. Small conferences are called symposia, and even smaller meetings are called workshops, often including some practical joint work or discussion sessions. If no paper is published and only the presentation slides are distributed, we call it a "presentation." Such presentations are challenging to find afterward. Usually, the newest information is available in recent workshops. In small conferences, it may be easier to create contacts. Small informal meetings, especially for young researchers, are called seminars.

Technical reports Finally, we have various technical reports, which often do not have any review process and are usually not even published. They belong to the "gray" literature, but authors should generally refer to publications that are available, at least through libraries. Public organizations often publish highly reliable reports. We divide published reports into standards, patents, and doctoral theses.

Standards describe working systems and thus include state-of-the-art integrated system knowledge. The purpose of standards is to guarantee interoperability of products from different manufacturers. Many standards are, however, a result of political consensus, and there are no explanations for why the authors made specific selections. Standards are sold by standardization organizations, for example, the International Organization for Standardization (ISO), the International Electrotechnical Commission (IEC), the International Telecommunications Union (ITU), and the IEEE. Only an active member of standardization groups has usually access to the newest knowledge. The most vital actors in standardization are large industrial companies. Some standards are freely available on the Internet.

A *patent* is a "government grant of the exclusive rights to make, use, and sell the substance of a recent invention" (Skolnik 1979; Mgbeoji 2003; Encyclopedia Britannica 2024). Patents are the only statutory exception to the principle of practicing legitimate business in countries governed by the rule of law. A patent examiner seeks limits to this monopoly and studies the scope of protection.

Patents are special reports describing new inventions, usually using an ambiguous writing style to make the scope or monopoly as large as possible. Although they are public, patents differ from other scientific reports since they aim to limit the industrial use of the knowledge. Patents are examples of intellectual property (IP) and should be a basis for an industrial product. We cannot patent published ideas. Generally, we should publish an invention only after submitting the patent application. Patents have a peer review process. We can find the patents through patent databases provided by patent offices, such as the European Patent Office (EPO). Companies are interested in *standard essential patents* (SEPs) that are considered mandatory for implementing systems described in standards. According to the European Telecommunications Standards Institute (ETSI), the SEPs are regulated so that the terms are "fair, reasonable, and non-discriminatory."

Other noteworthy reports include *doctoral theses*, which, by definition, should include literature reviews. Doctoral theses have a peer review that is usually not anonymous. We can use an Internet browser and reports from commercial publishers of commercial products and market research.

Publishers We divide publishers into nonprofit scientific societies and commercial publishers. Scientific societies publish many periodicals or journals, conference proceedings, and some books. An umbrella organization of scientific societies is the International Science Council (ISC), which was formed in 2018 from the International Council for Science (ICSU), originally the International Council of Scientific Unions (1931) and International Social Science Council (ISSC) (1952) (Table 2.2). In many countries, there are local umbrella organizations such as the American Association for the Advancement of Science (AAAS), which publishes the famous *Science* magazine founded in 1880.

The International Federation for Systems Research (IFSR) is the umbrella organization of systems science. The oldest society on general theory of systems is the International Society for the Systems Sciences (ISSS), originally the Society for the Advancement of General Systems Theory. The International Council on Systems Engineering (INCOSE) is a corresponding society in systems engineering. Both the ISSS and INCOSE are members of the IFSR. In interdisciplinary studies, the umbrella organization is the Global Alliance for Inter- and Transdisciplinarity (ITD Alliance), which includes natural and human sciences but so far excludes engineering. The Association for Interdisciplinary Studies (AIS) is an interdisciplinary society, originally coming from social sciences. The interdisciplinary field of science and technology studies (STS) covers the relationship between society, scientific research, and technological innovation. In history, systems thinking is represented by the International Big History Association (IBHA).

Scientific societies are usually discipline-specific. The most significant scientific society in engineering is the Institute of Electrical and Electronics Engineers (IEEE), a merger of the American Institute of Electrical Engineers (AIEE) and the Institute of Radio Engineers (IRE) in 1963 (Table 2.3). It has a database called the IEEE Xplore. The Institution of Electrical Engineers (IEE) is an even older society, originally the Society of Telegraph Engineers. In 1988, the IEE merged with the Institution of Electronic and Radio Engineers (IERE), which was originally the British Institution

Table 2.2 Scientific societies related to interdisciplinary systems view

Founded	Society
1848	American Association for the Advancement of Science (AAAS)
1931	International Council for Science (ICSU)
1952	International Social Science Council (ISSC)
1956	International Society for the Systems Sciences (ISSS)
1979	Association for Interdisciplinary Studies (AIS)
1980	International Federation for Systems Research (IFSR)
1990	International Council on Systems Engineering (INCOSE)
1995	Society for Design and Process Science (SDPS)
2004	Complex Systems Society (CSS)
2010	International Big History Association (IBHA)
2018	International Science Council (ISC)
2019	Global Alliance for Inter- and Transdisciplinarity (ITD Alliance)

of Radio Engineers. In 2006, the Institution of Engineering and Technology (IET) became a merger of the IEE and the Institution of Incorporated Engineers (IIE). Each discipline in engineering has its society. For example, a significant society in computing is the Association for Computing Machinery (ACM), founded in 1947, just after the invention of the digital computer. Later, new societies were founded in measurement, pattern recognition, signal processing, and AI. In Europe, the European Alliance for Innovation (EAI) has recently become active in publishing.

We list in Table 2.4 some of the best-known commercial publishers of scientific books in engineering (Lariviere et al. 2015; Johnson et al. 2018; Phillips 2018). Many of them also publish journals. The oldest university press is Cambridge University Press (1534). Oxford University Press was founded several decades after that (1586). Many of the other major publishers were founded in the 1800s. A recent study shows that commercial publishing of scientific papers is concentrated in the hands of a few companies (Lariviere et al. 2015). Many old book publishers have been merged recently. John Wiley & Sons (1807) is one of the oldest book publishers. It now owns D. Van Nostrand Company and Hindawi. Pearson was originally (1844) in the construction business but moved to publishing in 1921. It now includes Addison-Wesley and Prentice Hall. Springer was known initially as Springer-Verlag (founded in 1842) but has been known as Springer Nature since 2015. It includes Kluwer Academic Publishers, Macmillan Science and Education, and Plenum Publishing Corporation. Nature Research, owned by Springer Nature, publishes the famous *Nature* journal founded in 1869. Taylor & Francis was founded in 1852, but Taylor had been publishing since 1798. Taylor & Francis now owns Routledge. Elsevier (founded in 1880) includes the former Academic Press and CRC Press. In 1992, Elsevier was merged with Reed, and the new company was called Reed Elsevier. In

Table 2.3 Scientific societies and organizations related to the information concept

Founded	Society
1871	Institution of Electrical Engineers (IEE)
1884	American Institute of Electrical Engineers (AIEE)
1912	Institute of Radio Engineers (IRE)
1919	International Union of Radio Science (URSI)
1925	Institution of Electronic and Radio Engineers (IERE)
1947	Association for Computing Machinery (ACM)
1958	International Measurement Confederation (IMEKO)
1963	Institute of Electrical and Electronics Engineers (IEEE)
1972	International Association for Pattern Recognition (IAPR)
1978	European Association for Signal Processing (EURASIP)
1979	Association for the Advancement of Artificial Intelligence (AAAI)
2006	Institution of Engineering and Technology (IET), former IEE
2010	European Alliance for Innovation (EAI)

Table 2.4 Commercial publishers in engineering

Founded	Publisher
1534	Cambridge University Press
1586	Oxford University Press
1807	John Wiley & Sons
1832	Houghton Mifflin Harcourt
1842	Springer
1844	Pearson
1852	Taylor & Francis
1880	Elsevier
1888	McGraw-Hill

2015, the company changed its brand name to RELX. Elsevier owns large databases called Engineering Village, ScienceDirect, and Scopus.

There have been some attempts to rank publishers of journals and books, both scientific societies and commercial publishers (Johnson et al. 2018; Phillips 2018). However, there are various methodological problems in reaching an objective ranking. It can be based, for example, on the number of publications (books or journals) or the number of citations, and therefore, final conclusions are difficult to attain.

Open access (OA) publishers may have varying quality. In OA journals, the authors or their organizations pay the publishing costs, and the papers are accessible to everybody, whereas in conventional journals, the subscriber (often a library) pays for the subscription, and the authors do not pay. Some OA journals do not have a proper review process and are especially suspicious: they charge publication fees without providing editorial or publishing services, and we must use the ranking done by some organizations. High-quality OA publishers are listed in the Directory of Open Access Journals (DOAJ) offered by the Lund University Libraries. There are also some lists of predatory OA journals and publishers (Interacademy Partnership 2024). It is best to focus on OA journals published by reliable publishers. In some countries, publishers and journals are ranked according to quality. In the case of journals, the ranking is often based on journal impact factors. In some countries, conferences and journals are ranked separately.

2.3.3 Tools and Databases for Information Retrieval

Tools for information retrieval also form some kind of hierarchy, including discovery tools, general abstract and citation databases, and specific digital libraries (also called electronic libraries or e-libraries) published by scientific societies (Fig. 2.8). *Discovery tools* are a modern effort to collect information from various sources

Fig. 2.8 Tools and databases for information retrieval

Discovery tools
EDS
Primo
Summon
Digital libraries
Open Library
Journal Storage
ACM Digital Library
IEEE Xplore
Abstract and citation databases
Engineering Village
Scopus
Web of Science
Google Scholar

(Goodsett 2014). If they work well, no other tool is needed. The tool is "web software that searches journal-article and library-catalog metadata in a unified index and presents search results in a single interface." Examples include Elton B. Stephens Company Discovery Service (EDS), Primo, and Summon. The problem is that the discovery tools do not include any citations, but they will probably be available in the future.

Open Library is a general search tool for books. It also finds e-books, if there are any, on the Internet. Open Library is a service within the *Internet Archive* that also stores some books and old Internet pages in its Wayback Machine. Old books and papers are included in *Journal Storage (JSTOR).* Open Library and JSTOR thus form an online library, but the new contents are limited by copyright laws.

Many book publishers offer e-book services, and many other online book services, such as Google Books, also present sample pages from books. Specific complementary databases for books not covered by Open Library are included in online bookstores. The front cover, title page, copyright page, table of contents, index, back cover, and some sample pages are available from the books, but we cannot print the pages. We may still be able to search the whole book, but we cannot see all those pages, only the page numbers and samples of a few lines. The search is applicable even if we own the printed book and want to know on which pages a given term is mentioned. The index at the end of the book is incomplete because of space limitations. We can do a keyword search. A *keyword* is an index common term, abbreviation, or phrase that may include several words. We use keywords to classify a paper or book and to search for literature.

The abstract and citation databases generally include only journal and conference papers and some book reviews but not actual books. The most significant scientific databases in science and engineering include Web of Science, Scopus, and Engineering Village (Falagas et al. 2008; Tomaszewski 2021). The best databases are such that they contain various sorting tools, references, and citations. There are differences in time coverage, which is continuously improved. The best databases have coverage from the beginning of 1665, but full coverage may start much later. Citations are relatively recent, with the Web of Science having the longest traditions. Engineering Village includes three significant databases: Information Service for Physics, Electronics, and Computing (Inspec), Computerized Engineering Index (Compendex), and National Technical Information Service (NTIS) databases, which include only abstracts and originally no citations. There are also links to the full texts in digital libraries.

Generally, popular search engines such as Google (1998) and Bing (2009) exist. A scientific search tool is Google Scholar (2004) (Falagas et al. 2008), which searches for books and papers in the original databases but does not list books in online bookstores. The reliability depends on the location of the original publication. An extensive digital library is the IEEE Xplore. Other publishers also have similar databases, for example, ACM has the ACM Digital Library. The databases include portable document format (pdf) files of papers and a full-text search within the pdf files as an additional service. We can also try to find pdf files of papers and books especially in some open-access repositories of electronic preprints and post-prints such as arXiv, TechRxiv, and ResearchGate. Many universities and research institutes have their publication databases.

2.3.4 Practical Hints for Searching Literature

The best way to find existing knowledge is to follow citation networks. We use discovery tools, bibliographies, databases, other search tools, and references. We use *metadata* attached to the document, such as the author's name, the paper's title, the abstract, and keywords. One problem in information retrieval is that there are synonyms with the same meaning and homonyms with a different meaning. For example, the feedback concept has been invented using other terms such as the OODA loop. Furthermore, feedback is a technical term, but the same term may also mean constructive criticism in social sciences.

A citation has been made when a book or paper refers to an earlier publication. Using the lists of references, we can move only backward in time (Fig. 2.9). Many modern databases and search tools include citations with which we can move forward in time towards the present time. Ideally, one could find the newest state-of-the-art papers after a few iterations by using citations and references.

We can present a citation network (Newman 2010) as a *citation graph* to infer possible *invisible colleges* (de Solla Price 1986). Often, networks of authors form distinct schools that refer to each other, thus forming charmed circles. Robert Boyle (1646) introduced the term invisible college, which led to the foundation of the Royal Society. Boyle's group was the first invisible college. Initially, a small group of researchers met face-to-face and exchanged ideas. Price adopted the concept in 1963 and now, it designates informal groups as "that can be handled by interpersonal

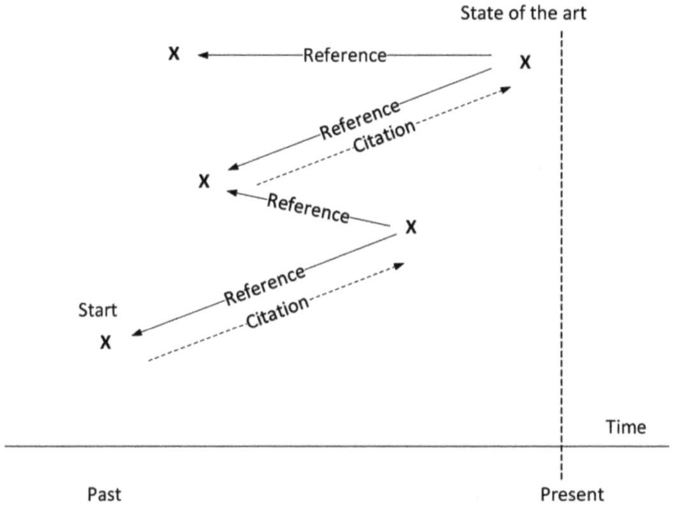

Fig. 2.9 Iterative use of references and citations presented as a simple citation graph

relationships." The groups are usually limited in size. Invisible colleges advance the research fronts of science.

According to statistics presented by Newman (2010), about half of all papers have never been cited. Only 20% of all papers have ten or more citations, and just 1% have 100 or more. The results imply a power-law degree distribution of the network. An alternative to a citation network is a *cocitation network*. Two papers are said to be cocited if the same third paper cites them. We take cocitation as an indicator that papers deal with related topics.

Citations form lines of thinking, creating *conceptual threads* (Richardson 1991); see Fig. 2.10. They often deviate from each other, forming independent parallel research that may use different terminology and not be aware of each other for decades. The idea's origin may come from independent discoveries or from the same discovery when the origin is forgotten, thus creating a *break* in the thread. An example of independent discoveries is related to the separation theorem. Robert Price discovered it in communications and called his receiver the estimator-correlator in 1956 (Kailath 1960). Later, Joseph and Tou (1961) found the same idea in control engineering, separating estimator and controller. After nine years, Conant and Ashby (1970) discovered it again, and we now sometimes call it the Conant-Ashby theorem (Skyttner 2005).

A break may be developed if the received information is only oral, and a researcher has no time to study the historical origin. These cases are unfortunate since the original discoverer needs to receive appropriate credit, and the presented information looks like an independent discovery, although this is always not the case. For example, in social sciences, two parallel threads using this concept, including the cybernetics thread and servomechanisms thread, have developed independently from each other. Sometimes, the distinct threads intersect. For example, Norbert Wiener, W. Ross

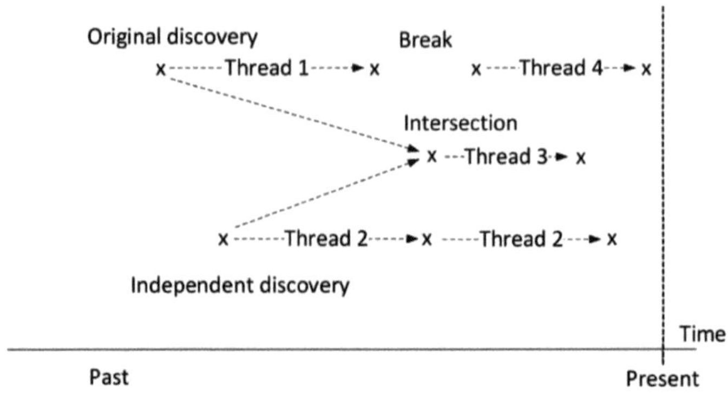

Fig. 2.10 Conceptual threads, breaks, and intersections. Independent threads are numbered

Ashby, and Jay Forrester used the feedback concept, and we can find the *intersections* using the names of these authors and some other relevant terms, such as cybernetics and systems dynamics, in the search. In this way, we often find review papers and books that may be anthologies. It is essential to find conceptual threads of landmark papers. In this way, it is easier to manage the ever-growing literature.

We divide science into various disciplines using different terms for similar concepts. Figure 2.11 shows the usage frequency of the term "multi-agent systems" in books (an alternative spelling is multiagent systems, which was more popular initially). Usage frequency is computed "by dividing the number of instances of the n-gram in a given year by the total number of words in the corpus in that year" (Michel et al. 2010). An n-gram is a phrase consisting of n words where n is a positive integer. The research on multiagent systems started in about 1977 using a name distributed artificial intelligence, but researchers realized the importance of multiagent systems in about 1987 (Russell and Norvig 2022), and the popularity has moved upwards and downwards, which is typical in such hot topics. Such a curve is sometimes called a "*hype cycle*" (Dedehayir and Steinert 2016). It resembles the step response of an underdamped control loop in control engineering (Ogata 2010). It is sometimes said that the popularity often changes over a period of twenty years. In this case, the distance from the first peak to the next valley is almost ten years, thus giving a period of twenty years for the popularity with a decreasing amplitude. People are often interested in topics that are fashionable.

It is best to use at least two databases or tools, for example, a general tool and a more specific tool of a scientific society of interest. Two databases are needed since they almost always include mistakes, and we may need help finding the relevant papers. We search using *keywords* combined with Boolean operators OR, AND, and NOT. If we want to find a keyword written precisely in the given form, we must write it in quotation marks. Citations are not complete in databases, especially citations from old papers. One way to find old citations is to use the paper's title in quotation marks in a full-text search using the whole publication, not just the metadata. The success of this method depends on the database.

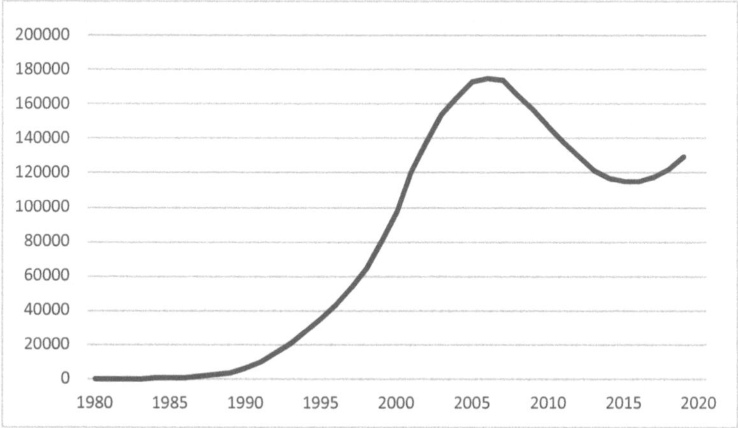

Fig. 2.11 Usage frequency of the term "multi-agent systems" in books from 1980 to 2019 showing a typical "hype cycle" (Google Books Ngram Viewer from the corpus English 2019 with smoothing of 3). The unit on the y-axis is 0.0000001%. For example, 20,000 means 0.002%

A search may include hundreds or thousands of papers; the problem is finding the most relevant ones. We can use different sorting methods to obtain a versatile view of the literature. The sorting tools include relevance, newest first, oldest first, and most cited. Relevance is estimated by the number of uses of the keyword and its location, for example, in the title, abstract, other metadata, and introduction. The newest papers include state-of-the-art information. They are the most advanced and complicated and may be difficult to read. The oldest papers are essential for understanding the origin of the field when the theories were in their simplest form. Since the terminology may have changed, we must also look at the reference list of the oldest papers. We can also use synonymous terms as alternatives. For example, the term "haptic" includes the terms "tactile" and "kinesthetic," and we have already three different terms. The best search tools may search for synonyms.

The most cited papers are the most popular and often review papers. A more advanced version of citation use is using the whole citation tree so that each citation is ranked according to its weight (Xing and Ghorbani 2004). If a paper is cited more, a citation given by it is weighted more. Two commonly used ranking algorithms are PageRank and Hypertext Induced Topic Selection (HITS), which have various more advanced versions.

Through citations, we can obtain links to the newest papers. The latest papers do not yet have many citations. There should be tools for finding reviews and bibliographies in the search tools. If not, one may use specific keywords such as review, survey, overview, tutorial, and history in addition to the standard particular keywords. Some English terms may have several meanings (such as "review"), so they may provide an unnecessarily long list of references. One way to locate new review papers is to start from an old landmark paper, which should be cited in a good review paper.

Some tools do not have comprehensive sorting methods. Sorting may be limited to relevance and the newest first. Relevance does not imply that the most cited papers are listed first. In that case, we need to find those papers by looking at the citations of, say, one hundred of the most relevant papers. Some tools may not include the "oldest first" sorting but may contain time limits. To find the oldest papers, we can customize the year range and move backward until we find the oldest paper. Automata may make some mistakes when inferring metadata from the actual data. The timestamp may be wrong since the automaton may use, for example, a page number as a time stamp. Therefore, we must check the time of publication separately for each paper. Initially, the terminology may have been different, so we must study the literature reviews in the oldest papers. For example, Dennis Gabor (1946) systematically used the complex envelope concept (Kailath 1966; Hill 2007). Still, the original paper did not use the exact term, but the terms "complex signal" and "complex time function."

2.3.5 Outlining a Literature Review

We write a literature review for experts in the field using a top-down approach unless we are writing a tutorial or textbook. In a paper, the review is usually relatively short to show the novelty of the research in the introduction, but it may be extended and included in a separate section. A review may consist of historical notes as additional information. It is best first to read only high-quality landmark or seminal papers, which good groups often produce. Papers collected in our files or even an annotated bibliography are not yet a review but are a reasonable basis for a review.

In the front and back matter of this book, you can find a chronology, a glossary, and a bibliography. In the literature, we may use different terms for the same concept. We can find definitions of new terms from reliable books and journal papers. It is essential to study the relationships of the concepts using hierarchical classifications or *taxonomies*, see Fig. 2.12. Landmark papers present new research. Although the history proceeds in a bottom-up way, the review uses a top-down organization. The terms and definitions may differ in different disciplines, which may look confusing, but the terminology must be unified in each paper. Etymological dictionaries may be helpful in conceptual analysis. General dictionaries, such as Oxford and Webster's dictionaries, often include clear definitions. History can be briefly and compactly presented as a chronology (Asimov 1994; Carlisle 2004). Usually, it is advisable to search for the origin of each idea to estimate the time frame in which the topic was discussed. We can present history as historical notes at the end of the review.

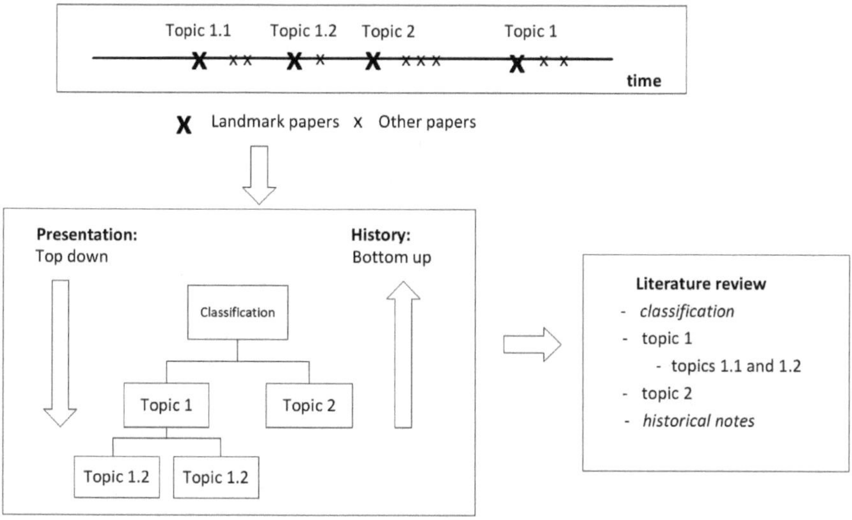

Fig. 2.12 Outlining a literature review

2.4 Final Result: Writing with Quality to Distribute Knowledge

2.4.1 Introduction

The research will be ready after we publish the results. Scientific papers improve the quality of the study and distribute new knowledge. Researchers and employers can use the papers since they measure scientific merit. Writing enhances thinking. While writing, new ideas come to our minds even though we did not know they existed.

Many excellent books on writing exist (Beer and McMurrey 2014; Turabian et al. 2018; Gastel and Day 2016). However, some problems exist, summarized in Wolfe (2009): Injunctions to avoid passive voice, there is a bias toward humanities citation practices, influential research in data visualization being ignored, and the absence of data, results, and numbers. Disciplines favoring Vancouver author-number style instead of the Harvard author-date style include electrical, computer, chemical, and mechanical engineering, mathematics, and physics. The passive voice and citation style de-emphasize people and shift attention to the phenomenon under study. For engineers, a significant problem is the missing detailed discussion on system models in the materials and methods section. For convenience, we briefly summarize all the parts of the manuscripts.

In writing, the experiments must be reproducible, emphasizing the importance of the materials and methods section without any implicit or silent assumptions. The length of the paper is usually strictly limited, which implies that the size of all the parts must be limited, and we must balance the size of each section using a page or word budget. In some journals, there are no page limits. Conference papers usually have five printed pages, but they may be shorter or longer, sometimes including only an abstract. For the manuscripts, conferences usually offer templates we must use in the submission.

The most common organization of a paper follows the introduction, materials and methods, results, and discussion (IMRAD) structure (Gastel and Day 2016). We often use the IMRDC structure where C refers to the conclusion. The R and D sections are usually combined. We often use the instructions of the IEEE since it is the largest engineering society in the world, and its writing instructions (IEEE 2012) are detailed and versatile. In the instructions, we discuss mainly original papers. Still, we can apply similar ideas in review papers and books, which should include, for example, a novelty claim, but the novelty is in integrating topics.

In addition to the IMRDC sections, a scientific original paper includes title, authors, abstract, keywords in the beginning and acknowledgment, appendices, references, and photographs and biographies of authors at the end. Some extensive papers include a list of abbreviations and symbols after the abstract and keywords. In IEEE papers, the corresponding headings may be nomenclature, glossary of terms, symbols and abbreviations, or notation. Some of them may be in a separate table or appendix. Symbols are sometimes defined at the end of the introduction.

We discuss only the most essential parts of a paper. The general structure is modeled as an hourglass (Fig. 2.13), where the introduction tries to attract as many readers as possible, and the conclusion gives a broader perspective on the results and the future. Some authors claim that the novelty of an original paper is presented four times: in the title, abstract, introduction, and conclusion.

Each section can be divided into several moves that are usually not explicitly stated in the text. Our summary of the moves in Table 2.5 and Fig. 2.14 is a more

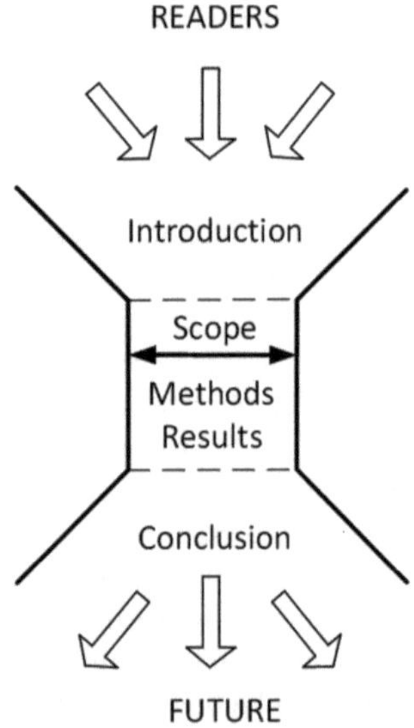

Fig. 2.13 Hourglass model of a paper

Table 2.5 General IMRDC structure of a paper

Section	Moves
Abstract	1. Research problem and its background 2. Research methods 3. Principal results and their significance and originality 4. Conclusion
Introduction	1. Motivation and orientation 2. Definition and scope of the problem 3. Previous related work and its limitations 4. Author's original contribution 5. Organization of the paper
Materials and methods	1. Detailed literature review (if needed) 2. Definitions, system model, and assumptions 3. Deductive and statistical methods 4. Experimental methods for verification and validation
Results and discussion	1. Numerical results in tables and figures 2. Verification and validation of results 3. New observations from the results 4. Discussion of the results with respect to earlier literature
Conclusion	1. Main results and their significance 2. Limitations and advantages 3. Applications of results 4. Recommendations for further work

detailed checklist of what to include in each section (IEEE Spectrum 1965; Skelton 1994).

Publishers of some books and most journals have *copy editors* who carefully review the language and finalize the published version to improve quality. In conferences, the authors prepare a camera-ready copy to be published in the conference proceedings, often using some template offered by the publisher.

2.4.2 IMRDC Structure of a Paper

After solving our problem, we should read the literature thoroughly to place our solution in a scholarly context. The organization of the original paper must be logical and straightforward, following the deductive top-down structure, which is just the opposite of the inductive or abductive bottom-up approach used in the research. We should outline before we start to write. We must organize the paper so that there are only a few cross-references to other parts of the text. We should not refer to future equations, figures, or tables. We treat each topic in detail in one place only. We avoid any repetitions except in the abstract and conclusion, which may include even wording similar to the other parts of the paper. However, the abstract and conclusion have a different structure, and they should not be identical since they have different purposes.

Fig. 2.14 General structure of a paper

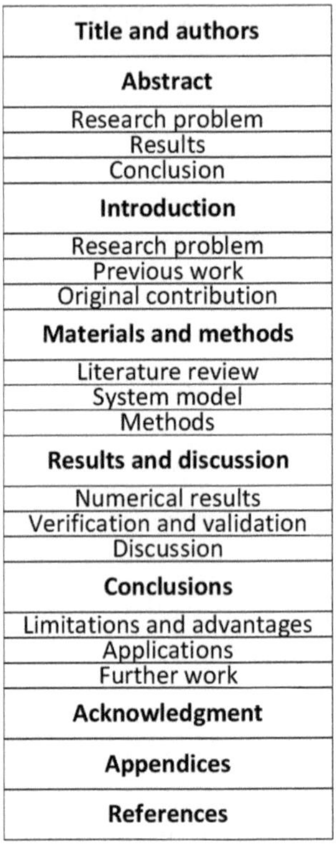

Title The title is the first place where we meet our readers. It should be brief, usually less than ten words, descriptive, and clear (IEEE Spectrum 1965). The title should emphasize the novelty and not be too general, which would reduce interest. The title should include keywords used in the paper to attract interested readers' attention. We do not make the title too arrogant or too underrated. If we plan to publish a series of papers, we should use different titles. If the readers find the title intriguing, they usually read the abstract, the introduction, and the conclusion next. We should make these parts enjoyable, emphasizing the novel and fresh results.

List of authors The list of authors should include all those who solved technical problems, i.e., had a scientific contribution to the paper (Michaelson 1990). Here, we give credit to our collaborators. There should not be any *ghost authors* who did contribute but whose names are not listed. On the other hand, do not write names of *honorary authors* who did not offer any contribution. The right place for some of them may be in the acknowledgment section. Some authors are highly productive, having over 50 papers per year, and this phenomenon has become more common (Ioannidis 2024). Such authors produce a paper every week on average. Some authors are suspected to be associated with overtly unethical practices such as paper mills or citation cartels. Honorary authorship may be used in the paper mills. Citation cartels, sometimes called citation doping, include extreme self-citations.

We select the order of the author names according to the importance of the contribution, but in some disciplines, the alphabetical order is always used. The author's name who contributed most should be in the first place. We use an alphabetical order if some of the authors have made an equal contribution. In general, the recommended maximum number of authors is 4–5 since the other authors are, in practice, neglected. In some disciplines, hundreds of names are used, which is unfair to other disciplines where only a few names are listed. We give the affiliation of all authors. If we changed the employer during the preparation of the paper, we write "NN was with X. He/she is now with Y." To identify authors, they are given an Open Researcher and Contributor Identification (ORCID), perhaps already during submission (ORCID 2022). To recognize organizations, they are given in some journals a Ringgold (2024). Some scientific societies have forbidden authors' use of AI tools and technologies: all authors must be humans (ACM Publications Board 2023). We must disclose their use in the acknowledgment section.

Abstract and keywords An abstract of a paper is a one-paragraph summary that presents the essential contents of the larger paper, including the research problem and its background, research methods, principal novel results, and conclusion (ANSI/NISO 2010). The abstract must be understandable independently and written concisely. It should be informative, not only descriptive, and contain significant words that identify the critical ideas. An *informative abstract* includes the essential information in the paper, especially the main novel results. A *descriptive abstract* presents only the thematic contents of the paper as a list of the covered general topics. Similar to an abstract, a summary, explanation, or comment in a reference is called an *annotation* (Skolnik 1979).

We start the abstract with a *topic sentence* that establishes the context and scope of the paper, thus presenting the paper's central thesis without repeating the words of the title of the paper (Weil 1970; Young 2002). Therefore, a good abstract should have an "explosive" start, moving straight to the paper's main point, and the background information is given later in the abstract. We must state clearly our new contribution. A common mistake is to present it at the end of the abstract or even not at all. We eliminate obscure abbreviations and use definite statements instead of generalities. We do not include concepts or conclusions beyond those discussed in the paper.

The abstract should be independently understandable in abstract databases and thus may not refer to figures, tables, or references. It may contain only simple one-line equations. We may refer to earlier important papers by giving the names of the authors and the year of publication in parentheses, for example, Smith (1990). The actual reference should be in the list of references.

The publisher usually limits the number of words in the abstract. The suitable length for full papers is 100–250 words, and for letters, it is 50–100 words. In conference papers, a typical size is 150 words. We usually describe the paper's contents using keywords below the abstract. The keywords are sometimes called index terms. Often, reviewers are selected based on the keywords.

In some conferences, only an abstract is submitted and if accepted, it is later published. Some conferences initially request an *extended abstract* for review, and after the acceptance, we submit the final full paper. This review process somewhat lowers the average quality of the papers if the full papers are not reviewed. The extended abstract is a detailed summary of the whole paper. It is usually 1–2 pages long, and we can use the IMRDC structure of the final paper. An *executive summary* is an abstract in some reports written for directors and managers, avoiding complicated concepts and terms.

Introduction The introduction motivates and orients potential readers so that they continue reading (Swales and Najjar 1987). Motivation is a desire to act in particular ways to achieve specific goals (McFarland and Bösser 1993). To attract many readers, we should emphasize significance and concreteness, include "hot topics," and have a suitable focus—not too broad or too narrow.

In the introduction, we define the problem we have solved. We should refrain from presenting any detailed new results in the introduction. We need at least a short literature review to show the state of the art, the original contribution beyond the state of the art, and the problem framing, usually called the *scope* in defining the problem. We must stay within the defined scope in the materials and methods, as well as results and discussion sections, otherwise the reader may be confused. A simple block diagram of the system model is often helpful for orientation as an integrating element. We should compare our contribution with that of the earlier relevant papers. A typical problem is that the author fails to present an explicit *novelty* or *originality claim*. We compare our results with the earlier ones and show what was improved. We cannot present results that have already been published. We cannot copy, for example, the structure of an earlier paper and paraphrase all the sentences using the same storyline. It is not a novel result.

The novelty usually lies in "original results, methods, observations, concepts, or applications, but may also reside in synthesis of, or new insights into, previously reported research" (IEEE Transactions on Information Theory 2021). The reviewers also assess the paper's significance, correctness, readability, and suitability or value to the journal's audience (Fig. 2.1). At the end of the introduction, the organization of the paper is presented.

Materials and methods The materials and methods section aims to guarantee the repeatability and reproducibility of the results. *Repeatability* means that the results can be produced again in the same laboratory within a particular uncertainty that should be estimated. *Reproducibility* means that the results can be repeated in an independent laboratory using only the information in the publication. In measurements, repeatability means "closeness of the agreement between the results of successive measurements of the same measurand carried out under the same conditions of measurement" (SE VOCAB 2024). Reproducibility means "closeness of the agreement between the results of measurements of the same measurand carried out under changed conditions of measurement."

Strictly speaking, we should present a statistical measurement result by defining measurement *uncertainty* that we describe by three numbers: average, coverage interval (i.e., confidence interval in statistics), and coverage probability (i.e., the confidence level in statistics), for example, 95% (Fig. 2.15) (JCGM 2012). The *error*

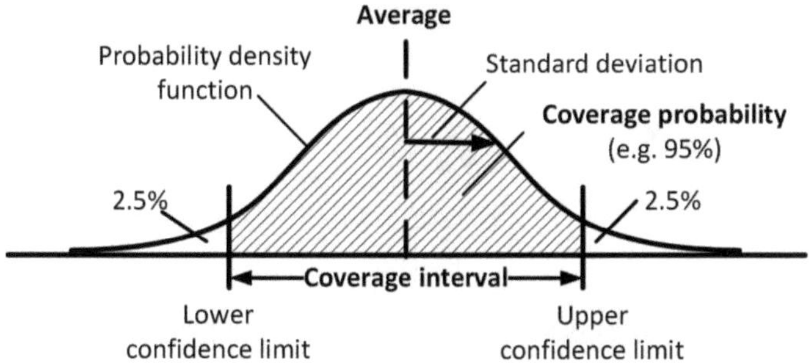

Fig. 2.15 Definition of uncertainty, coverage interval, and coverage probability

is the difference between the measured and the reference values representing the true value. With this definition, we have a situation where the sum of the reference value and the error is the measured value. To simplify notation, in some feedback systems, the definition of the error is the opposite (Ogata 2010; Haykin 2014), but we do this so that the feedback loop converges.

The error may include a systematic part called a bias and a random part where the error varies in an unpredictable manner (JCGM 2012). Sometimes, we assume that the error is normally distributed, and we estimate the standard deviation (denoted by σ) and define the coverage interval based on such knowledge. For example, if there is no bias, 68.27% of the measurement results are within one standard deviation, 95.45% are within two standard deviations, 99.73% are within three standard deviations from the average, 99.9937% are within three standard deviations from the average (Montgomery and Woodall 2008), see Table 2.6. In many areas of science, we consider events to be statistically significant when the coverage probability is 95%. The particle physics community uses a *five sigma rule* to declare something a discovery (Chekanov 2016). In communications, sometimes a *five-nines* requirement is defined for availability, which is claimed to correspond to carrier-grade requirements (Greene and Lancaster 2007). Five nines requirement corresponds to an availability of 0.99999 and an unplanned downtime of about 5 min a year. One year is often a suitable measurement interval when we need extremely high availability or reliability (Keyes 1987; Kish 2002).

Table 2.6 Coverage probabilities of normal distribution

Coverage interval	Coverage probability
$\pm 1\sigma$	68.27
$\pm 2\sigma$	95.45
$\pm 3\sigma$	99.73
$\pm 4\sigma$	99.9937
$\pm 5\sigma$	99.999943
$\pm 6\sigma$	99.9999998

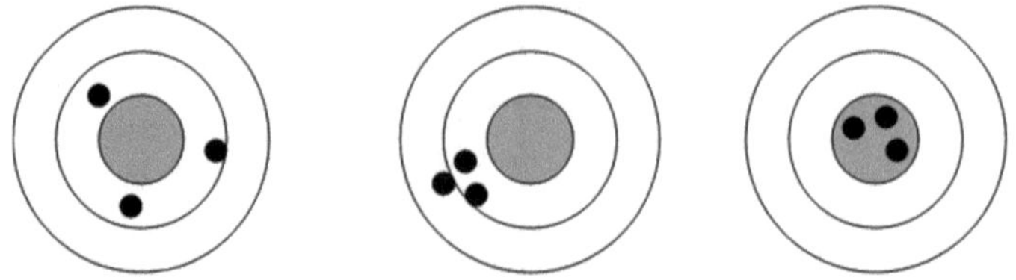

Fig. 2.16 Comparison of trueness, precision, and accuracy with respect to a reference value in the center

If the bias is uncertain, its upper bound must be estimated. In the common *six-sigma rule* developed for quality control in manufacturing, the maximum assumed bias is $\pm$ 1.5σ, and we use the worst-case estimates for the coverage probability (Montgomery and Woodall 2008; Watson and DeYong 2010). For example, with the maximum bias, the coverage probability within six standard deviations is 99.999660%, corresponding to 3.4 defects in a million products. Bill Smith developed this rule in 1986.

Trueness, precision, and accuracy are commonly used as qualitative descriptions (Fig. 2.16) (JCGM 2012). *Trueness* refers to a systematic error, *precision* refers to a random error, and *accuracy* refers a total error. It is a mistake to think that precision and accuracy are synonymous terms, and it is recommended that the terms are used only qualitatively. For quantitative numerical values, we should use the uncertainty concept to avoid ambiguities. Usually, we use the arithmetic average, especially if the distribution of the measurements is assumed to be symmetric. In cases where the distribution is skewed, a median is a more appropriate measure of the center of the distribution. Trueness, precision, and accuracy need a *reference value* used for comparison. The true value of a measurand is usually unknown, and we replace it with an agreed conventional quantity value as an estimate of the true value with small enough measurement uncertainty.

We can start the materials section with a more thorough literature review. We should not continue it elsewhere, so we separate the new contribution from the previous results. The materials section also includes definitions, a description of the system model, and the related assumptions, such as the performance criteria.

We describe the *system model* in its entirety, including the model of the environment in one place, so that the reader is not confused if we give new details later. We show clearly all the model's limitations. We present the variables and parameters with symbols. We use a simple enough system model. It is frustrating to read papers where significant overlap with other papers exists, the results are in the subordinate clauses, and the models are tangled with many inessential details. We mention explicitly all the assumptions we are using; there must not be any silent or implicit assumptions. We must state the assumptions and results clearly since they form the most important novel parts of the paper. Some readers would prefer to avoid going into the details of the analysis. For these readers, the organization of the text should be such that the analytical part can be treated as a "black box" with inputs (materials and methods) and outputs (conclusion) clearly shown. We give lengthy mathematical derivations in appendices.

The basic research methods include mathematical analysis, computer simulations, and practical experiments. We only briefly mention the methods in the introduction if they are well-known. The analysis is based on deduction or statistical methods. It is sometimes called "theory," but it belongs to the results and discussion section if it is new. Analytical results, in general, depend on the assumptions. Still, not all problems are mathematically tractable, especially those that include nonlinear relationships and feedback loops between parts (Casti 1994; Camazine et al. 2001; Thurner et al. 2018) and statistics that are not Gaussian or some of its derivatives (Simon 2002; Kim and Shevlyakov 2008). Sometimes, the optimization criterion creates a problem. For example, power or mean-square error may be tractable criteria for analysis (Wang and Bovik 2009), whereas error probability is not unless we assume interference that is additive Gaussian noise (Lucky 1973; Pulleyblank 1973).

Analytical results may be easier to reach after some simulations, and simulations and other measurements may improve our understanding of the model. We have a reasonable basis for our work if we use *optimal* systems as a reference, maximizing some performance criterion, and their *approximations*. Alternatively, we may consider some *suboptimal* systems.

Often, we can use theoretical models that are widely accepted or defined in a standard and no longer need verification. Otherwise, we need some experimental methods for verification and validation, described in such detail that the experiments are repeatable and reproducible. In communications, the environment is described using channel models, which include a distortion model corresponding to linear multipath fading, additive noise, and interference from other nearby systems (Proakis and Salehi 2008; Mämmelä and Wichman 2008).

Common noise forms in electronics include thermal, shot, flicker, and impulse noise. The amplitude of *thermal noise* is often assumed to have Gaussian distribution. The Gaussian distribution is also called a normal distribution. The thermal noise has a uniform spectrum and thus it is called white noise (Cohen 2005; Kim and Shevlyakov 2008; Ziemer and Tranter 2014). Gaussian distribution is a useful model since the central limit theorem of statistics leads to Gaussian distribution as in thermal noise. One reason to use Gaussian distribution is its mathematical tractability.

The term "white noise" was originally used by Vladimir K. Zworykin (1927). It refers to the uniform spectrum, but the term Gaussian noise refers to the probability density function of the amplitude. White noise is not always Gaussian. Thermal noise can be explained by assuming that a conductor is a box where some of the electrons behave randomly just like gas molecules in a room. The electrons have a speed distribution depending on the temperature. The higher the temperature, the wider the distribution. Since electrons have a discrete nature, they also result in another noise called *shot noise* that does not depend on temperature or frequency. The amplitude of the noise has a Poisson distribution. *Flicker noise* has a frequency spectrum inversely proportional to frequency. Another standard noise model is *impulse* or *burst noise* (Lucky 1973). Shot noise is continuous, while impulse noise occurs in short bursts. Often the arrival time is assumed to be Poisson distributed. Impulse noise is an example of human-made noise but may also come from nature. Some noise can also come from the atmosphere and space.

Multipath fading is commonly assumed to have complex Gaussian distribution, where the amplitude is either Rayleigh or Ricean distributed (Proakis and Salehi 2008). A common distribution is also Nakagami distribution. Distortion may also be nonlinear, representing the analog parts in the transmitter and the receiver, such as amplifiers, limiters, and mixers.

Practical measurements need a description of the measurement system and its environment. A challenging part is describing the environment. There are as many environments as there are places. Thus, reproducibility may only be possible if the measurements are done in many areas and averaged out. Sometimes, a simple map of the environment is useful. We can often use some standardized *environmental chambers* for product and material development to simulate various conventional and extreme environments using different environmental parameters (Xie et al. 2023). Such chambers include anechoic chambers and chambers for temperature, humidity, pressure, acceleration, vibration, and shock. In measurements, we use the International System of Quantities (ISQ), which includes the earlier International System of Units (SI).

Results and discussion We present novel results using equations, figures, and tables. It is usually most natural to discuss them immediately and not in a separate section. In the discussion, we elaborate on our findings and link the discussion back to the introduction (Shuttleworth 2009). Following the hourglass principle, we can expand on the topic later in the conclusion.

We present numerical results to illustrate the results of the analysis. The numerical results should include some idealized reference curves for limiting cases to verify that the results are correct. We should compare our results with the existing literature, measurements, or simulations with a reliable model.

We characterize systems by fundamental properties including functionality, performance, dependability, security, and cost (Hubka and Eder 1988; Avizienis et al. 2004). Performance indicates "the manner in which or efficiency with which the system works" (Random House Webster's College Dictionary 1999). We maximize the functionality ("benefits") and minimize the use of basic resources ("expenditures"). We measure system performance against a scale with a unit (for example, delay in seconds or temperature in kelvins) or by using efficiency = benefits/expenditures (for example, speed = distance/time).

We give numerical values of all parameters of the system model to guarantee reproducibility. The value of the results depends on how well we can generalize them. The bottom-up approach, from simple to more complex, helps us produce convincing generalizations.

Conclusion The conclusion is one of the sections that most readers read initially. In this section, we build on our discussion and relate our findings to other research (Shuttleworth 2009). The conclusion summarizes the main results, discusses their significance (IEEE Spectrum 1965), and offers a broader scope than defined in the introduction. It is also good to show the results' limitations, advantages, and applications and make recommendations for further work.

Acknowledgment In the acknowledgement section, we mention those contributing persons whose contribution was not enough to select them as coauthors. We also mention funding organizations and projects and those persons who acquired funding for our project. Often, even the project's contract number is mentioned. In some conference papers, the funding organizations are mentioned at the bottom of the first page.

Appendices An appendix is like an attic that includes relevant, important, additional information that we can neglect during the first reading. Possible appendices are usually located before the list of references since the appendices may also include citations. The appendices are numbered, and they are cited in the text using the numbers.

List of references The list of references is a must in a scientific paper. The list must be carefully compiled and written according to the publisher's instructions. We should include only relevant references. The instructions do not usually define the length of the list of references except in some tutorial papers. Still, there are limitations to the overall size of the manuscript, which also limits the length of the list of references. In the text, we cite the references so that the reader knows what we cited and what our contribution was. The authors should only refer to books and papers that they have seen. We should not generally refer to the Internet since there is no review process, and the contents may change or even disappear. Usually, the citation should be in the first sentence that we cited. Usually, the Harvard author-date style, for example (Smith 1990), or the Vancouver author-number style is used in citations, for instance, as a number in brackets such as [1]. In the Harvard style, the list of references is in an alphabetic order, but in the Vancouver style, they are usually in the order of use. It is generally best to refer to original journal papers and newest conference papers. In addition, we may also refer to a book or review paper to shorten the literature review, possibly using the phrase "and the references therein." It is in general advisable to give credit to the original discovery. If practical, we give relevant page numbers for books. If the list of references is extensive, an alphabetical order using the first author's surname may be better than the order of use.

Biographies The length of the biography is typically 150–200 words, depending on the journal. We do not include biographies in conference papers. Publishers usually have good instructions for writing biographies (IEEE Author Center 2024). The biography typically consists of the name, place and year of birth, education, major field of study, work experience, a short list of previous publications, research interests, memberships in scientific societies, awards, and positions of trust. In some journals, a photograph of each author is attached to the biographies.

2.4.3 Writing the Text

We list valuable tools for research in Table 2.7. When we conduct the research, we use the bottom-up approach, but we write a paper using the top-down approach from general to more specific. Originality, significance, correctness, and readability are the essential requirements for a scientific paper (Fig. 2.1). We do not write to ourselves but to our readers. We do not mix original and review papers. The text must be compact and unified. The text must not be implicit but explicit. We should not leave room for guesswork and interpretations. We do not describe the process of learning, only the final result. Define all new terms, symbols, and abbreviations when they occur for the first time. Some abbreviations may have over 100 definitions, and there is a danger that the text becomes ambiguous without explanations. Write a stand-alone document that is understandable without reading all the references. We number figures, tables, equations, appendices, and references separately, and we use those numbers when referring to them.

Plagiarism, including self-plagiarism, is strictly forbidden. *Plagiarism* is verbatim copying somebody else's work. *Self-plagiarism* is verbatim copying or reusing one's own work as if it were new. If we publish two journal papers, an overlap of more than, say, 25% may be interpreted as self-plagiarism (IEEE Journal of Selected Topics in Signal Processing 2024), see Fig. 2.17. We may need such an overlap in the materials and methods section for describing the system model. The other sections must, in general, be completely new. Recently, based on specific scientific databases, a *similarity index* or similarity score is measured in some journals before the review process to reveal plagiarism. The similarity index must be below a threshold such as 20% (IEEE Communications Magazine 2024).

Commonly, we present papers at various stages of its evolution, such as publishing early ideas in a workshop (often as a presentation), more developed work in a conference, and fully developed contributions in a journal (IEEE 2024). Suppose we submit an earlier conference paper to a journal. In that case, we must substantially revise the paper, and then the manuscript will be reviewed again. The authors will be required to cite the earlier own work. New results are not usually necessary compared to the earlier own conference paper, but the submission should contain "expansions of key ideas, examples, elaborations, and so forth, of the conference paper" (IEEE Design and Test 2022). In some journals, the journal paper must have, say, at least 30% new material (Fig. 2.17) (Offutt 2016a, b). We need a citation to the conference paper, and we must summarize the additional technical contributions in the introduction. The new manuscript should have a new title and abstract, a new idea, and further experimentation. It is best to rewrite everything, mainly if a similarity index is used in the review process. Some journals request "sufficient new technical material to justify a new paper" (IEEE Transactions on Microwave Theory and Techniques 2019). If the publisher of the conference paper and the journal paper differ, the publisher may own the copyright to the text, figures, and tables, which we must respect. Some letters journals do not publish earlier conference papers at all.

Table 2.7 Valuable tools for research

Tools for research	Explanation
Google Scholar	Search engine for scholarly literature
Google Books Ngram Viewer	Search engine for n-grams in books
Encyclopedia Britannica	Encyclopedia
Wikipedia	Encyclopedia based on crowdsourcing
Merriam-Webster Dictionary	English dictionary
Oxford English Dictionary	English dictionary
Oxford Advanced Learner's Dictionary	English dictionary
Online Etymology Dictionary	Etymology dictionary
Acronym Finder	Dictionary of acronyms
Software and Systems Engineering Vocabulary (SE VOCAB)	IEEE/ISO/IEC vocabulary
IEEE Standards Dictionary	IEEE vocabulary
International Vocabulary of Metrology	JCGM vocabulary
Electropedia (IEC Online)	IEC vocabulary
Open Library	Digital library
Internet Archive	Digital library
Google Books	Digital library
Journal Storage (JSTOR)	Digital library
IEEE Xplore	Digital library
ACM Digital Library	Digital library
Engineering Village	Scientific database
Scopus	Scientific database
Web of Science	Scientific database
Wolfram Public Resources	Resources for computation and knowledge
Eric Weinstein's World of Science	Resources for mathematics and science

Fig. 2.17 Relationship of two journal papers (left) and a conference and journal paper (right). The percentages refer to overlapping material and additional material, respectively

Intellectual property rights include patents, copyrights, trademarks, and trade secrets. *Copyright* is "the exclusive right to make and sell copies of an intellectual production" (Online Etymology Dictionary 2024). A *trademark* is a proprietary name protected by law (Skillin and Gay 1974).

If plagiarism is exposed, the editor-in-chief may request the plagiarist to publish a formal apology letter and return proper credit to the original authors. To avoid plagiarism, we must use quotation marks in verbatim citations or rephrase the sentences because of copyright restrictions and give the reference. According to the US Copyright Office, copyright protects "the form of expression rather than the subject matter of the writing." Copyright protection does not include ideas that are protected by *patents*. However, we must always credit earlier ideas by providing references.

The authors originally own the copyright but transfer it to the publisher for commercial purposes. Copyright law does not define the maximum length of a direct quotation, but it should not usually be longer than one paragraph or about 250 words (Higham 1998). Instead of quotation marks, we can use an indentation or a smaller font size. The quotation must be relevant to the manuscript that cannot be based on only quotations. For tables and figures, permission must be asked from the publisher unless we change them significantly (Higham 1998). We must paraphrase a long copyrighted text before a different publisher can publish it. *Creative Commons* is a nonprofit organization that can "give everyone from individual creators to large institutions a standardized way to grant the public permission to use their creative work under copyright law" (Creative Commons 2022). A Creative Commons (CC) license enables the free distribution of an otherwise copyrighted work.

It is easier for the reader to explain the objectives clearly; otherwise, the reader may need help in a text with endless topics and equations without any conclusions. We may use motivation and orientation in each new section to make the organization clear and easy to follow. All sections and paragraphs should have an apparent reason for existing. All paragraphs should present a single *topic*, and all sentences should present a single *thought*. Each paragraph, including the abstract, starts with a topic sentence, orienting the reader to that paragraph (Young 2002). The use of topic sentences corresponds to the general top-down approach in writing. Readers may browse the text by reading topic sentences; therefore, it is a good idea not to refer to the earlier paragraph in the topic sentence.

The table of contents and the organization represent the common thread of the text. Two approaches exist for the writing: drafting the whole text or drafting first the table of contents. In the former case, we write a draft and try to improve it iteratively, which is more manageable for beginners. In the latter case, we write a very detailed outline of the table of contents and then finish the sentences. This may lead to better organization since the unification is better done, including definitions of terms and symbols. We use this approach if we know the topic well.

Sometimes, people advise that we first write the body of the text and later the title, abstract, introduction, and conclusions. The latter parts are challenging to write, but we should start outlining them right from the beginning to have enough time to improve them. Otherwise, in the end, there may be no time to finalize them, and the quality of these more important parts may remain poor: they are not well linked to the body of the text but look glued at the top afterward. Furthermore, outlining the title and abstract makes it clear what is original and significant in the paper. Thus, we should outline them first.

We must unify the use of terms and symbols. We always use the same terms and symbols for the same concept. Using synonymous terms becomes evident if we clearly show their relationships. We define all the terms, symbols, and abbreviations the first time we use them in the paper. We can find definitions of terms in dictionaries such as Merriam-Webster, standards such as (SE VOCAB 2024; IEEE Standards Dictionary 2024; Electropedia 2024; JCGM 2012) or in good books and journal papers. We define also abbreviations, e.g., "signal-to-noise ratio (SNR)." The explanations are, for example, in the Acronym Finder.

The scientific text must be argumentative, logical, objective, and accurate. It must be correct, concise, and crystal clear (IEEE Transactions on Information Theory 1969). Specific jargon may make communication difficult (Ackoff 2006). Good grammar and style improve clarity. It is a pleasure to read good text. We ensure that each word used contributes to the sentence's meaning. We avoid verbosity, tautology, ambiguity clichés, overworked phrases, and repetitions. The grammar must be perfect (Huckin and Olsen 1991; Einsohn and Schwartz 2019). Do not jump tenses. In general, use the present tense except in the abstract and the materials and methods section, where the past tense is usually used (Higham 1998; IEEE 2012; Gastel and Day 2016). When we refer to existing knowledge, we use the present tense. We use the past tense when referring to our new results. The active voice is more exciting and less ambiguous than the passive voice, which can be used mainly if there is no agent (LoMaglio and Robinson 1985). We can avoid passive voice by using "editorial we" to represent a collective viewpoint (Random House Webster's Concise College Dictionary 1999). The "editorial we" should not be mixed with the "royal we," which refers to only one person.

We must avoid any explicit or implicit contradictory claims. If we always write everything accurately, we indeed find any weak points in our understanding. We use long complicated sentences sparingly since they are difficult to understand. A telegraphic style is irritating to read. We use only a few short or very long sections or paragraphs. If a section becomes prolonged, we can divide it by using subtitles. The division improves the readability of the text.

We group the sentences to form a consistent paragraph. There should be a link between all sentences. We can use different liaison words, such as however, therefore, hence, furthermore, etc., although the style may appear heavy if such words are used too often.

In general, we avoid boldface, italicized, or underlined sentences. Some new terms may be in italics when we define them for the first time. We should also avoid brief comments in parentheses. They may be inaccurate, especially if they do not form complete sentences. We should avoid using trade names, company names, and proprietary terms (IEEE Spectrum 1965). We should use footnotes sparingly, but they are common in human sciences.

Equations may appear either embedded within the text as *in-text equations* or set on separate lines as *displayed equations*. To conserve space, we can incorporate simple equations not subsequently referred to in the text without any equation number.

We number displayed equations. We locate the number close to the right margin. We refer to the equations only by using the numbers, for example (1). We do not refer to equations in other ways, such as "the equation above." The equations must be a logical part of a complete sentence with appropriate punctuation. We should write the displayed equations with the fewest possible lines.

We define all the symbols the first time they occur. Typically, we define them below the equation, for example, by using the word "where." If possible, use generally accepted symbols, for example, in standards or journal papers. Many symbols are defined in ISO 80000 standards on quantities and units (Thompson and Taylor 2008; Glavic 2021). The standards present the International System of Quantities (ISQ). Many standards are copyrighted and thus not freely available.

We present variables by letter symbols in italics everywhere, i.e., in the text, equations, figures, and tables (Thompson and Taylor 2008). We do not italicize numbers, brackets, functions, operators, signs such as +, −, ., /, etc., punctuation marks, or text unless we use it for a term that is defined. In general, we use only one-letter symbols with suitable subscripts and superscripts. If an index is an abbreviation, we write it as standard text or upright. Vectors and matrices are usually in boldface italic.

We number all the figures and tables separately and consecutively. We refer to the figures and tables only by using numbers. We refer to all the figures and tables in the text. We do not refer to them in other ways, such as "in the figure shown below." We should use self-explanatory captions, not merely labels. When we present numerical results, we should include the parameter values in the figures themselves or in the figure captions; then, there is no need to repeat them in the text.

The author in Harmon (1992) summarizes the problems in writing. The authors often hide the most exciting material deep in the text, they overestimate or underestimate the readers' knowledge of the subject, the authors may claim that well-known facts are new, and there may be gaps between the thoughts. Such mistakes show a poor understanding of history. Typical errors in writing include the following:

- Writing instructions are not strictly followed.
- Novelty is not clearly shown.
- The organization of the text could be better. There are repetitions, contradictions, or gaps in reasoning.
- Standard terminology is neither used nor defined. Terminology is not uniform.
- Not all abbreviations and symbols are defined, especially in tables and figures. Obscure abbreviations are used in titles and the abstract.
- There are grammatical mistakes in punctuation, spaces, articles, and use of lower-case and upper-case letters. There are spelling mistakes and long complicated sentences.
- Short, inaccurate comments in parentheses are used.
- Italicization and bolding rules are not followed in equations.

- Figures are inaccurately drawn.
- The author tries to write textbook text, although the target readers are experts in the field. The author writes for himself or herself.
- The author publishes only at low-level conferences, although the target should be in archival journal papers.
- The references are not properly used. Many references are not scientific or relevant. They may include web pages that disappear soon. The author probably does not know the relevant references, implying that no literature review has been done and the ideas may not be original.

2.4.4 Selection of Conference and Journal

After writing short internal reports, the following steps are conference and journal papers, usually in this order. Selection of the proper forum is crucial since an excellent manuscript may only be accepted if the topic matches the readership's interests. Suitable forums may be in your bibliography since they include similar earlier papers. Some countries rank book publishers, journals, and conferences according to quality. The most important ranking is the division into scientific and nonscientific forums.

The quality of conferences is sometimes estimated using the acceptance rates, although this is only partially objective. In a good conference, the acceptance rate is below 50%. In the best conferences, the acceptance rate is 10–30%. Conferences are usually organized annually or biannually, sometimes even twice a year. Therefore, the deadlines and dates of conferences are best remembered by developing a personal conference calendar since they usually repeat at the same time each year (Fig. 2.18), and we can get prepared early enough. A *deadline* is the date when the manuscript must be submitted at the latest, and it must be strictly followed. Similar deadlines are defined for special issues of journals, but regular papers can be submitted at any time. We should focus on a few relevant conferences so that we learn to know our colleagues in our discipline.

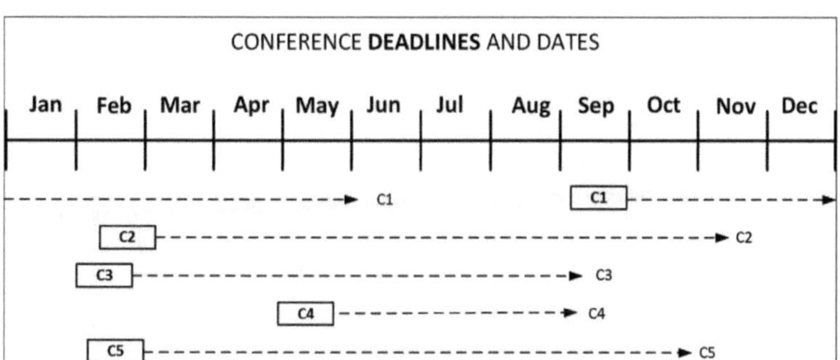

Fig. 2.18 A conference calendar for five conferences (C1–C5)

Journals are conventionally compared with *journal impact factors (JIFs)*, published by *Journal Citation Reports (JCR)*, and based on the Web of Science database. In any reference year, the JIF is the number of citations of papers published in a journal during the two preceding years, divided by the total number of papers published during those two years. Thus, the JIF is not the number of citations per paper but rather the average number of citations per year during the last two years. The impact factor may be misleading statistics since the index covers only two preceding years. However, the width of the *citation histogram* in good journals may be up to 20–25 years, and the maximum is after 2–6 years (Amin and Mabe 2000), see Fig. 2.19. Alternative indices include the 5-year impact factor, total cites, immediacy index, and cited half-life. The 5-year impact factor uses the cites in the reference year to papers published in the past five years. *Total cites* show the total number of citations to the journal in the reference year. The *immediacy index* is the number of citations in the reference year of papers published in a journal in the same year. The *cited half-life* is the median age of papers cited in a journal in the reference year. In good journals, the cited half-life may be over ten years. New journals must be separately examined based on the reputation of the publisher.

Eugene Garfield, one of the founders of bibliometrics and scientometrics, has also proposed another index called *journal performance indicator (JPI)*, whose purpose is to eliminate the discrepancies of the JIF to show the actual number of citations of an average paper (Garfield 2006, 2007; Kumar 2017). The JPI links each source item to its unique citations. It is possible to obtain cumulative impact measures covering longer time spans. If the period is increased, the JPI approaches an average paper's actual number of citations with the corresponding delay.

A journal ranking system is SCImago Journal and Country Rank based on Scopus. It uses three significant indices: SCImago Journal Rank (SJR), the journal citation h-index, and the number of citations per document, similar to Garfield's JPI (Bollen et al. 2009; Garfield 2007). The SJR index is based on the PageRank algorithm and

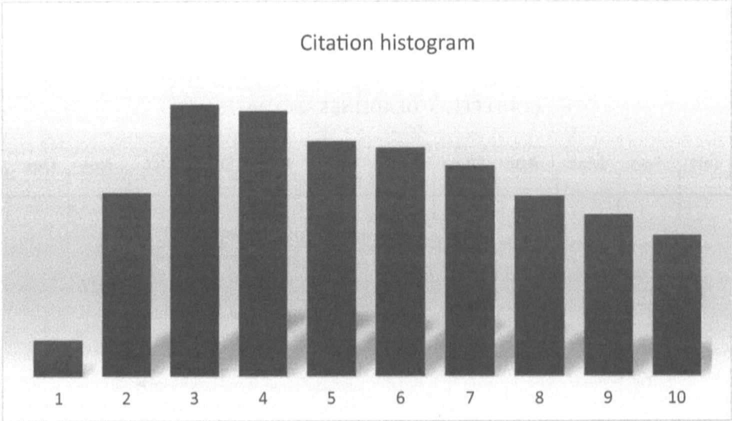

Fig. 2.19 The form of a typical citation histogram versus citation age in years

thus weights the citations using the scientific prestige of citing journals (Gonzalez-Pereira et al. 2010). Journal citation h-index in a given year is the number of papers h in a journal that received at least h citations. An additional measure is *the Eigenfactor*, an iterative ranking scheme that considers that a single citation from a high-quality journal may be more valuable than many citations from low-quality publications (Bergström 2007). Thus, citations and the citation network are used just like in some Internet browsers.

In Bollen et al. (2009), the authors compared 39 scientific impact measures for journals. The authors concluded that scientific impact cannot be measured by any single indicator. The JIF and SJR may not measure the actual scientific impact. According to the authors, usage-based measures may be better consensus measures. The trend is now to measure the impact of individual authors using the h-index (Hirsch 2005) or more comprehensive indices (Castelnuovo et al. 2010).

A conventional approach to evaluate an individual author's research output is to count the number of papers published in highly cited journals. The situation changed after Jorge E. Hirsch suggested the h-index of authors (Hirsch 2005); our h-index is h if we have h publications that are cited at least h times. The goal of the index is to measure the quantity and quality of a researcher's output at the same time. The h-index is now computed by Web of Science, Scopus, and Google Scholar, but all provide a different h-index. The h-index in Google Scholar is generally larger than in the scientific databases. Hirsch suggested that the value of $h = 12$ in a significant scientific database such as the Web of Science is a typical value for an associate professor, $h = 18$ is a typical value for a full professor, $h = 15 \ldots 20$ for a fellowship in a scientific society, and $h = 45$ for membership in a national academy of sciences.

The h-index has many shortcomings, as all indices based on citations. The nonlinearity of the index may be a problem. The h-index cannot be larger than the number of papers. For example, because of his short career, the famous mathematician Evariste Galois has an h-index $h = 2$, which will never increase. The authors in Waltnam and van Eck (2012) noticed the inconsistency of the h-index. According to the authors, the *highly cited publications indicator* does not produce inconsistent rankings, unlike the h-index. The indicator counts the number of publications with at least a certain number of citations forming a threshold. A question remains about how the threshold is selected since the indicator is a function of the threshold. For example, Google Scholar uses the i10 index, which has a threshold of ten citations.

The citations have several problems; some authors believe we should "stop the numbers game" (Parnas 2007). Eugene Garfield himself has stated: "In itself, the number of citations of a man's work is no measure of significance" (Meadows 1985). The number of citations depends on the size of the society doing research in the same discipline (Garfield 2006). Many authors may have similar names, or the same author is known with different names, especially in the case of transliteration according to spelling or transcription according to pronunciation. The citations include citations to the same journal or author. These are called *self-citations*. There may be a problem with charmed circles. One paper may include 500 authors, and all the authors receive the same credit, although there are usually only a few actual authors, and the others may be honorary authors.

Review papers are often easier to read and may receive more citations than original papers. Some significant papers may be challenging to understand or appreciate and may be forgotten for a long time. Such papers are called *Sleeping Beauties*. For example, the modern theory of genetics started from the studies of Gregor Mendel (1865), and his research was rediscovered 35 years later independently by three people (Rothman 2003), 16 years after Mendel's death. A more recent example is the theory of ambient backscatter communication invented by Harry Stockman (1948). The paper was rarely cited during the next 50 years or so until about 2001, when its relationship to radio frequency identification (RFID) was noticed (Bansal 2003).

Some citations may be negative and thus controversial. Even erroneous results may receive more citations than others. One famous example is (Sokal 1996), which received thousands of citations, but the author admitted later that the paper was a parody. His purpose was to demonstrate that the time's social scientific and philosophical discussion was too obscure. The paper is one of the author's most cited papers.

Citations often have a *skew* meaning that most of the citations are given to few papers, as expected by the Pareto principle extended to science: Vilfredo Pareto observed that 20% of the population owned 80% of the property. The remaining 20% of wealth was distributed in a similar way (Craft and Leake 2002). New journals have not yet received many citations, and thus, they must be separately considered, usually based on the contents and the reputation of the publisher and the author.

We all have heard the "publish or perish" principle. Authors are often advised to produce highly cited papers, which may restrict the topics researched and lead to a lack of motivation, innovation, and true collaboration (Calver 2015). Too much emphasis on citations may lead to incremental research and stagnation of science since it is too risky to focus on novel ideas (Parnas 2007; Bhattacharya and Packalen 2020). In addition to citations, some *novelty metrics* should be used to encourage pursuing more innovative and riskier projects. The number of citations is not a measure of significance since the citations may be superficial, and not all are equally valuable. The authors should be persistent, have a focused research program with a vision and sound methodology, and publish in relevant journals to advance career development and disciplinary and social impact (Calver 2015).

In summary, we should publish in a place where similar papers have been published earlier, using our literature review and bibliography. We select the best possible forum depending on our writing ability: a conference or a journal. In general, it is best to prefer good forums of scientific societies. Among scientific societies, the IEEE seems to have the best writing instructions in information technology.

2.4.5 Peer Review Process

After the manuscript is submitted to a journal or conference, it will go to an editorial board (editor, associate editor, or review organizer), which will organize a peer review process where at least two or three anonymous reviewers examine the manuscript, give comments, and a recommendation regarding the publication (Smith 1990; Senturia 2003). In books, a similar review is usually done for the book proposal. In peer review, the anonymous reviewers are at the same level regarding their abilities as the authors. A journal or conference without a peer review is not scientific. In some cases, the *double-anonymized review* is used so that the authors do not know the names of the reviewers, and the reviewers do not know the names of the authors. The reviewers provide criticism that is very valuable in improving the quality of our manuscript. In doctoral theses, the reviewers are usually not anonymous.

The reviewers are our peers, i.e., experts in the field, often selected using the keywords in the manuscript and from among the independent authors in the list of references. The reviewers usually have a template where they give numerical marks to the manuscript, general comments to the authors, and confidential comments to the editor. The editor or the associate editor makes a recommendation, and the editor-in-chief makes the final decision. The evaluation criteria are novelty, significance, correctness, readability, and suitability (Fig. 2.1).

Priority disputes As summarized in Rothman (2003), there have been many disputes on the priority of discoveries and inventions. Many of them have been made independently when the time was mature. It is important to patent or publish the idea as soon as possible to receive priority. In addition, it is as important as the invention itself to make the inventions practical and to market them.

Famous disputes concern the invention of the telephone and radio, initially the wireless telegraph (Salazar-Palma et al. 2011). One of the first to demonstrate the telephone was Antonio Meucci (1856), but Graham Bell and Elisha Gray (1876) had a dispute since Meucci was too poor to submit a patent application. Gray's caveat—a formal notice of work in progress—was filed two hours later than Bell's application, and the patent was granted to Bell, although, according to Rothman (2003), several curiosities were noticed. For example, Gray's caveat was much more detailed than Bell's application, and the patent officer had revealed to Bell the central idea in the caveat regarding the variable resistance. Somebody added the idea afterward in the margin of Bell's application. Gray eventually became convinced that he had been fooled.

Nikola Tesla gave a public demonstration of radio transmission in 1893 and submitted the first US patent applications for the invention in 1897, two years before Guglielmo Marconi. The patent was given to Tesla in 1899. However, the decision was reversed in 1903, and the patent was granted to Marconi. Furthermore, the Nobel Prize was given to Marconi in 1909. The Supreme Court decided in 1943 that Tesla was the true inventor of the radio, but at that time, both Marconi and Tesla had already passed away.

One dispute was about the invention of positive feedback, also known as regeneration (Bennett 1979a; Cotanis 1997). Edwin H. Armstrong invented positive feedback in 1913, and he also noticed that if the gain was too large, the amplifier started to oscillate. Lee de Forest claimed priority to the invention, and the US Supreme

Court decided in 1934 in favor of him. However, the scientific community was on Armstrong's side.

Modern parallel inventions or even disputes concerned packet switching used as the basis of the Internet (Huurdeman 2003), social networking services (Good 2012), and touch screens used in smartphones (Buxton 2010; Väänänen 2015). The touch screen was invented and demonstrated in 2002 years before Apple published its iPhone in 2007, but significant players did not believe in the idea.

Sometimes, it is impossible to define the original inventor, as in the case of short message service (SMS) (Lähteenmäki et al. 2017). The idea was not wholly new since characters have been sent wirelessly since the invention of the wireless telegraph using the Morse code.

Reviewers tend to prefer papers that follow the existing paradigm, a world view that is widely accepted in the discipline. New ideas are often rejected. Several classical examples concern the now-established theories on the theory of evolution, the Fourier series, the Doppler effect, alternating current (AC), negative feedback, and frequency modulation (FM). There are many other similar examples.

Charles Darwin (1859) is usually seen as the discoverer of the theory of evolution, but in fact, Georges-Louis Leclerc proposed it about one hundred years earlier (Roberts 2024). People were not receptive to his ideas, and he had to renounce publicly everything he had written.

Regarding the Fourier series (1807), contemporary mathematicians rejected the idea that an infinite sum of trigonometric functions can add up to an arbitrary function (Gonzalez-Velasco 1992). They failed to realize that a nonperiodic function could coincide with a periodic function over a bounded interval. At that time, there was no definition of convergence. Joseph Fourier himself gave one of the first definitions of convergence in 1811.

Christian Doppler's work (1842) created two controversies (Toman 1984). Christophorus H. D. Buys Ballot had verified Doppler's principle for sound. Still, he rejected the application of the principle to explain the color of stars since the human eye does not have the needed sensitivity to color, the known spectrum at that time was finite, and the known velocities were too small for the eye to perceive color changes resulting from the motion. Later, James Clerk Maxwell (1865) predicted the existence of the electromagnetic spectrum, and Edwin P. Hubble (1929) developed the concept of the expanding universe using the Doppler effect (Asimov 1994). Joseph Petzval rejected the correctness of Doppler's principle. It was later observed that Petzval's theory was valid only when the source and observer were at rest concerning each other.

Nikola Tesla (1883) constructed an alternating current (AC) induction motor, and William Stanley (1885) developed one of the first practical AC transformers for power transmission (Asimov 1994). Thomas A. Edison was a proponent of direct current (DC), opposed AC for safety reasons, and started a "war of currents." However, AC power transmission is far more practical than DC transmission and is now invariably used. Charles P. Steinmetz (1893) used complex numbers to analyze AC and completed the victory of AC over DC.

Harold Black from the Bell Laboratories developed the idea to reduce the distortion of amplifiers using negative feedback in 1927 (Bennett 1979a, b). The idea was to build an amplifier whose gain was much higher than needed and use negative feedback to throw away the excess gain. If we use feedback, nonlinear distortions are removed without knowledge of the amplifier dynamics (Gao 2014). The idea was too revolutionary, and people found it difficult to accept. Furthermore, the amplifier was thought to be unstable. His US patent application (1928) was approved only nine years later (1937). Even within the Bell Laboratories, people were doubtful. The director forbade using the idea but later had to relent. Black published his idea in 1934, seven years after his invention. Harry Nyquist (1932) published a paper concerning the stability of feedback systems.

The first broadcasting services were based on amplitude modulation (AM) (Lathi 1983). Frequency modulation (FM) was initially proposed as a method to reduce transmission bandwidth. John R. Carson (1922) showed that FM required more bandwidth than amplitude modulation (AM). Without much basis, he concluded that FM had no compensating advantages, and his authority set back the further development of FM. Edwin H. Armstrong (1936) later showed the noise-suppressing advantage of FM over AM because of bandwidth expansion. However, the Federal Communications Commission (FCC) started to resist the FM after an erroneous testimony by a technical expert. It abruptly shifted the allocated bandwidth for FM from 42–50 to 88–108 MHz, making the old equipment obsolete. Armstrong succeeded in 1947 in getting the expert to admit his error, but the frequency allocation was not changed. After strongly resisting FM, the broadcast industry started to use Armstrong's inventions without paying any royalties. Although he did not invent FM, he is considered the father of modern FM. Armstrong lost all his funds in patent suits, and he became depressed and died in 1954.

Ignaz Semmelweis (1847) found a solution to avoid childbed fever (Bencko and Schejbalova 2006; Tulodziecki 2013). He noticed that bad hygiene was related to the fewer, not bad air as many people assumed at that time. The colleagues rejected his ideas, and he became depressed and was forgotten. After Semmelweis had passed away, Joseph Lister (1867) also developed hygiene, and Louis Pasteur (1879) found the actual reason for the childbed fewer was streptococcus. The rejection of a new paradigm was later called the Semmelweis effect.

Charles S. Peirce invented abduction (Larson 2021). He was later described as "perhaps the most important mind the United States have ever produced." However, when he died, he was largely forgotten.

In the paper (Santini 2005), the author presents more recent case examples where famous papers by E. W. Dijkstra, E. F. Codd, A. Turing, C. E. Shannon, C. A. R. Hoare, and R. L. Rivest et al. were initially rejected. For example, Shannon, who invented the theory of information transmission (1948) as a theoretical basis for communications, received very negative comments: "I don't understand the relevance of discrete sources: No matter what one does, in the end, the signal will have to be modulated using good old-fashioned vacuum tubes, so the signal on the 'channel' will always be analogical." Now most wireless communications are done digitally using "discrete sources" although amplifiers and the propagation channel itself are still analog. Amplifiers are implemented with transistors, invented initially as bipolar transistors in 1947. As a confidential comment to the editor, the reviewer added: “Discrete channels with a finite number of symbols are good for telegraphy, but telegraphy is 100 years old, hardly a good research topic.” Many papers have been rejected, and they later received a Nobel Prize.

Ken Thompson and Dennis Ritchie invented the Unix operating system. Still, they had to do it secretly since their employer had withdrawn from the project in 1969 because it was behind schedule (Toomey 2011). They started using a discarded and outdated PDP-7 computer. Later, a new PDP-11 computer was bought, but the purpose of their work was kept secret. Richie also developed the C language (1972) for programming Unix, which was published in 1973. Both Thompson and Richie received many awards for their inventions.

M. Stanley Whittingham invented in 1972 the rechargeable lithium-ion battery and published it in 1976 in Science magazine (Murray 2023). The battery did not raise much interest, but it was developed further by John G. Goodenough and Akira Yoshino. It became a commercial product in 1991 or 19 years after the original invention. In 2019, the three inventors received a Nobel Prize in chemistry. Goodenough was the oldest recipient of the Nobel Prize in the history at the age of 97 years. The lithium-ion battery is now one of the most common batteries for example in smart phones in addition to alkaline battery used in everyday consumer devices due to their low cost and good availability.

Organization of peer review We often need to improve the manuscript before it can be published. If the manuscript is not rejected, the authors are usually asked to make corrections and send a response letter to each reviewer about the changes they made. In the letter, we may list each comment separately and our response as politely and accurately as possible. We must also make the appropriate corrections. It is best to react to all comments, although they may be small. If the author neglects some comments, the manuscript is most probably rejected in the second round of the review.

A similar peer review process is organized in conferences. There is a technical program committee (TPC) that organizes the review using anonymous reviewers. Usually, the decision on acceptance is made without any further examination. In some conferences, a *rebuttal process* is organized to allow a written discussion between the authors and the reviewers. The authors prepare a camera-ready copy of the accepted paper, which is published in conference proceedings.

The goal of the criticism given in the peer-review process is to show weaknesses and improve the work quality in international competition. We should not prevent criticism, although we may become angry because criticism may hurt. Criticism must be objective and impersonal.

If we act as a reviewer, we should offer constructive criticism. We start the feedback by summarizing the manuscript’s contribution to show we understood the message. The hamburger or sandwich method is a good general organization of the review. The organization means that positive feedback is given both in the beginning and end, and the “beef” or actual criticism is in the middle. The criticism is presented in a friendly and objective way to not discourage the author, who may be a young researcher. Minor comments can be given in general terms as a side note. A poor criticism is expressed in one sentence without any reason. For example, a typical comment is on the lack of numerical or simulation results. This comment is understandable when the reviewer needs help understanding the paper's contents and a numerical result to verify that the idea works. The reviewers much justify their comments. If the reviewers claim that the idea is not novel, they must clearly indicate the earlier publication. An example of a poor review is "this paper must be rewritten" unless explicit reasons are given.

A *copy editor* of the journal makes the final layout of the manuscript and prepares the camera-ready copy to be published. The time for the review of the copy-edited version or page proof is short, only a few days. The copy editor may have some questions forwarded to the authors. The paper is usually only accepted after the authors sign a *copyright form* with which they transfer the copyright to the publisher, and the authors must ask the publisher if they want to publish the material again with some other publisher. Sometimes, a fee must be paid to republish the material. We refer here to the commercial copyright. Ethically, copyright is always with the author. After publication, the manuscript is a commercial property of the publisher. The author can usually publish the final accepted version with a copyright notice, not the copy-edited version (IEEE 2012). Certain publishers may have special restrictions. For example, for some books, there may be an *embargo period* of a couple of years from the book's first publication.

Oral presentation of your ideas Here are some instructions on how to present your ideas in seminars, workshops, and conferences. In general, a good organization is the IMRDC structure. If the time is very limited, say, to a few minutes, you must give an "elevator pitch talk" where you use the needs, approach, benefits, and competition (NABC) structure from the Stanford Research Institute. If the audience is heterogeneous, it is incredibly challenging to give a talk. We must balance between trivial and unintelligible. Here is my advice:

- Prepare your presentation slides well in advance and make them mature so that the organization is good enough.
- Prepare the slides to the audience, not to yourself, to improve communication. Consider the question what the audience already knows about the topic. We can often safely assume that all people have a university degree, but it may not be from your discipline. However, it is best to demand a lot from the audience so that you do not underestimate it. There should be something for everyone. We must push the audience upwards in abstract thinking since abstractions have the most significant transfer effect (Epstein 2019).
- Explain your outline in the beginning, starting with orientation and motivation. Explain carefully why the topic is essential, using examples from everyday life. An alternative would be to delve deep into the details so that almost nobody can follow you. Your message should have a common thread that is uniform.
- Explain at least briefly the concepts that you use with some simplified definitions. Avoid ambiguous terminology. Explain the history with a simple timeline. This

way, you link your ideas to a bigger whole and history. Proceed from simple to complex especially in the case of complex ideas.

- Try to keep your presentation brief. An exhaustive talk is usually impossible in a limited time, but even a simple talk can raise the audience's interest in your ideas. You can use a list of keywords on a paper as a memory support so that you remember to say everything needed in a short time. Reading speech on paper may not sound natural, and you may speak too quickly.
- Summarize your *take-home lesson* that the audience should remember afterward (Rota 1997). This lesson is the novel idea you have explained in many words during your presentation. Concentrate on only a few ideas.
- Finally receive the feedback and criticism in a humble way since you may learn something. People in the audience are different. Even if you have done your best, you may receive a comment, "so what?" There is always somebody who knows things better than you. There is also somebody who knows less.

2.5 Chapter Summary and Recommended Reading

We summarized the practical methods to find existing knowledge. We presented the use of the most important databases. We showed the strength of using bibliographies, references (referring to the past), and citations (referring to the future) in literature reviews to find landmark books and papers. Own annotated bibliographies form the basis for the literature reviews. It is also important to thoroughly know the terminology and the field's history. We must classify the material using taxonomies and show the hierarchical relationships. The essential questions are: what the state of the art is, what kind of development or history led to it, and what type of vision for the future we can make based on the history.

We also discussed the IMRDC structure of a paper and the various moves that describe the contents of a paper. The author can use the moves as a checklist; there is no need to use the corresponding titles in the text. In addition, we emphasized the details of the materials and methods section, which is often overlooked in standard writing instructions, especially regarding the system concept. An apparent reason is that the system concept is not well-known in human sciences, and humanists often write the writing instructions.

The topics of this chapter are covered in some writing instructions and books on research methods, for example (Beer and McMurrey 2014; Gastel and Day 2016; Turabian et al. 2018; Repko and Szostak 2021). Information retrieval for interdisciplinary projects is well described in Repko and Szostak (2021). One of the most popular books on writing scientific papers is (Gastel and Day 2016), directly following the standard IMRAD structure and thus serving as a good starting point. An equally popular book presenting the Chicago style in detail is (Turabian et al. 2018). It emphasizes scientific papers rather than books unlike the *Chicago Manual of Style*. Writing instructions, especially for nonnative speakers, including English grammar, are presented in Huckin and Olsen (1991). Books on writing with style include (Strunk and White 1972; Young 2002). The English language is also changing (Louie 2010; Einsohn and Schwartz 2019). For example, there has been a shift from genitive ("the cover of the book") to possessive cases ("the book's cover"). We reserved the possessive case earlier for exceptional situations, such as humans. It is also a common practice to write "systems theory," whereas earlier, the recommended form was "system theory."

The IEEE style is presented in IEEE (2012), referring to some essential IEEE instructions, including operations manual, taxonomy, editorial style manual, reference guide, and editing mathematics. The IEEE gives more details in IEEE Computer Society Style Guide (IEEE Computer Society 2016). The IEEE instructions refer to the *Chicago Manual of Style* for detailed information. When writing mathematical papers, we recommend the books (Higham 1998; Krantz 2017). They present LaTeX, a modern document preparation system for mathematical texts, available for free in tools such as Overleaf. Good examples of the bolding and italicization rules of variables in equations following ISO standards are in Thompson and Taylor (2008, Sect. 10), available separately in NIST (2008), as a handy reference. We may find handbooks helpful when defining and using different mathematical functions (Abramowitz and Stegun 1970; Olver et al. 2010). In addition, Wolfram Public Resources (Wolfram 2024a) and Eric Weinstein's Wolfram MathWorld and Wolfram ScienceWorld (Wolfram 2024b) provide accurate information on mathematics and physical sciences.

Different publishers favor several famous English dictionaries. These include various versions of Oxford, Merriam-Webster's, Webster's New World, Random House Webster's, and American Heritage dictionaries (Higham 1998). Because of copyrights, they are all different and have dissimilar definitions. Many of the dictionaries are available online.

The most famous dictionary is the *Oxford English Dictionary*. With its 500,000 words, it is the world's largest dictionary of the English language. A popular dictionary for nonnative speakers is the *Oxford Advanced Learner's Dictionary* (Oxford Learner's Dictionaries 2024), available online. A famous book many publishers recommend is *Merriam-Webster*, which is also available online (Merriam-Webster 2024). The unabridged version is *Webster's Third New International Dictionary, Unabridged*, containing 475,000 entries, including the expanded and updated addenda section. The dictionary recommended by the IEEE is (Webster's New World College Dictionary 2001). A good alternative is (Random House Webster's College Dictionary 1999).

The abridged college dictionaries generally include 150,000–200,000 words and unabridged versions of about 500,000 words. Usually, they give the most common meanings first, but in some dictionaries, they use a historical order, which may be inconvenient. Good dictionaries also include the history and etymology of the words. The online versions include audio pronunciation in British and American English. Some dictionaries use the International Phonetic Alphabet (IPA) to express pronunciation. Many dictionaries of American English use some respelling approach where they indicate pronunciation phonemically. In some dictionaries, they separate countable and noncountable nouns. Sometimes, they show hyphenation. A dictionary may include grammar, examples, references, and encyclopedic information such as illustrations. A *thesaurus* contains synonyms and antonyms and explains their different meanings. Some ordinary dictionaries also include such information.

A good dictionary on etymology is (Online Etymology Dictionary 2024). The Time Traveler in the online version of Merriam-Webster's dictionary also gives the first known use of each word. Abbreviations are defined in Acronym Finder (2024). General engineering standard dictionaries include SE VOCAB (2024) about systems engineering, IEEE Standards Dictionary (2024) and Electropedia (2024) about electrical engineering, and JCGM (2012) about metrology.

Discussion Questions

1. How do we define science?
2. What are the most efficient ways to find scientific knowledge across many disciplines?
3. How do we organize a scientific paper? How do we select a conference or journal to publish our results?
4. What kind of peer review report should we write?
5. What are the desirable properties of a researcher? Why is ethics important in science?

References

Abramowitz M, Stegun IA (eds) (1970) Handbook of mathematical functions: with formulas, graphs, and mathematical tables. Dover Publications, New York

Ackoff RL (2006) Why few organizations adopt systems thinking. Syst Res Behav Sci 23:705–708. https://doi.org/10.1002/sres.791

ACM Publications Board (2023) ACM policy on authorship. https://www.acm.org. Accessed 13 Dec 2023

Acronym Finder (2024). https://www.acronymfinder.com. Accessed 17 Oct 2024

Albus JS, Meystel AM (2001) Engineering of mind: an introduction to the science of intelligent systems. Wiley, New York

Amin M, Mabe M (2000) Impact factors: use and abuse. Perspect Publ 1(1):1–6

Amyot D, Eberlein A (2003) An evaluation of scenario notations and construction approaches for telecommunication system development. Telecommun Syst 24(1):61–94

ANSI/NISO (2010) Guidelines for abstracts, Z39.14-1997 (R2009)

Arbnor I, Bjerke B (1997) Methodology for creating business knowledge, 2nd edn. Sage, London

Asimov I (1994) Asimov's chronology of science & discovery: updated and illustrated. Harper & Row, New York

Avizienis A et al (2004) Basic concepts and taxonomy of dependable and secure computing. IEEE Trans Dependable Secure Comput 1(1):11–33

Bansal R (2003) Coming soon to a Wal-Mart near you. IEEE Antennas Propag Mag 45(6):105–106

Barbour IG (1974) Myths, models, and paradigms: a comparative study in science & religion. Harper & Row, San Francisco, CA

Barbour IG (1997) Religion and science: historical and contemporary issues. HarperCollins, New York

Beer DF, McMurrey DA (2014) A guide to writing as an engineer, 4th edn. Wiley, Hoboken, NJ

Bencko V, Schejbalova M (2006) From Ignaz Semmelweis to the present: crucial problems of hospital hygiene. Indoor Built Environ 15(1):3–7

Bennett S (1979a) A history of control engineering, 1800–1930. Peter Peregrinus, Stevenage, UK

Bennett S (1979b) A history of control engineering, 1930–1955. Peter Peregrinus, Stevenage, UK

Bergström C (2007) Eigenfactor: measuring the value and prestige of scholarly journals. Coll Res Libr News 68(5):314–316

Bhattacharya J, Packalen M (2020) Stagnation and scientific incentives. Working paper 26752. National Bureau of Economic Research, Cambridge, MA

Bollen J et al (2009) A principal component analysis of 39 scientific impact measures. PLoS ONE 6(4):1–11

Boulton JG et al (2015) Embracing complexity: strategic perspectives for an age of turbulence. Oxford University Press, Oxford, UK

Buxton B (2010) A touching story: a personal perspective on the history of touch interfaces past and future. In: Proceedings of the society for information display (SID) international symposium seminar and exhibition 2010, Seattle, Washington, pp 444–448

Calver MC (2015) Please don't aim for a highly cited paper. Aust Univ Rev 57(1):45–51

Camazine S et al (2001) Self-organization in biological systems. Princeton University Press, Princeton, NJ

Carlisle R (2004) Scientific American inventions and discoveries: all the milestones in ingenuity-from the discovery of fire to the invention of the microwave oven. Wiley, Hoboken, NJ

Castelnuovo G et al (2010) A more comprehensive index in the evaluation of scientific research: the single researcher impact factor proposal. Clin Pract Epidemiol Ment Health 6:109–114. https://doi.org/10.2174/1745017901006010109

Casti JL (1994) Complexification: explaining paradoxical world through the science of surprise. Abacus, London

Checkland P (1999) Systems thinking, systems practice: includes a 30-year retrospective, rev. Wiley, Chichester, UK

Chekanov SV (2016) Numeric computation and statistical data analysis on the Java platform. Springer, Cham, Switzerland

Cohen L (2005) The history of noise [On the 100th anniversary of its birth]. IEEE Signal Processing Magazine 22(6): 20-45

Conant RC, Ashby WR (1970) Every good regulator of a system must be a model of that system. International Journal of Systems Science 1(2): 89-97

Cotanis N (1997) The radio receiver saga: an introduction to the classic paper by Edwin H. Armstrong. Proc IEEE 85(4):681–684

Craft RC, Leake C (2002) Pareto principle in organizational decision making. Manag Decis 40(8):729–733

Creative Commons (2022). https://creativecommons.org. Accessed 4 Mar 2022

de Bono E (2014) Lateral thinking: an introduction. Vermilion, London, UK

de Solla Price DJ (1986) Little science, big science… and beyond. Columbia University Press, New York

Dedehayir O, Steinert M (2016) The hype cycle model: a review and future directions. Technol Forecast Soc Change 108:28–41. https://doi.org/10.1016/j.techfore.2016.04.005

Einsohn A, Schwartz M (2019) The copyeditor's handbook: a guide for book publishing and corporate communications, 4th edn. University of California Press, Oakland, CA

Electropedia (2024) International Electrotechnical Commission (IEC). http://www.electropedia.org. Accessed 6 Nov 2024

Encyclopedia Britannica (2024). https://www.britannica.com. Accessed 5 Nov 2024

Epstein D (2019) Range: why generalists triumph in a specialized world. Riverhead Books, New York

Falagas ME et al (2008) Comparison of PubMed, Scopus, Web of Science, and Google Scholar: strengths and weaknesses. FASEB J 22(2):338–342

Fernandez-Cano A et al (2004) Reconsidering Price's model of scientific growth: an overview. Scientometrics 61(3):301–321
Feynman RP (1999) The pleasure of finding things out. Basic Books, New York
Gao Z (2014) Engineering cybernetics: 60 years in the making. Control Theory Technol 12(2):97–109
Garfield E (2006) The history and meaning of the journal impact factor. JAMA 295(1):90–93
Garfield E (2007) The evolution of the Science Citation Index. Int Microbiol 10(1):65–69
Gastel B, Day RA (2016) How to write and publish a scientific paper, 8th edn. Greenwood, Santa Barbara, CA
Glavic P (2021) Review of the international systems of quantities and units usage. Standards 1(1):2–16
Gonzalez-Pereira B et al (2010) A new approach to the metric of journals scientific prestige: the SJR indicator. J Informetr 3(4):379–391
Gonzalez-Velasco EA (1992) Connections in mathematical analysis: the case of Fourier series. Am Math Mon 99(5):427–441
Good KD (2012) From scrapbook to Facebook: a history of personal media assemblage and archives. New Media Soc 15(4):557–573
Goodsett M (2014) Discovery search tools: a comparative study. Ref Rev 28(6):2–8
Greene W, Lancaster B (2007) Carrier-grade: five nines, the myth and the reality. Pipeline 3(11):1–9
Harmon JE (1992) Evolution of the scientific paper. In: Proceedings of the IEEE international professional communications conference (IPCC'92), Santa Fe, NM, pp 468–475
Hawking S (2018) Brief answers to the big questions. John Murray, London
Haykin S (2014) Adaptive filter theory, 5th edn. Prentice Hall, Upper Saddle River, NJ
Hicks D (1999) Six reasons to do long-term research. Res Technol Manag 42(4):8–11
Higham NJ (1998) Handbook of writing for the mathematical sciences, 2nd edn. Society for Industrial and Applied Mathematics, Philadelphia, PA
Hill PCJ (2007) Dennis Gabor—contributions to communication theory & signal processing. In: Proceedings of the European conference on electrotechnics (EUROCON'07), Warsaw, Poland
Hirsch JE (2005) An index to quantify an individual's scientific research output. Proc Natl Acad Sci U S A (PNAS) 102(46):16569–16572
Honderich T (ed) (2005) Oxford companion to philosophy, 2nd edn. Oxford University Press, Oxford, UK
Hubka V, Eder WE (1988) Theory of technical systems: a total concept theory for engineering design. Springer-Verlag, Berlin
Huckin TN, Olsen LA (1991) Technical writing and professional communication for nonnative speakers, 2nd edn. McGraw-Hill, New York
Huurdeman A (2003) The worldwide history of telecommunications. Wiley, Hoboken, NJ
IEEE (2012) How to write for technical periodicals & conferences. IEEE, Piscataway, NJ
IEEE (2024) IEEE publication services and products board operations manual. IEEE, Piscataway, NJ
IEEE Author Center (2024) IEEE article templates. http://ieeeauthorcenter.ieee.org. Accessed 24 Oct 2024
IEEE Communications Magazine (2024) Manuscript submission policy. https://www.comsoc.org/publications/magazines/ieee-communications-magazine/author-guidelines/manuscript-submission-policy. Accessed 28 Dec 2024
IEEE Computer Society (2016) IEEE computer society style guide
IEEE Design and Test (2022) Author guidelines. http://www.eng.ucy.ac.cy. Accessed 15 Feb 2022
IEEE Journal of Selected Topics in Signal Processing (2024) Information for authors. https://signalprocessingsociety.org/publications-resources/ieee-journal-selected-topics-signal-processing/information-authors-jstsp. Accessed 28 Dec 2024
IEEE Spectrum (1965) Information for IEEE authors. IEEE Spectr 2(8):111–115
IEEE Standards Dictionary (2024). https://ieeexplore.ieee.org/browse/standards/dictionary. Accessed 5 Nov 2024

IEEE Transactions on Communications (2007) Information for authors. IEEE Trans Commun 55(12):2388

IEEE Transactions on Information Theory (1969) Advice to authors. IEEE Trans Inf Theory 15(2):338

IEEE Transactions on Information Theory (2021) Information for authors. https://www.itsoc.org/. Accessed 24 Oct 2024

IEEE Transactions on Microwave Theory and Techniques (2019) Author information—transactions. https://www.mtt.org/author-information-transactions. Accessed 15 Feb 2022

Interacademy Partnership (2024) Combatting predatory academic journals and conferences. https://www.interacademies.org. Accessed 5 Nov 2024

Ioannidis JPA (2024) Evolving patterns of extreme publishing behavior across science. Scientometrics 129:5783–5796. https://doi.org/10.1007/s11192-024-05117-w

Jain RK, Triandis HC (1997) Management of research and development organizations: managing the unmanageable. Wiley, New York

Jarke M et al (1998) Scenario management: an interdisciplinary approach. Requirements Eng 3:155–173. https://doi.org/10.1007/s007660050002

JCGM (2012) International vocabulary of metrology—basic and general concepts and associated terms (VIM), 3rd edn. Joint Committee for Guides in Metrology (JCGM)

Jinha AE (2010) Article 50 million: an estimate of the number of scholarly articles in existence. Learn Publ 23(3):258–263

Johnson R et al (2018) The STM report: an overview of scientific and scholarly journal publishing 1968–2018, 5th edn. International Association of Scientific, Technical and Medical Publishers (STM), The Hague, The Netherlands

Joseph PD, Tou JT (1961) On linear control theory. Transactions of the American Institute of Electrical Engineers, Part II: Applications and Industry 80(4): 193-196

Kailath T (1966) The complex envelope of white noise. IEEE Trans Inf Theory 12(3):397–398

Kailath T (1960) Correlation detection of signals perturbed by a random channel. IRE Trans Inf Theory IT 6(3):361–366

Keyes RW (1987) The physics of VLSI systems. Addison-Wesley, New York

Kim K, Shevlyakov G (2008) Why Gaussianity? [An attempt to explain this phenomenon]. IEEE Signal Process Mag 25(2):102–113

Kish LB (2002) End of Moore's law: thermal (noise) death of integration in micro and nano electronics. Phys Lett A 305(3–4):144–149

Kragh H (1999) Quantum generations: a history of physics in the twentieth century. Princeton University Press, Princeton, NJ

Krantz SG (2017) A primer of mathematical writing: being a disquisition on having your ideas recorded, typeset, published, read, and appreciated, 2nd edn. American Mathematical Society, Providence, RI

Kumar PKS (2017) Evaluation measures for academic research through citation analysis. Int J Multicult Lit 7(2):133–147

Lähteenmäki J et al (2017) Short-message service as a digital disruptor of industry. J Innov Manag 5(3):122–139

Lariviere V et al (2015) The oligopoly of academic publishers in the digital era. PLoS ONE 10(6):1–15. https://doi.org/10.1371/journal.pone.0127502

Larson EJ (2021) The myth of artificial intelligence: why computers can't think the way we do. Belknap Press, Cambridge, MA

Lathi BP (1983) Modern digital and analog communication systems. CBS College Publishing, New York

Li VOK (1999) Hints on writing technical papers and making presentations. IEEE Trans Educ 42(2):134–137

Lin L, Evans S (2012) Structural patterns in empirical research articles: A cross-disciplinary study. Engl Specif Purp 31(3):150–160

LoMaglio LJ, Robinson VJ (1985) The impact of passive voice on reading comprehension. IEEE Trans Prof Commun PC 28(4):26–27
Losee J (2001) A historical introduction to the philosophy of science, 4th edn. Oxford University Press, Oxford, UK
Louie AH (2010) Robert Rosen's anticipatory systems. Foresight 12(3):18–29
Lucky RW (1973) A survey of the communication theory literature: 1968–1973. IEEE Trans Inf Theory IT 19(6):725–739
Mämmelä A, Wichman R (2008) Cellular communications channels. In: Bidgoli H (ed) The handbook of computer networks, LANs, MANs, the Internet, global, cellular and wireless networks. John Wiley & Sons, New York, vol. 2, pp. 579-590
McFarland D, Bösser T (1993) Intelligent behavior in animals and robots. MIT Press, Cambridge, MA
Meadows AJ (1985) The scientific paper as an archaeological artefact. J Inf Sci 11(1):27–30
Merriam-Webster (2024). https://www.merriam-webster.com. Accessed 5 Nov 2024
Mgbeoji I (2003) The juridical origins of the international patent system: towards a historiography of the role of patents in industrialization. J Hist Int Law 5(2):403–422
Michaelson HB (1990) How to write and publish engineering papers and reports, 3rd edn. Oryx Press, Phoenix, AZ
Michel JB et al (2010) Quantitative analysis of culture using millions of digitized books. Science 331(6014):176–182
Montgomery DC, Woodall WH (2008) An overview of six sigma. Int Stat Rev 76(3):329–346
Murray CJ (2023) The lithium-ion battery's long and winding road. IEEE Spectr 60(8):40–45
Newman MEJ (2010) Networks: an introduction. Oxford University Press, New York
NIST (2008) Typefaces for symbols in scientific manuscripts. National Institute of Standards and Technology (NIST). https://physics.nist.gov/cuu/pdf/typefaces.pdf
Offutt J (2016a) Editorial: STVR policy on extending conference papers to journal submissions. Softw Test Verif Reliab 26(4):274–275
Offutt J (2016b) Editorial: how to extend a conference paper to a journal paper. Softw Test Verif Reliab 26(7):496–497
Ogata K (2010) Modern control engineering, 5th edn. Prentice Hall, Boston, MA
Olver FWJ et al (2010) NIST handbook of mathematical functions. Cambridge University Press, New York
Online Etymology Dictionary (2024). https://www.etymonline.com. Accessed 5 Nov 2024
ORCID (2022) Open researcher and contributor ID (ORCID). https://orcid.org. Accessed 17 Feb 2022
Oxford Learner's Dictionaries (2024). https://www.oxfordlearnersdictionaries.com. Accessed 25 Oct 2024
Parnas DL (2007) Stop the numbers game. Commun ACM 50(11):19–21
Phillips RL (2018) Book citations in PhD science dissertations: an examination of commercial book publishers' influence. Libr Trends 67(2):286–302
Poundstone W (1988) Labyrinths of reason: paradox, puzzles and the frailty of knowledge. Penguin Books, London
Proakis JG, Salehi M (2008) Digital communications, 5th edn. McGraw-Hill, New York
Proceedings of the IEEE (2024) Preparing and submitting your regular paper. https://proceedingsoftheieee.ieee.org. Accessed 24 Oct 2024
Pulleyblank R (1973) A comparison of receivers designed on the basis of minimum mean-square error and probability of error for channels with intersymbol interference and noise. IEEE Trans Commun 21(12):1434–1438
Pyenson L, Sheets-Pyenson S (1999) Servants of nature: history of scientific institutions, enterprises, and sensibilities. W. W. Norton & Company, New York
Random House Webster's College Dictionary (1999). Random House, New York
Ransome P (2010) Social theory for beginners. Policy Press, Bristol, UK

Repko AF, Szostak R (2021) Interdisciplinary research: process and theory, 4th edn. Sage, Thousand Oaks, CA
Richardson GP (1991) Feedback thought in social science and system theory. University of Pennsylvania Press, Philadelphia, PA
Riekki J, Mämmelä A (2021) Research and education towards smart and sustainable world. IEEE Access 9:53156–53177
Ringgold ID (2024) Ringgold Solutions. https://www.ringgold.com. Accessed 5 Nov 2024
Roberts J (2024) Every living thing: the great and deadly race to know all life. Random House, New York
Rosenberg A, McIntyre L (2020) Philosophy of science: a contemporary introduction, 4th edn. Routledge, New York
Rota GC (1997) Ten lessons I wish I had been taught. Notices AMS 44(1):22–25
Rothman T (2003) Everything's relative and other fables from science and technology. Wiley, Hoboken, NJ
Russell S, Norvig P (2022) Artificial intelligence: a modern approach, 3rd edn. Pearson Education, Harlow, UK
Salazar-Palma M et al (2011) The father of radio: a brief chronology of the origin and development of wireless communications. IEEE Antennas Propag Mag 53(6):83–114
Santini S (2005) We are sorry to inform you … Computer 38(12):127–128
Schoemaker PJH (2020) How historical analysis can enrich scenario planning. Futures Foresight Sci 2(3–4):1–13
SE VOCAB (2024) Software and systems engineering vocabulary. IEEE Computer Society and ISO/IEC JTC 1/SC7. https://pascal.computer.org. Accessed 5 Nov 2024
Senturia SD (2003) How to avoid the reviewer's axe: one editor's view. IEEE J Microelectromech Syst 12(3):229–232
Shuttleworth M (2009) Parts of a research paper. https://explorable.com/parts-of-a-research-paper. Accessed 27 Jan 2024
Simon MK (2002) Probability distributions involving Gaussian random variables: a handbook for engineers, scientists and mathematicians. Springer Science + Business Media, New York
Skelton J (1994) Analysis of the structure of original research papers: an aid to writing original papers for publication. Br J Gen Pract 44(387):455–459
Skillin ME, Gay RM (1974) Words into type, 3rd edn. Prentice-Hall, Englewood Cliffs
Skolnik H (1979) Historical aspects of patent systems. IEEE Trans Prof Commun PC 22(2):59–63
Skyttner L (2005) General systems theory: problems, perspectives, practice, 2nd edn. World Scientific Publishing, Singapore
Smith AJ (1990) The task of a referee. Computer 23(4):65–71
Sokal AD (1996) Transgressing the boundaries: towards a transformative hermeneutics of quantum gravity. Soc Text 14(46/47):217–252
Sternberg D (1981) How to complete and survive a doctoral dissertation. St. Martin's Press, New York
Strunk W Jr, White EB (1972) Elements of style. Macmillan, New York
Swales J, Najjar H (1987) The writing of research article introductions. Writ Commun 4(2):175–191
Thompson A, Taylor BN (2008) Guide for the use of the International System of Units (SI). NIST special publication 811. National Institute of Standards and Technology (NIST), Gaithersburg, MD
Thurner S et al (2018) Introduction to the theory of complex systems. Oxford University Press, Oxford, UK
Toman K (1984) Christian Doppler and the Doppler effect. EOS Trans Am Geophys Union 65(48):1193–1194
Tomaszewski R (2021) A study of citations to STEM databases: ACM Digital Library, Engineering Village, IEEE Xplore, and MathSciNet. Scientometrics 126:1797–1811. https://doi.org/10.1007/s11192-020-03795-w
Toomey W (2011) The strange birth and long life of Unix. IEEE Spectr 48(12):34–55

Tulodziecki D (2013) Shattering the myth of Semmelweis. Philos Sci 80(5):1065–1075
Turabian KL et al (2018) A manual for writers of research papers, theses, and dissertations: Chicago style for students and researchers, 9th edn. University of Chicago Press, Chicago, IL
Väänänen J (2015) The smart device. Vaka Väinämöinen
Waltnam L, van Eck NJ (2012) The inconsistency of the h-index. J Am Soc Inform Sci Technol 63(2):406–415
Wang Z, Bovik AC (2009) Mean squared error: love it or leave it? [A new look at signal fidelity measures]. IEEE Signal Process Mag 26(1):98–117
Watson GH, DeYong CF (2010) Design for six sigma: caveat emptor. Int J Lean Six Sigma 1(1):66–84
Webster's New World College Dictionary (2001) 4th edn. IDG Books Worldwide, Foster City, CA
Weil BH (1970) Standards for writing abstracts. J Am Soc Inf Sci 21(5):351–357
West G (2017) Scale: the universal laws of life and death in organisms, cities and companies. Penguin Books, New York
Wigner EP (1960) The unreasonable effectiveness of mathematics in the natural sciences. Commun Pure Appl Math XIII:1–14. https://doi.org/10.1142/9789814503488_0018
Wilson EO (1998) Consilience: the unity of knowledge. Vintage Books, New York
Wilson EO (2013) Letters to a young scientist. Liveright Publishing Corporation, New York
Wolfe J (2009) How technical communication textbooks fail engineering students. Tech Commun Q 18(4):351–375
Wolfram (2024a) Wolfram public resources. http://www.wolfram.com/resources. Accessed 6 Nov 2024
Wolfram (2024b) Eric Weisstein's world of science. http://scienceworld.wolfram.com. Accessed 6 Nov 2024
Xie D et al (2023) Analysis of application status and development prospect of environmental chambers: a review. Indoor Built Environ 32(2):305–322
Xing W, Ghorbani A (2004) Weighted PageRank algorithm. In: Proceedings of the annual conference on communication networks and services research (CNSR'04), Fredericton, NB, Canada
Young M (2002) The technical writer's handbook: writing with style and clarity, 2nd edn. University Science, Mill Valley, CA
Ziemer RE, Tranter WH (2014) Principles of communications: Systems, modulation, and noise, 7th edn. John Wiley & Sons, Hoboken, NJ

Chapter 3
Analytical Thinking

He who would climb the ladder must begin at the bottom. Proverb
The beginning of wisdom is the definition of terms. Socrates (c. 470–399 BCE)
There is no royal road to geometry. Euclid (c. 300 BCE)
There is nothing more practical than a good theory. Kurt Lewin (1891–1947)
You do not really understand something unless you can explain it to your grandmother. Richard P. Feynman (1918–1988)

Abstract We describe the whole research process using the conventional analytical thinking. Research is an advanced learning process that usually proceeds inductively bottom-up and from inside out. However, we present the results deductively top-down and from outside in. Research is different from development and innovation. Researchers must have specific properties, including independence and creativity, and follow high ethical standards. We divide research into the formation of concepts and theories. Conceptual analysis starts any research: we must understand the concepts and their definitions and relationships. The formation of theories consists of experimental-abductive and hypothetico-deductive methods, corresponding discovery, and verification or falsification.

3.1 Introduction

The analytical thinking has led to the success of Western culture, and thus, we often call this approach the scientific approach (Wilson 1998; Checkland 1999). We use a deductive structure to guarantee the coherence of our theories and verify them using observations and experiments. Verification confirms that the theory corresponds to reality.

The *scientific method* is "a method of research, in which a problem is identified, relevant data are gathered, a hypothesis is formulated [discovery], and the hypothesis is empirically tested [verification]" (Random House Webster's College Dictionary 1999). A research problem is a question proposed for discussion or solution. A

A. Mämmelä, *Unifying Systems*, https://doi.org/10.1007/978-3-031-85012-7_3

hypothesis is a tentative theory or model that we suggest as a solution to the problem. It may be either a correlation between random variables or a causal relationship. Correlation is not as strong an explanation as causality since the correlation between two effects can result from a common cause.

Any research includes forming or constructing concepts and theories (Niiniluoto 1983, 2002). Science does not fulfill its mission unless we follow ethical principles. The starting point is respect and fairness, which leads to trust, enables cooperation, and generates the feeling of safety. An equally important thing is to trust that the observations and experimental results were not tampered with or modified to support the claim, and we use sound reasoning to reach the conclusions. Thus, we trust the results and conclusions and do not need to repeat the experiments.

In science, we may observe a system by standing inside (at the bottom) or outside (at the top) the system (Umpleby 2016). Thus, we can view the system from inside out (from bottom up) or from outside in (from top down) or equivalently, "inside the box" or "outside the box." Both the approaches are helpful, and the history of science shows that they are usually used in the order "from inside out" as in the analytical thinking and "from outside in" as in the systems thinking since this makes our learning easier. However, the global understanding comes from the systems thinking. Often the theories are simplified by using the outside-in approach instead of the inside-out approach. An example of Ptolemy's geocentric model of the universe with all its epicycles and the much simplified Copernicus' and Kepler's heliocentric model without any epicycles. The three most critical methodological approaches are the analytical, systems, and actors approach (Fig. 3.1) (Arbnor and Bjerke 1997; Checkland 1999).

The analytical thinking is also called the *reductive*, *bottom-up*, or *inside-out approach*, and sometimes even the "atomistic" approach. The observer is inside the system. We assume that a whole is a sum of its parts isolated from the environment

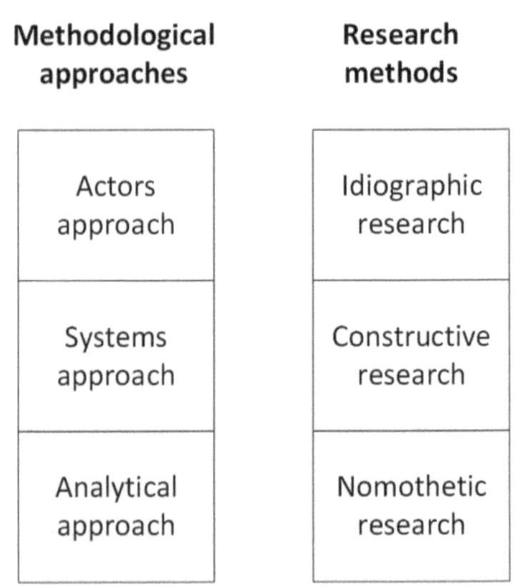

Fig. 3.1 Methodological approaches and research methods

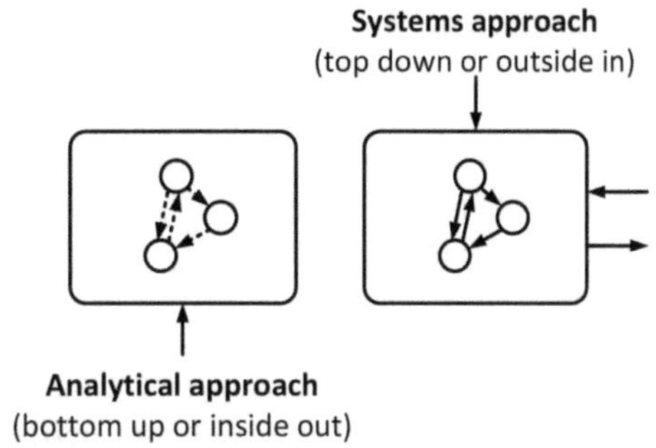

Fig. 3.2 Comparison of analytical and systems thinking. Dashed arrows refer to weak or linear relationships. Solid arrows refer to nonlinear relationships

(von Bertalanffy 1971; Wilson 1998). This property implies that the system is almost linear, see Appendix of this chapter. The reason for the term bottom-up approach is that it is easier for us to study the parts at the bottom of the hierarchy first and then the whole at the top of the hierarchy. The relationships between the parts are assumed nonexistent, linear, or so weak that we can neglect them (Fig. 3.2). If there are no relationships, the whole is not a system but a set of parts.

The emphasis in the analytical thinking is on details at the expense of the whole. Knowledge is independent of an observer, and we are interested in causal relationships in deterministic (i.e., nonrandom) phenomena and correlations in random phenomena. Preceding events or natural laws determine causally deterministic phenomena (Merriam-Webster 2024). Random phenomena are also called statistical, stochastic, nondeterministic, or probabilistic. Phenomena are defined as random if the causes are unknown or if it is unnecessary to specify them. An example is the movement of a single molecule in thermodynamics.

The analytical thinking is a good starting point for mathematical analysis, and we obtain general results. Still, we must initially make several idealizations and assume that the simplified models are perfect. We can apply the theories even to the whole universe as in the relativity theory. The analytical thinking is also used in learning. In analytical research, ideas evolve from simple to complex. For example, the Internet started from a connection between two computers. In many nonlinear systems, because of emergence, we cannot predict the global behavior from the local behavior, and a local optimum does not imply that we are closer to a global optimum (Bongaerts et al. 2000; Van Lange et al. 2013).

The term analytical thinking is inaccurate since we also use analysis in the systems thinking. Different terms describe the analytical thinking, depending on what part of the research one wants to emphasize (Fig. 1.8). Analysis refers to the reductive and deductive parts of the research. Simple deductions are called syllogisms and sorites (Poundstone 1988, pp. 14, 95). A *syllogism* consists of a major and minor premise and a conclusion, for example, "all humans are mortal, Socrates is a human, therefore Socrates is mortal." A sorites is a chain of linked syllogisms where the predicate of each statement is the subject of the next, for example, "All ravens are crows, all crows are birds, all birds are animals." In addition to deduction, the analysis may also be statistical.

In reduction, we study a system by breaking it into its components, which are more readily amenable to a rigorous scientific examination. We neglect emergence. Reduction also refers to dividing a problem into more minor problems on which one focuses. The bottom-up approach refers to the inductive and abductive generalizations from simple to complex. We look at the system "upwards" from the bottom or from inside out (Fig. 3.2).

The *systems thinking* is also called *holistic*, *top-down*, or *outside-in approach*, where a whole is not the same as the sum of its parts. The term holistic refers to the English word "whole," which is the same as a system. The term top-down approach refers to looking at the system "downward" from the top or from outside in. The observer is outside the system. Emphasis is on the whole, not on the details. The relationships between the parts often lead to emergent properties. The system is part of the environment. Just as in the analytical thinking, knowledge is independent of an observer. The analysis is difficult, if not impossible, and the results are often only descriptive, but they may still be deep because of their generality. The system may exchange materials, energy, and information with its environment. We may need simulations and experiments. We attempt global optimization, but there are contradictory goals. Examples of systems thinking include designing large complex systems, such as in the Apollo and Artemis programs, "Man to the Moon and Mars."

The *actors approach* corresponds to the systems approach when a human agent or *actor* is an essential part of the system (Arbnor and Bjerke 1997). A human is a conscious, reflective, and creative person. In the actors approach, observations become subjective. We are interested in understanding social wholes. The consciousness and free will of a human distinguish the actors approach from the traditional systems approach (Kline 1995). Modeling of the actor is not easy.

My focus is on the analytical and systems thinking. The systems approach includes the actors approach by emphasizing that a human is always at the top of the system hierarchy since machines do not understand anything. They "live" in their simulated world and may fail in the real world with uncertainties (Roberts 2020).

We can divide different research methods into nomothetic, constructive, and idiographic research (Fig. 3.1) (Nagel 1979; Iivari 1991). In social sciences, common research methods also include action research and case study research (Arbnor and Bjerke 1997). Methods are more concrete than approaches. We can use each method in many approaches, but usually, nomothetic research is an example of an analytical thinking.

The *nomothetic* or "lawgiving" research results in formal mathematical analysis. The ideal outcome is to find general theories (sometimes called "laws") to describe phenomena, but the theories can also be statistical. Scientific theories are usually deterministic and deductive, such as relativity theory, or statistical, such as quantum theory (Nagel 1979). According to Carl Hempel (1959), the corresponding models of explanation are *deductive-nomological*, using deterministic laws and deductive arguments, and *inductive-statistical*, using probabilistic generalizations (Hempel 1965; Rosenberg and McIntyre 2020). The deductive-nomological explanation model does not explicitly mention causality. In Hempel's opinion, all causal explanations are a subset of deductive-nomological explanations.

An example of deterministic causal theories is classical Newtonian mechanics. We characterize the system's state by values of specific quantitative characteristics of the parts of the system that are called the variables of the state (Fig. 1.2b). The relationships of the parts are called parameters of the state. In a system of point masses, we define the state by the positions and momenta $\boldsymbol{p} = m\boldsymbol{v}$ of the masses where m is the mass and $\boldsymbol{v}$ is the velocity whose magnitude is the speed (boldface letters refer to vectors). Given the state at any time, called the *initial condition*, the laws determine its state at any other time, earlier or later. Another example is Galileo's law of falling bodies. Such causal dynamic laws are called *laws of succession* (Hempel 1965).

Carl Hempel insisted that not all deterministic explanations are causal (Hempel 1965, pp. 347–354; von Wright 1971, pp. 15–16, 175–176, 184; Nagel 1979, pp. 77–78, 280, 292–293). Boyle's law is deterministic (the product pV is constant when the temperature T is constant where p is the pressure and V is the volume of gas) but does not explicitly show a causal relationship. The system is still causal, as we can see from statistical mechanics. Another example is Ohm's law. Such deterministic laws where causality is not explicit are called *laws of coexistence*. Usually, we see determinism and causality as synonymous (Merriam-Webster 2024).

Statistical generalizations include for example quantum mechanics, statistical mechanics, thermodynamics, and opinion surveys. Statistical theories are neither deductive nor causal, i.e., no prior cause exists or is not specified (Nagel 1979, p. 22, 77; Rosenberg and McIntyre 2020).

In *constructive research*, we not only show that the solution to a problem exists, as we sometimes do in mathematics (for example in information theory), but we construct the solution using conceptual or technical development, producing a prototype. In social sciences, we can build and study a social situation.

In *idiographic research*, the focus is on unique events, such as those in history without any general regularities, and we want to explain them. History may be seen as a series of random or cyclic events or as having a direction (Popper 1961; Fukuyama 1992; Diamond 1997). The assumption that history has a direction is sometimes called *historicism*.

Good examples of research are the journeys of exploration made by Christopher Columbus of Spain in 1492 and Vasco da Gama of Portugal in 1497–1499 (Asimov 1987, 1994). The problem was finding a new, easier, and safer route to India that had its spices and gold. Vasco da Gama discovered the route. Traditionally, people journeyed to India by land through the Silk Road, but this trip was laborious and dangerous. The sea formed a natural route that people had used locally since ancient times. Two competing hypotheses to solve the problem were over the Atlantic Ocean and around Africa. The two hypotheses were an example of strong inference on a large scale. Columbus used the former hypothesis, and da Gama used the latter hypothesis. Columbus had a map made by Paolo dal Pozzo Toscanelli (1474) (Asimov 1994). The map was inaccurate and did not include America. At that time, people knew that the world was a globe, but they underestimated its size, although Eratosthenes (276–194 BCE) had already accurately estimated the Earth's circumference. Columbus had an innovative and surprising idea that instead of traveling around Africa to the east, he could find a route to India by traveling in the opposite direction. Roger Bacon originally suggested this route two hundred years earlier (Asimov 1994), and according to a story, Toscanelli had the same idea, which people forwarded to Columbus. Columbus started the voyage by using three old ships and a crew of prisoners. He thought the trip from Europe to Asia would be only about 5000 km, but it was almost 20,000 km, and there was an unknown continent between Europe and Asia.

The example shows the uncertainties and surprises of research. Columbus had a poor map since nobody in the old continent knew about America, and the map's scale was utterly wrong. People inhabited America at least 20,000 years ago through what is now called the Bering Strait. A Viking called Leif Erikson had visited Labrador and Newfoundland already in about 1000 CE. Instead of India, Columbus found America without even being aware of himself during his lifetime of seeing the New World. Without starting the trip, he would have never found anything. He found no gold and not very many spices.

3.2 Research Is a Demanding Learning Process from the Bottom Up and from Inside Out

3.2.1 Learning

Research needs enthusiasm since it is a challenging and persevering learning process. Learning is remembering and generalizing beyond one's own experience to new situations (Nowak 2006). Thus, learning needs inductive inference. The learner is presented with data and has to infer the rules that generate the patterns in these data (Boulton et al. 2015). The method corresponds to learning the grammar of a language.

We should know how students learn to be able to advise them. They usually learn by using the inductive bottom-up approach (Felder and Silverman 1988). They start from something concrete and familiar and proceed towards abstract and unknown, from near to far or from inside out. They usually learn using simple examples from which they generalize the results. The generalization is sometimes called *forward reasoning* from data to hypothesis. We can read excellent general advice in the book (Engeström 1982): "Look for the origin, beginning, *primordial cell* of systems, which can help to understand why they are such as they are. In this way, you make students form high-quality cognitive structures and thought models with broad transfer effects. ... This kind of clear concrete model helps the learning process significantly. It gives the students a 'frame' or 'lens' to interpret, analyze, and use the new material they have learned." An example of a primordial or primary cell of a large oil refinery is a distillery, which one cannot see if one has not carefully studied the history and workings of the oil refinery. In this book, we try to find the "primordial cell" for each topic. For example, in this book, the primordial cell is the feedback loop in the form

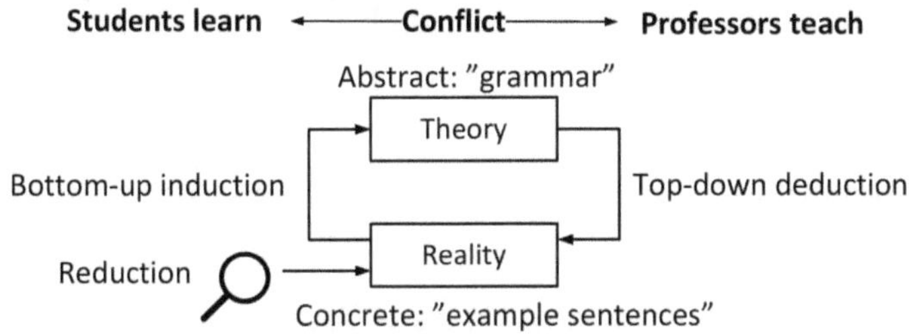

Fig. 3.3 Conflict between professors and students

of the learning loop; more specifically, in writing, the primordial cell is the top-down IMRDC structure.

Professors usually use in their teaching the deductive top-down approach (Fig. 3.3). Their starting point is some abstract principles, and they derive some more concrete results from the principles. The method is sometimes called *backward reasoning* from hypothesis to data. They find this approach natural since they already know the whole picture. They have forgotten how difficult learning is and how they learned themselves. However, the top-down approach is complex for the students. It resembles teaching grammar to a child who does not know the words. Children first learn some babbling sounds, words, and example sentences and do not know anything about grammar. They imitate what adults are saying. Later at school, the grammar supports learning. In practice, we combine bottom-up and top-down approaches to make learning efficient. Following Asimov (1984), my thesis is that knowledge of history is essential in learning and teaching.

As a student, I studied my lecture material, made summaries on a paper, used underlining, and recapitulated those underlines. Even now, I read a book with a pen page by page. Afterward, I reread the underlines and summarize the interesting broad ideas on the empty pages of the book with page numbers, thus effectively creating my index for the book. In this way, it is easy to find the ideas afterward, to reread them, and to use them in my book and other publications. Similarly, reading the table of contents and even the index is a way for me to rapidly absorb the essential contents of extensive books with too many pages to read carefully. We must read the landmark books thoroughly. An e-book is useful even if you have a printed book since you can make searches more efficiently. A printed book is the right place to read the detailed contents of the book. In learning, there is a danger of *confirmation bias*: we absorb information that supports our view, and we neglect the opposite views. Criticism is always needed.

Integrative learning is top-down learning divided into vertical and horizontal learning (Fig. 3.4) (Pearson and Hubball 2012; Rule 2006; Johri and Olds 2011; Symeonidis and Schwarz 2016). In *vertical learning*, we do integration within a subject or course. Each subject should include vertical integration, including motivation and orientation in the beginning and a summary in the end. In the more demanding *horizontal learning*, we do interdisciplinary integration between the

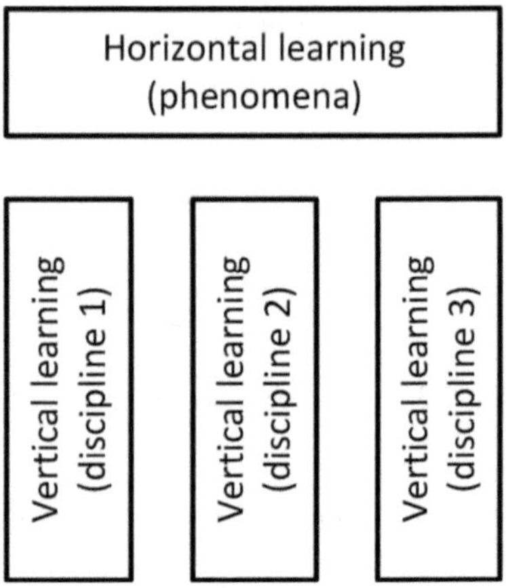

Fig. 3.4 We must do vertical integrative learning (within a discipline) and horizontal integrative learning (phenomena between disciplines) in this order since there is nothing to integrate otherwise

subjects or courses, which is a kind of systems thinking. Among horizontal integrative learning methods, we have phenomenon-based, problem-based, project-based, and situated learning. Situated learning is a form of authentic learning. It means "the notion of learning knowledge and skills in contexts that reflect how the knowledge will be useful in real life" (Herrington and Oliver 2000). Another example of horizontal learning is the thesis work at the end of the studies. All these horizontal methods are rather demanding for a student. Sometimes, people propose phenomenon-based learning as an alternative to conventional discipline-based learning. However, we should not start horizontal integrative learning too early because there is nothing to integrate. We must learn to walk before we can run.

Many horizontal learning methods mean we learn best by doing (Fig. 3.4). This works well in simple situations. But learning by doing is often misunderstood. The world is too complicated to be understandable as a whole. For an adult teacher, everything may look simple, but the results may be chaotic from the students' point of view since they should go through all the complexities that have taken thousands of years for the best scientists to understand. For a beginner, the world must be rationed in small portions to become easily understandable. The method emphasizes the concept of reduction to attain simplicity.

We proceed from the bottom up and from simple to complex, as Rene Descartes (1637) already proposed (Checkland 1999). Galileo also used this idea in his experiments. Therefore, reduction or orientation is needed before learning can start. We also need separate subjects or disciplines since, for example, we cannot explain sociology reductively by using physics due to the problem caused by emergence. Therefore, each discipline has its emergent properties and incomplete theories.

We should find simple principles and relationships. We compare the new knowledge to what we have learned earlier. We clarify possible conflicts and use criticism since there are mistakes even in the scientific literature. We should learn new terms and concepts from vocabularies or glossaries, dictionaries, the latest books, and journal papers. We also learn the standard spelling and pronunciation of new terms.

We should discuss with our colleagues and be active: we participate in teaching and seminars, ask questions, read different textbooks, compare references, go through algebra with all intermediate steps, and take exercises. We write our summaries as a form of reflections. We underline the important information in a textbook if we own it, concentrate on the essential points, and make notes.

A remarkable example of learning is Helen Keller (1880–1968) (Bohm and Peat 2000). Because of an illness, she was blind and deaf from her early childhood and thus unable to speak. From the age of seven, her teacher was Anne Sullivan, who learned how to communicate with her. Initially, she was some "wild animal" that she could not approach in any way. The determining step was to teach a concept with which to communicate. Sullivan asked Helen to touch the water in various cases and wrote "water" on her palm every time. Finally, Helen understood the connection between the different experiences, i.e., the concept of water and the word that Sullivan had written on the palm. She understood that everything has a name, but this took a long time. Helen learned to speak, read, and write and attended a college. She became a helper for the blind and other people with disabilities. She wrote several books and received many awards and honors.

3.2.2 Research, Development, and Innovations

According to the definitions of the Organisation for Economic Co-operation and Development (OECD), we carry out *research* to discover new knowledge, concepts, and paradigms (Jain and Triandis 1997). We improve our understanding by observing regularities and using models for dynamical explanations. *Understanding* occurs when the representation of the external reality in our mind is adequate to generate intelligent and rational behavior (Albus and Meystel 2001). In *basic research*, we do not have any specific application in mind; in *applied research*, we put ideas into an operational form (Jain and Triandis 1997). We do not consider a project a research project if we do not produce peer-reviewed publications.

In *development*, we use existing knowledge systematically (Jain and Triandis 1997). In constructive research, we often develop a prototype to demonstrate new ideas. A *prototype* is the first system design from which other designs are developed (Oxford Learner's Dictionaries 2024). A *focused prototype* is a partial prototype whose purpose is to demonstrate the novel aspects of system design. A *comprehensive prototype* is a full-scale, fully operational version of a product (Ulrich and Eppinger 1995). An alpha prototype is a comprehensive prototype used in in-house testing. A beta prototype is a comprehensive prototype tested externally by customers.

Working prototypes often include silent knowledge, which we call *tacit knowledge*, that is not documented (Honderich 2005). The tacit knowledge is unconscious, intuitive, or implied knowledge. It is a form of emergence. Tacit knowledge is the opposite of articulated or explicit knowledge. We understand many tasks intuitively how to perform but cannot explicitly define their rules. This kind of intuitive understanding is called *Polanyi's paradox*. For example, there are many Stradivarius violins, but we cannot produce a new one since there is no theory.

Inventions may be new concepts or implementations. Often, inventions are patented or published so that no one else can patent them. Sometimes, we keep them secret to gain a competitive advantage. *An innovation* is "the process of translating an idea or invention into a product or a service that creates value for the company or for which the customers will pay" (Vecchi and Brennan 2015). Not all inventions are innovations. For example, short message service (SMS) is an innovation since it is widespread in our society.

Our culture should produce innovations for the prosperity of society (Stonier 1992, 1997). We must improve the degree of processing of our natural resources to innovations. Different methods to support cultural innovations include easiness of exchange of knowledge (transportation and communication), storage and retrieval of knowledge (libraries and databases), creation of new knowledge (research), practical use of existing knowledge (development), and finally, sharing of existing cultural legacy (education system). The rate of cultural evolution depends on large populations and interconnectedness among individuals via urbanization, which increases the rate of evolution (Henrich 2020, pp. 436–474). Complex innovations arise from small additions or modifications, and many innovations were developed independently by many people since the ideas were already there. Most innovations are just novel recombinations of existing ideas. Serendipity or lucky coincidence plays a central role. Since about 1750, innovations have had a primary role in economic growth due to the Enlightenment and the Industrial Revolution.

Natural sciences and *technology* are different, although they use similar approaches and methods. For brevity, natural sciences are often called sciences. Technology deals with "the ways we provide ourselves with the material objects of our civilization" (Random House Webster's College Dictionary 1999). Technologies include for example agronomy, medicine, and engineering (Kline 1995). The author in Kline (1995) called them "working areas."

In natural sciences, the objects of study are the objects in nature, but in engineering sciences, they are methods, services, and products that we cannot find in nature although natural objects can act as a model for us. In science, we develop a theory for a phenomenon in nature. In engineering, we first define requirements that correspond to user needs and aim to provide a product or service that meets the requirements. A theory is often in the form of a model that we need to explain and predict the system behavior and performance.

The term "applied science" for engineering is incorrect since it implies that engineering only uses the methods and results of physical and other sciences (Kline 1995). In engineering, we follow the laws of nature (also called scientific laws) and fundamental limits and rely on basic resources such as materials and energy taken from nature.

Researcher and organization A researcher and organization have different roles, as explained in Fig. 3.5. The researcher's task is to carry out the actual research. The organization offers every possible support for the research, from the ideas, research problems, history, and the state of the art to the integration of the results. Using historical data, we can form a vision and a roadmap to the vision. The systems thinking should present a discipline's fundamental principles and open problems. We derive research problems and project plans from the vision and roadmap (Riekki and Mämmelä 2021). Marketing, recruiting, and investing are also tasks of the organization. We write project plans in cooperation with the researcher. The organization must continuously develop the research culture and education that transfers the cultural knowledge to the younger generation. Research culture includes knowledge of history. We integrate the results by creating a common testbed. The organization also offers funding for the research. Researchers gain experience and become more involved in the organization's duties.

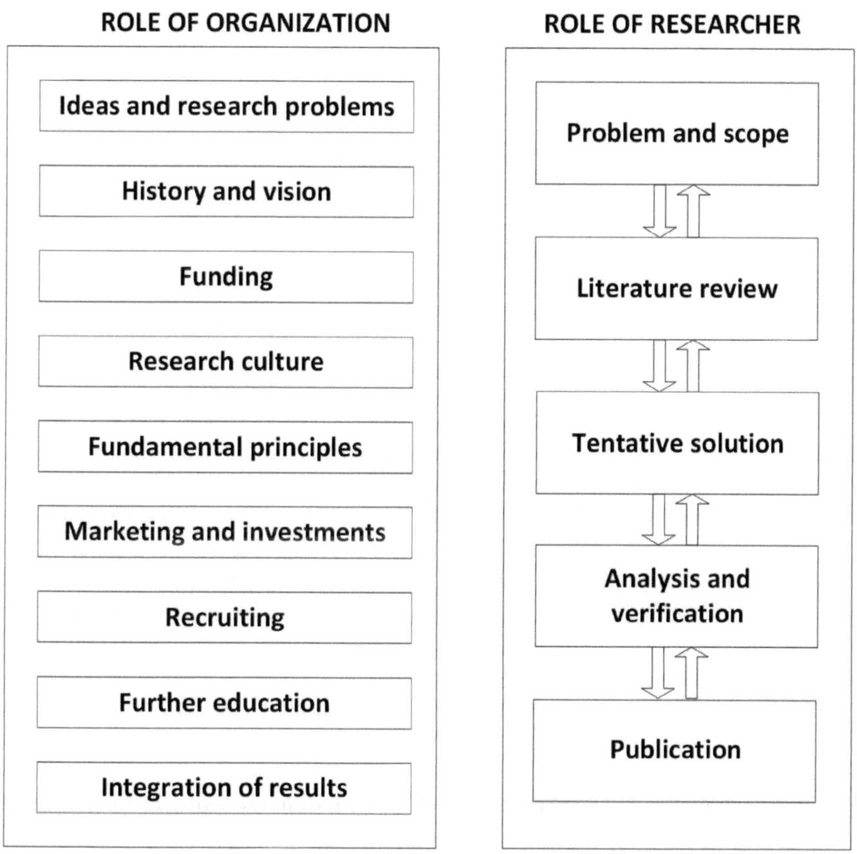

Fig. 3.5 The complementary roles of organization and researcher

3.2.3 How to Succeed as a Researcher

To succeed, we need talent, a suitable personality, hard work, and luck. Many ideas occur suddenly after years of hard work. Researchers should be analytical, curious, flexible, collaborative, tolerant of ambiguity, and critical to avoid groupthink: if the advisor is wrong, everybody in the group may be wrong (Loehle 1990; Jain and Triandis 1997). Researchers need autonomy, change, technical and communication skills, and knowledge of the relevant literature. Communication skills include social and pedagogical skills and knowledge of languages. Above all, they should have some creativity to enable original thinking. Successful researchers also have certain working habits. They always write notes in a notebook. They condense and find the essentials and summarize what they have learned. They make plans for the future all the time. They outline a paper or thesis right from the beginning. They discuss actively with colleagues, ask questions, and argue. Finally, they appreciate the ethical values of research.

A researcher should

1. have excellent oral and written knowledge of native language and English, which is the *lingua franca* of modern science
2. know the literature on a specific topic (big picture, history, state of the art, future trends)
3. know how to discover new knowledge (i.e., research methods)
4. contribute to the literature (i.e., publish original or review papers)
5. discuss and argue in seminars
6. guide younger researchers (i.e., they should have pedagogical skills).

Seminars are an excellent place to test our ideas. Most ideas come from discussions and dialogues (Jain and Triandis 1997; Senge 2006); thus, we should consider them. A seminar is a group of students studying under an advisor and exchanging results through discussions (Merriam-Webster 2024). There is a difference between discussion and dialogue, corresponding to competition and collaboration (Senge 2006). A *discussion* means heaving ideas back and forth, often resulting in a winner-takes-all competition. A *dialogue* means "thinking together," i.e., free-flowing information exchange to discover insights not attainable individually. Dialogue is the preferred method to exchange ideas.

Communication can be challenging. There is an anecdote that two prominent biologists, Robert Rosen and Francesco Varela, were once in the same meeting but found nothing to say to each other (Cornish-Bowden and Luz Cardenas 2020). There was also a famous dispute between physicists Niels Bohr and Albert Einstein about the statistical and deterministic world views, respectively, leading to nothing (Kragh 1999).

In seminars, we may receive necessary criticism. They also improve our oral abilities before presenting our first papers at a conference. Some researchers try to avoid seminar presentations, which is a big mistake since we need discussion abilities. When most of the potential questions are already dealt with in seminars, public discussions elsewhere are a much easier experience.

Look for a good advisor that should (Sternberg 1981):

1. be interested in the student's topic and give comments in a reasonable time
2. be a doctor and have experience in research in the same field
3. be a critical and tough methodologist; colleagues and also the student respect the advisor
4. have pedagogical skills, know literature and the big picture
5. be available for the whole project.

We must also know how to keep our advisor:

1. we orient our advisor using a table of contents and block diagrams of the system model
2. we discuss and argue and make notes and follow instructions
3. we make short progress reports, also called a learning diary, limit the scope, and organize the material well
4. we expect ways of thinking but not ready-made solutions
5. the advisors must have credit for their work in the form of publications
6. we must show initiative so the advisor knows we are interested in the topic.

Intelligence, rationality, creativity, and independence are beneficial in a researcher's work. Many of the old definitions of intelligence correspond to rationality, but now intelligence refers to analytical and algorithmic thinking, which is the ability to keep everything well organized (Jain and Triandis 1997; Pahl et al. 2007; Stanovich et al. 2016). An *algorithm* is a sequence of operations for solving a problem (Penrose 1999; Dewdney 2004, pp. 165, 185). It refers to any definite and clear process that proceeds in steps and eventually terminates with an answer.

Intelligent people are usually active and interested in their environment and others and tend to think critically. Research group members should take initiative, be curious, and be committed to the group's goals. We can find complementary knowledge by cooperating with other groups. It helps if there is some diversity in the same group so that not all people know the same things and only the same things. Thus, we should consider the educational backgrounds of different persons to encourage interdisciplinary thinking. Many good researchers are introverts, but this is a challenge for networking, which is also essential in research for information exchange. Superiors are typically extroverts who may need help understanding the potential of some of their best subordinates.

Rationality is the ability to efficiently attain goals in uncertain environments using available resources (Albus 1991; Robson 2019). Albus defined intelligence, what we would now call rationality, as "the ability of a system to act appropriately in an uncertain environment, where appropriate action is that which increases the probability of success, and success is the achievement of behavioral subgoals that support the system's ultimate goal" (Albus 1991). All purposeful behavior is a goal-directed operation using negative feedback systems (McFarland and Bösser 1993, p. vii; Ramage and Shipp 2020). The opposite is random or purposeless behavior.

Rational behavior has four requirements, including (McFarland and Bösser 1993, pp. 33–34):

1. *incompatibility*: specific tasks cannot be performed simultaneously
2. *common currency*: maximization of a utility function
3. *consistency*: the same decision is made in the same internal and external state and
4. *transitivity*: if decision A is preferred over B, and B is preferred over C, then A is preferred over C.

We should not mix up different interpretations of irrationality. The opposite of rationality is *irrationality*. A genuinely irrational person has beliefs that conflict with each other, are not adapted in the face of contrary evidence, and their assumptions are not open to question (McFarland and Bösser 1993, p. viii). Regarding consistency, the internal state may be changed through learning, and the decisions may be improved. In game theory, rationality is a form of selfishness, and from the game theory point of view, unselfish behavior would be irrational, which it is not. The definition of rationality is just a limitation of the game theory. Not all human behavior is rational and selfish, and more general evolutionary game theory is needed to cover such altruistic and philanthropic behavior (Nowak 2006).

A higher form of rationality is *wisdom*, which is "the ability to make sensible decisions and give good advice because of the experience and knowledge that you have" (Oxford Learner's Dictionaries 2024). Rationality seeks benefits, but wisdom takes ethics into account.

3.2.4 Creativity

According to the standard definition, *creativity* requires originality and effectiveness (Runco and Jaeger 2012). Creativity implies originality of thought: we must be able to define new problems and suggest novel solutions to them. Original ideas are novel, unusual, or unique. An effective solution is practical, appropriate, or valuable. Creativity refers to the ability of synthetic or systems thinking where the focus is on the goals and the ability to reach those goals, thus implying the need for rationality (Robson 2019). Creative people can summarize. They like to work at the edge of chaos and think that ambiguous problems are challenging. Highly intelligent people are not always very creative, although creativity requires a certain amount of intelligence (Jain and Triandis 1997; Robson 2019). Overspecialization may be dangerous for creativity (Epstein 2019).

Intuition is at the core of creativity: it is fast unconscious thinking, but it is not easy to define. There are at least 20 definitions (Epstein 2010). Seymour Epstein presented two working definitions: "Intuition involves a sense of knowing without knowing how one knows," and "intuition involves a sense of knowing based on unconscious information processing." He also discussed eight unresolved problems regarding intuition, including, for example, identifying the operating principles of intuitive processing, whether there is a source of intuition that determines the essence of intuitive processing, how vital the role of experience and emotion in intuition is, and what the relative advantages and disadvantages of intuitive and rational processing are. Conscious rational reasoning is much slower than intuition (Raami 2015; Stanovich et al. 2016; Penrose 1999). Intuition is the ability to make decisions with incomplete information. It is based on instincts, prejudice, experience, and expertise, although we might not see the connection to our knowledge. Intuition is useful when there is too much information or too little information. When the problem is complex and multidimensional, having nonlinear relationships, intuition may lead to a better solution than detailed analysis based on linear rational thinking. Dreams may reflect intuition. We must verify the results of intuition because of possible distortions of intuition.

Independence does not mean that we should avoid using the infrastructure around us. We must still show initiative since we must ourselves carry our research and write our paper. Too much independence may reduce quality since the advisors cannot do their work. A humble attitude is helpful. *Ethicality* is also at the core of research work. Otherwise, the results may not be reliable. Success implies tolerating loneliness and uncertainty, perseverance, good memory, extensive studies, and committed training for decades (Raami 2015).

Creativity exists at the edge of order and chaos, just as in natural evolution. In creativity, we are, in a way, walking on creaking ice. We use both continuity and flexibility, usually alternately (de Bono 2014). Pure order is not creative: we must have something we can build on, but we should not do the same that somebody has done many times before. We produce more chaos if we are too flexible. Often, creative moments are those when we are relaxed. Active doing may help creativity.

Sensitivity also supports creativity (Aron 1999; Aron Bridges and Schendan 2019). We know that many artists are sensitive people. They are people who see things that others do not see. They can see similarities in apparently different systems. In Bridges and Schendan (2019), the authors claim that *orienting sensitivity* is the most crucial trait that predicts high creativity. Open, sensitive people are more creative. The research in Bridges and Schendan (2019) was possible by using a more accurate definition of sensitivity. Orienting sensitivity means coping with sensory overload, which helps us manage adverse effects such as stress and enables a larger capacity for searching for new sensations and responding to subtle environmental cues. Such people can manage large amounts of materials, which is helpful for systems thinkers. This ability implies focusing on the most essential, choosing what to read according to the significance. Sensitivity is not enough, but also the ability to orient is needed since, otherwise, we would be overloaded. As always, we need concentration, but the object of concentration differs from analytical thinking.

There are some methods to improve our creativity. We must define the problem carefully. We should respect criticism to avoid *groupthink*, where somebody in a group says his or her solution is the best and everyone accepts it (Jain and Triandis 1997; Solomon 2006). A devil's advocate offering constructive criticism is always needed. Heterogeneous rather than homogeneous groups are more creative, can solve complex problems, and can avoid groupthink. An extreme form of groupthink is the *not-invented-here (NIH) syndrome*, where a group thinks it possesses a monopoly of knowledge in its field, thus rejecting all ideas from elsewhere. A related term is *Nobel disease*, when some recognized researchers trust their abilities too much and speak on topics outside their specific area of expertise (Robson 2019). We must emphasize integrity and follow ethical rules. We do not accept wildcat business, but we appreciate publicity. We accept dissimilarity and diversity and respect independence.

Ideas usually occur suddenly, so we must have a notebook (perhaps in a mobile phone) beside our bed or during our leisure time before we forget the idea. Often, ideas come when discussing and writing. On October 16, 1843, as William Rowan Hamilton was walking with his wife along the Royal Canal in Ireland, he had a flash of inspiration and invented a new system of mathematics using quaternions, which involved four dimensions to describe the rotation of a vector in space (Boyer and Merzbach 1991; Bruno and Baker 1999, p. 210). For that, he had to abandon the commutative law. The discovery was sudden, but he had been working toward it for about ten years and could not logically go further. He later described the moment: "An electric circuit seemed to close, and a spark flashed forth." He was on the Brougham Bridge and scratched the correct formula on a bridge stone. He always regarded the discovery of quaternions as his most outstanding achievement. —A similar occurrence happened on August 2, 1927, when Harold Black invented the feedback amplifier (Black 1977). The idea came in a flash while he was crossing the Hudson River on a ferry to work. After several years of hard work, Black now suddenly realized that if he fed the amplifier output back to the input in reverse phase, he could cancel the distortion in the output. He sketched a simple diagram and equations on a page of *the New York Times*.

We can concentrate better when there is silence, some weak background noise, or when we listen to music. A change of environment may be inspiring. Inspiration may come, for example, in a conference, during a walk, or in a long train journey. We can talk to a dog during the walk if we have a dog. One of my colleagues said that if his idea was good, his dog started to wag its tail. We can break our routines by doing something else. Dialogue in a safe environment in an interdisciplinary group is helpful (Edmondson 1999), for example, in seminars and brainstorming. In *brainstorming*, a small group has a problem, and solutions are offered without immediate criticism, thus simulating a group of brains and collective intelligence. In an extreme case, the group of brains is a global brain (Stonier 1997). Even writing may clarify our thoughts. When we start writing, we may not initially have a solution to a problem, but it appears during writing. This has happened to me many times.

Generally applicable methods for systematic work from a problem to a solution include analysis, synthesis, abstraction, method of persistent questions, use of negation or opposites, method of forward steps, method of backward steps, and use of computer support (Pahl et al. 2007). In analysis, also called reduction, we break down a complex system into parts and study the relationships. Ideally, in project work, analysis leads to strengths, weaknesses, opportunities, and threats (SWOT) analysis. Factorization is a method of analysis where we break down the problem or system into manageable individual problems or subsystems called *factors*. Factorization leads to a modular and possibly hierarchical solution.

In synthesis, we use systems thinking to produce a working system. We may use archetypes that produce desirable behaviors (Senge 2006; Meadows and Wright

2008). A *theory of inventive problem solving* called *TRIZ* is a systematic methodology or toolkit that provides an approach to developing creativity (Ilevbare et al. 2013). Genrich Altshuller developed the theory in the 1960s by drawing out certain regularities and basic patterns in technology patents to find out the processes of solving problems and creating new ideas.

In abstraction, we find higher-level interrelationships that are more generic and comprehensive. According to Arthur Eddington (1939), abstractions are essential since a scientific theory is a unified imaging of experimental data by abstract algebraic or geometrical structures, leading to maximum objectivity (Elsasser 1987). We can use question lists as checklists to remember relevant problems that are difficult to solve (Rota 1997). Open problems are helpful in project plans. Opposites are used in *reflective thinking*, such as in the thesis, antithesis, and synthesis methods (Robson 2019), and they are mainly used in human sciences, including social sciences and humanities (Smith 1997). The use of opposites corresponds to the Chinese yin (feminine) and yang (masculine) (Pan et al. 2013), which complement each other. The use of opposites is sometimes called *systematic doubting*. It is a unique form of *strong inference* (Chamberlin 1965; Platt 1964) that supports abduction.

Thinking based on straightforward deduction is called *vertical thinking*, and a more creative reflective thinking is called *lateral thinking*, proposed by Edvard de Bono (1967) (de Bono 2014). Lateral thinking is a form of sideways thinking, which may result in surprisingly simple, sound, and effective results. If you dig a well without success, rather than digging deeper, it makes sense to try somewhere else where water can be more easily found. Analytical thinking is linear *vertical thinking* with a focus on parts of a system, but nonlinear lateral thinking focuses on the relationships between the parts and is a form of systems thinking (Henrich 2020, pp. 53, 579). Vertical thinking is digging a hole deeper, lateral thinking is trying again elsewhere. Lateral thinking may also try different ideas without any systematic plan. Lateral thinking is "thinking outside the box." It was used for example by the person who invented the syphon that solved the problem how to move some liquid from a large and heavy container to a small one. A task that initially looks impossible is in fact easy using a flexible pipe, air pressure, and gravitation. Analytical thinking may create blind spots, for example an assumption that the current trend will continue instead of anticipating reversals or cycles.

Four principles exist in lateral thinking, including recognition of patterns, searching for different ways of looking at things, relaxation of the rigid control of vertical thinking, and the use of chance (de Bono 2014). It is best to alternate between periods of creative fluidity (i.e., flexibility) and periods of developmental rigidity (i.e., continuity). Edward Jenner (1796) shifted his attention from why people get smallbox to why dairymaids did not and invented vaccination. In 1901, Guglielmo Marconi wanted to transmit information using radio waves across the Atlantic Ocean, which experts saw an impossibility since you must transmit signals beyond the horizon. He succeeded and the reason was that the radio waves were reflected by the ionosphere whose existence was verified in 1925. Without doing own experiments, it is possible to look at the existing data and put it together in a new way as Albert Einstein did in his relativity theory (1905, 1915). The chance was used for example in the discovery of photography by Louis Daguerre (1839), radio waves by Heinrich Herz (1888), X-rays by William Röntgen (1895), and penicillin by Alexander Fleming (1928).

Examples of opposites include individualism and holism, analytic and synthetic, deductive and abductive (inductive), rational and emotional (intuitive), sequential (serial) and concurrent (parallel or distributed), verbal and preverbal (associative), objective and subjective, abstract and concrete, extrovert and introvert, vertical (deductive) and lateral (creative), temporal and spatial, light and dark, and active and passive (Skyttner 2005). Deductive logical reasoning and pattern recognition complement each other (Stonier 1992). Music corresponds to a sequential process, whereas a painting corresponds to a concurrent process. None of the opposites work alone; our rationality is bounded (Meadows and Wright 2008), so a good whole arises through collaboration between people with dissimilar personalities. In collaboration, we must stand different people that, on the other hand, provide us more strength.

Another form of strong inference is the method of forward steps, where we discover many paths from the problem to produce new solutions, thus using divergent thought. A version of strong inference is a systematic variation where we develop new solutions using classifications. In backward steps, the starting point is the goal or solution rather than the problem, thus using convergent thought. We use the method to retrace possible paths that may have led to the solution. Division of labor and collaboration are helpful since we all have different talents. We use collaboration, for example, in brainstorming. In computer simulations, we make our observations concrete.

The book (Pahl et al. 2007) classifies solution-finding methods into conventional, intuitive, discursive, and combining methods. Among the *traditional methods*, we have information gathering (related to literature review), analysis of natural systems, analysis of existing technical systems called reverse engineering (associated with a state-of-the-art review), analogies, and measurement and model tests called simulations and prototyping (related to the final result of research). Bionics or biomimetics is a synthesis based on natural systems (Vincent et al. 2006). Among *intuitive methods*, we have brainstorming, exchange of information in writing in a small group, a combination of individual work with group work (this is called the *Gallery method*), asking written opinions from experts (we call this the *Delphi method*), combining of various independent concepts (this is called *synectics*), and the combination of all these methods. *Discursive methods* include systematic study of physical processes, use of classification, and use of design catalogs.

Systems thinking is one way to improve our creativity. Some research groups are incredibly creative and can be called great groups (Bennis and Biederman 1997), for example, Disney and the group that discovered penicillin about ten years after the initial observation by Alexander Fleming. Properties of a good research group include, accorting to Jain and Triandis (1997) and Bennis and Biederman (1997):

1. An attainable, seductive, and clear vision and strategy
2. A strong leader with managerial and engineering skills

3. Co-operating, talented, and optimistic people, advisors, idea-generating and marketing people, and communicators: comfortable with abstract thinking, able to conceptualize, needing change and autonomy
4. Special spirit: avoid groupthink, unique communication network, and use of impersonal judgments
5. Triple hierarchy: we do not entirely separate management and professional hierarchies.

There are at least six myths regarding linearity and research organizations: (1) We assume that the world is linear (homogeneous and additive) without noticing the limitations of this assumption. (2) We assume that we can plan everything and that there are no overheads, for example, when we must change some project team members. We seldom know the results of a research project beforehand, although we can make hypotheses. A noticeable overhead comes from the learning phase needed by the newcomers. (3) We can measure everything with a single criterion, such as money, whereas any system has various mutually contradictory criteria above which survivability seems to be the most important one. (4) We assume that the distribution of work in geographically distant units is efficient, whereas distance makes communication challenging, causing delays and misunderstandings because of a lack of information exchange. (5) We assume that top-down management is efficient, but our bounded rationality would prefer distributed decision-making where information moves upwards and downwards as in a control system. Creativity is among the researchers. (6) We assume that we can differentiate research management and work, but we know how to manage only by participating in research all the time.

The *analogy* is "a form of reasoning in which one thing is inferred to be similar to another thing in a certain respect, based on known similarities in other respects" (Random House Webster's College Dictionary 1999). Although analogies help to find hypotheses, they may sometimes refer to superficial similarities (von Bertalanffy 1971). In biology, analogy is a functional similarity, but *homology* is a structural similarity (Encyclopedia Britannica 2024). Homologies have a common ancestral origin, but analogies have similar evolutionary pressure. A misleading analogy is when we compare the growth of an organism and a crystal with each other.

Similarly, if we view a society as an organism, it is misleading. Our biosphere is an ecosystem of organisms and not itself an organism (Boulding 1985). Homologies are analogies with formally identical laws, for example, in electric current and in the flow of a fluid such as gas or liquid. A kind of homology was used in information theory, where the concept of entropy was introduced from thermodynamics, but some authors consider the idea of using entropy in information theory controversial (Thims 2012; Gauvrit et al. 2017).

Some behaviors may be harmful to creativity (Bohm and Peat 2000). Paradigms and short-term profits may limit our thinking. Rewards and punishments do not encourage creativity. Competition, disagreement, and aggression may be obstacles to personal communication. Fragmentation of science also limits information exchange and, thus, our creativity.

A *paradigm* is the present worldview that consists of an unquestioned theory or set of beliefs (Honderich 2005). In physics, a present paradigm is the relativity theory developed by Albert Einstein. Before that, Newtonian mechanics was the dominating worldview. Tuomo Suntola has proposed an alternative paradigm called the dynamic universe (Suntola 2018, 2020). When a paradigm is changed, it is called a paradigm shift. The scientific community often rejects novel results outside the existing paradigm. If someone wants to replace an existing paradigm, we need a careful explanation of research methods and solid empirical evidence. For example, Louis Pasteur showed that spontaneous generation of life does not exist by explaining his methods in extreme detail (Gastel and Day 2016).

It is difficult to change the existing paradigms. The Sun consists mainly of hydrogen and helium (Bodanis 2000). Initially, assuming that the Sun consists of iron and other elements typical of the Earth was an accepted paradigm. Cecilia Payne was the first in 1925 to observe from a spectroscopic image that the Sun includes hydrogen. Still, one of her former supervisors, the famous Henry Norris Russell, and the other old guard "knew" that Payne was wrong. He forced her to write in her doctoral thesis that it is almost certain that the Sun does not include hydrogen. The addition was a requirement for the approval of the thesis. The opponents also attempted to hinder her in her career. Later, other groups showed that she was right and that the Sun was a massive nuclear plant. After that, Russell and others claimed they knew from the beginning that there was hydrogen.

Alfred Wegener (1910) was a meteorologist who discovered the continental drift hypothesis (Seselja and Weber 2012). He developed the idea of Pangaea, which states that the continents originally formed a supercontinent that started to break apart about 180 million years ago. The mainstream geologists assumed that the continents had been in the present place since the birth of the Earth. The geologists did not accept Wegener's hypothesis since no force was known to cause the drift. Wegener died in Greenland in 1930. Only in 1968 was the theory verified, almost 60 years after the discovery. Undersea volcanic eruptions cause the drift, and we see them as earthquakes and as the formation of mountains when the continents collide. Now, the coasts of Southern America and Africa fit together like a jigsaw puzzle. The appearance of the supercontinents appears to be cyclical. These observations were fruitful for the development of geology.

Other new ideas have also been rejected. For example, colleagues of chaos theory and fuzzy logic researchers belittled and discriminated against them until they succeeded through their persistent work (Gleick 1987; Zadeh 2015).

Visibility and networking with colleagues are crucial for success. Networking is usually most accessible with people in the same discipline having a common conceptual framework, but those people are generally also our competitors. Cooperation is more fruitful between different disciplines having complementary knowledge. We are practicing networking in all meetings. We need to keep trust and fairness by respecting others. We must develop ourselves broadly, especially in systems thinking (Boulding 1985; Checkland 1999; Ramage and Shipp 2020). We must write scientific papers so that we look convincing to others.

Inevitable mistakes are typical for young researchers. They often do not define the research problem correctly and cannot finish the work reasonably since it is too broad. They cannot test the hypothesis since it is not concrete enough. They are not open to new experiences and do not discuss with people from different backgrounds to find new ideas. They do not study existing literature, or, to one extreme, they spend all their time studying literature. We cannot read everything. Instead of publishing their original results, they either do not present intermediate results or concentrate on writing too comprehensive technical reports. They postpone the start of writing papers to wait for "better" times, although they should start outlining the paper at the beginning of the project. There will never be more time. After the present project, there will be another project with other topics. The researcher may always publish at low-level conferences where the requirements are modest; thus, they do not notice the possible problems. Their reporting may be ambiguous, and they cannot guarantee reproducibility.

3.2.5 *Ethical Rules*

We must attain the reliability of scientific results with ethical rules. Part of ethics is research integrity (ALLEA 2023; European Union 2024). Its four principles are reliability or quality of research, honesty, respect, and accountability or responsibility. Violations of research integrity include fabrication, falsification, and plagiarism. *Fabrication* is "making up results and recording them as if they were real." *Falsification* is "manipulating research materials, equipment or processes or changing, omitting or suppressing data or results without justification." *Plagiarism* is "using other people's work and ideas without giving proper credit to the source, thus violating the rights of the original author(s) to their intellectual outputs." Plagiarism is a theft in writing. We should not mix the term falsification in ethics with Popper's falsification, which is the opposite of verification and an appropriate scientific method (Rosenberg and McIntyre 2020). In the English language, the word falsify has two opposite meanings: (1) to prove or declare false (a meaning used in the philosophy of science) or (2) to make false or to represent falsely (a meaning used in research ethics) (Merriam-Webster 2024).

For motivation of actions, Immanuel Kant defined in *Groundwork of the Metaphysics of Morals* (1785) his categorical imperative: "Act only according to that maxim whereby you can at the same time will that it should become a universal law." According to Abraham Maslow, one of our deepest needs is physical safety against threat (Koltko-Rivera 2006). Therefore, we conclude that some of our society's most critical intrinsic values are fairness and trust; the corresponding norm is respect or love. The trust forms the cohesive force in our society. Trust is an enabler for the overall life satisfaction and happiness of citizens. Social problems such as unemployment and inequality weaken the trust. We present some of the most important values and their explanations in Table 3.1. Many values are apparent but challenging to assimilate unless our culture supports them.

Table 3.1 Summary of societal and scientific values[1]

Value	Explanation
Trust	Needed for cooperation and safety
Fairness	Needed for trust
Motivation	Make people to start new things
Creativity	Produce something new
Criticism	Obtain high quality
Objectivity	No bias, results correspond reality
Openness	Prevent intrigue
Integrity	Not to fabricate, falsify, or plagiarize
Communication	Clarity of expression, encourage dialogues
Diversity	Different people can do different things

3.3 Conceptual Analysis Starts Any Research: Know What You Are Talking About

Conceptual analysis is an integral part of research. For example, the authors in Bridges and Schendan (2019) noticed that research on orienting sensitivity became only possible after defining sensitivity more accurately. It is essential to conduct a conceptual analysis to thoroughly understand the problem, related concepts, and their definitions (Machado and Silva 2007). Conceptual analysis aims to increase "the conceptual clarity of a theory through careful clarifications and specifications of meaning."

English is the *lingua franca* of science. One problem is the ambiguity of this language: many words have several meanings, and we must infer the actual meaning from the context. This problem is unacceptable in scientific text, which must be crystal clear. Furthermore, different terms are used for the same concept, thus making understanding and learning more difficult. An example is a multiagent system in artificial intelligence (Russell and Norvig 2022), the same as a complex adaptive system in complexity theory (Holland 1995). Definitions are, therefore, fundamental. Researchers are often using abbreviations as new terms. Even they are not always defined that leads to ambiguities since some abbreviations have over one hundred definitions.

In computer engineering, conceptual analysis is often called *ontology*, a discipline within philosophy. Many scientists are not interested in conceptual analysis so that new concepts they propose may become contradictory. One reason is the research process itself, proceeding from the bottom up. Some general terms have too specific meanings. For example, *information theory* is a theory of information transmission, not really a theory of information. On the other hand, the term *information system* is usually limited to computer engineering, although the term information is more general, leading to the term *information and communication technology (ICT).*

[1] Falsification here does not refer to Karl Popper's falsification (ALLEA 2023).

It would be better to change the definition than invent new terminology that would contaminate the whole conceptual system. An excellent general term is a software-defined network (SDN). Still, it was defined so that the architecture of the network was included in the definition: the data plane and control plane were separated (Kreutz et al. 2015). A more general term, such as network automation, has been suggested.

People defined a self-organizing network (SON) as a distributed network until about 2008 (Prehofer and Bettstetter 2005; Dressler 2008). After this, we realized that the SON should be defined more generally so that internal centralized control is allowed in addition to distributed control (Di Marzo Serugendo et al. 2005; Ye et al. 2017). The 3rd Generation Partnership Project (3GPP) Rel. 8 (2008) stated this explicitly and defined centralized, distributed, and hybrid SONs (Fourati et al. 2021). The hybrid SON combines centralized and distributed control.

In a *semiotic triangle*, we include three descriptions or aspects of reality: an object, a term or sign, and a concept, see Fig. 3.6 (Honderich 2005). *Terms* are labels of concepts. A *concept* is the interpretation of the term. We form an idea behind the object by combining all its properties, which we summarize in a definition. We find the definitions of scientific terms in *vocabularies* that standardization organizations often prepare. However, different standards are not always unified.

We divide definitions into ostensive, dictionary, and stipulative definitions (Honderich 2005). *Ostensive definitions* are pseudo-definitions where we explain primitive or elementary terms by examples. We use ostensive definitions to avoid endless loops of definitions. For example, Newtonian mechanics does not define mass, space, and time. *Dictionary definitions* are descriptive: we describe how we understand the terms in natural language. For example, complexity is "the state of being formed of many parts" (Oxford Learner's Dictionaries 2024). *Stipulative* or working *definitions* are prescriptive; they are definitions by agreement. We use stipulative definitions in research to make a scientific text unambiguous.

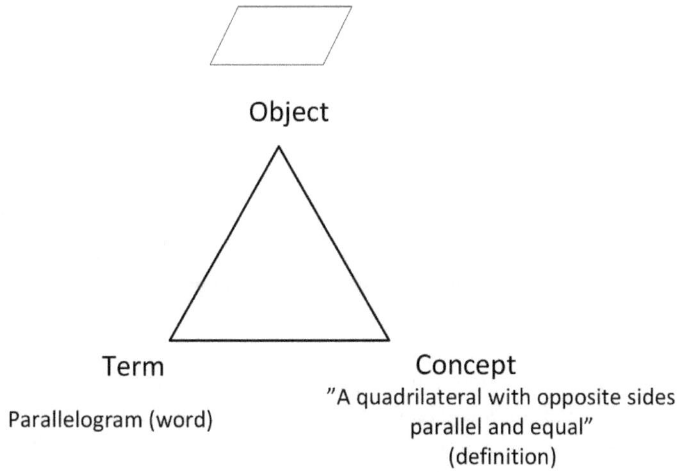

Fig. 3.6 Semiotic triangle

Pei Wang listed the requirements for a good definition: it must be similar to its common usage, draw a sharp boundary, lead to fruitful research, and be as simple as possible (Wang 2019). We often use stipulative definitions: we give a more specific meaning for a term in a dictionary or invent a new term from old languages such as Greek and Latin. For example, we now define a complex system as a complicated system with emergent properties (Kahlen et al. 2017, p. v), although they are synonymous in dictionaries.

A good definition is hierarchical. We name a wider class to which something belongs and the distinguishing properties. For example, "a parallelogram is a quadrilateral [a wider class] with opposite sides parallel and equal [distinguishing properties]" (Merriam-Webster 2024). Other parallelograms include, for example, a trapezoid, a rectangle and a square. In this way, we find a hierarchy of concepts in a classification called a taxonomy, used especially in biology. Some standardization organizations such as ISO, IEC, ITU, and IEEE provide stipulative definitions. Such efforts include Software and Systems Engineering Vocabulary (SE VOCAB) (SE VOCAB 2024), Electropedia by IEC (Electropedia 2024), and IEEE Standards Dictionary within the IEEE Xplore (IEEE Standards Dictionary 2024). We can also find reliable definitions from books and review papers. An excellent place to start is the SE VOCAB, which combines the efforts of the IEEE Computer Society and ISO/IEC technical committees. Still, it is focusing on software and systems engineering. A glossary of requirements engineering (Schneider and Berenbach 2013) is in Glinz (2017). There are also national standardization organizations that develop translations of terminologies.

3.4 Formation of Theories to Manage the World

In this section, we present the types of reasoning, a taxonomy of theories, methods of discovery, and methods of verification and falsification.

3.4.1 Types of Reasoning

In science, we use three basic types of inference or reasoning (Honderich 2005). They include deduction, induction, and abduction. We show them in Figs. 3.7 and 3.8. *Deduction* has the following property: if the assumptions or premises are true, the conclusions must be true. The property means that deduction preserves the truth, but only if the premises are true. If the premises are false, the conclusions may be either false or true. We use deduction especially in mathematics. The term *analysis* includes deduction and statistical analysis, especially in engineering (Hall 1962). We sometimes define deduction as proceeding from general to particular. The premises imply the conclusions (Casti 1994, p. 123). There is no new information in the

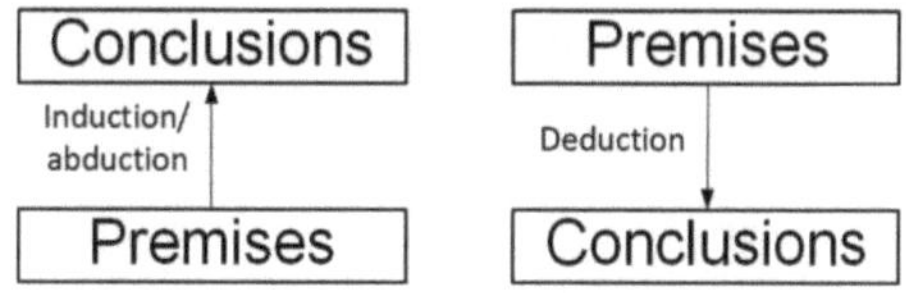

Fig. 3.7 Types of inference. Induction and abduction correspond to synthesis, and deduction corresponds to analysis

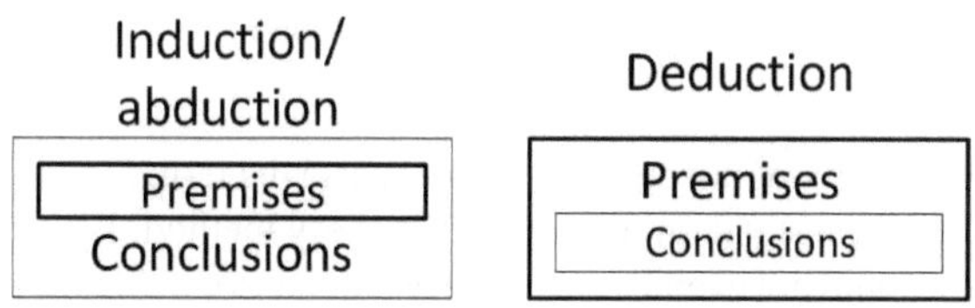

Fig. 3.8 Relationship of premises and conclusions in induction, abduction, and deduction

conclusions compared to the premises. The premises form a complete, but implicit summary of the conclusions, and deduction only makes the information explicit.

The term induction includes scientific induction and mathematical induction (Honderich 2005). *Scientific induction* is also called Bacon's induction. It is incomplete: it is reasoning where "the conclusion, though supported by the premises, does not follow from them necessarily." In scientific induction, the truth is not always preserved. This forms a problem called Hume's *problem of induction*, creating a weak point in science. *Underdetermination* is a view in which we cannot prove the truth of any theory but only verify or falsify by conducting scientific experiments because of the problem of induction (Honderich 2005); see Fig. 3.9.

Inductivism has been criticized. Science must proceed evolutionarily. Those theories are accepted that seem to work in practice. The conclusions contain more information than the premises: that is the basic idea of the generalization in induction. We often define induction loosely as proceeding from particular to general. We use extrapolation based on the unprovable assumption that the world is regular in time and space, and thus, we assume that predictions and generalizations are possible (Harre 1981). Induction is a form of synthesis (Hall 1962). Inductive reasoning may be also statistical (Rosenberg and McIntyre 2020). Sometimes, the new hypothesis or theory conflicts with an old theory: we cannot deduce the latest theory from the old theory, and a paradigm shift is needed, leading to a scientific revolution.

Scientific induction is usually called induction for brevity and is the basis for the experimental-inductive method (Fig. 1.6). It can be criticized since, as a form of synthesis, it does not lead to unique solutions, not to mention the best solution.

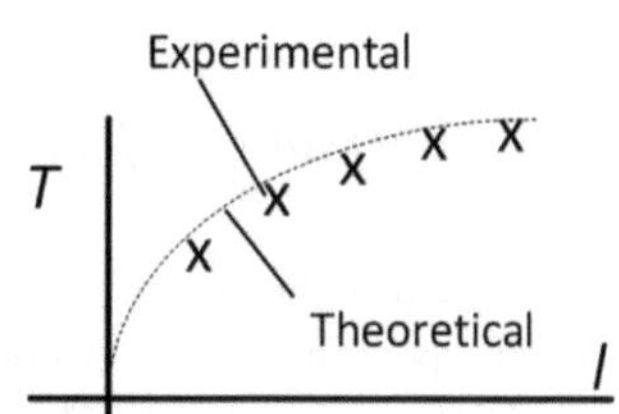

Fig. 3.9 Theoretical and experimental results (l and T are two parameters in the system)

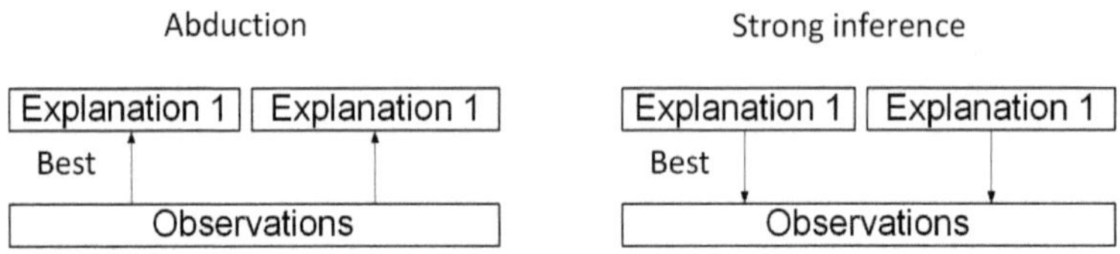

Fig. 3.10 Strong inference simulates abduction

Therefore, philosophers of science use the term *formation of hypotheses*, which does not take a stand on the actual discovery method. We need induction in everyday life. We could not even live without assuming some regularity in the world. The following quotation from Bernard Russell demonstrates the dangers of induction: "The man who has fed the chicken every day throughout its life at last wrings its neck instead, showing that more refined views as to the uniformity of nature would have been useful to the chicken" (Deutsch 1997; Larson 2021).

Mathematical induction is sometimes called Fermat's induction. We use it in mathematical proofs (Niiniluoto 1983). It is a particular case of *complete induction*, where we enumerate all the special cases of the generalization. We must differentiate mathematical induction from scientific induction. In mathematical induction, the statement dependent on a positive integer n is first shown to be true for $n = 1$. Next, we assume that the hypothesis is true for $n = k$, and we show that it is true also for $n = k + 1$. In this way, we have enumerated all possible n, and the hypothesis is true for all n.

Abduction is inference to the best explanation (Honderich 2005; Larson 2021), i.e., it is induction that has been somehow "optimized" (Fig. 3.10). Induction produces some explanation, which may be wrong, but abduction provides the best one. Abduction is the opposite of deduction. In practice, the explanation is the most plausible. In the method of multiple working hypotheses (Chamberlin 1965) or *strong inference* (Platt 1964), we approximate the abduction: select the best from several competing hypotheses, whereas in abduction, we choose the best from among all possible hypotheses. We are unsure about the best hypothesis and whether the theories are unique (Wigner 1960). If, according to experiments, the theories are equally good, we should select the simplest theory with the smallest number of definitions, concepts, and assumptions. This method is called the principle of parsimony or *Ockham's razor*, but for example, biology does not always follow this principle (Westerhoff et al. 2009).

3.4.2 Formation of Theories

We often use the word explanation loosely for scientific theories (Nagel 1979). Strictly speaking, they do not explain, i.e., answer to the question "why," which would refer to purposes. The theories only classify and describe, i.e., they answer to the questions "what" and "how." Theories may be deductive and deterministic, such as the theory of relativity, or random, such as quantum mechanics. A separate class of theories is chaos theory, which is based on deterministic models having some nonlinear feedback (Strogatz 2014). Such models are sensitive to initial conditions. In addition to theories and prototypes, engineers also use drawings, written descriptions, and tables.

We define science as the discovery of new knowledge. It is not defined as the search for truth since we cannot attain it but only approach it asymptotically. Still, three *theories of truth* are essential for us: coherence, correspondence, and pragmatism (Honderich 2005). A statement is coherent with other statements if we can derive it from the other true statements by mathematical deduction. Otherwise, it is false. *Correspondence* means agreement with reality that we verify with the hypothetico-deductive method. Experiments are not always accurate enough (Penrose 1999, p. 242). For example, Maxwell added a minor term in his equations that was not experimentally observed. This addition was an example of his masterstrokes and showed the limitations of induction that earlier researchers had made. Similarly, according to Tuomo Suntola, the equivalence principle, i.e., the equivalence of the gravitational and inertial mass, must be replaced with the energy conservation law (Suntola 2018).

Pragmatism is a view according to which the value of scientific knowledge is measured by its practical implications: knowledge is good if it is useful. Although our system models are approximations of the reality, the results may still be useful. We cannot verify hypotheses directly because of the problem of induction, but if a hypothesis produces something useful, it is an indirect verification. Charles S. Pierce (1877) favored pragmatism.

There has been a long-standing debate between rationalism and empiricism regarding the scientific method. *Rationalism* emphasizes the significance of rational reasoning and deduction in discovering knowledge. *Empiricism* or empirism emphasizes the importance of experiments and observations in discovering knowledge (Honderich 2005). *Positivism* is a view that emphasizes strict empiricism, rejecting, for example, metaphysics and ethics (Rosenberg 2018). Knowledge is based on definitions or derived by logic from sensory experiments. Positivism was later replaced by *logical empiricism*, also called logical positivism, which combined empiricism and rationalism: knowledge is based on definitions derived from sensory experiments and observations and unified by logical arguments. A modern version of positivism is analytic philosophy, which emphasizes conceptual clarity and rigor in arguments (Seebohm 2015). This view is used in physical sciences. *Naturalism* is a view that supports the use of the methods in natural sciences in the discovery of knowledge. We must still understand the difference between mechanisms, organisms, and social systems (Rosen 1991, 1996; Pan et al. 2013).

The debate between realism and antirealism is close to the discussion of whether science can attain the truth about the world or not (Bunge 1993). *Realism* or objectivism is inherent in science and engineering: we assume that the models represent reality accurately enough (Honderich 2005). The primary forms of realism are naive, critical, and scientific realism (Bunge 1993). In naive realism, we assume that things are as we observe them. In critical realism, we realize we cannot know the complete truth about the world. Critical realism is a middle kingdom between the physical and theoretical worlds (Ransome 2010). A form of critical realism is instrumentalism, where models are assumed to be instruments for making approximate predictions (Honderich 2005; Rosenberg and McIntyre 2020). Scientific realism is a version of critical realism where scientific research is the best mode of inquiry and can give us an increasingly true representation of the world.

Antirealistic philosophies have become popular in social sciences (Bunge 1993). Mario Bunge believes such philosophies are not beneficial for social sciences since they do not correspond to the scientific view, which aims at objectivity. For example, constructivism is one of the various antirealistic philosophies and is thus controversial. In *social constructivism*, we assume that a theory is a social construction.

Theories follow the definitions-assumptions-deduction-conclusions model (Honderich 2005). We call *assumptions* also premises, postulates, or axioms from which deduction starts. When we use assumptions, we simplify the problem, enable mathematical formulation, neglect or eliminate unnecessary factors, and focus on the most important ones. Typical simplifying assumptions include isolation from other systems and the environment (Young et al. 2012), hierarchy and modularity (Mämmelä et al. 2023), linearity and slow changes (Proakis and Salehi 2008), normal or Gaussian statistics for random variables (Simon 2002), and tractable criteria (Wang and Bovik 2009; Gao 2014).

Sometimes, it is not easy to see the difference between definitions and assumptions since a definition is, in fact, a form of assumption. For example, in Newtonian mechanics, the second law of motion or $F = ma$ can be interpreted as a definition or assumption (F is the force, m is the mass, and a is the acceleration). For Newton it was an axiom or an assumption, but it can be also interpreted as a definition since force is not defined in any other way (Nagel 1979).

We divide theories into axiomatic systems and model-based theories (Honderich 2005; Rosenberg and McIntyre 2020); see Fig. 3.11. In *axiomatic systems*, we derive theorems deductively from definitions and axioms. Such systems are an ideal form of theory. Axiomatic systems are either Hilbertian or hypothetico-deductive systems (Niiniluoto 2002). We use *Hilbertian axiomatic systems* in mathematics and other formal sciences. We do not make any interpretations of what the objects in the system mean in the real world. The tentative theorems are hypotheses or *conjectures*, which we prove by deducing them from the axioms. Examples of Hilbertian axiomatic systems are in logic, set theory, arithmetics, geometry, and probability theory. A famous conjecture or unproved theorem is Goldbach's conjecture: every even positive integer greater than 2 is equal to the sum of two prime numbers.

We use hypothetico-deductive systems in empirical sciences, such as physical sciences and engineering. The axioms are hypotheses that we interpret to show their correspondence with reality. We indirectly verify them using the hypothetico-deductive method, i.e., by comparing the theorems with the real world. Examples of hypothetico-deductive systems are Newtonian mechanics and relativity theory. We also use hypothetico-deductive systems in the social sciences and biology.

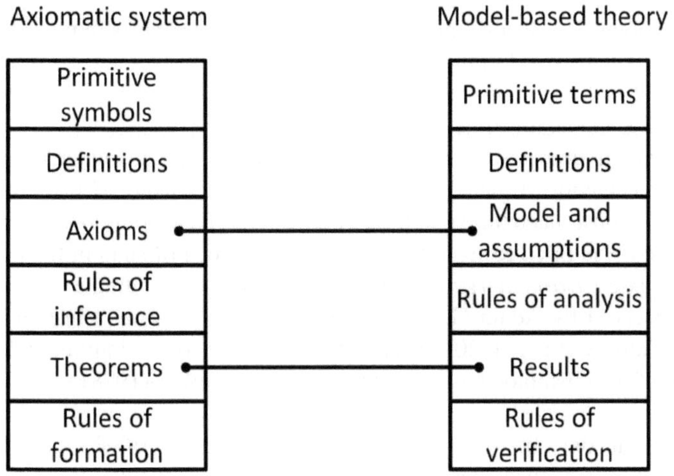

Fig. 3.11 Comparison of axiomatic systems and model-based theories

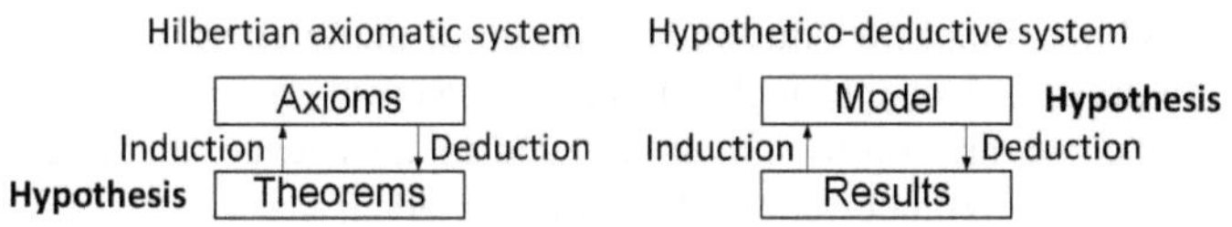

Fig. 3.12 Hilbertian axiomatic system and hypothetico-deductive system

We interpret the term "hypothesis" differently in formal and empirical sciences (Fig. 3.12). In formal sciences, the hypothesis is a tentative theorem or conjecture. In empirical sciences, the hypotheses are axioms or theoretical models. We verify them but do not prove them. The method verifies the correspondence between the real and theoretical world (Fig. 1.8) and gives semantic meaning to the theory that follows specific syntactical rules (Casti 1994, p. 123).

Verification is in practice impossible because we always use inductive reasoning (Rosenberg and McIntyre 2020). According to Karl R. Popper, only falsification is possible, which is the opposite of verification. A theory that has not yet been falsified has stood the test of time. An ambiguous theory that cannot even be criticized or falsified in principle is not a scientific theory but a *dogma*. The idea of falsification has been criticized since a theory can be "rescued" by using auxiliary assumptions or hypotheses, which are additional conditions for testing a hypothesis.

A historical example of *auxiliary hypotheses* is the phlogiston theory by Johann Joachim Becher (1667), which "explains" combustion and rusting, which is now called oxidation. Only after Antoine Lavoisier and, independently, Joseph Priestley discovered oxygen in the 1770s was the phlogiston theory rejected. Since Isaac Newton (1704), people used the ether theory to "explain" how electromagnetic waves could propagate in space just as mechanical sound waves. Later, it was shown that electromagnetic waves do not need matter to propagate, and no ether exists. An auxiliary hypothesis was also made to explain the discrepancies in the orbits of the known planets, which led to the discovery of Neptune and Uranus (Rosenberg and McIntyre 2020). Newtonian mechanics was not assumed to be falsified, but a new hypothesis was made, this time a fruitful one.

An auxiliary hypothesis still used is *dark matter* (also called hidden mass), which explains the behavior of galaxies using Newtonian mechanics (Chae 2023). Fritz Zwicky (1933) postulated the existence of dark matter. It cannot be observed directly, but its existence is inferred from the high rotation speed of stars in the outer parts of spiral galaxies. *Dark energy* is used to explain the accelerating expansion of the universe observed by Adam G. Riess et al. (1998) to "rescue" Einstein's general theory of relativity (Li et al. 2011). The idea of dark energy is implied in Einstein's (1917) use of the cosmological constant. Michael S. Turner (1998) coined the term dark energy.

A theory can only be discovered with creativity and verified or falsified by a sufficient body of evidence; therefore, science's progress is evolutionary. Old theories are falsified, and better theories replace them.

Models *Models* are the interpretations that make the theories concrete (Niiniluoto 2002). A model is a simplified causal description of the temporal and spatial regularities in the actual system through an analogy (Rosenberg and McIntyre 2020). Model-based theories are common in natural and social sciences and engineering—the models only approximate reality, for example, ideal gas and Bohr's model of the atom. The different parts of the theory are included in the IMRDC structure of a paper (Fig. 3.13). We cannot understand complicated systems without models. In science and engineering, a simplified model presentation is called a *system model*. In mathematical and theoretical models, we derive the results by deduction or statistical generalizations from definitions and assumptions. The structures of a model-based theory and an axiomatic system are similar. If we do not have any generalization in the form of a theory, all situations look entirely different. The theories improve our understanding of managing the real world since they reveal the underlying relationships.

In engineering, most theories are based on models. Axiomatic theories often belong to the formal sciences. Figure 3.13 shows how the IMRDC structure of a publication is related to model-based theories. The central part is the materials and methods section, which includes all other parts of the theory except the results, which belong to the results section.

We often use simpler and less accurate models than the best available model of a given physical process (Sandell et al. 1978). The first reason is to reduce the computations in simulations, analysis, and system design. The second reason is based on the realization that a simplified model leads to a simplified control system structure.

Models can be classified into scale, analog, mathematical, and theoretical models (Fig. 3.14) (Chestnut 1965; Achinstein 1968; Barbour 1974; Dutt and Gajski 1990; Bailer-Jones 2009; Gelfert 2017). This overarching classification is originally from Max Black (1962), as described in Gelfert (2017). *Scale models* are physical models

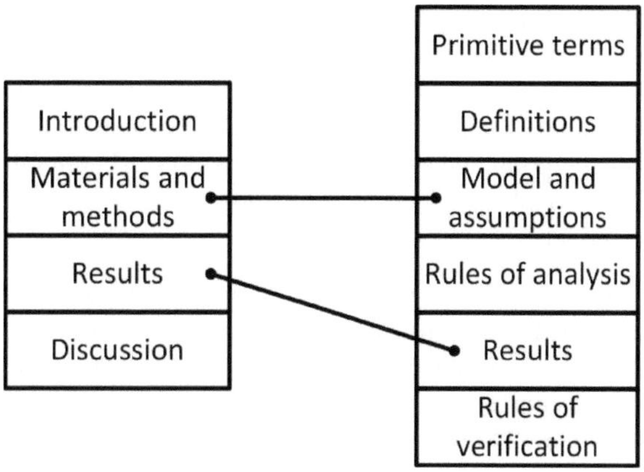

Fig. 3.13 Relationship of the IMRDC structure and a model-based theory

that increase or decrease the spatial features of the actual system. A physical model is also called an experimental model. The model is a miniature called a microscopic or micro model for large objects such as ships. Another example is a map such as a globe. We use macroscopic or macro models in prototypes for small objects that appear in electronics since such models are cheaper and easier to build than using integrated circuits in the final implementation used in products.

In *analog models*, we use a physical system as a model for another. The medium is changed, and often electronic circuits are used as models, for example, in systems involving potential energy in a power supply, energy flow in electric current, or energy storage in a capacitor. *A mathematical model* is a functional or black-box model expressed with mathematical and logical symbols that attempts to make predictions. It corresponds to the input–output relationships in physical and social systems and does not necessarily represent the internal dynamic behavior of the system. Examples include the economic relationship between supply and demand and population growth over time. *Theoretical models* are behavioral or structural models of a physical system presented by mathematical symbols, describing reality as well as possible by analogies. The theoretical models, such as flow charts or block diagrams, may

Theory		**Reality**
Axiomatic systems	**Theories based on models**	
Axioms Theorems	Mathematical models (functional models)	Physical models (scale and analogue models)
	Theoretical models (behavioral and structural models)	

Fig. 3.14 Classification of theories and models

also be conceptual. Examples include Bohr's model of an atom and the billiard-ball model of a gas. Mathematical and theoretical models based on equations are widely used in computer simulations. A new form of model is the *digital twin* whose goal is real-time simulation during a product lifecycle (Tao et al. 2019). A 3D *virtual model* is a temporal and spatial model of a physical entity. In a *metaverse*, avatars interact in a virtual 3D social world (Wang et al. 2023). A related concept is 3D printing (Jandyal et al. 2022).

Solving methods We can solve mathematical models using analytical methods, numerical deterministic methods, and random sampling (Chestnut 1965). By "solving," we mean finding the worst case or the optimum. For example, we can find a summary of various optimization methods in Michalewicz and Fogel (2004) and Talbi (2009). *Analytical methods* are helpful because we deduce an exact answer, but this method is valid only in relatively simple, mathematically tractable cases. In deterministic *numerical methods*, we apply some iterative methods. For example, we use Newton's method to find the roots of a nonlinear function iteratively. There may be local minima, and we must initially use an exhaustive search method with some resolution. We call this method the *grid search* (Kay 1993). In Monte Carlo simulations, we use *random sampling*, i.e., we repeat a random experiment many times and compute the average performance. We do not "solve" the model, but we can use approximate optimization by using exhaustive search if we vary the model's parameters, usually one at a time (Wohlin et al. 2000).

If we combine analytical and simulation methods, we call the combination *semi-analytical methods*. One example is importance sampling. Simulations may become faster if we do part of the computation using an analytical result instead of the slow Monte Carlo method. The semi-analytical method is especially valid for simulating the bit error rate in communications since the error rates are usually small and at least 100 errors must be measured to obtain small enough uncertainty (Portny 1966). The required error rate depends on the application. If the bit error rate is, for example, 10^{-4}, we must simulate about 10^6 bits to find about 100 errors, but if it is 10^{-10}, we must simulate 10^{12} bits. The simulations are much faster if we select another criterion such as mean-square error or study, for example, *eye pattern* or eye diagram, which is a synchronized superposition of consecutive amplitude-modulated symbol waveforms as explained in Newcombe and Pasupathy (1982) and Proakis and Salehi (2008, pp. 603–604). It resembles a human eye. If the signal also has phase modulation, the eye pattern is three-dimensional. However, we obtain a two-dimensional diagram if we take a synchronous sample from the middle of each symbol. The mean-square error measures the deviation of the pattern from its ideal value. We may use the opening of the eye pattern for rough estimates. The opening is the minimum distance between levels of the modulated signal in the middle of the eye pattern.

Simulations are conceptually between theory and experiment (Holland 1998, pp. 119–121). A simulation model is similar to a mathematical or theoretical model based on equations. Simulations differ from physical experiments since they do not manipulate the real world, but they are completely rigorous, thus forcing us to be

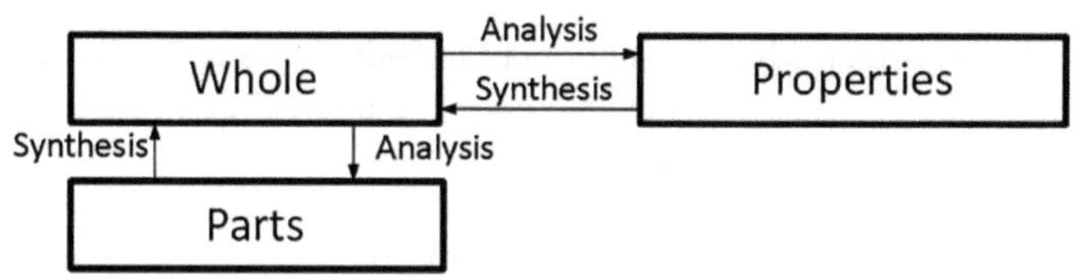

Fig. 3.15 A concrete whole with its parts and properties

careful in thinking. Through simulations, we can expand our intuition. They are similar to Einstein's *Gedanken* experiments, which were carried out only in thought.

We can break down a concrete *whole* in two different ways, either into parts or properties (Fig. 3.15). We can also replace the term "properties" with observations. In engineering they may be requirements. When we break down a whole, we call it *analysis*. We call it *synthesis* when we put together a whole from parts and required properties.

3.4.3 Causality and Forms and Reduction

Causality *Causality* in science is most often understood in a Newtonian way as a single causality, which always means forward causality based on the *efficient cause*, see Fig. 3.16 (Honderich 2005; Aaltonen 2007; Wang and Blei 2019). We can express the efficient cause with deduction (Nagel 1979, pp. 280, 292–293; von Wright 1971, pp. 15, 184). All deterministic physical systems are causal: the cause always precedes or coincides with the effect (Honderich 2005), implying that negative delays do not exist. Scientific theories describe (answer to the question how?) but do not strictly speaking explain (question why?) (Nagel 1979). Some authors prefer functional relationships instead of causal relationships (von Wright, pp. 36, 38).

In science, we focus on single causality, but there can be *multiple causes*, and the phenomenon is also called *multicausality* (Aaltonen 2007; Wang and Blei 2019). David Hume claimed that events are loose and separate, and there is no established link ("causal nexus") between the most probable cause and its effects, which ties

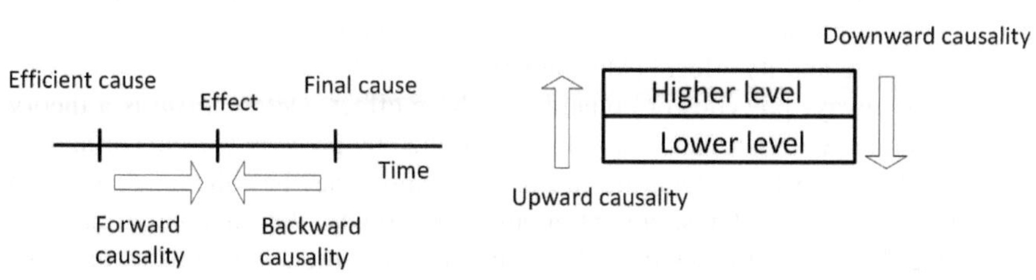

Fig. 3.16 Forms of causality. Modern science accepts only forward causality based on the efficient cause. Forward causality may also proceed upward or downward

cause and effect together. Multicausality may include linear or nonlinear feedback loops forming a network and causing emergence (Camazine et al. 2001).

In a hierarchical system, the causality may be same-level, downward, or upward causality (Kim 1999), but all of these are based on efficient causes. For example, birds' flocking patterns emerge from individual birds' local interactions. However, the overall flocking behavior is still reducible to and determined by the actions of the birds at the micro-level. Another example in control engineering is sense signals that move upwards and act or control signals that move downwards in a hierarchical system, thus forming a feedback loop (Mämmelä et al. 2023). The author in Kim (1999) shows that, except at the bottom level, both same-level and upward causality presupposes the possibility of downward causality. In natural systems, downward causality looks impossible but "is well established as a fact" (Bitbol 2012). An example of the use of downward causality is our brain that controls our body through the nerves.

Aristotle's final, material, and formal causes are not causes but explanations. In the final cause, we explain the effect by the purposes. In the *material cause*, we explain a whole by its parts. In the *formal cause*, we explain the parts by the whole.

The *final cause* sounds like backward causality. It is also called a purpose or goal. The finality is teleology: we explain an effect by its goals. In science, we do not accept teleological explanations based on final causes; for example, evolution has no goal. We can say that humans have two eyes to estimate the distance of an object better (this is a final cause), but the scientific explanation is that evolutionary pressure developed them: they were beneficial for our survival (this is an efficient cause). Although a negative feedback loop has a goal, it does not imply the existence of backward causality. The loop causes only an appearance of teleology, called "quasi-teleology," yet the loop operates according to causal laws (von Wright 1971, pp. 17, 156, 177).

There have been two traditions regarding causality. Actionists follow an Aristotelian tradition that uses final explanations and supports final causes (von Wright 1971, pp. viii, 2). Causalists follow a Galilean tradition that uses mechanistic explanations and supports efficient causes. Usually, mechanical explanations are defined so that they follow the physical and chemical laws of cause and effect, and they are opposite to biological explanations (Merriam-Webster 2024).

Possible explanations for something happening include causality, chance, and free will. Albert Einstein had a deterministic worldview and thought there was no such concept as chance, and free will was only an illusion. *Causality* is "the relation between a cause and its effect" (Merriam-Webster 2024). In causality, we assume that a cause always precedes or coincides with an effect. *Determinism* is a theory that all natural occurrences are "causally determined by preceding events or natural laws." All deterministic systems are causal. The causes may be either discrete, as in time-discrete control systems, or continuous, as in gravity. We can approximate the latter using discrete processes if we take samples from the continuous signals fast enough.

Gottfried Leibnitz believed that everything has an explanation: the state of the universe and the fundamental laws of physics determine history and evolution (Chen

2023). Chance and free will seem to start a new causality chain and have no prior causes (Nagel 1979, p. 22, 77). They are emergent phenomena in science, and thus, we do not have good theories for their causes. Free will is a part of consciousness that, as a whole, is itself an emergent phenomenon (Barrow 1998; Merriam-Webster 2024).

In engineering, noise is a typical example of *chance* or a random phenomenon (Chessin 1955; Mumford and Scheibe 1968; Cohen 2005). Some authors claim that free will is neither a deterministic nor random phenomenon nor a result of a specific cause (Cary 2007). We need free will to set our goals, and so far, there is no machine with consciousness and free will; thus, a machine cannot set its goals (Stonier 1992, p. 174). Similarly, Michael E. Hyland stated that people can create their own goals, but robots cannot (Schoemaker 1991).

We have three options to solve the dilemma with chance and free will, all leading to philosophical questions (Poundstone 1988):

1. Some people argue that all events can be ultimately traced back to prior causes, corresponding to strict determinism. In this mindset, chance and free will are illusions, and all phenomena are determined in advance in the big bang. This was the opinion that Albert Einstein had. We assume a phenomenon looks random if the causes are unknown or irrelevant to our study. Multicausality may sometimes look random. Free will may be assumed to be a result of multicausality. If our will is deterministic, a question arises whether we are morally responsible for our decisions, which seems to be an indefensible assumption.
2. Alternatively, we may think that determinism is an illusion and thus denies the existence of the laws of nature. If we accept free will, people can set goals for themselves and machines, but machines cannot do that without free will. Free will does not result from a specific cause, and we are responsible for our decisions. This is the basis for the punishments we receive if we break the law.
3. The third possibility is that determinism does not imply predictability and the absence of free will. Roger Penrose has stated that the world might be deterministic but still noncomputable since the action in our conscious mind is nonalgorithmic (Penrose 1999, p. 220). In this view, mechanisms are algorithmic, but organisms are not.

According to Benjamin Libet's famous study (originally in 1983), an electrical change in our brain begins 550 ms before the motor act (Libet 1999). A human becomes aware of the intention to act after this but 200 ms before the act. The process is, therefore, initiated unconsciously. But the conscious brain can still veto the act. Other researchers have also made Libet's observation. Some scientists believe free will cannot be excluded (Schurger et al. 2021).

Reduction We use the term reduction in three meanings: methodological, epistemological, and ontological reduction (Barbour 1997; Honderich 2005). *Methodological reduction* includes our analytical thinking, where we use ontological and epistemological reduction to study the behavior of complicated wholes by analyzing their parts and properties, respectively.

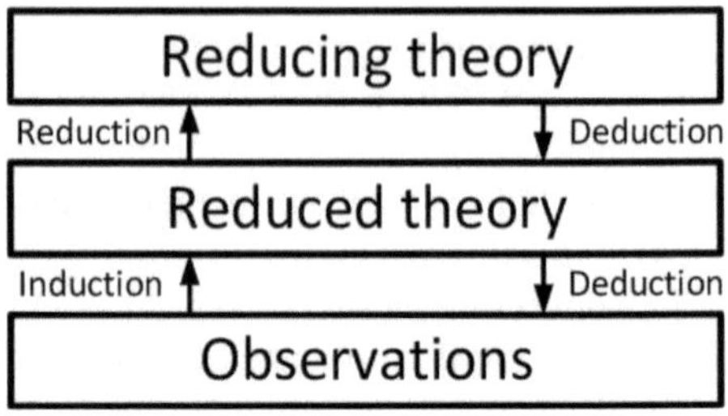

Fig. 3.17 Observations and theories in epistemological reduction

The *epistemological reduction* expresses a relation between theories in an abstract whole. The most general theory is at the top, and the most primitive theory is at the bottom, just above observations (Honderich 2005) (Fig. 3.17). We can reduce theories at any level to more general theories at a higher level (Rosenberg and McIntyre 2020). A good example is the reduction of Newtonian mechanics to the theory of relativity. The former is the reduced theory, and the latter is the reducing theory. As explained in Kline (1995) and Losee (2001), some authors in the past have thought that the most general theory should be at the bottom and the observations should be at the top, but that order would make our handy terms "top-down" and "bottom-up" meaningless.

In practice, the use of the epistemological reduction is limited by the concept of emergence. For example, we can see Newtonian mechanics (lower-level theory) as an approximation of Einstein's relativity theory (higher-level theory), and there is no possibility to derive relativity theory from Newtonian mechanics. Similarly, Stephen J. Kline claims we cannot derive thermodynamics from statistical mechanics (Kline 1995).

When we reduce the observations to a theory, this corresponds to synthesis. We usually call the formation of theories induction or abduction (Fig. 3.17). The opposite of epistemological reduction is deduction, which corresponds to analysis. Science proceeds upwards from observations to more and more general theories because this is how humans naturally learn, from simple to complex (Checkland 1999). We proceed upwards from the better known and specific, i.e., observations, to the less known and general, i.e., theories (Fig. 1.6). Since theories form a hierarchy, we proceed upwards from observations to theories (Fig. 3.17).

Figure 3.18 shows an example of Newtonian mechanics (Young et al. 2012; Rosenberg and McIntyre 2020). Newton reduced Galileo's and Johann Kepler's theories to Newtonian mechanics, and Einstein reduced Newtonian mechanics to general relativity theory, which covered high speeds and accelerated motion. Galileo's terrestrial mechanics and Kepler's celestial mechanics were formulated from observations. The theories are deterministic, causal, and symmetric in time.

Galileo introduced four physical ideas: (1) force determines acceleration, not velocity, corresponding Newton's first and second laws (2) relativity principle implying that there is no concept of the state of rest and the same laws are valid in uniform motion, (3) groping toward an understanding of the conservation of energy, which are included in Newton's laws although not explicitly, and (4) equivalence principle implied in the observation that all bodies fall at the same rate under gravity

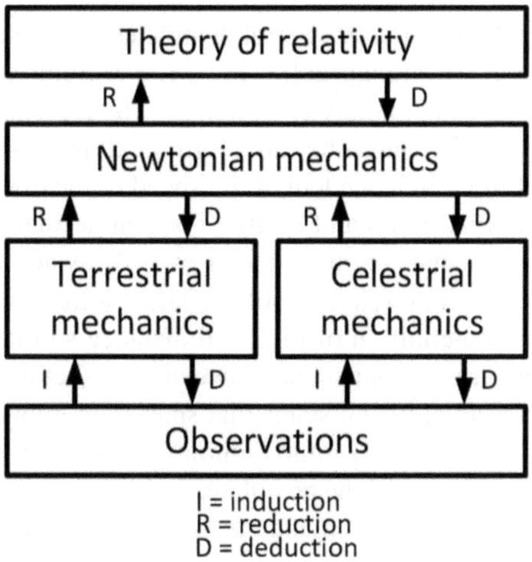

Fig. 3.18 An example of epistemological reduction

without air resistance (Penrose 1999, pp. 210–215, 262–263, 277). The equivalence principle means that the inertial mass in Newton's second law and the gravitational mass in Newton's fourth law are identical (Suntola 2018). Newton assumed that the equivalence principle is valid, although nothing in his theory demands that the two masses be the same. For example, charged objects dropping in an electric field do not fall at the same speed. Newton assumed that the gravitation force was instantaneous.

The Newtonian mechanics has the following structure in an isolated system (Young et al. 2012; Nagel 1979; Rosenberg and McIntyre 2020):

A. **Primitive concepts**: Mass m, space (length s or distance d), and time t.
B. **Definitions**: Velocity $\boldsymbol{v} = \mathrm{d}s/\mathrm{d}t$, acceleration $\boldsymbol{a} = \mathrm{d}\boldsymbol{v}/\mathrm{d}t = \mathrm{d}^2\boldsymbol{s}/\mathrm{d}t^2$, and momentum $\boldsymbol{p} = m\boldsymbol{v}$, G is constant of gravity.
C. **Axioms**: (1) Law of inertia: if $\boldsymbol{F} = 0$, $\boldsymbol{v}$ is constant, (2) Relationship of force and acceleration: $\boldsymbol{F} = \mathrm{d}\boldsymbol{p}/\mathrm{d}t = m\boldsymbol{a}$, (3) Law of action and reaction: $\boldsymbol{F}_1 = -\boldsymbol{F}_2$, (4) Law of gravitation $F = Gm_1m_2/d^2$.
D. **Theorems (some examples)**:

   I. *Galileo's terrestrial mechanics*: (1) Projectiles follow the path of a parabola. (2) Period of a simple pendulum is proportional to the square root of the length of the wire and is independent of the weight of the bob. (3) Law of free fall: all bodies fall with an acceleration that is constant and independent of their masses.
   II. *Kepler's celestial mechanics*: (1) Orbits of planets are elliptical. (2) A line from the Sun to a planet sweeps out equal areas in equal times. (3) The squares of the periods of planets are directly proportional to the cubes of the major axes of their orbits.

Newton's third law is a particular case of a more general law, the *conservation of momentum*, which is also valid in the theory of relativity.

Einstein used several postulates to derive his special and general theory of relativity (Rothman 2003, pp. 73, 79; Suntola 2018, p. 149). The central postulates include (1) relativity principle, which means that the equations describing the laws of physics have the same form in all frames of reference; (2) constancy of the speed of light, independent of the speed of the observer; (3) equivalence principle of gravitational mass and inertial mass in acceleration; and (4) Lorentz invariance which means that the fundamental laws of physics appear the same for all observers, regardless of their relative motion. There were also two additional postulates, including (5) the redefinition of time and distance so that they are functions of the velocity and the gravitational state between an object and the observer and (6) the cosmological principle, which states that space is homogeneous and isotropic on a cosmological scale. Finally, Tuomo Suntola, in his dynamic universe theory, reduced the relativity theory to only one postulate, i.e., the zero-energy principle, which replaced the theory of relativity and made the theory compatible with quantum mechanics.

The *ontological reduction* is a view of reality. We assume that reality comprises simple parts, such as elementary particles and atoms, organized hierarchically. The concrete whole is at the top, and its parts are at the bottom (Fig. 3.15). The whole is specific, and the parts are general. In an abstract whole, the observations are the most specific at the bottom and the most general theory at the top (Fig. 3.18). In a concrete whole, we proceed downwards from a whole, better known to us, to the parts less known to us. In engineering, the whole does not initially exist, and therefore, we start from the bottom, just like in evolution. We proceed from simple parts, such as transistors, to wholes, such as integrated circuits, not vice versa. We call the top-down approach in engineering "reverse engineering," and we can use it to learn how an existing system works when we do not have any documents.

Because of emergence, disciplines such as physics, chemistry, biology, psychology, sociology, economics, political science, history, and philosophy form a hierarchy from the bottom up (Boulding 1985; Kline 1995; Checkland 1999; Smith 1997). If there would be no emergence, we would need only one discipline. Although sciences are theories, we usually present them hierarchically, following the order in ontological reduction rather than epistemological reduction, so physics is at the bottom. We do not always follow this order; sometimes, the hierarchy is upside down, as in the original Comte's hierarchy (Kline 1995). People often claim that physics is the most fundamental of all sciences. Mechanics is a counterpart of physics in engineering (Weinberg 1975). In mechanics, the whole is always a sum of its parts. Some authors claim that biology is more general than physics since it covers organisms in addition to mechanisms, and organisms are not mechanisms (Rosen 1991, 1996).

It is still a philosophical question whether chemistry can be reduced to physics, not to mention that biology could be reduced to physics (Rosen 1996; Gribbin 2003; Szostak 2004). Reduction has not been possible because of emergence. For example, predicting a protein molecule's three-dimensional structure is impossible, even though we know all its atoms (Rosen 1996; Wilson 1998). This prediction would need the integration of energy relationships among thousands of atoms to form the whole. All this becomes even more complex when we move upwards in the hierarchy when we must consider new emergent properties.

3.4.4 Methods of Discovery

We divide empirical research into discovery and verification (Honderich 2005). In *discovery*, a hypothesis is formed or constructed from a problem that may consist of observations that need a theory (Fig. 3.19). However, in the philosophy of science, the main interest is in the problem of verification, although both discovery and verification imply uncertainties. We can refine the hypothesis when new data become available. No deductive methods exist for the discovery that corresponds to synthesis, and it is usually a nonlinear process. We can make it systematic only in particular cases, for example, estimating a linear system where we can find the optimum using a simple iterative method (Makhoul 1975). There is no emergence in linear systems. We learn by induction by generalizing from examples to theories (Felder and Silverman 1988). Discovery needs creativity, which can be supported by induction, abduction, history, analogies, symmetries, relations, opposites, extremes, taxonomies, or guessing.

There are three ways to acquire new information: talk to people who know, extrapolate from known things, and make new observations and experiments. Divide and conquer and iterative improvement are the traditional discovery methods (Pagels 1988). In *divide and conquer*, we use methodological reduction: we divide a large problem into simpler subproblems, which we solve, and finally combine the solutions. We use experiments and abduction, which we call the experimental-abductive method. Although the reductive method using idealizations is effective, its importance is not always understood: "Practical people often balk at this approach since the idealized situations may be so far removed from those of use as to appear highly academic" (Wilson 1990).

In *iterative improvement*, we guess a solution and then try to improve it using repetition. We show an example in a research project in Fig. 3.20. Most methods include iterative methods because the problem and hypotheses are initially unclear, and we find it challenging to understand solutions given in the literature since we must know the terminology thoroughly. We call this a chicken and egg problem. We gain experience through observations, experiments, and discussions with more

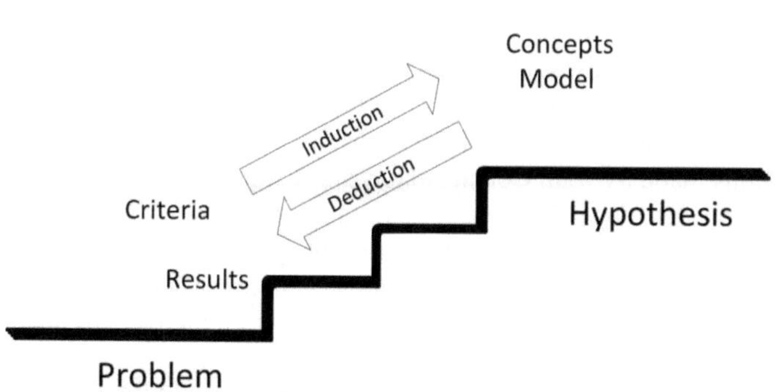

Fig. 3.19 From problem to solution or hypothesis

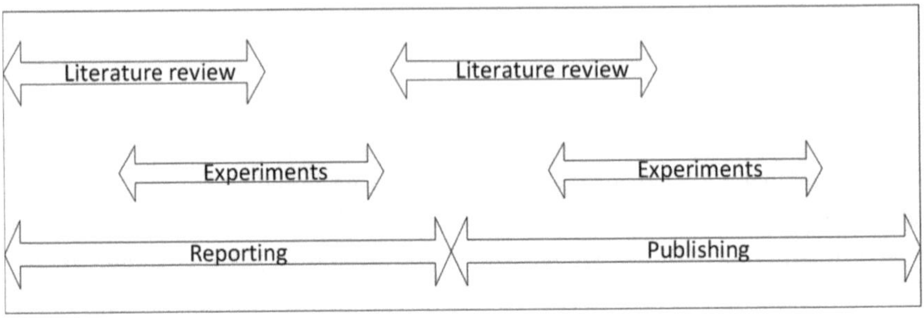

Fig. 3.20 Iterative improvement in research

experienced researchers, thus using collective intelligence (Stonier 1997). Scientific publishing improves the quality of research. Seminars are good places to exchange information.

We cannot formalize research skills, but there is good advice on getting started, for example in Bernstein (1999). For success in research, we need the right problem, timing, and approach (Loehle 1990; Hamming 1993). We must balance the difficulty of the problem and its likely payoff. The problem should neither be too easy nor too difficult. There is an opportunity for you if you notice that some other author is wrong. Publishing a correction is a delicate problem. We should not claim that the author is wrong but show what is right. There are possibilities if you find contradictory experiments or terminological confusion. You need to gain more experience to solve problems through dialogue (Jain and Triandis 1997; Senge 2006), observations and experiments, or literature. Experiments, for example, by simulations, should be started early in the research since we learn inductively.

Some books give good historical examples on discoveries (Derry 1999, p. 6). They have been classified as follows, including examples:

1. improved measuring instruments: Antonie van Leeuwenhoek's discovery of microbes using a microscope and Galileo's discovery of some moons of Jupiter using a telescope
2. understanding of patterns in data: Dmitri Mendeleev's discovery of the periodic table of elements
3. deduction from premises: Newtonian mechanics as an axiomatic system
4. hypothetico-deductive method: Edward Jenner's discovery of smallpox vaccine
5. clarification of discrepancies: Johan Gottfried Galle's discovery of Neptune using predictions made by John Couch Adams and Urbain Le Verrier
6. imagination: Nicolaus Copernicus' discovery of heliocentrism
7. intuition and dreams: Rene Descartes's discovery of reductionism (Wilson 1998), August Kekule's discovery of the structure of benzene (Hudson 1992), and Dmitri Mendeleev's discovery of the periodic system of elements (Strathern 2002) in their dreams, and
8. serendipity: Wilhelm Röntgen's discovery of X-rays and Alexander Fleming's discovery of penicillin.

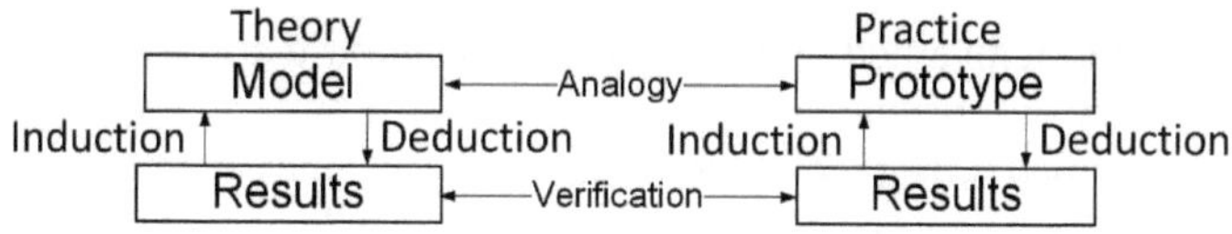

Fig. 3.21 Verification by hypothetico-deductive method. In science, the prototype is an object in the reality

Michael Polanyi believed that theories cannot be found by applying some explicitly known operation. Louis Pasteur said, "Chance favors only the prepared mind." This means that to see some weak signals, we must know what to look for.

3.4.5 Methods of Verification and Falsification

We gain experience through observations and experiments (Rosenberg and McIntyre 2020). In experiments, we affect the system under study and observe the results. In some sciences, such as astronomy, only observations can be made, and we rely on experiments offered by nature since we cannot affect nature by ourselves because of its large size and long distances. Sometimes nature provides an experiment, for example, during an eclipse of the Sun (Mota et al. 2009; Casetti 2021).

Verification, validation, and certification are different concepts (Calvez 1993). Verification generally means establishing a claim's accuracy or reality through experimentation and observation (Rosenberg and McIntyre 2020). In science and engineering, verification implies that we compare the results derived from the theory with the measurements in the real world (Fig. 3.21). We do this with the hypothetico-deductive method. The theoretical model acts as a hypothesis, which we verify or falsify when we compare the results given by the theoretical model with the corresponding experimental results given by the real world. Deduction provides internal coherence, and verification confirms the correspondence with reality.

In engineering, we verify the theoretical system model and the prototype against the requirements, and we finally validate the prototype in the field tests (JCGM 2012). Initially the requirements correspond to the theory. *Verification* is the "provision of objective evidence that a given item fulfils specified requirements" (JCGM 2012). Verification means that the measurement results fulfill the laboratory requirements. However, the requirements may not fully correspond to the user's actual needs because of a failure to define them. Therefore, in addition to laboratory measurements, we need measurements "in the field," and this phase is called *validation*. It is "verification, where the specified requirements are adequate for an intended use." In validation, we verify that the requirements correspond to the user's needs.

An accredited party does *certification* to confirm that the customer can accept a product after the validation (Calvez 1993). The ISO defines certification as a "procedure by which a third party gives written assurance that a product, process or service conforms to specified characteristics" (Balco 2001). *Accreditation* is "a procedure by which an authoritative body gives formal recognition that a body or person is competent to carry out specific tasks."

A theory is verified if the predictions of the theory and measurements correspond to each other. If they do not correspond to each other, the theory is falsified. Because of the problem of induction, verification is *not* a proof. For example, the term *proof of concept*, which is synonymous to *proof of principle*, is a misnomer in this sense. Data underdetermine theories since the data can support many competing theories. Thus, the *plausibility* of a theory is an important criterion. The principle of parsimony claims that a plausible theory is often the simplest of the alternatives. In addition to simplicity, a plausible theory is fruitful, resulting in new theories. Falsifications may improve plausibility since usually new theories are better than the old ones.

We describe a system by variables and parameters (Harre 1981; Kline 1995; Boulton et al. 2015), see Fig. 1.2b. *Variables* define the state of the system and its changes, which we call the *behavior* (Hubka and Eder 1988). We have independent and dependent variables (Fig. 3.22). An *independent variable* is manipulated directly. A *dependent variable* is affected by the changes in the independent variable. A property that is fixed in an experiment is called a *parameter*. For example, in Boyle's law, the temperature is kept as a constant parameter whereas pressure and volume are variables. Since they depend on each other, we can select one of them as an independent variable and the second one is then the dependent variable. More generally, parameters describe the *structure* of the system or network. A network consists of vertices or nodes and edges or links (Newman 2010). The parameters describe which links connect which nodes in a network graph. Each link may have a "weight," for example, distance or delay defined by the parameter. Since the structure can change, even the parameters can change; therefore, old links may disappear, and new links appear.

Tests are either deterministic or statistical. We use statistical tests in the Monte Carlo method. If there are many independent variables, we can change only one independent variable at a time and set the other independent variables at a fixed level (Fig. 3.22) (Wohlin et al. 2000). This way, we can determine the factors affecting the system. This idea works best for linear systems.

In the book (Harre 1981), the author describes twenty experiments that changed our worldview, including, for example, the experiments by Galileo, Isaac Newton, Robert Boyle, and Antoine Lavoisier. A famous negative result was Albert A. Michaelson and Edward W. Morley's (1887) measurement that falsified the ether

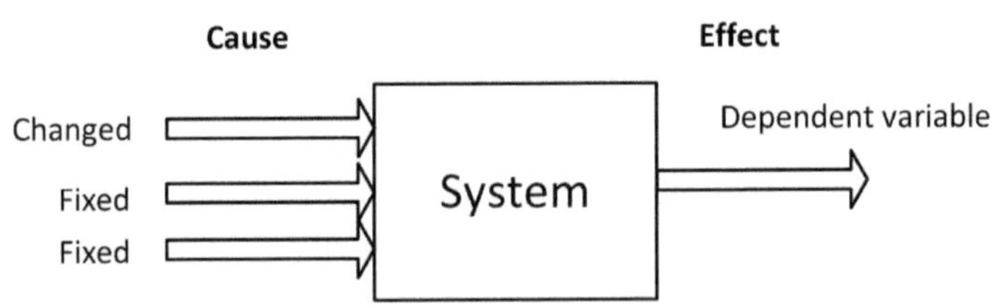

Fig. 3.22 A system with one dependent variable and several independent variables

theory. They measured the speed of light in different directions compared to the speed of the Earth and noticed no difference. The speed of light was constant, independent of the speed of the observer or source. Einstein used this as an assumption in his special theory of relativity (Rothman 2003).

Louis Pasteur (1861) made another necessary falsification (Porter 1961; Gastel and Day 2016). At that time, many biologists believed fanatically in the theory of spontaneous generation, but by reproducible experiments, Pasteur showed that diseases were caused by microorganisms called germs. Felix Archimede Pouschet had two years earlier claimed incorrectly that he had produced spontaneous generation (Roll-Hansen 1979). Now, the germ theory of disease is the foundation of Western medicine, belonging to reductionism (Pan et al. 2013).

Arthur Eddington (1919) verified a prediction made by Albert Einstein (1915) about the bending of the light rays near the Sun (Mota et al. 2009; Casetti 2021). The measurement had to be done during a solar eclipse using the light from a star. Eddington observed that the prediction of 1.75 arcseconds corresponded to the theory, thus verifying Einstein's general relativity theory in this experiment. The Newtonian mechanics predicted a bending of 0.875 arcseconds, half of that derived from the general relativity theory. Later, more accurate measurements were made, thus falsifying Newtonian mechanics, which is still accurate enough in normal circumstances and even during Moon flights. However, more accuracy is needed in Global Positioning System (GPS) navigation.

Reductionism may help us test our models. Performance is usually measured against the use of resources. We can find reference data from literature or simplified analysis and define several loss factors that increase resource use. The analysis may be intractable, and we often use lower and upper bounds to estimate performance (Proakis and Salehi 2008). The loss factors usually depend on the targeted performance level. Since the dependence is often approximately exponential, we use in these cases logarithmic scales to better visualize the loss factors.

We can verify or falsify hypotheses by using the hypothetico-deductive method (Rosenberg and McIntyre 2020), which is similar to a system identification problem where we want to identify the structure and parameters of an existing system (Eykhoff 1960; Widrow and Stearns 1985) (cf. Fig. 3.23a, b). In engineering, we initially do not have any system but only the user needs, which we convert to a set of *performance criteria* and finally to *performance requirements* (Fig. 3.23c). Therefore, we must modify the hypothetico-deductive method: we replace the natural object with the requirements. A research problem is often an optimization problem, and we find the optimum or worst case using an optimization criterion (Michalewicz and Fogel 2004; Talbi 2009). The requirements describe the properties of the expected system. Figures 3.23b, c show explicitly that the verification implies the use of feedback since the model can be improved during verification, cf. with Fig. 1.6.

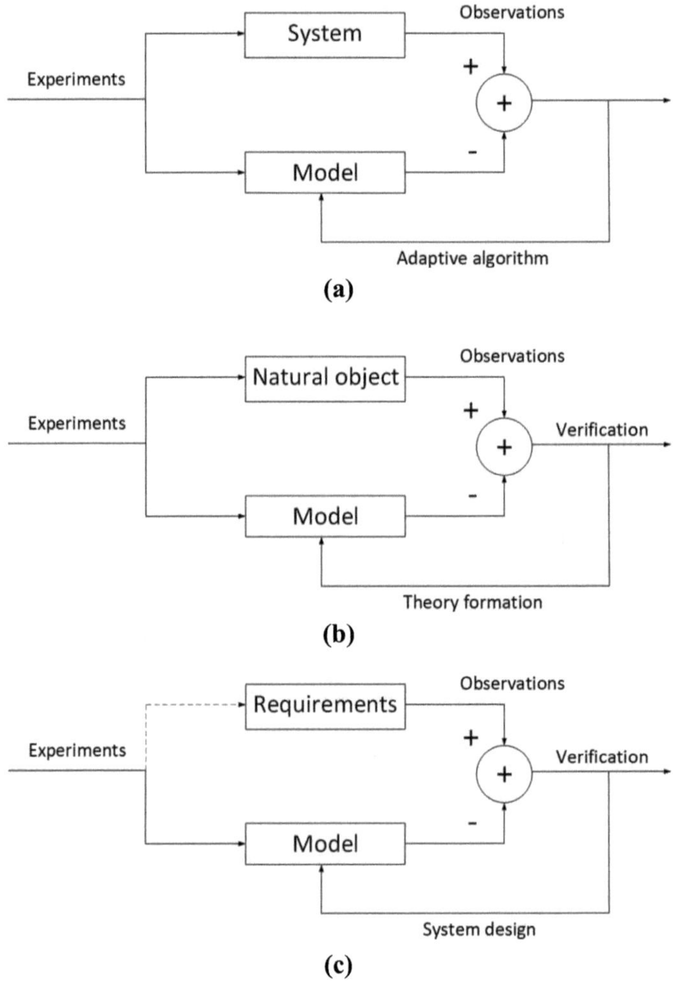

Fig. 3.23 **a** System identification problem. Difference of verification in **b** science and **c** engineering. In validation, requirements are replaced by user needs in the real world. The figure shows the use of feedback in the hypothetico-deductive method

3.5 Chapter Summary and Recommended Reading

We described the whole research process using the conventional analytical thinking or analytical approach. Research is an advanced learning process that usually proceeds inductively or abductively from the bottom up, although the results are presented deductively from the top down. Research is divided into the formation of concepts and theories. We also explained the different roles of a researcher and organization. Division of work in our society led to the need for experts. Although much information is now freely available to us in a liberal democracy, there is also much misinformation and disinformation. Experts are needed to select the most reliable information for each specific case. Experts act, for example, as teachers and researchers. We require generalists to see the forest for the trees when the world becomes more complex. They offer relevant information in the form of goals for research and the whole society.

General books on the analytical thinking include Thiel (2014), Morawski (2019) and Bock (2020). Philosophy of science is well described in the monograph (Rosenberg and McIntyre 2020). The encyclopedia of philosophy (Honderich 2005) also includes clear definitions. The role of the research organization is described in Jain and Triandis (1997). Exciting discussions on creativity are included in Bennis and Biederman (1997), Bohm and Peat (2000), Pahl et al. (2007) and de Bono (2014), and especially on intuition in Raami (2015). The importance of experts and generalists or systems thinkers in our society is emphasized in Nichols (2017) and Epstein (2019).

Discussion Questions

1. Define the tasks of a specialist and a generalist. Why are both needed? How are analytical and systems thinking different?
2. What is the difference between vertical and horizontal integration? What are their relationship to analytical and systems thinking?
3. Define research, development, and innovation.
4. What is the general structure of theories? Why are defining the scope and the conceptual analysis essential phases of research? What kind of definitions are there? Describe the methods of discovery and verification. What is the difference between verification, falsification, and validation?
5. Discuss efficient and final causes and multicausality.

Appendix

Linear systems are best analyzed using complex signals and systems that form a compact model of real signals and systems in the real world. Our purpose is not to present the linear system theory which many introductory books include Haykin and Moher (2014), Ziemer and Tranter (2014), Kay (1988) and Marple (2019). We present some results that are often neglected when summarizing the theory and that are a challenge for newcomers.

A complex number is an ordered pair of real numbers marked as (x, y). We can understand it best as a point in the complex plane where the number $z = x + jy$ has an amplitude /z/ and phase arg(z). The constant j is the imaginary unit. The amplitude is the distance from the origin, and the phase is the angle between the positive x-axis and the line segment from the origin to the point z. In a short-hand notation a sinusoid $A \cos(\omega t + \phi)$ with an amplitude A and a phase ϕ can be represented by a complex number $z = A \exp(j\phi)$ referred to the angular frequency $\omega = 2\pi f$ (in rad/s) where f is the frequency (in Hz). Such a number z is sometimes called a *phasor*. A complex number may be a function of time t, thus forming a signal. A real narrowband signal $A(t)\cos(\omega t + \phi(t))$ corresponds to the complex signal $z(t) = A(t)\exp(j\phi(t))$. Such signals represent narrowband modulated signals shifted to low frequencies in the baseband. The resulting complex signal is called the *complex envelope* of the original signal, thus preserving the knowledge of the amplitude and phase of the original signal with respect to the carrier $\cos(\omega t)$. The complex envelope concept is rigorously derived using the Hilbert transform, as explained by Franks (1969) and Haykin and Moher (2014). The use of the Hilbert transform is also the pedagogically correct approach to define the complex envelope.

In general, system models use complex signals having a real and imaginary part (Franks 1969; Haykin and Moher 2014). There are at least two reasons to use complex signals instead of real ones: eigenfunctions and complex envelopes. The eigenfunctions of a linear system are complex exponentials (Manley 1982), not real sinusoids. Complex envelopes are complex signals corresponding to real bandpass signals that may have both amplitude and angle modulation that can be phase or frequency modulation. Typically, we illustrate complex signals using two separate curves; for example, we show the amplitude and phase or real and imaginary parts separately. We can also use phasor trajectory on the complex plane called a *polar plot*. In control engineering, a transfer function presented as a phasor on the complex plane at different frequencies is a polar plot called a Nyquist plot (Ogata 2010).

Alternatively, complex signals can be presented graphically as three-dimensional curves projected on a plane (Boutin 1989, 1990a, b, c), and the geometrical insight is obvious. We can also see the relationships between different methods of representation. It is best to use the left-handed Cartesian coordinate system (from the word "co-order") where the three axes are the real part x and the imaginary part y of the signal and the time t. The x–y plane is the complex plane. In Fig. 3.24 we present the complex exponential $a\exp[j(2\pi f_0 t + \theta)]$, where a is the amplitude, $f_0 > 0$ is the frequency ($1/f_0$ is the period), and phase is θ. The projection of the complex signal on the complex plane is the polar plot. We use the left-handed coordinate system since, in this way, when the signal phase is increased, the phasor on the complex plane rotates counterclockwise, as in high-school mathematics. Using a right-handed coordinate system would be the opposite, resulting in potential confusion. Correspondingly, Fourier transforms are complex functions of frequency f, and the meaning of the polar plot is understandable as a projection on the complex plane when the frequency is changed.

We can analyze a linear system with integral transforms such as the *Fourier transform* (Haykin and Moher 2014; Ziemer and Tranter 2014), and the *Laplace transform* (Papoulis 1962). The former is helpful for the steady-state analysis of linear systems after all the transients have faded away, and the latter is helpful for the transient and steady-state analysis, using either periodic or aperiodic input signals (Nahin 1991). The transforms change differential equations into algebraic or polynomial equations that are much easier to solve. The Fourier transform is based on the work of Joseph Fourier (1822), and the Laplace transform is based on the work of Pierre-Simon Laplace (1812).

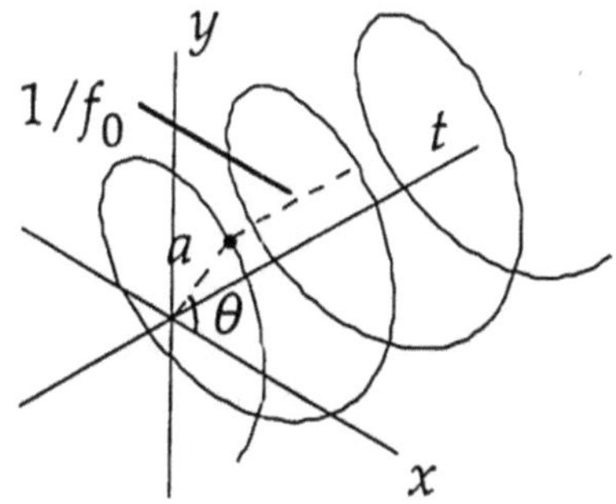

Fig. 3.24 Complex exponential as an example of complex signals

A discrete-time system is analyzed using the z-transform, which changes difference equations to algebraic equations, as explained in the books on digital signal processing (Proakis and Manolakis 2007; Oppenheim et al. 1999). Witold Hurewicz (1947) and John R. Ragazzini and Lotfi A. Zadeh (1952) developed the modern form of the z-transform.

An important observation is that the exponential time function exp(st) is an *eigenfunction* of any linear time-invariant system where s is a complex variable and t is time (Manley 1982). The eigenfunction corresponds to an eigenvector in matrix algebra (Kreyszig 2011; Kay 1988). In the Laplace transform, the exponential time function has the form exp(st), $t > 0$. The eigenfunction has the form exp(jωt) in the Fourier transform. The property leads to the concept of the *transfer function*, which is the Laplace transform $H(s)$ or Fourier transform $H(\omega)$ of the impulse response $h(t)$. The *impulse response* is the response of the linear system to a very narrow pulse called impulse, denoted by $\delta(t)$. The response contains all the necessary information about the system. In the time domain, the output $y(t)$ of a linear system is the *convolution* of the input signal $x(t)$ and the impulse response $h(t)$. In the transform domain, the convolution is changed to a product $Y(s) = H(s)\,X(s)$ or $Y(\omega) = H(\omega)\,X(\omega)$, which is much easier to compute. The product is a direct result of using the eigenfunctions in the transforms. Suppose input signal is exp(j$\omega_0 t$), where ω_0 is a real positive constant. In that case the output signal is $H(\omega_0)$ exp(j$\omega_0 t$), and thus the eigenfunction exp(j$\omega_0 t$) is simply multiplied by a complex number $H(\omega_0)$ and otherwise the eigenfunction keeps its form. This is the defining property of an eigenfunction.

For example, the signal cos(ωt) is not an eigenfunction of a linear system. We must use the expression cos(ωt) = ½ [exp(jωt) + exp(− jωt)] that consists of a sum of two eigenfunctions, and the corresponding output signal is ½ [H(ω) exp(jωt) + H(− ω) exp(− jωt)], which is a sum of two scaled versions of eigenfunctions. This property is why we have both negative and positive angular frequencies (− ω and ω, respectively) in the complex model. The function $X(\omega)$ is often called the spectrum of a signal. Similarly, $/X(\omega)/^2$ is the energy spectrum of a signal with finite energy. If the signal is periodic, its Fourier transform is equivalent to the Fourier series.

We can extend linear system theory to time-varying systems where both the impulse response and the transfer function are time-varying (Kailath 1960; Bello

1963; Proakis and Salehi 2008). In time-discrete systems, the time-varying case must be expressed as a matrix multiplication (Kailath 1960).

Matrix algebra is a tool for analyzing linear systems (Kay 1988; Marple 2019). A matrix is "a rectangular array of quantities (usually square)" (Online Etymology Dictionary 2024) or an ordered two-dimensional table of $N \times M$ real or complex numbers where N is the number of rows and M is the number of columns in the table. The numbers may correspond, for example, to samples of a discrete-time process. A special case of a matrix is a vector that has only one column or row. A special case of a real vector (x, y) corresponds to a complex number $z = x + jy$. We can show that an integral equation in continuous-time systems corresponds to a matrix equation in discrete-time systems, and the matrix equation is more straightforward to solve (Price 1954). We can express convolution as a product of a vector and a matrix, and this is now a standard approach in signal processing (Kay 1993) and communication systems (Proakis and Salehi 2008). Matrix equations can be generalized also to time-varying systems, as in Kailath (1960).

Since the system model usually includes a random part, in the analysis we also need the theory of probability for random variables and random or stochastic processes (Papoulis and Pillai 2002; Kay 2006) as explained for example in Kay (1988) and Marple (2019). A random process is a sequence of random variables, which is needed to compute ensemble averages such as a mean and variance, which may themselves be functions of time. An example is a *learning curve* of an adaptive algorithm (Widrow and Stearns 1985; Haykin 2014), presenting the reducing mean-square error as a function of time, thus showing the convergence of the algorithm.

References

Aaltonen M (2007) The return to multi-causality. J Futures Stud 12(1):81–86

Achinstein P (1968) Concepts of science: a philosophical analysis. John Hopkins Press, London

Albus JS (1991) Outline for a theory of intelligence. IEEE Trans Syst Man Cybern 21(3):473–509

Albus JS, Meystel AM (2001) Engineering of mind: an introduction to the science of intelligent systems. Wiley, New York

ALLEA (2023) The European code of conduct for research integrity, rev. edn. Berlin. https://allea.org/code-of-conduct/. Accessed 18 Oct 2024

Arbnor I, Bjerke B (1997) Methodology for creating business knowledge, 2nd edn. Sage, London

Aron EA (1999) The highly sensitive person: how to thrive when the world overwhelms you. Element, London

Asimov I (1984) The history of physics, rev. Walker and Company, New York

Asimov I (1987) Asimov's new guide to science, 4th edn. Penguin Books, Middlesex, England

Asimov I (1994) Asimov's chronology of science & discovery: updated and illustrated. Harper & Row, New York

Bailer-Jones DM (2009) Scientific models in philosophy of science. University of Pittsburgh Press, Pittsburgh, PA

Balco O (2001) A methodology for certification of modeling and simulation applications. ACM Trans Model Comput Simul 11(4):352–377

Barbour IG (1974) Myths, models, and paradigms: A comparative study in science and religion. Harper and Row, San Francisco, CA

Barbour IG (1997) Religion and science: historical and contemporary issues. HarperCollins, New York

Barrow JD (1998) Impossibility: the limits of science and the science of limits. Oxford University Press, New York

Bello PA (1963) Characterization of randomly time-variant linear channels. IEEE Trans Commun Syst CS 11(4):360–393

Bennis W, Biederman PW (1997) Organizing genius: the secrets of creative collaboration. Addison-Wesley, Reading, MA

Bernstein DS (1999) A student's guide to research. IEEE Control Syst Mag 19(1):102–108

Bitbol M (2012) Downward causation without foundations. Synthese 185:233–255. https://doi.org/10.1007/s11229-010-9723-5

Black H (1977) Inventing the negative feedback amplifier. IEEE Spectr 14(12):55–60

Bock P (2020) Getting it right: R&D methods for science and engineering, 2nd edn. Academic Press, San Diego, CA

Bodanis D (2000) $E = mc^2$: a biography of the world's most famous equation. Berkley Books, New York

Bohm D, Peat FD (2000) Science, order, and creativity, 2nd edn. Routledge, London

Bongaerts L et al (2000) Hierarchy in distributed shop floor control. Comput Ind 43(2):123–137

Boulding KE (1985) The world as a total system. Sage, Beverly Hills, CA

Boulton JG et al (2015) Embracing complexity: strategic perspectives for an age of turbulence. Oxford University Press, Oxford, UK

Boutin N (1989) Complex signals, part I. R.F. Design 12:27–33

Boutin N (1990a) Complex signals, part II. R.F. Design 13:57–65

Boutin N (1990b) Complex signals, part III. R.F. Design 13:109–115

Boutin N (1990c) Complex signals, part IV. R.F. Design 13:65–75

Boyer CB, Merzbach UC (1991) A history of mathematics, 2nd rev. Wiley, New York

Bridges D, Schendan HE (2019) Sensitive individuals are more creative. Pers Individ Differ 142:186–195. https://doi.org/10.1016/j.paid.2018.09.015

Bruno LC, Baker LW (eds) (1999) Math and mathematicians: the history of math discoveries around the world, vol 1 A-H. UXL, San Francisco, CA

Bunge M (1993) Realism and antirealism in social science. Theor Decis 35(3):207–235

Calvez JP (1993) Embedded real-time systems: a specification and design methodology. Wiley, Chichester, UK

Camazine S et al (2001) Self-organization in biological systems. Princeton University Press, Princeton, NJ

Cary P (2007) A brief history of the concept of free will: issues that are and are not germane to legal reasoning. Behav Sci Law 25(2):165–181

Casetti L (2021) Traveling towards fame: Albert Einstein and the Eddington eclipse expedition to Príncipe and Sobral in 1919. In: Graziani M et al (eds) Nel segno di Magellano tra terra e cielo: Il viaggio nelle arti umanistiche e scientifiche di lingua portoghese e di altre culture europee in un'ottica interculturale. Firenze University Press, Florence, Italy, pp 421–440

Casti JL (1994) Complexification: explaining paradoxical world through the science of surprise. Abacus, London

Chae KH (2023) Breakdown of the Newton-Einstein standard gravity at low acceleration in internal dynamics of wide binary stars. Astrophys J 952(2):1–33

Chamberlin TC (1965) The method of multiple working hypotheses. Science 148(3671):754–759

Checkland P (1999) Systems thinking, systems practice: includes a 30-year retrospective, rev. Wiley, Chichester, UK

Chen EK (2023) The preordained quantum universe. Nature 624(7992):513–515

Chessin PL (1955) A bibliography on noise. IRE Trans Inf Theory 1(2):15–31

Chestnut H (1965) Systems engineering tools. Wiley, New York

Cohen L (2005) The history of noise [on the 100th anniversary of its birth]. IEEE Signal Process Mag 22(6):20–45
Cornish-Bowden A, Luz Cardenas M (2020) Contrasting theories of life: historical context, current theories. In search of an ideal theory. Biosystems 188:1–50. https://doi.org/10.1016/j.biosystems.2019.104063
de Bono E (2014) Lateral thinking: an introduction. Vermilion, London, UK
Derry GN (1999) What science is and how it works, reprint. Princeton University Press, Princeton, NJ
Deutsch D (1997) The fabric of reality. Penguin Books, London
Dewdney AK (2004) Beyond reason: eight great problems that reveal the limits of science. Wiley, Hoboken, NJ
Di Marzo Serugendo G et al (2005) Self-organization in multi-agent systems. Knowl Eng Rev 20(2):165–189
Diamond J (1997) Guns, germs, and steel: the fates of human societies. W. W. Norton & Company, New York
Dressler F (2008) A study of self-organization mechanisms in ad hoc and sensor networks. Comput Commun 31(13):3018–3029
Dutt ND, Gajski DD (1990) Design synthesis and silicon compilation. IEEE Des Test Comput 7(6):8–23
Edmondson A (1999) Psychological safety and learning behavior in work teams. Adm Sci Q 44(2):350–383
Electropedia (2024) International electrotechnical commission (IEC). http://www.electropedia.org. Accessed 6 Nov 2024
Elsasser WM (1987) Reflections on a theory of organisms: holism in biology. The Johns Hopkins University Press, Baltimore, MD
Encyclopedia Britannica (2024). https://www.britannica.com. Accessed 5 Nov 2024
Engeström Y (1982) Perustietoa opetuksesta. Valtiovarainministeriö, Helsinki, Finland
Epstein S (2010) Demystifying intuition: what it is, what it does, and how it does it. Psychol Inq 21(4):295–312
Epstein D (2019) Range: why generalists triumph in a specialized world. Riverhead Books, New York
European Union (2024) Living guidelines on the responsible use of generative AI in research. European Commission
Eykhoff P (1960) Adaptive and optimalizing control systems. IEEE Trans Autom Control 5(2):148–151
Felder RM, Silverman LK (1988) Learning and teaching styles in engineering education. Eng Educ 78(7):674–681
Fourati H et al (2021) Comprehensive survey on self-organizing cellular network approaches applied to 5G networks. Comput Netw 199:1–24. https://doi.org/10.1016/j.comnet.2021.108435
Franks LE (1969) Signal theory. Prentice Hall, Englewood Cliffs, NJ
Fukuyama F (1992) The end of history and the last man. Free Press, New York
Gao Z (2014) Engineering cybernetics: 60 years in the making. Control Theory Technol 12(2):97–109
Gastel B, Day RA (2016) How to write and publish a scientific paper, 8th edn. Greenwood, Santa Barbara, CA
Gauvrit N et al (2017) The information-theoretic and algorithmic approach to human, animal, and artificial cognition. In: Dodig-Crnkovic G, Giovagnoli R (eds) Representation and reality in humans, other living organisms and intelligent machines. Springer International Publishing, Cham, Switzerland
Gelfert A (2017) The ontology of models. In: Magnani L, Bertolotti T (eds) Springer handbook of model-based science. Springer International Publishing, Dordrecht, The Netherlands
Gleick J (1987) Chaos: making a new science. Penguin Books, New York

Glinz M (2017) A glossary of requirements engineering terminology, version 1.7. https://expleoacademy.com/dach/wp-content/uploads/sites/4/2020/11/ireb_cpre_glossary_17.pdf
Gribbin J (2003) The scientists: a history of science told through the lives of its greatest inventors. Random House, New York
Hall AD (1962) A methodology for systems engineering. D. Van Nostrand Company, Princeton, NJ
Hamming RW (1993) You and your research. IEEE Potentials 12(3):37–40
Harre R (1981) Great scientific experiments: twenty experiments that changed our view of the world. Phaidon Press, Toronto, Canada
Haykin S (2014) Adaptive filter theory, 5th edn. Prentice Hall, Upper Saddle River, NJ
Haykin S, Moher M (2014) Communication systems, 5th edn. Wiley, Hoboken, NJ
Hempel CG (1965) Aspects of scientific explanation and other essays in the philosophy of science. The Free Press, New York
Henrich J (2020) The WEIRDest people in the world: how the west became psychologically peculiar and particularly prosperous. Picador, New York
Herrington J, Oliver R (2000) An instructional design framework for authentic learning environments. Educ Technol Res Dev 48(3):23–48
Holland JH (1995) Hidden order: how adaptation builds complexity. Perseus Books, Reading, MA
Holland JH (1998) Emergence: from chaos to order. Oxford University Press, Oxford, UK
Honderich T (ed) (2005) Oxford companion to philosophy, 2nd edn. Oxford University Press, Oxford, UK
Hubka V, Eder WE (1988) Theory of technical systems: a total concept theory for engineering design. Springer-Verlag, Berlin
Hudson J (1992) The history of chemistry. Chapman & Hall, New York
IEEE Standards Dictionary (2024). https://ieeexplore.ieee.org/browse/standards/dictionary. Accessed 5 Nov 2024
Iivari J (1991) A paradigmatic analysis of contemporary schools of IS development. Eur J Inf Syst 1(4):249–272
Ilevbare IM et al (2013) A review of TRIZ, and its benefits and challenges in practice. Technovation 33(2–3):30–37
Jain RK, Triandis HC (1997) Management of research and development organizations: managing the unmanageable. Wiley, New York
Jandyal A et al (2022) 3D printing—a review of processes, materials and applications in industry 4.0. Sustain Oper Comput 3:33–42. https://doi.org/10.1016/j.susoc.2021.09.004
JCGM (2012) International vocabulary of metrology—basic and general concepts and associated terms (VIM), 3rd edn. Joint Committee for Guides in Metrology (JCGM)
Johri A, Olds BM (2011) Situated engineering learning: bridging engineering education research and the learning sciences. J Eng Educ 100(1):151–185
Kahlen FJ et al (eds) (2017) Transdisciplinary perspectives on complex systems: new findings and approaches. Springer International Publishing, Cham, Switzerland
Kailath T (1960) Correlation detection of signals perturbed by a random channel. IRE Trans Inf Theory IT 6(3):361–366
Kay SM (1988) Modern spectral estimation: theory and application. Prentice-Hall, Englewood Cliffs, NJ
Kay SM (1993) Fundamentals of statistical signal processing, vol I: estimation theory. Prentice Hall, Englewood Cliffs, NJ
Kay SM (2006) Intuitive probability and random processes using MATLAB®. Springer Science + Business Media, New York
Kim J (1999) Making sense of emergence. Philos Stud 95(1):3–36
Kline SJ (1995) Conceptual foundations of multidisciplinary thinking. Stanford University Press, Stanford, CA

Koltko-Rivera M (2006) Rediscovering the later version of Maslow's hierarchy of needs: self-transcendence and opportunities for theory, research, and unification. Rev Gen Psychol 10(4):302–317

Kragh H (1999) Quantum generations: a history of physics in the twentieth century. Princeton University Press, Princeton, NJ

Kreutz D et al (2015) Software-defined networking: a comprehensive survey. Proc IEEE 103(1):14–76

Kreyszig E (2011) Advanced engineering mathematics, 10th edn. Wiley, New York

Larson EJ (2021) The myth of artificial intelligence: why computers can't think the way we do. Belknap Press, Cambridge, MA

Li M et al (2011) Dark energy. Commun Theor Phys 56(3):525–604

Libet B (1999) Do we have free will? J Conscious Stud 6(8–9):47–57

Loehle C (1990) A guide to increased creativity in research—inspiration or perspiration? Bioscience 40(2):123–129

Losee J (2001) A historical introduction to the philosophy of science, 4th edn. Oxford University Press, Oxford, UK

Machado A, Silva FJ (2007) Toward a richer view of the scientific method: the role of conceptual analysis. Am Psychol 62(7):671–681

Makhoul J (1975) Linear prediction: a tutorial review. Proc IEEE 63(4):561–580

Mämmelä A et al (2023) Loose coupling: an invisible thread in the history of technology. IEEE Access 11:59456–59482

Manley J (1982) The concept of frequency in linear system analysis. IEEE Commun Mag 20(19):26–35

Marple SL Jr (2019) Digital spectral analysis, 2nd edn. Dover Publications, Mineola, NY

McFarland D, Bösser T (1993) Intelligent behavior in animals and robots. MIT Press, Cambridge, MA

Meadows DH, Wright D (eds) (2008) Thinking in systems: a primer. Chelsea Green Publishing, White River Junction, VT

Merriam-Webster (2024). https://www.merriam-webster.com. Accessed 5 Nov 2024

Michalewicz Z, Fogel DB (2004) How to solve it: modern heuristics, 2nd edn. Springer, Berlin

Morawski RZ (2019) Technoscientific research: methodological and ethical aspects. Walter de Gruyter, Berlin

Mota E et al (2009) Einstein in Portugal: Eddington's expedition to Principe and the reactions of Portuguese astronomers (1917–25). Br J Hist Sci 42(2):245–273

Mumford WW, Scheibe EH (1968) Noise: performance factors in communication systems. Horizon House—Microwave, Inc., Dedham, MA

Nagel E (1979) Structure of science: problems in the logic of scientific explanation. Hackett Publishing Company, Indianapolis, IN

Nahin PJ (1991) Behind the Laplace transform. IEEE Spectr 28(3):60

Newcombe EA, Pasupathy S (1982) Error rate monitoring for digital communications. Proc IEEE 70(8):805–828

Newman MEJ (2010) Networks: an introduction. Oxford University Press, New York

Nichols T (2017) The death of expertise: the campaign against established knowledge and why it matters. Oxford University Press, New York

Niiniluoto I (1983) Tieteellinen päättely ja selittäminen. Otava, Helsinki, Finland

Niiniluoto I (2002) Johdatus tieteenteoriaan: Käsitteen- ja teorianmuodostus, 3rd edn. Otava, Helsinki, Finland

Nowak M (2006) Evolutionary dynamics: exploring the equations of life. The Belknap Press, Cambridge, MA

Ogata K (2010) Modern control engineering, 5th edn. Prentice Hall, Boston, MA

Online Etymology Dictionary (2024). https://www.etymonline.com. Accessed 5 November 2024

Oppenheim AV et al (1999) Discrete-time signal processing, 2nd edn. Prentice-Hall, Upper Saddle River, NJ

Oxford Learner's Dictionaries (2024). https://www.oxfordlearnersdictionaries.com. Accessed 25 Oct 2024
Pagels H (1988) The dreams of reason: the computer and the rise of the sciences of complexity. Simon & Schuster, New York
Pahl G et al (2007) Engineering design: a systematic approach, 3rd edn. Springer-Verlag, London
Pan X et al (2013) Systems thinking: a comparison between Chinese and Western approaches. Procedia Comput Sci 16:1027–1035. https://doi.org/10.1016/j.procs.2013.01.108
Papoulis A (1962) The Fourier integral and its applications. McGraw-Hill, New York
Papoulis A, Pillai S (2002) Probability, random variables, and stochastic processes, 4th edn. McGraw-Hill, New York
Pearson ML, Hubball HT (2012) Curricular integration in pharmacy education. Am J Pharm Educ 76(10):1–8. https://doi.org/10.5688/ajpe7610204
Penrose P (1999) The emperor's new mind: concerning computers, minds and the laws of physics, new. Oxford University Press, Oxford, UK
Platt JR (1964) Strong inference: certain systematic methods of scientific thinking may produce much more rapid progress than others. Science 146(3642):347–353
Popper K (1961) The poverty of historicism, 2nd edn. Routledge, London
Porter JR (1961) Louis Pasteur: achievements and disappointments, 1861. Bacteriol Rev 25(4):389–403
Portny SE (1966) Large sample confidence limits for binary error probabilities. Proc IEEE 54(12):1993
Poundstone W (1988) Labyrinths of reason: paradox, puzzles and the frailty of knowledge. Penguin Books, London
Prehofer C, Bettstetter C (2005) Self-organization in communication networks: principles and design paradigms. IEEE Commun Mag 43(7):78–85
Price R (1954) The detection of signals perturbed by scatter and noise. IRE Trans Inf Theory PGIT 4(4):163–170
Proakis JG, Manolakis DG (2007) Digital signal processing: principles, algorithms, and applications, 4rd edn. Pearson Education, Upper Saddle River, NJ
Proakis JG, Salehi M (2008) Digital communications, 5th edn. McGraw-Hill, New York
Raami A (2015) Intuition unleashed: on the application and development of intuition in the creative process. Ph.D. dissertation, Aalto University, Espoo, Finland
Ramage M, Shipp K (2020) Systems thinkers, 2nd edn. Springer, London
Random House Webster's College Dictionary (1999). Random House, New York
Ransome P (2010) Social theory for beginners. Policy Press, Bristol, UK
Riekki J, Mämmelä A (2021) Research and education towards smart and sustainable world. IEEE Access 9:53156–53177
Roberts S (2020) The power of not thinking: how our bodies learn and why we should trust them. Blink Publishing, London
Robson D (2019) Intelligence trap: why smart people make dumb mistakes. W. W. Norton & Company, New York
Roll-Hansen N (1979) Experimental method and spontaneous generation: the controversy between Pasteur and Pouchet, 1859–64. J Hist Med Allied Sci XXXIV(3):273–292
Rosen R (1991) Life itself: a comprehensive inquiry into the nature, origin, and fabrication of life. Columbia University Press, New York
Rosen R (1996) On the limitation of scientific knowledge. In: Casti JL, Karlqvist A (eds) Boundaries and barriers on the limits of scientific knowledge. Perseus Books, Reading, MA, pp 199–214
Rosenberg A (2018) Philosophy of social science, 5th edn. Routledge, New York
Rosenberg A, McIntyre L (2020) Philosophy of science: a contemporary introduction, 4th edn. Routledge, New York
Rota GC (1997) Ten lessons I wish I had been taught. Notices AMS 44(1):22–25
Rothman T (2003) Everything's relative and other fables from science and technology. Wiley, Hoboken, NJ

Rule AC (2006) Editorial: the components of authentic learning. J Authentic Learn 3(1):1–10
Runco MA, Jaeger GJ (2012) The standard definition of creativity. Creat Res J 24(1):92–96
Russell S, Norvig P (2022) Artificial intelligence: a modern approach, 3rd edn. Pearson Education, Harlow, UK
Sandell N Jr et al (1978) Survey of decentralized control methods for large scale systems. IEEE Trans Autom Control AC 23(2):108–128
Schneider F, Berenbach B (2013) A literature survey on international standards for systems requirements engineering. Procedia Comput Sci 16:796–805. https://doi.org/10.1016/j.procs.2013.01.083
Schoemaker PJH (1991) The quest for optimality: a positive heuristic of science? Behav Brain Sci 14(2):205–245
Schurger A et al (2021) What is the readiness potential? Trends Cogn Sci 25(7):558–570
SE VOCAB (2024) Software and systems engineering vocabulary. IEEE Computer Society and ISO/IEC JTC 1/SC7. https://pascal.computer.org. Accessed 6 Nov 2024
Seebohm TM (2015) History as a science and the system of the sciences: phenomenological investigations. Springer, Cham, Switzerland
Senge P (2006) The fifth discipline: the art and practice of the learning organization, rev. Doubleday, New York
Seselja D, Weber E (2012) Rationality and irrationality in the history of continental drift: was the hypothesis of continental drift worthy of pursuit? Stud Hist Philos Sci 43(1):147–159
Simon MK (2002) Probability distributions involving Gaussian random variables: a handbook for engineers, scientists and mathematicians. Springer Science + Business Media, New York
Skyttner L (2005) General systems theory: problems, perspectives, practice, 2nd edn. World Scientific Publishing, Singapore
Smith R (1997) The Norton history of the human sciences. W. W: Norton & Company, New York
Solomon M (2006) Groupthink versus the wisdom of crowds: the social epistemology of deliberation and dissent. South J Philos XLIV(S1):28–42
Stanovich KE et al (2016) The rationality quotient: toward a test of rational thinking. MIT Press, Cambridge, MA
Sternberg D (1981) How to complete and survive a doctoral dissertation. St. Martin's Press, New York
Stonier T (1992) Beyond information: the natural history of intelligence. Springer, Berlin
Stonier T (1997) Information and meaning: an evolutionary perspective. Springer, Berlin
Strathern P (2002) Mendeleyev's dream: the quest for the elements. Berkley Publishing, New York
Strogatz SH (2014) Nonlinear dynamics and chaos: with applications to physics, biology, chemistry, and engineering, 2nd edn. CRC Press, Boca Raton, FL
Suntola T (2018) The dynamic universe: toward a unified picture of physical reality, 4rd edn. Physics Foundations Society and The Finnish Society for Natural Philosophy. https://physicsfoundations.org
Suntola T (2020) Unification of theories requires a postulate basis in common. J Phys Conf Ser 1466:1–28. https://doi.org/10.1088/1742-6596/1466/1/012003
Symeonidis V, Schwarz JF (2016) Phenomenon-based teaching and learning through the pedagogical lenses of phenomenology: the recent curriculum reform in Finland. Forum Oświ 28(2):31–47
Szostak R (2004) Classifying science: phenomena, data, theory, methods, practice. Springer, Dordrecht, The Netherlands
Talbi EG (2009) Metaheuristics: from design to implementation. Wiley, Hoboken, NJ
Tao F et al (2019) Digital twin in industry: state-of-the-art. IEEE Trans Ind Inf 15(4):2405–2415
Thiel DV (2014) Research methods for engineers. Cambridge University Press, Cambridge, UK
Thims L (2012) Thermodynamics ≠ information theory: science's greatest Sokal affair. J Hum Thermodyn 8(1):1–120
Ulrich K, Eppinger S (1995) Product design and development. McGraw-Hill, New York

Umpleby SA (2016) Second-order cybernetics as a fundamental revolution in science. Constr Found 11(3):455–465

Van Lange PAM et al (2013) The psychology of social dilemmas: a review. Organ Behav Hum Decis Process 120(2):125–141

Vecchi A, Brennan L (2015) Leveraging business model innovation in the international space industry. In: Christiansen B (ed) Handbook of research on global business opportunities. IGI Global, New York

Vincent JFV et al (2006) Biomimetics: its practice and theory. J R Soc Interface 3:471–482. https://doi.org/10.1098/rsif.2006.0127

von Bertalanffy L (1971) General system theory: foundations, development, applications, rev. George Braziller, New York

von Wright GH (1971) Explanation and understanding. Cornell University Press, Ithaca, NY

Wang P (2019) On defining artificial intelligence. J Artif Gen Intell 10(2):1–37

Wang Y, Blei DM (2019) The blessings of multiple causes. J Am Stat Assoc 114(528):1574–1596

Wang Z, Bovik AC (2009) Mean squared error: love it or leave it? [A new look at signal fidelity measures]. IEEE Signal Process Mag 26(1):98–117

Wang H et al (2023) A survey on the metaverse: the state-of-the-art, technologies, applications, and challenges. IEEE Internet Things J 10(16):14671–14688

Weinberg GM (1975) An introduction to general systems thinking. Wiley, New York

Westerhoff HV et al (2009) Systems biology: the elements and principles of life. FEBS Lett 573(24):3882–3890

Widrow B, Stearns AD (1985) Adaptive signal processing. Prentice Hall, Englewood Cliffs, MA

Wigner EP (1960) The unreasonable effectiveness of mathematics in the natural sciences. Commun Pure Appl Math XIII:1–14. https://doi.org/10.1142/9789814503488_0018

Wilson EB (1990) An introduction to scientific research. Dover, Mineola, NY

Wilson EO (1998) Consilience: the unity of knowledge. Vintage Books, New York

Wohlin C et al (2000) Experimentation in software engineering: an introduction. Kluwer, Boston, MA

Ye D et al (2017) A survey of self-organization mechanisms in multiagent systems. IEEE Trans Syst Man Cybern Syst 47(3):441–461

Young HD et al (2012) Sears and Zemansky's university physics with modern physics, 13th edn. Addison Wesley, San Francisco, CA

Zadeh LA (2015) Fuzzy logic—a personal perspective. Fuzzy Sets Syst 281:4–20. https://doi.org/10.1016/j.fss.2015.05.009

Ziemer RE, Tranter WH (2014) Principles of communications: systems, modulation, and noise, 7th edn. Wiley, Hoboken, NJ

Chapter 4
Systems Thinking: Basics

If you want to go fast, go alone; if you want to go far, go together. African proverb
The most powerful natural species are those that adapt to environmental change without losing their fundamental identity which gives them their competitive advantage. Charles Darwin (1809–1882)
Democracy cannot succeed unless those who express their choice are prepared to choose wisely. The real safeguard of democracy, therefore, is education. Franklin D. Roosevelt (1882–1945)
Anyone who believes in indefinite growth in anything physical, on a physically finite planet, is either mad or an economist. Kenneth E. Boulding (1910–1993)
Only the truth is free from contradiction. Kurt Barnert (Never Look Away, Germany 2018)

Abstract We define a system in two ways: using a general definition as a set of parts and their relationships and a more specific definition as a set of interacting agents. The latter definition is helpful in self-organizing systems, called complex adaptive systems. We construct a roadmap and vision, usually for the next ten years. It is then easier to define the research problems and the actual research. The emergence phenomenon in complex systems makes reduction and deduction impossible, and the systems are analytically intractable. There are some limitations for human knowledge and fundamental limits of nature. We present a hierarchy of core sciences and information technology.

4.1 Introduction

Analytical thinking has various benefits, but it is also severely limited. If we want to understand, for example, the workings of the wings of an aircraft, it does not help if we study the chemical elements of which the wings are formed, but the aircraft and its wings must be treated as a system. The wings' form and the aircraft's speed make the aircraft fly. Another example is a helium balloon in a car. Typically, you

A. Mämmelä, *Unifying Systems*, https://doi.org/10.1007/978-3-031-85012-7_4

would expect that when the car is accelerating, the balloon would move backward, and when the car is slowing down, the balloon would move forward, but it is just the opposite. To explain this, we must consider the whole car as a system. The reason for the unexpected behavior is the fact that the density of helium is much smaller than the density of the air. The air is moving backward and forward, respectively, and the balloon must move in the opposite direction.

We must emphasize analytical thinking in project proposals since the reviewers usually appreciate it. We use systems thinking and history to show the proposal's novelty and prepare a vision for the future based on a broad knowledge of history. We must refer to recent original papers (max. ten years old, preferably 3–5 years old) to show the novelty. The literature review must be focused, especially with a little space for references. When the project budgets are limited, interdisciplinary work is demanding since it requires many researchers with reasonable workloads. As an alternative, we need a project portfolio. It is best to define a standard system model we study in the project portfolio from different aspects. This way, we divide a large project into smaller projects supporting the vision.

We can analyze two extremes (Fig. 4.1): simple deterministic systems and random systems (Weaver 1948; Checkland 1999). An important deterministic system is the feedback. A simple case is first-order feedback, which has an exponential behavior, either decay or growth (Ogata 2010; Strogatz 2014). Another example of simple deterministic systems is second-order feedback, which can be stable but may also oscillate. In physics, the second-order feedback corresponds to two-body systems. We can analyze random systems by using conventional statistics. If, in a multibody system, the bodies are weakly interacting with each other and move randomly, we can use the theory of statistical mechanics in the analysis.

No general theory exists for complex deterministic systems because of complicated, strong, nonlinear interactions between the parts. The existence of emergent properties implies analytical intractability. A limiting case is a chaotic system. Many deterministic nonlinear feedback systems tend to be chaotic, and we can analyze them

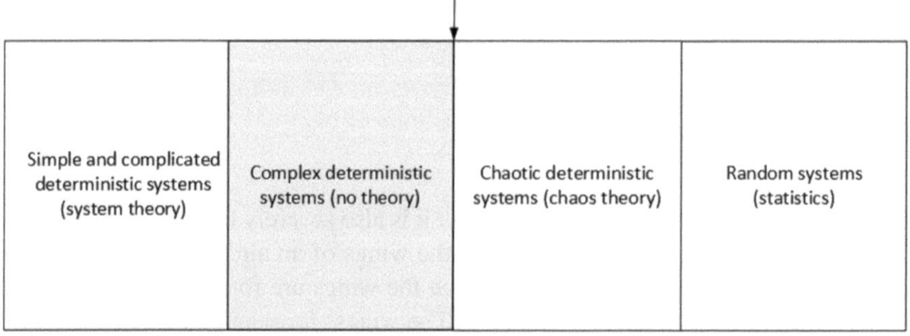

Fig. 4.1 Limitations of analysis

only statistically using chaos theory (Strogatz 2014). Already, a three-body system in physics is intractable and chaotic if there is no *mass hierarchy* where the mass of one of the bodies is much larger than the mass of the other two. With mass hierarchy, we can treat the three-body system as two almost isolated two-body systems.

Chaotic systems are, by definition, sensitive to initial conditions. Chaos is an emergent property in physics and elsewhere. There is a theory called *Lyapunov exponents* to separate unpredictable or chaotic systems from predictable or nonchaotic systems (Shin and Hammond 1998). A set of Lyapunov exponents characterizes a system. If a system contains at least one positive exponent, it is chaotic. It becomes soon unpredictable, so the nearby trajectories in the state space do not converge but diverge. Convergence is called damping, and in mechanical systems, damping is related to energy dissipation.

Technical systems, in general, should be neither random nor chaotic. Therefore, the edge of order and chaos is a significant turning point beyond which we should not move but where we can find creativity in research. A system is not easy to manage if we cannot analyze it. Complicated systems can, in practice, be implemented using a hierarchy and loose coupling between hierarchy levels and subsystems at each level (Simon 1973). Physical, biological, and social systems follow the idea. In a multibody system, a necessary condition for stability is mass hierarchy. For example, our solar system is so old that it has converged to one of the stable solutions to a multibody problem thus following mass hierarchy: the Sun has a much larger mass than all the planets, and each planet is much larger than all its moons. Biological systems are loosely coupled, a phenomenon called *near decomposability* (Simon 1962). Social systems often follow subsidiarity principle, also a form of loose coupling (Evans and Zimmermann 2014). We prefer deterministic systems that are analytically tractable at least approximately. Nature produces random phenomena, such as temperature-dependent thermal noise (Cohen 2005), which we can change only by reducing the temperature.

A concrete example of the need for systems thinking is the fall of the Broughton Suspension Bridge near Manchester, UK, on 12 April 1831 (Gazzola 2015). It is an example of unexpected resonance. The vibrations were caused by a group of soldiers who were marching over the bridge. No men were lost. After this, soldiers in many countries never march in lockstep over a bridge.

Tacoma Narrows Bridge collapsed on 7 November 1940 (Jenkins 2013; Gazzola 2015; Olson et al. 2015). The bridge was in Tacoma, west of Seattle, WA, USA. Initially, a resonance was suspected, but self-oscillation caused the collapse: specific dynamical systems give rise to various vibrations that may be useful or destructive. Fortunately, nobody died, but a car was lost. More research into bridge aerodynamics was needed.

We are not safe from disasters even nowadays. A large ship can fall over in certain conditions. An example is the *Costa Concordia* disaster on 13 January 2012 at Isola del Giglio, Tuscany, Italy, resulting in 34 deaths.

In the introduction, we defined disciplinary and interdisciplinary work. Now, we want to elaborate on this somewhat further using modern terminology. Research

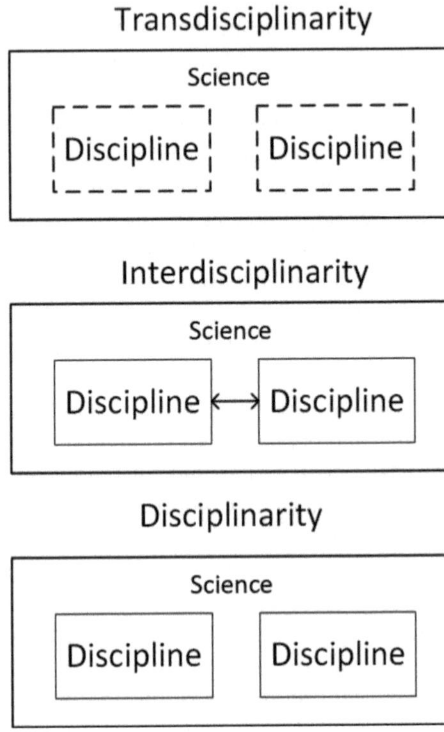

Fig. 4.2 Different approaches to scientific work

involving many disciplines has three levels, including multi-, inter-, and transdisciplinarity (Klein 1990; Choi and Pak 2006; Repko and Szostak 2021). They form a hierarchy from the bottom up (see Fig. 4.2). Systems thinking is helpful in both inter- and transdisciplinarity. Changes are usually fast in multidisciplinary work but slow in transdisciplinary work. Breakthroughs are possible in either way.

The conventional way of doing science is *multidisciplinary*: researchers from many disciplines are involved, but they work independently and do not cooperate significantly, leading to the fragmentation of science (Repko and Szostak 2021). We call this disciplinary work. An excellent example is an edited book, such as an encyclopedia with somewhat disconnected topics. Experts write the different chapters or articles independently; often, they do not make any unification. Another example is a typical university curriculum where courses are designed separately, and unification is again often missing. The progress is fast in disciplinary work since the researchers can focus on relatively narrow topics, but there may be much overlapping work using different terminology. For efficiency reasons, multidisciplinarity is mandatory because the amount of literature is vast, and we cannot produce any new results otherwise, but the danger is overspecialization. The term multidisciplinary is unfortunate since we easily mix it with interdisciplinary work.

The next level of studies among many disciplines is *interdisciplinarity*, where researchers from many different disciplines work interactively to solve a complex problem that we cannot solve in one discipline alone, and we present the solution, for example, in a unified report or an authored book. Such problems include, for example, the world population explosion, environmental contamination, climate change, and democracy crisis, which are some of the biggest problems of our time, but we must solve them to guarantee sustainability (Swilling 2020). In many developed countries the population has started to decline. We conclude that we can control population explosion mainly by education.

The highest level is *transdisciplinarity*. There are at least two schools that define the term differently. One of the schools (Hirsch Hadorn et al. 2008) sees that transdisciplinarity is a form of interdisciplinarity where different stakeholders are also included in the discussions when solving a complex problem. The other school (Nicolescu 2002; Choi and Pak 2006; Francois 2006; Repko 2008) has the opinion that transdisciplinarity means that the goal of all science is a unified view of science using common terminology and clear definitions by transcending the borders of all disciplines. Unity of science is the result of all science. Transdisciplinarity must be based on independent disciplinary studies. Unfortunately, many terms and definitions are discipline-specific. Historical and philosophical studies in systems thinking lead to a vision and shared goals that enable cooperation and improved effectiveness. The transdisciplinarity forms an attic, often resulting in Nobel Prizes (in science), Millennium Technology Prizes (in technology), and Field Medals (in mathematics). Tony Rothman has criticized the prizes since it is naive to assume that science is a collection of discoveries made by isolated geniuses, and some researchers think that the most significant credit is the satisfaction received from the discovery (Rothman 2003, p. 104). Success in inter- and transdisciplinarity requires talent to discriminate essential topics from nonessential ones to see the wood for the trees.

An excellent example of transdisciplinarity is the periodic table of chemical elements, which resulted from much analytical work with individual elements, without which one could not have developed the periodic table. The table made chemistry a modern integrated discipline. One could produce the table only with earlier detailed studies of elements. From them, one could see the periodicity of the properties of the 92 natural elements, and one could predict the existence and properties of some new elements, namely scandium, gallium, and germanium. One could find the physical reasons after the discovery of the elementary particles, including electrons, protons, and neutrons. Now we know that, in fact, from these, only an electron is an elementary particle, and a proton and neutron consist of three quarks. Transdisciplinary work is the area of generalists, who can define scientifically and societally significant goals for disciplinary and interdisciplinary work. In system design, we need a common goal given by systems thinkers or generalists to coordinate with the specialists, who must have the right and humble attitudes to cooperate (Barrow 1998).

Experts still do practical research in their discipline, but generalists can offer visions based on their broad knowledge of history (Barrow 1998; Surowiecki 2005; Epstein 2019, pp. 219–221). Sometimes, knowledge of history does not help, but we also need imagination. For example, many companies selling prospects could not forecast the success of online shopping.

According to Isaiah Berlin, experts are hedgehogs who know one big thing, but the generalists are foxes who know many little things. Hedgehogs have narrow but deep knowledge, but foxes have broad and shallow knowledge. Similarly, a decathlete cannot be anywhere as good as a specialist focusing on one sport only.

Some authors have noticed that experts are not good at forecasting progress (Surowiecki 2005; Nichols 2017; Epstein 2019). The reason for the trade-off made by experts and generalists is the brain's finite capacity (Gobet and Simon 1996): we cannot be deep and broad at the same time. Experts look at the world and each problem from their keyhole (Epstein 2019, pp. 219–221). According to some long-term research by Philip Tetlock (2005), experts perform poorly in short-term and long-term forecasting, even within their domain of expertise. Some individuals are *superforecasters* that are more accurate than the general public or experts. The superforecasters are immune to wishful thinking and prejudice.

Jack B. Soll and Richard Larrick (2006) claim that chasing an expert is a mistake, and often, a crowd can make better decisions than any individual (Surowiecki 2005, pp. xv, 32). A probable reason is that the crowd performs like a generalist when many people with different backgrounds are involved. No single person can become an expert in complex decision-making. A benefit of using the wisdom of the crowds is that we do not need to locate the best experts, which is a complex problem. Solomon (2006) concludes that aggregation of individual decisions produced anonymously can produce better decisions than those of either group deliberation to a consensus or individual expert judgment. In deliberation, the pressure to reach a consensus can lead to groupthink and data suppression. Decision-makers must use the wisdom of the crowds, superforecasters, and experts.

4.2 Basics of Systems Thinking

4.2.1 Definitions of a System

Control, computing, and communication systems in information technology are characterized by functionality, performance, dependability, security, and cost (Avizienis et al. 2004). Dependability and security are out of the scope of my book. After the functionality is defined, engineers usually focus on stability, scalability, and performance (Lee et al. 1998). Performance can be measured using efficiency, effectiveness, reliability, and agility (Mämmelä et al. 2023). Consumers measure the properties of a product by using functionality, reliability, convenience, and price in this order (Christensen 2006). This chapter focuses on functionality, stability, scalability, and performance.

A *system* is "a set or arrangement of things so related or connected as to form a unity or organic whole" (Webster's New World College Dictionary 2001). A pure *set* is not a system: the parts are isolated, and the relationships between the parts are nonexistent. Arthur D. Hall defined a system as "a set of objects with relationships between objects and between their attributes" (Hall 1962). The objects can be parts or components of the system, and their attributes are their properties. Eberhardt Rechtin proposed the following definition for a system: "A set of different elements so connected or related as to perform a unique function not performable by the elements alone" (Maier and Rechtin 2009). A system is thus essentially a function as in the functional, behavioral, and structural (FBS) model (Vermaas and Dorst 2007). In addition to stability, scalability, and performance, system has a model and general properties such as purpose, input, output, state, behavior, structure, and hierarchy (Hubka and Eder 1988). In engineering, we prefer modular hierarchical systems over integral architecture, which is challenging to design. An *architecture* is the structure of a system in terms of components, connections, and constraints (Maier and Rechtin 2009). *Systems of systems* are "systems that are composed of independent constituent systems, which act jointly towards a common goal through the synergism between them" (Gorod et al. 2008; Nielsen et al. 2015).

According to Claasen and Mecklenbäuker (1985), an information system has four features: a priori knowledge, quality criterion or metric, optimization and decision-making algorithm, and computing device, where we have generalized the terminology from adaptive signal processing. Any *prior knowledge* is helpful, otherwise, we must use a very general approach that leads to an overkill solution and would be less energy efficient. In control terms, we must use all the available environmental information. According to the separability principle, the controller has two parts: estimation and control of the environment (Skyttner 2005).

Lotfi A. Zadeh classified systems in the following way: linear and nonlinear, time-invariant and time-varying, continuous-time and discrete-time; continuous state, discrete state, and finite state; deterministic and random; differential and nondifferential; and small-scale and large-scale (Zadeh 1962). Linear systems are characterized by the superposition theorem, which substantially simplifies analysis. The system output generally depends on the current and previous inputs and the values of the internal parameters of the system characterizing the system's structure, see Fig. 1.2b. In a time-varying system, the parameters may also change, and the system state consists of the previous inputs and the values of the parameters. A system may be memoryless, and it may have a finite or infinite memory. The memory may be infinite if there are feedback loops. In a memoryless system, the output depends on the current input and some internal parameters but not on earlier inputs. We also make a distinction between continuous-amplitude and discrete-amplitude systems. Analog systems have both continuous time and continuous amplitude. Digital systems are both discrete-time (or sampled-data) and discrete-amplitude systems.

In mechanics, nonmoving systems are called *static*, and moving systems are called *dynamic* (Online Etymology Dictionary 2024). A static system is a system that shows little change, and a dynamic system is a system that is marked with change (Merriam-Webster 2024). In control systems, a static system is memoryless, and a dynamic system has memory (Ogata 2004, p. 2; 2010, pp. 14, 30). An example is a spring, which is dynamic, and its model has a memory, although the parameters in the corresponding differential equation are time-invariant. In signal theory, for example, a time-invariant filter usually has memory but is still static since nothing changes in the filter structure. A time-varying filter is dynamic in this case.

One or more ordinary differential equations characterize a differential system. Dynamic control systems that consist of linear time-invariant components may be described by linear time-invariant differential equations where the coefficients are constants. They are linear time-invariant (LTI) systems. If the coefficients are functions of time, such systems are linear time-varying systems. An example of the latter is a spacecraft control system since the mass of a spacecraft changes because of fuel consumption.

There is no clear distinction between small-scale and large-scale systems. A more common classification nowadays is simple, complicated, and complex systems (Kahlen et al. 2017), where the complex systems have emergent behavior. Dynamic nonlinear feedback systems are among the complex systems.

Modeling the system environment, which is also a system, can be divided into parameter estimation and system identification (Eykhoff 1960). In parameter estimation, we estimate the parameters of a model whose structure is known, but the parameters are unknown. In *system identification*, we determine the structure of a system about which we do not have much a priori information. System identification is a much more complex process than parameter estimation since initially the environment is completely unknown (Saridis 1979).

We can divide modeling approaches into deductive top-down and inductive bottom-up approaches. We can present models as a hierarchy of complexity (Table 4.1). In simple cases, we use simple *parametric models* that are useful in parameter estimation using the top-down deductive approach. The model is usually linear, but it may also be nonlinear. The model is selected based on some knowledge of the structure of the unknown system. Thus, there is no need to identify the structure; we must only estimate the model's parameters. This approach makes estimation fast. A simple and common linear model is a tapped delay line model whose parameters are the filter weights. The estimation fails if the model does not correspond to the unknown system (Claasen and Mecklenbäuker 1985).

Nonlinear systems are not generally commutative, i.e., their order cannot be changed without changing the input–output relationship (Mämmelä 2006). We must identify the nonlinearities, their location, the order of the various parts, and their couplings (Lasanen et al. 2008). We must also use some heuristic methods to classify the nonlinearities. Linear time-varying systems with memory are also not commutative since they correspond to a matrix operation (Kailath 1960) that is not, in general, commutative.

Table 4.1 Hierarchy of models

Model	Properties
Evolutionary models	Most general, structure defined from scratch though evolution
Neural networks	General model for intelligence produced by evolution
Parametric models	Simplest models if a priori information available

Neural networks are more general and complex parametric models for general purposes based on pattern recognition (Stonier 1992, p. 136) using the bottom-up inductive approach. Pattern recognition is a much more robust and reliable approach in uncertain environments than deductive logic. Neural networks resulted from evolution forming our brain; thus, a neural network is nature's solution to intelligence. We can also combine deductive logic and pattern recognition in *hybrid intelligent systems*, combining the best parts of both worlds (Medsker 1995; McGarry et al. 1999; Ovaska et al. 2006).

Evolutionary models are the most general system models since they initially have no structure. The use of evolutionary models is an inductive bottom-up approach. The evolutionary systems have a demanding task to identify the structure of an unknown system (this is called pattern recognition) or to form new patterns that survive in the environment (this is called pattern formation). Those agents survive best and have the best fitness in the environment. Structural identification is the most difficult and slowest of the optimization methods: we must identify the structure and estimate its parameters. A general approach uses a set of interacting agents, as in complexity theory (Benbya and McKelvey 2006). This way, we can form a self-organizing system, usually with hierarchy and loose coupling.

Estimation of a parametric model is fast, especially when the model is linear. Neural networks converge more slowly than ordinary parametric models because of the complexity of the network and the large number of parameters. If the network is extensive, the learning rate is slow because the network is tightly coupled instead of loosely coupled. Evolutionary models converge even more slowly since the model is formed bottom-up from scratch in the extreme case. The relevant changes in the environment must be much slower than in the parametric models and neural networks.

A system is separated from the environment, i.e., the rest of the universe by a *boundary* that an observer defines. A system may be part of a more comprehensive system. The broadest possible natural system is the universe. A technical system is a whole that has a *purpose*.

We call systems that follow known causal physical and chemical laws *mechanisms* (Rosen 1991, 1996). All machines are made of mechanisms. Living biological systems are called *organisms* that consist of organs, such as a heart, kidney, stem, or leaf. It is a philosophical question whether organisms are mechanisms. Organisms have emergent properties, such as life and consciousness, that mechanisms do not have. Still, organisms are assumed to follow physical and chemical laws some of which are unknown.

A system has a *state* that contains the numerical values of all properties (variables and parameters) at a given time, such as size, mass, velocity, energy, and stability (Hubka and Eder 1988). For example, in a linear time-discrete filter, the memory contents of the filter form the state. In an adaptive linear filter, in addition to the memory contents called variables, the state also consists the values of its weights called parameters (Haykin and Moher 2014). We often express the state in the form of a vector. We define *behavior* as the set of successive states of a system following a trajectory. In technical systems, we describe the desired behavior using algorithms, possibly including a feedback loop. The input–output behavior is a *function*.

Structure is a set of parts and their relationships connecting the parts. A complicated system is usually hierarchical (O'Neill et al. 1986; Pumain 2006; Wu 2013), and each hierarchy level consists of subsystems that are in engineering called *modules* (Russell 2012) and in biology subsystems (Simon 1962) or holons (Koestler 1967). The modular design in engineering shortens the development time and improves a system's flexibility and comprehensibility (Parnas 1972; Benbya and McKelvey 2006).

A *process* is "a series of changes with some sort of unity, or unifying principle" (Honderich 2005). Deterministic system models may include a random part, for example, in the form of noise caused by the environment. The inaccuracy of the computation may also cause internal noise. In digital processing, this is called quantization noise. The world is fundamentally stochastic, as in the quantum mechanics of the theory of the microworld. For most engineering purposes, the macro world looks deterministic and causal, although sometimes chaotic if studied carefully enough (Nagel 1979; Pagels 1988).

Order is "the arrangement or sequence of objects or of events in time" (Merriam-Webster 2024). We can divide order into static and dynamic order (Bohm and Peat 2000). We describe *static order* with different structures and classifications or taxonomies. *Dynamic* order is a temporal order that usually involves added iterations or repetitions. The *generative order* describes a dynamic creative process. The generative order is an overall order, which includes inherent bidirectional dynamism, and we cannot reduce it to a simple temporal order. The iterative version of the waterfall model, the V-model, and the spiral model are the primary models to approximate generative order for extensive system development (Calvez 1993; Bohm and Peat 2000; Ruparelia 2010).

A simple model for a temporal sequential process is a *waterfall model* where we divide the task or project into relatively independent phases (Calvez 1993; Ruparelia 2010). In the more advanced iterative waterfall model, we add feedback loops to revisit a preceding stage. The V-model is a variation of the waterfall model, where the specification and design phases are done top-down. Still, the implementation and validation phases are bottom-up (Fig. 4.3). The model's left leg includes project definition, and the right leg provides testing and integration. There is also feedback to the corresponding phase in the right leg from the left leg. The input may include verification, validation, and certification. We may repeat all the phases leading to a V-cycle where each new cycle improves the output. In practice, a research project is highly iterative and has complicated internal relations. A *spiral model* can approximate this process, which is essentially a form of V-cycle. We introduce several iterations to the V-cycle in a spiral form, starting from a small beginning. We can describe the idea as "start small, think big."

We use various hierarchical models of a system. We need a system model for analysis and simulations. A model describes the regularities in the system (Rosenberg and McIntyre 2020), including function, behavior, and structure. Such a model is called *functional, behavioral, and structural (FBS) model* (Vermaas and Dorst 2007). The structural model corresponds to the relationship of the physical parts in the system, thus forming the lowest level in the FBS model. The behavior is much

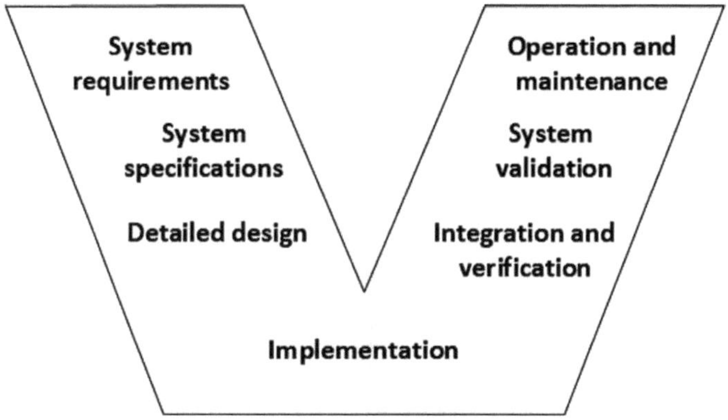

Fig. 4.3 V-model for system design

easier to change than the structure, and most automatic and autonomous systems change only the behavior. Only self-organizing systems change the structure, i.e., the parameters of the system.

A technical or artificial system cannot generally be completely autonomous, but humans must supervise it (Roberts 2020). However, humans may also cause problems since they can become ill and have limited knowledge. The latter is called *bounded rationality* (Meadows and Wright 2008). Thus, ideally, a system must be supervised by a group of people using the wisdom of crowds, but even this approach is not without problems. A related concept is the *Dunning–Kruger effect* or knowledge illusion (Sloman and Fernbach 2017), where people with limited knowledge significantly overestimate their understanding (Dunning 2011), which may in fact be based on collective intelligence resulting from the wisdom of the crowds (Stonier 1997; Surowiecki 2005).

In systems thinking, we admit that complex nonlinear interactions between parts of a whole can create emergent phenomena. In general, we cannot separate nonlinear systems into independent parts. Some simple nonlinear systems are separable for example into a memoryless nonlinear part and a linear part with memory (de Coulon 1986; Schetzen 2006). We can simulate a nonlinear dynamic network, but in chaotic systems, the results depend on the accuracy of the simulations, in addition to the initial conditions.

4.2.2 Isolated, Closed, and Open Systems

Systems are classified into isolated, closed, and open systems (Hall 1962; Lebon et al. 2008). Most systems studied in physics are isolated. *Isolated systems* exchange neither matter nor energy with the environment (see Fig. 4.4). This definition implies that there is also no energy in the form of external forces that would affect the system

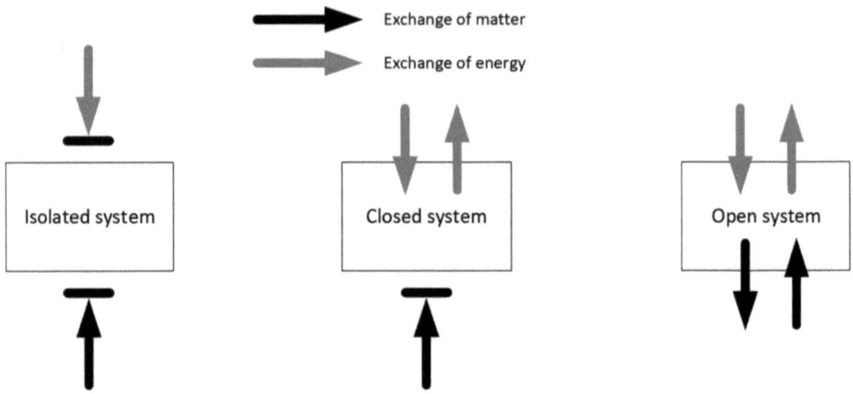

Fig. 4.4 Isolated, closed, and open systems

(Young et al. 2012). Physical forces are classified into weak and strong forces within an atom, electromagnetic force between charges, and gravitation between masses. All the forces except gravitation can be unified into a single theory.

If a system can exchange energy, but no matter with its environment, it is called a *closed system*. Therefore, isolated systems are not synonymous with closed systems. The difference is crucial since, for example, the second law of thermodynamics has a different form in an isolated, closed, and open system (Rosen 1991, p. 269; Kopicki et al. 2010; de Oliveira 2017; Lebon et al. 2008). Nearly all physical, biological, social, and technical systems are *open systems*, exchanging matter (materials) and energy with their environment (Hall 1962).

Energy in the form of heat may be transfered with convection, conduction, and radiation. We exchange information with energy or matter, for example, through a postal service (Cherry 1962). Another example is pneumatic mail, which is still used in large hospitals. The distances may be in the order of 10 km, speed in the order of 5 m/s, and the weight of the package may be in the order of 1 kg. In nature, matter is used for information exchange, for example, among ants, which use pheromones.

More generally, the input and output of an open system may matter, energy, or information, which are among the basic resources (Pahl et al. 2007); see Fig. 4.5. If the main flow through the system is materials, the system may be called an *apparatus*, but other similar terms are a factory, plant, and machine, for example, a car factory, a steel plant, or a paper machine. We call the system a *machine* if the main flow is energy. We have water, wind, and nuclear power plants producing electrical energy. An engine is a machine that converts various forms of energy into mechanical energy (Asimov 1974). Examples include a heat and combustion engine. A *motor* is an engine that converts electrical energy into mechanical energy. If the main flow is information, the system is called a *device*, for example, a mobile phone or a computer. Most often, electrical energy carries information.

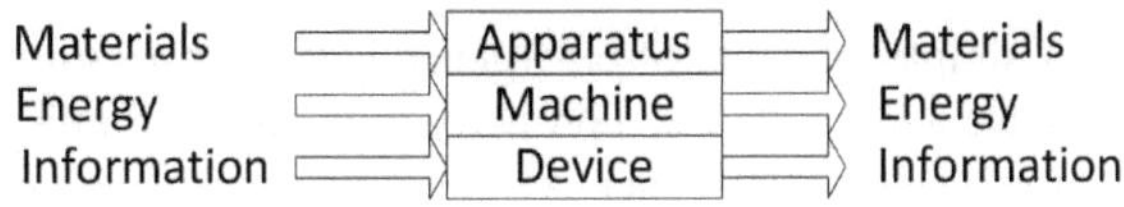

Fig. 4.5 Classification of open systems according to the main flow

4.2.3 Reductionism and Emergence

Reductionism Reductionism does not work in the presence of emergence, but there have also been claims of the opposite (Rosen 1996). Pierre-Simon Laplace described the reductionistic ideal best implemented in astronomy, where the solar system initially appeared to be a perfect machine. More recently, Jacques Monod claimed that all material systems are mechanisms.

An abstract form of a computer is called a Turing machine (Casti 1991, 1994). If one of the inputs is a program or algorithm, the machine is called a universal Turing machine. The universal Turing machine represents all possible computers. It suffices for all problems that are solvable using computation. Turing assumed that his computer has an infinite memory, an impossibility in practice, but can be usually approximated closely enough.

According to the *Church-Turing thesis* (1936),[1] we can translate everything that can be computed into an equivalent computation involving a universal Turing machine (Casti 1991; 1994, pp. 131, 137, 149). The translation is done without changing the complexity class such as polynomial and exponential complexity. Still, Roger Penrose claims that not everything is computable (Penrose 1999). Some things are not computable, and some can be computed. Things that can be computed can be computed with a universal Turing machine.

Peter Schor (1994) has recently shown that we can solve integer factorization in polynomial time in a quantum computer but not in a classical one since it is believed to have subexponential complexity (Arora and Barak 2009). Shor's algorithm has the potential to break through the Church-Turing thesis because the complexity class is changed from subexponential to polynomial.

Emergence Complex systems exhibit emergent properties that are not analytically tractable. Emergence means "new" or "unpredictable." Emergence also means that the behavior of the whole cannot be explained from the behavior of the parts (Frei and Di Marzo Serugendo 2011a), thus forming a clear motivation for systems thinking. Properties such as the mass of an object are additive, but emergent properties are not. If we combine two masses, there is no emergence. For example, the mass of two parts is the sum of the masses of those parts, based on the law of conservation of mass.

[1] The Church-Turing thesis is sometimes called the Church-Turing conjecture. There is a slight difference between a thesis and a conjecture. In a conjecture, all topics and concepts are precisely defined. In a thesis, some concepts are undefined. Alonzo Church did not rigorously define what some of his terms mean.

A simple example of emergence is the temperature of gas. Single molecules do not have a temperature, a property of many randomly moving molecules. This is an example where emergence is a consequence of the size of the system. Namely, many interacting molecules lead to emergent properties. Similarly, the pressure of gas or the taste of water are emergent properties. Additional examples of emergence include the swarming movement of a flock of birds and a traffic jam from the interactions of cars (De Wolf and Holvoet 2005).

In a society, the term *synergy* is used as an emergent phenomenon for achieving more power, energy, or success through cooperation (Oxford Learner's Dictionaries 2024). More generally, in physics, the emergent properties are the origin of mass and energy; in biology, the emergent property is life; and in psychology, the emergent property is consciousness since we have no theories for them (Barrow 1998). Emergence is a form of human ignorance resulting from the limits of our analytical tools. However, nature is using emergence seemingly effortlessly.

Emergence is often a property of self-organizing systems (Thurner et al. 2018). However, emergence and self-organization are separate concepts, but they can appear at the same time (De Wolf and Holvoet 2005). Thus, they can exist separately or coexist in the same system. An example of emergence without self-organization is the case where thermodynamics emerges from statistical mechanics (Kline 1995). An example of self-organization without emergence is a system with central control without distributed control. Four theories study emergence: complexity theory, nonlinear dynamics, synergetics, and nonequilibrium thermodynamics.

If a system would be linear, the whole would be a sum of its parts, and there would be no emergence. A prerequisite for emergence is nonlinearity (von Bertalanffy 1971; de Haan 2006). However, nonlinearity alone does not always produce emergence since simple nonlinear systems are analytically tractable. Emergence generally appears when nonlinearity and feedback are combined, especially in a self-organizing system (Camazine et al. 2001; Thurner et al. 2018). There have been attempts to use emergence for our benefit in a new field called *complexity engineering* or emergent engineering (Frei and Di Marzo Serugendo 2011a, b, 2012; Ulieru and Doursat 2011). This field uses positive emergence, resulting in a new system function (Pan et al. 2013). Negative emergence results in a system failure, such as chaos and instability.

A whole is not only a set of its parts but also of their relationships that may be nonlinear. We do not have good theories for emergence: our analytical tools do not work in many nonlinear feedback networks, and systems thinking is needed. Emergence may be a product of some unknown physical and chemical laws: "Because the global (collective) properties of the system often defy intuitive understanding of their origins, those properties may seem to appear mysteriously. There is nothing mystical or unscientific about their emergence, however" (Camazine et al. 2001, p. 91). Emergence may generate counterintuitive behavior, including catastrophes and chaos (Casti 1994). Not all emergent behavior is chaotic. We can simulate emergence if we have a good enough model of the physical world. In biological systems, the models have yet to be developed.

A *simple system*, in general, has predictable behavior, few interactions, and linear feedback loops, centralized instead of distributed decision-making, and it is decomposable with loose or weak interactions between its parts (Simon 1962, 1973; Casti 1994, pp. 271–272; Alon 2007). An intricate system is defined as *complex* if it includes emergent properties; otherwise, it is *complicated* (Kahlen et al. 2017, p. v). For example, an oil refinery is only complicated, but an organism is complex. Complex systems are mathematically intractable (Corning 2002; de Haan 2006). This makes the borderline between complicated and complex systems.

In Morowitz (2002), the author presents 28 observed instances that have emerged in physical, biological, and social sciences. It is an open question why there is something rather than nothing. Furthermore, it is an open question of how a dynamical system governed by time-symmetric equations of motion can exhibit irreversible behavior, as in the second law of thermodynamics (Pattee 1973; Kline 1995). In biology, we ask what life is (Rosen 1996). In psychology, a similar question is how we can be governed by the laws of nature and still choose to do whatever we wish.

4.2.4 Formation of Visions

Visions and roadmaps are essential in planning future work (Kostoff and Schaller 2001). According to Dufva and Rekola (2023), the future is always uncertain and surprising. Thinking of the future includes three phases: (1) Knowing what is happening (megatrends). (2) Knowing of challenges (weak signals). (3) Imagining alternative futures (planning). *Megatrends* are "directions of development, consisting of several phenomena, that describe broad arcs of change. They often occur at a global level and are often believed to continue in the same direction. Megatrends shed light on the phenomena around us that are currently prominent" (Dufva and Rekola 2023). The present megatrends in Dufva and Rekola (2023) are nature's limited carrying capacity, challenges to well-being, the battle for democracy, economic challenges, and the competition for digital power. According to Elina Hiltunen (2010), a *weak signal* is "the first symptom of change or a sign of an emerging phenomenon that may be significant in the future" (Dufva and Rowley 2022). Weak signals are thus possible emerging future megatrends.

James S. Albus and Alexander M. Meystel defined *planning* as a thinking process by which a human "imagines the future and selects the best course of action" (Albus and Meystel 2001, pp. xii–xiii). Similarly, Kenneth E. Boulding describes evaluations in social systems: "all choice-directed behavior involves the evaluation of alternative images of the future" (Boulding 1985, p. 28). Thus, in addition to knowing history, imagination is needed to anticipate turning points. For example, a turning point for mobile phones was smartphones just before 2010, and the market leader suddenly lost its position.

The image of the future is called *vision*; the best course of action is the *roadmap* to the vision. A roadmap without a vision does not lead to anywhere. Visions can lead to common and concrete system models from which new significant research problems and hypotheses can be formed. The visions must respect nature's fundamental limits. Accurate visions can be made for a maximum of ten years although it may still be inspiring to think about the future for several decades (Albus and Meystel 2001, pp. 353, 355), especially regarding the various potential risks.

Scenarios and use cases are part of the vision and are used to effectively discover user needs and define functional and nonfunctional requirements (Riekki and Mämmelä 2021). According to our interpretation, a *use case* is a particular case of a *scenario* (Jarke et al. 1998; Jacobson 2004), but an opposite view is also possible and sometimes used. Scenarios and use cases became popular in the 1990s (Jarke et al. 1998; Jacobson 2004), but the concepts have developed somewhat independently leading to contradictory definitions. The critique of purely model–based approaches started in the 1970s in operations research. Scenario-based approaches provide a response to the critique to share understanding of the contextual problems and to capture a vision that drives the changes.

The origin of the scenario concept is in theatrical studies, and it came to research via military and strategic gaming. Scenarios have been used also by economists, management scientists, and policy makers. Scenarios are used to stimulate thinking about possible events, assumptions relating these events, possible risks and opportunities, and courses of action.

Originally the term use case was developed by Ivar Jacobson in the 1980s (Jacobson et al. 1999; Jacobson 2004). He defined the use case as a piece of functionality in the system. All the use cases make up a scenario which describes the complete functionality of the system. The scenario provides a black-box view of the system; the system's internal structure would be of no interest in this model.

For constructing roadmaps, we have three approaches: expert-based and computer-based approaches and their hybrid form (Kostoff and Schaller 2001). Similar methods are used for scenarios and use cases (Jarke et al. 1998; Jacobson 2004). The expert-based approach is sometimes called the Delphi method according to the Oracle of Delphi consulted about important decisions in ancient Greece. Now, a group of experts is simulating the "oracle." In the computer-based approach, large databases that describe science, technology, engineering, and end products are subject to computer analyses. In the hybrid method, we combine the two approaches. Now, we can support the computer-based approach with artificial intelligence.

Forecasts are based on the observed regularities in the history. With knowledge of history, we can sometimes succeed in our predictions. The author in Schoemaker (2020) says that by examining the most significant changes during the last 30 years, we may get a view of what will happen during the next ten years with a 90% confidence interval (also called coverage interval). The suggested 30 years is enough in many cases, but we prefer to study the last 50–100 years to make reliable predictions for the next ten years. There may be a misunderstanding that the state of the art accumulates all the history, but new paradigms are often rejected, and they may come into use much later. There may be Sleeping Beauties, which have not been cited for decades. For example, based on the earlier work of Ktesibios in 270 BCE, Hero invented steam power in 50 CE, but it became an innovation in about 1750, almost two millennia later.

Science fiction makes long-term predictions for the future, but some may not follow nature's fundamental limits. Examples of science fiction include Herbert G. Wells' *The Time Machine* (1895), Aldous Huxley's *Brave New World* (1932), and George Orwell's *Animal Farm* (1945) and *Nineteen Eighty-Four* (1949). Many of the predictions were dystopia. Dennis Gabor and Isaac Asimov had more optimistic views. According to Joel N. Franklin, Gabor (1964), in his book *Inventing the Future*, claimed that the future cannot be predicted but invented. At that time, the primary concerns during the next 50 years until 2014 were the threat of nuclear destruction, overpopulation, automation and leisure, depletion of natural resources, and poverty and political immaturity. For Gabor, nationalism is our worst inheritance from the past.

Isaac Asimov independently attempted to make a forecast for the next 50 years (Asimov 1964). He had similar concerns as Gabor. In addition, Asimov expected that humans would continue to withdraw from nature to create an environment that would suit them better. There are even moon colonies with which we can communicate, but only uncrewed ships have landed on Mars. Communication is done with videophones; we can dial directly anywhere in the world through satellites. New energy sources are in use. Experimental fusion power plants exist, and solar power stations are commonly used. Transportation is improved so that it takes the least possible contact with the surface of the Earth. We can also remotely study documents and photographs and read books. Techniques in teaching advance, and new subjects include computer technology. Agriculture is turning to the more efficient micro-organisms. Oceans are exploited for resources such as food and minerals. The book (Hall 1962) shows that the core topics of systems thinking are relevant even after 60 years, although everything is much more elaborated.

Long-term predictions are possible if the changes are deterministic. Peter J. Denning and Robert M. Metcalfe made a prediction for the next 50 years (Denning and Metcalfe 1997), and Ray Kurzweil has predicted until 2100 (Kurzweil 1999). They all assumed that Moore's law for electronics would continue without saturation. Moore's law is not a law of nature but a prediction based on observation (Mämmelä and Anttonen 2017). In some cases, human learning follows an exponential law: the assumption is that having a line width is always as complex and can be done in the same time interval. The number of transistors on a chip has doubled every second year (initially every year) since the invention of the integrated circuit in 1959. This implies exponential growth. However, for silicon electronics, the exponential development was 2016 expected to discontinue in five years after about 60 years of development (Waldrop 2016; Courtland 2016; Mämmelä and Anttonen 2017). The law had problems already since 2004. The primary reason is the natural fundamental limit for energy efficiency caused by thermal noise and quantum phenomena (Zhirnov and Cavin 2013). The exponential increase of link bit rates in communications depends on Moore's law since higher bit rates generally require higher energy efficiency, and we must follow the limits for computing and communication, implying a *computing-communication trade-off* if the total energy remains constant (Mämmelä and Anttonen 2017). Still, Gerhard Fettweis predicted that bit rates would increase exponentially at least until 2035 (Fettweis 2014; Fettweis and

Alamouti 2014). Not all predictions will happen because of nature's fundamental limits.

We can make even longer-term predictions based on chaos theory and results from cosmology. For example, it has been predicted by simulations that one or more of the planets in our solar systems will fly off into space in the next 40 million years (Boulton et al. 2015, p. 74), probably by slowly increasing the excentricity of their elliptic orbits (Strogatz 2014). The time scale of such simulations may be highly unreliable because of the idealizations and the chaotic behavior of such multibody systems. Predictions can be made for several billions of years since the fate of stars is known, among them the fate of our Sun (Christian 2004).

A good vision is attractive and concrete enough to be expressed in engineering as a system model from which research problems can be defined. Too broad macro visions are quickly declined. If you discover "too much," other researchers may neglect you. Some phenomena are long-standing problems. For example, in communications, attenuation, distortion, and energy consumption have been problems since the start of its history and still are (IEEE 2002).

According to Senge (2006), innovative learning organizations should use five principles to achieve their goals. The principles include systems thinking, personal mastery, mental models, shared vision, and team learning, which form the author's five disciplines. The fifth discipline is systems thinking is the topic of our book, and it is well-grounded. *Personal mastery* means an exceptional level of proficiency that is enthusiastically improved all the time. Mastery also requires outstanding talent, including intelligence and creativity. *Mental models* are system models containing assumptions and generalizations about the world. The *vision* should be shared so that everybody works in the same direction. The system model is usually so comprehensive that we cannot study it in a single project, and we need a project portfolio sharing the same system model with different research problems. In *team learning*, we should use *dialogue* by "thinking together" instead of mere discussion, which may imply competition.

4.3 Hierarchy of Sciences and Technology

The sciences can be linked to the ecosystem and sociotechnical system, as shown in Fig. 4.6. The natural *ecosystem* consists of the natural world and is divided into inorganic and organic nature. Inorganic nature offers us the materials, energy, and laws of nature. It offers us all the six basic resources. After we use the resources, we either recycle them or transfer them back to nature as waste since there is no other place to site the waste. We live in a finite world that is sometimes compared to a spacecraft or even boat. The *sociotechnical system* comprises human society and products and services. Humans came initially from the organic nature.

As systems thinkers we must understand something about different disciplines to be able to communicate and to understand the similarities. We organize the sciences as a hierarchy of formal, natural, and social sciences and humanities (Fig. 4.6) (Cole

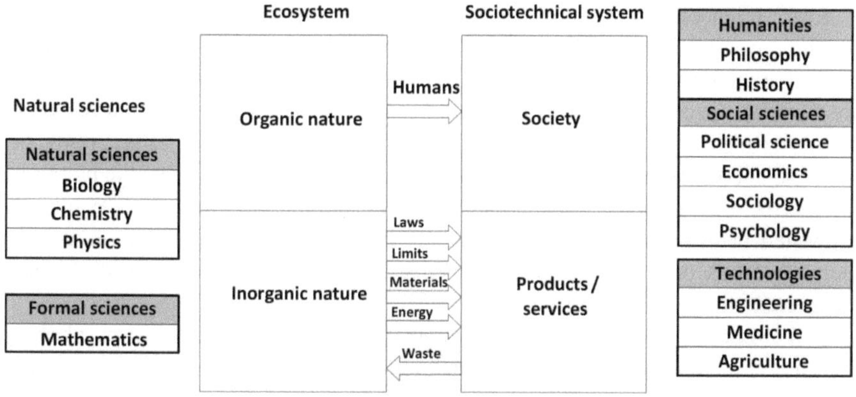

Fig. 4.6 Ecosystem and sociotechnical system and the related sciences and technologies

1983; Boulding 1985; Kline 1995; Wilson 1998; Schwanitz 1999; Smith et al. 2000; Fanelli and Glänzel 2013; Repko and Szostak 2021). The word science originally referred to natural sciences, and the humanities have been called liberal arts or letters.

We can use mathematics in natural and social sciences and technologies; history and philosophy cover all sciences. Technologies are a separate group. Social sciences were originally among humanities, but now they form a separate group between natural sciences and humanities (Wilson 1998). Social sciences and humanities are jointly called *human sciences* (Smith 1997).

Formal sciences are independent of experience and use abstract models, whereas *real sciences* focus on studying reality. The most crucial formal science is mathematics. It is usually taught at universities in the faculty of natural sciences. Human sciences focus on understanding rather than explaining, as in natural sciences, but strictly speaking, sciences do not answer the question "why" (i.e., they do not explain) but only to the questions "what" and "how" (Nagel 1979).

Some disciplines are interdisciplinary studies, often combining two or more traditional sciences (Klein 1990, p. 43). The oldest examples are biochemistry and social psychology, but there are many more, including physical chemistry, biophysics, ecological economics, materials science, environmental engineering, and systems engineering.

Technologies include engineering, medicine, and agriculture (Kline 1995, p. 210), but our focus among technologies is on engineering. Technologies are sometimes called "applied sciences" in contrast to pure or theoretical sciences as if technologies would only apply "pure sciences" and nothing else. The term "applied sciences" is a misnomer since technologies are another group of sciences. The interaction is bidirectional since both pure sciences and technologies benefit each other. Similarly, some authors claim that not all social sciences are sciences but practices (*Praktiken* in German) (Schwanitz 1999, p. 362). According to Dietrich Schwanitz, practices include, for example, political science, jurisprudence, pedagogy, and the science of communication. We present them among social sciences.

Real sciences form a hierarchy, including physics, chemistry, biology, psychology, and social sciences and humanities (Table 4.2). Physics is the most general at the bottom of the hierarchy, and social sciences and humanities at the top are the most specific. The order also roughly follows the order of the "hardness" of the disciplines, so physics is the hardest of all disciplines (Smith et al. 2000), but social sciences are the most complex. Although sciences are theories, the hierarchy follows the order of ontological reduction, not epistemological reduction, as initially suggested by August Comte (Checkland 1999, p. 61). Still, some authors use the hierarchy like Comte did: the natural sciences are at the top, and the social sciences are at the bottom (Cole 1983).

In the reductionist ideal, chemistry is physics, biology is chemistry, psychology is biology, sociology is psychology, economics is sociology, political science is economics, and history is political science (Boulding 1985; Checkland 1999, p. 52). We should consider this relationship loose. The sciences are separated from each other by the concept of emergence. If no emergence existed, we could combine all the sciences into a single science based on physics. For example, the emergent properties in physics are matter (mass), energy, and information; in chemistry, the emergent property is a chemical bond (Rosen 1991, p. 270; Wilson 1998, p. 91); in biology the emergent property is life, and in psychology it is consciousness (Barrow 1998), see Table 4.2. Because of emergence, we cannot reduce chemistry to physics, biology to physics and chemistry, and social sciences to biology.

Boulding (1985) states that there are two additional systems above the physical, biological, social, economic, and political systems. They are the communication and evaluative systems, the highest in his complexity hierarchy. Communication is needed to exchange information from and to the society. We see the evaluative system as a system for making decisions in a feedback loop. We conclude that the two uppermost systems in Boulding (1985) are not separate but subsystems in the social, economic, and political systems. However, Boulding's hierarchy emphasizes how vital communication, evaluation, and decision-making are.

Table 4.2 Hierarchy of some natural and social sciences and humanities

Discipline	Object of study	Emergent property
Philosophy	All disciplines	Unity of science
History	Past	Future
Political science	Political relationships	Sustainable politics, social dilemma
Economics	Economic relationships	Sustainable economy, social dilemma
Sociology	Social relationships	Social groups, social dilemma
Psychology	Human mind and behavior	Consciousness
Biology	Organisms	Life
Chemistry	Chemical compounds	Chemical bond
Physics	Mechanisms	Matter, energy, and information

Table 4.3 Information, feedback, and self-organization in natural and social sciences

Discipline	Information	Feedback	Self-organization
Political science	Laws and rules	Elections	Liberal democracy
Economics	Monetary values	Supply and demand	Free-market economics
Sociology	Ethical values	Human agent	Social contract
Psychology	Information in mind	Incremental learning	Learning in mind
Biology	Genotype	Homeostasis	Morphogenesis
Chemistry	Chemical bond	Electromagnetic forces	Molecules
Physics	State of universe	Gravity	Stars and galaxies

According to Kline, disciplines have different maturity phases or steps (Kline 1995, pp. 199–211). The phases include from the bottom up, (1) the domain or scope of the discipline, (2) concept formation, (3) taxonomies, (4) theory formation, (5) verification, (6) new theory formation, (7) generalization, and (8) simulations. Different disciplines develop at their own speed. Maturity is usually best at the bottom of the hierarchy of sciences, where the research problems are the simplest. Taxonomies describe static systems but modern science is also interested in dynamic nonlinear systems.

The basic concepts in our book are information, feedback, and self-organization, as shown in Table 4.3 for natural and social sciences. We present some details of each science in the following text. We can find competent broad reviews on the disciplines for example in *Encyclopedia Britannica.* We can find more information in the bibliography, which lists books on the history and philosophy of the core disciplines. Our emphasis is on systems view in the disciplines. In most disciplines, some form of system science exists; for example, in natural sciences, they are systems physics, systems chemistry, and systems biology. In social sciences, it is more common to use the prefix macro-, for example, macropsychology, macrosociology, and macroeconomics. Many of those subdisciplines are not yet well developed. From these, systems biology and macroeconomics are by far the most popular. In history, we have started to use the term big history starting from the big bang, but the term macrohistory is also common and a clear term usually with a more limited scope, for example focusing on human history.

4.3.1 Formal Sciences

Formal sciences are the opposite of real sciences. Examples include logic, mathematics, and statistics. We focus here on mathematics and see statistics as part of it. Statistics is the study of probability, random variables, and random or stochastic processes.

Mathematics

As Galileo has already noticed, the laws of nature are written in the language of mathematics, but it is a philosophical question of why mathematics can do this. Mathematics is not a natural science. With mathematics, many phenomena are easier to understand. Number theory, algebra, geometry, and analysis form the main pillars of all mathematics (Atiyah 2002). Analytic geometry merges algebra and geometry. Some authors think geometric thinking is a form of holistic thinking (Penrose 1999).

The essential thing about mathematics is that it deals with ideal objects and does so by forming deductive constructions in which one proceeds from one argument to another using formal logic. The basis of each theory is a small set of simple statements chosen as axioms that the theory assumes are valid. We describe objects using formal language sentences, but mathematicians, in most cases, also have an intuitive, often visual, or dynamic (e.g., stochastic) image in their mind.

Mathematical analysis is mainly based on deduction, but we also make inductive statistical generalizations. Alfred Tarski (1941) has claimed that logic is the common denominator of theoretical sciences, which are causal and deductive (Francois 2000). Willard Van Orman Quine believed any demonstration should be a chain of mechanical or logical arguments. A problem in all mathematics is the analysis of nonlinear dynamical networks, which are often mathematically intractable. Most of our analytical tools are limited to linear, possibly time-varying systems. Intractable problems appear, especially in complexity theory, where complex systems have a phenomenon called emergence, usually resulting from nonlinearity and feedback and probably involving multicausality (Camazine et al. 2001; Aaltonen 2007).

David Hilbert (1900) asked 23 questions about the limits of mathematics (Boyer and Merzbach 1991), such as whether mathematics is complete, whether mathematics is consistent, and whether mathematics is decidable (Larson 2021). The answers to all these three questions appear negative, as shown by Kurt Gödel (1931) for the first two questions and by Alan Turing (1936) for the third question. Gödel's two *incompleteness theorems* define the incompleteness of mathematics, saying that any finite formal logic system contains true propositions that are unprovable (Casti 1994, pp. 138–143). There is no finite set of axioms where we can solve all questions. Turing showed that mathematics is not decidable, i.e., no definite procedure exists to prove a statement is true or false.

4.3.2 Natural Sciences

Natural sciences, or briefly sciences, focus on the study of nature. They include physics, chemistry, and biology (Repko and Szostak 2021). Physics and chemistry are exact sciences since they use mathematics effectively, whereas biology and human sciences are nonexact. Earth science deals with the Earth, including geography, geology, meteorology, and oceanography. Geography is a broad discipline that is difficult to classify since part of it belongs to social sciences. It deals with "the diverse physical, biological, and cultural features of the earth's surface" (Merriam-Webster 2024). A complement to earth science is astronomy, which deals with the space outside the Earth's atmosphere. Physics and chemistry are physical sciences, and biology is among life sciences. Information theory has used some concepts from thermodynamics, and biological organisms contain information in physical and chemical form. Material systems are either mechanisms or organisms (Rosen 1991). Mechanisms follow physical and chemical laws, but biological organisms have primarily unknown principles (Rosen 1991; Westerhoff et al. 2009). We can see dynamic processes in the world as *evolution* having three great patterns, including physical, biological, and cultural or societal evolution (Boulding 1978). Physical evolution is the slowest, and cultural evolution is the fastest.

Physics

Physics is the scientific study of matter, its behavior in space and time, and the energy and force. The emergent properties of interest are matter, energy, and, to some extent also, information. We are interested in discovering the laws of inanimate nature in physics, but they still contain only a tiny part of our physical knowledge (Wigner 1960). The big bang was the beginning of matter and energy, the first emergent phenomenon about which we know. The age of the universe is 13.8 billion years or 10^{17} s, and the age of the Sun and the Earth is 4.57 and 4.54 billion years, respectively. The universe has an order of 10^{80} atoms (Elsasser 1987). A typical atom has a size of 0.1 nm. It is now possible to see an individual atom's elemental and chemical state with X-rays (Ajayi et al. 2023).

The oldest discipline is astronomy, where the regularities are most apparent (Hawking 2018). Classical physics focuses on *mechanisms* that follow deterministic physical and chemical laws (Rosen 1991, pp. xvii, 7; Merriam-Webster 2024). Since Newton, we have seen the universe as a causal machine, an enormous clock (Aaltonen 2007). We have assumed each event to have a single cause. If we know the present state, we can predict future behavior and retrodict the past behavior until the initial state. The laws are universal; they do not change, and we cannot break them. The universal regularity is called an *invariance*. We do not know the present state of the physical world accurately enough, and the theories in quantum mechanics are probabilistic and thus not causal (Nagel 1979). Physics offers the highest available accuracy. Recently, researchers measured an electron's magnetic moment at an accuracy of 13 digits (1.3 parts in 10 trillion) (Fan et al. 2023).

We divide physics into classical mechanics (inc. statics and dynamics), thermodynamics and statistical mechanics, electromagnetism, quantum mechanics, and special and general relativity (Young et al. 2012). The relativity theory is based on non-Euclidean geometry. The greatest theories are either deterministic, such as Newtonian mechanics and relativity theory, or statistical, such as statistical mechanics and quantum mechanics. Some theories conflict with each other. We do not know how to unite quantum mechanics and relativity theory. Experimental evidence shows quantum properties disappear in *quantum decoherence* (Schlosshauer 2019). Regarding information transmission, statistical mechanics and electromagnetism are the most useful in physics.

Table 4.4 includes a list of some great theories in natural sciences. Physics' general goal is the theory of everything, but the problem is the emergence concept (Penrose 1999). A possible theory of everything is the *standard model*, whose target is to explain the emergence of matter from fundamental particles (Schumm 2004). Self-organization can appear spontaneously in physics, as seen in snowflakes and galaxies.

According to one of the principles of special relativity theory, the speed of light in a vacuum is the largest possible speed and, therefore, forms a limit for the delay in transmitting information (Rothman 2003, p. 73). In some interpretations of special relativity theory, speed of light in vacuum is not property of light but property of the universe and it is called "speed of causality" and is the upper limit on the speed at which "cause" and "effect" can occur. For one event to cause another, information about the first event must be transmitted to the second.

Physics contains the concept of mass hierarchy in our solar system, making the system loosely coupled and highly stable (Mämmelä et al. 2023). Mass hierarchy is a consequence of the solar system converging to one of the stable solutions characterized by mass hierarchy. A mass and spring, a pendulum, and a two-body system form second-order feedback loops providing oscillations (Strogatz 2014; Ogata 2010).

One physical theory of interest is the dynamic universe (DU) theory since it represents a systems view of the scale of the universe. The theory of relativity is a mathematical description of observations that does not provide a physical explanation for the described phenomena unlike the DU theory. Suntola (2020) suggested that the DU theory replaces Einstein's relativity theory (Suntola 2018a, b, 2020, 2021).

Table 4.4 Some great theories in natural sciences

Year	Discoverer	Discovery
c. 250 BCE	Archimedes	Statics
1687 CE	I. Newton	Dynamics
1808	J. Dalton	Atomic theory
1838	M. Schleiden and T. Schwann	Cell theory
1859	C. Darwin	Theory of evolution
1865	J. C. Maxwell	Electromagnetics
1865	G. Mendel	Genetics
1869	D. Mendeleev	Periodic table of elements
1876	W. Gibbs	Thermodynamics
1905	A. Einstein	Special theory of relativity
1915	A. Einstein	General theory of relativity
1924	E. Hubble	Big bang theory
1925	W. Heisenberg et al.	Quantum mechanics
1939	L. Pauling	Bond theory
1955	I. Prigogine	Nonequilibrium thermodynamics
2020	T. Suntola	Dynamic universe

The DU theory is a significant paradigm shift and much more straightforward than the relativity theory: the latter is observer-oriented, representing the inside-out view, but the DU theory is system-oriented, representing the outside-in view. Similarly, the earlier complicated geocentric epicycle model was observer-oriented, and the much simpler heliocentric ellipse model is system-oriented since, in the latter, we move the observer from the Earth outside the solar system.

System-oriented theories are simpler than observer-oriented theories. The DU theory is an excellent example of the use of Occam's razor, and there is no discrepancy with observations. We do not make the various auxiliary assumptions of the theory of relativity. Time and distance are the same in real life: time dilation and length contraction are unnecessary; in the DU theory, relativity is a direct consequence of the overall energy balance in space. Similarly, the zero-energy principle replaces the equivalence principle, i.e., the gravitational and inertial mass equivalence. The dark matter can be interpreted as unstructured matter that is, in practice, radiation. The dark energy is unnecessary since the universe has no accelerating expansion. Direct measurement of acceleration or deceleration is impossible, and the question is about model-based interpretation. The dark energy is an auxiliary hypothesis that tries to rescue the relativity theory. The expansion slows down because the motion works against gravity, as does a ball's upward movement.

In the DU theory, we describe space as a 3-sphere, a 3-dimensional "surface" of a sphere with radius as the fourth dimension. The fourth dimension is not the direction of time but a metric dimension where the universe as the 3-sphere expands. This dimension is perpendicular to all conventional space dimensions, and presenting it as an imaginary dimension is convenient. In the DU theory, we have only one assumption: we conserve energy in all changes in a spherically closed universe. The conservation of energy, the first law of thermodynamics, is not included in the theory of relativity. The universe's total energy is zero when we interpret the potential energy caused by gravitation as negative and kinetic energy as positive. The modern form of energy conservation law, called the zero-energy hypothesis, was proposed by Dennis Sciama (1953) and Richard P. Feynman in his lectures in 1962–1963 (Sipilä 2014). The zero-energy principle allows for building up energy to the ongoing expansion phase. It links the speed of light in space to the expansion speed of the 3-sphere. We cannot surpass the speed of light, but the velocity depends on gravitation. There is a direct connection to quantum physics through the mass wave concept, whereas the theory of relativity is incompatible with quantum physics.

To summarize, the object of study in physics is mechanisms. The emergent properties include matter, energy, and information. Matter is a form of energy and fundamentally consist of atoms. Physics has studied mainly isolated systems but in thermodynamics also closed and open systems are under study. There are incompatible theories since the world looks both random and deterministic at the same time. Deterministic systems are causal, and the speed of light is the maximum speed of causality. Forces such as gravity form the basis for self-organization. The energy conservation law is one of the basic principles in physics. Some deterministic systems having nonlinear feedback loops are chaotic. Mass hierarchy is a form of loose coupling that is needed to avoid chaos in multibody systems and to form a stable environment for the evolution of life in our solar system.

Chemistry

Chemistry is the scientific study of matter's composition, structure, properties, and transformations (Merriam-Webster 2024), excluding nuclear reactions and radioactivity that are part of physics. The focus is on the chemical bond, which is "an attractive force that holds together the atoms, ions, or groups of atoms in a molecule or crystal" (Merriam-Webster 2024). Chemistry is divided into nonorganic and organic chemistry. Organic matter is based on carbon. Since chemistry is hierarchically between physics and biology, it also contains physical chemistry and biochemistry.

In addition to physical theories such as the atomic theory, the theory of thermodynamics, and quantum mechanics, some essential theories in chemistry include the periodic table of elements, the minimum energy principle, and the bond theory, see Table 4.4. The number of natural elements is 92, from which all matter in nature is formed. The periodic table of elements by Dmitri Mendeleev (1869) unified chemistry, thus defining the elements' natural order using a matrix hierarchy. We divide the elements into metals and nonmetals. Among the nonmetals, we have semiconductors, including, for example, silicon and germanium.

Mass is conserved in spontaneous chemical reactions in a closed system, not exchanging any matter with its environment (Treptow 2005), and energy is minimized in equilibrium (Rosen 1991, p. 269). Energy minimization is a form of the second law of thermodynamics for closed systems having constant entropy and constant external parameters such as volume. For example, molecules minimize their potential energy to find their most stable configuration.

Chemistry cannot be reduced to physics (Szostak 2004, p. 78), but there is a relationship between physics and chemistry in the form of Pauling's (1939) bond theory. Quantum mechanics now provides an exhaustive theory of chemical bonding (Elsasser 1987). Bonds are either strong or weak. Strong bonds include covalent bonds sharing electrons such as in organic molecules, ionic bonds between ions such as in salts, and metallic bonds between conduction electrons and metallic ions. We cannot, in practice, predict the three-dimensional structure of very large and complex molecules or macromolecules such as proteins, although all their atoms are known (Wilson 1998, p. 91). The needed accuracy for the thousands of energy contributions is beyond the grasp of physical sciences. Even a tiny polypeptide containing about 100 amino acids involves hundreds or thousands of atoms (Rosen 1991, p. 270). The formation of complex molecules is an example of self-organization and emergence in chemistry.

Genetic information in the deoxyribonucleic acid (DNA) protein of all cells in an organism is chemical information that can be changed between generations via mutations. The DNA contains all the information required to make the whole organism (Pattee 1973, s. 54; Kauffman 1995). A human genome includes 23 chromosomes and 20,000 genes, corresponding to 3 million base pairs.

To summarize, in chemistry the chemical bond is the core concept. Some organic molecules are so complex that they appear as examples of emergence, but the energy is minimized in equilibrium as in closed systems.

Biology

Biology is the scientific study of life in material objects called *organisms* that are assumed to differ from mechanisms (Rosen 1991, p. xvii). Walter Elsasser believed that after attaining a holistic understanding, biology would be the queen of all sciences (Elsasser 1987).

Athel Cornish-Bowden and Maria Luz Cardenas published an extensive summary of the definitions of *life* (Cornish-Bowden and Luz Cardenas 2020). They concluded that all definitions omit some essential elements. They all lack ideas of metabolic control and regulation and a mechanism to protect an organism from uncontrolled growth. Somewhat earlier, Kepa Ruiz-Mirazo and Alvaro Moreno also discussed the lack of a universal definition of life and defined it through autonomy and open-ended evolution: "Life is a complex network of self-reproducing autonomous agents whose basic organization is instructed by material records generated through the open-ended, historical process in which that collective network evolves" (Ruiz-Mirazo and Moreno 2011). National Aeronautics and Space Administration (NASA) has defined life as a "chemical system capable of Darwinian evolution" (Jacob 2016). Life is the collective behavior of interacting molecules and cells (Kauffman 1995). Life on the Earth contains the ideas of *photosynthesis*, *metabolism*, and *reproduction* (Christian 2004, pp. 79–84). It is an open question why the conditions (physical constants and laws) in our universe are suitable for the existence of intelligent life (Penrose 1999, pp. 458, 560–562). The idea is the *anthropic principle*, first discussed by Robert Dicke (1957) and extended by Brandon Carter (1973). An explanation is that we need to be present to observe it. In a universe where conditions are not suitable, there is nobody to observe it.

Life is an emergent phenomenon, and we do not know how life is formed spontaneously from nonlife when Louis Pasteur showed that life comes only from life (Kauffman 1995). The agility in how living organisms create new levels of complexity is greater than in mechanisms (Christian 2004). The rate of energy per time and mass unit is considerable. A *virus* is not an example of life since it does not have a metabolism and must act as a parasite in a cell. Living organisms adapt constantly to new environments. Linnean taxonomy organizes biology in a nested hierarchy (Wilson 1998). The taxonomy includes, from the bottom up, species, genus, family, order, class, phylum, kingdom, and domain. The original hierarchy included five levels, and modern hierarchy includes 21 levels (Roberts 2024). The taxonomy represents a static view to the species.

James G. Miller unified biological and social sciences using his hierarchical theory of living systems (Kalaidjieva and Swanson 2004). The eight hierarchy levels are cells, organs, organisms, groups, organizations, communities, societies, and supranational systems. According to Ahl and Allen (1996), levels in the science of biology can be derived either from definitions or from empirical observation. The conventional levels of organization derived from the definitions are cell, organism, population, community, ecosystem, landscape, biome, and biosphere. They form a nested hierarchy since organs contain cells, organisms contain organs, species contain organisms, communities contain populations of species, and so on. Miller did not include the community in the original hierarchy (Miller 1973) but introduced it later after the book (Miller 1978) was published. The hierarchy does not describe the material flows around the biosphere. For example, the host organism is larger than the population for a population of parasites, which is an empirical observation.

Biology is divided hierarchically into biochemistry, molecular, cellular, and organismic biology, ecology, and evolutionary biology (Wilson 1998). Systems biology unifies the theories (Trewavas 2006; Gatherer 2008; Westerhoff et al. 2009; Alon 2020). Presently, the focus of systems biology is on modeling. One crucial observation is that the survival of the fittest principle (Schoemaker 1991) has not led to maximal simplicity and efficiency (Westerhoff et al. 2009). Occam's razor is thus not valid. There has been some multiobjective optimization process that comes from Charles Darwin's theory of evolution, and the criterion is the fitness to the environment leading to survivability. The evolution must make various trade-offs between conflicting objectives, which implies that biological systems do not directly maximize only, for example, energy efficiency. However, they are often energy efficient since the energy is a scarce resource. Evolution may also have dead ends, and there have been many global species extinctions for natural reasons. Fitness is an optimization criterion in biological systems, and we can extend it to social and technical systems where the law of supply and demand is valid. Kenneth E. Boulding emphasizes that the actual criterion is the survival of the fitting, not the survival of the fittest (Boulding 1985, p. 65) since the environment is dynamic. Evolution is, in fact, coevolution since when we evolve, our competitors also evolve, and we must adapt to them (Kauffman 1995).

Ronald A. Fisher's fundamental theorem of natural selection (1930) is used in maximizing fitness (Frank and Slatkin 1992). It describes the rate at which an increase in fitness occurs in nature: it is proportional to genetic variance in the population. It means that a species adapts to its environment at a minimal cost by removing as few defects as necessary and as few early deaths as necessary. For example, foxes can catch the slowest rabbits, which results in a rapid increase in average speed of the remaining rabbit population. However, there is an optimally large pool of genetic diversity to form the basis of future evolution and respond to environmental changes. In other words, achieving as high fitness as possible is desirable but without overfitting. In engineering, we usually call it "robustness;" we want to achieve a trade-off between optimality and robustness.

Evolution may happen in two scenarios: an environment characterized by scarcity of resources and an environment characterized by abundant resources (Schuster 1996). To deal with scarcity, nature uses optimization. In times of scarcity, developing unknown properties and functions is too risky, and those who make such attempts are not likely to survive. To master unpredictability, nature uses the high flexibility of modularity and builds on the latest versions. Cooperation is also beneficial. On the other hand, nature takes advantage of abundance to create innovations, thus producing major transitions in evolution. In that case, the benefits for being cooperative are minor.

We must make an essential distinction in ecology: the biosphere is an ecosystem of organisms and not itself an organism (Boulding 1985). The distributed nature of the ecosystem is the reason for its high resilience. The largest organism on the Earth is a honey mushroom in the Malheur National Forest in Oregon, spanning about 890 ha. Animals and humans are tightly controlled systems by their brains at the bottom of the ecosystem, whereas the ecosystem is a distributed system, an example of loose coupling (Mämmelä et al. 2023). Thus, evolution as a distributed process has produced central control in the form of brains in animals and humans. Plants do not have a central nervous system.

The necessary elements for life are carbon, oxygen, hydrogen, nitrogen, phosphorus, and sulfur (Haas and Nikel 2023). The first four elements comprise about 99% of the organic material (Elsasser 1987). Researchers have discussed whether some other matter could be used as a basis for life (Cerceau 2010; Peng 2015; Jacob 2016; Haas and Nikel 2023). Julius Scheiner (1891) first proposed that life could be based on silicon. However, it does not have the advantages of carbon in universal abundance, bonding, and chirality. Carbon has a small atom and can form strong covalent bonds, thus creating complex molecules that are useful in forming life. Possible suggested alternatives for life include, for example, sulfur and ammonia.

There are two principal ways how life could have appeared on the Earth: (1) evolution from a single beginning initially from very simple, highly mechanistic systems, (2) life arose by a series of progressive chemical reactions that may have been likely or may have required highly improbable chemical events (Elsasser 1987; Stonier 1997, p. 77; Ladyman and Wiesner 2020, p. 27; Encyclopedia Britannica 2024).

According to Edward O. Wilson, the history of life has had four significant steps (Wilson 1998, p. 107). The first was the beginning of life about 3.77–4.28 billion years ago (Dodd et al. 2017) as simple organisms like bacteria, the simplest living cells that are at the bottom of the hierarchy of intelligence (Stonier 1997, p. 68). The second was the complex eukaryotic cell consisting of a nucleus and other organelles enclosed by a membrane. The third group was the multicellular animals with sense organs and a central nervous system. The fourth was human intelligence and culture, represented by cultural evolution.

About 50% of the oxygen is produced by algae (Chapman 2013). The atmosphere includes nitrogen but does not react easily with other elements. In the *Miller–Urey experiment* (1953) carried out by Stanley Miller and supervised by Harold Urey, they noticed that simulated lightning using an electric arc can produce organic acids (Lazcano and Bada 2003; Kauffman 2019). People later observed that nitrates were created by lightning near volcanoes (Navarro-Gonzalez et al. 1998). Lightning has enough energy to break nitrogen molecules in the air. The Belousov–Zhabotinsky (BZ) reaction by Boris Belousov (1958) and Anatol Zhabotinsky (1964) showed that a nonliving system can produce self-organization (Boulton et al. 2015, p. 167;

Ladyman and Wiesner 2020, p. 27). The reaction occurs in a mixture of potassium bromate and various acids.

William Harvey (1628) discovered the circulation of blood, which was one of the most outstanding results of all time in medicine (Neil 1962). Great theories in biology include cell theory, theory of evolution, and genetics (Table 4.4) (Morowitz 2002). A cell is a basic unit in living organisms, first observed by Robert Hooke (1665). Matthias Schleiden and Theodor Schwann (1838) proposed the cell theory. A typical cell has a size of 1 mm and contains over 10^{12} atoms, whose size is 0.1 nm (Elsasser 1987). There is little hope of predicting the character of a cell from its physical and chemical parts (Wilson 1998, p. 74). All cells are somewhat different and individual, although the elementary particles, such as electrons, are similar (Elsasser 1987). A human body consists of 37 trillion cells (Bianconi et al. 2013). The development of an adult organism is called *ontogeny*. There are 256 cell types in a human adult (Kauffman 1995). The set of genes in all cell types is identical, and the cells are different because different subsets of genes are active.

Georges-Louis Leclerc, Comte de Buffon, was one of the first to propose species' change and extinction outside the regular reproductive process in the 1749–1789 in his 36-volume book *Histoire Naturelle*, but he did not know how evolution actually took place (Roberts 2024). Leclerc suspected that the evolution had needed millions if not billions of years, and humans were part of nature. This was a dynamic view to species, but his contemporaries saw the change and extinction controversial, and the theory was rejected and forgotten. He is sometimes seen as the first ecologist. Independently, Charles Darwin (1859) developed the theory of evolution as a theory of natural selection, and Alfred R. Wallace (1858) had independently similar ideas. Later, Darwin realized that Leclerc had done similar work about one hundred years earlier. Gregor Mendel (1865) started the genetics theory in botany, but his results were forgotten until 1900 (Rothman 2003).

Modern theories of life developed after Erwin Schrödinger (1944) published his book *What is Life?* (Cornish-Bowden and Luz Cardenas 2020). The five major theories are metabolism-repair or (M, R) systems by Robert Rosen (1958), the hypercycle by Manfred Eigen (1971) and Peter Schuster (1977), the chemoton by Tibor Ganti (1971), autopoiesis by Humberto Maturana and Francisco Varela (1973), and autocatalytic sets by Freeman Dyson (1982), Stuart Kauffman (1986), and Karl Friston (2013). Most of the theories would require a whole book for their description. Furthermore, the various theories are very different; they do not influence each other, and there are unbridgeable gaps between them. Only Eigen and Schuster had a link to molecular biology. Eigen noticed a paradox: only specific enzymes could produce certain nucleic acids, but the enzymes could only be produced using the nucleic acids. Ganti's theories are most concrete but became available in English only in 2003. An organism can create and maintain itself. Organisms are closed to efficient causation, a fundamental difference between organisms and mechanisms. In metabolism, the efficient causes are enzymes. An organism synthesizes all of them by itself.

Organisms are divided into three domains: bacteria, archaea, and eukaryotes (Encyclopedia Britannica 2024; Woese et al. 1990). Bacteria and archaea are unicellular prokaryotes. The eukaryotes include fungi, plants, animals, and many others, most unicellular. Fungi are more like animals since they cannot photosynthesize and need material from other organisms for their living. In evolution, fungi appeared before plants (Wang et al. 1999). A microbe or microorganism is an organism of microscopic size of 10 nm–0.1 mm from all domains. The tiniest microbes are viruses, and the largest microbes are multicellular.

Biological evolution is based on changes over generations that appear by reproduction. Multicellular organisms appeared 570–590 million years ago (Christian 2004), resulting in the Cambrian explosion or diversification 550 million years ago. Mammals appeared 250 million years ago. Some natural threats, especially volcanos, earthquakes, and meteorites, have produced climate changes and mass extinctions. David M. Raup and J. John Sepkoski (1982) noticed that there have been five mass extinctions, the latest one 66 million years ago when the dinosaurs disappeared. We are now living in the sixth mass extinction because of human activities.

Primates arose at about the same time when the dinosaurs disappeared. Homo sapiens belongs to hominoids, which include the great apes, namely orangutans, gorillas, chimpanzees, and bonobos. Our closest relatives are chimpanzees and bonobos (physically similar to chimpanzees), whose lineage diverged from us 6.2–8.4 million years ago (Chen and Li 2001). The Homo genus started about 2 million years ago when *Homo habilis* appeared. Homo sapiens is about 200,000–300,000 years old. Our brain developed to its present form 30,000–70,000 years ago (Harari 2015). We have thus a hunter-gatherer's brain. Evolution has produced complexity, for example, our intelligence and the ability to cooperate, which are both critical for the success and survival of our species. The ability to speak, envision, make plans for the future improved cooperation, which has led to altruism since individuals who can cooperate and appreciate ethical values survive better than individuals who do not cooperate (Harari 2015; Korkman 2022). *Altruism* means that we are unselfish regarding the welfare of others (Merriam-Webster 2024) who are not necessarily strong enough. If a society wants to develop toward managing wholes with improved resilience, we need people who can cooperate and not only compete as individuals.

Life is based on three primary *biogeochemical cycles* through the atmosphere: nitrogen, carbon, and water cycles (Boulding 1985; Jorgensen 2012; Encyclopedia Britannica 2024). Without the cycles, plants cannot grow, and animals cannot live. In the *nitrogen cycle*, bacteria take nitrogen from the atmosphere and give it to plants. The nitrogen is turned into proteins and other substances within the plants that animals eat, and the nitrogen finally returns to the atmosphere. The *carbon cycle* is based on *photosynthesis*, a process where carbon dioxide and water are transformed into carbohydrates and oxygen using solar energy, and the entropy is reduced (Penrose 1999, p. 413). Energy is thus stored in carbohydrates that animals can consume. In *metabolism*, carbohydrates and oxygen change to carbon dioxide and energy within cells (Encyclopedia Britannica 2024). The *water cycle* is the continuous movement of water from one reservoir to another, using solar power, to be consumed by plants and animals.

Homeostasis is a self-regulating process by which biological systems tend to maintain stability while adjusting to optimal conditions for survival (Encyclopedia

Britannica 2024). Homeostasis is based on feedback. More generally, human motor control uses feedback to control movements in our body (Rosenbaum 2010). For example, if we pick up a pencil from a table, we are using feedback to reduce the distance between the hand and the pencil. *Morphogenesis* is the emergence of form, i.e., self-organization in biology.

The evolutionary process is enabled or made possible by empty *niches* that provide opportunities for either mutation or migration, and the complexity is increased against the entropy law in an open system (Boulding 1985; Kauffman 2019). When less complex niches are filled by mutation, this opens up new niches for still more complex organisms. The same happens in societal evolution. In evolution, the environment is a *selecting agent* that changes over time and from one region to another (Marcos and Arp 2013). Evolution has no goal, but humans and some animals can set goals for themselves using their free will (Schoemaker 1991). Optimality is not guaranteed since evolution is based on competition and, to a lesser extent, cooperation (Westerhoff et al. 2009).

Genotypes and phenotypes are generated by the constraints of a genetic code (Pattee 1973, p. 107). Some acquired properties may also be inherited. *Epigenetics* is the study of heritable changes in gene function that do not entail a change in a DNA sequence (Dupont 2009). A theory of inheritance of acquired characteristics was developed by Jean-Babtiste Lamarck (1802) before Darwin.

Organic molecules may have unknown physical laws that Walter Elsasser (1958) called *biotonic laws* (Gatherer 2008), and the corresponding creative selection algorithms to explain emergence are called unknown *pruning algorithms* (Elsasser 1966, 1987; Morowitz 2002). People often mix biotonic laws with the concept of *vitalism*, according to which life processes do not follow the laws of physics and chemistry alone. Elsasser himself rejected vitalism. Ludwig von Bertalanffy (1932) did the same and started organismic biology (Francois 2006). Elsasser's biotonic laws are assumed to be physical laws. Few pruning algorithms are known, including Pauli's exclusion principle in chemistry and the fitness in evolution theory. We can derive the exclusion principle from quantum mechanics.

Since biological systems are open systems, they follow *nonequilibrium thermodynamics*, developed by Ilya Prigogine (1955). New research is presented in Westerhoff et al. (2009), which shows that the fundamental principles of biology differ from those of physics, although physical laws are followed. Evolution has not selected structures with maximal simplicity, maximum entropy, minimum energy, or maximum thermodynamic efficiency (Boogerd et al. 2007; Westerhoff et al. 2009). Instead of minimizing energy or maximizing energy efficiency, organisms aim at maximal fitness, and energy is only part of it, albeit an important part.

Biological organisms follow some general principles, including nested hierarchy and modularity, feedback in homeostasis and morphogenesis, and near decomposability or loose coupling (Simon 1962, 1973; Gunawardena 2014; Alon 2020). Simon originally called loose coupling *near decomposability* and later used the terms *vertical loose coupling* between hierarchy levels and *horizontal loose coupling* between subsystems at the same level (Simon and Ando 1961; Simon 1962, 1973, 2002). In engineering, we call the subsystems modules.

We must separate the terms control and regulation, which both use feedback (Francois 2006). *Control* is a more complete and direct power over something, while *regulation* is a more systematic and indirect approach within certain limits or rules. For example, drivers can control their cars. Still, a thermostat regulates the temperature in a room, the body regulates its internal temperature, and, more generally, a regulatory agency regulates the use of the frequency spectrum.

According to some estimates, a human body includes over one thousand chemical feedback loops (Kline 1995, pp. 55, 160), for example, regulators of our heart, blood pressure, and respiratory rhythm (Francois 1999, 2006). Similar regulators exist in most organisms, in plants and animals. In addition, feedback appears in a society of animals (Strogatz 2014). For example, a predator–prey cycle corresponds to a feedback loop. Some of the feedback loops in organisms are positive feedback loops that discover changes in the environment so that the organism can learn, change its organization, and grow or shrink depending, for example, on the availability of food (Maruyama 1963; DeAngelis et al. 1986; Camazine et al. 2001). Time-scale separation is used between hierarchy levels (Gunawardena 2014). For example, the four timescales of a bacterium range from 1 ms to 1 h, and the last one corresponds to one cell generation (Alon 2020). The ratio of different time scales between consecutive hierarchy levels is 20–1000.

The human body includes three major parts: the brain and spinal cord, the vascular system and heart, and the intestines and entrails. All of them include nerves. The brain's left hemisphere is better at verbal information, such as grammar, whereas the right hemisphere is better at spatial information, such as visualization (Lilienfeld et al. 2010). Both hemispheres can manage verbal and spatial information. The hemispheres are more similar than different. The corpus callosum exchanges information between the hemispheres. Different parts of the brain have their own tasks (Penrose 1999). A hierarchical model is used in psychology (Stanovich et al. 2016), but the hierarchy is not linked to the physical parts of the brain, which have also hierarchy (Mämmelä et al. 2018).

The history of the research on the human brain is summarized in Wickens (2015). Neuroscience is "the science that deals with the structure and function of the brain and the nervous system" (Oxford Learner's Dictionaries 2024). Even simple organisms can learn. For example, an ameba or jellyfish can learn to avoid obstacles, although it does not even have a brain (Bielecki et al. 2023). An ameba can also distinguish a food particle from a particle of dust (Boulding 1985, p. 160). A dragonfly can respond in about 50 ms to a prey's maneuver (Chance 2021). Its neural network can then be about three layers deep if we consider the 10 ms delay in the eye, the 5 ms delay of the muscles, and the 10 ms delay of each neuron. Ants can build communities with their 250,000 neurons (Pietikäinen and Silven 2021). Flies having 150,000 neurons learn from the first flap attempt. A bumblebee with 850,000 neurons can show complex behavior (Loukola et al. 2017).

A typical *soma* or cell body in a neuron has a long tail called the *axon* (Fox 2011; Wickens 2015). The thickness of an axon is typically about 1 μm. The length of an axon depends on the type of the neuron and its function, and it can vary from several millimeters up to over 1 m. The sciatic nerves have the longest axons.

A *nerve* is a bundle of neurons and supporting cells called neuroglial cells. The propagation speed of an electrical signal or action potential in an axon is 10–100 m/s. An axon has branches, and the tips of the branches form contact points called *synapses* through the dendrites of other cells. According to *Hebb's rule* (1949), learning appears in the synapses where the weights of the neuronal connections are changed. Learning implies strengthening of the synapses, thus forming a distributed memory in the brain and the nervous system in the body (Roberts 2020). The synapses pass chemical messages to the next neuron through a synaptic gap, thus slowing information exchange. The synaptic delay is 0.5–4 ms (Dharani 2015). A recent study shows that learning is possible not only in our brain but also in some non-neural cells we have in our body (Kukushkin et al. 2024).

The physical properties of the human brain are summarized in Herculano-Houzel (2009) and Sarpeshkar (2010). The brain forms a neural network with 86 billion neurons, and each neuron is connected to other neurons through about 1000 synapses on average. The total number of synapses is about 10^{14}. Only about 3% of the neurons in the brain are active simultaneously, so the power consumption is about 20 W (Lennie 2003). Neurons work rather slowly, producing 1 ms pulses or spikes with an average rate of 5 Hz, and the high total speed of the brain is based on massive parallelism. The total processing speed is estimated at over 10^{16} operations per second (Sarpeshkar 2010). In Kurzweil (1999), the author estimates that the average rate of the pulses is 200 Hz, but that does not take the small duty cycle of the neurons (Lennie 2003) into account. If the average rate were 200 Hz, the brain's power consumption would be many times larger than it is now. In addition to neurons, the brain includes 40–140 billion glial cells supporting the neurons but not producing electrical pulses (Bartheld et al. 2016).

The average power of a human is 100 W, which includes the power of the brain of 20 W. The latter power is relatively large since the average mass of the brain (1.4 kg) is only about 2% of the total mass of a human, which implies that intelligence needs much energy. The maximum functional threshold power (FTP) a human can attain for one hour in various sports is about 6.4 W/kg (van Megen and van Dijk 2017). For example, Kenenisa Bekele, in his world record at the 10,000 m, had a power of about 380 W when his weight was 56 kg. The peak power over short intervals can be much larger.

The speed of the brain in complicated decisions, for example, in traffic, is in seconds, and in simple choices, at least 100 ms. Human reaction times are summarized in Kosinski (2013). For example, mean auditory reaction times are 140–160 ms. The current false start criterion the International Association of Athletics Federations (IAAF) uses is based on the assumed auditory reaction time of 100 ms. Still, there is evidence that some humans can have a shorter auditory reaction time (Pain and Hibbs 2007). The visual reaction times are 180–200 ms, thus longer than the auditory reaction times (Kosinski 2013). An auditory stimulus only takes 8–10 ms to reach the brain, but a visual stimulus takes 20–40 ms. Reaction time to touch is 155 ms.

There are various hierarchical theories of the brain, particularly of the cortex (Kiebel et al. 2008; Wang et al. 2009). The environment has different time scales, and the behavior must adapt to short-term and long-term changes. Temporal hierarchies in the environment "are transcribed into anatomical hierarchies in the brain." Thus, the brain uses time-scale separation between the hierarchy levels. The different time scales in the five cortical areas extend from milliseconds to tens of seconds and even more (Kiebel et al. 2008).

It is a common understanding that different brain locations have different tasks. The brain is a kind of *small-world network*, which is both globally and locally efficient between an ordered and random network (Buchanan 2002; Watts 2004; Liao et al. 2017; Mämmelä et al. 2023). The brain's neural representation is hyperdimensional, robust, independent from position, and random (Kanerva 2000). The brain is massive, having large numbers of neurons and synapses. Robust systems are tolerant to failures, and robustness comes from redundancy: many patterns are equivalent. Independence from position implies holographic or holistic representation. Although the brain is highly structured, its many details are determined by learning are left to chance, leading to randomness.

Learning in the brain is divided into incremental and one-shot learning (Lee et al. 2015). In *incremental learning*, new knowledge is acquired gradually through trial and error, thus based on the feedback concept. According to Karl J. Friston and Will Dabney et al., incremental learning in the brain may be reward-based in the form of reinforcement learning (Friston 2010; Dabney et al. 2020). In *one-shot learning*, the brain learns rapidly from only a single pairing of a stimulus and a consequence (i.e., cause and effect) (Lee et al. 2015). Information is stored in our memory as patterns of neural connections in synapses. We have a model of the world in our brains.

There have been many attempts to simulate the brain (Mämmelä et al. 2018; Einevoll et al. 2019). However, the operating principle of the brain remains unknown. The most recent attempts to emulate intelligence are based on natural language models in deep neural networks (Liu et al. 2023).

Some authors have estimated that the human brain is near its fundamental limits regarding processing speed, energy consumption, and reliability (Fox 2011). Thus, we cannot get much smarter. If the brain size is increased, more neurons can be used, but the delays are longer, the processing speed is slower, and the energy consumption is higher. More energy and space are needed if we add more links between distant neurons to communicate faster. If we make the axons thicker, we can increase the speed, but we need more energy and space. If we pack more neurons into the existing space by shrinking neurons or axons, they tend to fire randomly, and reliability is reduced.

To summarize, the object of study in biology is organisms, which are different from mechanisms. The emergent property in biology is life for which we have five incompatible theories. The great theories in biology are cell theory, theory of evolution, and genetics. Evolution is to maximize fitness to improve survivability. Organisms are open systems where nonequilibrium thermodynamics can be used. A human agent has senses, the brain for decision-making, and actuators, thus forming a feedback loop. The brain forms a hierarchical model of the world. There are over thousand feedback loops in our body, for example, in homeostasis for self-regulation and morphogenesis, an advanced form of self-organization.

4.3.3 Social Sciences

Social sciences study people in a society and their relationships and interactions. We focus on psychology, sociology, economics, and political science (Smith 1997, p. 9; Wilson 1998; Schwanitz 1999; Repko and Szostak 2021). The social sciences do not follow any hierarchy but consider society from different perspectives. Psychology is on the border of natural and social sciences, much closer to biology than sociology (Simonton 2004; Benjafield 2020). Biology and psychology form a pair of *life sciences*.

On the other hand, *behavioral science* denotes the unification of psychology and other social sciences (Smith 1997, p. 801), especially when the focus is on human behavior. There is some ambiguity about what social sciences are included in behavioral sciences. We use the term social sciences.

Sociology and anthropology are related since they examine society as a whole. Anthropology explores how cultures are formed, and sociology examines how that formation becomes a society. Some authors think anthropology is a general discipline that, with philosophy, encompasses virtually all established fields of knowledge regarding the study of humans, including natural and human sciences (Klein 1990, p. 66). However, anthropologists do not generally try to explain cultures after the rise of ancient states (Henrich 2020, pp. xi–xii).

The general problem is that we cannot do controlled experiments in social sciences; therefore, ideological prejudices may distort the results (Korkman 2022). Some basic values are needed since we cannot tell how things should be. The problem is called *Hume's law* or Hume's guillotine. Theories are accepted if they work and are efficient.

Social sciences are not concerned so much with human groups but with different relationships of humans in a society, such as securing human needs (economics), collective decisions (political science), resolution of conflicts (jurisprudence), exchange of information (communication studies or the science of communication), and learning and teaching (pedagogy) (Schwanitz 1999). Jurisprudence is guided by the theory of justice, which combines freedom and fairness in liberal democracy (Fukuyama 1992; Rawls 1999; Corning 2011; Haidt 2012). Sometimes jurisprudence is classified among humanities (Wilson 1998, p. 229).

Psychology

Psychology studies human behavior, the mind, its states, and interactions with the environment. The human mind is located in the brain and connected to the whole body through a neural network. Modern experimental psychology started when Wilhelm Wundt founded his psychological laboratory in 1879 in Leipzig, Germany. Psychology is a broad discipline since humans are biological, social, and cultural beings.

There have been some efforts to unify psychological theories. The book (Brennan and Houde 2018, p. 387) identified five streams of thought or paradigms from history, including biological, empirical, functional, humanistic, and idealistic paradigms.

They all have ancient origins. The corresponding subdisciplines in the twenty-first century are neuroscience and experimental, evolutionary, positive, and post-modern psychology. The authors found that, presently, no unification is possible. Some greatest psychologists are Wilhelm Wundt, Norman Ebbinghaus, Alfred Binet, Edward Thorndike, G. Stanley Hall, Sigmund Freud, John B. Watson, William James, Ivan Pavlov, Burrhus F. Skinner, and Jean Piaget. Skinner (1938) claimed that behavior can be modified through rewards and punishments, a form of reinforcement learning based on a feedback loop.

Human mind Psychology is separated from biology by the mind's emergent property called *consciousness*, which means awareness of one's existence, sensations, emotions, volition, thoughts,and axiology (Random House Webster's College Dictionary 1999; Merriam-Webster 2024). Thus, consciousness includes cognition (sensations), affection (emotions), and conation (volition or free will). We have no theory for consciousness, but it has had a survival value in evolution (Penrose 1999). Humans have seven basic emotions: happiness, surprise, fear, sadness, anger, disgust, and contempt (Ekman 2003). Emotions are linked to facial expressions. Later, more emotions were added, and not all have facial expressions. Emotions are expressions of our deeper needs.

An essential element in the human mind is memory. Free will is neither a deterministic nor random phenomenon but seems to start a new causality chain. Our thoughts do not follow only deduction but also induction and abduction (Nowak 2006; Larson 2021). Life and consciousness have so far only developed in organisms, and for the human species, consciousness has needed millions of years of evolution and a long childhood for each individual.

Self-consciousness means that one is aware of oneself as an individual. A self-conscious person is aware of one's mental states, such as perceptions, emotions, and attitudes (Newen and Vogeley 2003). Self-consciousness is sometimes measured by a mirror test developed by Gordon Gallup Jr. (1970). In the test, a red spot is placed on the forehead. Almost all animals respond to their images as to another individual of the same species. A human child above 18 months already has self-consciousness. Our closest relatives, the great apes, also pass the test, but monkeys generally fail the test.

Well before Sigmund Freud, there was a convention to divide our mind into the unconscious and conscious mind. The *unconscious mind* contains one's instincts, experience, expertise, and prejudice (Penrose 1999; Raami 2015). *Intuition* is located in the unconscious mind and is everything else than conscious thinking. After the birth of a child, the mind is not a blank writing-tablet that philosophers called *tabula rasa*, but we have received at least our instincts by heredity. Experience is gained already in the womb. Aristotle and John Locke (1590) discussed the concept of tabula rasa, but Locke used the term white paper.

The term unconscious mind is somewhat disputable, and modern researchers have replaced it with other terms, such as automatic mind (Kahneman 2011) and autonomous mind (Stanovich et al. 2016). According to Keith E. Stanovich (2011), the human mind has a *tripartite hierarchical structure*, which includes an

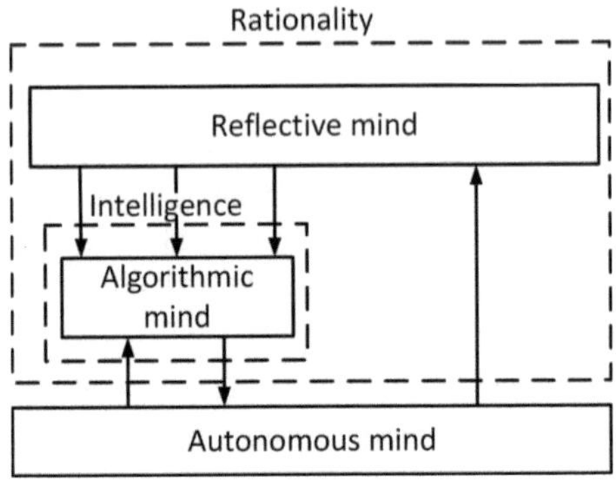

Fig. 4.7 Tripartite structure of the human mind

autonomous, algorithmic, and reflective mind from the bottom up (Stanovich et al. 2016); see Fig. 4.7. For brevity, we may call the autonomous mind intuitive mind, the algorithmic mind intelligent mind, and the reflective mind wise mind in its most advanced form. The model resembles the more complex hierarchical models of the brain (Kiebel et al. 2008; Wang et al. 2009). The tripartite structure differs from the old division into the unconscious mind ("System 1") and conscious mind ("System 2") (Kahneman 2011) so that the unconscious mind is called the autonomous mind, and the conscious mind is divided into two parts: algorithmic and reflective mind. According to Daniel Kahneman, System 1 includes automatic and often unconscious operations, and System 2 includes controlled conscious operations. System 1 is fast, intuitive, heuristic, and emotional in the old model, working in parallel at the bottom of the hierarchy (Kahneman 2011; Stanovich et al. 2016). System 2 is slower, more deliberative, and more logical. In works essentially in serial form.

In the model, we have a time-scale separation of the different levels so that the lowest level is the fastest and the highest level is the slowest. The algorithmic mind is slower than the autonomous mind. Analytic intelligence is located in the algorithmic mind. The reflective mind is even slower at the top of the hierarchy. Our rationality, i.e., the ability to attain goals, is based on the algorithmic and reflective mind. Therefore, one may be highly intelligent and irrational at the same time since the assumptions in the algorithmic mind may be selected stupidly (Robson 2019). Intelligent people may, thus, sometimes make silly mistakes. That has probably been the reason for dividing the conscious mind into two parts. Intuition is important in cases where we need fast decisions in dangerous situations, but reflections may result more probably in the right decision when we have enough time (Lilienfeld et al. 2010).

Rationality can be divided into two classes: *instrumental rationality* is the ability to reach one's goal efficiently using available resources, whereas *epistemic rationality* measures how closely one's beliefs correspond to reality (Robson 2019). Rationality needs both. If epistemic rationality is missing, one may act rationally or goal-directed and behave antisocially and violently if the goals are selected unwisely. Epistemic rationality is a result of enlightenment.

Even earlier, David Bohm divided the conscious mind into two parts (Bohm and Peat 2000). He called the static, deductive, and mechanical ability intellect. In contrast, true intelligence is dynamic and creative insight, the inductive or abductive ability to generalize and "read between the lines" (Bohm and Peat 2000; Larson 2021). This division looks similar to the one described in Stanovich et al. (2016).

Intelligence and rationality A confusion around the definition of intelligence and rationality is seen in the current literature (Albus 1991; Legg and Hutter 2007; Wang 2019). Intelligence and rationality are often seen a synonymous terms (Russell and Norvig 2022), but in Stanovich et al. (2016), rationality is a broader concept. It is essential to understand the definition of intelligence that each author is using. In this book, we use the definition in Stanovich et al. (2016) corresponding to the algorithmic mind, Alan Turing's ingenuity (Larson 2021) as in artificial intelligence, and David Bohm's intellect (Bohm and Peat 2000). Still, we understand that the broader definition in dictionaries is used in standard language. Stanovich has proposed a rationality quotient to complement the intelligence quotient (Stanovich et al. 2016).

There are various definitions of intelligence and rationality (Legg and Hutter 2007; Stonier 1992, 1997) and further discussed in Wang (2019). In dictionaries, a broad definition of intelligence is used. *Intelligence* is "the ability to learn, understand and think logically about things," or "the ability to learn or understand or to deal with new or trying situations" (Oxford Learner's Dictionaries 2024), or "the ability to apply knowledge to manipulate one's environment or to think abstractly as measured by objective criteria (such as tests)" (Merriam-Webster 2024).

The authors in Legg and Hutter (2007) have summarized the definitions in this form: "Intelligence measures an agent's ability to achieve goals in a wide range of environments." Pei Wang has the following working definition: "Intelligence is the capacity of an information-processing system to adapt to its environment while operating with insufficient knowledge and resources" (Wang 2019). Intelligence could be measured as a ratio of the ability to control our environment versus the tendency to be controlled by the environment (Stonier 1992, pp. 37–38; 1997, pp. 52, 97). An intelligent response is such that a system has enhanced its survivability and reproductive ability, and if the system is goal-directed, one has enhanced the achievement of that goal. Intelligence may thus be defined as the ability to survive (to continue living), to reproduce (to continue living of the family or more generally a society such as a state), and to attain one's goals (to make living more comfortable) (Stonier 1997). Reproduction offers a method to survive as a species and evolve. In modern terms, we would call this rationality rather than intelligence.

According to some definitions, all intelligent systems include at least one major feedback loop that controls the environment (Stonier 1992, p. 97; 1997, p. 38), and if they have goals, they are rational agents (Russell and Norvig 2022). Norbert Wiener (1948) and Herbert Simon (1954) noticed that a human is a feedback loop (Wiener 1961; Richardson 1991, pp. 3, 145, 147), implying an agent concept.

Intelligence is more narrowly measured by using the intelligence quotient (IQ). The average IQ is set to 100, and the IQ is assumed to be normally distributed with a standard deviation of 15. An IQ between 90 and 110 is treated as normal. International comparisons show that the average IQ depends on the cultural environment. Some authors think that a single parameter of intelligence, such as IQ, is wholly unjustified since it depends on cultural, environmental, and genetic forces, which form a multidimensional input (Stonier 1997, p. 53). Tom Stonier stated: "Very few of humanity's great insights were derived as a result of logical deductions."

The IQ measures intellect (Bohm and Peat 2000), not creative insight, although the concepts are mixed. In standard language, we often think of rationality when referring to intelligence. The authors (Bohm and Peat 2000) believe we should call artificial intelligence *artificial intellect*. Turing (1938) initially saw a difference between intuition and ingenuity, the latter of which Turing thought mechanical (Larson 2021). By 1950, the idea of intuition had disappeared from his writing, and he felt that minds and machines were fundamentally similar.

In addition to an IQ test, the brain's processing power can be measured using for example the digit-symbol substitution test (DSST) (Hartshorne and Germine 2015). The age for the peak performance of the brain depends on cognitive tasks. There is no age at which humans have a peak performance at all cognitive tasks. In general, fluid intelligence (e.g., short-term memory) peaks early in adulthood, whereas measures of crystallized intelligence (e.g., vocabulary) peak in middle age.

According to the threshold hypothesis, intelligence above the average is a necessary but not a sufficient condition for high creativity (Jauk et al. 2013). We must make a difference between creative potential and creative achievement, i.e., the actual realization of the potential, and the threshold hypothesis is valid only for the former. For achieving many original ideas, intelligence and creative potential correlate for IQs below 120, but above 120, there is no such correlation. Above the threshold, personality became more predictive of creativity. In this case, creative potential is positively related to openness to experience. In scientific work, conscientiousness may also improve creativity. On the other hand, intelligence and creative achievement correlate for all IQs, implying that creative achievement is enhanced when the IQ is higher. In summary, high intelligence and high openness predict creative potential, which, in turn, predicts creative achievement.

Howard Gardner (1985) classified human talent into eight classes, including linguistic, logical-mathematical, spatial, bodily-kinesthetic, musical, interpersonal, intrapersonal, and naturalist intelligence, the last of which was added later (Checkley 1997). Although Gardner used the term intelligence, these classes are usually considered as forms of talent.

Robert Sternberg (1999) divided intelligence into analytical, practical, and creative (Robson 2019), although in psychology, the term intelligence usually refers to analytical intelligence (Stanovich et al. 2016). According to Sternberg, one may be analytically highly intelligent without much practicality or creativity. IQ tests measuring analytical intelligence may be misleading, and some practical and creative people may be treated as "stupid."

Part of our intelligence is *memory*. The storage of new information proceeds through different stages, from short-term memory to permanent information storage in long-term memory (Aben et al. 2012). Many authors have claimed that our *short-term memory* is 3–5 concepts or "chunks," although George A. Miller (1956) declared it to be seven items plus minus two (Cowan 2000). In Doumont (2002), the estimate was five concepts. Some authors see a difference between short-term and *working memory*, where short-term memory covers maintenance, and working memory covers maintenance and manipulation (Aben et al. 2012).

There is a large discrepancy in the estimates of the size of our long-term memory, and some authors have claimed that it is nearly limitless (Landauer 1986). Herbert Simon and Kevin Gilmartin (1973) and William G. Chase and Herbert Simon (1973) proposed that our long-term memory is about 50,000 concepts that they called "chunks" (Gobet and Simon 1996). The memory is also unreliable and selective and depends on our attention to the information most relevant to us (Lilienfeld et al. 2010). The bounded memory is a clear sign of our bounded rationality (Meadows and Wright 2008). A minimum of 10,000 h or ten years of training is needed before reaching the expert level of having those 50,000 concepts (Ericsson 2006). For example, Shakespeare used 29,000 words with various meanings and perhaps over 100,000 concepts (Kurzweil 1999). In the *Oxford English Dictionary*, about 500,000 words are defined. Not all words can be defined since this would lead to endless definitions. For example, the *Oxford Advanced Learner's Dictionary* has a defining vocabulary of 3500 words with which most other words are defined. The defining words are chosen according to their frequency in the language, thus forming an assumed core vocabulary for the reader. The primary or most common meaning is used in the definitions.

By definition, a part of intelligence is *learning* where some model of the world in our brain becomes altered, and we change our behavior due to experience (Stonier 1992, pp. 60–61, 199; 1997, p. 56). Learning is inductive inference (Nowak 2006, pp. 262–263). We have to infer the rules that generate the data presented to us. For example, in the case of a language, those rules are the grammar. More generally, we call the rules a theory. That is the reason why research is a demanding learning process. Learning is memorization and the ability to generalize beyond one's experience to new circumstances. Thus, we can produce and understand sentences that we have never heard earlier.

Wisdom is the highest form of rationality (Robson 2019). According to Grossman, wisdom refers to successfully managing conflicts in social situations. It is based on six principles: (1) ability to take into account the points of view of all persons in conflict, (2) ability to recognize how a conflict can be developed following different scenarios, (3) ability to recognize a possibility for change, (4) ability to search for compromises, (5) ability to predict the solution of conflicts, and (5) intellectual humbleness, i.e., the awareness of the limitations of one's knowledge and uncertainty of one's evaluation abilities.

Personality *Personality* encompasses a broad range of traits and behaviors that develop over time. It is shaped by temperament and environmental factors: culture, education, and life experiences. *Temperament* refers to the biologically based characteristics that influence how individuals react to their environment, largely influenced by genetics.

The most popular classification of almost independent human traits is the big five (John and Srivastava 1999), initially suggested by Warren Norman in 1963 and named the big five by Lewis Goldberg in 1981 (John and Srivastava 1999). The traits are dependent and correlated in rural societies, but specialization in urban societies has shown greater independence and uncorrelatedness (Henrich 2020, pp. 381–387). People usually do not represent extreme traits but form a continuum, with each person having a personality profile. The traits are (John and Srivastava 1999)

- extroversion versus introversion
- openness to experience versus rigidity
- conscientiousness versus undependability
- agreeableness versus antagonism
- neuroticism versus emotional stability.

The classification is a summary of a more extensive earlier classification by Raymond P. Cattell in 1946, which finally produced the 16 personality factor test in 1970. Many good researchers are introverts (Jain and Triandis 1997), and superiors who are typically extroverts often do not appreciate their value.

Ethical values Our culture is value-based. Morality made civilization possible (Haidt 2012, p. xviii). Societies that do not respect ethics tend to decline (Fukuyama 1992). Science does not develop properly unless specific ethical rules are followed. Ethics is part of philosophy and, therefore, subject to speculation. However, ethics regarding fairness may have an evolutionary basis (Ryan 2012, p. 57).

There has been a long-standing discussion on whether humans are good or bad. The author (Bregman 2020) described two opposite images of humanity by Thomas Hobbes and Jean-Jacques Rousseau. Hobbes (1651) thought that a human is bad and only our culture can save us from animal instincts. Without a society, we would be in continual fear of danger of violent death, and the life of a human would be "solitary, poor, nasty, brutish, and short." Rousseau (1754) believed that a human is good, but our culture makes us bad.

William Golding wrote a novel, *The Lord of the Flies* (1954), trying to show how we are corrupted on a desert island. A group of six boys stayed in 1965–1966 for over a year on such an island, and just the opposite happened. Some researchers, including Stanley Milgram (1961) and Philip Zimbardo (1971), have tried to demonstrate the evil of humans, but their research has been criticized for manipulating the results. Roy F. Baumeister and his colleagues concluded that bad is stronger than good; for example, bad feedback has more impact than good (Baumeister et al. 2001). It generally benefits us to respond more strongly to bad than good events. Many people can still live happy lives since they have usually more often good than bad events.

The assumed evil is a self-fulfilling prophecy, and as Rutger Bregman suggests, it is a time for a new human image. We must be motivated to behave well through education and growing awareness. Richard Dawkins popularized the idea of a selfish gene that "wants" to survive and reproduce (Bregman 2020). In later editions of his book *The Selfish Gene*, he retracted his talk of our natural selfishness. The idea of selfishness is also criticized in Corning (2011), Acemoglu and Robinson (2020) and Aldred (2020).

Human needs and motivation Montesquieu (1748) defined "the laws of nature" (de Montesquieu 2001), which are essentially a hierarchy of human needs from the bottom up, including safety needs, physiological needs, belongingness needs, and desire to live in a society, referring to a social contract. Maslow (1943) independently proposed a different but overlapping hierarchy of needs that includes physiological or survival needs, safety needs, love and belongingness needs, self-esteem needs, self-actualization, and self-transcendence, the last of which is a later addition not so well known (Koltko-Rivera 2006). Maslow thus changed the order of the two lowest levels compared to Montesquieu. The hierarchy means that the most essential needs of an individual are at the bottom. For Maslow, the hierarchy of needs was, at the same time, also a hierarchy of motivation. *Motivation* is an experience that encourages us to engage in goal-directed behavior (McFarland and Bösser 1993).

Physiological needs are survival needs such as water, food, and sleep, which are necessities of life (Koltko-Rivera 2006; Taylor 2009). We should also add reproductive needs as survival needs over human generations (Corning 2011), as included in the definition of life (Christian 2004). Survivability and reproductive ability are sometimes included even in the definition of intelligence (Stonier 1992, p. 15). In *safety needs*, we want to feel safe and be able to relax. We want to experience fairness and seek safety through order and law. *Love and belonging* means a sense of well-being and community, i.e., affiliation with a group. Taylor (2009) reordered the hierarchy so that the physiological and safety needs, as well as love and belonging, are equally important, below all other needs, to emphasize the fragility of the needs above them (Taylor 2009). It is now clear why Adam Smith defined safety and justice as the basic tasks of a state (Siegfried 2006). Justice and fairness are overlapping concepts but not synonymous. While justice focuses on laws and regulations, fairness is broader and encompasses ethical aspects (Corning 2011).

Self-esteem needs mean feeling of worth in self and seeking recognition and achievement. *Self-actualization* implies fulfilling one's potential. Roy F. Baumeister has criticized Maslow's concept of self-actualization (Baumeister 1987). He saw three problems: how to form a specific idea of one's potential, how to fulfill the potential, and how to tolerate the disappointment associated with nonfulfillment. *Self-transcendence* seeks a further cause beyond the self and to experience a communion beyond the boundaries of the self, such as service to others and devotion to truth, art, social justice, environmentalism, or the pursuit of science. Our ultimate goal is participation in the life of our society (Corning 2011). The goal implies that our life's purpose is to survive, reproduce, and build our society. Similarly, the purpose of any society is collective survival.

We have combined the hierarchies in Koltko-Rivera (2006) and Taylor (2009) in Fig. 4.8. Louis Tay and Ed Diener have studied the needs in over one hundred countries (Tay and Diener 2011). They concluded that the needs are universal and not substitutable for each other. The fulfillment of needs is associated with subjective

Fig. 4.8 Hierarchy of needs

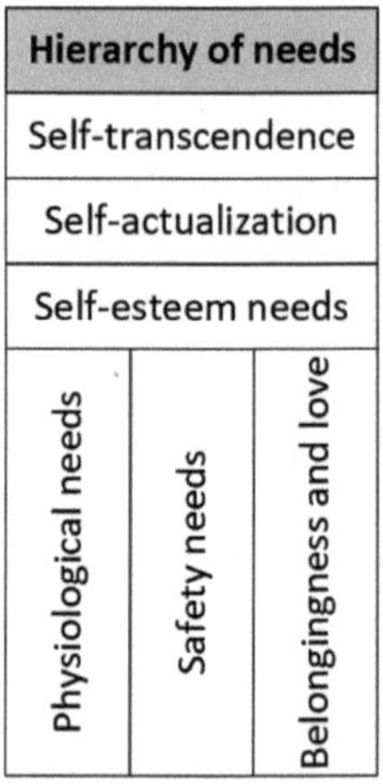

well-being everywhere. Positive feelings were most related to social and respect needs. The results indicated the desirability of living in a flourishing society.

Montesquieu (1748) assumed that we were initially in the *state of nature*, a term used already by Thomas Hobbes in his book *Leviathan* (1651). The state of nature is "a war of every man against every man" (Corning 2011). People are under the law of the jungle. Hobbes developed the modern concept of social contract, although similar ideas had been created since antiquity. Jean-Jacques Rousseau (1762) proposed the term social contract. The need for safety and fairness resulted in a *social contract* between individuals to form a state by giving part of one's freedom to the state to obtain physical safety. How the social contract is constructed is controversial, either bottom-up or top-down (Christian 2004). Revolutions sometimes replaced earlier inheritable monarchs with modern liberal democracies having free and fair elections. As John Locke noticed, the state of nature is now between nations (Pursiainen 1998, p. 220), which can also make contracts or pacts to reduce the threat.

Peter Corning has recently discussed human needs in more detail (Corning 2011). The Institute for the Study of Complex Systems developed a *Survival Indicators* paradigm. The paradigm distinguishes between primary, instrumental, and perceived needs, dependencies, and wants. None of the primary needs can be substituted by other primary needs. The instrumental needs are means to support the primary needs. The primary and instrumental needs form our *basic needs*. Satisfying basic needs is necessary but not sufficient. The primary needs include fourteen needs domains, including, in a somewhat arbitrary order, thermoregulation, waste elimination, nutrition, water, mobility, sleep, respiration, physical safety, physical health, mental health, communication, social relationships, reproduction, and nurturance of offspring. The perceived needs, dependencies, and wants form various motivational states.

Happiness After we have fulfilled our basic needs, we can lead a happy life. *Happiness* as overall life satisfaction is one of the most important, if not the most important, issue in our lives (Corning 2011, p. 90). According to Aristotle, the things we want are called good, and happiness consists of getting what we want. Our life is good if we achieve happiness approved by reason (Ryan 2012, pp. 79, 427). Happiness is a research subject in psychology and economics where it is called utility. Even the greatest happiness is always overshadowed by the fear of losing it. It is not possible to develop an objective measure of happiness. Happiness surveys are an indirect and unreliable measure of the satisfaction of our basic needs, the latter of which can be measured directly, but happiness is much more than that. According to Aristotle, happiness implies modesty and avoidance of extremes (Korkman 2022). Happiness also means fairness, even between generations, as understood in sustainability (Riekki and Mämmelä 2021).

In psychology, happiness is "a life marked by a preponderance of positive emotions derived from positive events and influences in life" (Vitali and Moran 2023). They include positive experiences, positive states and traits, and positive institutions. Six virtues are associated with well-being: wisdom and knowledge, courage, humanity, justice, temperance, and transcendence. According to the World Happiness Index, the ingredients for national happiness include income, freedom, healthy life expectancy, social support, trust, and generosity.

Our culture is based on values, norms, and beliefs leading to a shared vision (Boulding 1969; Guiso et al. 2006; Korkman 2022). The *values* are those which we view as valuable and desirable. The *norms* are rules of behavior used to protect our values. The *beliefs* are the assumed causal effects of our choices leading to visions, corresponding to our goal encouraging cooperation.

David Hume believed that trust is a central value to all social activities (Pursiainen 1998). The trust has prerequisites and consequences not usually presented together (Table 4.5). We believe in trust, and its opposite is threat (Boulding 1989). Trust is the glue that holds our democratic society together in a good climate. For that we need laws in addition to ethical norms. Understanding why trust is a much better starting point than threat is easy. In the state of nature, everybody threatens everybody else.

Trust means believing that others are good and honest and do not try to harm you (Merriam-Webster 2024). Trust also means that something is true and correct, and we can rely on it. According to Adam Smith, a government should provide fairness and safety to the citizens of a country (Siegfried 2006; Corning 2011). The game theory suggests that a workable society is based on a suitable balance between competition, cooperation, and punishments. Peter Corning discussed the fairness

Table 4.5 Ethical values and norms to provide overall satisfaction and happiness in our society

Ethical values and norms
Safety
Cooperation
Trust
Fairness
Respect

at length (Corning 2011). Trust can be destroyed if a government does not care for justice, which is essential in any constitutional state (Fukuyama 2014). Safety is in Abraham Maslow's hierarchy of needs (Koltko-Rivera 2006). The sense of self-preservation is one of our basic needs and for that we need a safe environment.

In general, in social situations, cooperation follows from trust, a prerequisite for safety to avoid the state of nature. Nature is our environment, without which we cannot survive for a moment, but which also contains threats such as natural disasters (earthquakes, volcanoes, storms, meteorites), predators, criminal people, and threatening countries. Organization of cooperation is challenging since cooperation is a voluntary act that needs some deep understanding of life: we must respect other people (Boulding 1985, 1989). Georg W. F. Hegel saw life as a struggle for recognition (Fukuyama 1992, pp. xvi–xvii). Without trust, we can only force cooperation that is more apparent than real. Trust requires fairness, which requires respect and love. Fairness means that we and the government follow laws and ethical norms. If we do not follow the laws, we are punished. If we do not follow the ethical norms, our society is shaken. Fairness, or justice in legal terms, is one of our deepest needs associated with our well-being (Corning 2011; Vitali and Moran 2023).

We know that friendship involves love and trust, and we are willing to cooperate with our friends. Threat does not belong to friendship. Love is related to the Golden Rule: "Treat others as you want to be treated." But it is possible that what I want is not wanted by others. Furthermore, the treatment must always be ethical and should not harm.

My conclusion is that there is the following chain of reasons (Table 4.5): respect and love enable fairness, which enables trust and, therefore, cooperation, and cooperation enables safety, and all of this enables satisfaction and happiness to citizens and not only to the elite. In our society, we do our best to make it an even better place. Respect, fairness, and trust provide a niche for cooperation and safety. Unfairness leads to a lack of trust, threats must force collaboration, and safety is lost. If country leaders respect their people, they bring about fairness, but even the leader is not safe without it. Building a safe and just society can thus be seen as the purpose of life in order for the life of the society to continue its existence (Corning 2011). The society must be in harmony with nature. Environmental protection is an essential part of our work.

Lawrence Kohlberg's (1971) stages of moral development include six levels (Kohlberg 1971) (Table 4.6). Kohlberg (1971) developed the stages of moral development using earlier ideas by Jean Piaget. The principles can be used both for individual people and for states. The levels describe different stages for internal commitment to social behavior, but there is not necessarily any development. Some cultures do not develop for centuries because of wrong idealism. In Europe, the slow growth of the Enlightenment needed a millennium of history. Individuals live only about a century in a thousand-year culture. They may lack models for proper moral behavior.

At the lowest level, people unquestionably respect power, and only punishments guide them. These principles are used in some medieval societies. At the second level, people instrumentally satisfy their own needs and think that there are different points of view on any problem. At the third level, people orient to behavior that helps

Table 4.6 Stages of moral development

Kohlberg's stages
Universal ethical principles
Social contract orientation
Orientation to authority
Interpersonal accord
Orientation to self-interest
Orientation to punishment

others. They want to be good people. At the fourth level, people think that what the authority says is right and do their duty according to the law. People understand the importance of democratically agreed-upon social contracts at the fifth level. They also appreciate the possibility that we can change the laws. The comprehensive, universal, and consistent ethical principles are fully understood at the highest or sixth level. People define principles in agreement so that they are most just. Many people and states never reach the two highest stages of morality, which may also slow down the development of those states.

To summarize, the research object of psychology is a conscious human, which makes this discipline one of the most complex. Humans can be seen as rational agents, i.e., feedback loops, but they cannot be modeled accurately. There is no unified theory in psychology, but altogether five paradigms. Just as the brain, the human mind has a hierarchical structure, and our rationality is bounded. Intelligence and rationality are related but not identical concepts. Personalities are classified into five traits, which we must understand to be able to cooperate. In social situations, humans must behave ethically. Trust as an ethical concept forms a glue in a happy society whose purpose is to fulfill our needs. Unfortunately, not all societies are at the same level in moral development.

Sociology

Sociology is a general interdisciplinary discipline with a broad scope, thus drawing from many other social sciences. Sociology is a pure science that does not focus on applications. In sociology, the research objects are human societies, their interactions, and the processes that preserve and change them. Sociology was initially defined as social physics and later the science of society since people thought societies follow natural laws (Fanelli 2010; Smith 1997, p. 427). Auguste Comte (1830) initiated sociology. He wrote that sociology was the ultimate goal of all research and the queen of all disciplines but also the least developed of the sciences because of its complexity. Thomas Schelling (1960) proposed that game theory can form a basis for social physics or sociophysics (Siegfried 2006).

The defining property in sociology is the human *role* in social groups, whereas in psychology, the focus is on an *individual* who may have many roles (Schwanitz 1999). Sociology is a broad discipline that includes various fields, such as theoretical and applied sociology, cultural sociology, historical sociology, sociology of knowledge, economic sociology, sociology of particular social groups (for example, a family, rural, urban, military), sociology of education, legal sociology, sociology of politics, demographic sociology, and social psychology. Kenneth E. Boulding divided the social system into three subsystems, including integrative, economic, and political systems, where the modes of interaction are respect, exchange, and threat, corresponding to three faces of power (Boulding 1985, 1989). We cover only some general results of sociological studies and then focus more on economics and political science, which are related to economic sociology and the sociology of politics, respectively.

Cultural evolution Fundamental theories of social change include the idea of degeneration, social cycle theory, and sociocultural evolution, also called cultural evolution. For example, circulation of the elites, Kondratiev cycles, and predator–prey model describe cyclic phenomena, not necessarily showing progress. Often, a delayed feedback loop generates the cycles, thus showing instability. Inspired by Auguste Comte's different stages of a society leading to the scientific stage that he called positivism, Herbert Spencer contributed to the biological evolution theory and defined the concept of *cultural evolution* (1862) (Stonier 1992), including the idea of social progress, seen as necessary since the times of Enlightenment. Social cycle theory and cultural evolution can be combined, thus showing the dynamics of a society. Cultural evolution differs from biological evolution in three respects: it is goal-directed because of our consciousness, the next generations inherit the cultural information though education, and its rate of change is much faster since it is not incremental.

There are four turning points in the cultural evolution leading to our collective intelligence. They were the invention of speech, writing, the printing press, and the Internet. The language as we know it now developed slowly in *Homo sapiens* about 70,000–100,000 years ago (Boe et al. 2019). At about the same time, humans started to use tools. Our brain evolved to its present form about 30,000–70,000 years ago, and thus there was also a dramatic change in symbolic thought only a few thousand generations ago (Morowitz 2002, p. 156; Harari 2015). We still have a hunter-gatherer's brain.

Most people speak Indo-European languages, which started to develop about 6000 years ago in Ukraine and Southern Russia north of the Black Sea and the Caspian Sea, from where they spread in all directions (Gnanadesikan 2009). Among Indo-European languages are, for example, Hellenic (Greek), Romance (Latin), Germanic, Slavic, and Indo-Aryan languages. English is one of the Germanic languages.

Writing was one of the most significant technological inventions of all time: the past can speak to the future (Gnanadesikan 2009). Other great ancient inventions were the controlled use of fire, agriculture, and the wheel. Writing was invented at least in three places: in Mesopotamia, China, and Mesoamerica. Sumerians were the first. They invented cuneiform writing in Mesopotamia in about 3500 BCE. Semitics invented letters in the Near East in 1800–1900 BCE but only used consonants. Now, the individual symbols stand for phonemes or particular sounds. At that time, alphabetic order also started to be formed. The idea was moved to Phoenicians who lived in the area that is now called Lebanon. They taught writing to the Greeks, who created the modern alphabet by including vowels in about 800 BCE. Etruscans in Tuscany, Italy, copied in 700 BCE the alphabet from the Greeks. The Latin alphabet we now use was developed in the Roman Republic in about 500 BCE. At that time, the left-to-right direction was settled. Initially, people used only capital letters. Small letters were invented during the Byzantine period in 330–1453 CE.

A positional system with base 60 was used in Babylonian numeration in about 1500 BCE (Ifrah 2000, p. 153). A zero was indicated by a space, which caused some ambiguities. Our Arabic numerals are initially from India, where the decimal positional system appeared about 500 CE in a book written by Aryabhata. The Indian numerals were adopted in Arabia in the 800s. In Europe, the numerals were first known in the 900s. Fibonacci in Italy recommended Arabic numerals in his book in 1202, but they replaced Roman numerals only in the 1500s.

Paper and printing press were invented in China, but the printing press was more successful in Europe, where the use of the alphabet made the printing press practical (Stonier 1992). Anybody can learn to write and read in a few weeks, leading to superior collective intelligence in Europe. Gutenberg (1440) used the printing press in Germany. Ted Nelson (1950) invented the *hypertext model*, which allows us to use hyperlinks to other text immediately. The first computer network was developed as Arpanet in 1969 and was later called the Internet in 1983. Tim Berners-Lee (1989) invented the *World Wide Web* for storing, updating, and finding files using the hypertext model. The Internet browsers were developed in the 1990s. Now, anybody who has an Internet connection can use the information on the Internet and use the network for video calls since the original computer network and mobile communication networks work together.

The success of a country depends on its ability to produce *collective intelligence*, which is supported by communication and transportation, information storage and retrieval (libraries, online databases), funding of science and research to discover new knowledge, and above all, the ability of its education system to distribute objective knowledge. Otherwise, our society declines (Stonier 1992, pp. 99, 210–211). The product of isolation and restrictions is that innovations are not produced (McNeill 1991; McNeill and McNeill 2003). We must know the past to understand the present and envisage the future. History is not only military history, but we must also teach it from the point of view of cultural evolution. Ignorant citizens can only lead to "cults of unreason."

Universal dimensions of culture Similar to the big five traits in psychology, there are five universal *dimensions of cultures* (Hofstede et al. 2010). The dimensions are measured with different indexes normalized between 0 and 100. The indexes include

- power distance index, measuring the degree of inequality
- individualism index, measuring the power of individuals
- masculinity index, measuring the importance of masculine values instead of feminine ones
- uncertainty avoidance index, measuring the tolerance to the ambiguous and the unpredictable, and

- long-term orientation index, measuring perseverance and thrift.

Masculine values include high earnings, recognition for good work, advancement to higher-level jobs, and challenging work. On the other hand, feminine values include good relationships, cooperation, a suitable living area, and employment security. Alex Inkeles and Daniel J. Levinson (1954) suggested the first four indexes, and Geert Hofstede (1991) proposed the last one.

The long-term orientation is correlated with economic growth, whereas individualism and, to some extent, small power distance are associated with national wealth. According to Sixten Korkman, understanding the reasons for long-term growth is the most exciting question in economic history (Korkman 2022). There are no commonly agreed answers, but he lists three possible multicausal reasons: (1) the growth depends on the available resources and technology even more than on the growth of labor force and capital, (2) the growth depends on the economic and political institutions of the society, especially on democracy, and (3) the culture affects the development of institutions, innovations, and technology.

There are also other indices, including the democracy index, happiness index, fragile states index, corruption perceptions index, and world press freedom index. The International Institute for Democracy and Electoral Assistance publishes a "Global state of democracy report" annually. The Economist Intelligence Unit (EIU) within the Economist Group has published the *democracy index*. Countries are rated full and flawed democracies, and hybrid and authoritarian regimes. In addition, the Sustainable Development Solutions Network formed by the United Nations is defining the Sustainable Development Goals (SDGs) and publishing annually "World happiness report," measuring the success of the states in their tasks, resulting in satisfaction and happiness of the citizens, summarized in a *happiness index*. The Fund for Peace organization in the United States publishes an annual report on the *fragile state index*. The index assesses vulnerability to conflict or collapse. The *corruption perceptions index* published by Transparency International measures the perceived levels of public sector corruption. Freedom House publishes the *world press freedom index* in its "Freedom of Press" report. The index measures the level of freedom and editorial independence of the press.

Wisdom of the crowds We can have about 150 stable social relationships, called *Dunbar's number*, proposed by Robin Dunbar (1992) (Dunbar 2011; West et al. 2020). The number is based on the size of our brain's neocortex as an extrapolation from group sizes of primates and their neocortexes, a sign of bounded rationality. The observation forms a theoretical link between psychology and sociology since this collective behavior is an enhanced form of *collective intelligence*, also called *collective* or *global brain* or *wisdom of the crowds* coming from a social network (Stonier 1992, 1997; Surowiecki 2005; Henrich 2020). The Dunbar number has experimental evidence from social media. The Dunbar number forms a limitation to our networking abilities: more networking is not always good networking.

According to Surowiecki (2005, pp. 10, 232, 278), the *wisdom of the crowds*, an idea developed by Francis Galton (1907), can be used if four conditions are satisfied: (1) there is diversity of opinion and each person has some private information, (2) to avoid groupthink, decisions are independently made and not determined by the opinions of those around them, (3) people can specialize and draw on local knowledge and thus decisions are decentralized, and (4) a suitable aggregation method is used to find a collective decision from individual decisions (Surowiecki 2005, p. 10).

Surowiecki makes a vague claim that random errors in decisions cancel themselves out (Surowiecki 2005, p. 10). If the decisions are random, there is much noise in the decisions, and the aggregate of the decisions is also random. We need an additional condition: the group members must be well informed, i.e., enlightened (Sloman and Fernbach 2017; Pinker 2018). Nicolas de Condorcet (1785) noticed that if a person independently makes correct decisions more often than wrong, the probability of correct decisions increases when the group size increases (Austen-Smith and Banks 1996; Edelman 2002). The phenomenon is called *Condorcet jury theorem*, and for independent binary choices, we can easily prove it using a binomial distribution. If the decisions are nonbinary, more general distributions are needed. The multinomial distribution is a natural extension of the binomial distribution for modeling outcomes with more than two categories (Wolfram 2024). It assumes that the outcomes are independent and identically distributed.

Our liberal democracy is essentially based on the wisdom of the crowds, but it has weaknesses and does not work without enlightened citizens. Otherwise, demagogies can mislead them in the "post-truth" politics, where the truth is no longer a value for some of those demagogies. Crowdsourcing is the process of obtaining new ideas or content from a large group of people.

Social dilemma There is a tension between individual and collective rationality, representing a paradox. *Social dilemmas* involve "a conflict between immediate self-interest and longer-term collective interests" (Dawes and Messick 2000; Van Lange et al. 2013). Robyn M. Dawes (1980) was one of the first to define the concept (Dawes and Messick 2000). An example is the prisoner's dilemma. We receive a higher immediate payoff for defecting than for cooperating. However, we would be better off if all cooperated than if all defected. The conclusion is that collective rationality implies irrational individual behavior leading to a better situation than individual rational behavior. A solution to the social dilemma links biological evolution to cultural evolution, where cooperation becomes essential. Individual rationality corresponds to partial optimization that does not generally lead to a global optimum since society is not linear. Thus, the dilemma is an example of the effects of emergence.

Advancing the interests of the society is overall optimization, which also promotes the interests of the individual in a conciliatory manner. An example is energy efficiency, referring to local optimization, and survivability, referring to global optimization; see Fig. 4.9. Organisms are highly energy efficient but not maximally energy efficient since, at the ecosystem level, we must trade off energy efficiency with survivability, where we must implicitly consider many other optimization criteria when all the resources are finite (Westerhoff et al. 2009). Understanding the social dilemma in general is called wisdom (Robson 2019), and the wisdom of nature comes from the survivability of species. We can scale the dilemma to relations between any societies. Those societies that are willing to cooperate will succeed better than those that are

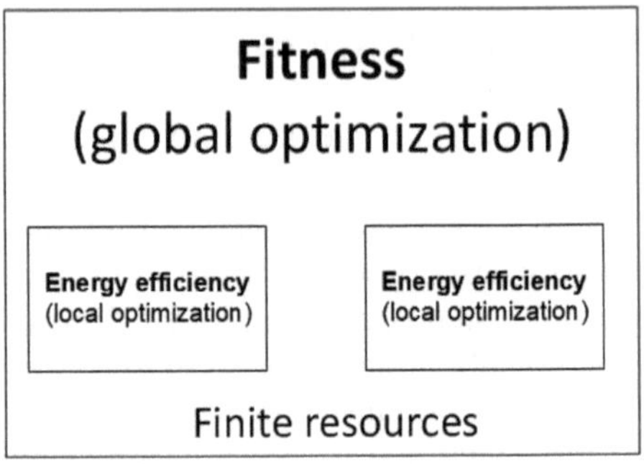

Fig. 4.9 Social dilemma in nature. Fitness does not lead to maximal energy efficiency

not. Jevons paradox is related to the social dilemma. Energy consumption cannot increase without limits in a finite world, and we must make compromises. Energy efficiency is not maximized since there are also other finite resources.

A general social dilemma is the *tragedy of the commons* by William F. Lloyd (1833), where the commons are the shared resources, originally a common pasture-land for cattle (Hardin 1968, 1998). Each herder tries to keep as many cattle as possible. The greediest herdsman would gain most—but only for a while. Freedom in using the commons brings ruin to all in a finite world. The tragedy is a side effect of free-market economics based on the assumption that separate selfish decisions are the best for society. Already, Aristotle noticed that a collectively owned property is cared for by nobody (Ryan 2012, p. 1010). If the commons are free to use, they are usually overused since if one is not using them, somebody else is using them. The most critical commons in the world are the atmosphere, oceans, and forests. The atmosphere and the seas are shared sinks for aerial and material garbage. A result of the pollution of the atmosphere is climate change. Marine fish are becoming scarce.

Thomas Hobbes proposed a *world government*, which could solve the tragedy between individual states as a form of international social contract: the states leave part of their freedom to obtain international safety and justice. The idea is impracticable and is against the present rights of the states, and the tragedy of the commons cannot be avoided. The freedom of the states is not unlimited, and we must change the concept of a sovereign state. A treaty between nations is a partial solution (Ryan et al. 2012, pp. 979, 1003). Regulation in corrupt and ignorant countries does not work.

There is no technical solution to the tragedy of the commons, but it is an ethical question (Hardin 1968). In Meadows and Wright (2008), the author offers three solutions: educate (i.e., enlighten) and exhort, privatize the commons, and regulate the commons. Elinor Ostrom (1990) developed the idea that to solve the tragedy of the commons, social control must work adequately (Bregman 2020). She received a Nobel Prize in economics in 2009. For example, the second solution corresponds to a private water meter for each household so that all households pay for what they have consumed. If we use a shared water meter, no one has the motivation to reduce water consumption. We cannot privatize all commons. The atmosphere and oceans are polluted, and the diversity of life disappears. Such commons are overused unless we have international regulations. Some suggestions regarding regulation have received heavy criticism, especially the attempts to limit population growth. Traffic is being regulated for safety reasons. An excellent example of a regulator is the International Telecommunication Union—Radiocommunication Sector (ITU-R), which governs the use of radio spectrum and satellite orbits. Another example is the International Commission on Non-Ionizing Radiation Protection (INIRP), which regulates the level of non-ionizing radiation, a form of pollution.

To summarize, sociology combines the results of all other social sciences and can be seen as fundamental as physics among natural sciences. We see instabilities in self-organizing social systems, but the situation is not so clearcut as in physics because the agents are now conscious people having free will. They cannot be modeled accurately. Cultural evolution is fundamentally based on the concept of writing and education and is faster than biological evolution. In a democratic society we can use collective intelligence in the form of the wisdom of the crowds to solve the bounded rationality of the individuals in a distributed manner. The social dilemma is, by definition, the main source for the conflict between an individual and the society.

Economics

A commonly accepted definition of economics by Lionel Robbins (1932) is "the science which studies human behavior as a relationship between ends and scarce means which have alternative uses" (Backhouse 2023). The defining property in economics is an *exchange* that benefits all parties (Boulding 1985). No economics can exist without using natural resources (Korkman 2022). If the resources would not be scarce, there would not be any need for economics. We also need ethics. Without a healthy economy, our culture cannot flourish, and we cannot protect our borders (Kennedy 1988). Table 4.7 lists some of the great theories in economics.

Economics can be divided into microeconomics and macroeconomics (Backhouse 2023). Microeconomics focuses on individual agents such as households and companies and their markets using individual commodities. *Macroeconomics* is the study of business cycles and growth. The economy is studied regarding resources, inflation, growth, and public policies. The behavior of the whole economy is dealt with, for example, national income, unemployment, and price level.

Exponential growth is a sign of instability, usually generated by a positive feedback loop. A delay in a stable negative feedback loop may also lead to an unstable positive feedback loop (Long et al. 1989; Sheridan 1993; Dorf and Bishop 2017). There are competing theories of short-term and long-term business cycles, and most economists are sceptical of the existence of long-term cycles. Short-term business cycles may be

Table 4.7 Some great theories in economics

Year	Discoverer	Discovery
1776	A. Smith	Free-market economics
1936	J. M. Keynes	Macroeconomics
1944	J. von Neumann and O. Morgenstern	Game theory

caused by overproduction or random shocks and the period is a few years (Forrester 2007; Sterman 2000, pp. 114–116, 784–785). Kondratiev cycles are assumed long-term cycles with peaks about 60 years apart on average with an amplitude much larger than the short-term business cycles. We can explain the cycles by the overinvestments and the delays in the system feedback loops, which cause long-term instability.

The essence of free-market economics is that selfish individuals engaging in market exchange can both benefit. The history of modern economics started with Adam Smith's work on free markets in his book *An Inquiry into the Nature and Causes of the Wealth of Nations* (1776) (Korkman 2022). Free-market economics is based on two simple principles: human selfishness and competition, leading to the law of supply and demand but, unfortunately, also to a social dilemma and the tragedy of the commons. One reason for the need for this law is that the products and services are incommensurate, and the prices are a partial solution. It is not an objective solution since, as the name of the law states, the prices depend on the availability of the products and services, which, on the other hand, depend on the available resources. Smith saw work as the origin of value. In his earlier book, *The Theory of Moral Sentiments* (1759), Smith explained that humans can restrain their selfishness for the common good.

Free-market economics is an evolutionary theory characterized by game theory, developed by John von Neumann and Oscar Morgenstern (1944). The theory hardly defines the whole discipline. A healthy economy benefits from ethical values such as trust and honesty. Later, game theory was generalized to evolutionary game theory, including cooperation (Nowak 2006). Selfishness does not work well elsewhere, for example, in politics.

In economics, we assume that humans are decision-making agents who rationally or selfishly maximize their profit (Korkman 2022); thus, we have forgotten Smith's moral sentiments (Siegfried 2006). After Smith, Max Weber, in his *The Protestant Ethic and the Spirit of Capitalism* (1905), was one of the first to realize that capitalism should be based on values and attitudes and not so much on the accumulation of capital or institutions.

Economics produces the needed goods and services for the members of society using scarce resources (Korkman 2022). *Market economy* means we organize production in the market through exchange. A market economy is efficient only in strict conditions and is not necessarily stable or fair. Efficiency is based on specialization that increases productivity, but Smith did not realize the importance of inventions and innovations that changed society even more than the division of work. We can see that the distributed market coordinating the economy's operation is the most excellent idea of all economics, emphasizing individual rationalism. *Capitalism* has many definitions. Usually it means that the capital needed for production is privately owned and the profits are reinvested. Still, the term is somewhat misleading since the promoter of new economics is not physical but human capital, including ideas and innovations (Korkman 2022). A problem is how the profits are divided in the society. Without liberal democracy, a market economy may lead to a corrupted form of capitalism called *kleptocracy*. Some authors think the free-market economy has corrupted us and has been "a license to be bad" (Aldred 2020). It alone does not solve the social dilemma, i.e., the conflict between interests of individuals and a society.

Market forces are a form of negative feedback unless there are long delays (Richardson 1991, pp. 60–64; Sterman 2000, pp. 798–800). Smith claimed that there is an *invisible hand* that offers products and services to everyone at a reasonable price without having the state intervene in the market. The invisible hand is a form of evolution and self-organization (Heylighen 2002). The producers act to maximize their gains. The effects of the invisible hand are not entirely positive since separate greedy "rational" decisions may lead to the tragedy of the commons when the resources are finite (Hardin 1968, 1998; Aldred 2020). In addition, the rich become rich, and the poor stay poor. There is thus a tendency towards *monopolies* that are not beneficial to ordinary customers, and in fact, the state must intervene in the market to remove the monopolies. Free-market economics does not offer Pareto optimality because of limited information exchange and, furthermore, Pareto optimality says nothing about fairness and thus allows monopolies (Siegfried 2006; Stiglitz 2000; Lasaulce and Tembine 2011; Wang et al. 2019). When we approach the limits of growth, cooperation is a must.

The virtue of capitalism is that it encourages and rewards innovation and entrepreneurship (Korkman 2022). Capitalism has several problems: income and other significant inequalities and unstable economics. Governments can use taxes for carbon oxide emissions and subsidies for green technology to fight against global climate change. Two primary tools exist to smooth economic cycles (Albus 2011). They are fiscal and monetary policy by the government. The *fiscal policy* includes spending, borrowing, and taxing. The *monetary policy* determines the interest rates and controls the supply of money and credit. The fiscal policy was influenced by John M. Keynes (1936) and the monetary policy by Milton Friedman (1936). Fiscal policy is used to stimulate an economy in recession, and monetary policy is used to control inflation.

John M. Keynes was one of the fathers of macroeconomics, which uses limited government interventions in the market (Korkman 2022). His magnum opus was *The General Theory of Employment, Interest and Money* (1936). Keynesian economics has been criticized and some economists prefer cancellation of all regulations. There is a continuous pendulum between centralized and distributed control by the government and the market. Sixten Korkman has noticed that Keynesian politics has saved capitalism since it can stop the economic tailspins caused by global finance crises.

An alternative to capitalism is socialism, in which "the means of production are owned and controlled by the state" (Merriam-Webster 2024). Socialism is based on the ideas of Jean-Jacques Rousseau and Karl Marx, whereas capitalism is based on John Locke and Adam Smith (Corning 2011). In capitalism, we focus on our material self-interest, and in socialism, we focus on everyday needs. According to Corning (2011), capitalism and socialism have failed to fulfill their promises since they are unfair and do not fulfill the needs of the present and future generations. The underlying assumptions are too simplistic, and an intermediate form is needed. A desirable society is based on *a mixed economy*, where a welfare state has a significant role (Korkman 2022). The mixed economy combines Smith's free-market economics and Keynes' macroeconomics, thus combining centralized and distributed control that we call hybrid control.

Welfare economics is a field that applies microeconomic techniques to maintain a society's overall welfare or well-being, maximizing the welfare of many individuals (Mishan 1960; Kesting 2010; Backhouse 2023). It has its roots in utilitarianism, but a new welfare economics culminated in the work of Arthur C. Pigou (1912, 1920), defined by John Hicks (1939), and systematized by Paul Samuelson (1947). *John Nash's bargaining solution* in a cooperative game is a theoretical basis for finding a unique, optimal, and fair solution when the agents have conflicting objectives (Lasaulce and Tembine 2011). Still, the incommensurability of the goals is a fundamental problem (Walasek and Brown 2023). Welfare economics has shown that "whenever information is imperfect or markets (including risk markets) are incomplete—that is, essentially almost always—competitive markets are not constrained Pareto efficient" (Stiglitz 2000; Siegfried 2006, p. 71). Welfare economics defines the strict requirements for obtaining a Pareto optimum in a free market, but optimal solutions are not always fair. Sharing information is a form of cooperation that has been further studied in game theory. An example of sharing perfect information is the game of chess (Siegfried 2006, p. 33). It is like playing poker with all the cards always face up.

In addition to the tragedy of the commons, severe problems in economy are Baumol's cost disease and Wagner's law (van der Ploeg 2007): we cannot automate people in many service roles. *Baumol's cost disease*, defined by William J. Baumol and William G. Bowen in 1965 (originally by Jean Fourastie in 1949), means that we cannot increase productivity significantly in services based on human work. Still, we must raise the salaries as in the industry where we can use automation. Otherwise, there would be no services in the end. *Wagner's law* by Adolph Wagner (1883) means that our demands rise when the standard of living increases. A result of this is the increase in the costs of the public sector, and some services must be periodically cut.

John M. Keynes saw that a problem in all societies is reconciling three societal requirements: efficiency of the economy, social fairness, and individual freedom (Korkman 2022). Peter Corning's ideas are almost identical to those of Keynes (Corning 2011). Corning's goal is to find a compromise between two extremes, which Jeremy Bentham and John Rawls, respectively, defined. Both extremes have drawbacks. In Bentham's case, the total utility is simply the sum of the utilities of individual people. Still, the utilities may differ for different individuals since only the average utility is maximized, implying inequality. Rawls' theory includes the greatest equal liberty, equal opportunity, and difference principles, which permit inequalities only if those inequalities benefit the underprivileged (Rawls 1999). In his case, welfare is maximized when the utility of the individuals who have the least is the largest.

Welfare is closely related to *fairness*. Fairness has two basic interpretations (Haidt 2012, p. 161): "On the left, fairness often implies equality, but on the right, it means proportionality—people should be rewarded in proportion to what they contribute, even if that guarantees unequal outcomes." According to Corning (2011), the concept of fairness includes equality, equity, and reciprocity, and they must be combined and balanced to achieve a truly fair society. *Equality* means equal share: we all have biological survival and reproductive needs, which must be satisfied in decent, modest living. *Equity* means rewards for merit, i.e., proportionality, but a significant income disparity between the rich and the poor is seen as unfair. Equity implies a proportional share. First, we must fulfill people's basic needs, and then equity can take a role. *Reciprocity* means that it is fair to expect social obligations in the form of contributions from us according to our ability to do so. It is a form of altruism. Reciprocity is based on the golden rule: "Do unto others as you would have them do unto you." However, other people's tastes may not be the same as ours. In game theory, there is the principle called "tit for tat" that implies reciprocity (Siegfrieds 2006).

An unfair society is organized to benefit only a tiny part of the population at the majority's expense (Acemoglu and Robinson 2020). John M. Keynes had the principles of equality and equity, and his third principle was to offer everyone the possibility to succeed, which is closely related to equality and education, as Adam Smith requested (Korkman 2022). Corning's third concept was already included in Smith's ideas since he emphasized progressive taxation. Smith also asked about banking regulation. There is a trade-off between social security and progressive taxation.

A recent trend in economics is *nonequilibrium* or *complexity economics*, based on Ilya Progogine's nonequilibrium thermodynamics (1955) (Swilling 2020; Arthur 2021). Society is dynamic since we have social rises and declines, and the theory covers those changes. The ideas have also been used in communication networks in information thermodynamics communications (Ge and Yan 2023).

To summarize, the essential role of feedback loops such as in the law of supply and demand is part of systems thinking relevant also in economics. Government interventions are a form of centralized control to improve the stability of the free-market economics, the latter of which is a form of self-organization in a distributed system. The mixed economy is a combination of centralized and distributed control that has been found useful also in engineering.

Political Science

In political science, the defining properties are trust and threat; the threat comes from conflicting objectives regarding especially the common resources (Boulding 1985, pp. 111–112). Threats are a part of political power in the form of law and war. Political science is a study of political and governmental institutions and processes (Merriam-Webster 2024), not only between different states but also within a state.

Social contract and liberal democracy Thomas Hobbes' magnum opus was *Leviathan* (1651), where he proposed the concept of social contract to avoid anarchy in the state of nature, which implies a war of all against all (Fukuyama 1992). John Locke presented his main ideas in *Two Treatises of Government* (1690). His opinions led to discussions on human rights, liberalism, and parliamentary democracy. In liberalism, the authorization to power comes from the citizens. He was one of the pioneers of Enlightenment and a founder of liberalism. However, he emphasized the rights of the majority and neglected the rights of minorities, which we now see as a distinctive feature of liberal democracy. David Hume emphasized the three natural laws of society: inviolate ownership, freedom of contract, and the principle that we must obey contracts.

According to Francis Fukuyama, *liberal democracy* is based on three principles: (1) a state that maintains law and order, (2) maintenance of such a constitutional state that monitors the observance of the law, protects human rights, and limits the state's exercise of power, and (3) democratic responsibility and a feedback mechanism through a voting system (Fukuyama 2014). Other characteristics of liberal democracy are the constitution, free media, and active citizens' dialogue. Liberalism supports tolerance of different opinions, respect for human rights, and a pluralist society. Freedom of speech does not mean we could discriminate other citizens, for example, because of their ethnical background. We should direct the criticism to the elite governing the country. Democracy is a method to achieve the common good or utility using public discussions and popular vote (Ryan 2012, p. 960).

Strengths of liberal democracy include freedom, rule of law, equality, responsibility, pluralism, peaceful power transitions, and protection of minority rights leading to overall satisfaction. Weaknesses include inefficiency in decision-making, vulnerability to populism, and possible instability during crises. The stability can be maintained with effective governance, strong institutions, economic growth, pluralism, and, legitimacy.

A state based on a free-market economy protects the freedom and rights of humans and enterprises (Fukuyama 1992). In addition, the state actively prevents the exclusion of citizens from the job market and ensures that all citizens have similar possibilities to get along. Free social mobility is necessary. Strengthening of inclusion supports economic growth when most people enjoy the benefits of the growth. If the income and wealth differences are too large, this often leads to societal disorder and, eventually, revolutions. Similar rules are also valid in international relationships. The developed countries must help people to live in developing countries.

For the ability to make correct decisions, a requirement is the ability to think critically, offered by the *enlightenment* of the citizens (Pinker 2018) so that they make rational decisions in complex situations. This idea is the basis for using majority votes in our Western democracy. If people are not well educated and independent, democracy does not work, resulting in chaos and anarchy. In a liberal democracy, the opposition and media are essential watchdogs of power. Thomas Hobbes, John Locke, Adam Smith, Voltaire, Jean-Jacques Rousseau, Immanuel Kant, and many others started the Enlightenment (Fukuyama 1992). It has been the reason for our prosperity and will do the same in developing countries.

Adam Smith (1776) defined the three tasks of a state, including defending the country, leading to safety, protecting individuals from injustice, and offering public services that are not profitable for private organizations (Siegfried 2006). Generally, the state takes care of at least part of education, employment, social security, health care, and the care of children and older people. Threats of a state are both internal and external. Just as in psychology, respect, fairness, and trust are requirements for peace, which is, in fact, cooperation. Lawrence Kohlberg's theories are also helpful when measuring the maturity of states, requesting the maturity and enlightenment of its citizens.

Model of ideologies Christopher Zeeman (1979) formed a geometrical model of ideologies shown in Fig. 4.10 where we have drawn Zeeman's original model upside down so that the people are at the bottom and leaders of a state at the top as in ordinary organization charts (Zeeman 1979; Casti 1994, pp. 48–49). The model has a reasonable justification, and the various aspects of political science are nicely combined. We have two conflicting pairs. The first is the horizontal *economic conflict* between equality and opportunity or proportionality, and the second is the vertical *political conflict* between political freedom and power. The former conflict is well known as a conflict between left- and right-wing thinking. The latter conflict was discussed in detail in Acemoglu and Robinson (2020). Zeeman's political conflict is orthogonal to the economic conflict since political power may be emphasized on the left and right. Each ideology can be placed in this double dichotomy. A danger of ideologies is that they may provoke people to engage in dogmatic action rather than thought (Ryan 2012, p. 913).

Jonathan Haidt has emphasized that in the United States, the word *liberal* refers to left-wing politics. Still, in Europe, the word liberal has its original meaning, valuing liberty, including economic activities (Haidt 2012). In the United States, the term *libertarian* roughly corresponds to the European word liberal. We are using the original meaning of the word liberal. In liberal democracy, we appreciate the opinions of the liberal left and liberal right. It is a solution to the social dilemma in the form of ambidexterity.

The economic conflict is an example of a social paradox. The feedback loop in the elections must be free and secret. Without a common goal, the feedback loop

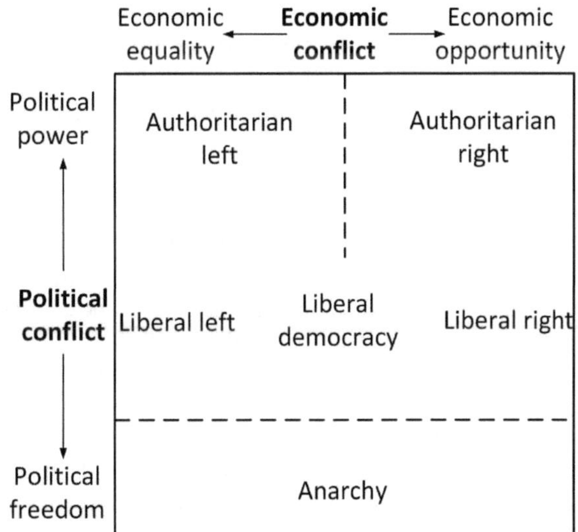

Fig. 4.10 Double dichotomy in Zeeman's geometrical model of ideologies

becomes unstable. In liberal democracy, the goal consists of shared beliefs on causal relationships, leading to appropriate visions. Kenneth E. Boulding (1969) and Guiso et al. (2006) defined a culture and corresponding vision using its values and beliefs that result in the best internal strength and innovativeness (Boulding 1969; Guiso et al. 2006). The development of our society depends on our collective decisions based on our experience, values, and beliefs, leading to the overall happiness of citizens over generations. Planning for the future starts from the imagination of the vision.

The United Nations is guided by three core values: integrity, professionalism, and respect for diversity. These values underpin the UN's mission to promote peace, human rights, and international cooperation among its member states. The European Union's core values are respect for human dignity, freedom, democracy, equality, rule of law, and respect for human rights. These values aim to promote peace, security, and social justice among member states.

In a multiparty system, at least three or four large parties are needed to obtain full democracy, and the opinions of the government's opposition are appreciated as a form of criticism to improve the quality of government. Left-wing politics promotes the interests of society, and right-wing politics promotes the interests of the individual. Ambidexterity here means that society changes dynamically and includes both left-wing and right-wing politics. Everyone is cared for in the former, and at least a minimum income is provided. In the latter, it is possible to succeed through work. A multiparty system corresponds to the conventional control system, where the feedback comes from the people through elections. Thus, a multiparty system works smoothly, especially if everyone behaves ethically. There is some oscillation, but the changes are smoother compared to a two-party system, let alone a one-party system.

Duverger's law by Maurice Duverger (1963) states that a simple majority single-ballot system favors a two-party system whose stability and strength have been discussed since the late 1960s (Riker 1982; Collet 1996). A block system where parties form rigid coalitions called blocks, usually two, is a form of a two-party system. The two-party systems may divide the nation to support the two extremes in the economic conflict (Haidt 2012).

The two extremes in political conflict are (1) anarchy or chaos when the state is too weak and there is too much freedom and (2) authoritarian regime when the state is too strong and there is no freedom. We need a balancing act so that the freedom of the elite at the top and people at the bottom is limited. A request for strict freedom may lead to discrimination. A citizen cannot be completely free since it could result in a social dilemma and eventually anarchy.

Our society is based on subsidiarity (Evans and Zimmermann 2014) and liberal democracy (Fukuyama 1992), which is in Fig. 4.10 the *narrow corridor* between the anarchy and the authoritarian regime, between too weak a state and too strong a state, respectively (Acemoglu and Robinson 2020). Democracy is at the edge of order at the top and chaos at the bottom. Modern democracy was a result of enlightenment. The "corridor" is narrow since it is difficult to reach, and it is difficult to stay there.

Even democratic elections can eventually lead to an authoritarian regime if the voters are not enlightened, and malicious leaders entice them.

Theories of power and institutions *Power theories* have four categories, including positional, pluralistic, structural, and relational views of power (Calhoun et al. 2022). The positional or legitimate power is based on positions and jurisdiction. The pluralistic power described by Robert Dahl is based on the idea that power is distributed and changes depending on the substance of the matter. The structural power described by Steven Lukes is based on the idea that power is structural and difficult to locate, leading to the exclusion of some groups. The relational power described by Manuel Castells assumes that power is in networks and relationships: we must know both the actors and their relationships to understand where the power is. The concept is an example of a system where the parts (actors) and relationships are essential, producing emergent phenomena.

Barbara Geddes (1999) classified authoritarian regimes into monarchies, single-party dictatorships (communism and fascism), personalist dictatorships, and military dictatorships. They are not democracies. *Communism* is an authoritarian socialist left-wing government in which a single party controls state-owned means of production (Merriam-Webster 2024). *Fascism* is an authoritarian right-wing government that has severe regimentation. Eco (1995) has defined 14 features of fascism, including incompatible messages, rejection of the modern world as depravity, action for action's shake, disagreement as treason, discrimination, appeal to social frustration, nationalism, feeling of humiliation, permanent warfare, contempt for the weak, thirst for power, heroism, populism, and impoverished talk (Eco 1995).

Authoritarian countries may make severe mistakes, leading to isolation, recession, injustice, persecution, famine, or want (McNeill 1991; McNeill and McNeill 2003). For example, in the 1440s, the Chinese emperor closed the shipyards, although the ships were part of the "Internet" of its time. Only within one generation shipbuilding skills disappeared, and the isolation gradually resulted in a recession compared to Western Europe. In 1086–1096, Su Song developed the first mechanical clock (Encyclopedia Britannica 2024), and the idea moved to Europe through the Arabs, but the Chinese forgot the discovery (Newth 1996). Later in the 1600s, they were impressed when the Europeans showed their clocks, but they did not realize that the clock was a Chinese invention. The event is an example of how important it is to know history. A democratic deficit may kill the citizens' initiative to develop something new.

An excellent example of how the liberal democracy between the two extremes of coercion and freedom is achieved is the Glorious Revolution in England in 1688 (Schwanitz 1999). The revolution was a nonviolent action of the intelligentsia. Jose Ortega y Gasset warned about the revolt of the masses (Ortega y Gasset 1932). By "masses," he meant uneducated demagogues. Those masses cannot see the difference between nature and technology and do not appreciate history and philosophy and they may even distort the history. History shows that a violent revolution of the masses results in an authoritarian regime. The most significant results of humans may disappear in a few generations. The elite must have a motivation to educate people and lead them to the enlightenment. Without enlightenment, democracy only leads to random decisions. A problem in democracy is that persevering policy is difficult to obtain because of the short terms between elections. In some countries, the parliament is divided into two houses, where the upper house has a longer term between the elections than the lower house.

Liberal democracy is not a natural order but needs a continuous battle between the elite and the citizens (Acemoglu and Robinson 2020). *Subsidiarity* is "the principle that a central authority should have a subsidiary function, performing only those tasks which cannot be performed at a more local level" (Oxford Learner's Dictionaries 2024). It seems to be the best and most efficient form of hierarchy (Bossel 2007, p. 47; Evans and Zimmermann 2014). It is a form of loose vertical coupling (Simon 1973) where the power is distributed, thus offering a similar resilience against catastrophes as in our biosphere (Boulding 1985, pp. 41, 68). For example, municipalities within a state are semiautonomous agents because of their power to collect taxes. The state has a subsidiary role in the system. Autonomy should be maximized to the point beyond which it becomes harmful. Subsidiarity has similarities with the hybrid control architecture used in hybrid self-organizing networks. Distributed control is not explicitly used in subsidiarity, although it is seen as desirable in the heterarchy (Crumley 2008). *Heterarchy* is the same as a distributed control architecture.

Kenneth E. Boulding presented the idea of subsidiarity for social systems with different terms (Boulding 1989). According to him, power must be well specified, and central control should not interfere with local problems too much. He saw three faces of power: destructive, productive, and integrative power. *Destructive power* is based on threat, as in international politics; *productive power* in exchange, as in economics; and *integrative power* in respect, as in social relationships. An organized threat system is also used in democratic countries in the form of punishments and taxes. Authority is always granted from the bottom of the hierarchy, as in democratic countries (Boulding 1985). Otherwise, the power would be very insecure.

Only democracy has a built-in self-correcting system. Liberal democracy contains two principles: liberty and equality (Fukuyama 1992). *Democracy* means a division of political power in the spirit of Montesquieu (Fukuyama 1992). A democracy is *liberal* if it respects human rights and the rights of minorities and offers protection against the power of the state and the majority. There are two theories for forming a state: top-down and bottom-up (Christian 2004, pp. 249–252). In the top-down theory, the government is based on coercion imposed by a privileged and influential minority, typical for communist and fascist countries. In the bottom-up theory, people need state-like structures to survive. Philosophers call this theory *social contract*. According to this theory, we were initially in the state of nature (Fukuyama 1992). In practice, the development was slow and complicated, using both top-down and bottom-up approaches.

History shows that implementing the bottom-up theory has led to prosperity, as evidenced in Europe after the collapse of the Roman Empire (Diamond 1997, p. 416). According to Walter Scheidel, the collapse was the best thing that has happened in Europe. After that, we had small competing states and innovation centers. Development has been fastest in regions that are only moderately connected, neither too tightly nor too loosely, thus representing the subsidiarity principle (Evans and Zimmermann

2014). There has been a long history leading to the present situation. In Europe, we had scholasticism, renaissance, and enlightenment (Pyenson and Sheets-Pyenson 1999; Ryan 2012; Pinker 2018), which led to the present liberal democracies.

Three political powers, including executive, judicial, and legislative, correspond to three political institutions: the state, the rule of law, and accountable democracy (Fukuyama 2011). The executive power is in the government, the judiciary power is in the court, and the legislative power is in the parliament. Montesquieu (1748) suggested that the three powers should be separated, and even in liberal democracies, there are different implementations of the separation of powers. The task of the executive power is to enforce laws and carry out policy; the judiciary and legislative powers constrain the power of the government and direct it to public purposes.

Scholasticism formed the basis of rational knowledge and for and against argumentation. It was affected by Aristotle and used in medieval schools and universities in Europe, characterized by a formal method of discussion (Online Etymology Dictionary 2024). The opposition is a valuable part of the whole.

It is usually understood that history and evolution do not generally have a direction (Popper 1961). The opposite thought is called *historicism*. According to Francis Fukuyama, liberal democracy is "the end of history," which means that history is moving in this direction (Fukuyama 1992). We know this change is slow and not straightforward: there seems to be always a fight between the citizens and the state. The citizens are strong enough if they are well educated.

If we consider evolution as a control problem, we immediately see that humankind does not have a common goal, but there are many conflicting goals. We have both economic and political conflict, forming four goals. The more dangerous conflict is the political conflict between the authoritarian regime (too strong a state) and complete freedom and anarchy (too weak a state) (Acemoglu and Robinson 2020). Chester Barnard (1938) observed that authority is always granted from below in the hierarchy (Boulding 1985, p. 111), i.e., from people who must experience the effects of decisions made at the top of the hierarchy. We need a delicate balance of power between the state and society (Acemoglu and Robinson 2012). Daron Acemoglu, Simon Johnson, and James A. Robinson received in 2024 the Nobel Prize in economics "for studies of how institutions are formed and affect prosperity." They have shown that societies in which the rule of law is poorly implemented and where institutions exploit the people do not generate growth or change for the better.

Although evolution does not have any direction, it has produced more complexity and intelligent, rationally behaving people who can cooperate. Liberal democracy gives the highest total satisfaction (Dorn et al. 2007), as measured, for example, by the happiness index and the fragile state index. It may take some time after the introduction of democratic structures before we can obtain the full benefits of democracy in the form of higher individual happiness.

According to the catastrophe theory, sudden changes between different extremes may occur. Our society is stable with a common goal that we must set. Only after humankind is enlightened enough can we approach the situation where liberal democracy is dominating since it provides us the highest possible total satisfaction in a state where people can fulfill their basic needs, including physiological needs, safety, and justice. Total satisfaction is a form of utility for humankind, which is the goal of cultural evolution. Since there is no common understanding of the utility, cultural evolution tends to have stop–go trends between different extremes. Somebody's happiness may be somebody else's misery.

Institutionalism is a traditional branch of political science (March and Olsen 1984). Institutions include social institutions such as family, education, and media; political institutions such as the legal system or legislature and the state; and economic institutions such as the firm. They have become larger, more complex, and more important to society.

It has been challenging to create and maintain political institutions that are simultaneously powerful, rule-bound, and accountable (Fukuyama 2011, pp. 10–16). According to Fukuyama, the three critical political institutions are the state, the rule of law, and accountable democracy. The state must offer safety and justice to citizens, just as Adam Smith proposed. History shows that a state must have military strength since "wealth is usually needed to underpin military power, and military power is usually needed to acquire and protect wealth" (Kennedy 1988, p. xvi). The leaders in a democracy are bound by a rule of law whose purpose is to offer justice to everyone (Fukuyama 2011), following John Rawls' theory of justice (Rawls 1999), complemented by Peter Corning's ideas on fairness (Corning 2011). Many authoritarian countries fail because they do not offer recognition, i.e., respect for the people (Fukuyama 1992). We must always revise the social contract in a liberal democracy. In liberal democracies, people are generally happy since their quality of life is high. Liberal democracies are also the least fragile.

In ancient Greece, Antiphon distinguished natural and conventional law concepts (Pursiainen 1998, pp. 218–221). Conventional law refers to the laws that are valid in different states. Laws aim at a common good, not the sum of various private goods but "the good of living in common the life of virtue" (Ryan 2012, p. 254). The natural law corresponds to our reason. The most essential requirement in the natural law is self-preservation, implying a need for safety. According to Callicles, the natural law includes the requirement for justice. Plato explained that we need a state that defines laws to guarantee justice and the rules for coexistence. The conventional laws are a compromise without any moral intrinsic value. Justice is originally between two extremes: either we can do someone an injustice without punishment, or we cannot take revenge for the suffered injustice. Conventional law is better for everyone than natural law without any order.

An outmoded cultural heritage has seen violence as a "solution" to problems with neighboring countries. Hugo Grotius (1625) formed the basis for international justice. After the Second World War, the United Nations (1945) defined human rights in the Universal Declaration of Human Rights (1948), but it does not deal with the environment. The declaration starts with: "All human beings are born free and equal in dignity and rights. They are endowed with reason and conscience and should act towards one another in a spirit of brotherhood." The United Nations founded the Human Rights Council in 2006. Only in 2021 did the Council recognize that a healthy and sustainable environment is part of human rights. They rely on human dignity and are becoming a universal value base.

The Convention Relating to the Status of Refugees (1951) was agreed upon by the United Nations. A *rule-based system* called the Liberal International Order (LIO) was developed in the 1940s using a basic norm prohibiting using force in international relations. It is a proposal to solve social dilemmas between governments. There are two international courts: the International Court of Justice (ICJ) (established in 1945) and the International Criminal Court (ICC) (established in 2002), both located in the Hague, The Netherlands. They consider disputes between states and war crimes of individual people, respectively. ICJ is one of the United Nations organs, and ICC is a separate intergovernmental organization.

After the Second World War, the crime of aggression (originally called a crime against peace) was defined as the supreme crime. Since 2018, the Statute of the ICC has included the primary crimes that are genocide, crimes against humanity, war crimes, and the crime of aggression. However, not all countries have ratified the Statute, and in those cases, those countries cannot be directly punished for their violent aggressions. Democratic countries follow the international laws, which makes them vulnerable to cyberattacks. They can only form alliances and use proclamations, sanctions, limitations of traffic abroad, and diplomatic exiles. A state's primary purpose is to guarantee its citizens' safety and fairness. David Hume noticed that if unprincipled villains surround people, they must live among the villains according to their own rules (Pursiainen 1998, pp. 21–22).

The question is about power, greed, and the fight for limited resources in politics. There is always the question of the "original" and fair borders between countries. They should be agreed internationally, not by war and retaliations, and the countries guilty of primary crimes must be punished so that we can live in a safe world. Threats, blackmail, and bribery do not belong to healthy, civilized relationships. International institutes often use unanimous decisions, which may paralyze their operations since they can be seen as a dictatorship of a minority, implying an assumption that certain members know the right choices better than others.

It seems that only a common external threat can make everybody understand that we are living on a finite planet. The biggest problems of our time are the use of fossil fuels, population explosion, the resulting climate change, and lack of resources.

In summary, political science must find a balance in the economic and political conflicts. The economic conflict is an example of a social dilemma. The political conflict between the citizens and the elite is more dangerous. Between the two extremes we have a narrow corridor that we call liberal democracy offering the greatest happiness to the citizens. Feedback appears in elections. Democracy works properly only if the citizens are well educated. The main tasks of a state include safety and justice. The main tools to solve the social dilemmas are social contract and ambidexterity. Subsidiarity is a form of loose coupling.

4.3.4 Humanities

Humanities investigate human constructs as opposed to natural processes in natural sciences and social relations in social sciences (Merriam-Webster 2024). In addition to humanities, *humanism* includes our culture and human-centric ideology that respects human dignity, freedom, fairness, and a sense of community (Korkman 2022). Since the rise of the Enlightenment in the 1700s, humanism has been a secular worldview based on science and rational reasoning. Culture is the whole consisting of our material and spiritual heritage.

Humanities include the core subjects of history, philosophy, languages, and comparative literature, as the Commission of the Humanities recommended in 1979–1980 (Wilson 1998, p. 229; Smith 1997). *Linguistics* is the scientific study of languages. Within linguistics, *philology* is the comparative science of languages (Smith 1997, p. 378). Our primary interest in humanities is in history and philosophy.

Fine arts are creative arts that are not sciences, but they are close to humanities and concerned with the creation of beautiful rather than valuable objects (Merriam-Webster 2024; Oxford Learner's Dictionaries 2024). Fine arts include literature, visual arts (painting, drawing, and sculpture), drama, music, and dance (Wilson 1998, pp. 128, 229, 238). Human sciences have a different identity from natural sciences (Smith 1997, p. 338). A joint property of science and art is the transmission of information since art communicates feeling directly from mind to mind. In this sense, the arts are the antithesis of science.

History

History is a study of events in the past and their explanation. History is an idiographic science, which means that the events in the past are unique. Just as in philosophy, we can consider the history of almost anything. Historians use written records, and the history before the invention of writing is called prehistory that is studied in archeology and is mainly based on material remains of early cultures. Prehistory can be studied also using genetics. Herodotus is sometimes called the father of history, but Leopold von Ranke started modern source-based history with his works in 1824 (Boldt 2017).

Big history is a system theory of history: a record of everything from the big bang to the present (Christian 2004). The focus in *macrohistory* is usually on the history of Homo sapiens that covers the last 300,000 years, which is only 1/50,000 of the age of the universe. If we would reduce the age of the universe to 24 h, Homo sapiens would appear only less than two seconds before the present. In big history, it is then natural to use a timeline where the time scale decreases, and the number of details increases when we approach the present. To understand the present social systems, we must know the world history of the last 500–1000 years.

William H. McNeill's book (McNeill 1991), initially published in 1963, challenged the earlier Sprengler–Toynbee view on separate civilizations and argued that human cultures interacted at every stage of their history. Sprengler published 1918–1922 his two-volume book *The decline of the west*, and Arnold J. Toynbee published

1934–1961 his 12-volume book *A study of history*. After a summary of the Stone Age, the history in McNeill (1991) starts from ancient Mesopotamia, where the first civilization was born. Good general summaries are also included in Jared Diamond's book *Guns, germs, and steel: The fates of human societies* (Diamond 1997), which similarly starts from the agricultural revolution but focuses on environmental effects and in Yuval Noah Harari's *Sapiens: A brief history of humankind* (Harari 2015) that starts from the development of the human brain and presents a fluid summary of the development human culture.

In his two-volume work, Francis Fukuyama explained how today's political institutions developed from the first tribal societies to the first modern state in China, the beginning of the rule of law in India and the Middle East, and the development of political accountability in Europe leading to the rise of democracy (Fukuyama 2011, 2014). Steven Pinker noticed that people worldwide are happier than before because of the gift given by the enlightenment of the citizens (Pinker 2018). David Graeber and David Wengrow's book *The dawn of everything* (Graeber and Wengrow 2021) took a different approach. The goal was to refute, using archeological and anthropological evidence, the social contract concept developed by Thomas Hobbes and Jean-Jacques Rousseau that was supported in Diamond (1997), Fukuyama (2011), Harari (2015) and Pinker (2018). According to Graeber and Wengrow (2021), there is no single original form of human society, and societies have developed without hierarchies and loss of freedom. Three sequels for *The dawn of everything* were planned to be written, but Graeber passed away in 2021.

History does not necessarily have a direction (Popper 1961). Karl R. Popper claimed that historicism is a poor method, not bearing any fruit. He claimed to have refuted historicism, which is "the theory that cultural and social events and situations can be explained by history" (Oxford Learner's Dictionaries 2024). However, there is evidence in many disciplines that evolution has a direction against the entropy law toward more complexity and more optimal or robust systems (Schoemaker 1991; Westerhoff et al. 2009). Thus, although evolution has no goal, it has proceeded, for example, in biology towards more complexity and intelligence because of environmental pressure that forces organisms to improve the probability of survival by maximizing fitness. Popper (1934) developed his falsification theory, which is based on improved scientific theories after successive falsifications or refutations.

Looking at history over hundreds of years, we can see the progress toward a better life in our Western culture (Pinker 2018; Rosling et al. 2018). Fukuyama assumes that history moves from the original state of nature toward liberal democracy (Fukuyama 1992). Furthermore, geography directs history, as was shown in Diamond (1997). The Eurasian geography was favorable for the development of culture. Mountains and waterways have affected the development of states in terms of safety (Marshall 2015).

East Asian culture, especially in China, Japan, and Korea, is more holistic than European culture (Nisbett 2003; Pan et al. 2013). The difference is seen even in Chinese writing, whereas in Europe, we use the alphabet, an example of reductive thinking. The alphabet favored cultural progress since letters were more useful in the printing press, and we could learn to read and write in a few weeks (Stonier 1992).

Therefore, western thinking proceeds bottom-up and is creative, individualistic, and model-oriented. It pays much attention to the emergence of complexity theory and rules, such as causality, feedback, specifications, and standards.

In contrast, Chinese thinking proceeds top-down and is goal-oriented, aiming at the big picture and emphasizing trade-offs and collective interests above personal interests (Pan et al. 2013). Western thinking approaches holism from individualism, and Chinese thinking approaches individualism from holism. In modern thinking, we need a dialectic unity of reductionism and holism since they both have advantages and disadvantages.

Historical investigations aim to bring order to history (Brennan and Houde 2018). We are interested in cultural history instead of war history, which are interconnected since we cannot develop any powerful culture without military power (Kennedy 1988). According to Edwin G. Boring (1950), historical investigation in sciences can be based either on great persons or the spirit of the time (*Zeitgeist* in German) (Brennan and Houde 2018). Thomas Kuhn (1962) proposed in his book *The structure of scientific revolutions* an approach using paradigms that are only changed in scientific revolutions. New paradigms are often mutually incompatible. The paradigms are a form of dogmas if they cannot be questioned and criticized.

Similarly, ideologies in political science can become dogmas. Robert I. Watson (1971) was interested in the relationship between scientific findings and prevailing cultural forces (Brennan and Houde 2018). Kuhn's and Watson's approaches can be seen as variants of the spirit of time view on the history of science. The actual history related to systems thinking is presented in a separate chapter in this book.

Philosophy

Philosophy is not easy to define, and often, we must content ourselves with its classifications. One definition is "a search for a general understanding of values and reality by chiefly speculative rather than observational means" (Merriam-Webster 2024). According to Rosenberg and McIntyre (2020), philosophy deals with the questions that science cannot answer and why science cannot answer these questions. Initially, all natural sciences were called natural philosophy. For example, the term physics appeared for the first time in 1715 instead of natural philosophy, meaning "science treating of properties of matter and energy" (Online Etymology Dictionary 2024). Some authors think that philosophy is now more boldly involving the unification of knowledge (Pyenson and Sheets-Pyenson 1999, p. 423). Philosophy has produced all the present disciplines after the problems in each discipline have found theoretical or experimental basis. Many modern sciences were developed during the second half of the 1800s. Socrates, Plato, and Aristotle were the first philosophers. Rene Descartes (1637) started modern philosophy, and Francis Bacon (1620) began the contemporary philosophy of science. Systems thinking is part of the philosophy of science and engineering.

Philosophy includes some somewhat disconnected subdisciplines, including logic, axiology, epistemology, and metaphysics (Random House Webster's College Dictionary 1999; Rosenberg 2018). They are all of the interest in scientific work and form ingredients of the philosophy of science (Ortega y Gasset 1932; Hall 1962;

Epstein 2019). *Logic* is a search for well-justified rules for reasoning. *Axiology* is a value theory that includes ethics and aesthetics. In *ethics*, our concern is what is right and wrong, good and bad, and justice and injustice for individuals and states. *Aesthetics* deals with the nature of beauty. *Epistemology* is a theory of knowledge. It studies the origin, nature, methods, and finiteness of knowledge. *Metaphysics* is the study of the first principles, including *ontology* or the science of being, and *cosmology*, which deals with the nature of the universe. Our book is a contribution to the philosophy of science and engineering.

4.3.5 Information Technology

Engineering includes various disciplines, such as construction, mechanical, and electrical engineering. In electrical engineering, four disciplines are essential from an information point of view. They are electronics, control, computer, and communications engineering. Control and communication were combined in cybernetics (Wiener 1961; Checkland 1999; Gao 2014). Later, cybernetics was extended to artificial intelligence by adding computing, finally in the form of interacting rational agents as also in complexity theory (Holland 1995; Benbya and McKelvey 2006; Ramage and Shipp 2020; Russell and Norvig 2022). The term artificial intelligence was used to separate it from cybernetics (Ramage and Shipp 2020, p. 22). We briefly describe electronics since it is the implementation method of most systems based on the information concept.

In addition, various system theories are relevant and will be described later. Decision theory is one of the more important ones since a decision block is necessary in a feedback system such as a rational agent. The decisions are usually based on optimization and robustification, which need a model of the environment (Conant and Ashby 1970). The uppermost level in the system hierarchy presented in Boulding (1985) is called *the evaluative system* and is based on decision theory. George N. Saridis combined control, artificial intelligence, and operations research in his intelligent control (Albus and Meystel 2001, p. 112; Saridis 2001, p. 1). Operations research was a precursor of decision theory. Saridis excluded communication since he focused on robotics using a single robot, but now we are also interested in socially interacting robots. Decision theory preceded artificial intelligence and is now part of the latter (Russell and Norvig 2022). Traditionally, artificial intelligence has not addressed the problem of dynamics, which is part of control engineering (Albus and Meystel 2001, p. 112).

In conclusion, in addition to decision theory and the general theory of systems, control, computing, and communication theories are essential for intelligent machines (Mämmelä et al. 2018). *Robotics* combines the results of control and computer engineering, thus covering dynamic situations (Bekey 2005). Common software architectures in robots are divided into the subsumption architecture by Rodney A. Brooks (1986) and the behavior-based architecture by Ronald C. Arkin (1986) (Bekey 2005, p. 3).

Information and communication technologies (ICT) combine the practical results of electronics and control, computer, and communications engineering (Mämmelä et al. 2018). For brevity, we call ICT information technology. In control engineering, a general goal is *self-organization* or the development of *spontaneous order*, as in complexity theory (Benbya and McKelvey 2006). A general goal in computer engineering *is artificial general intelligence (AGI)*, which emulates human intelligence and may be developed even beyond that (Casti 1994; Larson 2021).

In robotics, control, computer, and communications engineering work together, and the goal is to produce a robot that resembles a human. Another goal in computer engineering is a human in *virtual reality*, which is "an artificial environment which is experienced through sensory stimuli provided by a computer and in which one's actions partially determine what happens in the environment" (Merriam-Webster 2024). In communications, the final goal is *telepresence*, technology that "enables a person to perform actions in a distant or virtual location as if physically present in that location" (Merriam-Webster 2024). Telepresence is a complement of virtual reality, where a human has an experience of being in an environment that does not necessarily exist (Stone 2001). Ultimately, we need an evolutionary process and perhaps organic matter to attain the complexity required to achieve the goals.

Digital Electronics

Electronics includes analog and digital electronics. Our focus is on digital electronics, but there are some books on analog electronics in the bibliography. After Robert Noyce (1959) invented the planar integrated circuit, there was exponential development, so the number of transistors on a chip doubled initially every year and later every second year. Gordon Moore made this kind of prediction (Mämmelä and Anttonen 2017), and it is often called *Moore's law*, which describes the rate of our learning process and has become a self-fulfilling prediction. The law was valid for about 60 years, from the invention of the integrated circuit in 1959 until about 2020, but the energy efficiency of a transistor has not improved as expected since 2004. The most critical steps in developing electronics have been the invention of transistors, integrated circuits, microprocessors, digital signal processors, and multicore processors. All Boolean functions can be written with logical AND, OR, and NOT operations. All logic can be implemented with two-input NAND (NOT AND) or NOR (NOT OR) gates. That is why the complexity can be measured using the number of two-input NAND gates, called the gate count.

Quantum computers are a complementary technology to silicon electronics, but they are not general-purpose computers, and their energy and space efficiency have not yet developed significantly (Mämmelä and Anttonen 2017; Riekki and Mämmelä 2021). A quantum computer uses quantum mechanical phenomena. The needed superconductivity may need either an extremely low temperature or an extremely high pressure, which is impossible with small energy and size. Therefore, quantum computers are so far best suited to servers and supercomputers whose energy consumption and size are not critical. Only a few intractable algorithms in classical computers can be made tractable in quantum computers (Arora and Barak 2009). An important example is integer factorization.

Control Engineering

Control engineering is based on the feedback concept (Ogata 2010; Albus and Meystel 2001), a prerequisite to intelligent behavior (Stonier 1992, pp. 37–38; 1997, pp. 52, 97). Control systems have existed since ancient times, but modern control engineering started from Harry Nyquist's (1932) stability analysis, and systems based on feedback were called automatic. A system is *automatic* if it works without manual intervention but may receive some external control signals. An automatic system is *autonomous* or self-governing if it can achieve the externally given goal using sensing signals but without any other external control signals during operation (Bekey 2005; Nguyen et al. 2012). An autonomous agent must have the ability to set its goals, which is possible with free will (Schoemaker 1991). A technical system can only be *semiautonomous* since it cannot set its own goals and it always needs human supervision.

Generally, feedback consists of sense, decision, and action blocks, thus forming an agent. The action block controls the environment, sometimes called a plant or process. The environment depends on how the boundary of the control system is defined. For example, in communications networks, the environment is the network environment, but in the physical layer, it is the physical channel, also called medium, either wired or wireless. For stable operation, the decision block usually needs a goal.

The *order* of a control system indicates the degree of the denominator polynomial of a transfer function or the number of independent energy storage elements like capacitors or inductors in the system. Higher-order control systems exhibit more complex behavior (larger delays and oscillations and possible instability) compared to lower-order systems and are thus more difficult to manage. First- and second-order control loops are the most common loops. Negative second-order feedback loops may be overdamped or underdamped depending on system parameters (Ogata 2010, p. 166; Strogatz 2014). In the *underdamped* case, the step response initially shows exponential growth, but after an overshoot, there are some oscillations. The system is stable if bounded inputs produce bounded outputs; thus, the oscillations' amplitude does not grow to infinity. In the *overdamped* case, there are no oscillations, and the response resembles an s-curve: first, exponential growth and then saturation because of the feedback. All first-order loops are overdamped. Gardner's hype cycle (1995) is an example of an underdamped system (Dedehayir and Steinert 2016). A similar hype cycle can also be seen in the popularity of new research topics (Fig. 2.11). Many books include the theory of negative feedback, but positive feedback is seldom covered in detail, although it is important, especially in biology and economics. Some references on positive feedback include (Maruyama 1963; DeAngelis et al. 1986; Sterman 2000; Camazine et al. 2001; Lee 2004; Cosentino and Bates 2012; Ingalls 2013; Alon 2020).

A simple form of decision block called a controller is obtained by computing the difference between the goal and plant output as an *error signal*, whose power is minimized using the feedback. A common form is *the proportional-integral-derive (PID) controller* by Nicolas Minorsky (1922) (Gao 2014). It is simple to use and applies to most dynamic systems in practice. There are also shortcomings from limitations of the control law, complications associated with the integral action, and noise problems with the derivative action. An alternative is *model-predictive control* (MPC) by Charles R. Cutler and B. C. Ramaker (1979) using the name dynamic matrix control (Xi et al. 2013). MPC solves constrained control problems with a need for optimization and prediction for the future behavior of the dynamic system. Another viable alternative is *active disturbance rejection control* (ADRC), as proposed by Jingqing Han (1989) (Gao 2014). The disturbances are first estimated and canceled out, thus improving stability. In addition to feedback closed-loop control, we can use open-loop control without any sense block. If the act block is removed, the system is a monitoring system, which may also include feedback, but the environment is not controlled.

According to the *separation theorem*, control and estimation of the model parameters can be separated if the environment is linear or nonlinear, the metric is quadratic, and the noise is additive and Gaussian (Joseph and Tou 1961; Gunckel and Franklin 1963; Curry 1969). Some authors use the term Conant-Ashby theorem for the separation theorem (Skyttner 2005, p. 104), although it was discovered about ten years earlier. A quadratic metric has terms up to the second degree, as in mean-square error and least squares estimation.

Although not described in the standard textbooks such as (Ogata 2010; Dorf and Bishop 2017), control engineering has developed and classified the concepts of hierarchy (Mesarovic et al. 1970; Mesarovic 1970) and degree of centralization (Sandell et al. 1978; Frampton et al. 2010). The hierarchies are divided into nested and nonnested hierarchies; the nonnested hierarchies include dominance and layer hierarchies (Ahl and Allen 1996). The degrees of centralization, also called *control topology*, include centralized, decentralized, distributed, and hybrid, a combination of centralized and distributed control. Honeywell developed the first distributed control system in 1975 (Samad et al. 2007).

Computer Engineering

Computer science is a theory of computing and the design of computers. Information technology considers practical applications of computer science. Computer engineering is part of information technology. As can be seen, some related terms are computer-based, and some are information-based. We prefer the definition according to which *information technology* is "commonly a synonym for computers and computer networks but more broadly designating any technology that is used to generate, store, process, and/or distribute information electronically, including television and telephone" (Chandler and Munday 2011, p. 211).

Alan Turing (1938) started computer engineering as a separate discipline and defined a universal Turing machine that represents any digital computer (Larson 2021) well before the first practical digital computer was born (1946). Turing's theory led to the stored-program computer by John von Neumann (1946), now called the *von Neumann architecture*. The instructions share the same memory and pathways. A modified von Neumann architecture, often called the *Harvard architecture*, was developed in the context of microcontroller design. For speed advantage, the architecture has separate memories and pathways for instructions and data (Pawson 2022). The names of the architectures are still disputed.

Computing may be either local or distributed (Mämmelä et al. 2023). Computing is divided into sequential and concurrent computing, and the latter is divided into parallel and distributed computing (van Steen and Tanenbaum 2017). Local computing is sequential or parallel. The conventional form of computing is *sequential computing*, where the steps are sequential or in serial form. Almost all traditional computers are sequential since the implementation and programming are relatively straightforward. The computers execute one instruction at a time. According to Rajsbaum and Raynal (2020), not all computing tasks can be reduced to sequential computing. Among such tasks are applications that involve large amounts of data that are continually updated, resource allocation problems, clock synchronization, and distributed graph algorithms.

A shared memory, a global clock, and tight coupling between computing units characterize *parallel computing*. The memory may be a bottleneck in large systems where many agents use it simultaneously. Our brain is comparable to massively parallel computing without a clock (Kanerva 2000), and it seems that the brain cannot be represented using sequential computing (Rajsbaum and Raynal 2020). Part of the emergent properties of our mind may be hidden in this observation. Distributed computing uses a distributed memory using message passing, local clocks, and loose coupling between computing units. A benefit of distributed computing is independent failures of computing units (Coulouris et al. 2012). The fastest computers use concurrent computing to manage power consumption since development in electronics is no longer exponential.

Computing paradigms are divided into grid, cloud, fog, edge, and dew computing (Ray 2018). *Grid computing* is a form of distributed computing consisting of many loosely coupled computers in a network to perform a large task. In *cloud computing*, a carrier or a provider provides distributed computing services to users over the Internet. A *cloud* is a platform for distributed computing. *Edge computing* is done near the terminals at a network's edge. Since edge computing reduces delays, the stability of the network is improved compared to the older concept called cloud computing. Edge computing serves applications that include the Internet of Things (IoT). In *fog computing*, the computing resources are close to end users' devices in fixed communication. The basic idea in edge and fog computing is to offer computation close to the user. The purpose of *dew computing* is to solve the problem of cloud computing that it requires an Internet connection (Wang 2016). Cloud computing cannot be used when the connection is lost, and locally saved files are used instead. The update of the files called synchronization is done when the connection is again available.

An important theory in computer engineering is *computational complexity theory* (Dewdney 2004), which should not be mixed up with complexity theory, which originated in biology (Benbya and McKelvey 2006). Computational complexity theory considers fundamental limits, tractability, and complexity of computation. Decision problems are divided into *tractable* with polynomial complexity, *intractable* (i.e., intrinsically difficult) with exponential complexity without a quick solution, and *unsolvable* without any solution even in principle. All intractable problems can be reduced to a satisfiability problem with exponential complexity, which runs “screaming off into infinity” (Dewdney 2004, p. 190). Many such problems are related to using basic resources, such as the traveling salesman problem (shortest path problem), knapsack problem, or timetable design.

Artificial intelligence (AI), a theory of rational agents (Russell and Norvig 2022), is also a broad topic in computer engineering. Modern AI is based on deduction, inductive reasoning, and statistical analysis of big data without any real understanding (Larson 2021). Human thinking is a nonlinear multidimensional process based on massively parallel processing, which comes from the structure of our brain (Raami 2015; Stanovich et al. 2016).

Based on the Church-Turing thesis (1936) and the assumed increase in the speed of computers, some authors claim that machine intelligence may surpass human intelligence, thus producing artificial general intelligence (AGI) or strong AI (Kurzweil 1999; Moravec 1999; Casti 1994, pp. 150–166). However, intelligence is not only a question of speed since already existing supercomputers can surpass the computing speed of the human brain (Mämmelä and Anttonen 2017). It is more about the architecture of the computing. *Moravec’s paradox* by Hans Moravec tells us that humans and machines complement each other: the tasks that a human finds relatively straightforward, such as walking, cycling, or driving a car, are complex for a computer, but the functions that are complex for a human such as number crunching are accessible for a computer. As explained in Roberts (2020), intelligent behavior needs a body since we learn with our whole body, not only with our brain. The use of AI in decision-making may be dangerous since the objectivity of the decisions may be an illusion. The machine reflects the opinions of its programmer (O’Neill 2016).

Communications Engineering

At the core of communications engineering is the theory of information transmission, usually called *information theory*, which is at the statistical level of information (Gitt 1989) and only valid for a single isolated link. In standard language, the concept of information also includes semantics, but semantic information theory has been difficult to realize (Stonier 1992, 1997; Checkland 1999; Qin et al. 2023). In networks, a relevant theory is optimization decomposition.

One system-theoretical result is the Open Systems Interconnection (OSI) reference model (Tanenbaum and Wetherall 2011; Kurose and Ross 2013), which has seven layers, including physical, data link, network, transport, session, presentation, and application layers, from the bottom up. The tasks of each layer are described in Table 4.8 using (Walke 1999). The layer structure is defined so that Layers 5–7 can operate without knowing the details of the communication network formed in Layers 1–4. Furthermore, Layer 4 assumes that the information from Layers 1–2 is essentially error-free. Each layer has a different name for the protocol data unit (PDU) since additional control information is included when we move upwards in the hierarchy. The physical layer is responsible for the bits and symbols to be transmitted and received through a link. Bits are usually modulated to include several bits in a transmitted symbol. The data link layer transmits frames, and the network layer transmits packets or datagrams. Different layers have different times cales for time-scale separation, so the lowest layer is the fastest (Mämmelä et al. 2023). In a way, the application layer can be seen as part of the physical layer, although it is the highest in the hierarchy. The application layer is as fast as the physical layer. The newest version of the OSI standard is ISO/IEC 7498-1:1994 Information Technology—Open Systems Interconnection—Basic Reference Model: The Basic Model.

In practice, we use a simplified version of the OSI model, merging the session and presentation layers into the application layer (Tanenbaum and Wetherall 2011). Physical and data link layers are sometimes merged to form a link layer. In a practical implementation, separate processors for the application layer and physical layer base-band algorithms exist, respectively. The more complicated operations are done in the digital parts in the baseband before up-conversion and after down-conversion. A practical reference model is the Transmission Control Protocol/Internet Protocol (TCP/IP) model used on the Internet. The TCP and IP protocols are the major protocols in the transport and network layers, respectively.

In modern networks, an additional level, network service orchestration (NSO), is above network management (Mijumbi 2016; Saraiva de Sousa et al. 2019). NSO is based on three enabling technologies: cloud computing, software-defined networks,

Table 4.8 Layers and their tasks in the OSI model

Layer	Tasks of the layer
7. Application layer	The layer is the interface between the user and the network including services for data transmission between different processes (for example file transfer), for managing distributed systems such as distributed database access and allowing a process to be run in different computers
6. Presentation layer	The layer offers services to the application to transform data structures into a standard format and to compress and encrypt the data
5. Session layer	The layer controls the communication between user terminals, for example terminal identification and the form of data exchange
4. Transport layer	The layer offers network independent services for end-to-end data transport. The layer segments and reassembles the messages and controls the data flow. The PDU is a *segment*
3. Network layer	The layer includes management of the network, including routing, address interpretation, and optimal path detection. The PDU is a *datagram*, which is usually called a *packet*. The time scale is in the order of 1–10 s
2. Data link layer	The layer forwards the bits error free to the network layer. For that purpose, the layer uses systematic redundancy, and when errors are detected, an automatic repeat request (ARQ) message is transmitted. The PDU is a *frame*. The time scale is in the order of 1 ms
1. Physical layer	The layer transmits user bits bidirectionally over cable or wireless channels and defines the mechanical and electrical characteristics of the physical system. The layer modulates the signals in transmission and demodulates the signals in reception so that the bit errors are avoided as much as possible. The PDU is a *bit*. The time scale is in the order of 0.001 ms

and network function virtualization (NFV), signs of network softwarization (Popescu and Westerhagen 2022). *Network service orchestration* refers to "automated management and control processes involved in end-to-end services deployment and operations performed mainly by telecommunication operators and service providers, involving different types of resources and potentially multiple operators." In NFV, management creates and manages a virtual network infrastructure consisting of virtual resources: data links, routers, memory capacity, and processing capacity. Orchestration collects the virtual resources needed by an end-to-end service from the virtual resources provided by the manager.

Like Moore's law, there is *Cooper's law* (1997), according to which the wireless network capacity has doubled every 30 months since Marconi's time (Pietikäinen and Silven 2023). The number of simultaneous voice conversations and data transactions in the useful radio spectrum measures the wireless capacity. Most of the progress has been obtained by reducing the cell size. More minor improvements have been made by using a larger bandwidth and improving the spectral efficiency, thus resulting in a higher area spectral efficiency. Saturation is expected because of at least two reasons. We cannot reduce cell sizes without limits because of the complexity of interference management and the end of Moore's law. Charles A. Eldering et al. (1999) noticed that the link bit rates for a given distance have increased by a factor of 100 every ten years (Mämmelä and Anttonen 2017). Later, Phil Edholm (2004) and Gerhart Fettweis (2012) made similar observations. This trend must saturate because of a computation-communication trade-off caused by the Landauer and Shannon limits for a finite energy consumption, as shown in Mämmelä and Anttonen (2017).

As in control engineering, a separation theorem exists in communications where the theory leads to the estimator-correlator receiver (Kailath 1960, 1969). The channel is first estimated and then demodulated with a correlator.

4.4 Chapter Summary and Recommended Reading

In this chapter, we introduced the reader to the basics of systems thinking, which is complementary but not a replacement for analytical thinking. We defined a system in two ways: using a general definition as a set of parts and their relationships and a more specific definition as a set of interacting agents. The latter definition is helpful in self-organizing systems, called complex adaptive systems. We need a problem definition and a tentative solution for analytical and systems thinking. Therefore, we should construct a roadmap and vision after the literature review, usually for the next ten years. In this way, it is easier to define the research problems and the actual research. We can provide a reliable vision for the next ten years if we know the history of several decades, preferably of the last 50–100 years, but to understand social systems, our perspective should be 500–1000 years. We can find the history from books and review papers, but we must collect the most recent history for, say, the last ten years from original papers. We presented a hierarchy of core sciences and technology. The hierarchy of sciences includes physics, chemistry, biology, psychology, sociology, economics, political science, history, and philosophy. In addition, among formal sciences, we have mathematics.

All physical, biological, social, and technical systems are open, not isolated since they exchange materials, energy, and information with their environment. Nonlinear feedback loops produce a phenomenon called emergence, which makes reduction and deduction in the analytical thinking impossible. The system is then analytically intractable. We cannot predict the global behavior of a complex system from local behavior, and local optimization does not lead to global optimization. We presented the relevant disciplines as a hierarchy and gave a brief overview of each.

A good starting point for an overview of systems thinking is (Ramage and Shipp 2020), which provides a classification of system theories, the biographies of significant systems thinkers of the last century, and samples of their texts. In Checkland (1999), the author has a summary of systems thinking from ancient times until about 1980, since the book's first edition was published around that time. Otherwise, the emphasis is on soft systems thinking used in management science, and the recent engineering development is not included. Roger Penrose presented a holistic view on physics (Penrose 1999), Tom Stonier and Edward O. Wilson on biology (Stonier 1992, 1997; Wilson 1998), and George P. Richardson on social sciences (Richardson 1991).

Discussion Questions

1. How is a system defined?
2. Why do we need visions and roadmaps? How can we produce them?
3. What are the basic resources and why are they important in systems thinking?
4. In which ways is human knowledge bounded?
5. What are the core sciences, and how do they form a hierarchy?

References

Aaltonen M (2007) The return to multi-causality. J Futures Stud 12(1):81–86

Aben B et al (2012) About the distinction between working memory and short-term memory. Front Psychol 3:1–9. https://doi.org/10.3389/fpsyg.2012.00301

Acemoglu D, Robinson JA (2012) Why nations fail: the origins of power, prosperity, and poverty. Profile Books, London

Acemoglu D, Robinson JA (2020) The narrow corridor: how nations struggle for liberty. Penguin Books, London

Ahl V, Allen TFH (1996) Hierarchy theory: a vision, vocabulary, and epistemology. Columbia University Press, New York

Ajayi TM et al (2023) Characterization of just one atom synchrotron X-rays. Nature 618(7963):69–73

Albus JS (1991) Outline for a theory of intelligence. IEEE Trans Syst Man Cybern 21(3):473–509

Albus JS (2011) Path to a better world: a plan for prosperity, opportunity, and economic justice. iUniverse, Bloomington, IN

Albus JS, Meystel AM (2001) Engineering of mind: an introduction to the science of intelligent systems. Wiley, New York
Aldred J (2020) Licence to be bad: how economics corrupted us. Penguin, London
Alon U (2007) Simplicity in biology. Nature 446:497. https://doi.org/10.1038/446497a
Alon U (2020) An introduction to systems biology: design principles of biological circuits, 2nd edn. Chapman & Hall/CRC, Boca Ratoon, FL
Arora S, Barak B (2009) Computational complexity: a modern approach. Cambridge University Press, New York
Arthur WB (2021) Foundations of complexity economics. Nat Rev Phys 3:136–145. https://doi.org/10.1038/s42254-020-00273-3
Asimov I (1964) Visit to the world's fair of 2014. The New York Times, 16 Aug. https://archive.nytimes.com/. Accessed 6 Sept 2022
Asimov I (1974) Words of science and the history behind them, rev. Book Club Associates, London
Atiyah M (2002) Mathematics in the 20th century. Bull Lond Math Soc 34(1):1–15
Austen-Smith D, Banks JS (1996) Information aggregation, rationality, and the Condorcet jury theorem. Am Polit Sci Rev 90(1):34–45
Avizienis A et al (2004) Basic concepts and taxonomy of dependable and secure computing. IEEE Trans Dependable Secure Comput 1(1):11–33
Backhouse R (2023) The ordinary business of life: a history of economics from the ancient world to the twenty-first century, 2nd edn. Princeton University Press, Princeton, NJ
Barrow JD (1998) Impossibility: the limits of science and the science of limits. Oxford University Press, New York
Bartheld CS et al (2016) The search for true numbers of neurons and glial cells in the human brain: a review of 150 years of cell counting. J Comp Neurol 524(18):3675–3895
Baumeister RF (1987) How the self became a problem: a psychological review of historical research. J Pers Soc Psychol 52(1):163–176
Baumeister RF et al (2001) Bad is stronger than good. Rev Gen Psychol 5(4):323–370
Bekey GA (2005) Autonomous robots: from biological inspiration to implementation and control. MIT Press, Cambridge, MA
Benbya H, McKelvey B (2006) Toward a complexity theory of information systems development. Inf Technol People 19(1):12–34
Benjafield JG (2020) Vocabulary sharing among subjects belonging to the hierarchy of sciences. Scientometrics 125:1965–1982. https://doi.org/10.1007/s11192-020-03671-7
Bianconi E et al (2013) An estimation of the number of cells in the human body. Ann Hum Biol 40(6):463–471
Bielecki J et al (2023) Associative learning in the box jellyfish *Tripedalia cystophora*. Curr Biol 33(19):4150–4159
Boe JL et al (2019) Which way to the dawn of speech?: reanalyzing half a century of debates and data in light of speech science. Sci Adv 5(12):1–23
Bohm D, Peat FD (2000) Science, order, and creativity, 2nd edn. Routledge, London
Boldt AD (2017) Leopold von Ranke on Irish history and the Irish nation. Cogent Arts Humanit 4:1–19. https://doi.org/10.1080/23311983.2017.1314629
Boogerd FC et al (2007) Towards philosophical foundations of systems biology: introduction. In: Boogerd FC et al (eds) Systems biology: philosophical foundations. Elsevier, Amsterdam, pp 3–22
Bossel H (2007) Systems and models: complexity, dynamics, evolution, sustainability. Books on Demand, Norderstedt, Germany
Boulding KE (1969) Economics and a moral science. Am Econ Rev 59(1):1–12
Boulding KE (1978) Ecodynamics: a new theory of societal evolution. Sage, Beverly Hills, CA
Boulding KE (1985) The world as a total system. Sage, Beverly Hills, CA
Boulding KE (1989) Three faces of power. Sage, Beverly Hills, CA
Boulton JG et al (2015) Embracing complexity: strategic perspectives for an age of turbulence. Oxford University Press, Oxford, UK

Boyer CB, Merzbach UC (1991) A history of mathematics, 2nd rev. Wiley, New York
Bregman B (2020) Humankind: a hopeful history. Little, Brown and Company, New York
Brennan JF, Houde KA (2018) History and systems of psychology, 7th edn. Cambridge University Press, Cambridge, UK
Buchanan M (2002) Small world: uncovering nature's hidden networks. W. W. Norton and Company, New York
Calhoun C et al (eds) (2022) Contemporary sociological theory. Wiley, Hoboken, NJ
Calvez JP (1993) Embedded real-time systems: a specification and design methodology. Wiley, Chichester, UK
Camazine S et al (2001) Self-organization in biological systems. Princeton University Press, Princeton, NJ
Casti JL (1991) Chaos, Gödel, and truth. In: Casti JL, Karlqvist A (eds) Beyond belief: randomness, prediction and explanation in science. CRC Press, Boca Raton, FL, pp 280–327
Casti JL (1994), Complexification: Explaining paradoxical world through the science of surprise. Abacus, London
Cerceau FR (2010) What possible life forms could exist on other planets: a historical overview. Orig Life Evol Biosph 40:195–202. https://doi.org/10.1007/s11084-010-9200-7
Chance F (2021) Lessons from a dragonfly's brain. IEEE Spectr 58(8):29–33
Chandler D, Munday R (2011) A dictionary of media and communication. Oxford University Press, Oxford, UK
Chapman RL (2013) Algae: the world's most important 'plants'—an introduction. Mitig Adapt Strat Glob Change 18(1):5–12
Checkland P (1999) Systems thinking, systems practice: includes a 30-year retrospective, rev. Wiley, Chichester, UK
Checkley K (1997) The first seven … and the eighth: a conversation with Howard Gardner. Teach Mult Intell 55(1):8–13
Chen FC, Li WH (2001) Genomic divergences between humans and other hominoids and the effective population size of the common ancestor of humans and chimpanzees. Am J Hum Genet 68(2):444–456
Cherry C (1962) On communication before the days of radio. Proc IRE 50(5):1143–1145
Choi BCK, Pak AWP (2006) Multidisciplinarity, interdisciplinarity and transdisciplinarity in health research, services, education and policy: 1. Definitions, objectives, and evidence of effectiveness. Clin Investig Med 29(6):351–364
Christensen CM (2006) The innovator's dilemma. HarperCollins Publishers, New York
Christian D (2004) Maps of time: an introduction to big history. University of California Press, Berkeley, CA
Claasen TACM, Mecklenbräuker WFG (1985) Adaptive techniques for signal processing in communications. IEEE Commun Mag 23(11):8–19
Cohen L (2005) The history of noise [on the 100th anniversary of its birth]. IEEE Signal Process Mag 22(6):20–45
Cole S (1983) The hierarchy of the sciences? Am J Sociol 89(1):111–139
Collet C (1996) Trends: third parties and the two-party system. Public Opin Q 60(3):431–449
Conant RC, Ashby WR (1970) Every good regulator of a system must be a model of that system. Int J Syst Sci 1(2):89–97
Corning PA (2002) The re-emergence of 'emergence': a venerable concept in search of a theory. Complexity 7(6):18–30
Corning PA (2011) The fair society: the science of human nature and the pursuit of social justice. University of Chicago Press, Chicago, IL
Cornish-Bowden A, Luz Cardenas M (2020) Contrasting theories of life: historical context, current theories. In search of an ideal theory. Biosystems 188:1–50. https://doi.org/10.1016/j.biosystems.2019.104063
Cosentino C, Bates D (2012) Feedback control in systems biology. CRC Press, Roca Baton, FL

Coulouris G et al (2012) Distributed systems: concepts and design, 5th edn. Addison-Wesley, Boston, MA
Courtland R (2016) Transistors could stop shrinking in 2021. IEEE Spectr 53(9):9–11
Cowan N (2000) The magical number 4 in short-term memory: a reconsideration of mental storage capacity. Behav Brain Sci 24(1):87–185
Crumley CL (2008) Heterarchy and the analysis of complex societies. Archaeol Pap Am Anthropol Assoc 6(1):1–5
Curry RE (1969) A separation theorem for nonlinear measurements. IEEE Trans Autom Control 14(5):561–564
Dabney W et al (2020) A distributional code for value in dopamine-based reinforcement learning. Nature 577:671–675. https://doi.org/10.1038/s41586-019-1924-6
Dawes RM, Messick DM (2000) Social dilemmas. Int J Psychol 35(2):111–116
de Coulon F (1986) Signal theory and processing. Artech House, Deadham, MA
de Haan J (2006) How emergence arises. Ecol Complex 3(4):293–301
de Montesquieu B (2001) The spirit of laws. Batoche Books, Kitchener, ON, Canada
de Oliveira MJ (2017) Equilibrium thermodynamics, 2nd edn. Springer-Verlag, Berlin
De Wolf T, Holvoet T (2005) Emergence versus self-organisation: different concepts but promising when combined. In: Brueckner S et al (eds) Engineering self-organizing systems, methods, and applications. Springer-Verlag, Berlin, pp 1–15
DeAngelis DL et al (1986) Positive feedback in natural systems. Springer-Verlag, Berlin
Dedehayir O, Steinert M (2016) The hype cycle model: a review and future directions. Technol Forecast Soc Change 108:28–41. https://doi.org/10.1016/j.techfore.2016.04.005
Denning PJ, Metcalfe MR (1997) Beyond calculation. Springer-Verlag, New York
Dewdney AK (2004) Beyond reason: eight great problems that reveal the limits of science. Wiley, Hoboken, NJ
Dharani K (2015) The biology of thought: a neuronal mechanism in the generation of thought—a new molecular model. Elsevier, London
Diamond J (1997) Guns, germs, and steel: the fates of human societies. W. W. Norton & Company, New York
Dodd MS et al (2017) Evidence for early life in Earth's oldest hydrothermal vent precipitates. Nature 543:60–65. https://doi.org/10.1038/nature21377
Dorf RC, Bishop RH (2017) Modern control systems, 13th edn. Pearson, New York
Dorn D et al (2007) Is it culture or democracy? The impact of democracy and culture on happiness. Soc Indic Res 82:505–526. https://doi.org/10.1007/s11205-006-9048-4
Doumont JL (2002) Magical numbers: the seven-plus-or-minus-two myth. IEEE Trans Prof Commun 45(2):123–127
Dufva M, Rekola S (2023) Megatrends 2023: understanding an era of surprises. Sitra, Helsinki, Finland
Dufva M, Rowley C (2022) Weak signals: stories about futures. Sitra, Helsinki, Finland
Dunbar R (2011) How many 'friends' can you really have? IEEE Spectr 48(6):81, 83
Dunning D (2011) The Dunning–Kruger effect: on being ignorant of one's own ignorance. Adv Exp Soc Psychol 44:247–296. https://doi.org/10.1016/B978-0-12-385522-0.00005-6
Dupont C (2009) Epigenetics: definition, mechanisms and clinical perspective. Sem Reprod Med 27(5):351–357
Eco U (1995) Eternal fascism: fourteen ways of looking at a blackshirt. The New York Review of Books, 22 June, pp 12–15
Edelman PH (2002) On legal interpretations of the Condorcet jury theorem. J Legal Stud 31(2):327–349
Einevoll GT et al (2019) The scientific case for brain simulations. Neuron 102(4):735–744
Ekman P (2003) Emotions revealed: recognizing faces and feelings to improve communication and emotional life. Henry Holt and Company, New York
Elsasser W (1966) Atom and organism. Princeton University Press, Princeton, NJ

Elsasser WM (1987) Reflections on a theory of organisms: holism in biology. The Johns Hopkins University Press, Baltimore, MD
Encyclopedia Britannica (2024). https://www.britannica.com. Accessed 5 Nov 2024
Epstein D (2019) Range: why generalists triumph in a specialized world. Riverhead Books, New York
Ericsson KA (2006) The influence of experience and deliberate practice on the development of superior expert performance. In: Ericsson KA et al (eds) The Cambridge handbook of expertise and expert performance. Cambridge University Press, Cambridge, UK, pp 683–703
Evans M, Zimmermann A (eds) (2014) Global perspectives on subsidiarity. Springer, Dordrecht, The Netherlands
Eykhoff P (1960) Adaptive and optimalizing control systems. IEEE Trans Autom Control 5(2):148–151
Fan X et al (2023) Measurement of the electron magnetic moment. Phys Rev Lett 130(7):1–6
Fanelli D (2010) "Positive" results increase down the hierarchy of the sciences. PLoS ONE 5(4):1–10
Fanelli D, Glänzel W (2013) Bibliometric evidence for a hierarchy of the sciences. PLoS ONE 8(6):1–11
Fettweis GP (2014) The tactile Internet: applications and challenges. IEEE Veh Technol Mag 9(1):64–70
Fettweis GP, Alamouti S (2014) 5G: personal mobile Internet beyond what cellular did to telephony. IEEE Commun Mag 52(2):140–145
Forrester JW (2007) System dynamics—a personal view of the first fifty years. Syst Dyn Rev 23(2/3):345–358
Fox D (2011) Limits of intelligence. Sci Am 305(1):36–43
Frampton KD et al (2010) A comparison of decentralized, distributed, and centralized vibro-acoustic control. J Acoust Soc Am 128:2798–2806. https://doi.org/10.1121/1.3183369
Francois C (1999) Systemics and cybernetics in a historical perspective. Systems Research and Behavioral Science 16(3): 203-219
Francois C (2000) An exploration of the historical meaning of systemics in western thought. Systems 5(1–2):3–14
Francois C (2006) Transdisciplinary unified theory. Syst Res Behav Sci 23(5):617–624
Frank SA, Slatkin M (1992) Fisher's fundamental theorem of natural selection. TREE 7(3):92–95
Frei R, Di Marzo Serugendo G (2011a) Concepts in complexity engineering. Int J Bio-Inspired Comput 3(2):123–139
Frei R, Di Marzo Serugendo G (2011b) Advances in complexity engineering. Int J Bio-Inspired Comput 3(4):199–212
Frei R, Di Marzo Serugendo G (2012) The future of complexity engineering. Cent Eur J Eng 2(2):164–188
Friston K (2010) The free-energy principle: a unified brain theory? Nat Rev Neurosci 11:127–138. https://doi.org/10.1038/nrn2787
Fukuyama F (1992) The end of history and the last man. Free Press, New York
Fukuyama F (2011) The origins of political order: from prehuman times to the French revolution. Farrar, Straus and Giroux, New York
Fukuyama F (2014) Political order and political decay: from the industrial revolution to the globalization of democracy. Farrar, Straus and Giroux, New York
Gao Z (2014) Engineering cybernetics: 60 years in the making. Control Theory Technol 12(2):97–109
Gatherer D (2008) Finite universe of discourse: the systems biology of Walter Elsasser (1904–1991). Open Biol J 1:9–20. https://doi.org/10.2174/1874196700801010009
Gazzola F (2015) Mathematical models for suspension bridges: nonlinear structural instability. Springer, Cham, Switzerland
Ge X, Yan L (2023) Information thermodynamics communications. IEEE Wirel Commun 30(2):130–137
Gitt W (1989) Information: the third fundamental quantity. Siemens Rev 56(6):2–7

Gnanadesikan AE (2009) The writing revolution: cuneiform to the Internet. Wiley, Chichester, UK
Gobet F, Simon HA (1996) Recall of random and distorted chess positions: implications for the theory of expertise. Mem Cognit 24(4):493–501
Gorod A et al (2008) System-of-systems engineering management: a review of modern history and a path forward. IEEE Syst J 2(4):484–499
Graeber D, Wengrow D (2021) The dawn of everything: a new history of humanity. Farrar, Straus and Giroux, New York
Guiso L et al (2006) Does culture affect economic outcomes? J Econ Perspect 20(2):23–48
Gunawardena J (2014) Time-scale separation—Michaelis and Menten's old idea, still bearing fruit. FEBS J 281(2):473–488
Gunckel L, Franklin GF (1963) A general solution for linear, sampled-data control. J Basic Eng 85(2):197–201
Haas R, Nikel PI (2023) Challenges and opportunities in bringing nonbiological atoms to life with synthetic metabolism. Trends Biotechnol 41(1):27–45
Haidt J (2012) The righteous mind: why good people are divided by politics and religion. Pantheon Books, New York
Hall AD (1962) A methodology for systems engineering. D. Van Nostrand Company, Princeton, NJ
Harari YN (2015) Sapiens: a brief history of humankind. HarperCollins Publishers, New York
Hardin G (1968) The tragedy of the commons: the population problem has no technical solution; it requires a fundamental extension in morality. Science 162(3859):1234–1248
Hardin G (1998) Extension of "the tragedy of the commons." Science 280(5364):682–683
Hartshorne JK, Germine LT (2015) When does cognitive functioning peak? The asynchronous rise and fall of different cognitive abilities across the lifespan. Psychol Sci 26(4):433–443
Hawking S (2018) Brief answers to the big questions. John Murray, London
Haykin S, Moher M (2014) Communication systems, 5th edn. Wiley, Hoboken, NJ
Henrich J (2020) The WEIRDest people in the world: how the west became psychologically peculiar and particularly prosperous. Picador, New York
Herculano-Houzel S (2009) The human brain in numbers: a linearly scaled-up primate brain. Front Hum Neurosci 3:1–11. https://doi.org/10.3389/neuro.09.031.2009
Heylighen F (2002) The science of self-organization and adaptivity. In: Kiel LD (ed) Knowledge management, organizational intelligence and learning, and complexity, vol I. EOLSS Publishers, Oxford, UK, pp 184–211
Hirsch Hadorn G et al (eds) (2008) Handbook of transdisciplinary research. Springer Science + Business Media, Dordrecht, The Netherlands
Hofstede G et al (2010) Cultures and organizations: software of the mind: intercultural cooperation and its importance for survival, 3rd edn. McGraw-Hill, New York
Hubka V, Eder WE (1988) Theory of technical systems: a total concept theory for engineering design. Springer-Verlag, Berlin
Holland JH (1995) Hidden order: how adaptation builds complexity. Perseus Books, Reading, MA
Honderich T (ed) (2005) Oxford companion to philosophy, 2nd edn. Oxford University Press, Oxford, UK
IEEE (2002) A brief history of communications. IEEE, Piscataway, NJ
Ifrah G (2000) A universal history of numbers: from prehistory to computers. Wiley, New York
Ingalls BP (2013) Mathematical modeling in systems biology: an introduction. MIT Press, Cambridge, MA
Jacob DT (2016) There is no silicon-based life in the solar system. Silicon 8:175–176. https://doi.org/10.1007/s12633-014-9270-7
Jacobson A (2004) Use cases—yesterday, today, and tomorrow. Softw Syst Model 3(3):210–220
Jacobson A et al (1999) The unified software development process. Addison-Wesley, Reading, MA
Jain RK, Triandis HC (1997) Management of research and development organizations: managing the unmanageable. Wiley, New York

Jarke M et al (1998) Scenario management: an interdisciplinary approach. Requirements Eng 3:155–173. https://doi.org/10.1007/s007660050002

Jauk E et al (2013) The relationship between intelligence and creativity: new support for the threshold hypothesis by means of empirical breakpoint detection. Intelligence 41(4):212–221

Jenkins A (2013) Self-oscillation. Phys Rep 525(2):167–222

John OP, Srivastava S (1999) The big five trait taxonomy: history, measurement and theoretical perspectives. In: Pervin LA, John OP (eds) Handbook of personality: theory and research, 2nd edn. Guilford Press, New York, pp 102–138

Jorgensen SE (2012) Introduction to systems ecology. CRC Press, Boca Raton, FL

Joseph PD, Tou JT (1961) On linear control theory. Trans Am Inst Electr Eng Part II Appl Ind 80(4):193–196

Kahlen FJ et al (eds) (2017) Transdisciplinary perspectives on complex systems: new findings and approaches. Springer International Publishing, Cham, Switzerland

Kahneman D (2011) Thinking, fast and slow. Farrar, Straus and Giroux, New York

Kailath T (1960) Correlation detection of signals perturbed by a random channel. IRE Trans Inf Theory IT 6(3):361–366

Kailath T (1969) A general likelihood-ratio formula for random signals in Gaussian noise. IEEE Trans Inf Theory IT 15(3):350–361

Kalaidjieva MA, Swanson GA (2004) Intelligence and living systems: decision-making perspective. Syst Res Behav Sci 21(2):147–172

Kanerva P (2000) Hyperdimensional computing: an introduction to computing in distributed representation with high-dimensional random vectors. Cogn Comput 1(2):139–159

Kauffman S (1995) At home in the universe: the search for laws of self-organization and complexity. Oxford University Press, Oxford, UK

Kauffman S (2019) A world beyond physics: the emergence and evolution of life. Oxford University Press, New York

Kennedy P (1988) The rise and fall of the great powers: economic change and military conflict from 1500 to 2000. Unwin Hyman, London

Kesting S (2010) Boulding's welfare approach of communicative deliberation. Ecol Econ 69(5):973–977

Kiebel SJ et al (2008) A hierarchy of time-scales and the brain. PLoS Comput Biol 4(11):1–12

Klein JT (1990) Interdisciplinarity: history, theory, and practice. Wayne State University Press, Detroit, MI

Kline SJ (1995) Conceptual foundations of multidisciplinary thinking. Stanford University Press, Stanford, CA

Koestler A (1967) The ghost in the machine. Hutchinson & Co, London

Kohlberg L (1971) Stages of moral development as a basis for moral education. In: Beck CM et al (eds) Moral education: interdisciplinary approaches. University of Toronto Press, Toronto, Ontario, Canada, pp 23–92

Koltko-Rivera M (2006) Rediscovering the later version of Maslow's hierarchy of needs: self-transcendence and opportunities for theory, research, and unification. Rev Gen Psychol 10(4):302–317

Kopicki R et al (2010) Predicting workpiece motions under pushing manipulations using the principle of minimum energy. In: Proceedings of the workshop of robotics: science and systems, Zaragoza, Spain

Korkman S (2022) Talous ja humanismi. Otava, Helsinki, Finland

Kosinski RJ (2013) A literature review on reaction time. Technical note. Clemson University, Clemson, SC. http://www.cognaction.org/cogs105/readings/clemson.rt.pdf. Accessed 6 Dec 2024

Kostoff RN, Schaller RR (2001) Science and technology roadmaps. IEEE Trans Eng Manage 48(2):132–143

Kukushkin NV et al (2024) The massed-spaced learning effect in non-neural human cells. Nat Commun 15:1–10. https://doi.org/10.1038/s41467-024-53922-x

Kurose JF, Ross KD (2013) Computer networking: a top-down approach featuring the Internet, 6th edn. Addison-Wesley, Boston, MA
Kurzweil R (1999) The age of spiritual machines: when computers exceed human intelligence. Penguin Group, New York
Ladyman J, Wiesner K (2020) What is a complex system? Yale University Press, New Haven, CT
Landauer MK (1986) How much do people remember? Some estimates of the quantity of learned information in long-term memory. Cogn Sci 10(4):477–493
Larson EJ (2021) The myth of artificial intelligence: why computers can't think the way we do. Belknap Press, Cambridge, MA
Lasanen M et al (2008) Adaptive predistortion architecture for nonideal radio transmitter. In: Proceedings of the IEEE vehicular technology conference (VTC'08 spring), Singapore, pp 1256–1260
Lasaulce S, Tembine H (2011) Game theory and learning for wireless networks: fundamentals and applications. Academic Press, Oxford, UK
Lazcano A, Bada JL (2003) The 1953 Stanley L. Miller experiment: fifty years of prebiotic organic chemistry. Orig Life Evol Biosph 33:235–242. https://doi.org/10.1023/A:1024807125069
Lebon G et al (2008) Understanding non-equilibrium thermodynamics: foundations, applications, frontiers. Springer-Verlag, Berlin
Lee TH (2004) The design of CMOS radio-frequency integrated circuits, 2nd edn. Cambridge University Press, Cambridge, UK
Lee LC et al (1998) The stability, scalability and performance of multi-agent systems. BT Technol J 16:94–103. https://doi.org/10.1023/A:1009686016775
Lee SW et al (2015) Neural computations mediating one-shot learning in the human brain. PLoS Biol 13(4):1–36. https://doi.org/10.1371/journal.pbio.1002137
Legg S, Hutter M (2007) Universal intelligence: a definition of machine intelligence. Mind Mach 17(4):391–444
Lennie P (2003) The cost of cortical computation. Curr Biol 13(6):493–497
Liao X et al (2017) Small-world human brain networks: perspectives and challenges. Neurosci Biobehav Rev 77:286–300. https://doi.org/10.1016/j.neubiorev.2017.03.018
Lilienfeld SO et al (2010) 50 great myths of popular psychology: shattering widespread misconceptions about human behavior. Wiley, Chichester, UK
Liu P et al (2023) Pre-train, prompt, and predict: a systematic survey of prompting methods in natural language processing. ACM Comput Surv 55(9):1–35. https://doi.org/10.1145/3560815
Long G et al (1989) The LMS algorithm with delayed coefficient adaptation. IEEE Trans Acoust Speech Signal Process 37(9):1397–1405
Loukola O et al (2017) Bumblebees show cognitive flexibility by improving on an observed complex behavior. Science 355(6327):833–836
Maier MW, Rechtin E (2009) The art of systems architecting, 3rd edn. CRC Press, Boca Raton, FL
Mämmelä A (2006) Commutation in linear and nonlinear systems. Frequenz 60(5–6):92–94
Mämmelä A, Anttonen A (2017) Why will computing power need particular attention in future wireless devices? IEEE Circuits Syst Mag 17(1):12–26
Mämmelä A et al (2018) Multidisciplinary and historical perspectives for developing intelligent and resource-efficient systems. IEEE Access 6:17464–17499
Mämmelä A et al (2023) Loose coupling: an invisible thread in the history of technology. IEEE Access 11:59456–59482
March G, Olsen JP (1984) The new institutionalism: organizational factors in political life. Am Polit Sci Rev 78(3):734–749
Marcos A, Arp R (2013) Information in the biological sciences. In: Kampourakis K (ed) The philosophy of biology: a companion to educators. Springer Science + Business Media, Dordrecht, The Netherlands, pp 511–547
Marshall T (2015) Prisoners of geography: ten maps that explain everything about the world. Elliott & Thompson, London

Maruyama M (1963) The second cybernetics: deviation-amplifying mutual causal processes. Am Sci 5(2):164–179
McFarland D, Bösser T (1993) Intelligent behavior in animals and robots. MIT Press, Cambridge, MA
McGarry K et al (1999) Hybrid neural systems: from simple coupling to fully integrated neural networks. Neural Comput Surv 2(1):62–93
McNeill WH (1991) The rise of the west: a history of the human community with a retrospective essay. The University of Chicago Press, Chicago, IL
McNeill JR, McNeill WH (2003) The human web: a bird's-eye view of world history. Norton & Company, New York
Meadows DH, Wright D (eds) (2008) Thinking in systems: a primer. Chelsea Green Publishing, White River Junction, VT
Medsker LR (1995) Hybrid intelligent systems. Springer, New York
Merriam-Webster (2024). https://www.merriam-webster.com. Accessed 5 Nov 2024
Mesarovic MD (1970) Multilevel systems and concepts in process control. Proc IEEE 58(1):111–125
Mesarovic M et al (1970) Theory of hierarchical, multilevel systems. Academic Press, New York
Mijumbi R (2016) Management and orchestration challenges in network functions virtualization. IEEE Commun Mag 54(1):98–105
Miller JG (1973) Living systems. Q Rev Biol 48(2):63–91
Miller JG (1978) Living systems. McGraw-Hill, New York
Mishan EJ (1960) A survey of welfare economics, 1939–59. Econ J 70(278):197–265
Moravec H (1999) Robot: mere machine to transcendent mind. Oxford University Press, New York
Morowitz HJ (2002) The emergence of everything: how the world became complex. Oxford University Press, New York
Nagel E (1979) Structure of science: problems in the logic of scientific explanation. Hackett Publishing Company, Indianapolis, IN
Navarro-Gonzalez R et al (1998) Nitrogen fixation by volcanic lightning in the early Earth. Geophys Res Lett 25(16):3059–3213
Neil E (1962) Neural factors responsible for cardiovascular regulation. Circ Res 11(1):137–143
Newen A, Vogeley K (2003) Self-representation: searching for a neural signature of self-consciousness. Conscious Cogn 12(4):529–543
Newth E (1996) Jakten på sannheten. Tiden Norsk Forlag, Oslo, Norway
Nguyen CD et al (2012) Evolutionary testing of autonomous software agents. Auton Agent Multi-Agent Syst 25(2):260–283
Nichols T (2017) The death of expertise: the campaign against established knowledge and why it matters. Oxford University Press, New York
Nicolescu B (2002) Manifesto of transdisciplinarity. State University of New York Press, Albany, NY
Nielsen CB et al (2015) Systems of systems engineering: basic concepts, model-based techniques, and research directions. ACM Comput Surv 48(2):18:1–18:41
Nisbett RE (2003) The geography of thought: how Asians and Westerners think differently … and why. Nicholas Brealey Publishing, London
Nowak M (2006) Evolutionary dynamics: exploring the equations of life. The Belknap Press, Cambridge, MA
Ogata K (2004) System dynamics, 4th edn. Pearson Education, Harlow, Essex, UK
Ogata K (2010) Modern control engineering, 5th edn. Prentice Hall, Boston, MA
Olson DW et al (2015) The tacoma narrows bridge collapse. Phys Today 68(11):64–65
O'Neill C (2016) Weapons of math destruction: how big data increased inequality and threatens democracy. Penguin Books, London
O'Neill RV et al (1986) A hierarchical concept of ecosystems. Princeton University Press, Princeton, NJ
Online Etymology Dictionary (2024). https://www.etymonline.com. Accessed 5 Nov 2024

Ortega y Gasset J (1932) The revolt of the masses. W. W. Norton & Company, New York
Ovaska SJ et al (2006) Fusion of soft computing and hard computing: computational structures and characteristic features. IEEE Trans Syst Man Cybern Part C Appl Rev 36(3):439–448
Oxford Learner's Dictionaries (2024). https://www.oxfordlearnersdictionaries.com. Accessed 25 Oct 2024
Pagels H (1988) The dreams of reason: the computer and the rise of the sciences of complexity. Simon & Schuster, New York
Pahl G et al (2007) Engineering design: a systematic approach, 3rd edn. Springer-Verlag, London
Pain MTG, Hibbs A (2007) Sprint starts and the minimum auditory reaction time. J Sports Sci 25(1):79–86
Pan X et al (2013) Systems thinking: a comparison between Chinese and Western approaches. Procedia Comput Sci 16:1027–1035. https://doi.org/10.1016/j.procs.2013.01.108
Parnas DL (1972) On the criteria to be used in decomposing systems into modules. Commun ACM 15(12):1053–1058
Pattee HH (ed) (1973) Hierarchy theory: the challenge of complex systems. George Braziller, New York
Pawson P (2022) The myth of the Harvard architecture. IEEE Ann Hist Comput 44(3):59–69
Peng S (2015) Silicon-based life in the solar system. Silicon 7:1–3. https://doi.org/10.1007/s12633-014-9254-7
Penrose P (1999) The emperor's new mind: concerning computers, minds and the laws of physics, new. Oxford University Press, Oxford, UK
Pietikäinen M, Silven O (2021) Challenges of artificial intelligence: from machine learning and computer vision to emotional intelligence. Center for Machine Vision and Signal Analysis, University of Oulu, Oulu, Finland
Pietikäinen M, Silven O (2023) How will artificial intelligence affect our lives in the 2050s? Center for Machine Vision and Signal Analysis, University of Oulu, Oulu, Finland
Pinker S (2018) Enlightenment now: the case for reason, science, humanism, and progress. Viking, New York
Popescu A, Westerhagen A (2022) Network softwarization: developments and challenges. In: Proceedings of the 14th international conference on communications (COMM'22), Bucharest, Romania
Popper K (1961) The poverty of historicism, 2nd edn. Routledge, London
Pumain D (ed) (2006) Hierarchy in natural and social sciences. Springer, Dordrecht, The Netherlands
Pursiainen T (1998) Kymmenen (uutta) käskyä nykyajalle. Kirjapaja, Helsinki, Finland
Pyenson L, Sheets-Pyenson S (1999) Servants of nature: history of scientific institutions, enterprises, and sensibilities. W. W. Norton & Company, New York
Qin Z et al (2023) A generalized semantic communication system: from sources to channels. IEEE Wirel Commun 30(3):18–26
Raami A (2015) Intuition unleashed: on the application and development of intuition in the creative process. Ph.D. dissertation, Aalto University, Espoo, Finland
Rajsbaum S, Raynal M (2020) 60 years of mastering concurrent computing through sequential thinking. ACM SIGACT News 51(2):59–88
Ramage M, Shipp K (2020) Systems thinkers, 2nd edn. Springer, London
Random House Webster's College Dictionary (1999). Random House, New York
Rawls J (1999) A theory of justice, rev. Harvard University Press, Cambridge, MA
Ray PP (2018) An introduction to dew computing: definition, concept and implications. IEEE Access 6:723–737
Repko AF (2008) Interdisciplinary research: process and theory, 1st edn. Sage, Thousand Oaks, CA
Repko AF, Szostak R (2021) Interdisciplinary research: process and theory, 4th edn. Sage, Thousand Oaks, CA
Richardson GP (1991) Feedback thought in social science and system theory. University of Pennsylvania Press, Philadelphia, PA

Riekki J, Mämmelä A (2021) Research and education towards smart and sustainable world. IEEE Access 9:53156–53177

Riker WH (1982) The two-party system and Duverger's law: an essay on the history of political science. Am Polit Sci Rev 76(4):753–766

Roberts S (2020) The power of not thinking: how our bodies learn and why we should trust them. Blink Publishing, London

Roberts J (2024) Every living thing: the great and deadly race to know all life. Random House, New York

Robson D (2019) Intelligence trap: why smart people make dumb mistakes. W. W. Norton & Company, New York

Rosen R (1991) Life itself: a comprehensive inquiry into the nature, origin, and fabrication of life. Columbia University Press, New York

Rosen R (1996) On the limitation of scientific knowledge. In: Casti JL, Karlqvist A (eds) Boundaries and barriers on the limits of scientific knowledge. Perseus Books, Reading, MA, pp 199–214

Rosenbaum DA (2010) Human motor control, 2nd edn. Elsevier, London

Rosenberg A (2018) Philosophy of social science, 5th edn. Routledge, New York

Rosenberg A, McIntyre L (2020) Philosophy of science: a contemporary introduction, 4th edn. Routledge, New York

Rosling H et al (2018) Factfulness: ten reasons we're wrong about the world—and why things are better than you think. Flatiron Books, New York

Rothman T (2003) Everything's relative and other fables from science and technology. Wiley, Hoboken, NJ

Ruiz-Mirazo K, Moreno A (2011) The need for a universal definition of life in twenty-first-century biology. In: Terzis G, Arp R (eds) Information and living systems: philosophical and scientific perspectives. MIT Press, Cambridge, MA, pp 3–23

Ruparelia NB (2010) Software development lifecycle models. ACM SIGSOFT Softw Eng Notes 35(3):8–13

Russell AL (2012) Modularity: an interdisciplinary history of an ordering concept. Inf Cult 47(3):257–287

Russell S, Norvig P (2022) Artificial intelligence: a modern approach, 3rd edn. Pearson Education, Harlow, UK

Ryan A (2012) On politics: a history of political thought from Herodotus to the present. W. W. Norton, New York

Samad T et al (2007) System architecture for process automation: review and trends. J Process Control 17(3):191–201

Sandell N Jr et al. (1978) Survey of decentralized control methods for large scale systems. IEEE Trans Autom Control AC 23(2):108–128

Saraiva de Sousa NF et al (2019) Network service orchestration: a survey. Comput Commun 142–143:69–94. https://doi.org/10.1016/j.comcom.2019.04.008

Saridis GN (1979) Toward the realization of intelligent controls. Proc IEEE 67(8):1115–1133

Saridis GN (2001) Hierarchically intelligent machines. World Scientific Publishing, Singapore

Sarpeshkar R (2010) Ultra low power bioelectronics: fundamentals, biomedical applications, and bio-inspired systems. Cambridge University Press, Cambridge, UK

Schetzen M (2006) The Volterra and Wiener theories of nonlinear systems, 2nd edn. Krieger Publishing, Melbourne, FL

Schlosshauer M (2019) Quantum decoherence. Phys Rep 831:1–57. https://doi.org/10.1016/j.physrep.2019.10.001

Schoemaker PJH (1991) The quest for optimality: A positive heuristic of science? Behavioral and Brain Sciences 14(2): 205-245

Schoemaker PJH (2020) How historical analysis can enrich scenario planning. Futures Foresight Sci 2(3–4):1–13

Schumm BA (2004) Deep down things: the breathtaking beauty of particle physics. The Johns Hopkins University Press, Baltimore, MD

Schuster P (1996) How does complexity arise in evolution. Complexity 2(1):22–30
Schwanitz D (1999) Bildung: Alles, was man Wissen muß. Eichborn AG, Frankfurt am Main, Germany
Senge P (2006) The fifth discipline: the art and practice of the learning organization, rev. Doubleday, New York
Sheridan TB (1993) Space teleoperation through time delay: review and prognosis. IEEE Trans Robot Autom 9(5):592–606
Shin K, Hammond JK (1998) The instantaneous Lyapunov exponent and its application to chaotic dynamical systems. J Sound Vib 218(3):389–403
Siegfried T (2006) A beautiful math: John Nash, game theory, and the modern quest for a code of nature. Joseph Henry Press, Washington, DC
Simon HA (1962) The architecture of complexity. Proc Am Philos Soc 106(6):467–482
Simon HA (1973) The organization of complex systems. In: Pattee HH (ed) Hierarchy theory: the challenge of complex systems. George Braziller, New York, pp 1–27
Simon HA (2002) Near decomposability and the speed of evolution. Ind Corp Change 11(3):587–599
Simon HA, Ando A (1961) Aggregation of variables in dynamic systems. Econometrica 29(2):111–138
Simonton DK (2004) Psychology's status as a scientific discipline: its empirical placement within an implicit hierarchy of the science. Rev Gen Psychol 8(1):59–67
Sipilä H (2014) The zero-energy principle as a fundamental law of nature. La Nuova Crit Spec Issue 63–64:29–33
Skyttner L (2005) General systems theory: problems, perspectives, practice, 2nd edn. World Scientific Publishing, Singapore
Sloman S, Fernbach P (2017) The knowledge illusion: the myth of individual thought and the power of collective wisdom. Riverhead Books, New York
Smith R (1997) The Norton history of the human sciences. W. W: Norton & Company, New York
Smith LD et al (2000) Scientific graphs and the hierarchy of the sciences: a Latourian survey of inscription practices. Soc Stud Sci 30(1):73–94
Solomon M (2006) Groupthink versus the wisdom of crowds: the social epistemology of deliberation and dissent. South J Philos XLIV(S1):28–42
Stanovich KE et al (2016) The rationality quotient: toward a test of rational thinking. MIT Press, Cambridge, MA
Sterman JD (2000) Business dynamics: systems thinking and modeling for a complex world. McGraw-Hill, Boston, MA
Stiglitz JE (2000) The contributions of the economics of information to twentieth century economics. Q J Econ 115(4):1441–1478
Stone RJ (2001) Haptic feedback: a brief history from telepresence to virtual reality. In: Brewster S, Murray-Smith R (eds) Haptic human-computer interaction. Springer, Berlin, pp 1–16
Stonier T (1992) Beyond information: the natural history of intelligence. Springer, Berlin
Stonier T (1997) Information and meaning: an evolutionary perspective. Springer, Berlin
Strogatz SH (2014) Nonlinear dynamics and chaos: with applications to physics, biology, chemistry, and engineering, 2nd edn. CRC Press, Boca Raton, FL
Suntola T (2018a) The short history of science—or the long path to the union of metaphysics and empiricism, 3rd edn. Physics Foundations Society and The Finnish Society for Natural Philosophy. https://physicsfoundations.org
Suntola T (2018b) The dynamic universe: toward a unified picture of physical reality, 4rd edn. Physics Foundations Society and The Finnish Society for Natural Philosophy. https://physicsfoundations.org
Suntola T (2020) Unification of theories requires a postulate basis in common. J Phys Conf Ser 1466:1–28. https://doi.org/10.1088/1742-6596/1466/1/012003
Suntola T (2021) In a holistic perspective, time is absolute and relativity a direct consequence of the conservation of total energy. Phys Essays 34(4):486–501

Surowiecki J (2005) The wisdom of crowds: why the many are smarter than the few and how collective wisdom shapes business, economies, societies and nations. Anchor Books, New York
Swilling M (2020) The age of sustainability: just transitions in a complex world. Routledge, New York
Szostak R (2004) Classifying science: phenomena, data, theory, methods, practice. Springer, Dordrecht, The Netherlands
Tanenbaum AS, Wetherall DJ (2011) Computer networks, 5th edn. Prentice Hall, Englewood Cliffs, NJ
Tay L, Diener F (2011) Needs and subjective well-being around the world. J Pers Soc Psychol 101(2):354–365
Taylor AJW (2009) Justice as a basic human need. N Z J Psychol 3(2):5–10
Thurner S et al (2018) Introduction to the theory of complex systems. Oxford University Press, Oxford, UK
Treptow RS (2005) $E = mc^2$ for the chemist: when is mass conserved? J Chem Educ 82(11):1636–1641
Trewavas A (2006) A brief history of systems biology. Plant Cell 18(10):2420–2430
Ulieru M, Doursat R (2011) Emergent engineering: a radical paradigm shift. Int J Auton Adapt Commun Syst 4(1):39–60
van der Ploeg F (2007) Sustainable social spending and stagnant public services: Baumol's cost disease revisited. FinanzArchiv/Public Finance Anal 63(4):519–547
Van Lange PAM et al (2013) The psychology of social dilemmas: a review. Organ Behav Hum Decis Process 120(2):125–141
van Megen R, van Dijk H (2017) The secret of running: maximum performance gains through effective power metering and training analysis. Meyer & Meyer Sport, Aachen, Germany
van Steen M, Tanenbaum AS (2017) Distributed systems: principles and paradigms, 3rd edn
Vermaas PE, Dorst K (2007) On the conceptual framework of John Gero's FBS-model and the prescriptive aims of design methodology. Des Stud 28(2):133–157
Vitali V, Moran JA (2023) The pursuit of happiness: cultural and psychological considerations. In: Irtelli F, Gabrielli F (eds) Happiness and wellness biopsychosocial and anthropological perspectives. IntechOpen, London, pp 289–298
von Bertalanffy L (1971) General system theory: foundations, development, applications, rev. George Braziller, New York
Walasek L, Brown GDA (2023) Incomparability and incommensurability in choice: no common currency of value? Perspect Psychol Sci. https://doi.org/10.1177/17456916231192828
Waldrop MM (2016) More than Moore. Nature 530(7589):145–147
Walke BH (1999) Mobile radio networks: networking and protocols. Wiley, Chichester, UK
Wang Y (2016) Definition and categorization of dew computing. Open J Cloud Comput (OJCC) 3(1):1–7
Wang P (2019) On defining artificial intelligence. J Artif Gen Intell 10(2):1–37
Wang DYC et al (1999) Divergence time estimates for the early history of animal phyla and the origin of plants, animals and fungi. Proc R Soc Lond B Biol Sci 266(1415):163–171
Wang Y et al (2009) Contemporary cybernetics and its facets of cognitive informatics and computational intelligence. IEEE Trans Syst Man Cybern Part B Cybern 39(4):823–833
Wang J et al (2019) Thirty years of machine learning: the road to Pareto-optimal wireless networks. IEEE Commun Surv Tutor 22(3):1472–1514
Watts DJ (2004) Six degrees: The science of a connected age. W. W. Norton & Company, New York
Weaver W (1948) Science and complexity. Am Sci 36(4):536–544
Webster's New World College Dictionary (2001) IDG books worldwide, 4th edn. Foster City, CA
West BJ et al (2020) Relating size and functionality in human social networks through complexity. PNAS 117(31):18355–18358
Westerhoff HV et al (2009) Systems biology: the elements and principles of life. FEBS Lett 573(24):3882–3890

Wickens AP (2015) A history of the brain: from stone age surgery to modern neuroscience. Psychology Press, London
Wiener N (1961) Cybernetics: or control and communication in the animal and the machine, 2nd edn. MIT Press, Cambridge, MA
Wigner EP (1960) The unreasonable effectiveness of mathematics in the natural sciences. Commun Pure Appl Math XIII:1–14. https://doi.org/10.1142/9789814503488_0018
Wilson EO (1998) Consilience: the unity of knowledge. Vintage Books, New York
Woese CR et al (1990) Towards a natural system of organisms: proposal for the domains Archaea, Bacteria, and Eucarya. Proc Natl Acad Sci USA 87(12):4576–4579
Wolfram (2024) Eric Weisstein's world of science. http://scienceworld.wolfram.com. Accessed 6 Nov 2024
Wu J (2013) Hierarchy theory. In: Rozzi R et al (2013) Linking ecology and ethics for a changing world: values, philosophy, and action. Springer Science + Business Media, Dordrecht, The Netherlands, pp 281–302
Xi YG et al (2013) Model predictive control—status and challenges. Acta Autom Sin 39(3):222–236
Young HD et al (2012) Sears and Zemansky's university physics with modern physics, 13th edn. Addison Wesley, San Francisco, CA
Zadeh LA (1962) From circuit theory to system theory. Proc IRE 50(5):856–865
Zeeman EC (1979) A geometrical model of ideologies. In: Renfrew C, Cooke KL (eds) Transformations: mathematical approaches to cultural change. Academic Press, New York, pp 463–479
Zhirnov VV, Cavin RK (2013) Future microsystems for information processing: Limits and lessons from living systems. IEEE Journal of the Electron Devices Society 1(2): 29-47

Chapter 5
Systems Thinking: How Systems Work

All things in moderation, including moderation. Socrates (c. 470–399 BCE)
A new scientific truth does not triumph by convincing its opponents and making them see the light, but rather because its opponents eventually die, and a new generation grows up that is familiar with it. Max Planck (1858–1947)
What I cannot create, I do not understand. Richard P. Feynman (1918–1988)
Computers, who have no body, no childhood and no cultural practice, could not acquire intelligence at all. Hubert Dreyfus (1929–2017)
The world is its own best model - always exactly up to date and complete in every detail. Rodney Brooks (1954–)

Abstract We summarize the requirements for sustainable development, basic resources, finiteness of human knowledge, and the needs leading to system requirements. We present a general hierarchy of systems, including natural and technical systems. Self-organizing systems are the highest in the hierarchy of technical systems, thus providing, in special cases, all other systems lower in the hierarchy. We do not have a single system theory, but many theories complement each other. A modern form of general theory of systems is the complexity theory, a spin-off of cybernetics and artificial intelligence and related to system dynamics. The system archetypes include, for example, feedback, optimization and decision-making, hierarchy, and degree of centralization. The most advanced systems are nonlinear and dynamic such as nonequilibrium systems representing different whirlpools in nature.

5.1 Introduction

This chapter discusses the general requirements of sustainable systems, a general hierarchy of systems, and system theories and archetypes.

A. Mämmelä, *Unifying Systems*, https://doi.org/10.1007/978-3-031-85012-7_5

5.2 General Requirements of Sustainable Systems

5.2.1 Sustainable Development

The three concepts for ecologically responsible design in a finite world include sustainability, resilience, and regeneration (du Plessis 2022). The Brundtland Commission (1987) defined *sustainability* clearly: "Sustainable development is development that meets the needs of the present without compromising the ability of future generations to meet their own needs" (Riekki and Mämmelä 2021). The definition correctly includes the fairness between generations. *Resilience* is the "degree to which a service recovers its operational condition quickly after a failure occurs" (SE VOCAB 2024; Madni and Jackson 2009). *Regeneration* is a process where the system is formed or created again (Merriam-Webster 2024). It restores systems to what they were and to a better or higher state (du Plessis 2022).

The six principles leading to resilience include homeostasis, omnivory, high flux, flatness, buffering, and redundancy principle (Barnett 2001; Skyttner 2005). In *homeostasis*, the system is maintained through feedback between its parts, thus enabling adaptivity and learning. The *omnivory* principle uses diversification of resources and the means of their delivery. In the *high flux* principle, the resources are moved fast through the system to be available when needed. According to the *flatness* principle, hierarchical systems are less flexible and less able to change their behavior in surprising situations because of long chains of command. In the *buffering* principle, we use a system with a capacity larger than the needs, and we can use the surplus capacity when needed. In the *redundancy* principle, redundant parts can take on new functions and offer interchangeability. A form of omnivory, flatness, and redundancy principles is a distributed system on which the biosphere's resilience is based (Boulding 1985).

As explained in Swilling (2020), we are in the age of sustainability that is one of the great transformations equally significant as the agricultural revolution that started over 10,000 years ago and the industrial revolution that started about 250 years ago. Sustainable development must consider several areas of concern: population growth, use of resources, economics, and politics, all using systems thinking in decision-making (Bossel 2007).

Although biological processes generally improve their energy efficiency in evolution, they simultaneously increase the total use of energy (Buenstorf 2000). The increase also happens in technical systems: when their energy efficiency is improved, they become more popular, and the total energy consumption increases (Alcott 2005). The increase is called the *Jevons paradox* (1865). Humankind's energy consumption is growing faster than the size of the population, a consequence of the Jevons paradox. Energy is a finite resource and, thus, energy consumption cannot increase without limits.

The Club of Rome (1968) has pioneered the promotion of sustainable development. It published the report *Limits of Growth* (1972), forecasting the development for the next one hundred years using a system dynamics model. The report was updated in 1992 and 2004.

The *Earth Overshoot Day*, developed by the Global Footprint Network, is "the date when humanity's demand for ecological resources and services in a given year exceeds what Earth can regenerate in that year." The day has been estimated since 1969, when the day was close to the end of the calendar year. During the last 50 years, the world population has increased on average by 1.5% per year when sustainable development would have permitted an increase of only 0.4% per year (Mämmelä and Riekki 2022b). The world population is 70% too high for sustainable development. Now, the population is increasing less than 1% per year and the population is expected to saturate during the second half of this century (United Nations 2024). The United Nations provides other forecasts regarding sustainability. Berkeley Earth focuses on temperature data analysis.

The Earth forms essentially a closed system in terms of materials and energy together with the Sun (Mämmelä and Riekki 2022b). The world's annual energy consumption by humans is 0.01% of the annual energy radiated by the Sun toward the Earth. Part of the actually used energy is fission energy produced on and in the Earth. Energy consumption is increasing faster than the world population, 2.3% per year (IEA 2019).

Climate change is mainly a product of developed countries, although the population grows more rapidly in developing countries. In the atmosphere, some natural greenhouse gases, such as water vapor and carbon dioxide, keep the Earth warm enough for life. Still, the amount of greenhouse gases significantly increased in the 1900s, and for sustainability, the average temperature should stay within 1.5° compared to the preindustrial times 1850–1900. The developed countries and large developing countries use most of the fossil fuels that are the reason for climate change, which is because they emit greenhouse gases in the atmosphere. The most important of them are carbon dioxide and methane. The gases absorb the infrared radiation that the Earth emits. Water vapor is a greenhouse gas, but it does not have much effect on climate change. It just keeps the temperature moderate for living. Other greenhouse gases are more severe, resulting in the greenhouse effect. The problem is an example of the tragedy of the commons, where the commons include the atmosphere, seas, and forests that act as carbon sinks through photosynthesis. Forests can also be reflectors of the radiation from the Sun. Technologies that fight against the climate change by limiting for example the emissions of carbon dioxide are called green technologies.

Some phenomena in climate change include positive feedback loops that may lead to instability and rapid changes. For example, the ice cover of the Earth reflects the radiation of the Sun, but because of greenhouse gases, the heat does not get back into space, and the temperature increases, which results in further ice melting. There are also other such geophysical feedback mechanisms (Ramage and Shipp 2020). The Paris Agreement (2016) aims to keep the global temperature rise below 2 °C and preferably below 1.5 °C above preindustrial levels. The agreement did not define the preindustrial period, but 1850–1900 is often used. The agreement was negotiated at the 2015 United Nations Climate Change Conference.

Sustainability has three pillars: social, economic, and environmental (Purvis et al. 2019). The United Nations has sustainability in its long-term agenda (Riekki and Mämmelä 2021; Mämmelä and Riekki 2022b). Sustainability requires that exponential population growth end, only renewable energy sources are used, and pollution is controlled through recycling. Exponential economic growth cannot continue because of finite resources. We must move from quantitative to qualitative improvement.

We have assumed that the benefits offered by nature are free (Daily 1997; Caradonna 2014). Nature's ecosystem is an essential factor in economics. New systematic measures for sustainable development in the biosphere are needed. The costs are estimated using alternative costs in scenarios for the next 25 years. Economic operations are directed to the lowest environmental detriment. New charges are needed. The whole ecosystem in the biosphere is important. The gross domestic product (GDP) summarizes the aggregate value of economic activity (Ouyang et al. 2020). One new criterion is gross ecosystem product (GEP), which summarizes the aggregate value of nature's contributions to society.

5.2.2 Basic Resources

The basic resources include materials, energy, information, time, frequency, and space (Mämmelä and Anttonen 2017; Mämmelä et al. 2018), see Figs. 5.1 and 5.2. They are seldom presented together although in practice we must make a trade-off between them. Basic resources are scarce in our environment (Hall 1962; Chestnut 1965; von Bertalanffy 1971; Hubka and Eder 1988; Arbnor and Bjerke 1997; Checkland 1999; Pahl et al. 2007).

As a starting point for our list of basic resources we have used the concept of open systems (Hall 1962). Materials, energy, and information are exchanged through the

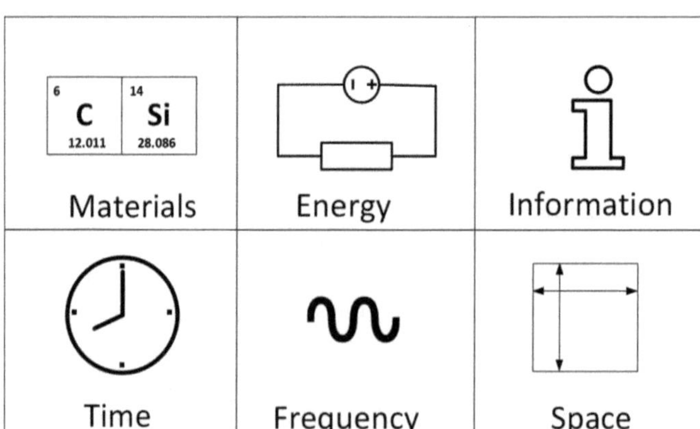

Fig. 5.1 Basic resources

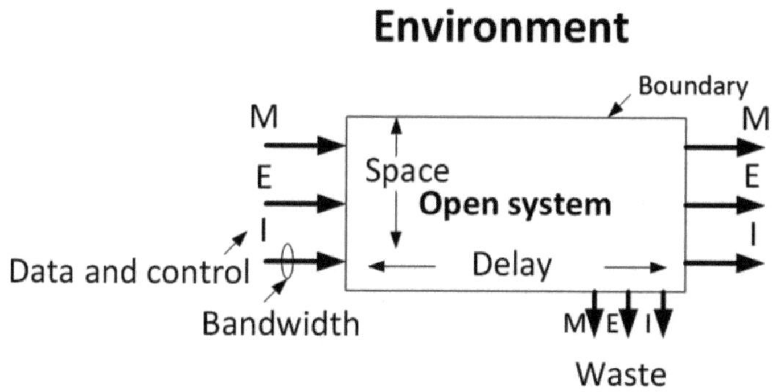

Fig. 5.2 Basic resources in an open system

boundaries of an open system. We have also used the earlier work in Ristenbatt (1973) where the basic resources in communications are energy and frequency bandwidth. Furthermore, we have used the work in Allen (1985) where the basic resources in computing are energy, time, and space. Time, frequency, and space are used in communications in diversity systems (Schwartz et al. 1966; Proakis and Salehi 2008), thus time and space must be added to the basic resources in communications.

We must use the scarce resources efficiently. One light bulb switched on in 1901 has worked for over one hundred years, although with a reduced power. In 1925 a cartel for incandescent light bulbs called Phoebus was started to limit competition and to start *designed aging* (Krajewski 2014). The light bulbs lasted "too long," and new ones could not be sold. People in the cartel agreed that the light bulbs should work a maximum of 1000 h. Similar principles were later applied to printers, mobile phones, and other electrical devices.

Our list of basic resources is almost the same as the *factors of production* in (Boulding 1978, pp. 27, 29, 69, 78, 150), including materials, energy, know-how, time, and space. The know-how is also called knowledge, which is information having a scientific basis. Only frequency is missing from this list since it is a specific resource in communications. We may add the cost of transportation as a replacement of frequency. The traditional factors of production are labor, land, and capital, but Kenneth E. Boulding finds them unsatisfactory from his evolutionary economics point of view.

The efficiency of material and energy use is always below 100%, which causes waste. Material waste must be recycled to obtain sustainability (Caradonna 2014). Typically, some of the energy is transformed into heat. Sustainability improves when this energy is used elsewhere. In a way, all other basic resources are intrinsically renewable, that is why the main focus in sustainability is presently in materials and energy, but in exponential growth of the world population all basic resources will be limiting factors.

Information and capital (money) are abstract resources without which no system can be produced. Systems use information for data and control needing bandwidth (Hubka and Eder 1988; Checkland 1999) so that some form of intelligence can be implemented with the control information. Information cannot be transmitted without any matter or energy; since physical systems are causal, there is always a delay, and time is a basic resource. The physical systems always need some materials and space.

The basic resources are *incommensurable*, and in practice, prices are used to make them commensurable (Boulding 1985; McFarland and Bösser 1993; Walasek and Brown 2023). Money is essentially a deposit of work that can be exchanged for new work to design and build a new system from its parts. Money is a measure to compare incommensurable resources. The find reasonable prices, we use an evolutionary approach based on the law of supply and demand. The prices are not objective measures, but they depend on the availability and need of the resources. For example, we cannot objectively compare 1 J of energy and 1 Hz of bandwidth, but this must be made through prices. The measurement units have been selected arbitrarily. Therefore, the question of prices is not strictly a scientific problem, although it is an essential problem in economics. We have not included money in Fig. 5.1.

Time and frequency are not entirely independent since there is a *time-frequency duality* (Bello 1964): a signal as a deterministic function of time with finite energy can be transformed into the frequency domain using the Fourier transform. A signal that exists in the time domain exists also in the frequency domain at the same time. Similarly, a random signal generally has a power spectrum without any phase information in the frequency domain. There is also a symmetry between frequency and spatial domains, and beamforming can be seen as spatial filtering (Van Veen and Buckley 1988). A signal in general needs time, frequency, and spatial domains for transmission.

In communication, the focus has traditionally been on energy and bandwidth (Ristenbatt 1973). Still, more recently, time in the form of delay has become critical, especially on the haptic or tactile Internet (Elhajj et al. 2001; Fettweis 2014). We must separate transmitted energy or power and signal processing energy or power (Mämmelä et al. 2010; Mämmelä and Anttonen 2017). The received power (excluding the power of the noise and interference) is a small portion of the transmitted power due to the high attenuation of the physical channel, especially in wireless communications, where we have a spreading loss: the signal is in general spread in all directions. There is a computation-communication trade-off between computing and transmission energies, as explained in Lettieri and Srivastava (1999), Cavalcante et al. (2014) and Mämmelä and Anttonen (2017). In Cavalcante et al. (2014), the descriptive terms *operating* and *radiated energy* are used, respectively. The latter is, in fact, a better division than the one in Lettieri and Srivastava (1999), which divides the energy between the digital and analog parts, which is dependent on the system architecture.

Materials Matter has mass and occupies physical space (Miller 1973). When selecting materials for electronics, we are interested in their physical, chemical, and electrical properties. They include linearity, resistance, capacitance, and inductance, and thermal and humidity stability. The materials are divided into metals, semiconductors, ceramics and polymers, and composites (Encyclopedia Britannica 2024; Smil 2014; Berger 2020). There are 92 chemical elements in nature, from hydrogen to uranium. The most common elements in the Earth's crust are oxygen, silicon, aluminum, iron, calcium, sodium, potassium, and magnesium, covering about 99% of the mass, usually in compounds. Important metals such as gold, silver, and copper are scarce. Noble metals, such as gold and platinum, are the most stable elements. The best conductor among the elements is silver. Still, copper, as the second-best conductor, is commonly used due to its lower costs and better sustainability since, in mining, the contamination is lower. Some chemical elements are considered strategic in using renewable energy, including cadmium, chromium, cobalt, copper, gallium, indium, lithium, manganese, nickel, silver, tellurium, tin, and zinc (Calvo and Valero 2022).

The most crucial semiconductor used in electronics is silicon. It is the second most common element in the Earth's crust. Silicon crystals form a diamond cubic lattice with a width (i.e., lattice constant) of 0.54 nm. Because of the crystal structure, the average distance between the silicon atoms is 0.27 nm. In a cube of 5 nm $\times$ 5 nm $\times$ 5 nm, there are about 18 $\times$ 18 $\times$ 18 silicon atoms. Philip R. Wallace started the theoretical study of *graphene* in 1947 (Encyclopedia Britannica 2024). In 2004, Konstantin Novoselov and Andre Geim rediscovered the material, consisting of a few layers of carbon atoms (Banerjee et al. 2010; Tiwari et al. 2020). It is 200 times stronger than steel. A graphene transistor has been demonstrated (Lin et al. 2010). *Carbon nanotubes (CNTs)* were reinvented in 1991, but their origin can be traced back to the 1950s. They are made by rolling a sheet of graphite or graphene into a cylinder (Awano et al. 2010). We can use them to build small mechanical machines, such as a radio (Jensen et al. 2007) or a computer (Shulaker et al. 2013). A recent trend is towards organic materials that should also be flexible, stretchable, and self-healing (Kelley et al. 2004; Frei et al. 2013; Brooks and Roy 2021).

Insufficient recycling and an inadequate share of renewable materials lead to a lack of scarce resources, such as some important metals. Waste collection and recycling are also important to prevent pollution, such as respirable particles in the air and microplastics in the water.

Energy Conventionally, energy has been the only universal currency (Smil 2017, 2020; Panwar et al. 2011). The unit of energy is 1 J, but a related measure is power in W, where 1 W = 1 J/s. Energy as a basic resource is more fundamental than power. It is not easy to define energy so that it would cover all situations (Domenech et al. 2007; Coelho 2009). In a mechanical context, energy is defined as the capacity to do work, but according to the second law of thermodynamics, not all energy can do work. In general, *energy* may be defined as the capacity to produce transformations.

The fundamental sources of energy are nuclear, tidal, and geothermal energy. Nuclear energy is divided into fusion and fission energy. Tidal energy is a result of the gravity of the Moon and the Sun. Geothermal energy is the thermal energy within the Earth. The most important energy source is the Sun, which provides fusion energy. Not all energy is renewable, and the use and production usually cause a carbon footprint (Caradonna 2014). Fossil fuels, including oil, coal, and natural gas, are nonrenewable energy sources. Microbes in the Earth's crust formed them in anaerobic decomposition from the remains of dead organisms over millions of years.

Renewable energy is divided into nuclear, water, wind, and solar power (inc. geothermal heat) and biofuels. Most of the renewable energy comes originally from the Sun. The majority of global energy used is still nonrenewable energy. In nuclear fission, atoms such as uranium or plutonium are divided into two fragments (Encyclopedia Britannica 2024). Fusion energy is produced when isotopes of hydrogen atoms are combined to form helium atoms. It is a possible future energy source that could also be made on Earth. The required temperature is over 100 million K. In contrast, in the core of the Sun, the temperature is about 15 million K since the high pressure can start the fusion reaction at a lower temperature.

The energy must be stored in batteries or fuel cells in portable and mobile systems. Most batteries are lithium batteries because of their high energy density, which is measured in gravimetric energy density (Wh/kg) and volumetric energy density (Wh/l) (Scrosati 2011; Liang et al. 2019). The energy density of a lithium-ion battery is 300 Wh/kg, and for diesel oil, it is 11,700 Wh/kg, implying a 40-fold difference (Smil 2020, pp. 166–169). It is a significant difference, which makes it more challenging to use batteries in truck traffic and ships only because of the large mass of the batteries when the needed energy is considerable. Furthermore, the energy density of batteries increases only 2–4% per year (Smil 2020; Whittingham 2012), implying an increase of 20–50% in ten years.

Lithium is among the alkali metals and constitutes about 0.002% of the Earth's crust. A possible future fuel is hydrogen (Smil 2020, p. 164; Thomas et al. 2020). It is not a primary source of energy since hydrogen is not in general freely available on Earth, except in some exceptional cases where hydrogen can be found in the crust (Stalker et al. 2022). Water can be decomposed by *electrolysis* or more integrated *solar water splitting* (Tachibana et al. 2012; Schmitt et al. 2023). The latter is also called artificial photosynthesis, a misnomer since carbon dioxide is combined with water in natural photosynthesis, and hydrogen is bound in carbohydrates. Even the air includes some water vapor that can produce hydrogen. If made practical, hydrogen can be used in *fuel cells*, producing water from hydrogen and oxygen and releasing energy. This process is the opposite of photosynthesis. Hydrogen as an energy source is in the research phase since it has safety threats because it is leakage- and explosion-prone.

The production of energy causes pollution in the form of greenhouse gases in the atmosphere and radioactive matter, which is the case with fission energy. For example, the half-life for the radioactive decay of plutonium-239 used in nuclear reactors is 24,110 years (Encyclopedia Britannica 2024). The waste must be saved in the bedrock for tens of thousands of years, up to 1 million years. The latter is a longer time than the age of Homo sapiens.

Although electronics is known to consume a minuscule amount of energy, because of the fundamental limits of nature, the switching energy must be well above the Szilard or Landauer limit formed by the noise power spectral density to guarantee reliable operation (Mämmelä and Anttonen 2017). The complexity of the implementations is increasing all the time. A practical limit exists for the number of components on a chip and the cooling efficiency (in W/cm^2) (Avila et al. 2007). Therefore, implementing a complex system must be divided into several chips. An example of how

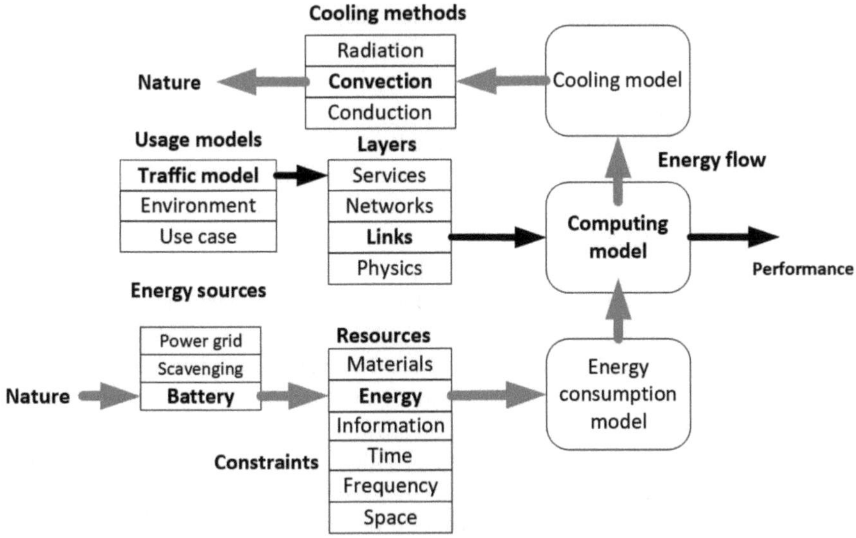

Fig. 5.3 Information and energy flows through a system

the information and energy flow through a system is shown in Fig. 5.3. Usage models are used to define network simulation scenarios for performance evaluation (Perahia 2008). A usage model is a model of services for network simulations, including applications, environments, and use cases.

Information Information is an immaterial resource, one of the basic resources used in feedback loops, initially called *information feedback* (Chang 1956; Harris and Morgan 1958; Love et al. 2008). In cybernetics we are mainly interested in information, and matter and energy are only bearers of information. The accuracy and timeliness of the information are relevant. According to Ian G. Barbour, information is an ordered pattern that can be communicated (Barbour 1997). Information is communicated when another system responds selectively. The meaning of the information depends on the broader context where it is interpreted. In a sense-decide-act feedback loop, the decision phase is essentially pattern recognition of the sensor outputs and pattern formation for the actuator inputs.

Information is usually carried by electrical energy, such as radio waves. Information may be transfered also with matter (Cherry 1962). An old example is the postal service that carries newspapers, letters, and books. Information includes data and control (Hubka and Eder 1988), measured in bits. Control bits are transmitted in addition to data bits to control and manage the transmission of the data bits (Tanenbaum and Wetherall 2011). Data is the new currency in addition to energy, as explained in Gates and Matthews (2014). Information is the capacity to organize things (Stonier 1997, p. 17). Peter Corning noticed that information theory is blind to information's functional properties, and cybernetics did not include any functional definition for information (Corning 2001). He defined control information as "the capacity (know-how) to control the acquisition, disposition and utilization of matter/energy in purposive (cybernetic) processes" (Corning 2001, 2011).

Information is part of the "wisdom hierarchy," which includes data, information, knowledge, and wisdom (DIKW) from the bottom up, a concept developed by Harlan Cleveland (1982), Milan Zeleny (1987), and Russell L. Ackoff (1989) (Meadow and Yuan 1997; Rowley 2007; Zins 2007; Gates and Matthews 2014). Information is defined in terms of data, knowledge in terms of information, and wisdom in terms of knowledge. The value is highest at the top of the hierarchy. Data means numerical facts, information understanding principles, knowledge understanding patterns, and wisdom understanding relationships. Data, information, and knowledge are the building blocks of information science (IS). The DIKW terms can be defined in various ways, as shown in Zins (2007), where 44 definitions are presented for each of these terms. Additional definitions are given in Meadow and Yuan (1997), where the impact and development of information are also discussed.

Data are now defined as "numerical facts collected for future reference" (Online Etymology Dictionary 2024). A *database* is a "structured collection of data in a computer." Data are symbols that represent properties of objects, events, and their environment (Rowley 2007). Data is the plural form of the Latin word datum, but the latter form is rarely used. Data can be seen as singular or plural in English since English grammar allows collective nouns. Originally, datum comes from the Latin verb "dare," which means "to give" (Online Etymology Dictionary 2024). Thus, data are things that were given.

Information is initially meant to be an "act of informing, communication of news" (Online Etymology Dictionary 2024; Marcos and Arp 2013). The word comes from the Latin noun *informatio* meaning "representation, idea, explanation" and the Latin verb *informare* (in + formare), which means "to give shape or form." Information is contained in descriptions and answers to questions that begin with what, where, and when. Information is inferred from data (Rowley 2007). Gitt (1989) presented a five-level hierarchy of the different interpretations of information (Gitt 1989), see Table 5.1, based initially on Charles S. Peirce's (1868) semiotics and further developed by Charles W. Morris (1938).

In semiotics, signs or symbols include three levels of interpretation including: syntactics (study of structure), semantics (study of meaning), and pragmatics (study of effects). The syntactic level deals with internal structural relations between symbols, just as grammar in a language where the symbols are words (Honderich

Table 5.1 Levels of information

Level	Meaning
Apobetic	Purpose of the action
Pragmatic	Practical action
Semantic	Meaning
Syntactic	Structural relationships
Statistical	Statistical relationships

2005). The semantic level considers information about reality or the meaning of the symbols, i.e., their relationship with reality in a particular context (Marcos and Arp 2013). The pragmatic level includes information to alter reality or the intention leading to practical action, thus implying an understanding of the meaning. All human-made technical products are at most at the syntactic level since, so far, a technical system cannot understand meanings. Technical systems can do practical things without any understanding. A similar hierarchy was used also in Shannon and Weaver (1998) without giving a reference. The authors used the terms technical problem (i.e., accuracy of communication), semantic problem, and effectiveness problem. They emphasized that information deals only with the technical problem.

Gitt (1989) divided the lowest and highest hierarchy levels into two parts (Gitt 1989); see Table 5.1. The lowest level has an additional lower level called statistics, i.e., statistical relationships of symbols. The highest level has an extra upper level called apobetics, i.e., the purpose of the symbols. If, for example, a military officer gives a command to soldiers, the command can be analyzed at the five levels. At the two lowest levels, we study statistical or grammatical relationships between the words in the command corresponding to a sentence. The semantic meaning links the command to the real world. Next, the soldiers can act accordingly and are at the pragmatic level, meaning they understand the command. Finally, the purpose of the command, such as winning a battle, is at the apobetic level. A robot may also act but does not understand the meaning and purpose of the command.

Shannon's statistical information theory (1948) does not cover the semantics of information. Semantic information theory is still under development (Stonier 1997; Checkland 1999; Qin et al. 2023). McCarthy and Hayes (1969) defined the *frame problem* as part of the semantic information theory: how a machine can decide the meaning and the context or frame of reference (McCarthy and Hayes 1969). The problem appears in the automatic translation of languages since a word may have many different meanings, and a machine cannot select the correct translation and may make stupid mistakes. Thus, a machine without semantical understanding always "lives" in a simulated world.

Knowledge is usually defined as an organized body of information. It makes possible the transformation of information into instructions and answers to questions that begin with the word 'how' and is thus a synonym for know-how (Rowley 2007). Knowledge can be obtained from experience and is a result of scientific research.

Wisdom is the ability to increase effectiveness (Rowley 2007). Wisdom answers to questions that begin with the word 'why.' Science cannot answer such questions. Bellinger et al. suggested in 2004 that moving from data to information involves 'understanding relations', moving from information to knowledge involves 'understanding patterns,' and moving from knowledge to wisdom involves 'understanding principles.' Milan Zeleny (1987) added the term *enlightenment* above the term wisdom. It goes beyond wisdom "attaining the sense of truth, the sense of right and wrong, and having it socially accepted, respected and sanctioned."

Time According to relativity theory, time forms the fourth dimension of our universe in addition to the three spatial dimensions. In signal theory, the concept of time includes both *duration* and *signal delay* (both measured in s). Delay is of the utmost importance in haptic Internet, also called tactile Internet (Elhajj et al. 2001; Fettweis 2014), and more generally in time-sensitive networking (Levesque and Tipper 2016).

In theory, strictly time-limited signals cannot be strictly band-limited and vice versa (Ziemer and Tranter 2014), which is a paradox explained in Slepian (1976). There is no universal definition for the duration. The definitions for bandwidth in Amoroso (1980) can also be used for the definition of signal duration because of the time-frequency duality (Bello 1964). In the case of deterministic signals with finite energy (i.e., energy signals), energy density in the time domain can be used in the definitions (Ziemer and Tranter 2014).

A delay can be unambiguously defined only in undistorted transmission in linear systems (Ziemer and Tranter 2014; Papoulis 1962). Signals are generally distorted, and the different frequencies experience different delays. We must separate phase, group, and signal-front delay. In undistorted transmission, all the three delays are equal. In general, the phase and group delays depend on frequency, and the signal-front delay is independent of frequency for a given signal. In a linear system, the delay of each frequency is called the *phase delay* of that frequency.

The *group delay* is a delay of a group of adjacent frequency components through a linear system. In undistorted transmission, the group delay for a pulse is the delay of the peak of a pulse (Stenner et al. 2003). Similarly, for an amplitude-modulated narrowband signal, the group delay evaluated at the carrier frequency is the delay of the envelope, and the phase delay is the carrier's delay (Ziemer and Tranter 2014). As a theoretical concept, the group delay in causal systems can even be negative, which looks like a paradox but does not mean the causality is violated (Stenner et al. 2003). The negative group delay is a consequence of the interference between its different frequency components (Wang et al. 2000). We should measure the delay in the time domain (Wang and Feng 2015). The group delay is compared experimentally with the energy center delay in Wang and Feng (2015). For a more detailed discussion on the group delay, see Fettweis (1977).

The signal pulse has a *leading edge* and *trailing edge* corresponding to the beginning and end of the pulse. The leading edge is also called the signal front or front edge. A band-limited signal cannot have a leading and trailing edge, which can be explained by the limitations of the Fourier transform concept (Slepian 1976). The leading-edge delay is theoretically the phase delay for an infinite frequency (Papoulis 1962, pp. 134–136, 187) and is thus different from the group delay. Arnold Sommerfeld (1914) has shown theoretically that the leading edge of an amplitude-modulated signal in physical systems cannot propagate faster than light, and the leading-edge delay corresponds to the information delay (Wang et al. 2000; Stenner et al. 2003).

Energy cannot be transfered faster than light. Just like electromagnetic waves, gravitational waves cannot propagate faster than light. In control engineering, the leading-edge delay is estimated using the step response. The delay time is required for the response to reach half the final value the first time (Ogata 2010, p. 170). Similarly, we define the rise time, the peak time, and the settling time from the response since the step response may be oscillatory in underdamped second-order systems.

Because of long geographical distances and complicated processing, the longest delays usually come from communication networks, where the *end-to-end delays* are most often of major interest. A data packet usually includes several bits, and the transmission is usually done in serial form. Thus, each bit and the packet itself have a certain duration. On the other hand, the whole packet is delayed during transmission since the system must be causal, and the operations take some time.

When defining a communication network's delay, we must define the layer, the protocol data unit (PDU) in the OSI reference model, its length, and whether it is *a one-way* or *round-trip delay*. The PDU is a bit or symbol in the physical layer, a frame in the data link layer, a packet or datagram in the network layer, a segment in the transport layer, and a message or a bit in the application layer (Tanenbaum and Wetherall 2011).

Suppose we are transmitting a packet of data. In that case, the total delay includes the latency and the transmission delay because of serial transmission (Sheldon 2001, pp. 337–341, 731; Bhunia 2005, p. 65; Briscoe et al. 2016) (Fig. 5.4). The terms have not been unified. We must select the best terms and their definitions. The *latency* is the initial delay between transmitting the first bit of the packet and receiving the first bit of the packet or any other protocol data unit. The term latency is also commonly used in electronics to describe delays in operations. The latency is sometimes called the *pipeline delay* (Ford 2019). The *transmission delay* is the time needed for the transmission of a packet from the transmission of the first bit to the transmission of the last bit. The *transfer delay* is the total delay, sometimes called the *transit delay* (ITU-T 1997). It is the time needed from the transmission of the first bit of a packet to the reception of the last bit, i.e., the sum of the latency and the transmission delays. In practice, unless otherwise specified, the delay refers to the end-to-end transfer delay of the PDU. The delay variation is called *jitter*, which is often more harmful than the delay itself.

The transfer delay includes processing, transmission, queuing, and propagation delays (Kwok 1997; Sheldon 2001). Processing delays are caused by inefficient processing, such as packetization, interleaving, and automatic repeat request (ARQ).

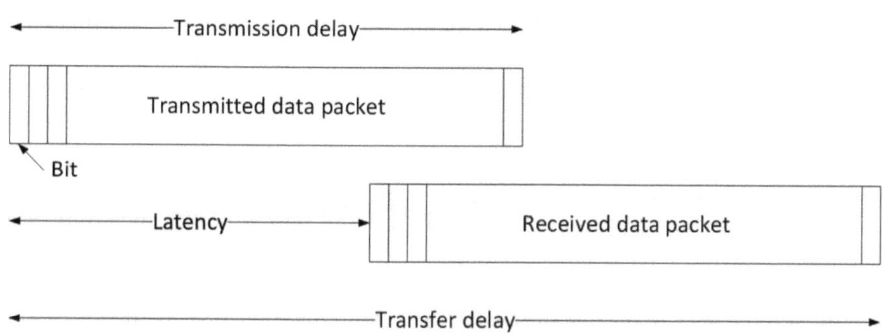

Fig. 5.4 Difference of latency, transmission delay, and transfer delay in one-way transmission

Packetization delay is incurred when filling up a packet with data symbols. Transmission delay is caused by serial transmission. Queuing delays occur when buffers in network devices become flooded. The physical medium causes propagation delay because of the finite speed of the electromagnetic waves, which cannot propagate faster than the speed of light in a vacuum. For example, in a vacuum and, in practice, also in the air, a distance of 0.3 m corresponds to a delay of 1 ns, which is the wavelength of a 1 GHz sinusoid. Delays can be reduced by affecting each of the delay factors and limiting the physical size of the network. In haptic or tactile Internet, the goal is to keep the round-trip delay below 1 ms to avoid cybersickness caused by the delay difference between sight and touch sensations (Elhajj et al. 2001; Fettweis 2014; Mämmelä et al. 2018). Cybersickness is a form of motion sickness that causes nausea. Haptic information includes kinesthetic information or sense of movement and tactile information on touch. A generalization to audio-visual and haptic communication is *human bond communication*, covering all five human senses (Prasad 2016).

Frequency The frequency interval used by a signal or available in a system is called the *bandwidth* (in Hz), corresponding to transportation capacity (or transport capacity) when humans or materials are transported instead of information. *Transport capacity* is sometimes used in communications, meaning the total bit-meters per second a network can reliably support (Gupta and Kumar 2000). In electronics, we have the product of the number of gates and the clock rates (gate-Hz) (Ward et al. 1984; Wu 1989). A similar measure is computing rate (in operations/s, OPs) (Kienle et al. 2011).

In communication networks, bandwidth sometimes refers to the throughput or bit rate (in bit/s), but this is an inaccurate terminology. The Shannon capacity equation limits the bit rate (Ziemer and Tranter 2014; Proakis and Salehi 2008). The maximum bit rate or capacity is directly proportional to the bandwidth and logarithmically dependent on the received signal-to-noise ratio. The signal-to-noise ratio can be measured as a ratio of signal power and noise power (Shannon 1948a, b) or as the ratio of symbol energy and noise power spectral density (Sklar 2001). At high signal-to-noise ratios, the bit rate (in bit/s) can be much larger than the bandwidth (in Hz) since we can use linear M-ary modulation in the form of phase-shift keying (PSK) and quadrature amplitude modulation (QAM) where usually $M = 2^k$ and k is a positive integer. M-ary modulation has M distinct waveforms, and each symbol corresponds to k bits. In spread-spectrum systems, the bandwidth is much larger than the bit rate. The increase is possible using a separate spreading code to modulate the signal before transmission. The primary purpose is an immunity to interference.

There are various definitions of bandwidth based on the power spectrum of a random signal with a finite power (Amoroso 1980). Such signals are called power signals that, in theory, have an infinite duration. The maximum of the spectrum is usually at the center or carrier frequency. The definitions include fractional power containment bandwidth, null-to-null bandwidth, bounded power spectral density, noise bandwidth, half-power bandwidth, and Gabor bandwidth. For the detailed definitions, see Amoroso (1980). A common but rough estimate is the half-power bandwidth, within which the spectral density is bounded to half of the maximum. In communications, the bandwidth must be strictly limited because of other users. The limitation is done using a *frequency mask* defining the relative power density for different frequencies with respect to the carrier frequency. A similar mask can be used in the time domain for the energy spectrum.

Space Space is the last basic resource. It refers to the size of the implementation. The size can be measured in terms of volume (in m^3) and in planar structures in area (in m^2). The mass is also essential. The mass density (in kg/m^3) links the mass and volume. In electronics, miniaturization is limited by the granularity of the material, for example, silicon. The transistor gate has a minimum length caused by quantum effects and noise (Zhirnov and Cavin 2013). The gate length cannot be much below 5 nm when electrons are used as charge carriers. The lower bound can be made smaller using heavier carriers.

Complexity The *complexity* of a system is generally measured by the number of parts and their relations (Barrow 1998, pp. 137; Random House Webster's College Dictionary 1999). In this case, complexity is a simple measure of the system's structure. *The algorithmic* or *Kolmogorov complexity* of an object is proportional to the shortest possible description of that object (Casti 1991, 1994, p. 9). An object is random or incompressible if its shortest description is the object itself. Unfortunately, the Kolmogorov complexity is uncomputable (Ladyman et al. 2013). An algorithm can compress a sequence by removing repetitions from the sequence. The length of the program implementing the algorithm is a reasonable estimate of the Kolmogorov complexity. The Lempel–Ziv complexity is the ratio of the program's length to the original sequence's length.

Systems can be classified in more detail in terms of "the amount of information needed to specify the structure completely and the rate at which that information needs to be changed in order for the system to change" (Barrow 1998, p. 145). A simple way to compare systems is to use the *power consumption* as a comparison criterion (Wu 1989; Mämmelä and Anttonen 2017), thus combining both the structure and the speed of change of the system. Since a switching operation needs a certain amount of energy depending on the maturity of the implementation technology, the power consumption is directly proportional to the switching speed of the implementation with a given structure. The switching speed does not need to be the same everywhere in the implementation. In practice, in the most complicated implementations, some of the logic gates are only used part of the time to save energy, and effectively, the clock rate in those parts is zero. Such parts are in a *sleep mode*. The power consumption also depends on the unavoidable load capacitances of the wires to be charged and uncharged in switching. In addition to this *dynamic power*, there is some *static power* that does not depend on the switching speed. Usually, the dynamic power dominates in high-speed electronics. Additional complexity measures can be found from Ladyman et al. (2013) and Ladyman and Wiesner (2020); see also the references therein.

Performance Our aim in engineering is to develop new functionalities and maximize resource efficiency so that we can improve performance and minimize complexity. These are somewhat conflicting aims. Performance is "the manner in which or the efficiency with which something reacts or fulfills its intended purpose" (Random House Webster's College Dictionary 1999). Practical performance measures include efficiency, reliability, and agility (Mämmelä and Riekki 2022a).

The basic resources received from nature are scarce (Pagels 1988; Checkland 1999); therefore, they must be managed well and recycled if possible. Legitimacy, effectiveness, and efficiency are criteria for system fitness (Hubka and Eder 1988, p. 50; Schwaninger 2001; Skyttner 2005; Zidane and Olsson 2017). They are different aspects of system performance. In addition, some authors use the term *efficacy*, but it has various interpretations (Skyttner 2005; Zidane and Olsson 2017); therefore, we follow Schwaninger (2001) and avoid using the term efficacy.

Markus Schwaninger defined *legitimacy* as "to fulfil a purpose at the service of a larger whole" (Schwaninger 2001). It is the highest-level concept above effectiveness and efficiency from top down and measures how well the system is fitted to the environment and thus how well the system can survive. Peter F. Drucker (1964) defined effectiveness as "doing the right things" and efficiency as "doing the things right." Effectiveness is a measure of "the extent to which a system achieves its intended transformation" (Skyttner 2005). Similarly, efficiency measures "the extent to which the system achieves its intended transformation with the minimum use of resources." The efficiency is useless if we are not doing the right things. Thus, hierarchically, effectiveness is a higher-level concept used externally to the system, including quality and long-term consequences. Efficiency is a lower-level concept used internally in the system (Zidane and Olsson 2017).

Unfortunately, effectiveness and legitimacy are subjective concepts and very hard to measure because of their multifaceted character, just as in multiobjective optimization with incommensurate resources (Marler and Arora 2004). We, therefore, focus on efficiency and keep effectiveness and legitimacy as necessary qualitative measures. In simple cases, legitimacy and effectiveness reduce to efficiency.

Efficiency In biology, the survivability of organisms is improved through improved efficiency (Westerhoff et al. 2009). Therefore, organisms are highly efficient although not maximally efficient. Nature can sometimes be used as a model for engineering. For example, engineers build load-bearing structures using tree forks (Amtsberg et al. 2020). Tree forks are efficient structures, and human manufacturing processes are incapable of replicating them. Efficiency is a side product caused by the fight for survival. The same is valid for products and services whose prices are defined evolutionally using the law of supply and demand. Fundamentally, in engineering, the goal is to minimize the use of basic resources for a given performance.

Efficiency is measured using the ratio of benefits and expenditures where the benefits correspond to some functionality such as number of bits transmitted, and the expenditures correspond to the use of some basic resources such as energy (Hubka and Eder 1988). The expenditures normalize the benefits. In Hubka and Eder (1988), this is the definition of effectiveness, but for us, this looks like a measure of efficiency when we remember the examples of energy and spectral efficiency (Proakis and Salehi 2008). Simple examples in physics are mass density, the ratio of mass and volume (in kg/m^3), which is a form of spatial efficiency, and speed, which is the ratio of distance and time (in m/s), a form of temporal efficiency. Biological systems do not necessarily aim at maximal efficiency (Westerhoff et al. 2009) since organisms optimize fitness to improve survivability. Since the resources are scarce (Checkland 1999), high energy efficiency is a necessary by-product.

The functionality may be, for example, the number of transmitted bits in communication or the number of performed operations (OPs) in computing. The bit rate has the unit bit/s, and the computing rate has the unit OP/s. These are also temporal efficiency measures. Energy efficiency is measured using the number of bits per energy unit (in bit/J) in communication and the number of operations per energy unit (in OP/J) in computing (Mämmelä and Anttonen 2017). Similar units are bit/s/W and OP/s/W, respectively, where the latter is usually abbreviated as OPS/W. An average is assumed if the bit rate or computing rate changes. In communications, spectral efficiency is measured in bit/s/Hz (Proakis and Salehi 2008). Normalization is not usually done in the case of delay, but it is measured in seconds. Sometimes efficiency is defined as output/input ratio; for example, in amplifiers, it is the ratio of output energy/input energy (Hubka and Eder 1988).

Efficiency is measured with a ratio. Thus, we have the problem of how a ratio of the form Y/X should be averaged, where X and Y are both random variables. If both X and Y are random variables, the average can be formed either using $E(Y/X)$ as in Darraji et al. (2011) or $E(Y)/E(X)$ as in Raab (1986), where E refers to an ensemble or group average. It is easy to show that the averages are generally different (Heijmans 1999). The averages are identical if X is nonrandom. The whole problem comes from the nonlinearity of the inversion operation and the randomness of X.

Another nonlinearity is the logarithm used in decibels in the form of $10 \lg(Z)$ where $Z = Y/X$ as in the measurement of attenuation (Rappaport 2002; Pahlavan and Levesque 2005). We can either average the actual values of X and Y or the decibel values. The result of the two approaches is different. If the goal is to measure the average of Y/X, we should not average the decibels. The correct approach is, thus, to form the average $10 \lg[E(Y)/E(X)]$. We conclude that the average $E(Y)/E(X)$ is, in general, more reasonable than $E(Y/X)$, as already claimed in Raab (1986), although no reasons were given there. The reason is the log-interval scale used in the ratio Y/X; see the description of measurement scales.

Measurement scales The commonly used measurement scales are nominal, ordinal, interval, ratio, and log-interval scales (Houle et al. 2011); see Table 5.2, where the properties of each scale are given, plus some examples where each scale is used. We call them types of the measurement scales. *Qualitative scales* include nominal and ordinal scales. *Nominal scales* typically classify objects as nominal scales preserve only equality property. In other words, the objects are either the same or not the same in nominal scale measurements. In biology, the nominal scale is used in a taxonomy where animals are classified into species. Such classifications are often seen as problematic when looked at more closely. An *ordinal scale* preserves equality and ordinality properties; that is, the order of the measurement values also reflects the order of the objects. However, we cannot say how much better one object is compared to the other. An example of an ordinal scale is the Mohs scale of mineral hardness by Friedrich Mohs (1812), which characterizes the scratch resistance of various minerals through the ability of harder material to scratch softer material. Another example of an ordinal scale is the absolute rating scale used in audio or video quality tests, often using a five-level scale.

Quantitative scales, on the other hand, include interval, log-interval, and ratio scales (Houle et al. 2011). *Interval scales* are linear scales that preserve equality, ordinality, and interval ratios among the objects. The interval scale is used, for example, in delays and temperatures. The interval ratio property means that one can make quantitative comparisons of intervals between measured values but not of the measured values themselves. Interval measures usually appear in temperature measurements. Suppose that we measure the temperature of objects A, B, and C. Suppose the temperatures are 15, 20, and 30 °C, respectively. Thus, the temperature difference between A and B is 5°, and between B and C, the difference is 10°. We also know that the difference in temperature between B and C is twice as much as between A and B. However, the statement that object C is twice as hot as object A makes no sense as if we change our measurement units from Celsius to Fahrenheit, we will obtain a different result.

Log-interval scales are minor variations of interval scales where intervals are replaced by ratios using the properties of logarithms. Consequently, the interval ratio property is replaced by a log-ratio property where one can make quantitative comparisons of ratios of measured values but not the measured values themselves. Log-interval measures are used, for example, in measurements of density and efficiency. Efficiency metrics are themselves ratios, but the scale is called the log-interval scale, i.e., it uses an interval scale when the ratio Y/X is expressed as a logarithm $\log(Y/X) = \log(Y) - \log(X)$. A logarithmic transformation converts any log-interval scale into an interval scale. This property is used in diagrams using logarithmic scales and decibels (dB) (Rappaport 2002).

Finally, in a *ratio scale* we define an absolute zero point, and we can compare different metrics using ratios. The scale is used, for example, in measurements of

Table 5.2 Measurement scales

Scale	Properties	Examples of use
Nominal scale	Equality	Species
Ordinal scale	Equality, ordinality	Mohs scale, absolute rating scale
Interval scale	Equality, ordinality, and interval ratios	Temperature in °C
Log-interval scale	Equality, ordinality, log-ratio property	Density, efficiency
Ratio scale	Equality, ordinality, interval ratios, and value ratios	Energy, time duration, bandwidth, absolute temperature

energy, time duration, bandwidth, and absolute temperature (in K). It preserves equality, ordinality, interval ratios, and value ratios. For that reason, one can make quantitative comparisons between the differences and ratios of the measured values themselves.

We can compare ratios of measured values if and only if the ratio Y/X does not depend on X. In that case, one system is, for example, twice as efficient as another one. In interval scales, addition and subtraction operations are meaningful, but in log-interval scales, multiplication and division operations are meaningful. The addition and subtraction operations do not have any meaning in the log-interval scale. Thus, there is a major difference between log-interval and ratio scales, which are often mixed.

The measurement values cannot be used arbitrarily. For example, one may obtain results that do not make sense by applying mathematical operations to measurement values. Each scale permits only certain types of transformations, commonly called admissible transformations, which transform one scale into another, for example, from the Celsius scale to the Fahrenheit scale (Houle et al. 2011). Admissible transformations do not change the type of the scale. Usually, there is some kind of nonlinearity in the group of metric transformations, which changes the scale from one type to another. Finally, a statement is meaningful in measurement theory if its truth is invariant against all admissible transformations.

Ideally, joint probabilities should be used for random variables. An arithmetic average is usually used for averaging variables, but if the distribution is skewed, the median may be a better measure. In utility functions, a weighted arithmetic or geometric average is usually used, and some authors prefer the weighted geometric average (Marler and Arora 2004; Stanczak et al. 2008; Saaty 2008; Krejki and Stoklasa 2018). A histogram that estimates the probability density function gives a more complete understanding of the changes.

Different performance measures are availability and reliability, which have no units (Avizienis et al. 2004; Al-Kuwaiti et al. 2009; Trivedi and Bobbio 2017). *Availability* refers to the readiness for correct service. Quantitatively, availability is the percentage of the time the end-to-end communication service is delivered according to an agreed quality of service (QoS), divided by the time the system is expected to provide the end-to-end service according to the specification in a specific area. The QoS refers to the quantitative performance metrics such as throughput, reliability, and delay. The quality of experience (QoE) is "service quality as subjectively perceived by the user" (Stankiewicz and Jajszczyk 2011).

Reliability refers to continuity of correct service (Avizienis et al. 2004; Zio 2009). The goal of reliability engineering is to reduce the probability of failure of a product. In communications, reliability is measured when the system is available. Reliability is the number of transmitted packets (or, more generally, PDUs such as bits) successfully delivered to the destination within the time constraint the targeted service requires, divided by the total number of transmitted packets (NGMN 2015; ITU-T 2016). Similarly, given a time constraint, the error rate is the number of erroneously received packets (or, more generally, PDUs such as bits) divided by the total number of packets. Thus, error rate = 1 − reliability. Low reliability may have similar effects as a large delay in some services (Shi et al. 2009).

The measurement of error rate is discussed in Newcombe and Pasupathy (1982). Since the errors are usually rare, measuring the error rate may take a long time. A rule of thumb is that during measurement, there should be at least one hundred errors if the errors are random. The errors may be clustered in a fading channel, and we need more time (Bello 1998); perhaps one hundred fades. In a slowly fading channel compared to the symbol rate, a possible solution in simulations is to use a random time-invariant model where the channel is independently and randomly selected for each measurement.

5.2.3 Finiteness of Human Knowledge

Human knowledge is finite because of the emergence concept and fundamental or principal limits of nature and existing open problems. We must follow some physical laws of nature (Copeland 1981; Barrow 1998; Meindl 2001; Lundheim 2002; Dewdney 2004; Cockshott et al. 2012; Markov 2014; Mämmelä and Anttonen 2017; Mämmelä et al. 2018). We present some fundamental and practical limits and related principles in Tables 5.3, 5.4 and 5.5. It is not possible to surpass the fundamental limits, but some of the limits are suspected. Initially, the limits came from the practical limits, but after the technology matured, fundamental limits became interesting. They were defined roughly between 1850 and 1950. Practical limits are related to speed-up in parallel computing using different constraints (Amdahl 2013; Gustafson 1988; Sun and Chen 2010; Woo and Lee 2008), transport capacity in an ad hoc network (Gupta and Kumar 2000), and cooling efficiency (Avila et al. 2007).

Table 5.3 Fundamental limits

Year	Discoverer	Discovery
1848	W. Thompson	Absolute zero temperature
1873	K. E. Abbe	Diffraction limit
1904	H. Poincare	Maximum speed
1927	W. Heisenberg	Uncertainty principle
1928	H. Nyquist	Maximum symbol rate
1929	L. Szilard	Minimum switching energy
1945	H. Cramer and C. R. Rao	Minimum variance
1946	D. Gabor	Uncertainty principle
1948	C. E. Shannon	Channel capacity
1949	M. J. E. Golay	Shannon limit
1949	C. E. Shannon	Minimum sampling rate

Table 5.4 Practical limits

Year	Discoverer	Discovery
1967	G. M. Amdahl	Fixed-size speedup
1988	J. L. Gustafson	Fixed-time speedup
1993	X.-H. Sun and L. Ni	Memory-bounded speedup
2000	P. Gupta and P. R. Kumar	Transport capacity
2007	A. Avila et al.	Limit for cooling
2008	D. H. Woo and H.-H. Lee	Energy-efficient speedup

Table 5.5 Fundamental principles

Year	Discoverer	Discovery
1687	I. Newton	Conservation of momentum and angular momentum
1789	A. Lavoisier	Conservation of mass
1814	P.-S. Laplace	Conservation of information
1843	J. Joule	Conservation of energy
1843	M. Faraday	Conservation of charge
1854	R. Clausius	Entropy law
1890	H. Poincare	Unpredictable systems
1905	A. Einstein	Conservation of mass-energy
1931	K. Gödel	Incompleteness theorems
1936	A. Church and A. Turing	Church–Turing thesis
1971	S. Cook and L. Levin	Intractable problems

Fundamental and practical limits The lowest possible temperature is *absolute zero* or 0 K (Young et al. 2012). Following the Boltzmann principle, the entropy has reached a constant value at this temperature. The residual entropy is usually but not necessarily close to zero. The universe's average temperature is 2.726 ± 0.01 K (Turner 1993), just above the absolute zero and about the hundredth part of the room temperature ($T = 300$ K). The temperature is a sign of background radiation from the big bang, as predicted by George Gamow (1948). It is possible to approach absolute zero temperatures well below 1 K. At those temperatures, matter exhibits superconductive properties. Due to the definition of temperature, we can in theory move even below the absolute zero (Braun et al. 2013). One may question whether the concept of temperature is even relevant in such extreme situations (Carr 2013).

Abbe's resolution or diffraction limit (also called Abbe-Rayleigh diffraction limit) can be used for lenses and antennas (Zheludev 2008; Berry et al. 2019). If one adjusts the distance of the radiating elements of an antenna array, there are no theoretical limits for antenna directivity. If we move below the resolution limit, we have a phenomenon called superresolution. The sensitivity of the practical antennas to manufacturing errors renders the concept impractical. Such superresolution can be attained in spectral analysis if we have additional knowledge of the second-order statistics (i.e., autocorrelation function) of the signal to be estimated (Kay 1988). Superresolution has also been suggested for radar systems, but in practice, targets cannot be modeled as point scatterers, and the approach is not practical (Rihaczek 1983).

The *speed of light* is an axiom in Einstein's special relativity theory, originally proposed as a limit by Henri Poincare (1904) (Rothman 2003). Maxwell (1865) was the first to show that electromagnetic waves propagate at the speed of light. There is some support for the maximum speed from the measurements by Albert A. Michelson and Edward W. Morley (1887), who observed that the speed of light does not depend on the speed of the observer. The mass of a particle increases towards infinity when we approach the speed of light. If we could surpass the speed of light, there would be a conflict with the causality principle (Penrose 1999, pp. 273–275, 369–371). Although the phase velocity of light may exceed the velocity of light (Chiao and Milonni 2002), the actual speed of causality does not exceed the speed of light (Wang et al. 2000; Stenner et al. 2003).

The speed of light is now used in the definition of the meter, our unit of length. Thus, the speed is precisely known, by definition, and it is 299 792 458 m/s. The maximum speed is valid for all electromagnetic waves, including radio waves, microwaves, infrared, visible light, ultraviolet, X-rays, and gamma rays. When the waves propagate in matter, the speed is generally smaller than in a vacuum, and the light can even be stopped for times in the order of milliseconds (Goss Levi 2001). The speed is about the same in the air; thus, the finite speed gives the minimum delay for the signal carried by the radio waves. Because of the delay, any network looks spatially distributed, not lumped. If there are reflections, the path length gives the delay for each reflected wave. The reflection result is a delay spread, and the reflections may be resolvable (Turin 1984).

So far, the warp drive proposed by John W. Campbell (1957) has remained a dream of science fiction (Elbehiery and Elbehiery 2022). A warp drive is an imaginary faster than the speed of light spacecraft propulsion system. Already, Albert Einstein wrote about quantum entanglement as "spooky action at a distance" without any delay, known as the Einstein–Podolsky–Rosen (EPR) paradox (1935) that was shown to exist in Shalm et al. (2015). In 2017, a quantum teleportation experiment was conducted with photons at a distance of 1400 km (Ren et al. 2017). It is believed that information connects cause and effect, and the speed of light in a vacuum is the maximum speed at which we can exchange information (Penrose 1999, pp. 273–275, 369–371), and so far, there is no experimental evidence on the opposite.

Isaac Newton's laws are axioms, some of which were shown inaccurate by Albert Einstein's relativity theories. Some observations cannot be explained by either of the theories, resulting in auxiliary hypotheses of dark matter and dark energy to "rescue" the theories (Li et al. 2011; Chae 2023). Alternatively, some modifications have been proposed to Newtonian mechanics, thus explaining that gravity is stronger than the theory predicts without the need for dark matter. Tuomo Suntola's dynamic universe theory does not need the assumption of dark energy (Suntola 2018). Some claims have been that Newton's third law can be violated, but such claims are still controversial (Wu 2018).

The *Heisenberg limit*, also called the *Heisenberg uncertainty principle*, gives a lower bound for the product $\Delta x\ \Delta p$ of the measurement uncertainty of the position Δx and the uncertainty of the momentum Δp of a particle. Since the momentum $p = mv$ is the product of mass m and speed v, the uncertainty is also valid for the speed. We cannot measure the position and the speed of a particle simultaneously with an arbitrary accuracy.

In signal theory, we have the *Gabor uncertainty principle*: the product of the duration and bandwidth called a time-bandwidth product of a signal has a minimum value where the actual minimum depends on the definition of the duration and bandwidth, but it is in the order of unity (Ziemer and Tranter 2014). This limit is a result of the time-frequency duality (Bello 1964).

In estimation theory, we have *the Cramer–Rao bound*: any unbiased estimate has a minimum variance depending on the form of the signal used for estimation (Skolnik 1970; Kay 1993). The limit depends on the signal-to-noise ratio. For time estimation, the limit depends on the bandwidth of the used signal. For frequency estimation, the limit depends on the duration of the used signal. A larger bandwidth or duration, respectively, improves the estimation of time and frequency.

Harry Nyquist (1928) derived the *maximum symbol rate* $R = 2W$ in an ideal noiseless channel with a bandwidth W (Landau 1967). The maximum rate is obtained with a unique pulse that has the form $\mathrm{sinc}(x) = \sin(\pi x)/\pi x$ (Proakis and Salehi 2008). There is no intersymbol interference (ISI) up to the maximum symbol rate. Above the Nyquist rate $2W$, we cannot avoid the ISI, but transmission is still possible with a somewhat reduced performance and increased complexity (Ishihara et al. 2021). We commonly assume that a signal band-limited to W cannot oscillate at frequencies higher than W (Ferreira and Kempf 2006; Berry et al. 2019). A signal band-limited to W cannot change substantially in an interval shorter than $1/2W$. However, localized high-frequency transients called *superoscillations* can occur only with amplitudes having widely different scales. We can produce fast-varying functions of any form in a limited bandwidth. The concept is closely related to superresolution and the Abbe diffraction limit (Zheludev 2008) because of frequency-space duality (Van Veen and Buckley 1988).

The Nyquist rate is closely related to the *Nyquist-Shannon sampling theorem*, which Shannon (1949) later proved rigorously. According to the theorem, we can reconstruct a band-limited signal with a bandwidth W from the samples if the uniform sampling rate is $f_s > 2W$. We can reconstruct the signal with the $\mathrm{sinc}(x)$ pulse. The average sampling rate can be reduced by periodic nonuniform sampling and random sampling using compressive sensing (Mishali and Eldar 2010). *Periodic nonuniform sampling* is used when the spectrum is fully occupied. *Random sampling* is used for multiband signals (Rani et al. 2018), which are sparse in the frequency domain. We can combine the two approaches.

In information theory, Shannon's (1948) *channel capacity* $C = W \log_2(1 + S/N)$ is the maximum bit rate in a linear ideal channel of bandwidth W having additive white Gaussian noise (AWGN) when the error probability of a long codeword is approaching zero. In the best case, there is only one erroneous bit in an erroneous code word. In general, we do not know how many bits are received in error. The complexity, computing energy, and delay of the system are assumed to be infinite. Ralph Hartley (1928) derived a similar approximate equation two decades earlier.

A network transports one bit-meter when one bit has been transported a distance of one meter toward its destination (Gupta and Kumar 2000). Gupta and Kumar (2000) derived the *transport capacity* of a multihop ad hoc network. The network's capacity is expressed in bit-meters per second as a function of bit rate and number of network nodes.

We can derive from the channel capacity the *Shannon limit*, which is the minimum received energy E_b per correctly received bit when bandwidth W is approaching infinity (Golay 1949; Shannon 1953). The signal power is $S = E_bC$, and the noise power is $N = N_0W$ where N_0 is the power spectral density of white noise. The Shannon limit is $E_{b,\min}/N_0 = \ln 2$, corresponding to $-$ 1.5917 dB, but this needs an infinite complexity, computing energy, and delay and unlimited M-ary modulation with infinite M. If the bandwidth is finite, the code rate should approach zero, and the bit rate would be minimal in a finite bandwidth. The code rate is the ratio of the information symbols and all symbols that include redundant symbols. We can approach the Shannon limit using low-density parity check (LDPC) codes when we use a finite code rate and, thus, a finite bandwidth. For a binary system with a code rate of ½, the Shannon limit is 0.1871 dB (Chung et al. 2001). For a nonbinary system, the corresponding limit is 0 dB. Some of the new codes such as Turbo codes have an error-rate bottoming effect, meaning that at large signal-to-noise ratios, the error probability saturates.

The *Szilard limit* (1929) is the minimum switching energy of a transistor of any form when the probability of error approaches the value of ½ (Mämmelä and Anttonen 2017). The limit is often called *Landauer limit* (1961) and sometimes also *von Neumann limit* (1949) or *Boltzmann limit* since the limit can be derived from the Boltzmann probability (1868) (Zhirnov et al. 2003; Meindl 2000; Zhirnov and Cavin 2013; Mämmelä et al. 2018). The limit is $E_{sw} = N_0 \ln 2$, where the noise spectral density $N_0 = kT$ depends on the Boltzmann constant k and absolute temperature T. At room temperature ($T = 300$ K), N_0 is about 4 zW/Hz, whereas the Szilard limit is about 3 zJ. In practice, the switching energy must be well above the Szilard limit to make the error probability small enough even for a larger number of transistors (Kish 2002). In Zhirnov et al. (2003) and Zhirnov and Cavin (2013), a lower limit was derived for the gate length of a transistor using the Heisenberg and Szilard limits. The limit depends on the switching energy (well above the Szilard limit) and the mass of the electric charge. We can surpass the limit by *reversible computing*, where no information is destroyed, and all the operations can be reversed. The process of destroying information has an energy cost. Due to limited memory, one has to destroy information to store new information. In reversible computing, there is no need to destroy any information, so it does not cost anything in energy. However, such computing seems to be very slow and thus impractical, and the possible gain can, in practice, be lost in the capacitances in wiring (Mämmelä and Anttonen 2017).

Numerically, the Szilard limit E_{sw} and the Shannon limit $E_{b,\min}$ are identical (Meindl 2000), although they are derived from different principles: the Szilard limit refers to the switching energy of a transistor, but the Shannon limit refers to the minimum received energy per bit for an infinite symbol sequence. Some authors think there is no conceptual difference (Meindl 2000; Zhirnov et al. 2003; Sarpeshkar 2010).

Fundamental principles David Hilbert thought that in a finite formal system, where the number of axioms and the number of rules are finite, every theorem should be provable in a finite number of steps (Casti 1991, 1994, pp. 138–143). Kurt Gödel defined two *incompleteness theorems* that state that mathematics would be limited if one could not add new axioms. One can extend the set of axioms and continue exploring. The theorems are: all finite formal systems remain incomplete (first theorem), and a formal system is too weak to prove its consistency or coherence (second theorem). A formal system is *complete* if every mathematical truth corresponds to a theorem and vice versa. A formal system is *consistent* if it does not include contradictory statements. According to Gödel, a finite formal system cannot be simultaneously complete and consistent. Essentially, Gödel showed that we will never get all the truth by following a simple set of rules; there is always something that deductive arguments cannot cover within a selected set of axioms.

Before Gödel's theorems were known, science based on axiomatic systems was led twice to a dead end. The first time this happened in ancient Greece, where deduction was assumed to be the only respectable means of attaining knowledge, axioms were considered to be "absolute truths," and other branches of knowledge could be developed from similar "absolute truths" (Asimov 1987, pp. 9–10). For the second time, there was a dead end when, at the beginning of the 1900s, positivists attempted to bring all the philosophy onto an axiomatic basis (Kline 1995, p. 227). Alfred North Whitehead and Bertrand Russell published the three-volume book *Principia Mathematica* in the USA in 1911–1913. In Europe, the Vienna Circle, chaired by Moritz Schlick at the University of Vienna in 1924–1936, had similar positivist ideas. Both attempts failed. There is an equivalence between a formal system of logic and a computer program and an equivalence between the computer program and a dynamic system, namely the halting problem and chaos, respectively (Casti 1991, 1994, pp. 141, 147).

Some of the laws coming from thermodynamics are the law of conservation of energy (first law), the entropy law (second law), and absolute zero (third law), which is, at the same time, a fundamental limit (Young et al. 2012). According to the energy conservation law, the energy is constant in an isolated system and can be neither created nor destroyed. The consumed energy must be transfered to the environment through heat by cooling, the efficiency of which is finite in W/m^2 (Mämmelä et al. 2018). Cooling may be based on conduction, convection, or radiation. Without cooling, the system's temperature may become too high, say, above 100 °C, which is dangerous to the system itself (Keyes 1987) and the users.

Classical physics has five *conservation laws*: energy, mass, momentum, angular momentum, and charge (Young et al. 2012). According to Emmy Noether (1915), conservation laws are signs of symmetry. The conservation of mass is valid only in chemical reactions, and it is not a universal law since mass and energy are equivalent, and mass can be changed to energy. The total mass-energy is conserved in all physical processes in an isolated system. Mass can be changed to energy, for example, in a nuclear reaction, either fission or fusion. Energy can also change to matter (Klein 1996, p. 46). For instance, if two protons collide, their kinetic energy may be changed to new protons and antiprotons.

There is also a law of *conservation of information*. Physical information means everything (velocity, momentum, angular momentum, etc.) needed to define the state of a system. In a deterministic world, we would know the past and could predict the future since we have all the information to determine the past and the future. This statement on causal determinism is originally from Laplace (1814). In quantum physics, the conservation of information is valid for a quantum state. A possible exception is a black hole, which may result in an information paradox (Hawking 2018).

We cannot predict the future of some deterministic systems since it is sensitive to the initial conditions (Strogatz 2014; Mämmelä et al. 2018). Such systems are *chaotic*. They contain a nonlinear feedback loop, and the nonlinearity may be based, for example, on quantization. Gravity representing feedback depends nonlinearly on the squared distance. The change of weather is a chaotic process; thus, the forecasts are a maximum of about ten days, and the forecast uncertainty increases for a longer time span. A nonlinear feedback loop may converge to a limit cycle or hang-up, one of the attractors in chaos theory. In *dithering*, noise is intentionally added to avoid the limit cycle (Ziemer and Peterson 1985). In a network, we can prevent chaotic situations caused by collisions by using random time intervals. Chaos may also occur if many feedback loops interact (Mämmelä et al. 2023). The problem can be avoided by decoupling the loops by interference avoidance (Pottie 1995). One form of decoupling in a hierarchical system is *time-scale separation*, where the time scale in the loop at the upper level is much larger than at the lower level.

The *entropy law* states that the degree of disorder (Checkland 1999, p. 114) called entropy $S = k \ln \Omega$ is consistently increased or kept constant and never decreased in an isolated system where Ω the number of microstates, which is a positive integer, implying that entropy is always nonnegative (Young et al. 2012). The entropy is zero if Ω is one. Entropy is a measure of the unavailability of energy (Asimov 1984). In an isolated system, the total energy is constant, but the available energy decreases when the entropy increases. In an open system, the situation is different since the entropy can be reduced locally if the environment's entropy is increased. Thus, an open system may receive energy from the environment. In our case, energy usually comes from the Sun, and the entropy of the Sun is increased, so the Sun-Earth system has increased entropy. Life is based on open systems, as explained by Ilya Prigogine (Boulton et al. 2015).

Open problems in engineering were summarized in Riekki and Mämmelä (2021). Emergence in complex systems is a long-lasting open problem. Open problems related to emergence include, for example, general theory of systems (von Bertalanffy 1971), semantic information theory (Stonier 1997; Checkland 1999; Qin et al. 2023), and network information theory (Cover and Thomas 2006). A crucial semantic problem is the frame problem. A partial solution to network information theory is network utility maximization (NUM) theory, which is based on the mathematical decomposition of the network into layers and functional modules, including vertical and horizontal decomposition (Chiang et al. 2007; Lin et al. 2006; Palomar and Chiang 2006; Johansson et al. 2006). The layers are loosely coupled, implying time-scale separation.

Some design problems are challenging to solve (Michalewicz and Fogel 2004). Sometimes, there is no unique performance criterion, and different requirements have different unknown priorities or weights. The complexity may depend exponentially on the size of the problem. Some problems may even have a factorial complexity (Woeginger 2008). The solutions are heavily constrained, and they may vary with time. The models may be too simplified, and the solutions may be useless.

Paradoxes *Paradoxes* are statements that look contradictory or oppose common sense and may be true (Merriam-Webster 2024). The word paradox comes from the Greek *paradoxon* 'incredible statement or opinion' (Online Etymology Dictionary 2024). We can call paradoxes also dilemmas or conflicts. A broad history of paradoxes is included in Sorensen (2003). Summaries of paradoxes are included in Poundstone (1988), Casti (1994), Klein (1996), Barrow (1998), Francois (2000), Sorensen (2003), Sainsbury (2009), Baldwin et al. (2010), Chang (2013), Van Lange et al. (2013), Yanofsky (2013) and Uusikylä and Jalonen (2023). We usually know the root causes of the paradoxes, but still, they cannot be solved. Paradoxes often come from a tension between opposites, for example, in the social dilemma between individual and collective rationality or the economic and political conflict in political science (Zeeman 1979; Dawes and Messick 2000). The dilemma leads to the need for trade-offs: there are no right or wrong answers to the conflicts. Systems are often dynamic and change smoothly between the opposite extremes as in thesis-antithesis-synthesis dialectic, a form of *ambidexterity* (O'Reilly and Tushman 2013; Uusikylä and Jalonen 2023) or "using both hands with equal ease" (Merriam-Webster 2024).

Interesting system paradoxes are conjunction systems paradox, equivalence systems paradox, and disjunction systems paradox (Baldwin et al. 2010; Uusikylä and Jalonen 2023). In the *conjunction systems paradox* or the paradox of opposite forces, forces drive the system in opposite directions. The left hand does not know what the right hand is doing. An example is the Jevons paradox. Another example is that nowadays, governments are trying to achieve a short graduation period for doctoral dissertations so that doctors can enter the labor market and influence society. Still, the opposite force lies in the fact that solving major problems requires extensive experience that cannot be achieved quickly.

In the *equivalence systems paradox*, the system has opposite properties, and there is a question of definition. An example is the sorites paradox, where it is difficult to say when a sandhill stops being a sandhill if separate sand grains are removed from it. The name of the paradox comes from a Greek word meaning 'heap.' In the *disjunction systems paradox*, also called the identity systems paradox, a system is more or less than the sum of its parts, a classic example of emergence. These and some other paradoxes mentioned elsewhere in this book are collected in Table 5.6. It is also a paradox that system theorists do not often know about each other.

Table 5.6 Paradoxes described in this book

Paradox	Explanation
Social dilemma	Tension between individual and collective rationality
Economic conflict	Conflict between equality and proportionality
Political conflict	Conflict between political freedom and power
Paradox of opposite forces	Forces drive a system in opposite directions
Jevons paradox	If energy efficiency of a species or product is improved, the total energy consumption is increased
Paradox of opposite properties	There is no strict border between two definitions
Paradox of emergence	A whole is different from the sum of its parts
Information paradox	Information is not conserved in a black hole
EPR paradox	Quantum entanglement has no delay
Polanyi's paradox	Intuition cannot be explained
Moravec's paradox	Humans and machines complement each other
Eigen's paradox	Only specific enzymes can produce certain nucleic acids, but the enzymes can only be produced using the nucleic acids
Chance and free will	Chance and free will do not follow the deterministic world view
Direction of time	Laws of physics do not depend on the direction of time, but in the entropy law, the time has a direction towards increased entropy
Negative group delay	The group delay in the frequency domain can be negative in causal systems
Finite time duration and bandwidth	A signal cannot have finite duration and bandwidth at the same time
Deadlock	A system reaches a state where it cannot continue
Attractor	Chaotic systems may generate order

John L. Casti presented five paradoxes in complex systems, all of which are relevant to us, including catastrophes, chaos, uncomputability, irreducibility, and emergence, leading to unpredictable nonintuitive behavior caused by the nonlinearity of the systems (Casti 1982, 1994), see Table 5.7. The paradoxes are presented in detail elsewhere in this book; including system theories (catastrophe theory, chaos theory, theory of computing) and the discussion of emergence (irreducibility and emergence). Paradoxes in scientific reasoning are also summarized in Poundstone (1988), Chang (2013) and Yanofsky (2013), complementing the discussion in Casti (1994).

Our thinking is developed best in a crisis (Klein 1996). As Etienne Klein explains, paradoxes are like an ingenious twist in a good drama and a valuable tool for teaching. Science led to a crisis at the end of the 1800s because paradoxes and the foundations of the classical scientific method were questioned (Francois 2000). There are three kinds of paradoxes (Poundstone 1988). The weakest type is a fallacy or a mistake

Table 5.7 Other major paradoxes of interest

Intuition	Paradox
Small, gradual changes in causes give rise to small gradual changes in effects	Catastrophe
Deterministic rules of behavior give rise to completely predictable events	Chaos
All true statements can be proved using deductive logic	Uncomputability
Complicated systems can be understood by breaking them down into simpler parts	Irreducibility
Surprising behavior is a result of complicated interactions among system parts	Emergence

in reasoning where we can "show," for example, that 1 = 2. The second type is "common sense is wrong," such as in the claim that heavier balls fall faster than lighter balls. Another example is the twin paradox of the relativity theory. In the third type, it is not clear which premises should be discarded, such as in the liar paradox, for example, "this sentence is false," which is self-contradictory, and the paradox cannot be solved.

Mathematicians found strange topological objects such as August F. Möbius strip, fractals (initially Helge von Koch snowflakes), Felix Klein's inside-outside bottles, and Waclaw Sierpinski's sieves (Francois 2000). In addition, non-Euclidean geometries and the infinity paradox in Georg Cantor sets were discovered. There were speculations of the fourth dimension. In logic, there were self-contradictory statements and self-including sets. The study of perception and observing systems led to Heinz von Förster's second-order cybernetics (Scott 2004; Ramage and Shipp 2020).

The entropy law was first seen as a paradox since life appeared impossible. Ilya Prigogine (1955) noticed that the entropy law is valid in isolated systems, and in open systems, order can be increased without violating the law. Henri Poincare (1890) studied the three-body problem, finally leading to the study of chaos theory and nonlinear dynamics. Planck introduced quanta, which led to a limitation of determinism and quantum physics in the form of matrix mechanics by Werner Heisenberg (1925) and wave mechanics by Erwin Schrödinger (1927) (Penrose 1999). Paul Dirac (1930) showed in his book *The Principles of Quantum Mechanics* that the theories were equivalent and provided a more general theoretical framework. The book became a landmark in the history of physics. Planck, Heisenberg, Schrödinger, and Dirac received Nobel Prizes in physics.

The paradoxes may reveal the finiteness of human knowledge, especially regarding something small or large where our common sense does not work correctly. Quantum mechanics in the microworld and relativity theory in the macroworld have different domains of validity, and it has been an open question of how they could be combined. The quantum properties disappear in quantum-to-classical transition in a process called *quantum decoherence*, observed for the first time by H. Dieter Zeh (1970) and having experimental evidence in Schlosshauer (2019). Wojciech Zurek (1991) introduced the decoherence theory to a broader audience of physicists. In quantum decoherence, the quantum states start to follow the equations of classical physics when more particles are added to the system. Quantum decoherence is known to be a barrier of implementing quantum computers. Tuomo Suntola has shown that his dynamic universe concept is directly linked to quantum physics through the mass wave concept (Suntola 2018).

The relativity theory combines the three spatial dimensions and time into a four-dimensional space, which we find difficult to imagine. Furthermore, the space-time is curved because of masses and does not follow the conventional Euclidean geometry.

In quantum physics, there is *an information paradox*, which means that the law of conservation of information is not valid in black holes where information seems to disappear (Hawking 2018). The information paradox has not yet been solved.

Wave-particle duality means that electromagnetic waves behave simultaneously like waves and particles (Klein 1996). Christiaan Huygens (1691) proposed that light consists of waves, but Isaac Newton (1703) claimed that light consists of particles. Thomas Young demonstrated with his double-slit experiment that the wave theory is valid. Also, Albert Einstein suggested that light consists of particles. The wave-particle duality was accepted after the work of Louis de Broglie (1924).

In signal theory, strictly time-limited signals cannot be band-limited and vice versa (Ziemer and Tranter 2014; Papoulis 1962; Slepian 1976). The property is a paradox since it is difficult to imagine that signals in the real world could be unlimited in the time and frequency domain, and still, in the theoretical world, a signal cannot be limited in both the domains simultaneously. David Slepian explains that the theoretical model is just an approximation of the real world, and not all phenomena in the theoretical world can be transfered to the real world. For example, the Fourier transform used to transform signals from the time domain to the frequency domain is based on a complex exponential $\exp(j2\pi ft)$, which has an infinite duration, an impossibility in the real world.

Physical laws in Newtonian mechanics do not depend on time's direction (Klein 1996). The equations are reversible. However, in practice, time only proceeds forward. For example, in thermodynamics, the molecules follow the laws of physics that do not depend on the direction of time, but paradoxically, in the entropy law, the time has a direction towards increased entropy, and the equation is irreversible although the macroscopic behavior is a combination of the microscopic behavior. According to Kline (1995, pp. 223, 302), it is not possible to derive the entropy law of thermodynamics (a high-level macroscopic theory) from statistical mechanics (a low-level microscopic theory). The direction of time is called the *arrow of time*, a term suggested by Arthur S. Eddington (1927) since time proceeds always forward and never backward, and all systems are causal. According to relativity theory, time is not the same for all observers, but it depends on the observer's speed and the gravitational potential. When the speed is large or the gravitational potential is low, time proceeds slower, leading to a twin paradox.

Fractals, invented by Benoit Mandelbrot (1961), are special patterns found in mathematics and nature (West 2017). Most biological networks are fractals that look approximately the same at all scales. The length of the border of fractals increases when the resolution is increased and does not converge to a certain value. The length of our circulatory system, including arteries, veins, and capillaries, is about 100,000 km. The area of the alveoli of our lungs is almost the size of a tennis court.

The fractal dimension may be noninteger. A smooth line has a dimension 1, a smooth surface has a dimension 2, and a smooth volume has a dimension 3, but for example, a line may have a fractal dimension close to 2, and thus it behaves as if it would be an area. For example, Norway's coast is fractal, with a dimension of 1.52. With an additional dimension, an organism may function as if operating in four dimensions. Almost no artifact uses the power of fractals to optimize performance, and the artifacts are, in this sense, very primitive. Fractals have been applied in wireless communications, such as antennas, spreading codes, modulation, compression, and watermarking (El-Khamy 2004).

5.2.4 Needs and System Requirements

Our systems are characterized by functionality, performance, and cost (Avizienis et al. 2004). Engineers are also interested in stability and scalability (Lee et al. 1998). Performance can be measured using efficiency, reliability, and agility (Mämmelä and Riekki 2022a).

Quality goals can be defined using different bases: technology, market, benchmarking, or history (Juran and Godfey 1999). A *benchmark* is a commonly agreed standard test to measure the performance of a system (Merriam-Webster 2024). Old benchmarks in computer engineering included the number of operations per second (OPS) and the number of instructions per second (IPS). Still, they are very rough unless the operations and instructions are carefully defined. In electronics, a standard benchmark has been Moore's law (1975) for the number of transistors on a chip, valid until about 2020. Similar predictions included Dennard's (1974) scaling rules (Mämmelä and Anttonen 2017) and House's (1975) and Keyes's (1981) predictions for the energy efficiency of the switching operation. Modern benchmarks must take resource efficiency into account. For example, energy efficiency would be the number of operations per energy unit (in OP/J) (Kienle et al. 2011). Good benchmarks can be formed using the fundamental limits of nature (Mämmelä et al. 2018). Another interesting comparison can be made using a human as a reference (Sarpeshkar 2010; Kosinski 2013). Machines can easily beat humans in specific tasks, but our versatility is unbeatable, a sign of Hans Moravec's paradox.

Example benchmarks in computing include Standard Performance Evaluation Corporation (SPEC) benchmarks (1988). More generally, for global optimization, 175 test functions are available to be used in benchmark programs (Jamil and Yang 2013). In communications, benchmark tests for system design include traffic models (Botta et al. 2010), channel models, algorithms, and protocols. In fair comparisons, a benchmark task and the hardware platform with its hardware accelerators and word lengths must be carefully defined (Kuon and Rose 2006).

System *requirements* describe human needs as well as possible. The requirements can be divided into functional and nonfunctional requirements. Functionalities are

Table 5.8 Performance metrics for different basic resources

Basic resource	Performance metric	Unit
Materials	Density	kg/m^3
Energy	Energy efficiency	bit/J, OP/J
Information	Energy efficiency	bit/J
Time	Duration, delay	s
Frequency	Bandwidth efficiency	bit/s/Hz
Space	Area efficiency	$bit/s/m^2$, $OP/s/m^2$

application-specific. Scenarios and their particular cases, called use cases, are part of the vision and are used to discover user needs and define functional and nonfunctional requirements (Riekki and Mämmelä 2021). A roadmap shows the methods of reaching the vision, and planning proceeds from system requirements to a system concept and specifications. The roadmap is a trajectory to the vision. These topics are detailed in books like (Belliveauet al. 2002; Kossiakoff et al. 2011).

The nonfunctional requirements usually focus on efficiency since effectiveness and legitimacy are difficult to measure (Schwaninger 2001). Performance or efficiency metrics measure the efficiency of using the basic resources; see Table 5.8. The mass measures the use of materials but materials are sometimes included in their space requirements. For example, in electronics, we use the area in mm^2 (Kienle et al. 2011). Delays are measured without normalization, usually in ms. Depending on the most limiting basic resource, systems can be divided into bandwidth-, energy-, delay-, space-, and reliability-limited or -sensitive systems (Mämmelä et al. 2018). Availability and reliability are dimensionless ratios that are estimates of corresponding probabilities.

5.2.5 *System Verification and Validation*

System design is a form of synthesis and, therefore, a creative process. It may be based on system archetypes. New system models must be verified and validated. Verification has a different meaning in science and engineering since, in science, we do not have requirements. Verification is the opposite of falsification (Rosenberg and McIntyre 2020). In engineering, verification is confirmation that an object fulfills the specified requirements (JCGM 2012). Validation is more demanding than verification. In *validation*, the future product or service confirms that the specified requirements are suitable for the intended purpose and correspond to user needs (JCGM 2012). In nature, evolution is a validation process. In biology, experiments are done in vivo (in a test tube) or in vitro (in a living organism) (Elsasser 1987), corresponding to verification and validation, respectively.

Verification can be done using three complementary methods: analysis, simulations, and experiments. Verification is best done from simple to complex and from analysis to simulations and finally to experiments. The analysis is based either on deterministic models using deduction or on random models using statistics or their mixed forms. In constructive research, we build a prototype and make experiments with it. We can use the prototype both for verification and validation.

5.3 Forming a General Hierarchy of Systems

5.3.1 Properties of Systems

There are various definitions of a system. As discussed in Hubka and Eder (1988), it can be characterized by purpose, behavior, structure, environment, input, output, property, and state. All technical systems have a purpose for their users, but natural systems do not have a purpose; they just exist. The purpose describes a final cause that is denied in the philosophy of science and science in general. A human gives the purpose and goals to a system. A system has a *structure* that shows the relationships between the parts and the environment. The structure may be time-invariant or time-varying. A system can be isolated, closed, or open. An open system has inputs and outputs using materials, energy, and information. Information is usually carried with energy. All physical systems are causal but chance and free will seem to be exceptions.

A *property* describes or characterizes a system (Hubka and Eder 1988). It is measured quantitatively using a numerical value. Properties include, for example, bit rate, delay, and reliability. The *state* measures all properties at a given time. *Behavior* is a set of successive states of a system.

A system may be concrete or abstract, such as an axiomatic system. It has a *model* that is a simplified description of the system's regularities (Rosenberg and McIntyre 2020). Complex systems may be hierarchical and distributed. They may also be deterministic (i.e., nonrandom) or random (i.e., stochastic). A system may be natural or technical.

Different forms of *similarity* are analogy, homology, homomorphy, and isomorphy (Hubka and Eder 1988). As mentioned earlier, analogy is a functional similarity in biology because of convergent evolution, but homology is a structural similarity because of a common origin (Encyclopedia Britannica 2024; Merriam-Webster 2024). The definitions may be different in different disciplines.

Another pair of terms includes homomorphy and isomorphy. *Homomorphy* is, in biology, the "superficial resemblance between organisms of different groups due to evolutionary convergence" (Merriam-Webster 2024). *Isomorphism* is "similarity in organisms of different ancestry resulting from convergence." Homomorphism and isomorphism are thus both synonymous to analogy. In mathematics, isomorphism is "one-to-one correspondence between two mathematical sets" (Merriam-Webster 2024). In Hubka and Eder (1988), the terminology is used so that only isomorphy includes symmetry, such as in the interpretation of mathematics. Usually, isomorphy

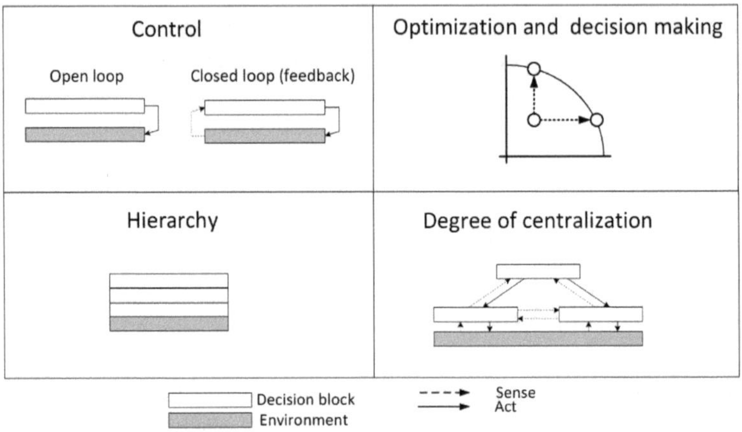

Fig. 5.5 Basic system archetypes

is assumed to correspond between a physical system and its model (Francois 2006), but strictly speaking, the models are always approximations of reality and sometimes may even predict phenomena that do not exist in the real world (Slepian 1976).

A *function* describes the transformation of a system's input to its output. *Coupling* between systems and subsystems is sometimes called interaction (Glassman 1973), which is implemented using materials, energy, and information (Hubka and Eder 1988). Qualitatively, the coupling may be full, tight, loose, or uncoupled (McGarry et al. 1999). The systems can be in series or parallel. Alternatively, feedback from the output to the input can be used.

Basic system archetypes Some basic system archetypes are summarized in Fig. 5.5 (Mämmelä and Riekki 2022b). They include control, optimization and decision-making, hierarchy, and degree of centralization. These are the building blocks of more complex systems, and they are thus system archetypes.

Control loops include open-loop control, which is a more rudimentary form of control, and closed-loop control (Ogata 2010). Figure 5.6 shows a general form of closed-loop feedback control: a sense-decide-act loop. The subsystem implementing the sense operation is called the *sensor* and the subsystem that implements the act operation is called the *actuator*.

Feedback loops are classified into negative and positive feedback loops, where positive feedback is generally considered unstable but may be used within a negative feedback loop if the latter dominates the system so that the whole system forms a negative feedback loop (DeAngelis et al. 1986; Ogata 2010). The control loop changes the state of the environment or plant from the present state to the desired state or a better performance (McFarland and Bösser 1993, pp. x–xi). If we remove the sense block, the system is called an *open-loop control system* (Ogata 2010). If we alternatively remove the act block, the system is called an *adaptation or monitoring system*, depending on the application (Widrow and Stearns 1985; Caripe et al. 1998).

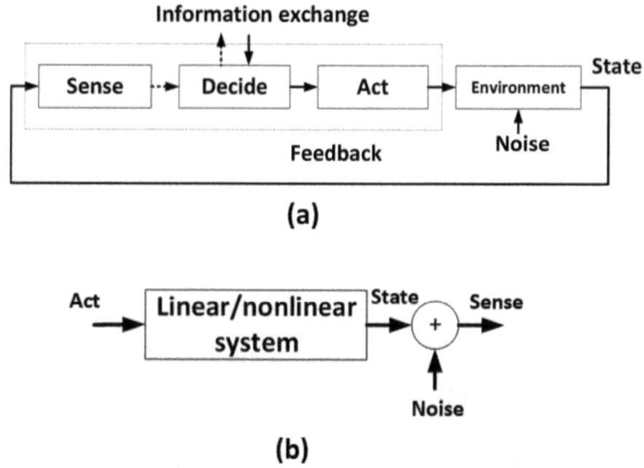

Fig. 5.6 **a** Closed loop feedback control. **b** Model of the environment

In a monitoring system, the decision maker may be a human who implements the needed actions, and this closes the loop. Such a system is using a *human in the loop* as, for example, in driving a car.

The desired state or performance is the *goal* of the feedback loop (Albus and Meystel 2001, p. 93). A human operator or supervisor sets the goal. We need free will to set a goal (Stonier 1997, pp. 174, 177). Negative feedback causes an appearance of teleology or "quasi-teleology" since the system has a goal or "purpose" yet operates according to causal laws (von Wright 1971, pp. 17, 156, 177).

In a communication network, the network state consists of node and link states and topology information. The node state includes, for example, processing capacity, memory usage, energy levels, and queuing lengths. The link parameters include, for example, transmission power, delay, error rate, bandwidth or bit rate, and signal-to-noise ratio. In the 2020s, a typical node in a wireless network was estimated to have about 2000 parameters to be configured and optimized (Imran et al. 2014).

The environment includes some noise, and thus, the sensing results are inaccurate. We also have a limited view of the state of the environment, and not everything in the environment can be controlled. We say we have limited observability and controllability, respectively (Ogata 2010, p. 675). A system is *observable* if we can determine the present state by observing the output over a finite time interval. The purpose of monitoring is to observe the state of a system. In social sciences, the term *transparency* corresponds to observability. A system is *controllable* if we can transfer the system from any initial state to any other state in a finite time interval. Rudolf E. Kalman (1960) introduced the concepts.

If the distance of sensors from the decision block is large, as in communications, the feedback signals are incomplete. Such feedback signals are an example of limited observability. Similarly, the distance to the actuator may be large and have limited controllability. Limited observability and controllability are problems, especially in networked control systems (NCSs). In Zhang et al. (2001), the effect of delays and packet errors is analyzed. Errors may be packet dropouts and multiple packet transmissions. In Sipahi (2011), the focus is on delays. In Zhang et al. (2009),

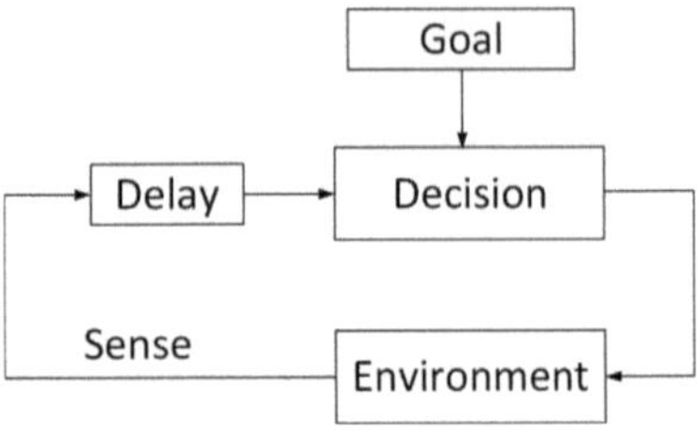

Fig. 5.7 Delay in a feedback loop

the analysis includes delays, packet losses and disorder, time-varying transmission intervals, competition of multiple nodes accessing networks, and data quantization.

The reviews (Love et al. 2004, 2008) give an overview on the limited information feedback in specific adaptive transmission systems. The limitations include bit rate, error rate, and delay. For example, we can use the information feedback in transmitter power control. The results show that limited information feedback can perform well if properly designed. However, stability problems are not discussed in Love et al. (2008). A delay may significantly affect the stability (Fig. 5.7) (Dorf and Bishop 2017).

Different forms of control and adaptation are shown in Fig. 5.8 (Mämmelä and Riekki 2022b). In open-loop control; we do not have any sense block (Ogata 2010; Mämmelä et al. 2018). *Open-loop control* tries to find its goal directly in one shot or iteratively. Such systems are working blindly, using, for example, a predefined time, such as in a washing machine or in traffic control. In open-loop control, disturbances may cause errors, and frequent calibration may be needed. In open-loop *feedforward control*, we use prediction, which is helpful if the changes are deterministic or slow (Rosenbaum 2010). A simple predictor is based on averaging. Open-loop control is more straightforward than closed-loop control; there is no stability problem and no need to measure the process output. Moreover, open-loop control has the benefit of being faster than closed-loop control, which is essential in many applications since closed-loop algorithms may be slow, especially when there are many variables to be controlled. For closed-loop feedback control, the convergence time may not be easy to predict and depends on the number of degrees of freedom or the number of parameters (Widrow and Stearns 1985).

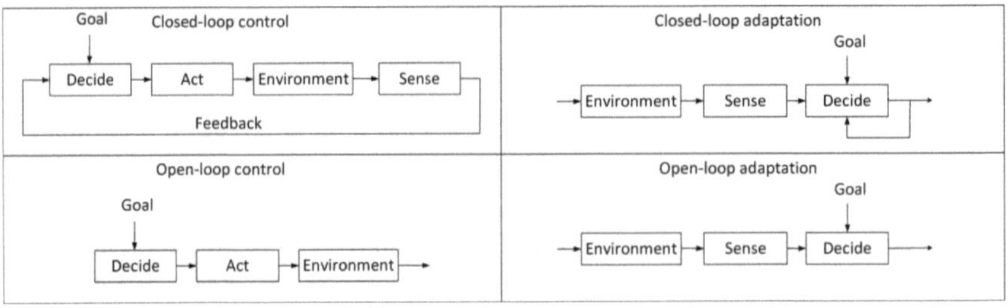

Fig. 5.8 Different forms of control and adaptation

In communications, open-loop control is sometimes used in synchronization, channel estimation, and transmitter power control, where we rely on the channel's reciprocity (Mämmelä et al. 2018). In transmitter power control, closed-loop control may be impractical if the delay in the feedback channel is excessive, and open-loop control is preferred. Open-loop control is also used in some biological systems, such as the human brain (Kanerva 2000), in addition to closed-loop control.

In an adaptation or monitoring system (Mämmelä et al. 2018; Mämmelä and Reikki 2022b), the environment is not necessarily controlled at all. A monitoring system model is common in data science, pattern recognition, and machine learning. An adaptation system can be closed-loop or open-loop. In communications applications, closed-loop adaptation is usually used based on an iterative or recursive algorithm. If a system is an open-loop system, it is sometimes called a *one-shot system* (Tyukin et al. 2021).

Hierarchies are vertical subsystem arrangements divided into nested and nonnested hierarchies (Mesarovic 1970; Mesarovic et al. 1970; O'Neill et al. 1986; Ahl and Allen 1996; Pumain 2006; Wu 2013). A hierarchy consists of several levels, which are called strata, layers, or echelons, depending on the type of hierarchy, either nested, layer, or dominance hierarchy; see Fig. 5.9. The term *level* is used as a general term when referring to any of the hierarchies. The terms strata and echelons are not very common in the present technical literature. In communications, the term layer is used even for levels in the dominance hierarchy. Each level may interact with the environment, but the interaction often occurs at the lowest level. Each level consists of subsystems called *modules* in engineering. In biology, the modules are sometimes called holons (Koestler 1967). The levels and modules are loosely coupled with each other. The environment is outside the system but hierarchically "below" the system in nonnested hierarchies.

Biological systems use a *nested* or *stratified* (multistrata) *hierarchy* where the levels are sometimes called *strata.* An organism consists of organs, cells, organelles, molecules, atoms, and elementary particles within each other. Social organizational

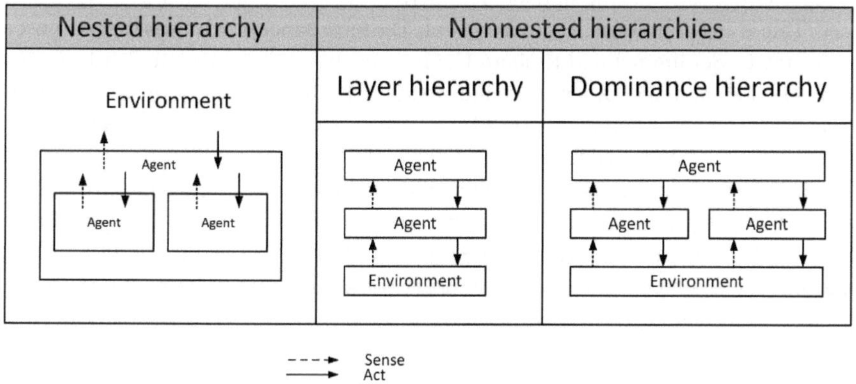

Fig. 5.9 Different forms of hierarchies

units also form nested hierarchies. In *nonnested hierarchies*, lower levels offer services to upper levels but are not inside the upper levels. Social reporting hierarchies are *dominance*, organizational, or multiechelon (echelon) *hierarchies* where the levels are sometimes called *echelons*. An example is the military command hierarchy. The army's organizational units form a nested hierarchy, but its commanders and leaders create a nonnested hierarchy.

A particular case of the dominance hierarchy is a *layer hierarchy* where the levels are called *layers*. An example is the Open Systems Interconnection (OSI) reference model used in communications (Tanenbaum and Wetherall 2011; Kurose and Ross 2013). The seven layers are physical, data link, network, transport, session, presentation, and application layers (Table 4.8). In practice, the simpler five-layer reference model is used where session and presentation layers are included in the application layer. The protocols of the different layers are called the protocol stack, which forms vertical interfaces. The OSI model also defines each layer's *application programming interfaces* (APIs) (Pautasso and Wilde 2009). They form the horizontal interfaces. The Internet protocol stack forms the TCP/IP model that was developed at the same time as the OSI model. The TCP/IP model specifies only the vertical interfaces.

Noise and interference Disturbances in the environment can be additive or multiplicative (Yu et al. 2021), reducing system performance. In the latter case, interference is called *distortion*. Usually, by noise and interference, we mean additive disturbances. In this case, we have a superposition of waves carrying the information in the channel. Such interference may appear if two packets collide in the channel. If two reflections of a wave coming from the same source interfere with each other and the delays are randomly changing, this results in fading, an example of multiplicative interference. Multipath fading is a linear phenomenon. More generally, the distortion produced by multiplication or convolution is called multiplicative interference. In the case of convolution with an impulse, the convolution reduces to multiplication. The distortion can be linear or nonlinear (de Coulon 1986; Schetzen 2006).

Anomalies Anomalies are also called outliers. In some disciplines, *concept drift* or concept shift means that the statistical properties of the environment are changed over time. This is an anomaly in the environment, The term concept drift was first proposed by Jeffrey C. Schlimmer and Richard H. Granger, Jr. (1986) (Lu et al. 2019). It may be a network anomaly. Other anomalies include deadlocks and conflicts (Coulouris et al. 2012; Hennessy and Patterson 2017). A deadlock means that the system reaches a state where it cannot continue. Deadlocks and conflicts are commonly found in distributed systems. We can detect anomalies and use some methods to avoid them such as randomization. Centralized control, in the form of priority of the upper levels over lower levels in a hierarchy, helps to avoid deadlocks (Mesarovic et al. 1970, p. 57).

5.3.2 Description Levels of Systems

Systems are described hierarchically using the functional, behavioral, and structural levels from the top down. This model is called John S. Gero's *FBS model* (1990) (Vermaas and Dorst 2007). We have extended the model to include a description of the physical level (Mämmelä et al. 2018), as seen in Table 5.9. The *functional level* describes the relationship between the system input and output as a black box without any details of the internal behavior. In a linear system, the function can be expressed by an impulse response and a transfer function (Haykin and Moher 2014; Ziemer and Tranter 2014). The system's internal behavior is usually described at the behavioral level using algorithms. The behavior is defined using the internal state changes located in the system's memory (Hubka and Eder 1988). A simple system is a discrete-time transversal filter whose state is the contents of the memory at a given time. The filter may also be time-varying, as in an adaptive filter, and the state also contains the values of the weights called parameters. In addition to the inputs, the internal functions change the state.

The parts and their relationships are described as internal functions at the structural level. The parts may be agents as in a complex adaptive system. In our solar system, the sun, planets, and moons are the parts, and the relationships include the geometrical relationships and the gravitational forces. In this case, the state consists of the locations, velocities, accelerations, etc., of the bodies. When the parts move, we say that the state has changed, and this is called behavior.

Since most, if not all, technical systems are open systems, we must also define the relationships of the parts with the environment. The changes in the structure form an additional complication in the analysis of systems. There is an extra level below the structural level, namely the *physical level*. It can be justified by Daniel D. Gajski's *Y-chart* concept in Dutt and Gajski (1990). In information technology, the implementation is done with electronics.

Some authors see a difference between organization and structure (Ramage and Shipp 2020, p. 206). According to Humbert R. Maturana and Francisco J. Varela, the organization means the relationships between parts, which we have defined as a structure (Hubka and Eder 1988). For Maturana and Varela, the structure means the parts' particular physical form. In our thinking, the physical structure belongs to the physical level of description, which is an additional level below Gero's FBS model (Vermaas and Dorst 2007). Two systems may differ at the physical level but may

Table 5.9 Description levels of a system

Description levels	Explanation
Functional level	Relationship between input and output
Behavioral level	Algorithms and protocols
Structural level	Parts and relationships
Physical level	Physical implementation

be similar at the structural level (Ramage and Shipp 2020, p. 209). Thus, there is a reasonable basis for using the additional physical level.

In digital electronics, we have a more detailed hierarchy for the description of the physical level (Gajski 1988), slightly overlapping with the FBS model, see Table 5.10. We must thus find the connections between Gero's and Gajski's models, which the authors developed independently. Gajski's system level in Table 5.10 corresponds to the functional level, the algorithmic level to the behavioral level, and the microarchitectural level corresponds to the FBS model's structural level. The levels are abstract at the higher levels and more concrete at the lower levels. The system level defines the overall performance but is not interested in which algorithms we use. The algorithmic level describes only the order of execution in the algorithms. There is no clock at the algorithmic level. The microarchitectural level specifies the time in terms of clocks and states. The microarchitectural level is often called the register-transfer level (RTL). The logic level defines how we implement Boolean operations and what gates we use. All digital machines have a finite number of states because the memory that contains the state is finite. Flip-flops are simple one-bit memories. Finally, the circuit level defines the signals in continuous time. The core component is a transistor, which is essentially a switch. Even digital systems are analog at the circuit level, but the transistors within the logic gates and the clock at the microarchitectural level make the system behave digitally. Sometimes, the layout level is a separate level below the circuit level. In Gajski's thinking, all the levels have structural, behavioral, and physical domains (Gajski 1988; Dutt and Gajski 1990) whose details are out of the scope of our book.

The *changes* in the system may be dynamical, self-organizing, or evolutionary (Table 5.11). For the definition of dimension, state, variables, and parameters, see Fig. 1.2b. In a *dynamical* or unfolding *change*, the variables change, but the dimension of the network and the parameters do not change (Boulton et al. 2015). In a *self-organizing change*, the dimensions do not change, but the parameters do change. In an *evolutionary change*, both the dimensions and the interactions change. A communication network consists of nodes (parts) and links (interactions). A self-organizing change happens, for example, when we use transmitter power control. An evolutionary change occurs in an ad hoc network where the number of nodes changes: some nodes appear, and others disappear.

In physics, many problems are analytical: the system's state may change through the interactions that do not change (Thurner et al. 2018, pp. 6–7). In complex systems,

Table 5.10 Gajski's hierarchy for the physical level in a simplified form

Hierarchy level	Corresponding FBS level and examples
System level	Functional level: processors
Algorithmic level	Behavioral level: algorithms
Microarchitectural level	Structural level: arithmetic logic units, registers
Logic level	Structural level: finite-state machines, logic gates, flip-flops
Circuit level	Physical level: timing, transistors, wires, layouts

Table 5.11 Different types of systems and their changes

Type of system	Type of change	Variable	Parameter	Dimension	Examples
Evolutionary system	Evolutionary change	Change	Change	Change	Ad hoc network
Algorithmic system	Self-organization	Change	Change	No change	Power control
Analytic system	Dynamical change	Change	No change	No change	Filter

also the interactions and parameters can change over time. Such systems change their structure, and thus, they are self-organizing systems. In such complex systems, the next state depends not only on the earlier state but also on the changes in the interactions, which makes the analysis difficult. This problem appears already in an adaptive filter that is not self-organizing. Using an algorithm, it changes its parameters, which are called the weights, and the analysis becomes more difficult.

In complexity theory, systems with dynamical changes in the parts' state follow the *analytical paradigm* (Thurner et al. 2018). Such systems are analytically tractable. Systems with self-organizing changes between the interactions of the parts have an *algorithmic* description. The algorithms describe both the changes in the variables and the parameters. A self-organizing system corresponds to a complex system that is analytically intractable. Such systems are called complex adaptive systems (CAS), consisting of interacting agents (Holland 1995; Benbya and McKelvey 2006). The systems with algorithmic descriptions may be chaotic unless designed carefully. Usually, some loose coupling is needed to improve the system's stability (Mämmelä et al. 2023).

5.3.3 Principles of Hierarchical Systems

Future network architectures will be hierarchical, modular, and loosely or weakly coupled (Simon 1973; Mämmelä et al. 2023); see Table 5.12. The hierarchy uses different speeds and amplitude, time, frequency, spatial ranges and resolutions (Saridis 1979; Albus and Meystel 2001; Meystel and Albus 2002). *Range* or scope defines the limits in amplitude, time, frequency, and spatial domains using some resolution. *Resolution* is the smallest resolved change within a specific range in the measured quantity (JCGM 2012). In Turin (1980), the author used the term resolution bin for the quantizing interval defined by resolution. It can also be called a *resolution cell*. In imaging it is called a pixel. We say that the resolution is *high* when it corresponds to a relatively small change within the range. On the other hand, we say that the resolution is *low* when it corresponds to a relatively significant change within the range.

Table 5.12 Properties of hierarchical systems

Hierarchy level	Degree of coupling	Speed	Range	Resolution
High	Loose	Slow	Broad	Low
Low	Tight	Fast	Limited	High

The amplitude range is called the *working range* in analog-to-digital conversion, the time range is roughly the *time scale* in hierarchical systems, and the frequency range is called *bandwidth*. By time scale, we mean "the period of time that it takes for something to happen or be completed" (Oxford Learner's Dictionaries 2024). The spatial range may refer to the spatial working area, such as a network or cell coverage area (in m^2). In beamforming, spatial resolution is called *beamwidth* (in degrees). In communication networks, the cellular system for frequency reuse and interference avoidance was developed by D. H. Ring in 1947 (Young 1979). A typical frequency reuse pattern consists of seven cells; each cell has a base station. We can avoid interference if each cell in the seven-cell pattern uses a different frequency band.

Generally, the range is broad or long at the higher hierarchy levels, but the resolution is low (i.e., the resolution cell is large). On the other hand, the range is narrow or short at the lower levels, but the resolution is high (i.e., the resolution cell is small). The range increases (from narrow to broad) geometrically, and the resolution decreases (from high to low) geometrically from level to level when moving from bottom up so that the complexity of each level is balanced (Albus and Meystel 2001; Meystel and Albus 2002, p. 23). The range and resolution cell ratio is approximately constant at different levels for a particular dimension (Albus and Meystel 2001, pp. 110–111, 323). In other words, the number of resolution cells is the same at all hierarchy levels. We can minimize the complexity of the whole system by optimizing the number of resolution cells in adjacent layers. In Wu (1989), the author was interested in amplitude resolution in the physical implementation and concluded that when the speed is high (i.e., the time resolution is high and the bandwidth is large), the amplitude resolution must be low and vice versa.

We want to minimize vertical coupling between feedback loops to improve stability. Usually, a major focus is on time resolution. In *vertical loose coupling*, the high layers work slowly, and the lower layers work fast (Mesarovic et al. 1970). The difference between the speeds of different levels is called time-scale separation (Kawadia and Kumar 2005; Gunawardena 2014), which is also called separation of time scales (Simon 1973; Sandell et al. 1978; Kuehn 2015; Mämmelä et al. 2023). For example, in a communication network, in the physical layer, the time resolution is in the order of 1 μs (inverse of 1 MHz); in the data link layer, the time resolution is in the order of 1 ms (inverse of 1 kHz), and in the network layer, the time resolution is in the order of 1–10 s (inverse of 0.1–1 Hz). Generally, the time-scale separation between the adjacent layers must be at least two or three orders of magnitude to guarantee stability. It can be smaller, but then stability must be compromised. In time-scale separation, the lower hierarchy level of a system is assumed to be operating fast enough compared to the higher level so that the lower level has reached a steady state from higher layer point of view. The changes at the higher level are slow, and because of the slowness of the higher level, it sees the changes of the lower level in an averaged form. The hierarchy achieves a steady state from the bottom up (Mämmelä et al. 2023).

Modules at each hierarchy level should be loosely coupled. To minimize horizontal coupling between different power control and other loops and to improve stability, *horizontal loose coupling* in the form of interference avoidance between network users is used (Simon 1973; Mämmelä et al. 2023). Interference is avoided best by using *orthogonal signals* that are separable in different domains, including time, frequency, and space (Peterson et al. 1954; Gabor 1954; Pasupathy 1979; Madhow 2008; Anttonen et al. 2011). In a decentralized system, interference avoidance methods are not straightforward, especially in the time domain, unless some common timing synchronization is used.

Mihajlo D. Mesarovic and George N. Saridis proposed a three-level control system commonly used also elsewhere (Mesarovic 1970; Mesarovic et al. 1970; Saridis 1979, 2001); see Table 5.13. The number of levels can also be smaller or larger depending on the complexity of the system to be controlled (Antsaklis et al. 1989). The three levels apply to most architectures of automatic and autonomous controllers. Using the entropy concept, George N. Saridis (1988) derived optimal control (Saridis 2001). The entropy is minimized by using a three-level hierarchy if the process has different time scales, making the hierarchical control possible using time-scale separation.

The three levels are called control or execution, coordination, and organization or management level. The controller has low complexity, high speed, wide bandwidth, high accuracy, no memory, and narrow spatial extent (Saridis 1979; Albus and Meystel 2001; Mämmelä et al. 2018). Automatic systems belong to this level. Coordinators have short-term memory and are based on autonomous systems. Managers have high complexity, low speed, small bandwidth, low accuracy, long-term memory, and wide spatial extent. Managers are self-organizing systems. They have been also called organizers.

The layers in robotics are called behavioral, executive, and task-planning layers. The behavioral layer is closest to sensors and actuators and is responsible for movement and avoiding obstacles (Kortenkamp and Simmons 2008). The executive layer coordinates the behavioral layer and chooses the current movement to achieve a task. The task planning layer defines the long-term goals of the robot within resource

Table 5.13 Hierarchical control in robotics and communications

Hierarchy level	Properties	Example from robotics	Example from communications
Manager	Long-term memory	Task-planning layer	Network layer
Coordinator	Short-term memory	Executive layer	Data link layer
Controller	No memory	Behavioral layer	Physical layer

constraints, taking priorities, order of tasks, and recharging into account. The goals may have a priority queue that fluctuates when the environment changes (Carver and Scheier 2002).

In communications, the corresponding layers are called physical, data link, and network layers. The physical layer transmits bits or symbols, the data link layer transmits frames, and the network layer transmits packets called datagrams. There are also other similar hierarchies. For example, there is an automation pyramid in ANSI/ISA-95.00.05-2018 Enterprise-Control System IntegrationPart 5: Business-to-manufacturing transactions standard, including the levels field, control, supervisory, planning, and management from bottom up (ANSI, American National Standards Institute; ISA, International Society of Automation).

5.3.4 *Hierarchy of Everything*

We present a hierarchy of everything in Table 5.14 with explanations of each hierarchy level. The table is partially based on (Ahl and Allen 1996), covering living systems between cells and the biosphere. Higher-level systems include planets, solar systems, galaxies, galaxy groups, galaxy clusters, galaxy superclusters, and the universe. Galaxy superclusters are the largest known objects bound by gravity. Above our universe is a hypothetical multiverse, which means that there are many parallel universes (Deutsch 1997), and our universe is one of them. The idea originated in ancient Greece, but Hugh Everett (1957) proposed it as an interpretation of quantum physics. So far, there is no experimental evidence to support the hypothesis. A related concept is a cyclic universe, where the universe starts with a big bang and ends in a big crunch, followed by the next big bang, thus forming a series of universes. One of the first to propose a cyclic model was Alexandr Friedman (1922) (Encyclopedia Britannica 2024). Edwin Hubble (1929) showed that our universe is expanding.

Hierarchies of living systems can be formed from definitions or empirical observations. Living systems cannot be ordered by spatial extent, as we would assume from definitions in Table 5.14, and their hierarchy does not tell much about the material flows in biological material as we would expect from observations (Ahl and Allen 1996). Many organisms are much larger than many populations. For example, for a parasite, the host organism may be a landscape. A biome is a significant ecological community such as a rainforest or a desert. A landscape contains ecosystems close to each other characterized by spatial heterogeneity.

Below the cell level, we have organelles, molecules, atoms, elementary particles, and quarks. Organelles are functional units within a cell, such as the mitochondrion and nucleus. In an inanimate matter, we have crystals instead of cells and organelles. At the bottom of the hierarchy, we have quarks that form certain small particles, such as protons and neutrons. Quarks cannot exist alone but are always combined with other quarks. Murray Gell-Mann and George Zweig (1964) independently proposed the theory.

Table 5.14 Hierarchy of everything

Hierarchy level	Explanation
Universe	Everything known to exist
Galaxy supercluster	Group of galaxy clusters
Galaxy cluster	Group of galaxy groups
Galaxy group	Group of galaxies
Galaxy	Group of stars
Solar system	Star and its planes and their moons
Planet	Large body orbiting a star
Biosphere	Organisms and their environment
Biome	Major ecological community
Landscape	Area containing interacting ecosystems
Ecosystem	Community of organisms and its environment
Community	Interacting population of species
Population	Organisms of the same species
Organism	Living being
Cell	Protoplasm bounded by a membrane
Organelle	Functional unit in a cell
Molecule	Smallest particle of a substance
Atom	Smallest particle of a chemical element
Elementary particle	Smallest particle of matter
Quark	Part of elementary particle

Kenneth E. Boulding presented a general hierarchy of complexity in Boulding (1956) and updated it in Boulding (1985). The updated version is shown in Table 5.15. Here, ecological systems differ from evolutionary systems in that in ecological systems, there are no changes over generations, and in evolutionary systems, there are changes over generations, implying that evolutionary systems are reproductive systems. Similarly, ecology and evolutionary biology are separate subdisciplines in biology (Wilson 1998). The term "creodic systems" is not commonly used. Now, we would use the term morphogenetic systems. Conrad H. Waddington (1962) used the term "creodes," which he developed from two Greek words meaning "necessary path."

5.3.5 *Hierarchy of Natural and Technical Systems*

We present a general hierarchy of natural and technical systems in Table 5.16 (Mämmelä et al. 2018, 2023). We have separated natural and technical systems since they are different in many respects, and the natural systems are more advanced:

Table 5.15 Boulding's hierarchy of complexity

Boulding's hierarchy	Explanations
Social systems	Interacting human beings
Human systems	Self-conscious human beings
Evolutionary systems	Interacting populations with changes
Ecological systems	Interacting populations without changes
Demographic systems	Isolated populations of species
Reproductive systems	Organisms
Creodic systems	Morphogenetic systems
Positive feedback systems	Deviation-amplifying systems
Cybernetic systems	Negative feedback systems, homeostasis
Mechanical systems	Static and dynamic systems

they have even some higher hierarchy levels that technical systems do not have. The essential references used in the hierarchy are Boulding (1956, 1985), Mesarovic et al. (1970) and Stonier (1992, pp. 37, 53–54, 203; 1997, pp. 184–185), but we have changed the terminology to correspond with the current terminology. In Boulding (1956), the hierarchy is mainly for natural systems, and in Mesarovic et al. (1970), it is primarily for control systems.

In Mesarovic et al. (1970), self-organizing systems are highest in the hierarchy of technical systems; we have learning and adaptive systems below it. W. Ross Ashby (1947) first separated adaptive and self-organizing systems (Ramage and Shipp 2020) and thus set the oldest basis for the hierarchy. He was interested in regulation, adaptation, learning, and self-organization (Umpleby 2009). The difference between control, adaptive, and learning systems is from Claasen and Mecklenbräuker (1985) and Landau et al. (2011), defining their order in the hierarchy. Control and adaptive systems are called automatic systems, and learning systems

Table 5.16 Hierarchies of natural and technical systems

Natural systems	Technical systems
Social systems	
Conscious systems	
Reproductive systems	
Morphogenetic systems	Self-organizing systems
	Learning systems
Homeostatic systems	Adaptive systems
	Control systems
Simple dynamic systems	Simple dynamic systems
Static systems	Static systems

Table 5.17 Alternative terminology for technical systems

First terminology	Second terminology
Self-organizing systems	Self-organizing systems
Autonomous systems	Learning systems
Automatic systems	Adaptive systems
	Control systems

are called autonomous systems unless there is external supervision, which in practice makes them only semiautonomous. Structure and organization are synonymous terms (Hoffman 1964).

We have received additional inspiration from Kline (1995, pp. 89–94). Still, for example, Stephen J. Kline used the term "autonomous" where we would use the term "adaptive," and he used the term "self-restructuring" in place of "self-organizing." An important observation in Kline (1995) is the central role of the feedback concept and its set-point value or more generally a goal from control systems upwards. Alternative hierarchies exist, for example, in Miller (1973), Bossel (2007, pp. 3–5) and Aliu et al. (2013), but we believe that the hierarchies in Table 5.16 best correspond to the state-of-the-art terminology of the hierarchies. Autopoietic and reproductive systems are related concepts (Ramage and Shipp 2020) but are not synonymous. Autopoietic systems are self-producing and self-maintaining, while reproductive systems produce offspring or copies of themselves (Cornish-Bowden and Luz Cardenas 2020).

We present alternative terminologies in Table 5.17 (Mämmelä et al. 2018). Automatic systems are control and adaptive systems which use an external control signal during operation. Such systems do not need any manual control. Some learning systems are also automatic, especially those using supervised learning and reinforcement learning (Marsland 2015). Autonomous systems do not require external control signals during operation, especially those using unsupervised learning. Also, many systems produced by evolution are autonomous. In evolutionary systems, a form of control comes from environmental pressure, which improves survivability.

In technical systems, the simplest systems are at the bottom, and the most complex systems are at the top (Table 5.18). At the first level, we have *static systems* where everything is fixed as in a passive filter that does not even need any energy from the outside: all the energy comes from the input signal, and the filter cannot amplify the signal according to the energy conservation law. The energy of the output signal is always smaller than that of the input signal. An active filter is usually based on an operational amplifier. Here, "active" means that some energy is consumed. Other examples of static systems are a bridge and a building. They are static during their life cycle except during renovation.

The second level includes *simple dynamic systems* where all the changes are predetermined motions or changes, as in a mechanical clock. It also has a structure: it has hands and their relationships. When the hands move, the structure changes. The clock is a simple dynamic system whose structure is changed periodically. It

Table 5.18 Hierarchy of technical systems

Hierarchy level	Explanation	Examples
Self-organizing systems	Structural changes	Complex adaptive systems
Learning systems	Behavioral changes, memory	Reinforcement learning
Adaptive systems	Reference signal, performance criterion, algorithm	LMS algorithm
Control systems	Feedback, set-point value	PID control
Simple dynamic systems	Periodic deterministic changes	Clock
Static systems	Everything fixed	Filter

comes back to the same state every 12 h. In modern clocks, the energy comes from a battery, but in pendulum clocks, it comes from gravity.

In mechanical systems such as celestial mechanics, the equations describing the changes rarely go beyond the third degree (Boulding 1985). The changes include speed, acceleration, which is the derivative of the speed, and jerk, which is the derivative of the acceleration (Mehrotra and Mahapatra 1997). At the third level, we have *control systems* based on feedback. They have a goal defined by a set-point value or a reference input. A simple example is a thermostat, where the set-point value is the desired temperature. Another more complicated example is the PID controller.

A control system is an *automatic system* acting upon controlled variables to eliminate the effect of disturbances (Landau et al. 2011). It does not need any manual intervention during operation, although it needs, in general, a goal. An *adaptive system* at the fourth level is an advanced automatic system that includes a performance criterion optimized using an algorithm in the feedback loop (Landau et al. 2011). The iterative least-mean square (LMS) algorithm is a form of integrative (I) controller where the proportional (P) and derivative (D) controllers of the PID controller are not used. We use adaptive systems for example as channel estimators and linear equalizers that are essentially inverse estimators (Proakis and Salehi 2008).

Learning systems can change their behavior based on earlier experience (Stonier 1992, 1997). For this, they need a memory to store the experience. Machine learning algorithms are learning systems (Bishop 2006; Marsland 2015). Supervised learning systems belong to automatic systems. For example, we can use pattern recognition with much slower convergence than supervised and unsupervised learning. An unsupervised learning system is *autonomous*. In communications, decision-directed and blind algorithms are simple autonomous systems (Proakis and Salehi 2008). In decision-directed algorithms, the reference signal is replaced by the decisions of the receiver, which needs the decisions to be reliable enough. In blind algorithms, some other nonlinearity is used instead of a detector. Reinforcement learning is not entirely autonomous. Evolutionary learning is the most general type of reinforcement learning, and it does not necessarily use any model as a starting point.

Self-organizing systems The sixth level includes the *self-organizing systems*. They are autonomous systems that can change not only their behavior but also their structure, which is deeper in the FBS description hierarchy. Among the self-organizing systems are social agents and robots.The methods are not as mature as those changing only behavior (Bongaerts et al. 2000; Cao et al. 2013; Silk et al. 2016). The agents and robots can cooperate or compete and may be punished if needed as in game theory (Siegfried 2006). An essential aspect of a self-organizing system is the ability to recover from an arbitrary state automatically (Schneider 1999; Dolev and Tzachar 2009). Such systems are called self-stabilizing, a beneficial property for resilience.

The prefix self- refers to autonomous operation (Mesarovic et al. 1970, pp. 55–56). Autonomous systems are automatic, and self-organizing systems are automatic and autonomous (Mämmelä et al. 2023). Autonomy means that there is no external agent that would change the structure. Self-organization is the broadest and most complex decision problem that a technical system must solve and, therefore, is often based on heuristics. Since self-organization has a finite decision-making capacity, it must take longer to arrive at its decisions than in learning systems. An external agent can set goals and constraints for the system, and only a humans with their free will have that capability. Complexity theory is a theory of self-organization (Benbya and McKelvey 2006; Kauffman 1995). No machine is truly autonomous but needs human supervision. Nature has been able, through evolution, to change even the physical level below the structural level.

We can now explain the difference between automatic and autonomous systems more concretely with an example. An automatic ship is a ship that proceeds from one harbor to another without manual control but with a reference trajectory that defines the route on a map. The trajectory is the needed control signal during operation. If there is an unexpected obstacle, the ship would stop and go around the obstacle. An autonomous ship is a ship that proceeds from one harbor to another without any reference trajectory. However, the next harbor must be defined as a goal since a machine cannot determine its goals. The ship is thus goal-directed (McFarland and Bösser 1993). Without a goal, we should use a goal-seeking or goal-achieving system, which would not work in the case of a ship; at least, it would be very slow. The early robots were goal-seeking in the sense that they used random search: when they ran into an obstacle, they turned and proceeded again (Bekey 2005). In agent theory, such an agent is either a simple reflex agent or a model-based reflex agent (Russell and Norvig 2022).

Humans, with their free will, give a goal or performance requirement in the form of utility to any machine to improve, for example, its stability. An example is a car and its driver.

There are some similarities in natural systems compared to technical systems (Table 5.16). Homeostasis corresponds to control and adaptive systems. We cannot separate them in natural systems. Morphogenesis corresponds to learning and self-organizing systems. There are also three additional levels that technical systems do not have. They include reproductive, conscious, and social systems; see Boulding's complexity hierarchy in Table 5.15, where evolutionary systems are reproductive. Reproduction has been essential in the evolution of consciousness. No machine can reproduce itself (Cornish-Bowden and Luz Cardenas 2020); thus, no machine has reached consciousness. Conscious, intelligent organisms can form social systems. Machines and robots can simulate social behavior but only in a rudimentary form, and we have classified them as self-organizing systems. Natural systems do not have an explicit goal, but evolution has produced conscious organisms that can set their goals (Schoemaker 1991). Evolution does have an implicit goal. The implicit goal is the fitness to the environment.

Self-organizing systems are at the highest level of technical systems. They are the least mature technical systems (Bongaerts et al. 2000; Cao et al. 2013; Silk et al. 2016). Despite their benefits in technical systems, self-organizing systems are not widely exploited since they can become the primary source of failure (Silk et al. 2016). The reason is the emergence due to nonlinear feedback in the system: the global behavior cannot be predicted from local behavior, and the global optimum cannot be found from local optimization (Bongaerts et al. 2000). In general, some weak centralized control is needed to offer a goal to the self-organizing system using a hybrid combination of centralized and distributed control (Mämmelä et al. 2023). Without a goal, a system using feedback may easily become unstable. An example is a social system based on free-market economics leading to instability in the form of business cycles (Korkman 2022).

In computing, the term *autonomic* has become popular (Kephart and Chess 2003), and this terminology has also moved to communications, as proposed by Mikhail Smirnov in 2004 (Dobson et al. 2010). The term was initially used in physiology for the nervous system, which acts involuntarily. In engineering, autonomic roughly means the same as autonomous; in some cases, it is also distributed (Schaefer 2016) or self-organizing. Autonomic systems are self-managing, i.e., they have self-configuring, self-optimizing, self-healing, self-monitoring, and self-protecting properties. Many self- terms were collected in Brooks and Roy (2021), for example, self-healing materials. In the European Telecommunications Standards Institute (ETSI) terminology, *autonomic networking* is defined as a "networking paradigm enabling network devices and the overall network architecture to exhibit the so-called self-managing properties, namely: auto-discovery, self-configuration (auto-configuration), self-diagnosing, self-repair (self-healing), self-optimization, etc." (ETSI 2014).

There are attempts to compare and unify the terms "self-organizing" and "self-managing" (i.e., autonomic). For example, the authors in Lynn et al. (2016) think that the terms are complementary methods of managing complexity, and they have their own roots. They are two parallel properties of a complex system. On the other hand, the authors in Mühl et al. (2017) think that the terms are hierarchical. The hierarchy is from the bottom up: adaptive, self-manageable, self-managing, and self-organizing. A system generally has *regular inputs* and *control inputs*, where the regular inputs are sensing information from the environment. An adaptive system is a system that performs acceptably for various inputs. The reference signals form control inputs. In a self-manageable system, an *external controller* is used, but the control inputs can be computed from the past and current regular inputs and the past and current outputs. Thus, the control unit is *separated* from the other parts of the system. The separation is just an intermediate step from adaptive systems to self-managing systems needed for conceptual analysis. A self-managing system is a self-manageable system without any control input, i.e., the controller mentioned above is included in the system. A self-organizing system is a self-managing and structure-adaptive system having distributed control.

There are seven general principles in self-organizing systems (Benbya and McKelvey 2006); see Table 5.19. The adaptive tension by Ilya Prigogine (1955) includes any tension imposed on an agent, such as energy differentials, the difference between supply and demand, or new technology. In an adaptive system, the tension is caused by an error signal in the feedback loop. The requisite complexity by W. Ross Ashby (1956) means that internal complexity must, in general, exceed the complexity of the environment, which can be understood using the separability principle where the estimation and control of the environment are separated (Ashby 1956). According to Ronald A. Fisher (1930), the internal rate of change must be higher than the rate of change in the environment. This property is common in adaptive systems used in slowly fading channels (Monsen 1980). Loosely coupled hierarchies and subsystems can increase the adaptive response rate, as Herbert Simon (1962) suggested. Positive feedback by Maruyama (1963) can result in significant order creation from insignificant environmental changes. Complexity is generated by using many causes and thus using multicausality according to the causal intricacy by Charles E. Lindblom (1959). Closely related to multicausality is the coordination rhythm by Louis Dumont (1966), which means that alternation of causal dominance offers a creative force.

Hybrid self-organizing systems An interesting question is whether a self-organizing system needs a goal like an ordinary control loop. Many authors believe that self-organizing systems are distributed without centralized control or goal (Prehofer and Bettstetter 2005; Dressler 2008). This definition has been recently changed since an internal central controller is now allowed (Di Marzo Serugendo et al. 2005; Ye et al. 2017). The change happened around the time when 3GPP Rel. 8 (2008) defined three kinds of self-organizing systems, including centralized SON (C-SON), distributed SON (D-SON), and their combination hybrid SON (H-SON) (Fourati et al. 2021).

As mentioned earlier, the need for centralized control comes from emergence: global behavior cannot be predicted from local behavior, and we cannot find

Table 5.19 Principles of self-organizing systems

Year	Discoverer	Discovery
1930	R. A. Fisher	Change rate
1955	I. Prigogine	Adaptive tension
1956	W. R. Ashby	Requisite complexity
1959	C. E. Lindblom	Causal intricacy
1962	H. Simon	Hierarchical and modular systems
1963	M. Maruyama	Positive feedback
1966	L. Dumont	Coordination rhythm

the global optimum from local optimization due to nonlinearities in the system (Bongaerts et al. 2000). If we could manage emergence, we could do it with a distributed system, and this kind of system would be at the top of all self-organizing systems with the least assumptions. An alternative would be a distributed system where the different control units negotiate with everyone else. The negotiations lead to a Nash bargaining solution (Bacci et al. 2016). Usually, in distributed systems, negotiations are made only with the nearest neighbors since otherwise, the system's complexity and delays would be overwhelming (Lin et al. 2012).

Although often suggested (Prehofer and Bettstetter 2005; Dressler 2008), spontaneous order using local interactions is difficult to attain in technical systems since we have no theory for emergence. Just as in a rational agent (Russell and Norvig 2022), the goal of a self-organizing system can be either in the form of a desirable state or as a utility function to be maximized. Without any goal, the result is a random behavior. A good example is a flock of birds or a shoal of fish. Using swarm intelligence, the swarm can rapidly avoid predators. However, without a leader, the swarm moves randomly without any goal, which may be tiring for the swarm. We need a *leader* who is more intelligent than all others and leads the swarm from danger to a safe place and not to a downfall. The use of the leader corresponds to a hybrid self-organizing system.

There are various reasons to use hybrid self-organizing systems, which combine centralized and distributed control. Centralized and distributed control alone is unsatisfactory. Because of complexity, we must decompose an optimization problem into more minor problems, leading to vertical and horizontal decomposition (Whitney and Milley 1974; Chiang et al. 2007). We cannot decompose tightly coupled problems with conflicting objectives, and we must solve them using optimization methods, such as evolutionary methods, for example, game theory or genetic algorithms (Marler and Arora 2004).

Adaptive systems are goal-directed, goal-seeking, or goal-achieving (McFarland and Bösser 1993). In goal-directed systems, an explicit goal is defined externally. In goal-seeking systems, the goal is only implicit and corresponds to an equilibrium such as minimum energy (Kauffman 1995). In goal-achieving systems, the goal is implicit and achieved by random search. Eventually, the goal may show up as fitness. Darwin's principle, i.e., the survival of the fittest, is crucial (Schoemaker 1991), and biological systems do not always seek maximal efficiency (Westerhoff et al. 2009), an example solution to the social dilemma.

A centrally controlled system may, in principle, find a global optimum, but distributed systems generally have better resilience, and therefore, a hierarchical solution combining the benefits of both central and distributed control may be more satisfactory (Mämmelä et al. 2023). Therefore, a pure centrally controlled system is against the ideas of systems thinking.

Usually, the desirable state is unknown, and we cannot form any proper error signal. We must find the desirable state indirectly using a utility function (McFarland and Bösser 1993). In practice, global optimization is not often possible or even desirable because of existing constraints, the exponential complexity of the exhaustive search, and the need for robustness in addition to optimality (Mämmelä et al.

2023). We must find a satisfying solution for complex problems with our bounded rationality and memory, thus pointing to a partially distributed solution (Simon 1956; Gorod et al. 2017).

Distributed control has problems in providing globally optimized performance, and the behavior of a system under distributed control can be unpredictable (Bongaerts et al. 2000). In general, distributed control performs better than decentralized control and can sometimes approach the performance of centralized control (Frampton et al. 2010). The relationship between the local rules and the global behavior remains elusive, and no systematic procedure is known to engineer a specific global result (Roy 2008). However, the author (Roy 2008) expects that a distributed multiagent system with swarming could achieve a nearly optimal global state with only a modest amount of local signaling.

Distributed systems tend to have stability problems because of the delays in the feedback loops within the system (Forrester 2007a; Dorf and Bishop 2017). The stability problems must be solved using centralized control (Korkman 2022). We can improve stability by using loose coupling (Skyttner 2005) vertically and horizontally.

Hybrid control combines the best properties of hierarchical and distributed control, including high and predictable performance with a high robustness against disturbances. As special cases of hybrid systems, we get all major degrees of centralization, including centralized, decentralized, and distributed systems (Mämmelä et al. 2023). The hybrid system adds flexibility to the system with some reduced efficiency.

Especially in social systems, forced cooperation in a centralized system tends to drift towards decentralized systems, and competition in decentralized systems tend to drift towards centralized systems (Boulding 1981). Thus, the natural solution is hybrid (Fourati et al. 2021; Mämmelä et al. 2023; Hugoson 2009). In practice, objectives are usually incommensurate (Walasek and Brown 2023), and we must solve the problem through cooperation (i.e., negotiation) or competition.

The *Nash equilibrium* in a noncooperative game is not generally optimal, fair, or unique (Lasaulce and Tembine 2011) and thus does not solve the social dilemma without any information exchange. A noncooperative game corresponds to competition in a decentralized system. The *Nash bargaining solution* in a cooperative game is optimal, fair, or unique and suggests that the system should be distributed, but all the players must be willing to cooperate with everybody else, providing a solution to the social dilemma. A Stackelberg game using a leader and a set of followers is a hierarchical approximation of the Nash bargaining solution when there are too many geographically distributed players to negotiate efficiently (Haddad et al. 2011; Luong et al. 2019).

An interesting new interdisciplinary concept is *guided self-organization*, where the self-organization is guided using constraints (Prokopenko 2009). Thus, the system can have a goal, and in addition, there are some constraints so that collisions are avoided. Guided self-organization is a form of hybrid control combining centralized and distributed control.

Complex systems Typical properties of complex systems in nature are (Dooley 1997; Heylighen 2002; Ladyman et al. 2013; Ladyman and Wiesner 2020)

- organizational boundary
- large number of parts and their interactions
- hierarchy and emergent properties
- nonlinearity and feedback that may be sensitive to initial conditions as in chaotic systems
- seemingly random behavior may be a result of simple nonlinear feedback loops
- distributed control
- robustness and resilience
- bifurcations and symmetry breaking
- ability to self-organize
- nonequilibrium dynamics far from equilibrium.

The sensitivity to initial conditions results in a re-examination of causality, which may proceed in a hierarchical system from one hierarchy level to another, and the effects may be determined by multiple causes (Dooley 1997). In natural self-organizing systems, the global order is formed from many local interactions and distributed control. The system is loosely coupled with the environment. It has a hierarchy with emergent properties. The system is highly robust and resilient. Self-organization and emergence can appear simultaneously but are conceptually different (De Wolf and Holvoet 2005).

Nonlinear systems have, in general, many stable states. A *bifurcation* is a possibility for branching of a stable state to two or more states when some parameter changes, eventually leading to some chaotic states. The bifurcation point marks the transition between ordered and disordered configurations. *Symmetry breaking* means that one configuration dominates all others after self-organization, and the symmetry is lost. The system has made a choice: initially, it treated all configurations equally, but then it preferred one possibility. A *thermodynamic equilibrium* is a state where no entropy is produced. An increasing input of energy pushes the system farther from its thermodynamic equilibrium. A *dissipative structure* is an organized pattern of activity that dissipates matter or energy and exhibits dynamic self-organization towards a far-from-equilibrium system described in Ilya Prigogine's *nonequilibrium thermodynamics*.

5.4 System Theories and Archetypes

5.4.1 System Theories

System theories have been hard to develop, and no single unified theory exists. We summarize the theories in Table 5.20 based on the discussions in von Bertalanffy (1971), Bahg (1990), Francois (1999), Ramage and Shipp (2020) and Uusikylä and Jalonen (2023). The table also shows the kinships of the theories. For example, artificial intelligence, system dynamics, and complexity theory are spin-offs of cybernetics at least implicitly. In our view, Norbert Wiener (1948) devised the agent concept using feedback through our brain, and Herbert Simon (1954) later elaborated the idea that finally became the central concept in artificial intelligence and complexity theory (Wiener 1961; Richardson 1991; Holland 1995; Russell and Norvig 2022). Agent-based modeling is also useful in system dynamics (Sterman 2000). The theories have developed independently, although they have a common root in the feedback concept in cybernetics.

Chang-Gen Bahg classified the theories according to each author's discipline, including mathematics, physics and chemistry, biology and psychology, social sciences, philosophy, cybernetics, and information theory (Bahg 1990). Magnus Ramage and Karen Shipp classified systems thinkers according to the subject (Ramage and Shipp 2020). The taxonomy includes early cybernetics, general systems theory, system dynamics, soft and critical systems, later cybernetics, complexity theory, and learning systems. The book seems to have the broadest existing view of systems thinking. Still, since its focus is on systems thinkers, it lacks details of some critical theories such as evolutionary methods, artificial intelligence, and systems engineering.

Lars Skyttner has done an excellent job collecting basic ideas in the general theory of systems and a selection of system theories (Skyttner 2005). Gerald M. Weinberg has a collection of systems laws (Weinberg 1975). In his view, the main ingredient of systems thinking is the art of simplification. Xing Pan et al. have an excellent summary of different approaches to holistic systems thinking and the necessary references, including foundations of systems methodologies, different learning disciplines, systems thinking laws, critical skills in systems thinking, and systems thinking competencies (Pan et al. 2013).

Linear system theory and circuit theory Linear system theory is the simplest form of system theories described in many books on mathematics (Papoulis 1962; Kreyszig 2011), circuit theory (Smith and Dorf 1991; Maloberti and Davies 2024), analog filter theory (Schaumann and Van Valkenburg 2001), and communications engineering

Table 5.20 Some great theories in systems thinking

System theory	Related system theories
Theory of evolution	Cultural evolution and theories of life
Linear system theory	Circuit theory
Nonlinear system theory	Chaos theory and catastrophe theory
Nonequilibrium thermodynamics	Thermodynamics, low energy equilibrium, synergetics, and stigmergy
Optimization and decision theory	Game theory, detection theory, and estimation theory
Cybernetics	System dynamics, artificial intelligence, and complexity theory
Network theory	Hierarchy theory and theory of information transmission
Theory of computing	Computational complexity theory
Complexity theory	General theory of systems

(Haykin and Moher 2014; Ziemer and Tranter 2014). In linear systems, the superposition theorem is valid. Just as in scalar multiplication, linear time-invariant systems are commutable: the order of the blocks can be changed without affecting the output (Mämmelä 2006), but in the time-varying case, this is not possible since the needed model corresponds to matrix multiplication, which is not in general commutable (Kailath 1960). Similarly, we need matrix multiplication in multiple-input multiple-output (MIMO) systems such as multiantenna systems. A generalization of a linear transformation is an *affine transformation* (Kay 1993; Wolfram 2024), including translations and rotations. More specifically, adding a constant direct current (DC) signal to an input signal is not a linear but an affine operation. In most practical applications, a radio channel is linear if the additive noise at its output is ignored.

Nonlinear system theory Nonlinear systems do not follow the superposition theorem (de Coulon 1986; Schetzen 2006; Widrow and Walach 1996). Nonlinearities and feedback in complex systems may result in emergent behavior leading to mathematical intractability (Camazine et al. 2001). In biological systems, emergence appears in self-organizing systems, which are based on positive and negative feedback. Nonlinear systems are not, in general, commutable, i.e., the order of two nonlinear blocks cannot be changed without changing the output (Mämmelä 2006).

Nonlinear system theory includes the theory of time-invariant and time-varying nonlinear systems. The theory of time-varying nonlinear systems is called nonlinear dynamics, which consists of chaos theory, catastrophe theory, and complexity theory. Simple time-invariant nonlinear systems used intentionally include envelope detectors, square-law detectors, soft and hard limiters, and frequency multipliers (Haykin and Moher 2014). Unintentional nonlinearities come from the saturation of the electrical components. Nonlinear phenomena are generally challenging to analyze and compensate (Proakis and Salehi 2008). Compensation should be provided close to the place where the nonlinearity is generated. In communications, the power amplifier in a transmitter is the most crucial source of nonlinearity. Often, some predistortion is used so that the predistorter and amplifier form an almost linear system over a reasonable amplitude range.

Chaos theory Chaos theory is a theory of nonlinearly interacting agents (Strogatz 2014; Casti 1994). Chaotic systems are systems that are sensitive to their initial conditions. A simple example is the three-body system, where the bodies (A, B, and C) have roughly equal masses. The system is deterministic, but because of the three feedback loops between all the bodies (A–B, A–C, and B–C), the behavior looks random and, therefore, chaotic. Chaotic systems generate only an appearance of randomness. A proper random process has no deterministic basis. Thus, randomness is an extreme case of chaos (Bohm and Peat 2000). In practice, knowing a chaotic system's initial state is impossible, and thus, the system is effectively incomputable.

A chaotic system always includes some nonlinear feedback loop producing emergent properties. In general, we should avoid chaotic systems by using loose coupling. For example, in a multibody system, stability can be obtained by using mass hierarchy, as in our solar system. If the distances are large compared to the sizes of the bodies, the latter can be considered point masses.

Some patterns in the state space are called *attractors*, including fixed points, limit cycles, and strange attractors (Casti 1991, p. 283). Some authors also mention a fourth type of attractor, namely a quasiperiodic attractor. The attractors are the points in the state space where the state space trajectory moves.

The *fixed point* is a single point in the state space, and the *limit cycle* is a closed loop in the state space, such as an ellipse. *Strange attractors* have aperiodic trajectories in the state space. The *quasiperiodic attractor* is a combination of limit cycles that almost intersect. An example is a solenoid-like curve winding around the surface of a torus. The attractors also appear in cellular automata. Dynamical chaotic systems are related to Gödel's incompleteness theorem and computational complexity theory (Casti 1991, pp. 281, 317; 1994, pp. 137, 141, 147). Examples of chaotic phenomena are the behavior of the weather and the stock market.

Catastrophe theory Like chaos theory, catastrophe theory is a theory of unstable nonlinear dynamic systems (Casti 1994). The focus is on fixed-point attractors because of mathematical tractability. A catastrophe is an abrupt, significant change caused by a small, gradual change in the inputs, which is against our intuition and can be seen as a paradox. There is a change in a catastrophe point from one initially stable fixed-point attractor to another.

An example of a catastrophe is a threatened dog that suddenly decides to attack or flee (Simon 1996). The theory is similar to the evolutionary theory in that it explains past events rather than predicts them. The theory gives possibilities but does not tell when something will happen.

Catastrophe theory has been used in various disciplines, such as physics, biology, economics, and political science (Casti 1994). Mechanical structures, for example, columns or beams, can collapse. Similar phenomena occur in reflecting rays when several rays come together and cause rippling patterns seen at the bottom of a swimming pool. The phenomenon is called *light caustics.* Catastrophes in social sciences include the collapse of old civilizations, ideological revolutions, stock market crashes, the fall of the Berlin Wall in 1989, and the downfall of communism in 1991. The theory explains why the authoritarian left can suddenly change to an authoritarian right or vice versa, and why political freedom may change to anarchy.

Theory of evolution Evolution is one unifying biological principle (Morowitz 2002; Nowak 2006; Bowler 2009), useful also elsewhere. We can see three forms of evolution having different time scales: physical, biological, and cultural or social (Boulding 1989), where physical evolution is the slowest. An example of physical evolution is the continental drift observed by Alfred Wegener (Seselja and Weber 2012). Herbert Spencer (1862), in his book *First Principles of a New System of Philosophy*, developed the concept of *cultural evolution* independently of Darwin's biological evolution (Stonier 1992). The rate of change in cultural evolution is now much faster than that of biological evolution. Culture cannot evolve without ethical development.

Cultural evolution shows evolution within and between species at various levels, including economy and politics. *Social Darwinism* is a pseudoscience that means that we apply evolution theory to social relationships in the form of brainwashing or human breeding. The side effects of evolution in social systems include instability and monopolies such as large companies in economy and superpowers in politics leading to unhealthy phenomena. We must fight against them at least with international contracts that, however, superpowers do not always respect. Without laws and moral rules, even a complete state can decline to a rogue state, whose development can be prevented only with enlightenment. Ethically valuable influencing on human relationships is called wisdom.

Thomas R. Malthus (1799) predicted exponentially growing populations when resources were unlimited. Jean-Baptiste Lamarck (1809) noticed that species change. Only a fraction of individuals survive if the resources are a limiting factor. Charles Darwin (1859) and independently Alfred R. Wallace (1858) developed the theory of evolution. The basic idea is the survival of the fittest, i.e., those that reproduce fastest, an expression created by Herbert Spencer (1864) for natural selection (Kampourakis 2013). It was Spencer who saw natural selection as a pruning force. Walter M. Elsasser (1958) introduced the term "biotonic laws" much later to describe the unknown physical laws in biology. Gregor Mendel (1865) started the theory of genetics in botany, which eventually led to John Holland's (1975) genetic algorithms to simulate evolution in technical systems and John Maynard Smith's evolutionary game theory (1973). William D. Hamilton (1864) discovered that selfish genes can favor altruistic behavior among relatives.

According to Tom Stonier, five basic processes are prerequisites for establishing intelligent systems: resonance, feedback, duplication, differentiation, and recombination (Stonier 1997, pp. 77–79). Evolution consists of the introduction of variation into systems and the selection of those systems that work. *Resonance* produces oscillations and favors stability as in a spinning gyroscope but allows minor variations. Resonating systems set the stage for feedback loops. *Feedback* allows a system to interact with the environment and enhances survivability. The system is divided or multiplied into many identical units in duplication or reproduction. *Differentiation* introduces variations into the systems. It is an ontogeny process where unspecialized cells attain their adult form and function (Merriam-Webster 2024; Kauffman 1995). *Recombination* is the primary source of significant evolutionary advances in addition to mutations. Recombination is the formation of new combinations of genes in progeny that do not occur in parents (Merriam-Webster 2024).

A modern general theory, integrating earlier theories, is *evolutionary dynamics*, whose primary ingredients are reproduction, mutation, selection, random drift, and spatial movement (Nowak 2006). Individuals change over time, but only populations evolve. Ordinary game theory is based on rational agents, but evolutionary game theory is based on agents that are "irrational": fitness and reproductive success are the key concepts and ideas that are sometimes included in the concept of intelligence (Stonier 1992, p. 15). In game theory, cooperation can be studied by using a game called *prisoner's dilemma*, where the dilemma is that cooperation is "irrational" but produces a larger payoff than competition, which is seen as "rational" (Nowak 2006). The observation explains why humans do not always behave rationally but altruistically (Robson 2019): the question is about the poor definition of rationality. Merrill Flood and Melvin Dresher (1950) were the first to define the prisoner's dilemma, and Albert W. Tucker (1950) named the dilemma as the most famous game-theoretic paradox.

The theory of living systems is a theory of systems based on the observation that biological and social systems form a hierarchy, and each hierarchy level is based on the feedback concept (Richardson 1991; Kalaidjieva and Swanson 2004). James G. Miller bridged the natural and social sciences with the open system concept from cells to supranational systems.

Thermodynamics Thermodynamics includes three laws (Young et al. 2012). The *first law of thermodynamics* is about energy conservation in the universe. Conservation of energy means that energy can neither be created nor destroyed but only transformed (Domenech et al. 2007; Coelho 2009). Thus, if we use energy in electronics, the produced heat must be removed by cooling so that the temperature does not become too high since, otherwise, the components may be destroyed. Since mass m and energy E are equivalent via the equation $E = mc^2$, where c is the speed of light, we must more generally refer to the conservation of mass-energy.

The *second law of thermodynamics* has three forms for isolated, closed, and open systems, respectively (Rosen 1991; Kauffman 1995; Lebon et al. 2008; Kopicki et al. 2010; de Oliveira 2017); see Table 5.21. Entropy increases and order decreases or stays constant whereas the energy is constant in an isolated system. This is usually the only second law of thermodynamics presented in the literature. In a closed system, the total energy is minimized, order may be increased, and the rest of the energy is transferred to the environment. In an open system, the system behaves as a nonequilibrium system using constant flow of matter and energy, and the order may be increased.

Entropy refers to disorder, which is unavailable energy that we cannot use (Asimov 1984, pp. 238–239). Entropy is a measure of the evenness with which energy is distributed. Heat is motion spread out as evenly as possible and has the maximum entropy (Penrose 1999, p. 412). Using and transferring energy always produces heat as a side-product. Heat can only be used for work if there is a temperature difference, as in a steam engine. A temperature difference implies that the entropy is not yet maximized. Similarly, potential energy can only be used for work if there is a height difference.

In closed systems the minimum energy principle has at least three forms depending in the assumptions (Lebon et al. 2008, pp. 21–24): (1) When the entropy and the external parameters such as the volume are constant, Rudolf Clausius stated that the total internal energy is minimized at equilibrium, (2) when the temperature and

Table 5.21 Three forms of the second law of thermodynamics

Type of system	Second law
Isolated system	Entropy is increased and order is decreased
Closed system	Energy is minimized and order is increased leading to self-organization
Open system	Order is increased in nonequilibrium systems leading to self-organization

pressure are constant, the free energy defined by Willard Gibbs is minimized at equilibrium, (3) when the temperature and volume are constant, the free energy defined by Herman von Helmholtz is minimized at equilibrium. The total internal energy includes the kinetic and potential energies of the particles. Thus, there is a symmetry: for an isolated system with fixed internal energy, the entropy is maximized at equilibrium, but for a closed system with fixed entropy, the energy is minimized at equilibrium. In chemical reactions usually the temperature and pressure are kept constant, and Gibbs free energy is minimized. Minimization of the potential energy is valid for molecules.

Entropy law is not valid for open and closed systems. Thus, entropy can decrease locally if the entropy is increased globally. For example, on Earth, the Sun is a constant source of energy; thus, the entropy can be decreased since the entropy in the Sun is increased even more. Organisms are open systems, and Prigogine's nonequilibrium thermodynamics explains the local decrease of entropy (Boulton et al. 2015). Entropy law does not consider the effect of forces between the particles and their inelastic collisions (Corning 2002; He and Kang 2010). For example, gravity has created stars and galaxies, thus reducing entropy (Wallace 2010). Similarly, molecules are formed using electrical forces.

The *third law of thermodynamics* states that entropy is zero at absolute zero temperature. Later, the *zeroth law of thermodynamics was* defined concerning thermal equilibrium: if systems A and B are in thermal equilibrium with system C, they are in thermal equilibrium with each other.

According to Pierre-Simon Laplace (1814), information is conserved in deterministic physical systems in the sense that the present state includes information on the initial state. The state consists of the properties of all particles, such as location, velocity, acceleration, etc. Laplace assumed that the universe is one big clock whose past and future can, in principle, be computed.

Nonequilibrium thermodynamics Ilya Prigogine (1955) started the European school of complexity theory, focusing on *nonequilibrium thermodynamics* (Boulton et al. 2015). He claimed to have discovered the universal law of evolution (Corning 2002). He published his first results in French in 1947. Prigogine received a Nobel Prize in 1977 for this discovery. Some authors think he was the most influential scientist of the twentieth century because of the potential impact on human sciences (Francois 2006). The theory is based on the observation that organisms are open systems that exchange matter and energy with their environment, whereas, in physics, only isolated systems were considered. Therefore, organisms are not mechanisms and do not follow the deterministic laws of Newtonian mechanics (Rosen 1991). Furthermore, they do not follow the entropy law of isolated systems: entropy is not always increased locally.

Evolution is based on three principles: variation, selection, and establishment of selections, thus generating order, which was initially improbable (Schwanitz 1999). In addition to evolution, order is generated with two primary principles: energy minimization in closed systems and nonequilibrium thermodynamics in open systems (Kauffman 1995). Organisms can resist the entropy law by accessing external material and energy resources and operating far from equilibrium (Prigogine 1997; Swilling 2020). We can compare nonequilibrium systems with a whirlpool in a bathtub where the drain is open, and water is continuously added (Kauffman 1995). The whirlpool is an example of the flux of matter and energy, where the energy comes from the gravitation force. Prigogine called such systems *dissipative structures* that dissipate matter and energy. The system may be called a whirlpool dissipative system, which is robust and stable and corresponds to an attractor in chaos theory (Kauffman 1995, p. 187).

Cells, ecosystems, and economic systems are complex metabolic whirlpools (Kauffman 1995). Similarly, our biosphere is an open system that receives energy from the Sun and generates three significant cycles, including nitrogen, carbon, and water cycles, which are necessary for life, offering an always-changing environment with rises and declines. In open systems, there is "a never-ending battle between energy-powered order creation and entropy-driven order destruction" (Swilling 2020). At the core of this fight is *photosynthesis*, where carbon dioxide is combined with water, generating carbohydrates and oxygen. In this way, the energy from the Sun is retained for future use in *metabolism*.

There are three obstacles to finding general laws in self-organization (Kauffman 1995). The first is quantum physics, according to which nature is random by its very nature. The second is chaos theory, where deterministic systems behave as if they were random. The third obstacle is that some phenomena are nonalgorithmic and cannot be implemented on a computer (Penrose 1999).

Synergetics by Herman Haken (1971) is a theory of self-organization in distributed cooperative systems, closely related to nonequilibrium thermodynamics, but there are also substantial differences (Haken 1988; Bahg 1990). An example is ant colony optimization, which is based on *stigmergy* by Pierre-Paul Grasse (1959) (Theraulaz and Bonabeau 1999), a form of indirect communication where agents (in this case ants) coordinate their actions through modifications in their environment, such as pheromone trails left on paths. This method allows for the emergence of complex patterns and solutions from simple local interactions among the agents, a key concept in synergetics.

In engineering, a synergetics-related concept is self-replicating agents in the form of cellular automata that may simulate artificial life (Goldstein 1999). They are advanced forms of self-organizing systems. Self-replicating machines have never been built so far, and the gap between machines (mechanisms) and organisms seems unbridgeable (Cornish-Bowden and Luz Cardenas 2020).

Cybernetics and system dynamics Control engineering is based on closed-loop feedback control, which generally uses the sense-decide-act loop (Ogata 2010; Mämmelä et al. 2023). Open-loop control does not include any sense block. Because of the feedback, stability is an essential problem in control systems, but in general, it is not easy to analyze. Alexandr M. Lyapunov (1892) and Harry Nyquist (1932) have presented a general analysis of the stability of the feedback. Feedback is a prerequisite to intelligence (Stonier 1997, p. 48). In addition to engineering, feedback is used in natural and social sciences. In natural sciences, feedback is in the form of homeostasis and morphogenesis (Riekki and Mämmelä 2021). An important separability principle means that estimation of the environment can be separated from control if the optimization criterion is quadratic and the additive noise is Gaussian.

George P. Richardson saw two parallel threads in feedback systems, starting between 1943 and 1953, including cybernetics and servomechanisms threads with overlapping origins (Richardson 1991). Cybernetics combines control and communications in machines and animals (Wiener 1961). Cybernetics uses the universal principle of feedback and links various fields, including control, regulation, servomechanism, and mere feedback (Gao 2014). The origin of servomechanisms is in self-regulated steam engines using James Watt's flyball governor. Cybernetics is an engineering science, and servomechanism is an engineering practice. Norbert Wiener connected physiology, psychology, sociology, and engineering with cybernetics.

System dynamics was originally called industrial dynamics. It is similar to cybernetics, but its focus is on social systems rather than on biology and engineering, as in cybernetics (Richardson 1991; Meadows and Wright 2008). It is inside the servomechanisms thread. System dynamics uses both positive and negative feedback (Sterman 2000). In addition, it uses nonlinearities and Herbert Simon's ideas on bounded rationality and satisfying principles. System dynamics does not focus on individual agents in the same way that agent-based modeling does. Instead, it provides tools for analyzing complex systems through feedback mechanisms and aggregate behavior over time.

Wiener did not use positive feedback in his cybernetics because of its instability. Wiener's research suggested that positive feedback is dangerous and unstable. For Magoroh Maruyama, negative feedback is deviation-counteracting, and he called it the first cybernetics (Maruyama 1963; Arbnor and Bjerke 1997). He developed the idea of second cybernetics using positive and negative feedback. He often used the term deviation-amplifying since the positive feedback amplifies the deviation between the current and goal states. The idea is helpful in morphogenesis and evolution, where the structure must change when the environment changes. The system can learn and self-organize and grow or shrink. We use negative feedback to protect the system from minor disturbances and positive feedback to discover severe environmental deviations to find a new structure that better fits the environment. Maruyama's idea is now used in system dynamics, which is a form of the second cybernetics.

Wiener's first-order cybernetics is for observed systems (Scott 2004). Heinz von Förster (1981) developed second-order *cybernetics* for observing systems: the observer is included in the feedback loop. Von Förster first introduced the term in 1974. Stuart A. Umpleby emphasizes that in second-order cybernetics, the observer is within the system, and the system is looked from inside out whereas in first-order cybernetics the system is looked from outside in Umpleby (2016). The second-order cybernetics is also called cybernetics of cybernetics. Von Förster published his theory in 1981 in the book *The Second Order Cybernetics of Observing Systems*. The idea of *human in the loop* is historically rooted in W. R. Ashby's double feedback and von Förster's second-order cybernetics (Dautenhahn 1998; Ramage and Shipp 2020).

Optimization and decision theories Optimization is complicated when the environment is dynamic, and we must do adaptive optimization at different levels of a hierarchy. *Optimization theory* is used in various disciplines, including physics, chemistry, biology, and engineering (Gottfried and Weisman 1973; Schoemaker 1991; Forst and Hoffman 2010). According to Bahg (1990), operations research (OR), also called operational research, is a general theory that includes optimization theory (for example, linear and nonlinear programming, game theory, and queuing theory), and decision theory. Operations research means scientific control of existing systems, which can consist of, for example, humans, machines, and materials (von Bertalanffy 1971). Estimation and detection theories are a subset of optimization theory.

Decision theory is a theory of rational choice that uses optimization theory (Peterson 2009). Each decision is preceded by optimization, but the optimum is generally not unique. Some other criterion selects one optimum, usually fairness (Han et al. 2005), which in decision theory means equality, leading to the Nash bargaining solution. A global optimization problem is usually a multiobjective optimization (MOO) or joint optimization problem with mutually conflicting objectives (Marler and Arora 2004; Björnson et al. 2014; Fei et al. 2017). If there are many objectives or criteria, we have a problem called *multiple-criteria decision-making (MCDM)* (Figueira et al. 2005).

A simple form of optimization is scalar optimization, where only one parameter is optimized, and the optimum is unique for convex problems. Optimization implies that we maximize our objective or performance criterion, and if the objective is an efficiency metric, we maximize the efficiency of our system. The most essential efficiency metrics in engineering are called key performance indicators (KPIs).

According to Michael Byron, optimizing means "implementing the best means towards the desired result, and following the steps of itemizing all available options, assessing each one, and then selecting the best" (Gorod et al. 2017). Optimization is often possible only for simple situations.

Optimal systems are efficient, but they are not necessarily robust. A *robust*, insensitive system can function correctly in stressful environments or invalid inputs (SE VOCAB). Thus, we must consider robustification to complement optimization (Arvidsson and Gremyr 2008). Robust design is part of quality engineering. Robust design methodology means "systematic efforts to achieve insensitivity to noise factors." Four principles of robust design have been identified: awareness of variation, insensitivity to noise factors, application of various methods, and application in all stages of a design process. Noise factors are factors that are uncontrollable or hard to control. They cause the performance to deviate from its desired or specified level. They are divided into external, internal, and unit-to-unit noise. Genichi Taguchi developed the first robust design method using a three-step procedure including system, parameter, and tolerance design in the 1940s. The method was translated into English in 1979.

According to Herbert Simon, we do not have infinite rationality but *bounded rationality* and also bounded memory using 50,000 concepts, and we often use a simplified decision model based on the *satisficing principle*, see Fig. 5.10. We accept a satisfactory result, which is not necessarily optimal since there is no choice in complex problems (Simon 1956, 1996; Sterman 2000; Gorod et al. 2017). Thus, we select a solution that is good enough. We reduce the complexity by goal setting. Proper optimization using exhaustive search is only possible in simple problems. In unbounded rationality, we would maximize our utility. Our rationality is bounded due to constraints such as the complexity of the problem, our limited computational power and memory, incomplete information, limited time, and biased objectives that are incommensurate. If we are satisfied, it does not matter if we have not reached the best solution. Mathematically intractable problems show that also computers have bounded rationality.

Human choices are often inconsistent, intransitive, and thus "irrational" (Simon 1996; McFarland and Bösser 1993). Contrary to utility, which is always positive, human satisfaction may also be negative, corresponding to different degrees of dissatisfaction. Herbert Simon suggests that we should use the concept of *aspiration* from psychology. A solution is satisfactory if it meets aspirations along all dimensions or objectives, i.e., satisfaction is positive in all dimensions. This approach is far better than utility maximization. People use heuristics or rules of thumb in their decision making.

In engineering, a satisfactory solution is often a solution that is better than the existing ones, especially if the optimal solution with which to make comparisons is unknown. The robustness of the solution is also crucial (Arvidsson and Gremyr 2008).

The *performance criterion* has many alternative terms in the literature, somewhat depending on the discipline, for example, metric or objective (Marler and Arora 2004), cost function (Gao 2014), figure of merit (Haykin and Moher 2014), measure of goodness (Boulding 1985), or utility (Yi and Chiang 2008; Russell and Norvig

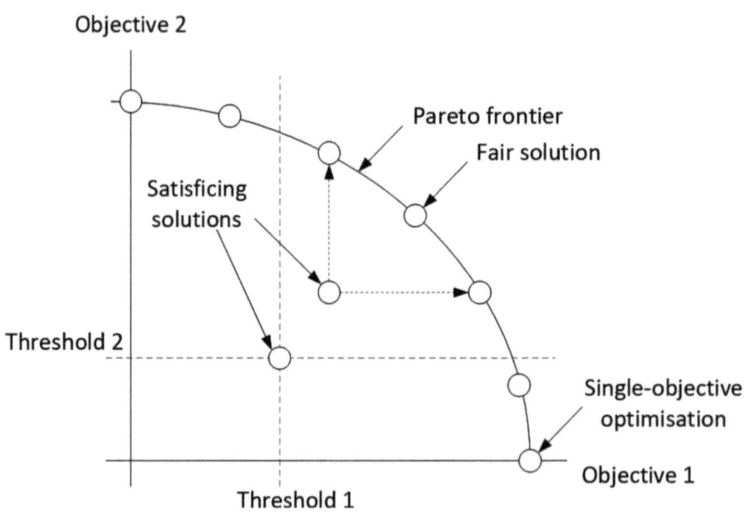

Fig. 5.10 Pareto optimality and satisficing principle

2022) that tries to measure total goodness, satisfaction, or happiness in social situations (Corning 2011). In the optimization, the result is as good as the selected criterion. In nature, the implicit optimization criterion is fitness, which is the capacity to survive and reproduce (Schoemaker 1991). It is perhaps the most significant criterion since it is helpful in technical and social systems and leads to a definition of intelligence (Boulding 1985, p. 174; Stonier 1997, p. 52).

Fitness is helpful in evolutionary methods, which are usually slow, but we also need other criteria. According to Lotfi A. Zadeh, the selection of the optimization criterion is always somewhat arbitrary (Zadeh 1958). We may select a mathematically tractable criterion, such as the minimum mean-square error, that is optimal for a broad class of criteria. However, this does not resolve the problem since it may be poor in some other sense (Gao 2014). We may consider a set of criteria and select a system that is optimal under a majority of the criteria, but the ordering of the systems may be intransitive (Merriam-Webster 2024). Furthermore, the optimization must be global since local optimization does not generally lead to a global optimum because of the phenomenon of emergence. There are cases where the optimum is valid for "any reasonable criterion of goodness" (Ericson 1971).

We may oversimplify the problem by using a scalar metric when, in fact, a vector-valued metric is preferred (Zadeh 1958). Multiobjective optimization is complex since the objectives are generally incommensurate: we do not have a common "currency." Closest to that in natural and technical systems is energy, but more generally, the ability to fit into the environment for improved survival is important (Boulding 1985). There is no objective method to define the utility function to combine different metrics, and the function must often be selected by reverse engineering from successful solutions (Chiang et al. 2007). Various metrics may also depend nonlinearly on each other. Suppose the problem involves many mutually conflicting objectives and constraints. In that case, the optimization becomes "foggy" since, in general, we must abandon one-dimensional optimization and cannot easily say what a "good" design is.

The authors in Walasek and Brown (2023) discuss the incommensurability in much detail. In decision-making, we assume that there is a common currency, such as fitness, happiness, or utility. However, there is no universal approach to solving the problem, and most decision-making models in economics and psychology are fundamentally limited. As in the satisficing principle (Simon 1996), we abandon the common-currency assumption and use analytic hierarchy process (Saaty 2008) and other heuristic rank-based strategies that radically differ from conventional utility-based approaches. The heuristic strategies lead to inconsistencies in decision-making, such as preference reversals, also observed in experimental studies. It appears that it will never be possible to develop consistent single-quantity-maximizing models for decision-making (Walasek and Brown 2023).

Table 5.22 presents traditional optimization methods. Their details can be found in Michalewicz and Fogel (2004). Scalarization and multipolicy algorithms are alternatives to multiobjective optimization (Vamplew et al. 2008; Van Moffaert and Nowe 2014; Radulescu et al. 2020). Scalarization searches for a single optimal solution, whereas multipolicy algorithms search for a set of optimal solutions in a single run.

A conventional reinforcement learning (RL) algorithm receives a scalar feedback signal for its behavior, but more generally, a multiobjective reinforcement algorithm called Pareto Q-learning (PQL) is needed.

Exhaustive search is an optimization method where all solutions in the search space are checked until the best global solution has been found using the selected objective function (Michalewicz and Fogel 2004, pp. 58–64). The exhaustive search is out of the question when the search space is large. *The direct method* is an optimization method where the optimum is found directly using a closed-form equation, mainly when matrix inversion is used in linear systems (Makhoul 1975). *Local search* means optimization in a local neighborhood of some particular solution (Michalewicz and Fogel 2004, pp. 64–76).

Divide and conquer is a solution to a complicated problem by breaking it up into smaller, simpler problems, often in a recursive manner (Michalewicz and Fogel 2004, pp. 90–92). The process continues until the problems are reduced to trivial so they can be solved "by hand." The algorithm then spirals "upward," combining solutions to construct the final solution. The idea has been known since antiquity, but John Mauchly (1946) was the first to describe it clearly.

Linear programming or simplex method is a method to find the maximum or minimum of a linear combination of variables subject to some equality and inequality constraints (Michalewicz and Fogel 2004, pp. 76–80). Any vector that satisfies all the constraints is said to be feasible. The feasible region or solution space is called the simplex. The goal is to find the best result regarding the objective function. The optimal solution lies at one of the vertices of the simplex. Linear programming has been studied since Joseph Fourier (1827). *Scalarization* combines the components of a vector of objective functions to form a single scalar objective function (Marler and Arora 2004). The combining is formed by using a utility function. Optimality is guaranteed, for example, by using a weighted sum or weighted product as the utility function. In *vector optimization*, we treat each objective function independently (Stadler 1986; Marler and Arora 2004).

Optimization problems may be decoupled, weakly or loosely coupled, and strongly or tightly coupled (Sandell et al. 1978). We can use optimization and decomposition to solve large problems (Whitney and Milley 1974). In *optimization decomposition*, an optimization problem is made simpler by decomposition:

Table 5.22 Traditional optimization methods

Traditional optimization methods	Examples
Exhaustive search	Direct method, grid search
Local search	Iterative algorithms, greedy algorithms, simulated annealing, tabu search
Divide and conquer	Recursive algorithms, branch and bound
Linear programming	Simplex method
Scalarization	Weighted sum, weighted product
Optimization decomposition	Dynamic programming

we use decomposition before optimization. Decomposition reduces a large loosely connected problem into smaller tightly connected subproblems that conventional optimization methods can then solve. The size of each subproblem is reduced to a minimum, but the size may still not be manageable. Tightly coupled problems are the hardest to solve since everything depends on everything, and no decomposition can be made.

The optimization methods work best if only one objective represents the overriding design goal. In practice, many mutually conflicting objectives may also be incommensurate, such as in the selection of apples and oranges. When there are conflicting objectives, the solution must be evolutionary-based, possibly using game theory or genetic algorithms (Marler and Arora 2004). Natural systems are usually nearly decomposable or loosely coupled (Simon and Ando 1961; Simon 1962, 1973; Mämmelä et al. 2023). Optimization decomposition is a basis for division of work and specialization in our society (Sterman 2000).

A general decomposition algorithm is *dynamic programming* (Bellman 1957; Köksalan et al. 2011). Richard E. Bellman was able to analyze hundreds of optimization problems. A complicated problem is decomposed into simpler subproblems recursively. In this recursive multistage optimization method, the overall solution is found by operating on an intermediate point between where you are now and where you want to go (Michalewicz and Fogel 2004, pp. 93–101). The method is helpful for problems where time plays a significant role, and the order of operations may be crucial, thus the term "dynamic." The term programming conveyed the notion of finding an optimal program for planning and decision-making, and the term dynamic means that the problems were time-varying.

A problem must have two critical attributes for applying dynamic programming: optimal substructure and overlapping subproblems. If a problem can be solved by combining optimal solutions with nonoverlapping subproblems, the strategy is called divide and conquer instead of dynamic programming. Dynamic programming is used in various algorithms, such as an exact or approximate solution to the traveling salesman problem, the knapsack problem, the shortest path problem including Dijkstra's algorithm and Bellman–Ford algorithm, Viterbi algorithm for finding the maximum likelihood sequence that is closest to the received sequence using the Hamming or Euclidean distance, and recursive least squares (RLS) method for minimizing the exponentially weighted squared error sum.

Standard optimization techniques can be applied to optimization of functions or problems with finitely many parameters. *Calculus of variations* goes one step further and works with functionals, i.e., functions of functions (Bellman 1957; Gottfried and Weisman 1973). In other words, it optimizes the space of functions. The optimal trajectories in control theory are found using optimal control theory which has its roots in calculus of variations. Bellman's dynamic programming has its roots in calculus of variations and optimal control theory.

Optimization may be constrained or unconstrained. A *constraint* is a forcible limitation of freedom in optimization (Pattee 1973). A constraint makes the optimization more complex, and the desired performance may be unattainable within the constraints (Whitney and Milley 1974). Anyhow, the constraints prevent the achievement of the best performance. Fundamental constraints are the fundamental limits of nature (Mämmelä et al. 2018). Constraints can also simplify the optimization, thus transforming multiobjective optimization into single-objective optimization. In communications, delay and throughput may be constrained, and energy minimized, representing Herbert Simon's satisficing principle.

Optimization is generally exponentially complex (Talbi 2009, pp. 14, 22). The problem is called the *curse of dimensionality* (Bellman 1957). As the number of variables increases, the need for computer memory rises exponentially. The complexity implies that large general optimization problems can only be solved approximatively. A generally good method to approximate the solution is the use of a hierarchy and loose horizontal and vertical coupling, especially when the problem is decomposable (Chiang et al. 2007).

Optimization criteria are listed in Table 5.23. The most significant criterion is survivability, which has led to the satisficing principle because of our bounded rationality. Other criteria may be utility, resource efficiency, entropy minimization (Saridis 2001), signal-to-noise ratio (SNR), signal-to-interference ratio (SIR), signal-to-interference and noise ratio (SINR) (Newcombe and Pasupathy 1982; Proakis and Salehi 2008), probability of error (Pulleyblank 1973), and entropy (Saridis 2001). In estimation theory, we use minimum mean-square error (MMSE), maximum a posteriori probability (MAP), maximum likelihood (ML), and least squares (LS) criteria (Kay 1993). In control engineering, a linear quadratic (LQ) cost function is common where the controller is linear (Gao 2014), corresponding to the LS criterion.

There are many reasons for the popularity of quadratic metrics, including MMSE, LS, and LQ (Wang and Bovik 2009): they are simple and memoryless; they satisfy many convenient conditions, including nonnegativity, identity, symmetry, and triangular inequality; they have a physical meaning related to the power or energy of an error signal; in optimization, they are mathematically tractable; and sample average

Table 5.23 Different optimization criteria

Criterion	Properties
Fitness	Survival of the fittest
Satisficing	Bounded rationality
Utility	Multi-objective optimization
Resource efficiency	Single-objective optimization
Entropy minimization	Order maximization
MMSE, LS, LQ	Mathematically tractable quadratic metrics
SNR, SIR, SINR	Fast to measure
MAP, ML	Used in receiver optimization
Probability of error	Often intractable, takes long time to measure
Minimax principle	Zero-sum game

can be replaced with a statistical expectation. Since each error is affected in proportion to its squared magnitude, significant errors have a more considerable influence on the total squared error than the more minor errors. Weighting can be used in different parts of the signal.

Because of implicit solid assumptions, the quadratic metrics are not optimal for all applications. The assumptions include the independence of the relationships between the samples of the original signal and the error signal and of the signs of the error signal samples, and all signal samples are equally crucial for signal quality. Good alternatives exist for different applications. For example, in signal processing, the minimum fourth error criterion has been proposed (Walach and Widrow 1984).

The quadratic metric is helpful in noise filtering, but it has some limitations in control engineering (Gao 2014). For example, the metric may lead to stability problems in cases where we select the best transfer function that yields a fast response with a slight overshoot. Efforts with robust control have addressed the deficiencies with limited success.

A solution to an optimization problem with conflicting objectives is Edgeworth-Pareto optimal or simply *Pareto optimal* if no improvement in any objective can be made without worsening some other objective (Marler and Arora 2004). The Pareto optimum is generally neither socially fair nor unique except in the particular case of a single objective. A selection must be made using additional criteria, usually fairness (Han et al. 2005). It is a common practice, however, to separate fairness from optimality. Suppose, for example, a dictator takes all the resources. In that case, the situation is Pareto optimal since any change would lead to a worse situation from the dictator's point of view. This is an example of a monopoly that the Pareto optimum allows if fairness is not taken into account. The set of Pareto optima forms a *Pareto frontier* beyond which we cannot move but which shows the necessary trade-offs between the objectives, see Fig. 5.10. The frontier demonstrates the effect of the social dilemma: the maximum of a single objective is not a social optimum where many objectives must be traded off. Fairness is an ethical choice.

Game theory is an approach to finding solutions to optimization problems, but in general, the optimum is only found with cooperation. Based on a *cooperative game, Nash bargaining solution* forms a Pareto optimal, unique, and fair solution to multiobjective problems (Lasaulce and Tembine 2011; Salami et al. 2011; Bacci et al. 2016). The idea is to negotiate with all other agents or players to find a fair solution in a distributed way. In a geographically distributed system, the communication would be imperfect, the needed communication would be overwhelming, and there would be delays (Siegfried 2006). Thus, in practice, the game must be approximated using a Stackelberg game or by negotiating only with the nearest neighbors (Lin et al. 2012). In the former case, the negotiations are coordinated hierarchically (Luong et al. 2019). In the latter case, the neighbors have their neighbors, and the situation is similar to a small-world network (Buchanan 2002; Watts 2004) where an exponentially increasing number of members in the network is contained in the optimization using an evolutionary approach.

The combination of objectives is called *utility* if several criteria are combined using a linear or nonlinear utility function (Marler and Arora 2004; Yi and Chiang 2008;

Zhao et al. 2009). It measures the degree of satisfaction. Initially, the utility was the same as money. It is an open question of how to define a utility function objectively. The designer must understand the problem well before selecting the utility function (Whitney and Milley 1974). It could be "discovered" by reverse-engineering existing systems (Chiang et al. 2007). The other possibility is to focus on a particular class of functions with desirable properties, as discussed in Kelly et al. (1998) and Marler and Arora (2004). The utility function should express a decision-maker's preferences. Ideally, the utility function should be an increasing, strictly concave, and continuously differentiable function that leads to a Pareto optimal solution. Typical utility functions are a weighted sum and a weighted product (Krejki and Stoklasa 2018), but there are many more, as summarized in Marler and Arora (2004).

Different criteria are usually incommensurate and mutually conflicting. Decisions involving incommensurate quantities are always subjective (Saaty 2008). It is not straightforward to set the weighting factors in a utility function. In our free market economy, the law of supply and demand is a method to find the prices for incommensurate resources, products, and services (Boulding 1985). In engineering, we usually assume that the prices are defined before the planning starts. If the weighted sum can be used as the utility function, the weights are the prices of each objective, and the utility is the total price, which should be minimized.

A recent review on metaheuristic algorithms is in Katoch et al. (2021). A metaheuristic is a high-level framework that provides guidelines to develop heuristic optimization algorithms. The algorithms may find a single solution or be based on a population of solutions. In *single-solution algorithms*, a single candidate solution is improved by local search but may be stuck in a local optimum. Such algorithms include simulated annealing, tabu search, microcanonical annealing, and guided local search. *Population-based algorithms* use many candidate solutions. Such diversity is used to avoid local optima. The algorithms include genetic algorithms, particle swarm optimization, ant colony optimization, spotted hyena optimizer, emperor penguin optimizer, and seagull optimization. The genetic algorithm is a well-known algorithm that simulates the Darwinian evolutionary theory and was proposed by John Holland (Srinivas and Patnaik 1994). A popular multiobjective evolutionary algorithm (MOEA) solves many of the problems of earlier algorithms (Deb 2002), but even it has shortcomings, and some solutions to the problems have been found (Katoch et al. 2021).

A practical approach for hierarchical optimization is *the analytic hierarchy process* (AHP) (Saaty 2008; Krejki and Stoklasa 2018; Shukla et al. 2016), which has various applications in different fields. In the AHP, an optimization problem is first defined, a decision hierarchy is defined, pairwise comparisons are made, and a weighted average is used to find the overall global utility. The two most common utility functions have been considered to combine different criteria: the weighted product corresponding to the weighted geometric mean and the weighted sum corresponding to using the weighted arithmetic mean. Due to normalizations, according to Krejki and Stoklasa (2018), the weighted product should be preferred over the weighted sum. The weighted product makes the ranking normalization-independent.

Game theory Game theory is a theory of solving optimization problems having mutually conflicting objectives (Siegfried 2006; Lasaulce and Tembine 2011; Bacci et al. 2016). The theory is an example of evolutionary methods. In game theory, agents are called players. Each of the agents is based on feedback. A game is thus a generalization of the feedback concept for many agents. As an evolutionary method, a game offers, in general, a slow approximate solution to the problem with trading but does not always lead to an optimal solution. Furthermore, it does not necessarily approximate natural selection in evolution. Games may be noncooperative, cooperative, and evolutionary. Most often, when discussing games, we refer only to noncooperative games although this is not explicitly mentioned.

Game theory was originally invented to explain economic behavior but may become a unifying theory between disciplines (Siegfried 2006). Some authors think game theory represents a code of nature, describing how nature and social systems work. There is a connection between game theory, statistical mechanics, and quantum theory. The most obvious connection is to agent theory. In artificial intelligence, games can be implemented with multiagent systems (MASs).

Games are divided into noncooperative and cooperative, and the players can be rational or irrational (Nowak 2006), resulting in different equilibria. In a *noncooperative game*, the players are assumed to be *rational*, thus maximizing their utility. A stable, noncooperative game with rational players converges to a *Nash equilibrium*, which is a situation where players cannot gain anything by unilaterally changing their strategy (Lasaulce and Tembine 2011; Bacci et al. 2016). The Nash equilibrium is stable since no one can do better. It is generally not particularly good; it is neither Pareto optimal, unique, nor fair. That is the reason why Nash equilibrium is not called an optimum. Without cooperation, Pareto optima are not stable unless they are Nash equilibria. A noncooperative game without information exchange results in some players taking a majority of resources, implying a birth of monopoles (Boulding 1985). Some animals, such as ducks, follow the game theory in simple situations and find the Nash equilibrium (Siegfried 2006, pp. 73–75). A noncooperative game based on rational players is only a rough approximation of how humans behave. Humans do not act rationally (i.e., selfishly) but altruistically (Nowak 2006, p. 46; Aldred 2020). Noncooperative game theory can be extended to coalitions (Saad et al. 2009). A *coalition* is a set of players cooperating and thus playing as a single player.

In general, convergence to the Pareto optimum requires that all players cooperate. Cooperation corresponds to a single-player game (Marler and Arora 2004). Since there are conflicting goals, we need negotiations. In a *cooperative game*, all the players form a coalition. The solution is called the Nash bargaining solution (NBS). All players negotiate with everyone else; thus, the NBS is distributed and not centralized. Not all distributed solutions are optimal without negotiations. Information exchange is a form of cooperation. Cooperation is less probable if there are many players, when communication is limited, or when time is short (Siegfried 2006, p. 71). In practice, such negotiations are challenging to organize since the number of them would be overwhelming. The distances may be significant; in such cases, even decentralized systems may be preferred (Sandell et al. 1978). The NBS is a good baseline when different methods are compared in terms of optimality and fairness.

One problem is the incommensurability of the resources (Boulding 1985; Walasek and Brown 2023).

An approach to approximate a cooperative game is a hierarchical *Stackelberg game* with a leader (sometimes called an arbitrator) and a group of followers competing on specific resources (Luong et al. 2019), thus combining centralized and distributed decision-making as a hybrid solution. The game can be optimal (Migdalas 1995) or fair (Liu 2021). The NBS has been applied to network optimization, bandwidth allocation, and radio resource management (Salami et al. 2011; Bacci et al. 2016). The Stackelberg game has been used, for example, in wireless networks (Haddad et al. 2011).

Evolutionary game theory by John Maynard Smith (1973) approximates natural selection in evolution. It considers that fitness depends on the environment, and thus, the selections cannot be fixed, although individuals may have fixed strategies (Nowak 2006, pp. 46, 73). The evolutionary game theory is an approach to *evolutionary dynamics* and contains constant selection as its particular case. The theory does not rely on rationality. Strategies that do well reproduce faster and others are out-competed.

The evolutionary game theory explains why people do not act "rationally," which in game theory means selfishly. The problem is in the narrow definition of rationality. The problem can be explained by applying evolutionary game theory to a prisoner's dilemma game. Although cooperation is "irrational," according to the theory, cooperation leads to a higher payoff than mutual defection. Thus, evolutionary game theory is a more accurate description of human behavior and a way to welfare economics. The prisoner's dilemma has become the most influential game in game theory (Aldred 2020). It expresses the social dilemma or the conflict between private and collective interests. The tragedy of the commons is an example of the prisoner's dilemma.

Cooperation is not stable since an always-defect strategy can invade it (Siegfried 2006, pp. 90, 220). A simple winning strategy is *a tit-for-tat* proposed by Anatol Rapoport (1980) where a player first cooperates, but if the other player defects, the first player also defects until the second player cooperates. This strategy is stable. The best strategy to maximize winnings and minimize losses is a *mixed* or *hybrid strategy*, which combines cooperation, competition, and punishments. Nature and the human race play mixed strategies since this is the direction in which evolution has guided us. The mixed strategy approximates an evolutionary game. Punishments are needed since some people always break the rules and may win, which is seen as unfair.

Detection and estimation theory Detection and estimation theories are parts of statistical signal processing (Whalen 1984; Mendel 1995; Kay 1993, 1998, 2013). They are particular forms of optimization and decision theories. We can also see detection theory as a specific case of estimation theory. In detection, we estimate data with a finite number of discrete values, sometimes distorted, whereas, in estimation, the parameters are often continuous (Proakis and Salehi 2008).

In *estimation theory*, unknown parameters must be estimated in a noisy environment by optimally filtering the noise. After optimal estimators are defined, they are sometimes too complicated and must be approximated, or we must find other suboptimal estimators with some reduced performance. Estimation theory consists of classical and Bayesian estimation (Kay 1993). Classical estimation assumes that the unknown parameter to be estimated is a deterministic (i.e., nonrandom) constant. Bayesian estimation assumes that the unknown parameter is random. Usually in the latter case, the second order statistics is assumed to be known in the form of the mean and autocorrelation function that correspond to the power spectrum through the Fourier transform. Although the classical and Bayesian methods are based on different models, in some cases, they are similar in form. In general, adaptive systems as estimators can track only slow changes compared to the symbol rate (Schwartz et al. 1966; Monsen 1980).

The optimal estimators must follow the Cramer–Rao lower bound for the variance of any unbiased estimator. An estimator is *unbiased* if the mean of the estimate of a parameter is the actual value of the unknown parameter. Usually the Cramer–Rao lower bound and unbiased estimators are used for deterministic parameters, but they can be extended and modified to random parameters. Typical estimators include maximum likelihood (ML) and least squares (LS) estimators for deterministic parameters and minimum mean-square error (MMSE) and maximum a posteriori probability (MAP) for random parameters (Kay 1993). The term *likelihood* differs from the term probability since likelihood always refers to a posteriori probabilities (after observation), not prior probabilities (before observation). ML estimation is a particular case of MAP estimation when the a priori probabilities of the parameter to be estimated have a uniform distribution.

Estimation algorithms may be *batch* or *sequential estimators* (Kay and Marple 1981). In the former case, the algorithm computes a solution by directly processing a block of data without recursions or iterations. Sequential algorithms update the estimate on a sample-by-sample basis, i.e., when the data block becomes larger. Sequential estimators may be iterative, such as the least-mean square (LMS) algorithm, time-recursive, such as the recursive least-squares (RLS) algorithm in a transversal filter, or order-recursive as the recursive least-squares lattice algorithm (Makhoul 1975; Qureshi 1982, 1985; Proakis and Salehi 2008). The *transversal filter* is a finite impulse response filter, also called a *tapped delay line*, where the taps are the different intervening outputs of the delay line. The output is a weighted sum of the samples in the memory of the delay line. The state changes when a new signal sample is received as an input, the old samples are shifted one step forward, and the oldest sample is removed from the memory. The taps are turned on or off, but they may also be "partially open" so that the weight (i.e., the unknown parameter to be estimated) may be any real or complex number.

An *iterative algorithm* is based on a process that makes repetitive steps to find a solution. It can often overshoot or undershoot the solution and sometimes does not converge if the stability conditions are unmet. A *recursive algorithm* usually finds an exact solution, obtained in stages and leading to the same solution as the corresponding batch algorithm.

Detection theory is another part of statistical signal processing (Kay 1998). The channel through which the data are transmitted causes distortion and additive noise.

Distortion may be interpreted as multiplicative noise (Yu et al. 2021), corresponding to the convolution of the transmitted signal with the channel impulse response in a linear channel. Nonlinear distortion also corresponds to multiplicative noise. A Viterbi algorithm can implement the optimal maximum likelihood sequence detector recursively. If there is no interference between symbols, the optimal receiver is the matched filter. If the additive noise is Gaussian, the optimal estimator in an unknown channel is an estimator-correlator (Kailath 1960). The estimator-correlator represents one form of the separation theorem.

Artificial intelligence John McCarthy (1955) proposed the term AI as the name of a new field that combines control and computing. Game theory was originally developed in economics, but now it is also included in decision theory and AI.

The five critical paradigms of artificial intelligence in engineering include knowledge-based systems, neural networks, fuzzy logic, genetic algorithms, and rational agents (Song and Johns 1998; Bezdek 2016; Russell and Norvig 2022). Rational agents will dominate the future. Expert systems are a particular case of knowledge-based systems. Genetic algorithms are a form of evolutionary computation. Conventional artificial intelligence is regarded as *hard computing*. The primary forms of *soft computing*, also called *computational intelligence (CI)*, include neural networks originally devised by Warren McCulloch and Walter Pitts (1943), fuzzy sets and fuzzy logic by Lotfi A. Zadeh (1965, 1973), and genetic algorithms by John H. Holland (1975) as a form of evolutional computing (Chaturvedi 2008; Bezdek 2016). Soft computing also includes swarm intelligence and artificial immune systems (Engelbrecht 2007). Some computers have a hybrid form, combining hard and soft computing, see Medsker (1995) and McGarry et al. (1999) and independently in Ovaska et al. (2006). Initially, Larry R. Medsker combined expert systems and neural networks and called them the combination hybrid intelligent systems (Medsker 1995).

Modern AI is a theory of interacting agents called multiagent systems (Stone and Veloso 2000; Rizk et al. 2018; Russell and Norvig 2022). The central role of agents was realized only in about 1987, whereas earlier, AI studied lower-level components of the theory (Russell and Norvig 2022, p. 79). Agents are divided into *reactive*, *proactive*, and social agents and their hybrid forms (Mämmelä et al. 2018). Some common hybrid robot architectures combine lower-layer reactive and higher-layer proactive behavior (Bekey 2005, pp. 107–110). Social or interacting agents can be either competitive or cooperative. AI and machine learning algorithms can be seen as optimization algorithms. Machine learning is a subset of artificial intelligence, often not based on feedback: they observe the environment without trying to control it (Marsland 2015). In this sense, they are monitoring systems, whereas AI systems are more complete feedback control systems.

The interaction in multiagent systems forms a game whose equilibria are studied in game theory. Since an agent is based on a sense-decide-act feedback loop, AI is based on control engineering, and in addition, the AI uses optimization and decision theories. The most important new thing was the integration of computing to provide a more advanced feedback loop than in cybernetics. Game and decision theories predated AI by a decade. Complexity theory is a spin-off of artificial intelligence, just as artificial intelligence was a spin-off of cybernetics. AI may be based on deduction or induction (Larson 2021). Human creativity is based on abduction, but according to Larson (2021), a machine cannot use abduction.

The learning algorithms are classified into supervised, unsupervised, reinforcement, and evolutionary learning (Bishop 2006; Marsland 2015). In *supervised learning*, we use a training set, and the corresponding correct responses are used as teachers. The algorithm can generalize so that all possible inputs result in the proper response. In control engineering, we call such a system an automatic system that uses a reference signal, which may be a simple set-point value. *Unsupervised learning* does not need any training set, but we use for example pattern recognition to find regularities in the data, such as anomaly detection, clustering, or density estimation. In anomaly detection, we identify unusual patterns in the form of deviations from normal behavior in data. Clustering is a form of dimensionality reduction where we discover groups of similar examples within data. In density estimation, we estimate an unknown probability distribution in the data.

Reinforcement learning is a simple form of supervised learning where the supervision is at a minimum level. It is learning with a critic. Reinforcement learning is based on the same principle as a children's game called scavenger hunt, also called treasure hunt, where we have a list of items (a key, a book, a toy car, a wooden spoon, etc.) and one of us hides all the items and the other persons find them. When someone struggles to find an item, we say: "Do you want a hint?" If the seeker says "yes," we then say "hot… hotter… boiling" as they get closer and "cold… colder… freezing" as they move farther away. The scavenger hunt is an example of positive and negative reinforcement. Reinforcement learning is essentially a negative feedback goal-directed system where the critic knows the goal and guides the system in the right direction.

Evolutionary learning is a form of reinforcement learning in which the environment provides all the supervision, but more directly than in reinforcement learning. In evolution, those systems survive than have the best fit in the environment. In a way, the environment acts as a reinforcing agent without any clear goal, but the result is increased complexity, survivability, intelligence, rationality, and finally wisdom.

Some of the results of artificial intelligence include computers that can play chess or Go games, personal digital assistants displaced by smartphones, a chatbot, and a self-driving car (Roberts 2020; Larson 2021). Computers work best in known, perfect, and static environments such as the Go game, and unknown, uncertain, and dynamic environments such as real traffic are still an open problem for autonomous self-driving vehicles.

In 1997, Deep Blue Computer could beat the world champion in chess (Roberts 2020; Pietikäinen and Silven 2021). It has been estimated that there are at least 10^{120} possible chess games (Bernstein and de Roberts 1958). Similarly, the AlphaGo machine beat the world champion in Go in 2016. In 2009, an attempt to make science automatic was published (King et al. 2009). A machine generated autonomously hypotheses and experimentally tested these hypotheses by using laboratory automation. In 2011, Watson machine won humans in the TV quiz show Jeopardy

(Pietikäinen and Silven 2021). In 2016, the average performance of humans was in verbal IQ tests lower than that of a machine (Wang et al. 2016).

Now *large language models* (LLMs) are popular in artificial intelligence using a deep learning neural network architecture (Corchado et al. 2023; Liu et al. 2023). They often use transformers that are effective for natural language processing (NLP). The method is essentially based on statistical analysis of big data produced by humans, not on any kind of understanding. The transformer has also been used as a pixel-generative model for high-quality art and videos.

Statistical analysis may lead to gross mistakes, and human supervision is always needed. The need for supervision is an example of a frame problem: a machine does not understand semantics, i.e., the relationship between abstract symbols and reality. One problem is that because of a self-consuming loop, the quality and diversity of the generative models decrease without reliable real data (Alemohammad et al. 2023). The phenomenon is called model collapse (Shumailov et al. 2014). AI should be based on reliable scientific papers produced and reviewed by humans without a self-consuming loop, which would dumb the AI down. An additional problem is the large amount of energy consumed. The focus is on the decision block of a rational agent, whereas complex adaptive systems are made of a large set of agents.

According to Larson (2021), the future of AI is unknown, but biological and artificial intelligence are radically different. The present AI does not understand anything. So far, human-level self-consciousness can be reached only through evolution using carbon-based organic matter. Consciousness is an emergent property, but there is nothing mystical (Camazine et al. 2001, p. 91). Furthermore, a human needs a childhood to mature and become an adult. Silicon is an inorganic matter that cannot form complex molecules like carbon, which is a major stumbling block in AI.

Significant problems in artificial intelligence are complexity and the need for real-time operation since learning is slow (Hu et al. 2021). There is no guarantee that an algorithm will converge. Heuristics is often used, and there are no systematic ways to select the parameter values. In Q-learning, a problem is the large size of the Q-table (Jang et al. 2019). There are examples where the number of rows in the table is larger than the number of atoms in the universe, and the time for convergence is larger than the universe's age (Tan et al. 2017). Deep Q-learning aims to solve some of these problems.

Theory of information transmission Information theory is a statistical theory of information transmission developed by Claude E. Shannon (1948) (Shannon 1948a, b, 1949; Shannon and Weaver 1998). The theory provides a quantitative and logarithmic information measure based on probability. A more advanced semantic information theory is yet to be developed (Stonier 1997; Marcos and Arp 2013, p. 518; Qin et al. 2023). Shannon did not like the term "information theory" (Rioul 2021). It is not a theory about information but a theory about the transmission of information. Hartley (1928) used the term "theory of information transmission." The term "bit" (binary unit) was introduced in Shannon (1948a, b).

Shannon used the term entropy from thermodynamics according to a suggestion made by John von Neumann based on mathematical similarity (Thims 2012; Gauvrit et al. 2017). According to some claims, thermodynamics forms a basis for information theory, but this relationship has also been criticized. One of the first critics was Dirk ter Haar (1954). Mathematical similarity does not yet show that there is some relationship. It is also counterintuitive that random sequences would contain most statistical information (Marcos and Arp 2013). The reason is that statistical information has nothing to do with the meaning. At the semantic level, most of the information is in a complex sequence that looks random and thus has high entropy, but that complex sequence must be related to something that has a meaning to us humans. For example, a standing house contains a lot of semantic information for humans in its order. That information is increased with complexity, but a collapsed house includes no semantic information, although it includes much statistical information. Thus, although we are not directly interested in random sequences at the semantic level, the fact that complex deterministic sequences look random makes statistical information theory relevant to us. Shannon's information depends on the probability of a symbol. It does not represent the level of surprise as is sometimes claimed since, in statistical information theory, the symbols do not have any meaning in the real world.

Shannon divided the perturbations in a channel into linear distortion and additive Gaussian noise, representing thermal noise. The Shannon information theory offers the upper limits for the bit rate in a band-limited linear channel, including additive Gaussian noise. The theory is an existence proof, i.e., it does not directly tell the optimal coding and modulation methods, and they must be found in other ways. The capacity has also been derived for a nonideal channel with additive colored or nonwhite noise, leading to the water-filling principle. The principle means that if the signal power is distributed in time, frequency, and spatial domains, most of the power is transmitted where the channel is best regarding signal-to-noise ratio. Some crucial results exist for nonlinear channels, such as optical communications (Secondini and Forestieri 2017) and analog-to-digital converters (Ranjbar 2020).

Shannon decomposed or separated the information transmission problem into source and channel coding. In source coding, any redundancy is removed, and in channel coding, we add systematic redundancy in parity symbols so that the received signal can be efficiently demodulated. The maximum bit rate is called the channel capacity (in bit/s). The capacity is the bit rate below which a zero-error probability can be obtained if the complexity and the system's delay are unlimited. The capacity can be achieved closely in a binary channel using, for example, low-density parity-check (LDPC) codes with reasonable complexity and delay.

Ideally, we would need *network information theory*. The problem is the interference between the links. The interference is not Gaussian since the signals are not Gaussian, leading to mathematical intractability (Simon 2002). We have different solutions to this problem. We can assume that the interference is Gaussian (which it is not), we can use other criteria in optimization, for example mean-square error (MSE) or signal-to-interference ratio (SIR) (Newcombe and Pasupathy 1982; Wang and Bovik 2009), we can use multiuser receivers to reduce interference and assume that the interference does not exist (Proakis and Salehi 2008), or we can assume loose coupling between the layers and subsystems in each layer (Simon 1973; Mämmelä et al. 2023), for example, we can avoid interference by using orthogonal signals (Pottie 1995). All of these are approximations. Orthogonal frequency division multiplexing (OFDM) used in modern communication systems is approximately complex Gaussian based on the central limit theorem in mathematics (Proakis and Salehi 2008).

Queuing theory (sometimes also called queueing theory) is a theory of queues started by Agner K. Erlang (1909) (Stordahl 2007). It is a network optimization theory when there is a crowding condition in the network. A model is constructed so that queue lengths and waiting times can be predicted.

Network or graph theory Network theory and graph theory are synonymous terms, and the theories were developed already before communication networks. A network consists of nodes (also called vertices) and links (also called edges or branches) that are paths that connect the nodes (Poundstone 1988, p. 165; Newman 2010). An extension of graph theory is *random graph theory*, which combines graph theory and probability theory and is used to analyze the properties of typical graphs (Newman 2010). In a random graph, a set of nodes is connected randomly by a set of edges. The way the nodes are connected is called *topology*, which is the structure of the network. The focus is on the number of links between two users, and the delays and errors in the links are usually neglected.

A maze or labyrinth is an example of a graph (Poundstone 1988, p. 172). In a labyrinth, a node is a point similar to a fork where paths meet, and we must decide. Finding a simple route not crossing itself through a maze from an entrance to a goal is a nondeterministic polynomial (NP) complete problem (Dewdney 2004). Still, if an oracle tells the answer, verifying the solution is a simple task.

A relevant problem in network theory is knowing how many links or "hops" there are between two arbitrary nodes (Buchanan 2002; Watts 2004). In a human society, the nodes are assumed to be humans, and the links are considered the relationships between humans. Humans form a *small-world network* in that each human in the world is separated from any other human only by six links. The idea is called the *six degrees of separation*. If each human knows about $N = 150$ friends (which is the Dunbar number) and each of them knows 150 other friends, etc., after L links, we have contact with N^L persons by assuming that the new friends are always different. There is thus an exponential growth of contacts. We can also see the small world as a hierarchy that solves a decomposable problem with exponential complexity in a simple, distributed manner. This leads to the efficiency of the division of work in our society. With $L = 5$ links, we already have a number of N^L exceeding the world population. However, there is a significant overlap among the friends of our friends. This overlap is also essential since it offers suitable shortcuts that are a property of small-world networks. Because of the exponential growth of contacts, there is a logarithmic relation between the average distance between the nodes and the network radius (Ogras and Marculescu 2006).

Some people have an exceptionally high number of friends. They are called *hubs* of the network. In practice, $L = 6$ is an excellent estimate for covering the whole world population. However, it is not valid for isolated tribes that do not have any contact with the outside world.

Small-world networks have high local and global efficiencies (Latora and Marchiori 2001). They are intermediate between a regular and random network (Liao et al. 2017). A human brain is an example of a small-world network. Small-world networks can also be applied to wireless communication networks, where the basic idea is to use shortcuts (Helmy 2003). Small-world networks appear also in integrated circuits (Ogras and Marculescu 2006). Recently, some researchers have found deterministic small-world networks where the number of nodes is either fixed or growing (Guo et al. 2012). The benefit is that the network structure can be found analytically, whereas the older models construct networks probabilistically and do not explain how each link is formed.

Hierarchy theory Hierarchy theory can be seen as an extension of network theory to hierarchical systems (Wu 2013). The theoretical basis comes from the optimization decomposition using network utility maximization (Chiang et al. 2007). Chiang et al. (2007) present a mathematical theory of network architectures (Chiang et al. 2007). Corresponding tutorial presentations are in Palomar and Chiang (2006) and Lin et al. (2006). The theory is based on *network utility maximization* (NUM) theory, which leads to the decomposition of the NUM problem into hierarchical layers and modules within layers. The decomposition is vertical decomposition into layers and horizontal composition into modules so that the network can manage geographically disparate network elements using distributed computing.

The optimization starts with maximizing a utility function, whose selection is subjective. The utility is defined in an ordinal scale rather than a ratio scale. Thus, the actual values of the utility function are meaningless and used only to establish the order for comparison purposes. The clean-slate optimization-based approach naturally results in a vertical loosely coupled solution (Simon 1973; Mämmelä et al. 2023) with only a limited degree of cross-layer coupling (Lin et al. 2006; Johansson et al. 2006; Chiang et al. 2007). The small degree of coupling corresponds to the time-scale separation of layers, but this needs that the environment has similar time-scale separation. In addition, although not mentioned in Chiang et al. (2007), Lin et al. (2006) and Johansson et al. (2006), we expect that horizontal loose coupling is needed. It corresponds to interference avoidance between network users; for example, power control loops in the uplink from a terminal to the base station must be loosely coupled or decoupled. Some vertical coupling is needed; otherwise, layers have no control.

A set of systems can be arranged into a complexity hierarchy where the more complex systems are higher in the hierarchy. Such hierarchies have been proposed for biological systems and technical systems (Boulding 1985; Mämmelä et al. 2023). Different disciplines, from physics to philosophy, can also be presented as a hierarchy.

Theory of computing and computational complexity theory The theoretical study of computing is called the *automata theory*. *Computing problems* are classified into decision, optimization, and search problems (Sipser 2006; Talbi 2009). In *decision* *problems*, we find a yes or no answer (Dewdney 2004). In *optimization problems*, we find the best solution out of all feasible solutions. All optimization problems can be reduced to decision problems (Talbi 2009, p. 12; Dewdney 2004, p. 191). For example, we can find a minimum length through a network by asking binary questions regarding different maximal lengths until the optimum is found. Optimization problems are, in general, more complex than decision problems.

Verifying an optimization problem is generally more complex than verifying a decision problem, even if the solution is known. In decision problems, we verify whether a given solution is or is not a solution. In optimization problems, to verify whether the solution is optimal, we need to compare it with all other solutions to confirm that the best was found. If we can show that the problem is convex, then verification of an optimization problem is simpler due to the uniqueness of the global optimum.

In *search problems*, we look for a sequence of actions that reaches a goal (Pearl and Korf 1987; Russell and Norvig 2022). A search algorithm returns a solution as an action sequence, also called an algorithm. Typical search problems include seven bridges of Königsberg, solving puzzles such as Rubik's cube, and playing games such as chess or Go. Search problems are generally more complex than decision and optimization problems (Arora and Barak 2009, p. 51).

The difficulty of computing problems is classified into three groups, including tractable, intractable, and unsolvable problems (Dewdney 2004; Woeginger 2008). The difficulty is measured by the needed time in steps and space in the form of memory to solve them. The complexity may be a polynomial or exponential function of the size of the problem. For example, the *size* may be the number of puzzle pieces or nodes in a maze, graph, or network (Poundstone 1988, pp. 177–178).

Ordinary algorithms are deterministic and determined in advance, implying that the outcome is also determined if the problem is time-invariant (Dewdney 2004). Solving a problem is generally more complex than verifying the solution after we know the solution. *Tractable problems* are easy problems that can be solved in polynomial (P) time $O(n^k)$ at the maximum where O(·) means the order of complexity, n is the size of the problem, and $k \geq 0$ is an integer. Tractable problems include, for example, constant time $O(1)$, linear time $O(n)$, quadratic time $O(n^2)$, and logarithmic time $O(\log_2(n))$ problems. *Intractable problems* cannot be solved in polynomial time, and they have at least exponential time complexity $O(k^n)$, where k is a positive integer. Intractable problems include factorial time $O(n!)$ problems (Woeginger 2008). *Unsolvable problems* are problems for which no solution can be found with any computer, i.e., the computer will never terminate. The existence of intractable and unsolvable problems shows that also computers have bounded rationality leading to the need for satisficing principle defined by Herbert Simon (Simon 1996).

Nondeterministic, polynomial time (NP) problems are problems that can be verified in polynomial time but cannot always be solved in polynomial time; see Fig. 5.11 and Table 5.24. NP problems include P, NP-intermediate, and NP-complete problems. Exhaustive search can solve every NP problem in exponential time (Woeginger 2008). If we had a computer that could check all solutions simultaneously in parallel, it would terminate in polynomial time since the time needed is for verifying the solution, which is a P problem among the NP problems (Casti 1994). Such a computer is *nondeterministic* (Wolfram 2024). The parallel computers do not communicate with each other. Since, in practice, we cannot do such a simultaneous check, a nondeterministic algorithm would need guessing or the use of an oracle, also called a clairvoyant or a genie. Polynomial time problems are a subset of NP problems.

Intractable problems can in principle be solved, i.e., the algorithm will eventually terminate. Still, depending on the size of the problem, the solution may take an enormous amount of time, even in the order of the universe's age. The number of memory elements may even be in the order of the number of atoms in the universe (Poundstone 1988). Thus, a computer of the size of the universe using the time of the age of the universe cannot solve them.

NP-complete problems are the most complex problems among NP problems (Johnson 2012). All the NP-complete problems can be transformed into satisfiability problems regarding the consistency of a given set of statements (Poundstone

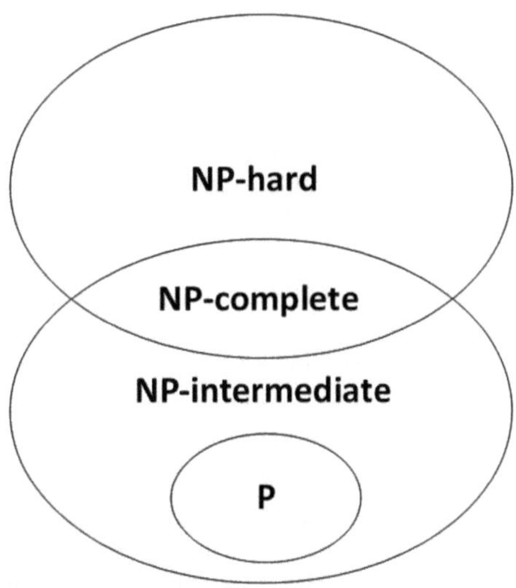

Fig. 5.11 A Venn diagram of computing problems that are solvable in principle. NP problems include P, NP-intermediate, and NP-complete problems

Table 5.24 Classification of problems based on their difficulty

Problem type	Solution complexity	Verification complexity	Examples
Unsolvable problems	Unsolvable	Unsolvable	Halting problem
NP-hard problems	Exponential	Exponential	Optimization problems
NP-complete problems	Exponential	Polynomial	Satisfiability problem
NP-intermediate problems	Polynomial	Polynomial	Integer factorization
P problems	Polynomial	Polynomial	Sorting problem

1988, p. 21, 188). The set of statements is *satisfiable* when they are true in some possible world that is not necessarily our own. We do not understand the statements if we cannot see the contradictions. Jigsaw puzzles and simple arithmetic problems are P problems, but solving mazes is an NP-complete problem. The satisfiability problem delimits our knowledge (Casti 1994, p. 141).

If we must reveal possible contradictions, the nth statement must be compared against every possible subset of the current $n - 1$ statements (Poundstone 1988, p. 184). The number of comparisons needed in the satisfiability problem is $2^n - 1$, corresponding to (2^n), where n is the number of statements. For example, if $n = 100$, the number of comparisons is 1.3×10^{30}, and if $n = 330$, the number of comparisons is almost 10^{100}. The number of protons in the universe is 10^{80} (initially estimated in 1940 by Arthur Eddington), and the universe's age is about 10^{17} s. Walter Elsasser and William Poundstone independently estimated that even though we would use the whole universe as a computer, the number of operations that can be done during the lifetime of the universe would be finite, say 10^{100} (Elsasser 1987, p. 51; Poundstone 1988, p. 187). The number 10^{100} is called googol in mathematics, as Edward Kassner (1940) suggested. Walter Elsasser calls numbers larger than googol *immense numbers*. For all practical cases they are infinite numbers. The number of statements we can fully understand is much smaller than $n = 330$. An immensely small number is smaller than 10^{-100}.

There are thousands of NP-complete problems, for example, traveling salesman (shortest path) problem, knapsack problem, timetable design, and computer circuit fault detection problem (Dewdney 2004, pp. 184, 193). It is an open question whether they can be solved in polynomial time, i.e., whether NP = P. If the satisfiability problem can be solved in polynomial time, all other NP-complete problems can be solved in polynomial time. However, it is suspected that the NP-complete problems cannot be solved in polynomial time. This has far-reaching consequences, not only in computational complexity theory. Because of NP problems, acts of creation are difficult and time consuming. If NP problems were P problems, doing science or engineering would be simple and everyone could do it. Everyone could paint a masterpiece, compose an opera, write a good book, and succeed in information retrieval. Verification of a theory is rather straightforward when you have P problems: you can tell whether a painting is good or not, appreciate good music, etc.

NP-complete problems are approximately solved in polynomial time in different ways (Upadhyaya and Dhingra 2010; Tse 2010). *Approximation*: Instead of searching for an optimal solution, search for an "almost" optimal one. *Randomization*: Use randomness to get a faster average running time and allow the algorithm to fail with some small probability. Evolutionary approaches, such as genetic algorithms, belong to this class. *Restriction*: By restricting the input structure, faster algorithms are usually possible. *Parameterization*: There are often fast algorithms if specific parameters of the input are fixed. Fixing the parameters is a form of constraint. *Heuristic*: An algorithm that works "reasonably well" in many cases but for which there is no proof that it is always fast and produces a good result.

NP-hard problems are a more general class of hard problems which includes NP-complete problems as a particular case (Talbi 2009) (Fig. 5.11). Although a problem would be NP-complete or NP-hard, it can be solved when the size n of the problem is small (Talbi 2009, p. 29). NP-complete problems are NP and NP-hard problems at the same time. In NP-hard problems, solutions cannot be always verified in polynomial time and thus not all NP-hard problems are NP problems. Most optimization problems in practice are NP-hard and require exponential time to be solved (Talbi 2009, pp. 14, 22), which is called the curse of dimensionality (Bellman 1957). Some NP-hard problems cannot even be approximated in polynomial time.

It is unlikely that quantum computers can solve NP-complete problems in polynomial time (Yanofsky 2013, pp. 120, 136). It is suspected that there are NP problems between the P and NP-complete problems, as suggested by Richard E. Ladner (1975) (Hamadi and Wintersteiger 2012). Such problems are called *NP-intermediate problems*. Among them, quantum computers can solve only a few problems in polynomial time (Arora and Barak 2009, p. 188; Aaronson 2008). Problems that can be solved in polynomial time with a quantum computer are called bounded quantum polynomial (BQP) problems (Monroe 2019). This class was defined by Ethan Bernstein and Umesh Vazirani (1997). Soon after this, Peter Shor (1997) discovered a method for factoring integers on a quantum computer in polynomial time. It has subexponential complexity in a classical computer but polynomial complexity in a quantum computer.

The *halting problem* means whether a solution is ever found and whether the algorithm eventually stops (Casti 1994, p. 136). The halting problem is forever unsolvable. It is the computer-theoretic counterpart of Gödel's first incompleteness theorem. Similarly, the existence of strange attractors in dynamical systems in chaos theory shows that there are states that cannot be attained from any given initial state, which is a form of Gödel's theorem (Casti 1991, pp. 218, 317). There is a deterministic logical route to chaos.

General theory of systems The theory was initially called a general system theory (from German *Allgemeine Systemtheorie*), but some authors think it is a misnomer since there are no general systems (Francois 2000; Ramage and Shipp 2020). von Bertalanffy (1950) noticed that different disciplines converge to similar solutions without much interaction: "As we survey the evolution of modern science, we find a remarkable phenomenon that similar general conceptions and viewpoints have evolved independently in the various branches of science" (von Bertalanffy 1950). The ideas are either invented independently or somehow "leaked"—perhaps orally—from one discipline to the other, and often, those links are not documented in citations. Complexity theory is a modern form of the general theory of systems (Thurner et al. 2018; Mobus 2022). No mathematical expression exists for how cells, individuals, or societies act (Casti 1994).

The similarity of ideas implies that only a finite number of generic structures or *system archetypes* have stood the test of time (Senge 2006; Meadows and Wright 2008). The archetypes produce some desirable behavior and they are mainly used in system dynamics. Systems architects (Maier and Rechtin 2009) should use the system archetypes as their primary tool. Jay Forrester estimated that a relatively small number of simple structures are found in different problems in various fields

(Forrester 2007a, b). He estimated that 20 archetypes would cover more than 90% of different situations in management. Peter M. Senge presented nine archetypes and one special case in his book (Senge 2006). Meadows presented eight archetypes, some similar to those of Senge (Meadows and Wright 2008). Thus, we estimate that most of the time, we can do with 10–20 archetypes. A core set of four generic two-loop archetypes in system dynamics was presented in Wolstenholme (2003).

For our purposes, the most critical archetypes include positive and negative feedback, hierarchy, optimization and decision-making, and communication and control topologies (Mämmelä et al. 2018), set of interacting agents (Benbya and McKelvey 2006; Thurner et al. 2018; Mobus 2022), sequential and concurrent computing (Mämmelä et al. 2023), and nonequilibrium thermodynamics (Boulton et al. 2015). Communication and control topologies include small-world systems (Buchanan 2002; Watts 2004; Newman 2010), degrees of centralization, and degrees of coupling (Mämmelä et al. 2023). Information is exchanged using shared memory or message passing (Decker 1987).

Complexity theory Complexity theory is a modern version of a general theory of systems and essentially a spin-off of cybernetics and artificial intelligence (Holland 1995; Benbya and McKelvey 2006; Thurner et al. 2018; Mobus 2022; Russell and Norvig 2022). It is a theory of *complex adaptive systems* (CASs) (Holland 1995), which George E. Mobus calls complex adaptive and evolvable systems (CAESs) (Mobus 2022). The researchers at Santa Fe Institute developed the CAS concept (Holland and Miller 1991; Holland 1992, 1995, 1998, 2006; West 2017). Complexity theory is a theory of self-organization. CASs include biological, ecological, social, economic, and political systems, and traffic and weather (Kauffman 1995; Dooley 1997). Some of them are chaotic. Complexity theory started to use multiagent systems but with a different name and focus on self-organization, usually excluded from conventional AI (Russell and Norvig 2022), which has been mainly interested in static systems (Albus and Meystel 2001).

A system also needs some hierarchical structure. For an *agent*, we use a broad definition: it can be, for example, a human, a robot, or a software agent. Agents are implemented as *sense-decide-act feedback loops*: we first sense the environment, make decisions, and control action (Albus and Meystel 2001, p. 7; Kline 1995, p. 188; Russell and Norvig 2022). Some agents do not have any sense block but are based in open-loop control. In the former times, intelligence and rationality were often assumed to be synonymous. In modern psychology, intelligence refers to the ability to reason using the rules of logic. In contrast, rationality is a higher-level concept that means agents can efficiently reach their goals with the available resources in an uncertain environment (Albus 1991; Stanovich et al. 2016; Robson 2019). However, a machine's ability to act appropriately in uncertain dynamic environments such as traffic is limited (Roberts 2020; Larson 2021). Even modern deep neural networks are based on statistical regularity but do not work reliably in busy streets.

5.4.2 System Archetypes

Different disciplines have converged towards similar system models (Mämmelä et al. 2018; Riekki and Mämmelä 2021). We have networked control systems (NCSs) and autonomous, cooperative, and self-organizing robots in control engineering. In NCSs, control is done remotely through a network, perhaps including haptic control using the sense of touch. In computer engineering, we have distributed and autonomic computing, multiagent systems, and cloud and edge servers, which are used in different forms of distributed computing. In communications engineering, we have network automation and self-organizing networks (SONs). Self-organization can be realized with programmable networks (Mämmelä et al. 2023). They are divided into active networks and software-defined networks (SDNs) (Feamster 2013). In software-defined networks (SDNs), the data or user plane and the control plane are separated, but now network automation is done through application programming interfaces (APIs). However, SDN is a good term for network automation, including network service orchestration, if we change the definition. The active networks were used in the first programmable networks, which were later replaced by SDNs and more general network automation since SDNs were narrowly defined. Generic system archetypes are presented in Table 5.25.

Feedback The feedback loop including the present sense-decide-act phases appeared only slowly. The decision phase is now often preceded by the processing phase (Kline 1995, pp. 55–56, 188, 316). Still, we use the term "decision" to emphasize the most central task in this phase of the feedback loop, and the processing of sensing information is assumed to be included in the decision phase. Feedback is called the agent in artificial intelligence.

If two feedback loops are *sequential* (Ingalls 2013), as in a hierarchical system, there must be time-scale separation between the loops to guarantee stability (Mämmelä et al. 2023). In practice, the feedback loop at a higher hierarchy level must act much more slowly than at a lower level. Two feedback loops may also be *nested* (Ingalls 2013). If we use positive feedback, it is usually the inner of the two loops, and a negative feedback loop is the outer of the loops so that effectively, the whole loop behaves as a negative feedback loop (DeAngelis et al. 1986; Ogata 2010; Ford 2019). Thus, the positive feedback loop may initially dominate, producing exponential growth. Then, there is a shift in dominance from the positive feedback loop to the negative feedback loop, producing saturation, thus forming a behavior that resembles an s-curve.

Research is an advanced learning process, often identifying a model for the environment needed in the decision phase in the feedback loop. In this sense, the learning and research process can be seen as a particular case of the general sense-decide-act loop. Reliable decisions are possible if we have a model of the environment (Conant and Ashby 1970); see Fig. 5.12. The model of the environment is first identified and verified. *Perception* is a process where sensing results are transformed into environmental knowledge (Albus and Meystel 2001). Next, using the model, a decision is made to shift the environment from the present state to the desired state or improved

Table 5.25 System archetypes

System archetype	Explanation
Feedback	Positive and negative feedback loops. Some control loops are based on open-loop control without any sensors
Hierarchy and modularity	Hierarchies are classified into nested and non-nested hierarchies. The hierarchy levels and the modules are usually loosely coupled
Optimization and decision-making	Optimization methods are based on parametric models, neural networks, and evolutionary methods. The optimum is called a Pareto optimum, which is not unique or fair and decision-making is necessary. Nash bargaining solution is a distributed solution in a cooperative game, which is optimal, unique, and fair. In optimization decomposition, horizontal and vertical loose coupling is used. In dynamic programming, recursion provides an exact solution using a set of nested solutions
Degrees of centralization	The degrees of centralization include centralized, decentralized, distributed, and hybrid, which is a combination of centralized and distributed systems. A hybrid network can be made both locally and globally optimal and it includes all other degrees of centralization as special cases
Small-world network	A locally and globally optimal network between random and ordered networks
Multiagent system	A set of interacting agents forming a complex adaptive system
Message passing and shared memory	Methods to exchange information
Degrees of coupling	The degrees of coupling include uncoupled and loosely, tightly, and fully coupled
Forms of electronics	Combinational and sequential logic and finite state machines
Forms of computing	Computing may be local or distributed and sequential or concurrent. Concurrent computing is divided into local parallel computing and distributed computing. Von Neumann architecture is used in computing. Interacting rational agents are called multiagent systems or complex adaptive systems. Neural, evolutionary, and fuzzy computing are soft computing methods
Principles of adaptive systems	Adaptive feedback systems may be goal-directed, goal-seeking, and goal-achieving
Principles of self-organization	In nature, the major known principles include energy minimization in closed systems and nonequilibrium systems in open systems corresponding to a whirlpool dissipative structure
Hierarchy of technical systems	The hierarchy includes static, simple dynamic, control, adaptive, learning, and self-organizing systems

performance, which is generally done iteratively. Sometimes, a goal is attained immediately from a single action. Usually, the agent has to consider "long sequences of twists and turns" to find a way to achieve the goal (Russell and Norvig 2022).

Goal in a feedback loop Agents can be divided into those with or without a goal. In Russell and Norvig (2022), intelligent agents are divided into simple reflex agents,

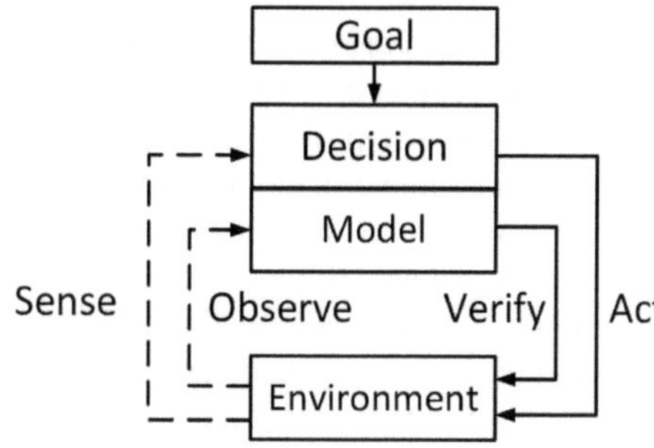

Fig. 5.12 Relationship of the sense-decide-act loop and the observe-model-verify learning and research process that produces a model of the environment

model-based reflex agents, goal-based agents, and utility-based agents from the simplest to the most advanced. A *simple reflex agent* reacts to external obstacles. Reflex agents are goalless unless one wants to define the goal as a range, such as the borders of a robot's working area. An example is a robot lawnmower that proceeds in a random direction, and when it hits an obstacle such as a border, it turns to another direction until its battery is almost used and it moves to the charging station. It does not necessarily have any memory. The garden's borders must be marked with a wire sensed by the robot as an obstacle. A *model-based reflex agent* has some internal model of the world, such as a map, so that it knows where it has already been within its working area, as in a robot vacuum cleaner. Now, the robot has a memory: it knows where it has been and when to stop cleaning. A *goal-based agent* has a desirable state towards which it is moving. The desirable state may be the destination of an autonomous ship or car. Often, the desirable state is not known (McFarland and Bösser 1993). A more advanced alternative is to use a *utility-based agent* that maximizes its utility.

A system where an explicit goal is defined is called a *goal-directed system* (also the terms goal-based or goal-oriented are used) (McFarland and Bösser 1993; Stonier 1992; Russell and Norvig 2022). The goal can be, for example, a set-point value. More generally, the goal can be a reference signal in adaptive systems or a reference trajectory in moving systems (Albus and Meystel 2001). Alternatives to goal-directed systems are goal-seeking and goal-achieving systems.

In *goal-seeking systems*, the system seeks a goal that is not explicitly defined but is found in an equilibrium (McFarland and Bösser 1993). Many physical systems try to reach the minimum energy, which is the natural equilibrium of the system, as in the second law of thermodynamics in a closed system (Rosen 1991, p. 269; Kopicki et al. 2010; Friston et al. 2006; Friston 2010; Lebon et al. 2008). Another example of a goal-seeking system is an adaptive algorithm in a linear transversal filter, whose optimization criterion is a mean-square error (MSE), and the algorithm is the iterative least-mean square (LMS) algorithm (Widrow and Stearns 1985; Widrow 2005). If the algorithm is stable, with a small enough feedback gain or step size, the algorithm converges to the minimum MSE solution from any initial state. We do not know the optimal state beforehand; thus, the goal-directed system cannot be used.

In *goal-achieving systems*, we rely on serendipity (McFarland and Bösser 1993). The system recognizes when the goal is attained. An example is the random search algorithm, which improves its performance by making random changes in system parameters in a linear random search (LRS) algorithm (Widrow and McCool 1976). Biological systems are a product of evolution and have no explicit set-point values or optimization criteria (Bekey 2005, pp. 9, 30, 42). Our homeostatic system maintains, for example, our temperature almost constant, but there is no reference value for the temperature. Natural systems are either goal-achieving or goal-seeking, not goal-directed. Evolution does not have any explicit goal (Schoemaker 1991).

More advanced human-made agents are either goal- or utility-directed. They have a goal since the utility can be seen as an example of a goal. Goals are externally given to a machine (Stonier 1997; Schoemaker 1991). The actual goal can also be computed from an externally given input.

The *goal* is a desired state of the environment or a desired performance or utility of the system in the environment (Ogata 2010; Russell and Norvig 2022). Evolution or design builds the goal into a system (Albus and Meystel 2001, pp. 7, 84). In biological systems, the goal can be generated internal to the system in response to a need, drive, or urge. In technical systems, the goal may come from an engineer's design. Setting a goal by design needs consciousness and, therefore, free will (Stonier 1992, p. 174; Albus and Meystel 2001, p. 122). In engineering, human needs are goals translated into system requirements, producing system specifications, and finally, the system itself. User *satisfaction* tells whether the user's needs are fulfilled.

A goal is necessary to improve the stability of a negative feedback system (Kline 1995; Ogata 2010; Albus and Meystel 2001). In goal-directed systems, the goal may be a set-point value, a reference signal, or a reference trajectory. For example, a *set-point value* or set point is a constant given to a thermostat as a target temperature. The heater starts heating when the measured temperature is lower than the set-point value. When the measured temperature is higher than the set-point value, the heater stops heating. The thermostat is an example of binary negative feedback with continuous control. The same idea can be used in cooling. When the changes in the environment are dynamic, such as in a cruise control on a car, we need a more complicated PID feedback control that may include a proportional, integrative, and derivative part. The positive P factor adjusts the speed of convergence. The I factor integrates the error signal and pushes it towards an average equal to zero using the feedback. The D factor is the derivative factor that anticipates future trends, minimizes the error signal using the estimated trend, and thus improves the sensitivity of the loop. The D factor may be sensitive to noise, and the PI controller is typical in noisy applications.

A *reference signal* is needed in a more complicated situation, such as an adaptive filter (Widrow and Stearns 1985). Now, the reference signal is used as a training signal again using negative feedback. An error signal is formed between the reference signal and the filter's output. In the feedback, we need an adaptive algorithm such as the LMS algorithm, which is an example of an integral (I) controller if we use the terms of control systems. Thus, the error signal is attenuated and integrated.

A *reference trajectory* is a goal used in physical movements, such as an automatic ship. Therefore, it is usually a smooth curve. When we drive a car, our reference trajectory is in the middle of the lane we are driving in. When the lane is turning, we correct the error between the car and the center of the lane. When we want to change lanes, for example, to pass another car, we change our reference trajectory to the middle of the next lane according to traffic regulations.

An example of the use of feedback is a feedback amplifier. The input signal can be interpreted as the goal. The output signal should be an amplified version of the input signal. The feedback may be positive or negative; see Fig. 5.13, where we initially assume for brevity that $A > 0$ and B are real constants. If the input signal is x and the output signal is y, and the error signal is $e = x + By$, the output is $y = A(x + By)$, and therefore the system gain is $H = y/x = A/(1 - AB)$. Thus, positive feedback ($B > 0$) increases the gain, and negative feedback ($B < 0$) reduces the gain when $AB < 1$; otherwise, the feedback cannot be made stable (Nyquist 1932; Lee 2004). If we change the sign of the error signal, the system gain is $H = y/x = -A/(1 + AB)$. If now $B < 0$, the feedback is positive. The change of the sign of the error signal has changed the negative feedback to positive feedback. This is the reason why in feedback systems the error signal is the difference between the reference input and the feedback signal.

In practice, amplification A is not a real number but a complex constant that depends on the frequency. Its magnitude decreases above a specific cut-off frequency, and a negative phase shift is generated because of the delay of the amplifier and the actual feedback may be changed from negative to positive and the amplifier may become instable. A simple amplifier model is presented in Gershenfeld (2000, pp. 205–206). The most important stability criterion is the Nyquist criterion described in Nyquist (1932).

The reason for the asymmetric stability region $AB < 1$ in the real analog case is explained in Belevitch (1962). The transients in the amplifier must be considered, and the terms in the geometric series generated by the loop become convolution products, which do not appear in the time-discrete case. In the time-discrete case, $A = 1$, but the stability region is different from the analog case and symmetric concerning the origin, i.e., $/B/ < 1$. In this case, positive and negative feedback have similar properties regarding the stability.

Positive feedback is no longer used in amplifiers since the *operational amplifiers* have a very large gain ($A >> 1$). Positive feedback is usually used in oscillators. The negative feedback is used to improve the amplifier's stability, reduce noise and

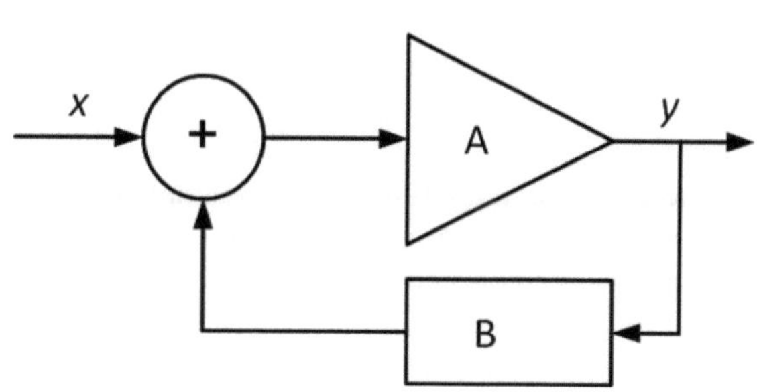

Fig. 5.13 Feedback amplifier

distortion, and thus improve the linearity of the amplifier (Black 1934). We can use an approximation $H \approx -1/B$ if A is large. In the case of negative feedback, we usually have $-1 < B < 0$, resulting in a desirable amplification, and the constant B can be implemented with a passive attenuator.

In time-discrete systems, a simple feedback is expressed with the equation $y_n = ax_n + by_{n-1}$ where x_n is the input sample, y_n is the output sample, n is the time index, and a and b are constants. If the input signal at time $n = 0$ is a constant x_0, and otherwise zero and $y_{-1} = 0$, the output signal is the scaled impulse response $y_n = ax_0 b^n$, which corresponds to a geometric series and the system memory is exponential. The stability condition is now /b/ < 1 since in this case the geometric series converges. The impulse response has an infinite memory with exponential decay. If /b/ > 1, the impulse response has a memory with exponential growth, and the system is unstable.

Hierarchy Complicated systems are hierarchical and modular. The opposite would be an integral or integrated architecture without any obvious hierarchy or modularity (Ulrich and Eppinger 1995; Belliveau et al. 2002). Hierarchy and modularity imply, in general, an approximate form of optimization unless the problem can be ideally decomposed hierarchically and vertically (Chiang et al. 2007). Integral *architecture* could be the most efficient, but it is not flexible, and it is challenging to design. Thus, it is not seen as a practical alternative to hierarchical modular design. An example of integral architecture is a neural network, as in our brain. It is a networked architecture using massively parallel processing having some hierarchy and modularity (Kanerva 2000).

Degrees of coupling In a hierarchical system, each hierarchy level consists of subsystems called modules. Hierarchical and modular systems should generally be loosely coupled or loosely connected (Mämmelä et al. 2023). The loose coupling has various desirable properties, including generality, simplicity, stability, scalability, efficiency, fairness, reliability, comprehensibility, flexibility, locality, and agility (Mämmelä et al. 2023). For example, according to the system *separability principle*, systems with loose coupling are more stable than those with tight coupling (Skyttner 2005, p. 102).

The degree of coupling C is usually defined only qualitatively. However, in network theory, it has been described quantitatively as a real number between 0 and 1 (Caplan 1966). The qualitative classification is uncoupled, loosely coupled, tightly coupled, and fully coupled (Yourdon and Constantine 1978; McGarry et al. 1999; Pautasso and Wilde 2009). Qualitative classification is also used in distributed software systems (Decker 1987; Walker 1995). Loose coupling corresponds to information exchange via message passing, tight coupling to shared memory, and full coupling corresponds to function calls.

The *uncoupled* case is also called noninteracting or *decoupled*, and the degree of coupling is $C = 0$. The subsystems are isolated from each other in this sense. Since there are no interconnections, no system is formed, but we have a set of subsystems (Hall 1962; Hubka and Eder 1988). The interactions are loose or relatively slow in *loose* or *weak coupling*, and the degree of coupling is $0 < C << 1$. Loose coupling is a common term in computer engineering and social sciences (Pautasso and Wilde

2009). The term weak coupling is common in control engineering. In a *fully coupled* or interleaved system, the interconnections are strong, and the degree of coupling is $C = 1$. In a *tightly coupled* system, the degree of coupling is $0 << C < 1$.

The horizontal degree of coupling can be defined in the physical layer of communication networks as the inverse of the received signal-to-interference ratio (SIR) (Chaoub et al. 2023; Mämmelä et al. 2023). Loose coupling means that the SIR is high, and the degree of coupling is close to zero. Tight coupling means that the SIR is low, and the degree of coupling is close to unity. In vertical coupling, the degree of coupling is the ratio of the speed of the higher layer and the speed of the lower layer. The speed corresponds to the bandwidth of the corresponding changes. In loose coupling, the feedback loops in the different layers and the same layer work as if the other loops do not exist. Coupling metrics for layered and modular software design are discussed in Yu et al. (2009).

According to Cesare Pautasso and Erik Wilde, the degree of coupling is a multifaceted phenomenon that includes 12 facets (Pautasso and Wilde 2009). Not many systems are loosely or tightly coupled according to all the facets. For example, one of the facets is interaction, which can be *asynchronous*, corresponding to loose coupling, or *synchronous*, corresponding to tight coupling. In asynchronous systems, a lower-level system does not wait for responses from the higher level. For service-oriented architectures, loose coupling means that software modules and services share only a small set of assumptions. Therefore, the impact of change is limited, and the software modules and services can evolve independently and rapidly and scale easily. Modern service-oriented architectures are based on microservices (Dragoni et al. 2017). *Service-oriented computing* is a computing paradigm that uses services as fundamental elements (Papazoglou 2003). *Service-oriented architecture* (SOA) is a software-construction model, whereas *software as a service* (SaaS) is a software-delivery model (Laplante et al. 2008).

Shared or distributed agent memory and partial isolation of control loops are two examples of facets of hierarchical multiagent systems (Pautasso and Wilde 2009). According to Yu et al. (2009), the *types of coupling* can be classified into parameter coupling, external medium coupling, inheritance coupling, and common coupling. If one module passes a parameter to another, the modules have parameter coupling. If two modules access the same external medium, for example, a file, they have external medium coupling. If one module descends from another module, as in object-oriented programming, the two modules have inheritance coupling. If two modules use the same global variable, they have a common coupling.

In communication networks, vertical loose coupling can be implemented with time-scale separation (Kawadia and Kumar 2005) and horizontal loose coupling with interference avoidance (Pottie 1995). Different users should use orthogonal signals for interference avoidance, which may need additional control, for example, in time-division multiple access (TDMA) systems but improves capacity. Orthogonality is especially important in the physical layer. In self-organization, a system must be neither too loosely nor too tightly coupled vertically (Tzafestas 2018). In a decentralized system, there should be no interference between different agents.

Control topologies and degrees of centralization The *degree of centralization* is divided into centralized, decentralized, distributed, and hybrid forms; see Fig. 5.14 and Table 5.26 (Sandell et al. 1978; Frampton et al. 2010; Fourati et al. 2021). Centralized and hybrid forms are always combined with the hierarchy concept. In *centralized systems*, all decision-making is done by a central agent: a *network manager* in self-organizing networks, a *leader* in game theory and multiagent systems (Lasaulce and Tembine 2011; Dorri et al. 2018), and an *arbitrator* in game theory and welfare economics (Lasaulce and Tembine 2011). The lower-level agents (i.e., followers) follow the control signals moving downwards from the central agent. The lower-level agents can send some sensing signals upwards to the central agent. The system has a good performance.

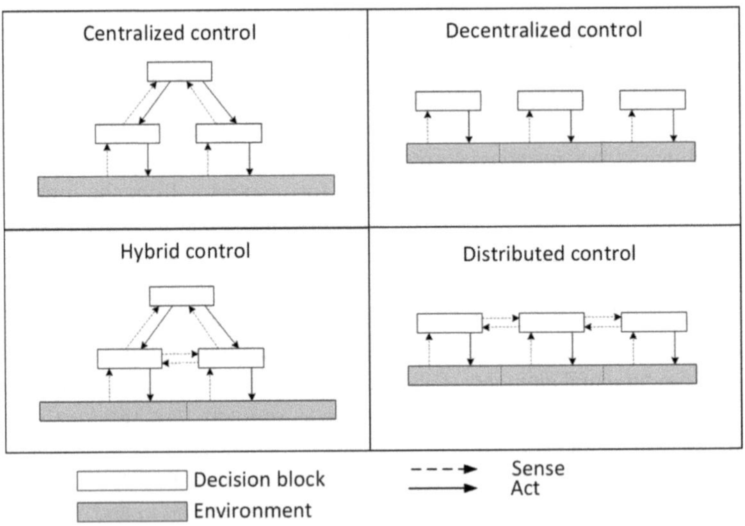

Fig. 5.14 Degrees of centralization

Table 5.26 Degrees of centralization

Degree of centralization	Properties
Centralized	A central control unit is used to force cooperation, sensing information proceeds upwards and control information downwards in hierarchy
Decentralized	Competitive autonomous rational agents that may be reactive or proactive; information is not exchanged with other agents
Distributed	Interacting semiautonomous cooperative agents exchanging information, possibly forming clusters
Hybrid	A combination of centralized and distributed systems, special cases include all other degrees of centralization

Another extreme is the *decentralized system*, which does not include any hierarchy; thus, the network architecture is flat (Sandell et al. 1978). The decentralized system consists of many agents working autonomously to maximize a global performance metric (Frampton et al. 2010). The agents sense their environment and make autonomous decisions. The system is easy to implement, scalable, and robust, but its performance could be better. Nils R. Sandell et al. have called a decentralized system a completely decentralized system, whereas a distributed system is partially decentralized (Sandell et al. 1978). Decentralized systems are used when centrality is not an option due to a lack of centralized information or computing capability. Such systems often have geographical separation, leading to high economic costs and poor communication reliability.

The *distributed system* is an intermediate form between the centralized and decentralized systems. Distributed systems are sometimes called *heterarchical systems* (Bongaerts et al. 2000). The architecture is also flat. Now, the agents exchange information with all other agents. In practice, information is exchanged only with the nearest neighbors. Distributed systems may have the high performance of centralized systems and maintain the scalability, ease of implementation, and robustness of decentralized control (Frampton et al. 2010). In principle, distributed systems can be optimal if all the agents negotiate with all network members (Frampton et al. 2010). Still, since communication is limited, the optimal solution is found only slowly after the global state is distributed to the whole system. If, in a distributed system, all agents negotiate with each other, we can have an optimal, unique, and fair system called the Nash bargaining solution (Lasaulce and Tembine 2011; Bacci et al. 2016). Distributed systems may not find the global optimum and may be slow in providing overall reactions since they do not have any central control (Bongaerts et al. 2000). A decentralized system can be seen as a particular case of a distributed system where no information exchange is done between the agents (Frampton et al. 2010).

A *hybrid system* combines centralized and distributed control as defined initially by 3GPP in Rel. 9 (2008) (Fourati et al. 2021). Hybrid systems are sometimes called *holonic systems*, especially in nested hierarchies from where the term holon originally came (Bongaerts et al. 2000; Dorri et al. 2018). The reason for preferring the hybrid form to other degrees of centralization is the problem with emergence: local optimization does not lead to global optimization, and global behavior cannot be predicted from local behavior (Bongaerts et al. 2000). A hybrid system is a generic form since all other degrees of centralization can be obtained from it as special cases. Thus, the system is highly flexible, but flexibility always implies reduced efficiency, as we know from programmable systems. A hybrid system can do both *global* and *local optimization*. If an external threat is local and fast, the central control may be too slow, and distributed control is better. For a global and slow threat, we need centralized control.

Defining the balance between centralized and distributed control is a challenging task. It is known that, at least in social systems, centralized systems in practice tend to drift towards decentralization, and decentralized systems tend to drift towards centralization since the extremes are unstable (Boulding 1981, pp. 106, 137). Human organizations are becoming less hierarchical and more decentralized for increased flexibility and competitive advantage (Kauffman 1995). In his *Essays of Government*, James Mill (1823) concluded that representative democracy is a necessary element of good government (Encyclopedia Britannica 2024). Fukuyama (1992) expected society to drift toward liberal democracy (Fukuyama 1992). Still, according to Acemoglu and Robinson (2020), there is always a struggle between a state that is too weak to lead to anarchy and one that is too strong to lead to an authoritarian regime. In game theory, one conclusion is that we should use a hybrid strategy combining competition and cooperation with punishments (Siegfried 2006, p. 220).

We also know that a multiparty system is generally better in a state than one-party or two-party systems. One-party systems lead to an authoritarian regime, and two-party systems may divide a country into two competing and extreme views. As in nature, the world should form an ecosystem where every country understands that it does not succeed without cooperation. The international system must be such that it is also using a mixed strategy, and there must be an international punishment system. Imperialism and colonialism do not belong to modern international collaboration.

Organizations have evolved so that the state of nature was initially decentralized. A straightforward alternative is centralized (first locally and then more globally), whereas a distributed system is an intermediate step to hybrid organizations.

5.5 Chapter Summary and Recommended Reading

We summarized the most crucial system theories. There is no single system theory, but many theories complement each other. A modern form of general theory of systems is now the complexity theory, a spin-off of cybernetics and artificial intelligence. The definition of system requirements starts by describing user needs translated into functional and nonfunctional requirements. The former requirements are application-dependent, but they may use system archetypes. The latter requirements define the efficiency of using basic resources and, preferably, the system's effectiveness and legitimacy.

The system archetypes include feedback, optimization and decision-making, hierarchy, and degree of centralization. A vital system archetype is a network where data are transmitted in a small-world network, and control is organized as a vertically and horizontally loosely coupled hierarchical network. A universal model for controlling a system is a hybrid self-organizing system, which combines centralized and distributed control. It has high flexibility since, as its special cases, it can represent a centralized, decentralized, and distributed system. Self-organizing systems are the highest in the hierarchy of technical systems, thus providing, as special cases, all other systems lower in the hierarchy.

Donella Meadows presents the principles of system dynamics where the feedback concept is heavily used independently from cybernetics (Meadows and Wright 2008). George P. Richardson used system dynamics in social sciences (Richardson 1991). In engineering, interesting general books include (Hubka and Eder 1988; Kline 1995;

Kossiakoff et al. 2011). Complexity theory is described in the books (Thurner et al. 2018; Mobus 2022).

Discussion Questions

1. How do we define sustainable development?
2. What does bounded rationality mean? How do we define satisficing principle?
3. Discuss the Nash equilibrium and Nash bargaining solution and its approximations. How are they related to Pareto optimality?
4. What are the most essential system theories? Why are there so many and not only one?
5. What are the most essential system archetypes? Describe a hierarchy of natural and technical systems? Now are they different?

Simulation Exercises

The exercises aim to provide tools to manage complicated systems, for example, to eliminate harmful coupling of feedback loops. Examples of corresponding simulations can be found in Dorf and Bishop (2017). In the simulations, the purpose is to study phenomena; therefore, you can select the values of the parameters at your will. Similar system models are in Sterman (2000).

1. Study the step response of the first-order positive and negative feedback and their combination (positive feedback usually only as an inner loop).
2. Study the step response of the second-order feedback.
3. Study the effect of a delay in the step response of a feedback loop.
4. Study the step response of two parallel coupled feedback loops and their decoupling. Study the step response of two feedback loops with different loop delays using time-scale separation.
5. Study the agent-based modeling of a simple network with vertical and horizontal loose coupling.

References

Aaronson S (2008) The limits of quantum computers. Sci Am 298(3):62–69

Acemoglu D, Robinson JA (2020) The narrow corridor: how nations struggle for liberty. Penguin Books, London

Ahl V, Allen TFH (1996) Hierarchy theory: a vision, vocabulary, and epistemology. Columbia University Press, New York

Albus JS (1991) Outline for a theory of intelligence. IEEE Trans Syst Man Cybern 21(3):473–509

Albus JS, Meystel AM (2001) Engineering of mind: an introduction to the science of intelligent systems. Wiley, New York

Alcott B (2005) Jevons' paradox. Ecol Econ 54(1):9–21

Aldred J (2020) Licence to be bad: how economics corrupted us. Penguin, London

Alemohammad S et al (2023) Self-consuming generative models go MAD. Preprint at arXiv:2307.01850 [cs.LG]

Aliu OG et al (2013) A survey of self organisation in future cellular networks. IEEE Commun Surv Tutor 15(1):336–361
Al-Kuwaiti A et al (2009) A comparative analysis of network dependability, fault-tolerance, reliability, security, and survivability. IEEE Commun Surv Tutor 11(2):106–124
Allen J (1985) Computer architecture for digital signal processing. Proc IEEE 73(5):852–873
Amdahl GM (2013) Computer architecture and Amdahl's law. Computer 46(12):38–46
Amoroso F (1980) The bandwidth of digital data signals. IEEE Commun Mag 18(6):13–24
Amtsberg F et al (2020) Structural up-cycling: matching digital and natural geometry. In: Baverel O et al (eds) Advances in architectural geometry 2020. Presses des Ponts, Paris, pp 486–505
Antsaklis PJ et al (1989) Towards intelligent autonomous control systems: architecture and fundamental issues. J Intell Robot Syst 1(4):315–342
Anttonen A et al (2011) Low complexity phase-unware detectors based on estimator-correlator concept. In: Matin M (ed) Ultra wideband communications: novel trends—system, architecture, and implementation. InTech, Rijeka, Croatia, pp 65–88
Arbnor I, Bjerke B (1997) Methodology for creating business knowledge, 2nd edn. Sage, London
Arora S, Barak B (2009) Computational complexity: a modern approach. Cambridge University Press, New York
Arvidsson M, Gremyr I (2008) Principles of robust design methodology. Qual Reliab Eng 24:23–35. https://doi.org/10.1002/qre.864
Ashby WR (1956) An introduction to cybernetics. Chapman & Hall, London
Asimov I (1984) The history of physics, rev. Walker and Company, New York
Asimov I (1987) Asimov's new guide to science, 4th edn. Penguin Books, Middlesex, England
Avila A et al (2007) Fundamental limits of heat transfer. In: Proceedings of the thermal challenges in next generation electronic systems (THERMES'07), Santa Fe, NM, pp 25–32
Avizienis A et al (2004) Basic concepts and taxonomy of dependable and secure computing. IEEE Trans Dependable Secure Comput 1(1):11–33
Awano Y et al (2010) Carbon nanotubes for VLSI: interconnect and transistor applications. Proc IEEE 98(12):2015–2031
Bacci G et al (2016) Game theory for networks: a tutorial on game-theoretic tools for emerging signal processing applications. IEEE Signal Process Mag 33(1):94–119
Bahg CG (1990) Major system theories throughout the world. Behav Sci 35(2):79–207
Baldwin CW et al (2010) A typology of systems paradoxes. Inf Knowl Syst Manag 9(1):1–15
Banerjee SK et al (2010) Graphene for CMOS and beyond CMOS applications. Proc IEEE 98(12):2032–2046
Barbour IG (1997) Religion and science: historical and contemporary issues. HarperCollins, New York
Barnett J (2001) Adapting to climate change in Pacific Island countries: the problem of uncertainty. World Dev 29(6):977–993
Barrow JD (1998) Impossibility: the limits of science and the science of limits. Oxford University Press, New York
Bekey GA (2005) Autonomous robots: from biological inspiration to implementation and control. MIT Press, Cambridge, MA
Belevitch V (1962) Summary of the history of circuit theory. Proc IRE 50(5):848–855
Belliveau P et al (eds) (2002) The PDMA toolbook for new product development. Wiley, New York
Bellman R (1957) Dynamic programming. Princeton University Press, Princeton, NJ
Bello PA (1964) Time-frequency duality. IEEE Trans Inf Theory 10(1):18–33
Bello PA (1998) Sample size required in error-rate measurement on fading channels. Proc IEEE 86(7):1435–1441
Benbya H, McKelvey B (2006) Toward a complexity theory of information systems development. Inf Technol People 19(1):12–34
Berger LI (2020) Semiconductor materials. CRC Press, Boca Raton, FL
Bernstein A, de Roberts M (1958) Computer v. chess-player. Sci Am 198(6):96–107
Berry M et al (2019) Roadmap on superoscillations. J Opt 21(5):1–35

Bezdek JC (2016) (Computational) intelligence: what's in a name? IEEE Syst Man Cybern Mag 2(2):4–14
Bhunia CT (2005) Information technology network and Internet. New Age International, New Delhi, India
Bishop CM (2006) Pattern recognition and machine learning. Springer, Singapore
Björnson E et al (2014) Multiobjective signal processing optimization: the way to balance conflicting metrics in 5G systems. IEEE Signal Process Mag 31(6):14–23
Black HS (1934) Stabilized feedback amplifiers. Bell Syst Tech J 13(1):1–18
Bohm D, Peat FD (2000) Science, order, and creativity, 2nd edn. Routledge, London
Bongaerts L et al (2000) Hierarchy in distributed shop floor control. Comput Ind 43(2):123–137
Bossel H (2007) Systems and models: complexity, dynamics, evolution, sustainability. Books on Demand, Norderstedt, Germany
Botta A et al (2010) Do you trust your software-based traffic generator? IEEE Commun Mag 48(9):158–165
Boulding KE (1956) General systems theory. Manage Sci 2(3):197–208
Boulding KE (1978) Ecodynamics: a new theory of societal evolution. Sage, Beverly Hills, CA
Boulding KE (1981) Evolutionary economics. Sage, Beverly Hills, CA
Boulding KE (1985) The world as a total system. Sage, Beverly Hills, CA
Boulding KE (1989) Three faces of power. Sage, Beverly Hills, CA
Boulton JG et al (2015) Embracing complexity: strategic perspectives for an age of turbulence. Oxford University Press, Oxford, UK
Bowler PJ (2009) Evolution: the history of an idea, 25th anniversary. University of California Press, Berkeley, CA
Braun S et al (2013) Negative absolute temperature for motional degrees of freedom. Science 339(6115):52–55
Briscoe B et al (2016) Reducing Internet latency: a survey of techniques and their merits. IEEE Commun Surv Tutor 18(3):2149–2196
Brooks S, Roy R (2021) An overview of self-engineering systems. J Eng Des 32(8):397–447
Buchanan M (2002) Small world: uncovering nature's hidden networks. W. W. Norton and Company, New York
Buenstorf G (2000) Self-organization and sustainability: energetics of evolution and implications for ecological economics. Ecol Econ 33(1):119–134
Calvo G, Valero A (2022) Strategic mineral resources: availability and future estimations for the renewable energy sector. Environ Dev 41:1–11. https://doi.org/10.1016/j.envdev.2021.100640
Camazine S et al (2001) Self-organization in biological systems. Princeton University Press, Princeton, NJ
Cao Y et al (2013) An overview of recent progress in the study of distributed multi-agent coordination. IEEE Trans Ind Inf 9(1):427–438
Caplan SR (1966) The degree of coupling and its relation to efficiency of energy conversion in multiple-flow systems. J Theor Biol 10(2):209–235
Caradonna JL (2014) Sustainability: A history. Oxford University Press, New York
Caripe W et al (1998) Network awareness and mobile agent systems. IEEE Commun Mag 6(7):44–49
Carr LD (2013) Negative temperatures? Science 339(6115):42–43
Carver CS, Scheier MF (2002) Control processes and self-organization as complementary principles underlying behavior. Pers Soc Psychol Rev 6(4):304–305
Casti JL (1982) Recent developments and future perspectives in nonlinear system theory. SIAM Rev 24(3):301–331
Casti JL (1991) Chaos, Gödel, and truth. In: Casti JL, Karlqvist A (eds) Beyond belief: randomness, prediction and explanation in science. CRC Press, Boca Raton, FL, pp 280–327
Casti JL (1994) Complexification: explaining paradoxical world through the science of surprise. Abacus, London

Cavalcante RLG et al (2014) Toward energy-efficient 5G wireless communications technologies: tools for decoupling the scaling of networks from the growth of operating power. IEEE Signal Process Mag 31(6):24–34
Chae KH (2023) Breakdown of the Newton–Einstein standard gravity at low acceleration in internal dynamics of wide binary stars. Astrophys J 952(2):1–33
Chang S (1956) Theory of information feedback systems. IRE Trans Inf Theory 2(3):29–40
Chang M (2013) Paradoxes in scientific inference. CRC Press, Boca Raton, FL
Chaoub A et al (2023) Hybrid self-organizing networks: evolution, standardization trends, and a 6G architecture vision. IEEE Commun Stand Mag 7(1):14–22
Chaturvedi DK (2008) Soft computing: techniques and its applications in electrical engineering. Springer, Berlin
Checkland P (1999) Systems thinking, systems practice: includes a 30-year retrospective, rev. Wiley, Chichester, UK
Cherry C (1962) On communication before the days of radio. Proc IRE 50(5):1143–1145
Chestnut H (1965) Systems engineering tools. Wiley, New York
Chiang M et al (2007) Layering as optimization decomposition: a mathematical theory of network architectures. Proc IEEE 95(1):255–312
Chiao RY, Milonni PW (2002) Fast light, slow light. Opt Photonics News 13(6):26–30
Chung SY et al (2001) On the design of low-density parity-check codes within 0.0045 dB of the Shannon limit. IEEE Commun Lett 5(2):58–60
Claasen TACM, Mecklenbräuker WFG (1985) Adaptive techniques for signal processing in communications. IEEE Commun Mag 23(11):8–19
Cockshott P et al (2012) Computation and its limits. Oxford University Press, Oxford, UK
Coelho RL (2009) On the concept of energy: how understanding its history can improve physics teaching. Sci Educ 18:961–983. https://doi.org/10.1007/s11191-007-9128-0
Conant RC, Ashby WR (1970) Every good regulator of a system must be a model of that system. Int J Syst Sci 1(2):89–97
Copeland JA (ed) (1981) Special issue on fundamental limits in electrical engineering. Proc IEEE 69(2):147–282
Corchado JM et al (2023) Generative artificial intelligence: fundamentals. ADCAIJ Adv Distrib Comput Artif Intell J 12(1):1–43. https://doi.org/10.14201/adcaij.31704
Corning PA (2001) 'Control information': the missing element in Norbert Wiener's cybernetic paradigm? Kybernetes 30(9/10):1272–1288
Corning PA (2002) Thermoeconomics: beyond the second law. J Bioecon 4:57–88. https://doi.org/10.1023/A:1020633317271
Corning PA (2011) The fair society: the science of human nature and the pursuit of social justice. University of Chicago Press, Chicago, IL
Cornish-Bowden A, Luz Cardenas M (2020) Contrasting theories of life: historical context, current theories. In search of an ideal theory. Biosystems 188:1–50. https://doi.org/10.1016/j.biosystems.2019.104063
Coulouris G et al (2012) Distributed systems: concepts and design, 5th edn. Addison-Wesley, Boston, MA
Cover TM, Thomas JA (2006) Elements of information theory, 2nd edn. Wiley, Hoboken, NJ
Daily GD (ed) (1997) Nature's services: societal dependence on natural ecosystems. Island Press, Washington, DC
Darraji R et al (2011) A dual-input digitally driven Doherty amplifier architecture for performance enhancement of Doherty transmitters. IEEE Trans Microw Theory Tech 59(5):1284–1293
Dautenhahn K (1998) The art of designing socially intelligent agents: science, fiction, and the human in the loop. Appl Artif Intell 12(7–8):573–617
Dawes RM, Messick DM (2000) Social dilemmas. Int J Psychol 35(2):111–116
de Coulon F (1986) Signal theory and processing. Artech House, Deadham, MA
de Oliveira MJ (2017) Equilibrium thermodynamics, 2nd edn. Springer-Verlag, Berlin

De Wolf T, Holvoet T (2005) Emergence versus self-organisation: different concepts but promising when combined. In: Brueckner S et al (eds) Engineering self-organizing systems, methods, and applications. Springer-Verlag, Berlin, pp 1–15

DeAngelis DL et al (1986) Positive feedback in natural systems. Springer-Verlag, Berlin

Deb K (2002) A fast and elitist multiobjective genetic algorithm: NSGA-II. IEEE Trans Evol Comput 6(2):182–197

Decker KS (1987) Distributed problem-solving techniques: a survey. IEEE Trans Syst Man Cybern 17(5):729–740

Deutsch D (1997) The fabric of reality. Penguin Books, London

Dewdney AK (2004) Beyond reason: eight great problems that reveal the limits of science. Wiley, Hoboken, NJ

Di Marzo Serugendo G et al (2005) Self-organization in multi-agent systems. Knowl Eng Rev 20(2):165–189

Dobson S et al (2010) Fulfilling the vision of autonomic computing. Computer 43(1):35–41

Dolev S, Tzachar N (2009) Empire of colonies: self-stabilizing and self-organizing distributed algorithm. Theoret Comput Sci 410(6–7):514–532

Dooley KJ (1997) A complex adaptive systems model of organization change. Nonlinear Dyn Psychol Life Sci 1(1):69–97

Domenech JL et al (2007) Teaching of energy issues: a debate proposal for a global reorientation. Sci Educ 16:43–64. https://doi.org/10.1007/s11191-005-5036-3

Dorf RC, Bishop RH (2017) Modern control systems, 13th edn. Pearson, New York

Dorri A et al (2018) Multi-agent systems: a survey. IEEE Access 6:28573–28593

Dragoni N et al (2017) Microservices: yesterday, today, and tomorrow. In: Mazzara M, Meyer B (eds) Present and ulterior software engineering. Springer, Cham, Switzerland, pp 195–216

Dressler F (2008) A study of self-organization mechanisms in ad hoc and sensor networks. Comput Commun 31(13):3018–3029

du Plessis C (2022) The city sustainable, resilient, regenerative—a rose by any other name? In: Roggema R (ed) Design for regenerative cities and landscapes: rebalancing human impact and natural environment. Springer Nature, Cham, Switzerland

Dutt ND, Gajski DD (1990) Design synthesis and silicon compilation. IEEE Des Test Comput 7(6):8–23

Elbehiery H, Elbehiery K (2022) Gravitational energy: aerospace's future technology. In: Magdi DA et al (eds) Digital transformation technology: proceedings of ITAF 2020. Springer Nature Singapore, Singapore, pp 3–27

Elhajj I et al (2001) Haptic information in Internet-based teleoperation. IEEE/ASME Trans Mechatron 6(3):295–304

El-Khamy SE (2004) New trends in wireless multimedia communications based on chaos and fractals. In: Proceedings of the 21st national radio science conference (NRSC'04), Cairo, Egypt

Elsasser WM (1987) Reflections on a theory of organisms: holism in biology. The Johns Hopkins University Press, Baltimore, MD

Encyclopedia Britannica (2024). https://www.britannica.com. Accessed 5 Nov 2024

Engelbrecht A (2007) Computational intelligence: an introduction, 2nd edn. Wiley, New York

Ericson T (1971) Structure of optimum receiving filters in data transmission systems. IEEE Trans Inf Theory 17(3):352–353

ETSI (2014) Network technologies (NTECH); autonomic network engineering for the self-managing future Internet (AFI); scenarios, use cases and requirements for autonomic/self-managing future Internet. ETSI TS 103 194 V1.1.1

Feamster N (2013) The road to SDN: an intellectual history of programmable networks. ACM Queue 11(12):1–21

Fei Z et al (2017) A survey of multi-objective optimization in wireless sensor networks: metrics, algorithms, and open problems. IEEE Commun Surv Tutor 19(1):550–586

Ferreira PJSG, Kempf A (2006) Superoscillations: faster than the Nyquist rate. IEEE Trans Signal Process 54(10):3732–3740

Fettweis A (1977) On the significance of group delay in communication engineering. Arch Elektron Übertrag 31(9):342–348
Fettweis GP (2014) The tactile Internet: applications and challenges. IEEE Veh Technol Mag 9(1):64–70
Figueira J et al (eds) (2005) Multiple-criteria decision analysis: state of the art surveys. Springer, Boston, MA
Ford DN (2019) A system dynamics glossary. Syst Dyn Rev 35(4):369–379
Forrester JW (2007a) System dynamics—a personal view of the first fifty years. Syst Dyn Rev 23(2/3):345–358
Forrester JW (2007b) System dynamics—the next fifty years. Syst Dyn Rev 23(2/3):359–370
Forst W, Hoffman D (2010) Optimization—theory and practice. Springer Science + Business Media, New York
Fourati H et al (2021) Comprehensive survey on self-organizing cellular network approaches applied to 5G networks. Comput Netw 199:1–24. https://doi.org/10.1016/j.comnet.2021.108435
Frampton KD et al (2010) A comparison of decentralized, distributed, and centralized vibro-acoustic control. J Acoust Soc Am 128:2798–2806. https://doi.org/10.1121/1.3183369
Francois C (1999) Systemics and cybernetics in a historical perspective. Syst Res Behav Sci 16(3):203–219
Francois C (2000) An exploration of the historical meaning of systemics in western thought. Systems 5(1–2):3–14
Francois C (2006) Transdisciplinary unified theory. Syst Res Behav Sci 23(5):617–624
Frei R et al (2013) Self-healing and self-repairing technologies. Int J Adv Manuf Technol 69:1033–1061. https://doi.org/10.1007/s00170-013-5070-2
Friston K (2010) The free-energy principle: a unified brain theory? Nat Rev Neurosci 11:127–138. https://doi.org/10.1038/nrn2787
Friston K et al (2006) A free energy principle for the brain. J Physiol Paris 100(1–3):70–87
Fukuyama F (1992) The end of history and the last man. Free Press, New York
Gabor D (1954) Communication theory and cybernetics. Trans IRE Prof Group Om Circuit Theory 1(4):19–31
Gajski DD (1988) Introduction to silicon compilation. In: Gajski DD (ed) Silicon compilation. Addison-Wesley, Reading, MA, pp 1–48
Gao Z (2014) Engineering cybernetics: 60 years in the making. Control Theory Technol 12(2):97–109
Gates C, Matthews P (2014) Data is the new currency. In: Proceedings of the new security paradigms workshop (NSPW'14), Victoria, BC, Canada
Gauvrit N et al (2017) The information-theoretic and algorithmic approach to human, animal, and artificial cognition. In: Dodig-Crnkovic G, Giovagnoli R (eds) Representation and reality in humans, other living organisms and intelligent machines. Springer International Publishing, Cham, Switzerland
Gershenfeld N (2000) The physics of information technology. Cambridge University Press, Cambridge, UK
Gitt W (1989) Information: the third fundamental quantity. Siemens Rev 56(6):2–7
Glassman RB (1973) Persistence and loose coupling in living systems. Behav Sci 18(2):83–98
Golay MJE (1949) Note on the theoretical efficiency of information reception with PPM. Proc IRE 37(9):1031
Goldstein J (1999) Emergence as a construct: history and issues. Emergence 1(1):49–72
Gorod A et al (2017) Systems engineering decision-making: optimizing and/or satisficing? In: Proceedings of the 2017 annual IEEE international systems conference (SysCon'17)
Goss Levi B (2001) Researchers stop, store, and retrieve photons—or at least the information they carry. Phys Today 54(3):17–19
Gottfried BS, Weisman J (1973) Introduction to optimization theory. Prentice-Hall, Englewood Cliffs, NJ

Gunawardena J (2014) Time-scale separation—Michaelis and Menten's old idea, still bearing fruit. FEBS J 281(2):473–488
Guo SZ et al (2012) A tree-structured deterministic small-world network. IEICE Trans Inf Syst E95-D(5):1536–1538
Gupta P, Kumar PR (2000) Capacity of wireless networks. IEEE Trans Inf Theory 46(2):388–401
Gustafson JL (1988) Reevaluating Amdahl's law. Commun ACM 31(5):532–533
Haddad M et al (2011) A hybrid approach for radio resource management in heterogeneous cognitive networks. IEEE J Sel Areas Commun 29(4):831–842
Haken HPJ (1988) Synergetics. IEEE Circuits Devices Mag 4(6):3–7
Hall AD (1962) A methodology for systems engineering. D. Van Nostrand Company, Princeton, NJ
Hamadi Y, Wintersteiger CM (2012) Seven challenges in parallel SAT solving. In: Proceedings of the AAAI conference on artificial intelligence (AAAI'12), Toronto, Ontario, Canada, pp 2020–2125
Han Z et al (2005) Fair multiuser channel allocation for OFDMA networks using Nash bargaining solutions and coalitions. IEEE Trans Commun 53(8):1366–1376
Harris B, Morgan KC (1958) Binary symmetric decision feedback systems. Trans Am Inst Electr Eng Part I Commun Electron 77(4):436–443
Hawking S (2018) Brief answers to the big questions. John Murray, London
Haykin S, Moher M (2014) Communication systems, 5th edn. Wiley, Hoboken, NJ
He P, Kang DB (2010) Entropy principle and complementary second law of thermodynamics for self-gravitating systems. Mon Not R Astron Soc 406:2678–2688. https://doi.org/10.1111/j.1365-2966.2010.16869.x
Heijmans R (1999) When does the expectation of a ratio equal the ratio of expectations? Stat Pap 40(1):107–115
Helmy A (2003) Small worlds in wireless networks. IEEE Commun Lett 7(10):490–492
Hennessy JL, Patterson DA (2017) Computer architecture: a quantitative approach. Elsevier, Waltham, MA
Heylighen F (2002) The science of self-organization and adaptivity. In: Kiel LD (ed) Knowledge management, organizational intelligence and learning, and complexity, vol I. EOLSS Publishers, Oxford, UK, pp 184–211
Hoffman JG (1964) Self-organizing systems 1962. Phys Today 17(5):85–86
Holland JH (1992) Complex adaptive systems. Daedalus 121(1):17–30
Holland JH (1995) Hidden order: how adaptation builds complexity. Perseus Books, Reading, MA
Holland JH (1998) Emergence: from chaos to order. Oxford University Press, Oxford, UK
Holland JH (2006) Studying complex adaptive systems. J Syst Sci Complex 19:1–8. https://doi.org/10.1007/s11424-006-0001-z
Holland JH, Miller JH (1991) Artificial adaptive agents in economic theory. Am Econ Rev 81(2):365–370
Honderich T (ed) (2005) Oxford companion to philosophy, 2nd edn. Oxford University Press, Oxford, UK
Houle D et al (2011) Measurement and meaning in biology. Q Rev Biol 86(1):3–34
Hu S et al (2021) Distributed machine learning for wireless communication networks: techniques, architectures, and applications. IEEE Commun Surv Tutor 23(3):1458–1493
Hubka V, Eder WE (1988) Theory of technical systems: a total concept theory for engineering design. Springer-Verlag, Berlin
Hugoson MÅ (2009) Centralized versus decentralized information systems: a historical flashback. In: Impagliazzo J et al (eds) History of Nordic computing 2 (HiNC 2007). IFIP advances in information and communication technology, vol 303. Springer, Berlin, pp 106–115
IEA (2019) Global energy & CO_2 status report. International Energy Agency. https://www.iea.org/geco. Accessed 13 July 2020
Imran A et al (2014) Challenges in 5G: how to empower SON with big data for enabling 5G. IEEE Netw 28(6):27–33

Ingalls BP (2013) Mathematical modeling in systems biology: an introduction. MIT Press, Cambridge, MA
Ishihara T et al (2021) The evolution of faster-than-Nyquist signaling. IEEE Access 9:86535–86564
ITU-T (1997) Network general structure—terminology, series I: integrated services digital network, vocabulary of terms for broadband aspects of ISDN, June 1997
ITU-T (2016) Internet protocol aspects—quality of service and network performance, Internet protocol data communication service—IP packet transfer and availability performance parameters, July 2016
Jamil M, Yang XS (2013) A literature survey of benchmark functions for global optimization problems. Int J Math Model Numer Optim 4(2):150–194
Jang B et al (2019) Q-learning algorithms: a comprehensive classification and applications. IEEE Access 7:133653–133667
JCGM (2012) International vocabulary of metrology—basic and general concepts and associated terms (VIM), 3rd edn. Joint Committee for Guides in Metrology (JCGM)
Jensen K et al (2007) Nanotube radio. Nano Lett 11(7):3508–3511
Johansson B et al (2006) Mathematical decomposition techniques for distributed cross-layer optimization of data networks. IEEE J Sel Areas Commun 24(8):1535–1547
Johnson DS (2012) A brief history of NP-completeness, 1954–2012. In: Documenta mathematica, pp 359–376. https://elibm.org/article/10011465
Juran JM, Godfey AB (1999) Juran's quality handbook, 5th edn. McGraw-Hill, New York
Kailath T (1960) Correlation detection of signals perturbed by a random channel. IRE Trans Inf Theory 6(3):361–366
Kalaidjieva MA, Swanson GA (2004) Intelligence and living systems: decision-making perspective. Syst Res Behav Sci 21(2):147–172
Kampourakis K (ed) (2013) The philosophy of biology: a companion to educators. Springer Science + Business Media, Dordrecht, The Netherlands
Kanerva P (2000) Hyperdimensional computing: an introduction to computing in distributed representation with high-dimensional random vectors. Cogn Comput 1(2):139–159
Katoch S et al (2021) A review on genetic algorithm: past, present, and future. Multimed Tools Appl 80:8091–8126
Kauffman S (1995) At home in the universe: the search for laws of self-organization and complexity. Oxford University Press, Oxford, UK
Kawadia V, Kumar PR (2005) A cautionary perspective on cross-layer design. IEEE Wirel Commun 12(1):3–11
Kay SM (1988) Modern spectral estimation: theory and application. Prentice-Hall, Englewood Cliffs, NJ
Kay SM (1993) Fundamentals of statistical signal processing, vol. I: estimation theory. Prentice Hall, Englewood Cliffs, NJ
Kay SM (1998) Fundamentals of statistical signal processing, vol. II: detection theory. Prentice Hall, Englewood Cliffs, NJ
Kay SM (2013) Fundamentals of statistical signal processing, vol. III: practical algorithm development. Pearson Education, Upper Saddle River, NJ
Kay SM, Marple SL Jr (1981) Spectrum analysis: a modern perspective. Proc IEEE 69(11):1380–1419
Kelley TW et al (2004) Recent progress in organic electronics: materials, devices, and processes. Chem Mater 16(23):4413–4422
Kelly FP et al (1998) Rate control for communication networks: shadow prices, proportional fairness and stability. J Oper Res Soc 49(3):237–252
Kephart JO, Chess DM (2003) The vision of autonomic computing. Computer 36(1):41–50
Keyes RW (1987) The physics of VLSI systems. Addison-Wesley, New York
Kienle F et al (2011) On complexity, energy- and implementation-efficiency of channel decoders. IEEE Trans Commun 59(12):3301–3310
King RD et al (2009) The automation of science. Science 324(5923):85–89

Kish LB (2002) End of Moore's law: thermal (noise) death of integration in micro and nano electronics. Phys Lett A 305(3–4):144–149

Klein E (1996) Conversations with the sphinx: paradoxes in physics. Souvenier Press, London

Kline SJ (1995) Conceptual foundations of multidisciplinary thinking. Stanford University Press, Stanford, CA

Koestler A (1967) The ghost in the machine. Hutchinson & Co, London

Köksalan M et al (2011) Multiple criteria decision making. World Scientific Publishing, Singapore

Kopicki R et al (2010) Predicting workpiece motions under pushing manipulations using the principle of minimum energy. In: Proceedings of the workshop of robotics: science and systems, Zaragoza, Spain

Korkman S (2022) Talous ja humanismi. Otava, Helsinki, Finland

Kortenkamp D, Simmons R (2008) Robotic systems architectures and programming. In: Siciliano B, Khatib O (eds) Springer handbook of robotics. Springer, Berlin, pp 187–206

Kosinski RJ (2013) A literature review on reaction time. Technical note. Clemson University, Clemson, SC

Kossiakoff A et al (2011) Systems engineering: principles and practice, 2nd edn. Wiley, Hoboken, NJ

Krajewski M (2014) The great lightbulb conspiracy. IEEE Spectr 51(10):56–61

Krejki J, Stoklasa J (2018) Aggregation in the analytic hierarchy process: why weighted geometric mean should be used instead of weighted arithmetic mean. Expert Syst Appl 114:97–106. https://www.sciencedirect.com/science/article/pii/S0957417418303981

Kreyszig E (2011) Advanced engineering mathematics, 10th edn. Wiley, New York

Kuehn C (2015) Multiple time scale dynamics. Springer, Cham, Switzerland

Kuon I, Rose J (2006) Measuring the gap between FPGAs and ASICs. In: Proceedings of the 2006 ACM/SIGDA 14th international symposium on field programmable gate arrays (FPGA'06), Monterey, CA, pp 21–30

Kurose JF, Ross KD (2013) Computer networking: A top-down approach featuring the Internet, 6th edn. Addison- Wesley, Boston, MA

Kwok TC (1997) Residential broadband Internet services and applications requirements. IEEE Commun Mag 35(6):76–83

Ladyman J, Wiesner K (2020) What is a complex system? Yale University Press, New Haven, CT

Ladyman J et al (2013) What is a complex system? Eur J Philos Sci 3:33–67. https://doi.org/10.1007/s13194-012-0056-8

Landau HJ (1967) Sampling, data transmission, and the Nyquist rate. Proc IEEE 55(10):1701–1706

Landau ID et al (2011) Adaptive control: algorithms, analysis and applications, 2nd edn. Springer-Verlag, London

Laplante PA et al (2008) What's in a name? Distinguishing between SaaS and SOA. IT Prof 10(3):46–50

Larson EJ (2021) The myth of artificial intelligence: why computers can't think the way we do. Belknap Press, Cambridge, MA

Lasaulce S, Tembine H (2011) Game theory and learning for wireless networks: fundamentals and applications. Academic Press, Oxford, UK

Latora V, Marchiori M (2001) Efficient behavior of small-world networks. Phys Rev Lett 87(19):1–4. https://doi.org/10.1103/PhysRevLett.87.198701

Lebon G et al (2008) Understanding non-equilibrium thermodynamics: foundations, applications, frontiers. Springer-Verlag, Berlin

Lee TH (2004) The design of CMOS radio-frequency integrated circuits, 2nd edn. Cambridge University Press, Cambridge, UK

Lee LC et al (1998) The stability, scalability and performance of multi-agent systems. BT Technol J 16:94–103. https://doi.org/10.1023/A:1009686016775

Lettieri P, Srivastava MB (1999) Advances in wireless terminals. IEEE Pers Commun 6(1):6–19

Levesque M, Tipper D (2016) A survey of clock synchronization over packet-switched networks. IEEE Commun Surv Tutor 18(4):2926–2947

Li M et al (2011) Dark energy. Commun Theor Phys 56(3):525–604
Liang Y et al (2019) A review of rechargeable batteries for portable electronic devices. InfoMat 1(1):6–32
Liao X et al (2017) Small-world human brain networks: perspectives and challenges. Neurosci Biobehav Rev 77:286–300. https://doi.org/10.1016/j.neubiorev.2017.03.018
Lin X et al (2006) A tutorial on cross-layer optimization in wireless networks. IEEE J Sel Areas Commun 24(8):1452–1463
Lin YM et al (2010) 100-GHz transistors from wafer-scale epitaxial graphene. Science 327(5966):662
Lin F et al (2012) Optimal control of vehicular formations with nearest neighbor interactions. IEEE Trans Autom Control 57(9):2203–2218
Liu Z (2021) Game-based approach of fair resource allocation in wireless powered cooperative cognitive radio networks. Int J Electron Commun (AEÜ) 134:1–11. https://doi.org/10.1016/j.aeue.2021.153699
Liu P et al (2023) Pre-train, prompt, and predict: a systematic survey of prompting methods in natural language processing. ACM Comput Surv 55(9):1–35. https://doi.org/10.1145/3560815
Love DJ et al (2004) What is the value of limited feedback for MIMO channels? IEEE Commun Mag 42(10):54–59
Love DJ et al (2008) An overview of limited feedback in wireless communication systems. IEEE J Sel Areas Commun 26(8):1341–1365
Lu J et al (2019) Learning under concept drift: a review. IEEE Trans Knowl Data Eng 31(12):2346–2363
Lundheim L (2002) On Shannon and 'Shannon's formula.' Telektronikk 98(1):20–29
Luong NC et al (2019) Applications of economic and pricing models for resource management in 5G wireless networks: a survey. IEEE Commun Surv Tutor 21(4):3298–3339
Lynn T et al (2016) Cloudlightning: a framework for a self-organising and self-managing heterogeneous cloud. In: Proceedings of the international conference on cloud computing and services science, Rome, pp 333–338
Madhow U (2008) Fundamentals of digital communication. Cambridge University Press, Cambridge, UK
Madni AM, Jackson S (2009) Towards a conceptual framework for resilience engineering. IEEE Syst J 3(2):181–191
Maier MW, Rechtin E (2009) The art of systems architecting, 3rd edn. CRC Press, Boca Raton, FL
Makhoul J (1975) Linear prediction: a tutorial review. Proc IEEE 63(4):561–580
Maloberti F, Davies AC (eds) (2024) A short history of circuits and systems, 2nd edn. River Publishers, Gistrup, Denmark
Mämmelä A (2006) Commutation in linear and nonlinear systems. Frequenz 60(5–6):92–94
Mämmelä A, Anttonen A (2017) Why will computing power need particular attention in future wireless devices? IEEE Circuits Syst Mag 17(1):12–26
Mämmelä A, Riekki J (2022a) New network architectures will be weakly coupled. IEEE Future Netw Tech Focus, Apr 2022. https://futurenetworks.ieee.org/tech-focus/april-2022. Accessed 10 Dec 2024
Mämmelä A, Riekki J (2022b) Systems view in engineering research. In: Rezaei N (ed) Transdisciplinarity. Springer Nature Switzerland, Cham, Switzerland, pp 105–130
Mämmelä A et al (2010) Relationship of average transmitted and received energies in adaptive transmission. IEEE Trans Veh Technol 59(3):1257–1268
Mämmelä A et al (2018) Multidisciplinary and historical perspectives for developing intelligent and resource-efficient systems. IEEE Access 6:17464–17499
Mämmelä A et al (2023) Loose coupling: an invisible thread in the history of technology. IEEE Access 11:59456–59482
Marcos A, Arp R (2013) Information in the biological sciences. In: Kampourakis K (ed) The philosophy of biology: a companion to educators. Springer Science + Business Media, Dordrecht, The Netherlands, pp 511–547

Markov IL (2014) Limits on fundamental limits to computation. Nature 512:147–154. https://doi.org/10.1038/nature13570
Marler RT, Arora JS (2004) Survey of multi-objective optimization methods for engineering. Struct Multidiscip Optim 26(6):369–395
Marsland S (2015) Machine learning: an algorithmic perspective, 2nd edn. Chapman & Hall/CRC, New York
Maruyama M (1963) The second cybernetics: deviation-amplifying mutual causal processes. Am Sci 5(2):164–179
McCarthy J, Hayes P (1969) Some philosophical problems from the standpoint of artificial intelligence. In: Meltzer B, Michie D (eds) Machine intelligence 4. Edinburgh University Press, Edinburgh, UK, pp 463–502
McFarland D, Bösser T (1993) Intelligent behavior in animals and robots. MIT Press, Cambridge, MA
McGarry K et al (1999) Hybrid neural systems: from simple coupling to fully integrated neural networks. Neural Computing Surveys 2(1):62–93
Meadow CT, Yuan W (1997) Measuring the impact of information: defining the concepts. Inf Process Manage 33(6):697–714
Meadows DH, Wright D (eds) (2008) Thinking in systems: a primer. Chelsea Green Publishing, White River Junction, VT
Medsker LR (1995) Hybrid intelligent systems. Springer, New York
Mehrotra K, Mahapatra PR (1997) A jerk model for tracking highly maneuvering targets. IEEE Trans Aerosp Electron Syst 33(4):1094–1105
Meindl JD (2000) Beyond Moore's law: the interconnect era. Comput Sci Eng 5(1):20–24
Meindl J (ed) (2001) Special issue on limits of semiconductor technology. Proc IEEE 89(3):223–393
Mendel JM (1995) Lessons in estimation theory for signal processing, communications, and control. Prentice Hall, Englewood Cliffs, NJ
Merriam-Webster (2024). https://www.merriam-webster.com. Accessed 5 Nov 2024
Mesarovic MD (1970) Multilevel systems and concepts in process control. Proc IEEE 58(1):111–125
Mesarovic M et al (1970) Theory of hierarchical, multilevel systems. Academic Press, New York
Meystel AM, Albus JS (2002) Intelligent systems: architecture, design, and control. Wiley, New York
Michalewicz Z, Fogel DB (2004) How to solve it: modern heuristics, 2nd edn. Springer, Berlin
Migdalas A (1995) When is a Stackelberg equilibrium Pareto optimum? In: Pardalos PM et al (eds) Advances in multicriteria analysis. Springer, Boston, MA, pp 175–181
Miller JG (1973) Living systems. Q Rev Biol 48(2):63–91
Mishali M, Eldar YC (2010) From theory to practice: sub-Nyquist sampling of sparse wideband analog signals. IEEE J Sel Top Signal Process 4(2):375–391
Mobus GE (2022) Systems science: theory, analysis, modeling, and design. Springer Nature, Cham, Switzerland
Monroe D (2019) Quantum leap. Commun ACM 62(1):10–12
Monsen P (1980) Fading channel communications. IEEE Commun Mag 18(1):16–25
Morowitz HJ (2002) The emergence of everything: how the world became complex. Oxford University Press, New York
Mühl G et al (2017) On the definitions of self-managing and self-organizing systems. In: Proceedings of the ITG/GI symposium communication in distributed systems, Bern, Switzerland
Newcombe EA, Pasupathy S (1982) Error rate monitoring for digital communications. Proc IEEE 70(8):805–828
Newman MEJ (2010) Networks: an introduction. Oxford University Press, New York
NGMN (2015) 5G white paper. https://www.ngmn.org/5g-white-paper.html. Accessed 2 Feb 2023
Nowak M (2006) Evolutionary dynamics: exploring the equations of life. The Belknap Press, Cambridge, MA
Nyquist H (1932) Regeneration theory. Bell Syst Tech J 11(1):126–147

Ogata K (2010) Modern control engineering, 5th edn. Prentice Hall, Boston, MA
Ogras UY, Marculescu R (2006) "It's a small world after all": NoC performance optimization via long-range link insertion. IEEE Trans Very Large Scale Integr (VLSI) Syst 14(7):693–706
O'Neill RV et al (1986) A hierarchical concept of ecosystems. Princeton University Press, Princeton, NJ
Online Etymology Dictionary (2024). https://www.etymonline.com. Accessed 5 Nov 2024
O'Reilly CA III, Tushman ML (2013) Organizational ambidexterity: past, present, and future. Acad Manag Perspect 27(4):324–338
Ouyang Z et al (2020) Using gross ecosystem product (GEP) to value nature in decision making. PNAS 117(25):14593–14601
Ovaska SJ et al (2006) Fusion of soft computing and hard computing: computational structures and characteristic features. IEEE Trans Syst Man Cybern Part C Appl Rev 36(3):439–448
Oxford Learner's Dictionaries (2024). https://www.oxfordlearnersdictionaries.com. Accessed 25 Oct 2024
Pagels H (1988) The dreams of reason: the computer and the rise of the sciences of complexity. Simon & Schuster, New York
Pahl G et al (2007) Engineering design: a systematic approach, 3rd edn. Springer-Verlag, London
Pahlavan K, Levesque AH (2005) Wireless information networks, 2nd edn. Wiley, New York
Palomar DP, Chiang M (2006) A tutorial on decomposition methods for network utility maximization. IEEE J Sel Areas Commun 24(8):1439–1451
Pan X et al (2013) Systems thinking: a comparison between Chinese and Western approaches. Procedia Comput Sci 16:1027–1035. https://doi.org/10.1016/j.procs.2013.01.108
Panwar NL et al (2011) Role of renewable energy sources in environmental protection: a review. Renew Sustain Energy Rev 15(3):1513–1524
Papazoglou MP (2003) Service-oriented computing: concepts, characteristics and directions. In: Proceedings of the fourth international conference on web information systems engineering (WISE'03)
Papoulis A (1962) The Fourier integral and its applications. McGraw-Hill, New York
Pasupathy S (1979) Minimum shift keying: a spectrally efficient modulation. IEEE Commun Mag 17(4):14–22
Pattee HH (ed) (1973) Hierarchy theory: the challenge of complex systems. George Braziller, New York
Pautasso C, Wilde E (2009) Why is the web loosely coupled? A multi-faceted metric for service design. In: Proceedings of the 18th international conference on world wide web (WWW'09), Madrid, pp 911–920
Pearl J, Korf RE (1987) Search techniques. Annu Rev Comput Sci 2:451–457. https://doi.org/10.1146/annurev.cs.02.060187.002315
Penrose P (1999) The emperor's new mind: concerning computers, minds and the laws of physics, new. Oxford University Press, Oxford, UK
Perahia E (2008) IEEE 802.11n development: history, process, and technology. IEEE Commun Mag 48–55
Peterson M (2009) An introduction to decision theory. Cambridge University Press, Cambridge, UK
Peterson W et al (1954) The theory of signal detectability. Trans IRE Prof Group Inf Theory 4(4):171–212
Pietikäinen M, Silven O (2021) Challenges of artificial intelligence: from machine learning and computer vision to emotional intelligence. Center for Machine Vision and Signal Analysis, University of Oulu, Oulu, Finland
Pottie GJ (1995) System design choices in personal communications. IEEE Pers Commun 2(5):50–67
Poundstone W (1988) Labyrinths of reason: paradox, puzzles and the frailty of knowledge. Penguin Books, London
Prasad R (2016) Human bond communication. Wireless Pers Commun 87(3):619–627

Prehofer C, Bettstetter C (2005) Self-organization in communication networks: principles and design paradigms. IEEE Commun Mag 43(7):78–85
Prigogine I (1997) The end of certainty: time, chaos, and the new laws of nature. Free Press, Kinston, NC
Proakis JG, Salehi M (2008) Digital communications, 5th edn. McGraw-Hill, New York
Prokopenko M (2009) Guided self-organization. HFSP J 3(5):287–289
Pulleyblank R (1973) A comparison of receivers designed on the basis of minimum mean-square error and probability of error for channels with intersymbol interference and noise. IEEE Trans Commun 21(12):1434–1438
Pumain D (ed) (2006) Hierarchy in natural and social sciences. Springer, Dordrecht, The Netherlands
Purvis B et al (2019) Three pillars of sustainability: in search of conceptual origins. Sustain Sci 14:681–695. https://doi.org/10.1007/s11625-018-0627-5
Qin Z et al (2023) A generalized semantic communication system: from sources to channels. IEEE Wirel Commun 30(3):18–26
Qureshi S (1982) Adaptive equalization. IEEE Commun Mag 20(2):9–16
Qureshi SUH (1985) Adaptive equalization. Proc IEEE 73(9):1349–1387
Raab FH (1986) Average efficiency of power amplifiers. In: Proceedings of the RF technology expo 86, Anaheim, CA, pp 473–486
Radulescu R et al (2020) Multi-objective multi-agent decision making: a utility-based analysis and survey. Auton Agent Multi-Agent Syst 34:1–52. https://doi.org/10.1007/s10458-019-09433-x
Ramage M, Shipp K (2020) Systems thinkers, 2nd edn. Springer, London
Random House Webster's College Dictionary (1999). Random House, New York
Rani M et al (2018) A systematic review of compressive sensing: concepts, implementations and applications. IEEE Access 6:4875–4894
Ranjbar N (2020) Capacity region and capacity-achieving signaling schemes for 1-bit ADC multiple access channels in Rayleigh fading. IEEE Trans Wireless Commun 19(9):6162–6178
Rappaport TS (2002) Wireless communications: principles and practice, 2nd edn. Prentice-Hall, Upper Saddle River, NJ
Ren JG et al (2017) Ground-to-satellite quantum teleportation. Nature 549:70–73
Richardson GP (1991) Feedback thought in social science and system theory. University of Pennsylvania Press, Philadelphia, PA
Riekki J, Mämmelä A (2021) Research and education towards smart and sustainable world. IEEE Access 9:53156–53177
Rihaczek AW (1983) The maximum entropy of radar resolution. IEEE Trans Aerosp Electron Syst 17(1):144
Rioul O (2021) This is IT: a primer on Shannon's entropy and information. In: Duplantier B, Rivasseau V (eds) Information theory: Poincaré seminar 2018. Birkhäuser, Cham, Switzerland, pp 49–86
Ristenbatt MP (1973) Alternatives in digital communications. Proc IEEE 6(6):703–721
Rizk Y et al (2018) Decision making in multi-agent systems: a survey. IEEE Trans Cogn Dev Syst 10(3):514–529
Roberts S (2020) The power of not thinking: how our bodies learn and why we should trust them. Blink Publishing, London
Robson D (2019) Intelligence trap: why smart people make dumb mistakes. W. W. Norton & Company, New York
Rosen R (1991) Life itself: a comprehensive inquiry into the nature, origin, and fabrication of life. Columbia University Press, New York
Rosenbaum DA (2010) Human motor control, 2nd edn. Elsevier, London
Rosenberg A, McIntyre L (2020) Philosophy of science: a contemporary introduction, 4th edn. Routledge, New York
Rothman T (2003) Everything's relative and other fables from science and technology. Wiley, Hoboken, NJ

Rowley J (2007) The wisdom hierarchy: representations of the DIKW hierarchy. J Inf Sci 33(2):163–180

Roy S (2008) Minimalist self-organization in wireless networks. In: Proceedings of the international conference on advanced technologies for communications 2008, Phoenix Park, Korea, pp 451–456

Russell S, Norvig P (2022) Artificial intelligence: a modern approach, 3rd edn. Pearson Education, Harlow, UK

Saad W et al (2009) Coalitional game theory for communication networks. IEEE Signal Process Mag 26(5):77–97

Saaty TL (2008) Decision making with the analytic hierarchy process. Int J Serv Sci 1(1):83–98

Sainsbury M (2009) Paradoxes, 3rd edn. Cambridge University Press, Cambridge, UK

Salami G et al (2011) A comparison between the centralized and distributed approaches for spectrum management. IEEE Commun Surv Tutor 13(2):274–290

Sandell N Jr et al (1978) Survey of decentralized control methods for large scale systems. IEEE Trans Autom Control 23(2):108–128

Saridis GN (1979) Toward the realization of intelligent controls. Proc IEEE 67(8):1115–1133

Saridis GN (2001) Hierarchically intelligent machines. World Scientific Publising, Singapore

Sarpeshkar R (2010) Ultra low power bioelectronics: fundamentals, biomedical applications, and bio-inspired systems. Cambridge University Press, Cambridge, UK

Schaefer M (2016) Multi-agent traffic simulation for development and validation of autonomic car-to-car systems. In: McCluskey TL et al (eds) Autonomic road transport support systems. Springer, Cham, Switzerland, pp 165–180

Schaumann R, Van Valkenburg ME (2001) Design of analog filters. Oxford University Press, New York

Schetzen M (2006) The Volterra and Wiener theories of nonlinear systems, 2nd edn. Krieger Publishing, Melbourne, FL

Schlosshauer M (2019) Quantum decoherence. Phys Rep 831:1–57. https://doi.org/10.1016/j.physrep.2019.10.001

Schmitt EA et al (2023) Photoelectrochemical Schlenk cell functionalization of multi-junction water-splitting photoelectrodes. Cell Rep Phys Sci 4(10):1–14

Schneider M (1999) Self-stabilization. ACM Comput Surv 25(1):45–67

Schoemaker PJH (1991) The quest for optimality: a positive heuristic of science? Behav Brain Sci 14(2):205–245

Schwaninger M (2001) Intelligent organizations: an integrative framework. Syst Res Behav Sci 18(2):137–158

Schwanitz D (1999) Bildung: Alles, was man Wissen muß. Eichborn AG, Frankfurt am Main, Germany

Schwartz M et al (1966) Communication systems and techniques. McGraw-Hill, New York

Scott B (2004) Second-order cybernetics: an historical introduction. Kybernetes 33(9/10):1365–1378

Scrosati B (2011) History of lithium batteries. J Solid State Electrochem 15:1623–1630. https://doi.org/10.1007/s10008-011-1386-8

SE VOCAB (2024) Software and systems engineering vocabulary. IEEE Computer Society and ISO/IEC JTC 1/SC7. https://pascal.computer.org. Accessed 6 Nov 2024

Secondini M, Forestieri E (2017) Scope and limitations of the nonlinear Shannon limit. J Lightwave Technol 35(4):893–902

Senge P (2006) The fifth discipline: the art and practice of the learning organization, rev. Doubleday, New York

Seselja D, Weber E (2012) Rationality and irrationality in the history of continental drift: was the hypothesis of continental drift worthy of pursuit? Stud Hist Philos Sci 43(1):147–159

Shalm LK et al (2015) A strong loophole-free test of local realism. Phys Rev Lett 115(25):1–10. https://doi.org/10.1103/PhysRevLett.115.250402

Shannon CE (1948a) A mathematical theory of communication. Bell Syst Tech J 27(3):349–423

Shannon CE (1948b) A mathematical theory of communication. Bell Syst Tech J 27(4):623–656
Shannon CE (1949) Communication in the presence of noise. Proc IRE 37(1):10–21
Shannon CE (1953) General treatment of the problem of coding. Trans IRE Prof Group Inf Theory 1(1):102–104
Shannon CE, Weaver W (1998) The mathematical theory of communication. University of Illinois Press, Chicago, IL
Sheldon T (2001) McGraw-Hill encyclopedia of networking & telecommunications. Osborne/McGraw-Hill, Berkeley, CA
Shi Z et al (2009) Effects of packet loss and latency on temporal discrimination of visual-haptic events. IEEE Trans Haptics 3(1):28–36
Shukla V et al (2016) Multicriteria decision-making methodology for systems engineering. IEEE Syst J 10(1):4–14
Shulaker MM et al (2013) Carbon nanotube computer. Nature 501:526–530. https://doi.org/10.1038/nature12502
Shumailov I et al (2014) AI models collapse when trained on recursively generated data. Nature 631:755–760. https://doi.org/10.1038/s41586-024-07566-y
Siegfried T (2006) A beautiful math: John Nash, game theory, and the modern quest for a code of nature. Joseph Henry Press, Washington, DC
Silk H et al (2016) Design of self-organizing networks: creating specified degree distributions. IEEE Trans Netw Sci Eng 3(3):147–158
Simon H (1956) Rational choice and the structure of the environment. Psychol Rev 63(2):129–138
Simon HA (1962) The architecture of complexity. Proc Am Philos Soc 106(6):467–482
Simon HA (1973) The organization of complex systems. In: Pattee HH (ed) Hierarchy theory: the challenge of complex systems. George Braziller, pp 1–27
Simon HA (1996) The sciences of the artificial, 3rd edn. MIT Press, Cambridge, MA
Simon MK (2002) Probability distributions involving Gaussian random variables: a handbook for engineers, scientists and mathematicians. Springer Science + Business Media, New York
Simon HA, Ando A (1961) Aggregation of variables in dynamic systems. Econometrica 29(2):111–138
Sipahi R (2011) Stability and stabilization of systems with time delay: limitations and opportunities. IEEE Control Syst Mag 31(1):38–65
Sipser M (2006) Introduction to the theory of computation, 2nd edn. Thomson Course Technology, Boston, MA
Sklar B (2001) Digital communications, 2nd edn. Prentice-Hall, Upper Saddle River, NJ
Skolnik MI (ed) (1970) Radar handbook. McGraw-Hill, New York
Skyttner L (2005) General systems theory: problems, perspectives, practice, 2nd edn. World Scientific Publishing, Singapore
Slepian D (1976) On bandwidth. Proc IEEE 64(3):292–300
Smil V (2014) Making the modern world: materials and dematerialization. Wiley, Chichester, UK
Smil V (2017) Energy and civilization: a history. MIT Press, Cambridge, MA
Smil V (2020) Numbers don't lie: 71 things you need to know about the world. Penguin Books, New York
Smith RJ, Dorf RC (1991) Circuits, devices, and systems: a first course in electrical engineering, 5th edn. Wiley, Hoboken, NJ
Song YH, Johns AT (1998) Application of fuzzy logic in power systems. Part 2: comparison and integration with expert systems, neural networks and genetic algorithms. Power Eng J 12(4):185–190
Sorensen R (2003) A brief history of the paradox: philosophy and the labyrinth of the mind. Oxford University Press, New York
Srinivas M, Patnaik LM (1994) Genetic algorithms: a survey. Computer 27(6):17–26
Stadler W (1986) Initiators of multicriteria optimization. In: Jahn J, Krabs W (eds) Recent advances and historical development of vector optimization. Springer-Verlag, Berlin, pp 3–47

Stalker L et al (2022) Gold (hydrogen) rush: risks and uncertainties in exploring for naturally occurring hydrogen. APPEA J 62(1):361–380
Stanczak S et al (2008) Fundamentals of resource allocation in wireless networks: theory and algorithms, 2nd edn. Springer-Verlag, Berlin
Stankiewicz R, Jajszczyk A (2011) A survey of QoE assurance in converged networks. Comput Netw 55(7):1459–1473
Stanovich KE et al (2016) The rationality quotient: toward a test of rational thinking. MIT Press, Cambridge, MA
Stenner MD et al (2003) The speed of information in a 'fast-light' optical medium. Nature 425:695–698. https://doi.org/10.1038/nature02016
Sterman JD (2000) Business dynamics: systems thinking and modeling for a complex world. McGraw-Hill, Boston, MA
Stone P, Veloso M (2000) Multi-agent systems: a survey from a machine learning perspective. Auton Robot 8:345–383. https://doi.org/10.1023/A:1008942012299
Stonier T (1992) Beyond information: the natural history of intelligence. Springer, Berlin
Stonier T (1997) Information and meaning: an evolutionary perspective. Springer, Berlin
Stordahl K (2007) The history behind the probability theory and the queuing theory. Telektronikk 103(2):123–140
Strogatz SH (2014) Nonlinear dynamics and chaos: with applications to physics, biology, chemistry, and engineering, 2nd edn. CRC Press, Boca Raton, FL
Sun XH, Chen Y (2010) Reevaluating Amdahl's law in the multicore era. J Parallel Distrib Comput 70(2):183–188
Suntola T (2018) The short history of science—or the long path to the union of metaphysics and empiricism, 3rd edn. Physics Foundations Society and The Finnish Society for Natural Philosophy. https://physicsfoundations.org
Swilling M (2020) The age of sustainability: just transitions in a complex world. Routledge, New York
Tachibana Y et al (2012) Artificial photosynthesis for solar water-splitting. Nat Photonics 6:511–518. https://doi.org/10.1038/nphoton.2012.175
Talbi EG (2009) Metaheuristics: from design to implementation. Wiley, Hoboken, NJ
Tan F et al (2017) Deep reinforcement learning: from Q-learning to deep Q-learning. In: Liu D et al (eds) Neural information processing. Springer International Publishing, Cham, Switzerland, pp 475–483
Tanenbaum AS, Wetherall DJ (2011) Computer networks, 5th edn. Prentice Hall, Englewood Cliffs, NJ
Theraulaz G, Bonabeau E (1999) A brief history of stigmergy. Artif Life 5(2):97–116
Thims L (2012) Thermodynamics $\neq$ information theory: science's greatest Sokal affair. J Hum Thermodyn 8(1):1–120
Thomas JM et al (2020) Decarbonising energy: the developing international activity in hydrogen technologies and fuel cells. J Energy Chem 51:405–415. https://doi.org/10.1016/j.jechem.2020.03.087
Thurner S et al (2018) Introduction to the theory of complex systems. Oxford University Press, Oxford, UK
Tiwari SK et al (2020) Graphene research and their outputs: status and prospect. J Sci Adv Mater Devices 5(1):10–29
Trivedi KS, Bobbio A (2017) Reliability and availability engineering: modeling, analysis, and applications. Cambridge University Press, Cambridge, UK
Tse D (2010) It is easier to approximate. Inf Theory Soc Neswlett 60(1):6–11
Turin GL (1980) Introduction to spread-spectrum antimultipath techniques and their application to urban digital radio. Proc IEEE 68(3):328–353
Turin GL (1984) The effects of multipath and fading on the performance of direct-sequence CDMA systems. IEEE Trans Veh Technol 33(3):213–219
Turner MS (1993) Why is the temperature of the universe 2.726 kelvin? Science 262(5135):861–867

Tyukin IY et al (2021) Demystification of few-shot and one-shot learning. In: Proceedings of the 2021 international joint conference on neural networks (IJCNN), Shenzhen, China
Tzafestas SG (2018) Energy, feedback, adaptation, and self-organization: the fundamental elements of life and society. Springer International Publishing, Cham, Switzerland
Ulrich K, Eppinger S (1995) Product design and development. McGraw-Hill, New York
Umpleby SA (2009) Ross Ashby's general theory of adaptive systems. Int J Gen Syst 38(2):231–238
Umpleby SA (2016) Second-order cybernetics as a fundamental revolution in science. Constructivist Foundations 11(3): 455-465
United Nations (2024) United Nations world population prospects. https://population.un.org/wpp. Accessed 20 Oct 2024
Upadhyaya S, Dhingra G (2010) Exploring issues for QoS based routing algorithms. Int J Comput Sci Eng 2(5):1792–1795
Uusikylä P, Jalonen H (2023) Epävarmuuden aika: Kuinka ymmärtää systeemistä muutosta? Into Kustannus, Helsinki, Finland
Vamplew P et al (2008) On the limitations of scalarisation for multi-objective reinforcement learning of Pareto fronts. In: Wobcke W, Zhang M (eds) AI 2008: advances in artificial intelligence. Springer, Berlin, pp 372–378
Van Lange PAM et al (2013) The psychology of social dilemmas: a review. Organ Behav Hum Decis Process 120(2):125–141
Van Moffaert K, Nowe A (2014) Multi-objective reinforcement learning using sets of Pareto dominating policies. J Mach Learn Res 15(1):3663–3692
Van Veen BD, Buckley KM (1988) Beamforming: a versatile approach to spatial filtering. IEEE ASSP Mag 5(2):4–24
Vermaas PE, Dorst K (2007) On the conceptual framework of John Gero's FBS-model and the prescriptive aims of design methodology. Des Stud 28(2):133–157
von Bertalanffy L (1950) An outline of general system theory. Br J Philos Sci 1(2):134–165
von Bertalanffy L (1971) General system theory: foundations, development, applications, rev. George Braziller, New York
von Wright GH (1971) Explanation and understanding. Cornell University Press, Ithaca, NY
Walach E, Widrow B (1984) The least mean fourth (LMF) adaptive algorithm and its family. IEEE Trans Inf Theory 30(2):275–283
Walasek L, Brown GDA (2023) Incomparability and incommensurability in choice: no common currency of value? Perspect Psychol Sci 19(6):1011–1030
Walker DW (1995) An introduction to message passing paradigms. In: Proceedings of the CERN school of computing, Arles, France, pp 165–184
Wallace D (2010) Gravity, entropy, and cosmology: in search of clarity. Br J Philos Sci 61(3):513–540
Wang Z, Bovik AC (2009) Mean squared error: love it or leave it? [A new look at signal fidelity measures]. IEEE Signal Process Mag 26(1):98–117
Wang JW, Feng ZH (2015) Time-domain nature of group delay. Chin Phys B 24(10):1–5. https://doi.org/10.1088/1674-1056/24/10/100301
Wang LJ et al (2000) Gain-assisted superluminal light propagation. Nature 406:277–279. https://doi.org/10.1038/35018520
Wang H et al (2016) Solving verbal questions in IQ test by knowledge-powered word embedding. In: Proceedings of the 2016 conference on empirical methods in natural language processing, Austin, Texas, pp 541–550
Ward JS et al (1984) Figures of merit for VLSI implementations of digital signal processing algorithms. IEE Proc F 131(1):64–70
Watts DJ (2004) Six degrees: the science of a connected age. W. W. Norton & Company, New York
Weinberg GM (1975) An introduction to general systems thinking. Wiley, New York
West G (2017) Scale: the universal laws of life and death in organisms, cities and companies. Penguin Books, New York

Westerhoff HV et al (2009) Systems biology: the elements and principles of life. FEBS Lett 573(24):3882–3890
Whalen AD (1984) Statistical theory of signal detection and parameter estimation. IEEE Commun Mag 22(6):37–44
Whitney DE, Milley MK (1974) CADSYS: a new approach to computer aided design. IEEE Trans Syst Man Cybern 4(1):50–58
Whittingham MS (2012) History, evolution, and future status of energy storage. Proc IEEE 100(Special Centennial Issue):1518–1534
Widrow B (2005) Thinking about thinking: the discovery of the LMS algorithm. IEEE Signal Process Mag 22(1):101–102, 106
Widrow B, McCool J (1976) A comparison of adaptive algorithms based on the methods of steepest descent and random search. IEEE Trans Antennas Propag 24(5):615–637
Widrow B, Stearns AD (1985) Adaptive signal processing. Prentice Hall, Englewood Cliffs, MA
Widrow B, Walach E (1996) Adaptive inverse control. Prentice Hall, Upped Saddle River, NJ
Wiener N (1961) Cybernetics: or control and communication in the animal and the machine, 2nd edn. MIT Press, Cambridge, MA
Wilson EO (1998) Consilience: the unity of knowledge. Vintage Books, New York
Woeginger GJ (2008) Open problems around exact algorithms. Discret Appl Math 156(3):397–405
Wolfram (2024) Eric Weisstein's world of science. http://scienceworld.wolfram.com
Wolstenholme EF (2003) Towards the definition and use of a core set of archetypal structures in system dynamics. Syst Dyn Rev 19(1):7–26
Woo DH, Lee HH (2008) Extending Amdahl's law for energy-efficient computing in the many-core era. IEEE Comput 41(12):24–31
Wu YS (1989) "Constant capacity", DSP architecture—an historical prospective. In: Chan YT (ed) Underwater acoustic data processing. Kluwer Academic Publishers, Dordrecht, The Netherlands, pp 609–627
Wu J (2013) Hierarchy theory. In: Rozzi R et al (2013) Linking ecology and ethics for a changing world: values, philosophy, and action. Springer Science + Business Media Dordrecht, The Netherlands, pp 281–302
Wu CW (2018) Comments on theoretical foundation of "EM drive." Acta Astronaut 144:214–215. https://doi.org/10.1016/j.actaastro.2018.01.006
Yanofsky NS (2013) The outer limits of reason: what science, mathematics, and logic cannot tell us. MIT Press, Cambridge, MA
Ye D et al (2017) A survey of self-organization mechanisms in multiagent systems. IEEE Trans Syst Man Cybern Syst 47(3):441–461
Yi Y, Chiang M (2008) Stochastic network utility maximisation – a tribute to Kelly's paper published in this journal a decade ago. European Transactions on Telecommunications 19(4): 421-442
Young WR (1979) Advanced mobile phone service: introduction, background, and objectives. Bell Syst Tech J 58(1):1–14
Young HD et al (2012) Sears and Zemansky's university physics with modern physics, 13th edn. Addison Wesley, San Francisco, CA
Yourdon E, Constantine LL (1978) Structured design: fundamentals of a discipline of computer programs and systems design, 2nd edn. Yourdon Press, New York
Yu L et al (2009) Multiple-parameter coupling metrics for layered component-based software. Softw Qual J 17:5–24. https://doi.org/10.1007/s11219-008-9052-9
Yu X et al (2021) Physical anti-collision in RFID systems: theory and practice. Springer Nature, Singapore
Zadeh LA (1958) What is optimal? IRE Trans Inf Theory 4(1):3
Zeeman EC (1979) A geometrical model of ideologies. In: Renfrew C, Cooke KL (eds) Transformations: mathematical approaches to cultural change. Academic Press, New York, pp 463–479
Zhang W et al (2001) Stability of networked control systems. IEEE Control Syst Mag 21(1):84–99

Zhang L et al (2009) Network-induced constraints in networked control systems—a survey. IEEE Trans Ind Inf 9(1):403–416

Zhao Y et al (2009) Performance evaluation of cognitive radios: metrics, utility functions, and methodology. Proc IEEE 9(4):642–659

Zheludev NI (2008) What diffraction limit? Nat Mater 7:420–422. https://doi.org/10.1038/nmat2163

Zhirnov VV, Cavin RK (2013) Future microsystems for information processing: limits and lessons from living systems. IEEE J Electron Devices Soc 1(2):29–47

Zhirnov VV et al (2003) Limits to binary logic switch scaling—a gedanken model. Proc IEEE 91(11):1934–1939

Zidane YJT, Olsson NOE (2017) Defining project efficiency, effectiveness and efficacy. Int J Manag Proj Bus 10(3):621–641

Ziemer RE, Peterson RL (1985) Digital communications and spread spectrum systems. Macmillan, New York

Ziemer RE, Tranter WH (2014) Principles of communications: systems, modulation, and noise, 7th edn. Wiley, Hoboken, NJ

Zins C (2007) Conceptual approaches for defining data, information, and knowledge. J Am Soc Inform Sci Technol 58(4):479–493

Zio E (2009) Reliability engineering: old problems and new challenges. Reliab Eng Syst Saf 94(2):125–141

Chapter 6
History for Understanding the Present

If I have seen further, it is by standing on the shoulders of Giants. Isaac Newton (1642–1727)
What is the use of a new-born child? Benjamin Franklin (1706–1790)
The farther back you can look, the farther forward you are likely to see. Sir Winston Churchill (1874–1965)
If all human beings understood history, they might cease making the same stupid mistakes over and over. Isaac Asimov (1920–1992)
The purpose of life is to stay alive. Michael Crichton (1942–2008)

Abstract Knowledge of history belongs to the general knowledge of all researchers and is, therefore, essential for understanding the present and envisioning the future. We present the history of information retrieval and the writing of scientific papers. Many modern concepts were invented before the scientific revolution of the 1600s, but their significance was not widely understood. Galileo, Francis Bacon, Rene Descartes, and Isaac Newton developed the modern analytical thinking combining rationalism and empiricism. The newest idea is the system concept of the last century by Ludwig von Bertalanffy, Norbert Wiener, Kenneth E. Boulding, and many others since about 1950. Analytical thinking is about 400 years old, but systems thinking is about 75 years old.

6.1 Introduction

Isaac Asimov was a popularizer of science who explained scientific ideas historically, going as far back as possible to a time when the science in question was at its simplest stage (Asimov 1984). For him, facts, laws, and rules were unbearably dull without history. Furthermore, we need to know the history of the last 50–100 years to understand the present, see the trends, and forecast the future. Visions are generally developed only for the next ten years because of the rapid and often unpredictable changes (Albus and Meystel 2001; Schoemaker 2020). Further details on the history

A. Mämmelä, *Unifying Systems*, https://doi.org/10.1007/978-3-031-85012-7_6

of different disciplines can be found in the bibliography of the books in one of the appendices.

6.2 Beginning and End of the Research Process

The history of scientific societies, publishing, and information retrieval is presented in Tables 6.1 and 6.2.

6.2.1 Information Retrieval

Since the first scientific papers in 1665, the literature has expanded exponentially, and efficient methods to manage literature are needed. In the past, until about 1995, it took a lot of work to find information, especially about books that were and still are published by separate commercial publishers. Now, Internet browsers and online bookstores offer interdisciplinary information independently of publishers. Initially, we had to rely on abstract journals and separate card files of libraries that were clumsy to use. Later, information retrieval could be made using large general computerized databases since the 1970s and electronic libraries since the 1990s. Scientific societies offer the latter.

Table 6.1 History of scientific societies and publishing

Year	Discoverer	Discovery
1624	England	Patent law
1660	Royal Society	Scientific society
1665	Royal Society	Scientific journal
1752	Royal Society	Peer review
1785	Manchester Literary and Philosophical Society	Conference proceedings
1788	Linnean Society	First specialist society
1790	USA	Copyright law
1818	Institution of Civil Engineers	First engineering society
1822	GDNÄ	Nationwide umbrella society
1822	J. J. Berzelius	Review journal
1860	F. A. Kekule	International conference
1865	International Telegraph Union (ITU)	International standardization organization
1876	L. Pasteur	Methods section in papers
1931	International Council of Scientific Unions (ICSU)	First international umbrella organization

Table 6.2 History of major sources for information retrieval

Year	Discoverer	Discovery
1714	C. G. Hoffman	Abstract journal
1768	C. Macfarquhar et al.	Encyclopedia Britannica
1828	N. Webster, Jr.	An American Dictionary of the English Language
1860	H. J. Labatt	Citation index
1884	Oxford University Press	The Oxford English Dictionary
1884	J. B. Johnson	Engineering Index
1898	IEE and Physical Society of London	Science Abstracts (now Inspec)
1938	IEC	International Electrotechnical Vocabulary
1946	NTIS	Government Reports Announcements and Index
1964	E. Garfield	Science Citation Index (now Web of Science)
1971	M. S. Hart	Digital library of books
1972	IEEE	IEEE Standard Dictionary of Electrical and Electronics Terms
1973	IEEE	Index to IEEE Publications
1984	ISO	International Vocabulary of Metrology (VIM)
1994	National Academies Press	Scientific open access book
1995	Elsevier	Engineering Village
1995	W. G. Bowen	Journal Storage (JSTOR)
1996	IEEE and IEE	IEEE/IEE Electronic Library (now IEEE Xplore)
1996	B. Kahle	Internet Archive
1996	A. Varki	Scientific open access journal
1996	AMS	MathSciNet
1997	ACM	ACM Digital Library
1999	E. Weinstein	Wolfram MathWorld
1998	M. K. Molloy	Acronym Finder
2001	D. R. Harper	Online Etymology Dictionary
2001	J. Wales and L. Sanger	Wikipedia
2002	E. Weinstein	Wolfram ScienceWorld
2004	Elsevier	Scopus
2004	Google	Google Scholar
2004	Google	Google Books
2006	A. Swartz	Open Library
2006	E. M. Izhikevich	Scholarpedia
2009	Wolfram	Wolfram Alpha
2009	Many discoverers	Discovery tool

(continued)

Table 6.2 (continued)

Year	Discoverer	Discovery
2010	Google	Google Books Ngram Viewer
2010	ISO/IEC/IEEE	Software and Systems Engineering Vocabulary

The general databases and electronic libraries are commercial products, and they originally included few books and there were no citations. Google Scholar (2004) made a significant change for interdisciplinary and transdisciplinary systems thinking since the searches were free of charge. Open-access publishing is becoming more popular. An important change was the publication of general books on systems thinking such as Ramage and Shipp (2020). Another difficulty is that systems thinking, as interdisciplinary and transdisciplinary thinking, is challenging and requires a lot of experience. Often, systems thinkers are experienced researchers, many of whom have already retired. In general, engineering education is an excellent background to systems thinking since, for example, the essential concept of feedback is not commonly included in other curricula such as social sciences (Richardson 1991). Systems biology has appeared since about 2000 and is proceeding in the right direction (Westerhoff et al. 2009; Alon 2020).

Publishers Initially, the scientific societies were local, and the scientists had society meetings where some important correspondence was read aloud (Mason 1962). Some short-living scientific societies, such as Academia Secretorum Naturae (Naples, Italy, 1560–1578) and Academia dei Lincei (Rome, Italy, 1601–1651), existed. Francis Bacon suggested a National Academy in his *New Atlantis* (1626). John Wilkins was the leading spirit in the philosophical college in London (1644), also called the invisible college, which had ten members whose names are known. Robert Boyle joined the group in 1646. Its successor, the Royal Society of London for Improving Natural Knowledge, was one of the first scientific societies, founded on November 28, 1660. Wilkins was the first chairman of the Royal Society. Two years later, King Charles II sealed the charter. The first president was William Brouncker, and Wilkins was one of the two secretaries. The Royal Society published *Philosophical Transactions*, one of the first scientific journals (1665) and still existing. Similar societies were also founded elsewhere, including the Paris Academy of Sciences (1666), the Berlin Academy (1700), and the American Philosophical Society (1743). Societies such as the Lunar Society (1766) collected scientists in industrial regions, but the first engineering society was the Institution of Civil Engineers (1818).

The authors and readership became more specialized (Harmon 1992). Linnaean Society (1788) was one of the first specialist societies devoted to natural history that we would now call biology, a term used since 1819 (Online Etymology Dictionary 2024). In 1831, William Whewell proposed that a new society should limit membership to experts who published scientific papers. Admission to the Royal Society was limited to scientists in 1847. The foundation of the Society of German Natural Scientists and Physicians (Gesellschaft Deutsches Naturforscher und Ärzte (GDNÄ) in German) (1822) started nationwide umbrella societies (Mason 1962). It organized its first national meeting in Leipzig and acted as a model for other countries. Similar societies were later founded in the UK, Italy, the USA, and France. For example, the American Association for the Advancement of Science (AAAS) was founded in 1848. Verband der Elektrotechnik, Elektronik und Informationstechnik (VDE) is now one of the most significant European technical-scientific associations, founded in 1893. The International Science Council (ISC) is an international umbrella organization founded in 1931 using the name the International Council of Scientific Unions (ICSU).

Manchester Literary and Philosophical Society started the tradition of recording conferences and, four years later, in 1785, started publishing the conference papers (Mason 1962, p. 286). We now call these records conference proceedings. Lorenz Oken recommended in 1823 a lively and impromptu delivery instead of reading the paper out loud, but this rule was not initially followed. One researcher gave his talk in Latin as late as 1832. August Kekule organized the first international conference in 1860 in chemistry (Asimov 1994).

The first electronic scientific journals were published in the 1980s (Harmon 1992). They offer more flexibility regarding the length and content of papers. The National Academies Press started to publish open-access books in 1994, and Ajit Varki published the first scientific open-access journal in 1996. We expect hypertext versions of papers and books will become more common.

Abstract and citation journals and databases Abstracts have been used since ancient times (Witty 1973; Skolnik 1979). They were much later collected in abstract journals. Initially, they were published in printed form only. The first abstract journals were published in 1670, after the first archive journals (Kronick 1976, p. 152). One influential abstract journal was C. G. Hoffman's *Aufrichtige* in 1714–1717; another was L. F. F. von Crell's *Chemisches journal* 1778–1781 (Houghton 1975, p. 82). Such journals became common during the next century (Harmon 1992). The most influential was *Pharmaceutisches central-platt*, published by the Berlin Academy 1830–1849 and edited by G. T. Fecher, acting as a model for the subsequent abstracting services (Houghton 1975, p. 82). In science and engineering, the significant abstract journals (in fact, books) were *Engineering Index (EI)* (1884) and *Science Abstracts* (1898), which was later called *Inspec* (1967). J. B. Johnson founded the EI, and the IEE and the Physical Society of London founded *Science Abstracts*. The *National Technical Information Service (NTIS)* was initially called the Publication Board (Bolin 1999). In 1946, it published US-sponsored research in *Government Reports Announcements and Index*, first under various other names. In their last issue of the year, many IEEE journals published an author and subject index annually. Later, they published cumulative indices over many years, often starting from the journal's beginning. IEEE published its *Index to IEEE Publications* (1973) as a printed book. It was later replaced by the IEEE/IEE Electronic Library (IEL) (1996), the IEL Online (1998), and the IEEE Xplore (2000).

Abstract journals were published as books and included bibliographic data. Author and subject indexes were also provided, referring to the numbered abstracts that were published separately using a certain classification according to the subject. Paper copies had to be ordered as inter-library loans unless the papers were not available in print in the local library.

Information retrieval closely followed the development of electronics, computers, and communications (Neufeld and Cornog 1986). The digital computer was invented in 1946. Databases were developed from numerical to bibliographical and full-text databases. A significant bottleneck was the storage that developed from Herman Hollerith's punched cards (1890) and its predecessors to magnetic tapes (1965) and finally to disc storage systems (1970). In the beginning, the search used batch processing that was replaced by random access processing with the disc storage systems, and there was no longer any need to locate information by reading the entire tape. In about 1970, everything became computerized after the digital computer and appropriate memories had been developed.

The references link the papers to some older papers but can also be used as citations to find links to new papers, the idea behind citation indices. Henry J. Labatt's *A Table of Cases in California as Affirmed, Overruled, Modified, Commented upon, or Altered by Statutory Enactment* in 1860 is the first true citation index. Still, similar attempts have been made since 1743 in legal literature (Shapiro 1992). Eugene Garfield from the Institute for Scientific Information (ISI) started the *Science Citation Index* in 1964 after developing the concept of *the journal impact factor* (1955) (Burnham 2006; Garfield 2006, 2007). Later, the database covered human sciences. It was available in electronic form in 1974 and online in 2000. The name was changed to *ISI Web of Knowledge* and later to *Web of Science (WoS)*, which Clarivate Analytics now produces. It is one of the largest citation databases. *Journal Citation Reports (JCR)* started in 1975. Since 2011, WoS has included a *Book Citation Index*.

Engineering Index was distributed on magnetic tapes since 1967, and *Inspec* followed two years later. The name *Compendex* came into use in 1969. Elsevier created the web-based *Engineering Village* in 1995, including *Inspec* (initial coverage since 1969), *Compendex* (initial coverage since 1970), *NTIS*, and many more. The EI Backfile inside the Engineering Village covers papers starting from 1884. The Inspec Archive covers documents from 1898. Citations in the Engineering Village are from Scopus.

González-Pereira et al. developed SCImago Journal Rank (SJR) index used in Scopus. Scopus started operating in 2004 as a direct competitor of *WoS*, but initially, abstracts of the citations were limitedly available (Burnham 2006). Links to the full texts are available in the corresponding digital libraries both in WoS and Scopus. In 2024, Scopus AI merged generative AI with the Scopus database.

IEEE Xplore was initially 1996 called *IEEE/IEE Electronic Library (IEL)* and was first distributed on CD-ROMs. Two years later, an online version was available, and in 2000, the name of the database was changed to *IEEE Xplore*. The original coverage was from 1988. The database now covers AIEE papers since 1884, IRE papers since 1913 (IRE was founded one year earlier), and IEEE papers since 1963. The database also includes IEEE standards and documents from some other publishers. IEEE Xplore now includes citations, but citations from old papers may be missing. Many different scientific societies now have a digital library. For example, *ACM Digital Library* started in 1997.

The oldest digital library of books is *Project Gutenberg* (1971), founded by Michael S. Hart. William G. Powen launched *JSTOR* as a library of journal papers in 1995, covering later documents since 1665. *JSTOR* now also includes books. Brewster Kahle founded the Internet Archive in 1996. *Open Library*, as a library of books, started in 2006. The originators were Aaron Swartz and others. A particular database for mathematical literature is MathSciNet, founded in 1996. It is based on *Mathematical Reviews* published since 1940 by the American Mathematical Society (AMS). *Mathematical Reviews* is a journal that includes brief synopses of papers in mathematics.

Google Search, better known as simply Google, started as a search engine in 1998 using the PageRank algorithm developed by Larry Page and Sergey Brin. One of Google's competitors is Bing, launched in 2009 and based on some earlier similar tools. New Google services were Google Scholar and Google Books in 2004, and Google Books Ngram Viewer in 2010. More recently, discovery tools such as Summon (2009), Primo (2010), and EDS (2010) started their operation (Goodsett 2014).

Derek J. de Solla Price (1961) was one of the founders of the field of *scientometry* (Matricciani 1991; Fernandez-Cano et al. 2004). He noticed that the scientific literature, in terms of the number of scientific papers, has been growing exponentially since the 1600s. The number of researchers is a small fraction of the world population, and the number of publications per researcher per year is limited. A fundamental question is, therefore, how long the number of researchers can increase exponentially.

Price says that the doubling time for "very high quality" work is about 20 years (Fernandez-Cano et al. 2004). Still, Nicholas Rescher (1978) believed that although the total number of papers is growing exponentially, the number of essential outcomes grows only linearly (Wagner-Döbler 2001). This implies that if the resources grow exponentially, productivity grows only logarithmically. Scientific progress will decelerate if exponential investment reaches its limits of growth. The deceleration is assumed to have happened during the second half of the last century. Emilio Matricciani noticed that the age of references in all fields may be modeled according to a lognormal probability density function (Matricciani 1991).

Copyright Copyright law was developed first in the USA (1790), after which other countries followed, and the need for an international code began (Encyclopedia Britannica 2024). Copyright is granted automatically without any formal registrations. There are two important international conventions protecting copyright. According to the Berne Convention (1886), all contracting countries shall provide automatic protection for works first published in other countries. The minimum level of protection was the author's lifetime plus 50 years. In some countries, the minimum copyright period is now the author's lifetime plus 70 years. The Universal Copyright Convention (1952) in Geneva defined "national treatment" as each country treating the works from other countries as it would those of its citizens.

The details of the copyright law depend on the country. The U.S. copyright law has a separate rule for anonymous and pseudonymous works and for works whose authors worked for hire in those cases. After the copyright has expired, the work is in the *public domain* as a work free for all to use, but the origin must be acknowledged.

Suppose a work cannot be interpreted as an "original work of authorship," such as catalogs, tables, databases, programs, and photographs. In that case, it may still have a *related right* whose protection period is usually shorter than that of the copyright. Trademarks can last indefinitely but must be continually renewed depending on the trademark law.

Patents The word patent is an abbreviation of Anglo-French *lettre patent*, "open letter," and Latin *patentem*, "open," since the patent is open to everyone (Online Etymology Dictionary 2024). The patent must be useful and advance significantly the state of the art. The patent may be sold to others, and others can be authorized by a license to use the patent, and the owner can receive royalties.

The first recorded patent was granted in Florence (1421), and the idea moved to other countries, most notably England, Germany, France, and the United States. The first lasting patent law was accepted in England (1624), and a patent was defined as a privilege, not a right of the inventor. The patent law was accepted in the USA in 1790, using the English patent law as a model. Inventors must apply for patents in every country in which they wish for patent protection.

The patent system was harmonized in 1883 by the *Paris Convention for the Protection of Industrial Property*, which is still valid, and each country must follow the Paris Convention as a member of the Patent Cooperation Treaty (PCT). It is managed by the World Intellectual Property Organization (WIPO). The inventors who filed a patent application in one country received the first filing date for application in other member countries. It is cheaper to get geographically extensive patent protection in this way. More recently, the PCT simplified the filing of patent applications. The PCT does not grant any patents but is responsible for the patentability research.

The European Patent Office (EPO) was created in 1977. Patent applications are submitted to the EPO. Within it, we have had a Unitary Patent (UP) system and a Unified Patent Court (UPC) since 2023. Each patent granted by the EPO must be validated in all European Patent Convention (EPC) member countries. The litigation is also done in the member countries. In the future, all patents should be unitary patents. The EPC system follows EU legislation.

The International Patent Classification (IPC) system was approved in 1968 to serve reviewers examining patent applications. The 1995 Agreement on Trade-Related Aspects of Intellectual Property Rights (TRIPS) specified that in all member countries of the World Trade Organization (WTO), the minimum patent term should be 20 years from the filing date. In general, the term cannot be extended. An annual maintenance fee must be paid; otherwise, the patent expires.

Standards In standardization, we can see a general trend toward international unification and specialization (Kearsey and Jones 1985). The ITU was founded in 1865 with the name International Telegraph Union. This organization is much older than other global organizations and has established working methods. It is now a specialized agency of the United Nations (UN). The International Electrotechnical Commission (IEC) was founded in 1906 to formulate electrical and electronics engineering standards. In 1938, the IEC started to publish the International Electrotechnical Vocabulary (IEV). Its one-line version is now called the Electropedia or IEV Online. The ISO is the IEC's sister organization, founded in 1947. It covers almost all fields except those covered by the ITU and the IEC. In addition to these international organizations, there are many regional organizations in specific areas. Within the EU, only standards developed by the European Committee for Standardization (CEN), the European Committee for Electrotechnical Standardization (CENELEC), and the European Telecommunications Standards Institute (ETSI) are recognized as European Standards (ENs).

The ISO published in 1984 the first *International vocabulary of basic and general terms in metrology* (VIM). The Joint Committee for Guides in Metrology (JCGM) was formed in 1997 and continued to publish *the International vocabulary of metrology: Basic and general concepts and associated terms* (VIM) (JCGM 2012). In addition, it is publishing *Evaluation of measurement data: Guide to the expression of uncertainty in measurement* (GUM). JCGM works below ISO and has representatives from various organizations, including the International Bureau of Weights and Measures (BIPM), ISO, and IEC.

The IEEE started in 1972 to publish the *IEEE Standard Dictionary of Electrical and Electronics Terms*. Its seventh edition, *IEEE 100: The Authoritative Dictionary of IEEE Standards Terms*, was published in 2000 and is available in the IEEE Xplore. It is a collection of almost 35,000 terms. *IEEE Standards Dictionary* is a collection of words defined in IEEE standards and also available within the IEEE Xplore. The ISO, IEC, and IEEE have published since 2010 the SE VOCAB. The different definitions are not always unified in different standards. There is a need to do this unification for systems thinking across all disciplines. Often, different disciplines use their terminology with some more profound meaning. For example, in biology, we have the term "morphogenesis," which corresponds to the technical term "self-organization," but in a much more complex form.

6.2.2 Publishing of New Knowledge

The history of scientific papers is summarized in Houghton (1975), Kronick (1976) and Harmon (1992). Scientific writing started after the first scientific societies were founded. Books were written by hand already before the paper (105 CE) and printing press (1454) were invented (Asimov 1994). Thus, initially, all published material was in books. Galileo's *Two New Sciences* (1638) was the first modern scientific textbook.

Encyclopedias were published in antiquity since Pliny the Elder, also called Gaius Plinius Secundus (77 CE), whose 37-volume work was *Naturalis Historia* (*Natural History*) (Encyclopedia Britannica 2024). It was the first scientific encyclopedia, but the author did not distinguish speculation, opinion, and fact. It was, for centuries, the primary source of scientific information. The first modern encyclopedia was Denis

Diderot's *Encyclopédie* (1751–1772). The encyclopedia started an encyclopedist movement, but the existing knowledge expanded exponentially.

Encyclopedia Britannica started in 1768. It was initially published by private publishers C. Macfarquhar, A. Bell, and A. Constable in Edinburgh, UK. The last 32-volume printed book was published in 2010, after which only the online version has been updated. In his book *World Brain*, Herbert G. Wells (1938) proposed a world encyclopedia as a universal information source. He wrote: "It is no doubt true that literature is a kind of overmind of the race" (Stonier 1992, 1997). Tom Stonier used the terms global brain, global intelligence, and collective intelligence, forming a hyper brain based on a worldwide network. Jimmy Wales and Larry Sanger founded Wikipedia in 2001. Eugene M. Izhikevich conceived Scholarpedia in 2005. Michael K. Molloy compiled the Acronym Finder in 1998 and Douglas R. Harper the Online Etymology Dictionary (2024) in 2001.

Noah Webster originally published his dictionary in 1828. George and Charles Merriam received the publishing rights after Noah Webster died in 1843. The company and the dictionary have been called Merriam-Webster since 1982. The *Oxford English Dictionary* began to be published in 1884. The *Oxford Advanced Learner's Dictionary* was first published in 1948.

Scientific papers have existed since 1665 when the first scientific journals were published, including the *Le Journal des sçavans* in France and the *Philosophical Transactions of the Royal Society* in the UK (Skolnik 1979). Literature formed a hierarchy that includes books and review papers above original papers. Books are often extended review papers; thus, the concept has been there for a long time. The first review journal was J. Jacob Berzelius' (1779–1848) *Jahresbericht ueber die Forschritte der physischen Wissenschaften* in 1822 with an emphasis on chemistry. He is known as the last person to know all chemistry. In the IEEE literature, *Proceedings of the IEEE* (formerly *Proceedings of the IRE*) started to publish review papers in 1913 (Brittain 1996).

IMRDC structure Initially, people did not standardize the structure of papers. They were either learned letters or experimental reports that were descriptive and usually proceeded chronologically (Day 1989; Sollaci and Pereira 2004).

The topical IMRDC structure (originally IMRAD) is widely used in papers to facilitate modular reading (Gastel and Day 2016). The order of the sections may differ. For example, the methods section may be at the end of the paper. The structure has a long history (Day 1989; Harmon 1989; Sollaci and Pereira 2004). Christiaan Huygens (1690) was the first to explicitly define the *hypothetico-deductive method* to verify the hypothesis (Nola and Sankey 2007, p. 170; Encyclopedia Britannica 2024). Louis Pasteur (1876) developed the methods section to the present form and used the whole IMRAD structure, although it had different titles in his book *Etudes sur la Biere* (Day 1989). The method section was vital for him to falsify the assumed spontaneous generation of life, which had fanatic proponents. He described his experiments in such detail that any reasonable person could reproduce them. The IMRAD structure was described in the style books *The Writing of Medical Papers* by Maud H. Mellish-Wilson in 1922 and *Preparation of Scientific and Technical Papers* by Sam F. Trelease and Emma S. Yule in 1927 (Sollaci and Pereira 2004; Harmon 1989, 1992), but not yet used by all authors.

Peter B. Medawar claimed in 1964 that the IMRAD structure was fraudulent and did not present the discovery process (Meadows 1985; Harmon 1989; Wu 2011). Everything is made easy, simple, and inevitable. He proposed that discussion should be placed at the beginning, followed by results and methods. Present thinking is that the presentation should not describe the discovery process, only the essential part of the creative process. Franz J. Ingelfinger criticized in 1967 the inflexibility of the formula, which he called "IMRAD" for the first time (E. J. H. 1967; de Haen 1968; Soffer and Weinberg 1975). Some authors saw that the redundancy involved in the structure made papers longer than they would be otherwise.

The IMRAD structure was used extensively in physics only in the 1950s (Sollaci and Pereira 2004). ANSI published in 1972 and updated in 1979 the "American national standard for the preparation of scientific papers for written and oral presentation" (ANSI 1979). After this, the IMRDC structure was spread to all sciences. The Institute of Radio Engineers (IRE), later merged with the IEEE, recommended a structure for the abstract, introduction, and conclusion in 1960 (IRE 1960), including 13 moves. Later, many authors (Skelton 1994; Nwogu 1997; Hartley 1999; Schulz et al. 2010) proposed the idea of such a generally structured paper.

For mathematical papers, there is no standard structure (Harmon 1992). Still, the organization usually includes the introduction, including the problem, definitions, assumptions, theorem or conceptual framework derived from the assumptions, proof of the theorem using deductive logic, and conclusion, including recommendations on future work. For details, see Higham (1998) and Krantz (2017). A document preparation system for mathematical texts called LaTeX is based on the TeX typesetting program by Donald E. Knuth (1978) and was developed further by Leslie Lamport (1984).

Abstract The word abstract comes from the Latin *abstractus*, "drawn away" (Online Etymology Dictionary 2024). The first journals published abstracts of new developments and annotations of books.

Gordon S. Fulcher developed modern scientific abstracting in his paper "Preparation of abstracts" in 1920 "to enable a reader to tell at a glance what the article is about." Still, the abstracts became common only in the 1950s (Harmon 1989). A recent development is the structured abstract, which sometimes includes subtitles. An ANSI standard Z39.14-1971, "Guidelines for abstracts" (ANSI/NISO 2010), described the contents of an abstract. The standard was updated in 1979 and 1997 and reaffirmed in 2010 (ANSI 1977; ANSI/NISO 2010). The abstract should contain five moves, including purpose, methodology, results, conclusions, collateral, and other information, thus including the idea of IMRDC structure. The ISO standard "International standard on abstracts for publications and documentation" (ISO 214-1976) was a revision of ISO Recommendation R 214-1961 but was based mainly on ANSI Z39.14-1971.

Figures and tables Tables were used at the beginning of the 1600s, but data plots became common after Johann H. Lambert and William Playfair reinvented them by

1786 (Harmon 1989). Until that time, drawings were used. The Cartesian coordinate system had been invented independently many times earlier by Nicole Oresme (1325–1382), by Rene Descartes in 1637, and by Pierre de Fermat at about the same time in the 1630s (Mason 1962; Lapaine 2017). By the early twentieth century, the results section has centered on the figures and tables. A good piece of advice is: "Structure your story around the graphs and enable the captions to capture the key points of your paper" (Wu 2011).

References References have been used from the beginning, but their regular use started in the middle of the nineteenth century (Harmon 1989, 1992). In the beginning, the references were in the text or as footnotes. Two common citation styles exist. *Harvard style* was developed by Edward L. Mark of Harvard University in 1881 using an author-date format (Chernin 1988). The style is used in human sciences. The *Vancouver style* is an author-number system. The references in the text are identified as numbers in parentheses, brackets, or superscripts referring to footnotes or endnotes. The style is used in physical sciences and engineering. The style was defined in Vancouver, Canada (1978), but it has been known for over a century.

The information in the list of references was standardized in the early twentieth century. A major style guide in engineering is *The Chicago Manual of Style*, initially published by the Chicago University Press in 1906. The *AIP Style Manual* by the American Institute of Physics, first published in 1951, refers to the Chicago style. The IEEE style is also based on the Chicago style (IEEE 2012). The IEEE style was published in 1965 (IEEE Spectrum 1965, 1966). The instructions were partially based on the earlier instructions of the IRE published in 1954 and updated in 1960, but the style was slightly changed (Proceedings of the IRE 1954, 1960). The AIEE style was different. Later, the instructions became more extensive, as summarized in IEEE (2012), citing various other IEEE instructions.

Peer-review process Few journals and proceedings had in the beginning a peer-review process (Harmon 1992; Spier 2002). The review was the responsibility of the editor. Peer review started in 1675, but it took a long time before it became a common practice. Finally, peers from the scientific community were used. John Hill criticized the Royal Society for publishing trivial papers; the following year, a committee was selected for the review process (1752). This year is usually regarded as the start of the peer review process, but the Royal Society of Edinburgh had already used the peer review process in 1731. The reviewers have been anonymous to the authors since the 1750s. One reason for the late start of the peer review was technology's immaturity. The typewriter became available in the 1890s and the Xerox photocopier in 1959. For example, *Science* started to use external reviewers in the 1940s. In physics, peer review became common in the 1950s (Sollaci and Pereira 2004).

In 1936, Albert Einstein refused to accept peer review. He wrote to the editor (Kennefick 2005): "We (Mr. Rosen and I) had sent you our manuscript for publication and had not authorized you to show it to specialists before it is printed. I see no reason to address the—in any case erroneous—comments of your anonymous expert. On the basis of this incident I prefer to publish the paper elsewhere." Recently, some journals have started to use a double-anonymized review process. The process means that also the reviewers do not know the identity of the authors.

6.3 Analytical Thinking

Human culture was initially developed slowly by new transportation and communication methods. The greatest innovations in transportation included the wheel, ship, train, car, and aircraft. In communication, the innovations included writing, the alphabet, paper, the printing press, the postal service, the telegraph, the telephone, radio, television, the copy machine, and the Internet.

6.3.1 Development of Scientific Thought

The principles of science are now included in general texts on the philosophy of science such as Rosenberg and McIntyre (2020). Its history is summarized in Losee (2001). There are also chronologies of science (Asimov 1994; Carlisle 2004) and biographies of scientists (Asimov 1982; Simmons 1996). Scholasticism, Renaissance, and Enlightenment were necessary to develop European scientific thought. *Scholasticism* was a philosophical movement from the ninth until the seventeenth century, forming the basis for the modern understanding of rational knowledge and the thesis-antithesis-synthesis argumentation on which the Western world is built. The opposition is a valuable part of the whole. Later, the Renaissance and the Enlightenment formed the basis for modern liberal democracies and their human rights. The *Renaissance* (1400–1530) started the interest in ancient Greece. It was a movement in Europe between medieval and modern times marked by a humanistic revival of classical influence by the beginnings of modern science (Merriam-Webster 2024).

The *Enlightenment* (1715–1800) was another critical step in developing European scientific thought in addition to scholasticism and Renaissance and is still vital. It was a philosophical movement of the eighteenth century that emphasized rationalism (Merriam-Webster 2024). The critical ideas of Enlightenment are reason, science, humanism, and progress, thus strengthening the citizens (Pinker 2018). The rule of law exists only when even the rulers feel bound by the law (Fukuyama 2011). The *law* is "a body of abstract rules of justice that bind a community together."

The word science comes from the Latin *scientia*, "knowledge" (Online Etymology Dictionary 2024). Science was initially called natural philosophy until about 1737 (Gribbin 2003, p. 286). The change is a sign that all science was philosophy from which the modern disciplines separated. The term "research" resembles the term "discovery" in its meaning, but research also covers inventions (Bernstein 1999). The word research comes from the old French *recercher* "seek out, search closely" (Online Etymology Dictionary 2024). *Theory* is "an intelligible explanation based on observation and reasoning." A model is a "likeness made to scale." The word technology is from the Greek word *tekhnologia*, "systematic treatment of an art, craft, or technique." The word engineer comes from the Latin *ingenium*, which means "inborn qualities, talent."

The word nomological comes from the Greek word *nomos*, "law" and *logos*, "reason" (Online Etymology Dictionary 2024). The word nomothetic is derived from the Greek word *nomothetes*, "lawgiver," and the word idiographic is from *idios*, "personal, private," and *graphein*, "to write, to draw." The word paradigm comes from the Greek *paradeigma* "pattern, model."

The word analysis comes from the Greek word *analyein*, "unloose, resolution of anything complex into simple elements," and the word synthesis from *syntithenai*, "put together, combine, composition, a combination of parts into a whole" (Online Etymology Dictionary 2024). The word deduction comes from the Latin word *deducere*, "lead down, derive," the phrase induction from *inducere*, "lead into," and the word reduction from *reducere*, "to bring back, reversion to a simpler form." The word abduction comes from the Latin *abducere*, "to lead away, take away, arrest" (often by force). The word intelligence comes from the Latin *inter* "between" and *legere* "choose, pick out, read" (Online Etymology Dictionary 2024). An intelligent person can thus "read between the lines."

6.3.2 Science in the Antiquity and Middle Ages

There was little science before the Greeks since no generalizations were used. Mathematics was developed in ancient Babylon and Egypt (Boyer and Merzbach 1991). At that time, no theory was used, but a large number of numerical examples were used. The emphasis was on computation ("practice"), possibly with numerical tables. In the Greek tradition, the emphasis was on "theory."

The first Egyptian scholar known by name was Imhotep, who lived near Memphis, Egypt, around 2980–2950 BCE (Asimov 1982). He was the architect of one of the earliest pyramids, called "step pyramids," near Memphis.

Many modern ideas were invented in antiquity, but often in a rudimentary form, and they were not commonly accepted; for example, feedback, see Table 6.3. The first proper researcher, known by name, was Thales of Miletus (c. 600 BCE), who was listed as the first of the seven wise men in Greece. He noticed some regularity in nature: it is not entirely capricious (Asimov 1982, 1994; Checkland 1999, pp. 3, 25). He visited Egypt and probably Babylon in Mesopotamia, where some of his knowledge came from. He predicted the eclipse of the Sun that happened on May 28, 585 BCE. The eclipse is the first historical event whose time is known precisely. He measured the height of a pyramid using the length of its shadow and the concept of trigonometry; he knew that the moon reflected sunlight. He was able to think of imaginary lines with zero thickness.

Table 6.3 Science in the antiquity and Middle Ages

Year	Discoverer	Discovery
c. 600 BCE	Thales	Scientific inquiry, deduction
550	Anaximander	Universal laws, evolutionary theory
500	Pythagoras	Spherical Earth
450	Leucippus	Causality
450	Leucippus and Democritos	Atom theory
400	Horodotus	Method of hypothesis
400	Socrates	Dialectic method
350	Plato	Political structures
350	Aristotle	Study of logic
300	Euclid	Axiomatic system
270	Ktesibios	Feedback in water clock
260	Aristarchos	Heliocentric world view
50 CE	Hero	Steam power
140	Ptolemy	Geocentric universe using epicycles
1021	Alhazen	Analytical and experimental method
1247	R. Bacon	Observation and experiments
1327	W. of Ockham	Ockham's razor

Thales was the first to use deductive arguments. His student was Anaximander of Miletus (c. 550 BCE), who started to look for universal principles and had an evolutionary view. Leucippus (c. 500 BCE) discovered atomism and causality. Herodotus (c. 450 BCE), the father of history, used the method of hypothesis (Losee 2001).

Socrates developed the dialectic method, a commonly used tool in a wide range of discussions, now called the Socratic method, which finally led to John Dewey's (1910) reflections. Socrates also contributed to the field of ethics, epistemology, and logic. His ideas survived through the writings of his students, especially those of Plato. Socrates died a martyr's death, as described in de Botton (2000). He was convinced that he was innocent of the claims to be responsible for the loss in a war, but he had to drink a poisoned chalice.

Plato was the founder of the Academy in Athens (c. 387 BCE). It was the first institution of higher learning in the Western world. He discovered the foundations of natural philosophy and rationalism. In rationalism, "reason alone is a source of knowledge and is independent of experience" (Random House Webster's College Dictionary 1999). Empiricism is a complement and opposite of rationalism, where the "sensory experience is the primary source of knowledge and justification for the truth of propositions" (Barbour 1997). Rationalism and empiricism together form the modern scientific method.

Plato realized that we observe only a shadow of reality with our senses. His allegory of the cave related to this idea is famous (Ryan 2012, p. 66): humans are sitting confined in a dark cave, seeing only flickering shadows cast by people walking behind them, and the shadows are taken for reality. Plato's student Aristotle used induction and deduction, the axiomatic system, and classification. He defined four causes, including the efficient, final, material, and formal causes. He developed the Aristotelian geocentric worldview. Aristotle's main work was *Organon* ("instrument"), written in the 300s BCE. Euclid (c. 300 BCE) discovered axiomatic systems and deductive mathematics for his geometry. The axiomatic system was one of the greatest inventions in ancient Greece.

The Greeks invented abstraction or idealization and generalization (Asimov 1987). Euclidean geometry was based on five axioms (Poundstone 1988, p. 9). It integrated the ancient knowledge of mathematics. The nonessentials are stripped off in *abstraction*, also called idealization or undermodeling. In *generalization*, general solutions for classes of problems are derived. The Greeks committed two grave errors: (1) They considered deduction as the only respectable means to attain knowledge, and observations and experiments were undervalued, and (2) They thought axioms were "absolute truths" and other branches of knowledge could be developed from similar "absolute truths." The errors, encouraged by the success in geometry, eventually led to a dead end. We now think that the truth is unattainable but can be approached asymptotically. A similar dead-end happened in mathematics until Kurt Gödel (1931) discovered his incompleteness theorem (Kline 1995, p. 227). Plato's Academy was closed in 529, and the scholars dispersed (Boyer and Merzbach 1991). Some philosophers moved to Persia. The Romans were more interested in practical knowledge to create great architecture and technology.

The use of models has a long history, especially in astronomy. Aristotle (c. 300 BCE) assumed a geocentric model where the orbits of the Sun and the planets were circles since such a trajectory was believed to be perfect. Ptolemy (c. 140 CE) insisted that the orbits must consist of circles and explained the observed retrograde motions using 80 epicycles, each having its radius and velocity. This model resembles a Fourier series (Acosta et al. 2020).

After the Greek culture declined, Arabic culture flourished, and the Arabs translated many Greek books into their language. Many of them are known only as Arabic translations. Baghdad was founded in 762, and at the beginning of the 800s, a famous library called the House of Wisdom was built. It existed until Baghdad was destroyed by Mongols in 1258. Hasan Ibn al-Haytham, better known as Alhazen, was the most influential physicist in the Middle Ages (Gorini 2003). He developed analytical and experimental methods in his *Book of Optics* in 1011–1021, well before Galileo. Alhazen invented the modern scientific method, which became commonly used in the 1600s. Hippocrates (c. 400 BCE) in Greece had earlier similar ideas, including rationalism and careful observation (Asimov 1982).

Arabic culture declined in the 1400s. Fortunately, Europe was again open to scientific knowledge. The first modern university was founded in Bologna in 1088 (Perkin 2006). The Europeans translated the results of the Greek and Arabic cultures from Arabic to Latin.

The English philosopher Robert Grosseteste (c. 1200) recommended the use of competing hypotheses (Losee 2001, p. 59), which Aristotle had already employed.

He also systematically applied the method of falsification, which had been used since Euclid's time. Roger Bacon was Grosseteste's student. They were both influenced by Alhazen's work. Alhazen also had an important influence, for example, on Kepler, who corresponded with Galileo.

Roger Bacon used experiments to increase knowledge of phenomena. He also wrote a summary of existing scientific knowledge. William of Ockham (sometimes spelled as Occam) used *Ockham's razor*, also called the principle of parsimony or the principle of economy: we should select the simplest theory if several competing theories predict the observations. Simple theories are thought to be beautiful. However, there is no theoretical or experimental demonstration for the validity of Ockham's razor (Westerhoff et al. 2009). For example, control of biological organisms is not as simple as possible.

6.3.3 Scientific Method Since the Scientific Revolution

Christopher Columbus (1492) started the time of exploration using the idea that the world is a globe, see Table 6.4. Nicolaus Copernicus (1543) developed the heliocentric system and assumed that the orbits of planets around the Sun were still circles, but the number of epicycles was reduced. The original idea of the heliocentric system is from Aristarchus (260 BCE). Based on accurate observations of Tycho Brahe, Johann Kepler (1609, 1619) used an ellipse as a model of planetary motion. Now, no epicycles were needed, and the model was significantly simplified by moving the observer from the Earth to outside the solar system. Carl F. Gauss (1795) developed the least squares method and later predicted the location of the asteroid Ceres, which had been lost after some observations (Boyer and Merzbach 1991). The asteroid was found close to the place indicated by his calculations. Since then, models have been widely used in natural and social sciences (Bailer-Jones 2009). John Locke (1590) noticed the possibility of an endless loop of definitions; therefore, we need ostensive definitions (Honderich 2005).

Modern science started when researchers refused to respect ancient authorities. Francis Bacon (1620), William Whewell (1840), John Stuart Mill (1843), William Stanley Jevons (1874), Karl Pearson (1892), and E. Bright Wilson, Jr. (1952) published classical works on the scientific method (Wilson 1990). The modern research method based on the analytical thinking using experiments was developed in the 1600s by several people, including Galileo Galilei, Francis Bacon, Rene Descartes, and Isaac Newton (Arbnor and Bjerke 1997; Wilson 1998; Checkland 1999; Ramage and Shipp 2020), based on the earlier work by Nicolaus Copernicus and Johann Kepler. The discovery of the scientific method was the start of the scientific revolution. That century started scientific research at full speed; the first scientific societies and journals were founded, and exponential growth of knowledge started.

Galileo Galilei is usually considered the first modern scientist (Wilson 1998; Losee 2001). He started reductionism and combined experiments and analysis, used idealizations in analysis, and demonstrated the inadequacy of Aristotle's physics.

Table 6.4 Science leading to the scientific revolution

Year	Discoverer	Discovery
1100s	Europe	Scholasticism
1400s	Florence	Renaissance
1473	C. Copernicus	Heliocentric world view
1492	C. Columbus	Age of discovery
1576	T. Brahe	Astronomical observations
1609	J. Kepler	Laws of planetary motion
1620	F. Bacon	Experimental-inductive method
1637	R. Descartes	Axiomatization and reductionism
1638	Galileo	Scientific method
1687	I. Newton	Newtonian mechanics
1690	C. Huygens	Hypothetico-deductive method
1700s	France	Enlightenment
1739	D. Hume	Problem of induction
1750s	England	Industrial revolution
1765	J. Watt	Modern steam engine
1789	J. Bentham	Utilitarism
1830	A. Comte	Positivism
1843	J. P. Joule	Energy conservation law
1860	R. J. E. Clausius	Entropy law
1875	G. H. Lewes	Emergence
1878	C. S. Peirce	Abduction
1897	T. C. Chamberlin	Competing hypotheses
1910	J. Dewey	Reflective thinking

Galileo's work led to the breakthrough of the Copernican worldview. Galileo's final book and scientific testament was *Discourses and Mathematical Demonstrations Relating to Two New Sciences* (1638), published a few years before his death. The two new sciences were materials science and kinematics, i.e., the geometry of motion, a part of classical mechanics. Christoph Clavius suggested the plausibility requirement for science at the time of Galileo (Harre 1981).

Francis Bacon (1561–1626) was the first in 1620 to write thoroughly about the principles of modern research methods in his *Novum Organum* (*New Method*), emphasizing the experimental-inductive method. However, he only did a few experiments himself. The title of the book refers to Aristotles' *Organum.* Bacon started the modern philosophy of science. He rejected other Aristotle's causes except the efficient cause. He suggested a divorce between science and theology, which was later stated in the founding document of the Royal Society of London (1660): "We will not deal with matters of religion and personal preferences" (Kline 1995). Bacon aimed to publish a much larger book called *Instauratio Magna* (*The Great Instauration*) to summarize human scientific knowledge, but it was not finished.

Galileo used methodological reduction, but Rene Descartes rigorously described the reductive research method in his *Discourse on the Method* (1637) (Wilson 1998, p. 31; Checkland 1999, p. 46). He founded modern philosophy and supported rationalism, which is complementary to empiricism. He described reductionism using the words "to divide each of the difficulties that I was examining into as many parts as might be possible and necessary in order best to solve it." He also used a deductive hierarchy of propositions and hypotheses based on analogies. He was a mathematician, and thus, he was not very interested in verifying the results. Christiaan Huygens (1690) formulated in his *Treatise on Light* the hypothetico-deductive method for verification (Shapiro 1989; Nola and Sankey 2007; Encyclopedia Britannica 2024), thus complementing the experimental-inductive method. Still, already Robert Boyle (1662) and other serious experimentalists such as Robert Hooke (1665) and Isaac Newton (1687) described all aspects of experiments. They realized that a theory can be tested only by examining its consequences. In the hypothetico-deductive method, the crucial third part is unmentioned, where the outcomes are compared with the experiments or observations.

Isaac Newton derived Newtonian mechanics (1687) from only four axioms or laws. He combined analysis and synthesis in his method. He reduced Galileo's laws of terrestrial motion and Kepler's laws of planetary motion to Newtonian mechanics. He made a distinction between an axiomatic system (abstract) and its experimental application (concrete). His major work was *Philosophiae Naturalis Principia Mathematica* (1687), one of the greatest books in the history of physics.

The discussion on the research method continued for centuries. Finally, there was the famous debate between John Stuart Mill and William Whewell (Losee 2001, p. 136). Mill favored inductive arguments, but Whewell supported the free invention of hypotheses and coined the term hypothetico-deductive method to verify hypotheses. In contrast, earlier, it was called the method of hypothesis (Encyclopedia Britannica 2024) and was used in ancient times (Nola and Sankey 2007). Now, the hypothetico-deductive view is the standard view on research. Still, it does not tell anything about forming hypotheses, which is as essential as verification. The term experimental-inductive method has been used at least since the late 1800s. The terms inductive-experimental, empirical-inductive and inductive-empirical method are also common. David Hume (1748) was the first to realize the problem of induction. Charles S. Peirce (1878) developed the idea of abduction. Therefore, we have replaced the term experimental-inductive method with the more general term experimental-abductive method whose special case is experimental-inductive method. The term experimental-abductive reasoning has been used in the literature only recently.

David Hume (1739) discussed the problems of induction and causality. Since Newton's time, we have been limited to a single cause, which is Aristotle's efficient cause. However, causality in complex systems having nonlinear feedback loops is circular, and we must return to multicausality and emergence (Aaltonen 2007; Wang and Blei 2019).

William Whewell (1840) stressed the unity of science based on epistemological reduction. He analyzed the history of the scientific method, proposed new scientific terminology (for example scientist and physicist to replace natural philosopher, consilience for unification of knowledge, and O as the chemical notation for oxygen), and emphasized the discovery as the free invention of hypotheses. He published two books, *History of the Inductive Sciences, From the Earliest to the Present Time* (1837) and *The Philosophy of the Inductive Sciences, Founded Upon Their History* (1840). George Sarton was the founder of the discipline of the history of science, inspired by the work of Leonardo da Vinci (Garfield 1985). His goal was an integrated philosophy of science, "the new humanism," that connected the sciences and the humanities. His major book series was *Introduction to the History of Science* (1927–1948) in three volumes consisting of altogether five parts and 4296 pages, covering history until the fourteenth century and thus not including da Vinci.

At the turn of the eighteenth century, Johann Gottlieb Fichte developed the thesis-antithesis-synthesis dialectic, and Charles S. Peirce (1878) developed abduction. Thomas C. Chamberlin (1897) devised the method of multiple hypotheses, which was later promoted by Platt (1964) using the term strong inference (Platt 1964). Strong inference is a form of reflection. At the end of the 1800s, many disciplines found their present form, such as biology and psychology.

There have been competing views on the nature of scientific knowledge (Leon 1999). The modern scientific method combines rationalism and empiricism: knowledge is based on definitions, conceptual clarity, and rigor in arguments (i.e., rationalism), and knowledge is based on sensory experiments (i.e., empiricism). In rationalism, we emphasize coherence, and in empiricism, we rely on correspondence with reality. They are now seen as complementary views, equally important.

Auguste Comte (1830) developed *positivism*, and Karl Popper (1934) criticized it. Popper developed the falsification theory, anticipated by Aristotle and Robert Grosseteste (Losee 2001, p. 59), which led to the idea of the evolution of theories. Popper claimed to have solved the problem of induction using falsification. In this way, the plausibility of the theories can be improved but never proved. His main work was *Logic of Scientific Discovery* (in German in 1935). Pierre Duhem (1906) and Willard Quine (1951) discussed the role of auxiliary assumptions that may make even falsification impossible (Rosenberg and McIntyre 2020).

Thomas Kuhn (1962) presented a theory on the development of scientific theories in the progress of science in the form of revolutions described in his book *The Structure of Scientific Revolutions*. He also introduced the term *paradigm* to explain the present worldview of scientists, which they unconsciously defend, although it is perhaps eventually shown to be wrong. New paradigms led to scientific revolutions, such as those by Isaac Newton and Albert Einstein.

Lakatos (1970) defined the concept of *research programs* to combine and revise Popper's and Kuhn's views (Lakatos 1970; Losee 2001). In Popper's view, criticism must always exist, and commitment to a paradigm is a crime. In Kuhn's view, criticism of normal science is an anathema. According to him, the transition from criticism to commitment is where progress and normal science begin. In research programs, the two different positions are combined: we must accept the existence of paradigms.

Still, we must also be open to criticism, which does not happen even nowadays, but Kuhn's vision is mainly followed. Research programs must be based on well-founded visions.

Paul Feyerabend (1975) denied the possibility of finding any method for scientific research (Losee 2001). In his view, "anything goes," and creativity is demonstrated by the proliferation of theories. Thus, he claimed that there is no need for a philosophy of science apart from the practice and history of science.

We have now moved from a prescriptive to a descriptive philosophy of science because we think that scientists know better than philosophers how research is done, as the former conduct practical research. Philosophers' important contribution is in conceptual analysis.

Simulations became possible in 1946 with the electronic computer called the Electronic Numerical Integrator and Computer (ENIAC). However, the world's first working programmable, fully automatic digital computer was Konrad Zuse's Z-3, completed in 1941. It was an electromechanical computer. Modeling became popular in the 1950s after the computer was invented, and the idea of systems thinking started to gain interest. There has been a breakthrough in numerical methods using computer simulations and later big data to complement but not to replace mathematical analysis and prototypes. Chris Anderson claimed 2008 that big data was the end of scientific theories, but practical examples so far show that this is not the case (West 2017, pp. 439–448; Larson 2021).

Jim Gray summarized that there have been four paradigms in scientific research (West 2017, p. 443):

- Empirical observation before Galileo
- Theory-based models after Isaac Newton
- Computation and simulation after the invention of the digital computer, and
- Unification of theory, experiment, and simulation with added data gathering and analysis.

Geoffrey West believes the last paradigm is more like part of the third paradigm rather than a new one. Large language models (LLMs) in artificial intelligence support scientific work using big data since they can help find existing knowledge and revise authors' texts. Researchers always have full responsibility for the quality of the research results. New discoveries are now often the result of group work.

6.3.4 Development of Researcher Education

The first modern university is the University of Bologna, founded in 1088 and still active (Perkin 2006). The university system took its model from Plato's Academy, closed in 529. The academy was the name of the public garden outside ancient Athens where Plato taught his school from c. 387 BCE (Online Etymology Dictionary 2024). The word university comes from the Latin *universus*, "whole, entire." The first university of technology was founded in Budapest in 1782.

Doctors must have shown that they can independently discover new scientific knowledge. The word "doctor" comes from the Latin word *doctor*, which refers to a teacher (Online Etymology Dictionary 2024). The word was first used for a holder of the highest degree in a university in 1375. The abbreviation Ph.D. is an abbreviation of the Latin word *philosophiæ doctor*, "teacher of philosophy," thus showing the origin of all science in philosophy.

Education views developed in European universities can be divided into two general complementary groups: the German *Bildung* system and British *liberal education* (Holford 2014). *Bildung* is a German word that means general knowledge. The idea was developed by Wilhelm von Humboldt (1767–1835) in his book *The Limits of State Action*, written in 1792 but published posthumously in 1852. He was one of the founders of the University of Berlin (1809), now called the Humboldt University of Berlin. Humboldt's ideas were initially resisted. The Humboldtian system is based on four principles: Freedom of teaching and learning, unity of education and research, preference for pure science over specialized professional training, and unity of science, implying transdisciplinarity. There is no fundamental distinction between natural and human sciences. Education has been mainly professor-centric. This view has been vital in countries using the German language and in the Nordic countries.

John Henry Newman developed liberal education in his book *The Idea of a University* (published in 1858) (Holford 2014). Universities are more for education than research. Education is more student-centric, and the interaction between students and professors is essential. Universities work closely with society. Ethics and aesthetics are emphasized. The differences between the two views have been reduced and are now seen as complementary elements of Western universities. Professors as experts in their disciplines must say what is learned and not the students (Nichols 2017).

University education should find a good compromise between the Humboldtian and Newmannian university models (Holford 2014) so that the university has general and professional education components, respectively. The compromise is now even more critical when our systems are becoming more complex, and we are approaching the fundamental limits of nature with limited resources. Our goal has been to present a hierarchical and evolutionary worldview produced by consecutive falsifications (Rosenberg and McIntyre 2020) that guides future research as a new paradigm or worldview for the intelligent, sustainable, and resilient world. According to Georg Henrik von Wright, a *worldview* is the understanding of the birth and structure of the world, the intelligibility and explanations of natural events, and the right way of life adopted by a particular era or group of people (Korkman 2022). We are in the age of sustainability comparable to the industrial revolution (Swilling 2020).

The Bologna process is now harmonizing the university systems to ensure compatible degrees, transferable credits, and equal academic qualifications in the European Union (EU) (Holford 2014). The *Bologna declaration* was signed in 1999 at the University of Bologna.

6.4 Systems Thinking

The systems thinking was created in the last century, although significant systems thinkers have existed since ancient times (Kline 1995; Checkland 1999; Ramage and Shipp 2020). The modern systems thinking was developed by Norbert Wiener, Ludwig von Bertalanffy, Kenneth E. Boulding, Ilya Prigogine, Herbert A. Simon, and others, and more system theories started to appear. Some systems thinkers such as Ilya Progogine and Herbert Simon later received Nobel Prizes. The systems thinking was developed because of the limitations of our analytical tools. David Silverman developed the actors approach in his book *The Theory of Organizations* (1970) (Arbnor and Bjerke 1997). He used earlier work by Edmund Husserl, Alfred Schultz, and Max Weber.

6.4.1 Beginning of Systems Thinking

Alexander Bogdanov (1912) was one of the less-known pioneers in systems thinking (Dudley 1996). His real name was Alexander Malinovsky. He developed a field called *tektology*, or universal organizational science. Another forgotten pioneer was Erwin Bauer (Brauckmann 2000). In 1920, he stated, "All living systems, and only living systems, exist by maintaining themselves in a non-equilibrium state." He thus anticipated the nonequilibrium thermodynamics.

The founding father of the systems thinking is generally thought to be Ludwig von Bertalanffy, a biologist (von Bertalanffy 1971). His early writings are in German. He started to write in English in 1950 (von Bertalanffy 1950a, b) after moving from Austria to Great Britain in 1948, to Canada, and finally to the USA. He summarized his work in *General System Theory* (von Bertalanffy 1971), first published in 1968. He defined open systems in organisms in 1932 and outlined the general theory of systems at the University of Chicago in 1937 before cybernetics, but at that time the theory had a bad reputation in biology. He published his first paper "Zu einer allgemeinen Systemlehre" in 1945.

Norbert Wiener, a mathematician, developed cybernetics in his book *Cybernetics: Or Control and Communication in the Animal and the Machine* (Wiener 1961), first published in 1948. He studied negative feedback and thought that positive feedback was not helpful since it was unstable.

Kenneth E. Boulding, an economist, was interested in the general hierarchy of systems (Boulding 1956, 1985). He developed an evolutionary hierarchical worldview. His most important book in this sense was *The World as a Total System* (Boulding 1985), where he elaborated his hierarchy of natural systems published in Boulding (1956). In addition, he developed a more general hierarchy of the systems in the world.

The foundation of the International Society for the Systems Sciences (ISSS) was a landmark in developing systems thinking. In 1954, von Bertalanffy, Boulding,

Ralph W. Gerard, a physiologist, and Anatol Rapoport, a mathematician, conceived the Society for the Advancement of General Systems Theory (Checkland 1999, p. 93). The name was changed to the Society for General Systems Research in 1955. The society was formally established in 1956 in collaboration with James G. Miller, a biologist. The name was changed again in 1986 to the International Society for General Systems Research. From 1988 the name has been the ISSS.

One of the pioneers in systems engineering was Hall (1962). Much later, in 1990, the International Council on Systems Engineering (INCOSE) was founded. In the social sciences, the emphasis was on interdisciplinary research (Klein 1990), and the Association for Interdisciplinary Studies (AIS) was founded (1979), initially with the name Association for Integrative Studies.

At the beginning of the 1900s, the generality of the feedback concept was better understood, and some system theories were developed, including game and information theory and cybernetics. The word system comes from the Greek *systema*, "organized whole, a whole compounded of parts" (Online Etymology Dictionary 2024). Jan Smuts (1926) coined the word holism in his book *Holism and Evolution*, and it comes from the Greek word *holos*, "whole." Science can be seen as a struggle between reductionists and holists, although the two approaches are complementary rather than mutually exclusive (Elsasser 1987).

6.4.2 History of Information Technology

Information technology includes electronics and control, computer, and communications engineering. The branches have progressed hand in hand. We have observed a tradition that started with Harry Nyquist's control engineering (1932), Norbert Wiener's cybernetics (1948), John McCarthy's artificial intelligence (1956), Jay Forrester's system dynamics (1958), and John Holland's complexity theory (1992). There were also many other developers, but we want to define the birth year and a significant contributor to each of these disciplines. Although the feedback concept has an ancient origin, Nyquist started control engineering because he described the stability conditions of a feedback loop (Nyquist 1932), and researchers understood the generality of the feedback concept. Wiener is commonly understood as a pioneer in cybernetics, which combines control and communications (Wiener 1961). McCarthy invented the term artificial intelligence, which combined cybernetics and computing. He was also the main organizer of the first workshop on AI (1956). In about 1987, an agent became the core component of AI (Russell and Norvig 2022). Holland was the first to define complexity theory as a theory of complex adaptive systems (Holland 1992), which are multiagent systems already known at that time in artificial intelligence in the form of distributed artificial intelligence (Hewitt 1977). The pioneers of complexity theory defined it as a theory of self-organization that was initially a research topic in AI.

The exponential development of digital electronics has made the development of control, computer, and communication technologies possible, all ingredients of information technology. The history started with practical applications, and the theoretical research began afterwards. Some of the most advanced concepts are virtual reality and telepresence (Mämmelä et al. 2018). Morton Heilig (1962) developed one of the first *virtual reality* prototypes called Sensorama, but the idea became more popular in the 1980s. Marvin Minsky (1980) coined the term *telepresence.* He outlined his vision from the older concept of teleoperation that focused on giving a remote participant a feeling of being present at a different location. A recent trend since the late 1980s is cooperative robots in *multirobot systems* (Yan et al. 2013). Their roots are in multiagent systems developed in computer engineering (Hewitt 1977). A closely related concept is swarm intelligence (1993). A robot swarm is essentially a distributed system, which may need a leader for stable operation.

Mature measurement theory started with Patrick Suppes (1951), who integrated the two earlier lines of research (Diez 1997a, b). Stanley S. Stevens focused on the study of scale types (Stevens 1946, 1957; Krantz et al. 1971; Narens and Luce 1986; Houle et al. 2011). He initially used nominal, ordinal, interval, and ratio scales. He later introduced the logarithmic interval scale, whose name is shortened to the log-interval scale.

Digital electronics According to Dummer (1997), there are three fundamental inventions in electronics on which the others depend, including Faraday's (1831) discovery of electromagnetic induction, Lee de Forest's triode (1906), and Bell Laboratories' transistor (1947). Our focus here is on digital electronics, but analog electronics is important in radio frequency design and wide bandwidths where digital electronics is not energy efficient (Hosticka 1985).

The first electrically operated switches were *relays.* Joseph Henry (1835) and Samuel Morse (1840) invented the modern relay for their telegraphs. Joseph J. Thomson (1897) discovered the electron. Electronics started with the invention of vacuum tubes (or valves in British English) in the form of a diode by John A. Fleming (1904) and a triode by Lee De Forest (1906). The term *electronics* has been used since 1910 for science about electrons (Online Etymology Dictionary 2024). The first digital computers, such as Z-3 developed by Konrad Zuse (1941), Mark 2 Colossus by Tommy Flower (1944), and ENIAC by John Mauchly and J. Presper Eckert (1946), advanced the practical use of electronics.

John Bardeen, Walter Brattain, and William Schockley at Bell Laboratories invented the transistor using germanium (1947) (Dummer 1997). The name transistor combines the words transfer and resistor since the transistor transfers an electrical current across a resistor (Online Etymology Dictionary 2024). In the paper, the authors used the term transistor only in the title; otherwise, it was called a semiconductor diode. The inventors received a Nobel Prize in 1956. Jack Kilby (1958) and Robert Noyce (1959) invented an integrated circuit that can include many transistors on the same chip (Mämmelä and Anttonen 2017; Riekki and Mämmelä 2021). Noyce's version was an actual monolithic, single-crystal planar integrated circuit since it did not use jumper wires. Kilby received a Nobel Prize in 2000 when Noyce had already passed away.

George Boole (1848) invented Boolean algebra, and logic within philosophy became part of mathematics. In his letter, Charles S. Peirce (1886) described how logical electrical switching circuits could carry out operations. Akira Nakashima (1934–1936), Claude E. Shannon (1938), and Victor Shestakov (1938) developed independently *combinational logic*, which was at that time implemented with relays and called switching circuits (Dummer 1997). Shannon's paper was based on his master's thesis, "A symbolic analysis of relay and switching circuits," prepared one year earlier. The term "gate" was not yet used for a logic gate but became common at the beginning of the 1950s. In vacuum tubes, the gate terminal acts as a gate to control the current flow, similar to how a logic gate controls the flow of signals based on its inputs.

The bibliography in Netherwood (1958) is an early history of logic systems. The first semiconductor logic gates were diode gates, but they can implement only AND and OR gates. We need an active element for a NOT gate, first in the form of diode-transistor logic. The first monolithic gates used resistor-transistor logic (1961), and soon after that, transistor-transistor logic (TTL) (1963). Mohamed Atalla and Dawon Kahng (1960) demonstrated the first metal-oxide-semiconductor (MOS) field-effect transistor. Based on this, Frank Wanlass and Chih-Tang Sah (1963) published the complementary metal-oxide-semiconductor (CMOS) logic, which is now the mainstream technology because of its energy efficiency. It had a slow start because of manufacturing problems.

Combinational logic has no memory, whereas *sequential logic* has a memory. The bistable multivibrator is the most crucial element in sequential logic (Dummer 1997). It is a simple one-bit memory based on feedback and the basis of finite-state machines. It can change its state by using an external trigger pulse. Using two vacuum tubes, William Henry Eccles and Frank Wilfred Jordan (1919) invented a bistable multivibrator, initially called the Eccless-Jordan trigger circuit, that would now be called a latch. We use the term flip-flop for edge-triggered storage elements and the term latch for level-triggered storage elements. The paper (Harris 1952) already includes a modern description of a shift register, a monostable and bistable multivibrator, and different logic gates, only five years after the invention of the transistor. The bistable multivibrator is now better known as an RS flip-flop (S means set, and R means reset). An edge-triggered D flip-flop is a one-bit memory and includes two inputs, data and clock, and two outputs, Q and its logical negation (D refers to delay). RS flip-flop is a component in the D flip-flop.

The degree of integration has improved significantly, but since about 1980, all integrated circuits have been large-scale integrated (VLSI) circuits with at least 100,000 transistors. Implementing microprocessors (1971), digital signal processors (1980), and multicore processors on a single chip has been possible. Federico Faggin, Marcian E. Hoff, Jr., and Stanley Mazor developed the first microprocessor, Intel 4004, a four-bit processor with 2300 transistors using 10 μm line width.

The first successful digital signal processor (DSP) chips were NEC μPD7720 (1980) and Texas Instruments TMS32010 (1983). Multicore processors appeared at the beginning of the 2000s. In addition to general-purpose processors, application-specific integrated circuits (ASICs) are also available. The term ASIC became popular at the beginning of the 1980s. At about the same time as ASICs, the term system-on-chip (SoC) was introduced, emphasizing the possibility of implementing whole systems on a chip. The ASICs have used gate arrays, standard cells, and structured hardware design (Jess 2000). ASICs are designed for one customer, but application-specific standard products (ASSPs) are off-the-self components with a broad market. SoCs became the dominant technology in about 2005. A network-on-chip (NoC) is a concept presenting a unification of on-chip communication solutions (Bjerregaard and Mahadevan 2006; Ogras and Marculescu 2006). The NoC is a packet switching network between SoC modules based on routers. Thus, the largest network in the world (the Internet) and the smallest network (the NoC) are based on the same principles. In the 2020s, separate chips can be combined to form chiplets, which can be stacked in 3D integrated circuits. The development of integration is summarized in Liu and Wong (2024).

Initially, the circuit diagrams were drawn by hand until design automation started to develop in the 1980s. The chips are designed with hardware description languages such as Very High-Speed Integrated Circuit Hardware Description Language (VHDL) (1983) and Verilog (1984), which the IEEE later standardized (Jess 2000). In the 1990s, logic synthesis tools became common, and the tools automatically generate combinational and sequential logic. The logic is synchronous, and all state changes are made simultaneously using a master clock. System-level modeling languages such as SystemC (2000) are now available. It is a hardware description language that produces some more overhead than lower-level modeling.

Gordon Moore (1965) noticed that after the invention of the integrated circuit, the number of transistors in 2D digital electronics increased exponentially and initially doubled every year (Mämmelä and Anttonen 2017). Ten years later (1975), he updated the prediction: the number of transistors doubled every second year. The prediction is now known as Moore's law. The miniaturization followed Robert H. Dennard's (1974) scaling rules.

More fundamentally, David House (1975) predicted that the computing rate would double in 18 months with a constant power consumption since, because of miniaturization, also the clock rate increases (Mämmelä and Anttonen 2017). Keyes (1981) noticed that energy efficiency had doubled every 18 months, following House's observation (Keyes 1981). Energy efficiency increased by a factor of one hundred in ten years.

There have been predictions that Moore's law will continue until at least 2050–2100 (Mämmelä and Anttonen 2017). However, there is a fundamental limit called the Szilard or Landauer limit for the required energy of a switch, independently of the structure of the switch. Moore's law for silicon electronics has had problems since 2004. Because of power consumption, not all the transistors could be used simultaneously; the clock rates were frozen to 3–4 GHz, and parallel computing had to be used. The maximum power consumption of an integrated circuit is now about 200 W because of cooling problems. Cooling efficiency is expected to improve only slowly. Hand-held devices can consume about 3 W.

The Semiconductor Industry Association (SIA) published since 1993 a national technology roadmap for semiconductors. From 1998 to 2016, an international group of semiconductor industry experts published the International Technology Roadmap for Semiconductors (ITRS). In 2016, ITRS predicted that Moore's law would result in a thermal noise death in five years (Waldrop 2016; Courtland 2016). Since 2017, the IEEE has published a new International Roadmap for Devices and Systems (IRDS). The roadmaps offer a 15-year vision of systems and devices. This development is an example of how systems progress from the bottom up, from semiconductor devices to systems. After the semiconductor devices have matured close to the fundamental limits of nature, the interest has moved to the upper levels of the hierarchy and systems.

The interest in the reliability of electronics started with an American Institute of Electrical Engineers (AIEE) standard in 1913, but it did not include time-dependent degradation (Ryerson 1962; Dummer 1997). Three years later, a reliability program was started at the Bell Telephone Laboratories and the Western Electric Company to provide good-performing telephone equipment. An authoritative treatise on all aspects of quality control was written by Joseph M. Juran (1951) in the first edition of his *Quality Control Handbook*. The 1950s meant a significant upsurge in reliability in quality control. Reliability engineering became a scientific discipline. Juran and A. Blanton Godfrey published the fifth edition of *Juran's Quality Control* in 1999 (Juran and Godfrey 1999). They presented two definitions of quality: *Quality* means (1) "those features of products which meet customer needs and thereby provide customer satisfaction" and (2) "freedom from deficiencies." Customer satisfaction is "a state of affairs in which customers feel that their expectations have been met by the product features." Juran and Frank M. Gryna (1993) defined *reliability* as the "chance that a product will work for the required time." Later, the definition also included the operating environment. W. Grant Ireson (1996) stated that reliability is "the ability or capability of the product to perform the specified function in the designated environment for a minimum length of time or minimum number of cycles or events."

Availability and reliability are essential measures of system effectiveness (Barlow and Proschan 1976; Tillman et al. 1982; Saleh and Marais 2006). The measurements can be divided into nonparametric and parametric, and the parameters to be estimated are assumed to be deterministic unknown constants or statistical with known statistics. In general, when the data are scarce, and the measurements are expensive, the statistical approaches are useful instead of the deterministic approaches, resulting in smaller uncertainty. When the sample size is large, the statistical methods are less valuable. Multivariate distributions have been used since 1975 in statistical techniques.

Control engineering Control engineering is based on the feedback concept, although open-loop control is sometimes used if rough control is enough (Mämmelä et al. 2018). We present the history of feedback, cybernetics, artificial intelligence, and self-organization separately in this chapter.

Control systems have advanced from automatic to adaptive and autonomous control systems. The term adaptive control (1957) was borrowed from biology. The term autonomous control became popular after Panos J. Antsakis et al. (1988) introduced it whereas King-Sun Fu (1971) initially called it intelligent control. An important branch of robotics is *microrobotics* in the micrometer range and nanorobotics in the nanometer range. Recent developments are summarized in Cao et al. (2013), Yan et al. (2013) and Ye et al. (2017).

Computer engineering Blaise Pascal (1642) and Gottfried W. Leibnitz (1672) developed the first mechanical calculators for addition, and multiplication and division, respectively. Charles Babbage (1822) is usually considered the father of the computer. He made a design for a mechanical computer. Alan Turing (1936) presented an abstract machine later called the Turing machine. In 1938, he generalized it to the universal Turing machine that could simulate any digital computer using a program. General-purpose computers are Turing machines (Penrose 1999, p. 75).

The first programmable computer, ENIAC (1946), could also be used for simulations (Dummer 1997). Its main purpose was to compute firing and ballistic tables by integrating a system of ordinary differential equations. The computer occupied a space of 9 m $\times$ 15 m and contained 18,000 vacuum tubes. It consisted mainly of decade ring counters, flip-flops, and pentodes. A pentode is a vacuum tube with five electrodes.

A supercomputer was proposed only two years later. Real-time computing started in 1973 (Kim and Kumar 2012). John von Neumann (1946) invented the stored-program computer architecture, now called the von Neumann architecture, in his report "Memorandum on the program of the high speed computer" (Dummer 1997). The term Harvard architecture was most likely used in the early 1970s and later applied in digital signal processors.

The history of distributed computing started with the first computer networks, although the first conference was organized in 1982, and distributed computing eventually led to autonomic computing. Jeffrey O. Kephart and David M. Chess (2001) proposed autonomic computing, a form of self-organizing computing. The idea was developed in a Defense Advanced Research Projects Agency (DARPA) project (1997) called Situational Awareness System. The aim was to create personal communication and location devices for up to 10,000 soldiers on the battlefield. Decentralized multihop ad hoc routing was used in a challenging environment to keep round-trip latency below 200 ms.

The end of Moore's law was expected, and John Casti and Christian S. Calude (1994) proposed a new term *unconventional computing* (Adamatzky 2017; Calude 2017). The idea led to a series of conferences and, eventually, books. Initially, unconventional computing included biological, molecular, DNA, and quantum computing, neural networks, cellular automata, reversible computation, genetic algorithms, and any models of computation that go beyond the *Turing barrier*. The barrier is derived from the Church-Turing thesis (1936), according to which all computations are equivalent to Turing machines, but in Penrose (1999, pp. 46, 62), the author claims that there are mathematical operations that are not mechanical as required by the Turing machine. In about 2006, the term *cyber-physical systems* was introduced to describe systems at the interface of the cyber and physical worlds.

The concept of cloud computing can be traced back to John McCarthy (1961) (Surbiryala and Rong 2019). Ramnath K. Chellappa (1997) used the term for the first time, and more recently, Cisco (2015) suggested fog computing for fixed networks (Ray 2018). Edge computing of Akamai Technologies (1999) was initially called content delivery (Dilley et al. 2002). Yingwei Wang (2015) proposed dew computing.

The history of computational complexity theory is summarized in Cook (1983), Dewdney (2004) and Fortnow and Homer (2014). A distinction between polynomial and exponential complexity was made first by John von Neumann in 1953 (Cook 1983). Jack Edmonds (1965) expressed the tractability of polynomial complexity problems. Donald E. Knuth (1974) discussed the terms NP-complete and NP-hard, after which the terms have been widely used. Stephen A. Cook (published in 1971) and Leonid Levin (published in 1973) independently discovered the existence of NP-complete problems. The term NP-complete was popularized later by Alfred V. Aho et al. in their book *The Design and Analysis of Computer Algorithms* in 1974. Cook did not use this term.

Communications engineering The history of communications engineering from the practical application point of view is included in Huurdeman (2003). The history started with the optical telegraph by Claude Chappe (1792). It was a mechanical system. Electronic communication started with the wired telegraph by Samuel Morse (1837), but there were also earlier similar inventions. His telegraph became practical in 1844. The next step was the wireless telegraph, usually called the radio. Commonly, the credit is given to Guglielmo Marconi, but there was a dispute regarding priority between Nikola Tesla and Marconi.

Theoretical research on communications started much later. Harry Nyquist (1924) and Ralph Hartley (1928) defined the maximum transmission speed in a noiseless and noisy channel, respectively. A rigorous theory was given by Claude E. Shannon (1948, 1949) in his information theory and sampling theorem. Dwight North (1943) devised the matched filter corresponding to a correlator, thus maximizing the signal-to-noise ratio at its output with additive white noise. If the noise is also Gaussian, the error probability is minimized. The concept was also used in defining the maximum a posteriori probability (MAP) receiver and, finally, in maximum likelihood sequence detection (MLSD). Simpler solutions exist, including linear and decision-feedback equalizers.

We obtain reliability in fading channels using space, frequency, or time diversity (Schwartz et al. 1966; Proakis and Salehi 2008). A. de Haas (1927) and H. H. Beverage et al. (1928) implemented the first diversity systems as a countermeasure for channel fading (Schwartz et al. 1966; Dummer 1997). The latter group used three antennas spaced about 300 m apart. Donald G. Brennan (1955) was the first to discuss optimal diversity combining, an extension of correlation. The modern version of space diversity is called a MIMO system, where many antennas are used both in the transmitter and the receiver (Yang and Hanzo 2015). A hybrid frequency-space diversity was already common in tropospheric scatter networks in 1955, using two antennas in the transmitter and receiver (Schwartz et al. 1966, pp. 424–425).

The information theory is an existence proof but does not give the actual algorithms with which the limits are approached. The channel coding methods were developed in the work of Richard W. Hamming (1950) and Peter Elias (1955) for block and convolutional codes, respectively. Channel coding is a form of diversity. G. David Forney, Jr. (1966) developed concatenated codes using two codes, one is an inner code, and another one is an outer code. Powerful codes are Reed-Solomon codes by Irving S. Reed and Gustave Solomon (1960) that can be used as outer codes in concatenated coding schemes, which are practical because of their modularity. The inner code is often a convolutional code. Channel coding and modulation were combined in trellis-coded modulation (TCM) by Gottfried Ungerboeck (1976). Eventually, the low-density parity-check (LDPC) codes by Robert G. Gallager (1963) and the turbo codes by Claude Berrou (1991) were shown to be close to optimal. LDPC codes became practical only after the maturity of implementation technology.

Optimality in an unknown channel needs adaptive transmission and reception. The first books on adaptive, learning, and pattern recognition systems were (Mendel and Fu 1970; Tsypkin 1972; Widrow and Stearns 1985). The first adaptive receiver in a multipath fading channel was the adaptive correlator or matched filter called the Rake receiver by Robert Price and Paul E. Green, Jr. (1958). The authors called it automatic since the term adaptive reception was not yet commonly used. Another practical solution for adaptive reception has been the least-mean square (LMS) algorithm by Bernard Widrow and Marcian E. Hoff, Jr. (1960). Various alternatives now exist, and the recursive least squares (RLS) algorithm is close to optimal convergence when the received samples are highly correlated (Widrow and Walach 1984). Adaptive transmission started from adaptive power control by Jeremiah F. Hayes (1968). The idea was extended to various adaptive modulation and coding (AMC) schemes. According to the information theory, most energy should be transmitted where the channel has the highest gain in time, frequency, and spatial domains.

The information theory is valid only for isolated links. Communication networks have been much more demanding to optimize since the interference is not Gaussian. A practical and close to optimal solution is to use loose coupling: avoid interference between links using orthogonal signals and to use time-scale separation in hierarchical management and control (Mämmelä et al. 2023). The optimality can be shown using optimization decomposition (Chiang et al. 2007). In the spatial domain, a cellular system is the most practical solution. Interference is minimized by using channel attenuation. Adaptivity can be used even in the spatial domain, for example, *cell breathing*, where some traffic is offloaded to neighboring cells, a form of *load balancing* used in computing. Essentially, the service area of the cells is adapted to the traffic situation. Overloaded cells are made smaller, and less loaded cells are made larger. Cell breathing is useful especially in code-division multiple access (CDMA) networks where quasi-orthogonal spreading codes separate user signals.

6.4.3 History of Sustainability

Sustainability has a long history, but in Caradonna (2014), it started in the 1600s. After the Industrial Revolution since about 1750, the use of fossil fuels became common in the industry, which started climate change, a multicausal phenomenon.

Thomas R. Malthus (1798) noticed that unlimited resources led to an exponential growth in population. Pierre-Francois Verhulst (1838) expected limited growth in case of limited resources and developed a logistic function similar to the s-curve to describe the growth. After Adam Smith (1776) proposed the free market economy, William F. Lloyd (1833) was one of the first to describe the tragedy of the commons (Feeny et al. 1990; Meadows and Wright 2008). Later the tragedy has been discussed by H. Scott Gordon (1954), Anthony D. Scott (1955), and Hardin (1968). Kenneth E. Boulding (1966), influenced by Henry George's (1879) work, compared the Earth with a spacecraft. The Earth is a closed system with limited material resources, and there is no place to throw the waste.

In 1967–1968, some critical writings were published, including Lynn White's paper "The historical roots of our ecological crisis," Paul R. Ehrlich's book *The Population Bomb*, and Garett Hardin's paper "The tragedy of the commons" (Hardin 1968; Caradonna 2014). Later, Hardin used a controversial metaphor: We live on a lifeboat with finite resources, and there is no place for everyone (Hardin 1974). Elinor Ostrom (1990) noticed many reasons for climate change and proposed methods to govern the commons (Bregman 2020). The social control must work properly. Aurelio Peccei and Alexander King founded the Club of Rome in 1968 and started publishing reports titled *The Limits of Growth*. Since 1971, Global Footprint Network has defined the Earth Overshoot Day.

The term sustainable comes from the Latin *sustinere* and has meant "capable of being continued or maintained at a certain level" since 1965 (Online Etymology Dictionary 2024). The term resilience comes from Latin *resiliens* and has had since the 1620s the meaning "the act of rebounding or springing back." The term regeneration comes from the Latin *regenerates*, "to bring forth again" (du Plessis 2022).

Crawford Stanley Holling (1973) was one of the first to discuss the theory of resilient systems (Barnett 2001; Skyttner 2005). He defined resilience as "the persistence of relationships within a system and is a measure of the ability of these systems to absorb changes of state variables, driving variables, and parameters, and persist." Later, K. Watt and P. Craig (1988) prepared a list of several principles in their book chapter "Surprise, ecological stability theory" of the book *The Anatomy of Surprise* edited by C. S. Holling. Brundtland Commission developed in its report "Our common future" (1987) the first well-developed definition for sustainability (Caradonna 2014). United Nations published in 2015 its 2030 sustainable development agenda and sustainable development goals (SDGs) (Riekki and Mämmelä 2021). The EU has similar goals.

In our biosphere and its ecosystems, the phenomena are exceptionally complex. In Cuddington et al. (2007), the authors present the history of ecosystem engineering.

Clive G. Jones et al. (1994) developed the term *ecosystem engineering*. Its history started in 1868 from the observation by Lewis H. Morgan that beavers affect stream ecosystems. In 2021, Syukuro Manabe and Klaus Hasselmann were awarded a Nobel Prize "for the physical modelling of Earth's climate, quantifying variability and reliably predicting global warming." Giorgio Parisi was awarded a Nobel Prize "for the discovery of the interplay of disorder and fluctuations in physical systems from atomic to planetary scales." A theory of technical ecosystems is summarized in Jacobides et al. (2018).

6.4.4 Principles of Systems and System Theories

According to Dori et al. (2020), Aristotle was the first systems thinker. He had ideas about emergence and subsidiarity (McCarthy et al. 2006; Evans and Zimmermann 2014). Among the successors were Rene Descartes on reductionism, Sadi Carnot and Rudolf Clausius on thermodynamics, Ludwig von Bertalanffy on the general theory of systems, Norbert Wiener and W. Ross Ashby on cybernetics, and James G. Miller on living systems, finally converging to the concept of CASs, which many key figures developed but one important contributor in engineering was John Holland (Dori et al. 2020).

System development life cycle Software development life cycle (SDLC) models have heavily affected system development (Ruparelia 2010; Misra et al. 2012). The idea of division of labor for efficiency improvement started with the agricultural revolution. Production lines were developed, and Frederick W. Taylor (1909) wrote about highly mechanistic "scientific management" (Checkland 1999, pp. 105, 128). By 1913, Henry Ford had developed the moving assembly line. Production and moving assembly lines were precursors of the waterfall model where everything works sequentially step by step as in an algorithm. New models support creativity better and include iterations where new experience is used.

Herbert D. Benington (1956) was the first to document the waterfall model, also called the stagewise method, for software development, and Winston W. Royce (1970) described its iterative version where each preceding stage could be revisited using a feedback loop (Ruparelia 2010). David J. Bohm and F. David Peat (1987) introduced the generative order for creative work (Bohm and Peat 2000). NASA (1991) developed the V-model as a variation of the waterfall model. Barry W. Boehm (1986) modified the V-model by introducing several iterations in a spiral form, thus forming the spiral model. The Rapid Application Development (RAD) model by James Martin (1991) uses prototyping for iterative development (Ruparelia 2010). Agile software development (ASD) is one of its spin-offs (Misra et al. 2012). A group of 17 software practitioners developed a lightweight software development method in 2001 to rationalize their common philosophy called "agile." The ASD lays less emphasis on process and documentation and pays more attention to developing products quickly and incorporating the changing customer needs. Group members have flexible roles and responsibilities, which helps to create innovations in the dynamic interactions between group members.

One major tool in the systems thinking is the concept of system archetypes, developed in system dynamics (Senge 2006; Meadows and Wright 2008). The history is described in Akers et al. (2015). The idea is seen already in Plato's works, and the term archetype appears for the first time in the works of Francis Bacon (1605) and Thomas Browne (1658). The significance of the archetypes was first observed by Carl Jung in psychiatry (1917). The term *system archetype* became highly popular through the book (Senge 2006), first published in 1990. We are interested in archetypes where feedback and self-organization are used, especially in control, computer, and communications engineering. The word archetype comes from the Greek *arkhein*, "to be the first," and *typos*, "model, type" (Online Etymology Dictionary 2024). Among system archetypes are different system hierarchies (Akers et al. 2015) presented in Boulding (1956, 1985), Miller (1978), Ackoff and Gharajedaghi (1996), Martinelli (2001), Bossel (2007) and Mämmelä et al. (2023). In Martinelli (2001), the author discussed and classified altogether 18 hierarchies and proposed an additional hierarchy.

Basic resources Many researchers, such as Joseph Black, Henry Cavendish, and Mikhail V. Lomonosov, assumed the conservation of *mass* in chemical reactions. Antoine Lavoisier (1789) made quantitative measurements and is one of the founding fathers of chemistry (Whitaker 1975; Asimov 1984, p. 487). The words matter and material come from Latin *materia*, which means "substance from which something is made" (Online Etymology Dictionary 2024). The word mass comes from the Latin *massa*, "kneaded dough, lump." The mass has had the modern meaning "quantity of a portion of matter" since 1704.

Isaac Newton did not use the concept of energy, only momentum. James Watt used horsepower to compare steam engines as a measure of power, which was one step towards the energy concept. He later gave his name to the unit of power or energy per time unit. Gottfried Leibniz (1686) was the first to anticipate the energy conservation law using his *vis viva* ("living force") and *vis mortua* ("dead force") concepts that correspond to the kinetic and potential energies, respectively (Suntola 2018). Thomas Young (1807) was the first to use the term energy in the modern sense. Gustave Coriolis (1829) described kinetic energy, and William Rankine (1853) used potential energy. Robert Mayer (1842) and James Joule (1843) developed the concept of conservation of energy (Coelho 2009). Hermann von Helmholtz (1847) formulated the corresponding first law of thermodynamics. Usually, physicists think that Mayer and Joule discovered the concept of energy. Joule also gave his name to the unit of energy. Energy comes from the Greek *energeia*, "activity, action, operation" (Online Etymology Dictionary 2024). The conservation energy corresponds to the zero-energy principle (Sipilä 2014).

After Albert Einstein (1905) published his special relativity theory, Gilbert N. Lewis (1908) stated that mass and energy have different names and different measures of the same quantity (Treptow 1986, 2005). Thus, the conserved quantity is *mass-energy*. The conservation of mass principle is generally assumed to be valid in chemical reactions, but since energy is emitted in chemical reactions, the mass must decrease accordingly.

The word information comes from the Latin *informare*, "to shape, give form to" (Online Etymology Dictionary 2024). The meaning "knowledge communicated concerning a particular topic" is from the mid-1400s. Pierre-Simon Laplace (1814) defined the conservation of information in physical deterministic systems. Charles S. Peirce (1868) founded semiotics, the philosophical study of signs. The meaning "study or doctrine of signs and symbols with special regard to function and origin" has been used since about 1880. Peirce developed the triadic theory of signs, thus distinguishing between a sign, object, and interpretant, often expressed as a semiotic triangle. Morris (1938) divided semiotics into three branches, including syntactics, semantics, and pragmatics (Morris 1938), which form a hierarchy from the bottom up. He focused on dyadic relationships sign–sign (syntactics), sign–object (semantics), and sign–interpretant (pragmatics) (Kauppinen-Räisänen and Jauffret 2018). The *interpretant* is a mental concept that is the "receiver's reaction" to the sign.

In Claude E. Shannon's (1948) work, information became a scientific concept that can be measured in bits (Shannon 1948). Shannon and Warren Weaver (1949) divided the communication problem into three levels: technical, semantic, and effectiveness problem (Shannon and Weaver 1998), which seem to correspond to the three branches of semiotics. Gitt (1989) extended the three-level semiotics to five levels (Gitt 1989). Shannon's information is at the statistical level, and semantic communication is an active research area (Qin et al. 2023).

Time has been measured since ancient times. Initially, the calendars were based on the Earth's and the Moon's rotation periods, resulting in solar and lunar calendars, respectively. Our present calendar is a solar calendar, which has the benefit that the four seasons do not shift from year to year. The spring equinox is always at the same time in a year with small shifts because of the leap years. Time has had the sense of "an indefinite continuous duration" since the late 1300s (Online Etymology Dictionary 2024).

Egyptians were the first to use the solar calendar. The modern calendar was developed in the Roman Empire, and the years were counted from the assumed foundation of Rome that happened according to a legend on 21 April 753 BCE. The Julian calendar (45 BCE) proposed by Julius Caesar included leap years every fourth year, and the average length of the year was 365.25 days. Leap years are needed since the average solar day and year are not synchronized. Pope Gregory XIII of the Catholic Church changed the calendar in 1582. Since then, we have used the Gregorian calendar in most countries, sometimes introduced with a significant delay. The number of leap years was reduced so that every 400 years, one leap year is passed over, and the average calendar year of 365.2425 days matches better with the average solar year of 365.2422 days. The division of a day into 24 h is from Egyptians and Sumerians, and the smaller divisions are from Babylonians who used them in angular measurements (Asimov 1960). Arabic scholars (c. 1000) subdivided the mean solar day into 24 h, each of which was subdivided sexagesimally, and the modern concepts of hour, minute, and second were born. The length of the solar day slowly increases by approximately one second in 100,000 years as the Earth's rotation slows. Christiaan Huygens (1656) built the first pendulum clock after Galileo had noticed the regularity in the swing of a pendant (Mämmelä et al. 2023). After this invention, the measurement of time became more and more accurate.

Frequency comes from the Latin *frequentem*, "often, regular, repeated" (Online Etymology Dictionary 2024). In physics, frequency has had the modern meaning "rate of recurrence" since 1831 in the case of vibrations. The frequency is the inverse of a *period*. The word period is from the Greek *periodos*, "cycle, period of time." Heinrich Hertz (1888) was the first to experiment with radio waves (initially called Hertzian waves), and his name is now in the unit of frequency, the inverse of the unit of time.

Measurement of *space* has an ancient origin. Egyptians are credited for the start of geometry. The Greek mathematician Archimedes (c. 260 BCE) studied the area of polygons and a circle and volumes of a sphere almost two thousand years before Newton (1687) invented calculus. Eratosthenes (c. 240 BCE) was the first to measure the circumference of the Earth with remarkable accuracy (Asimov 1987). The present unit of length, the meter, was defined in 1799 using the circumference of the Earth as a yardstick. Thus, Eratosthenes showed the way.

Measurement units The decimal metric system was initiated in 1792 in France, and the prototypes of meter and kilogram were standardized in 1799 (Klein 1988; Glavic 2021). The metric system has become popular in most countries of the world. Recently, there has been an attempt to define the units using natural constants without needing any prototypes that may be destroyed or changed as a function of time. The accuracy is also not good enough when using prototypes. Thus, the prototypes have only some historical significance. For brevity, we present the original starting point of the measures of length, mass, and time from where everything started, and the present definitions can be found in the literature.

The meter prototype was initially defined as the fraction 1/10,000,000 of the distance from the equator to the North Pole along a great circle. The actual circumference of the Earth through its poles is 40,007,863 m. Thus, the meter is slightly shorter than initially planned. The kilogram prototype had a mass of one liter (1 dm^3) of water at the temperature of 4 °C, where the water is densest at normal or standard atmospheric pressure (Klein 1988, pp. 199–200). In 1861, coherent measurement units were introduced with centimeter, gram, and second units, and the cgs system was born. The second was the fraction 1/86,400 of the average solar day ($24 \times 60 \times 60 = 86{,}400$).

The central units of measurement are related to the parts of the human body (Agnoli and D'Acostini 2005). The meter is close to the human biological scale. The unit of time is in the order of the human heart rate interval. The meter and second are approximately interconnected since the length of the *second's pendulum* is 99.35 cm. The period of the second's pendulum is 2 s. If the period should be 1 s, the pendulum's length would be approximately 25 cm, which would be less practical. The word meter comes from the Greek *metron* "measure" (Online Etymology Dictionary

2024). The word gram comes from the Greek *gramma* "small weight," and the word second comes from Latin *secundus* "second," meaning that the second is the second subdivision of an hour. The measures are somewhat arbitrary. The original yardsticks for measurements were taken from the Earth and water and scaled so that humans could easily understand them.

The International Bureau of Weights and Measures (BIPM) was established in 1875. In 1889, the BIPM defined the MKS system. The acronym MKS comes from the units meter, kilogram, and second. The next version was the MKSA system, proposed by G. Giorgi in 1901 but approved only in 1954. The additional unit was ampere. The BIPM approved the International System of Units (SI) in 1960 and is continuously updating it. The units were now meter, kilogram, second, ampere, kelvin, and candela for length, mass, time, electric current, temperature, and luminous density, respectively. Later, in 1971, the mole was added as a seventh base unit for the amount of substance. The SI units are now part of the International System of Quantities (ISQ). The latest standard is ISO/IEC 80000 Quantities and units, having several parts since about 2010. Part IEC 80000-13 is on information science and technology.

Open systems Open systems were first observed at least implicitly in celestial mechanics (Mämmelä et al. 2023). Isaac Newton (1687) applied an idealization in our solar system: the Sun and each planet, respectively, form an isolated two-body system (Boulton et al. 2015) that corresponds to a second-order feedback loop (Diacu and Holmes 1996; Strogatz 2014). The model is additive, thus making analysis simple. Higher-order effects appear since the two-body systems are open, and each planet affects every other. Pierre-Simon Laplace (1786) analyzed the higher-order effects caused by the interactions using his perturbation theory (Bell 1986). The theory is also relevant in satellite communications since the Earth is an imperfect, inhomogeneous globe. The model must include the aerodynamic drag, solar radiation pressure, and the attraction of the Moon.

David Bernoulli (1738) started the research on the kinetic theory of gases that later resulted in statistical mechanics by James Clerk Maxwell (1866), Ludwig Boltzmann (1877), and Willard Gibbs (1876, 1878). Boltzmann's version of statistical mechanics influenced Alfred J. Lotka (Pouvreau and Drack 2007; Drack 2009). Gibbs published an extensive paper, "On the equilibrium of heterogeneous substances," in 1876 and 1878, comparable to Newton's *Principia*. The year 1876 is often called the year of the birth of thermodynamics. In addition to isolated systems, Gibbs studied also closed systems.

William Stanley Jevons (1865) introduced *the Jevons paradox* in the growing energy sector, and Alfred J. Lotka (1922) later applied it to biological processes (Buenstorf 2000; Alcott 2005). Rudolf Clausius introduced the concept of *the environment* (Dori et al. 2020), which is essential in the definition of open systems. Henderson (1913) observed that living systems must exchange matter and energy with the environment without using the term "open system" (Henderson 1913). He wrote: "Finally a living being must be active, hence its metabolism must be fed with matter and energy, and accordingly there must always be exchange of matter and energy with the environment."

Debora Hammond referred to Lotka's 1925 work on population dynamics and wrote that Lotka is "credited with the introduction of the open-system concept, which was further developed in Bertalanffy's work" (Hammond 2003, pp. 34, 38). von Bertalanffy (1932) introduced the open system concept in German to biology for matter and energy: "It is immediately apparent that a system in dynamic equilibrium can only exist as an open system. A closed system would transition to rest as quickly as possible. The transition does not happen to the organism because the energies released during decay, as well as the products of degradation, leave the system, but on the other hand, materials constantly enter it from the outside world that provides energy to maintain the distance from the equilibrium" (Bertalanffy 1932, p. 93).

Bertalanffy published his results in English in 1950 (von Bertalanffy 1950a, b), but in von Bertalanffy (1950a) the exchange of only matter was included in the definition, not the energy. The open system concept is best known from this paper, although the idea is at least 25 years older.

In the early 1900s, it was an open problem why biological systems follow neither Newtonian mechanics nor the entropy law (Boulton et al. 2015). Ilya Prigogine (1955) developed the theory of nonequilibrium thermodynamics for open systems, thus solving the problem. Biological systems are far from equilibrium.

In 1955, a Report of Automation Committee A, Radio-Electronics-Television Manufacturers Association, proposed a definition of automation, including the terms materials, energy, and information (Mämmelä et al. 2023). The term open system was not used. Eventually, information, in addition to matter and energy, was included in the definition of open systems (Hall 1962).

Claude E. Shannon's (1948) statistical information has no semantic content. Norbert Wiener (1948) defined semantic information as the quantity that can increase order and reduce uncertainty (Wiener 1961). Communication is exchanging information or patterns to improve order and reduce entropy. The importance of information became apparent after the invention of the modern model of deoxyribonucleic acid (DNA) (1953). Gregor Mendel (1865) was the first to suggest the existence of discrete inheritable units (Rothman 2003). Oswald T. Avery, Colin M. MacLeod, and Maclyn McCarty (1944) discovered that DNA carries the genetic message (Elsasser 1987, p. xx). Rosalind Franklin and Maurice Wilkins studied the structure of DNA by using X-ray crystallography, and James D. Watson and Francis Crick (1953) published a model of the double-stranded DNA molecule (Bookstein 2009). Watson, Crick, and Wilkins received a Nobel Prize for the discovery since Franklin had already passed away. Marshall W. Nirenberg (1961), Robert W. Holley, and H. Gobind Khorana discovered the actual genetic code and received a Nobel Prize for their discoveries (Marcos and Arp 2013).

James H. March and Herbert Simon (1958) were the first to recognize that human management organizations are open systems (Thompson 2017). Later, Daniel Katz and Robert L. Kahn (1966) presented a detailed analysis. Miller (1978) offered a comprehensive hierarchy of natural and social systems using the open system concept (Miller 1978), an idea he initially published in 1965.

Emergence In Aristotle's opinion, a whole is more than the sum of its parts, a sign of emergence (Dori et al. 2020; Mämmelä et al. 2023). The word emergence comes from the Latin *emergere*, "rise up" (Online Etymology Dictionary 2024). The meaning "unforeseen occurrence" is from the 1640s. In a scientific context, John Stuart Mill (1843) and Thomas H. Huxley (1868) noticed the idea, and George Henry Lewes (1875) started to use the term (Mayr 1982; Ali and Zimmer 1998; Goldstein 1999). However, C. Lloyd Morgan (1894) was the first to recognize the importance of the concept. Later Morgan (1923) and Charlie Dunbar Broad (1923) discussed it in more detail (Checkland 1999; Morowitz 2002). Michael Polanyi (1966) developed the concept of tacit knowledge, which implies the existence of emergence.

System Theories

System theories are a product of the twentieth century (Kline 1995), see Table 6.5. The timing of each theory is challenging since maturity is reached much later than the first discoveries. One possibility is to use the popularity of the basic terms, which can be studied using, for example, Google Books Ngram Viewer. Usually, after a long precursor phase, accelerated progress starts, and it is interesting to find out when that happened compared to the original discovery. We can also use essential review papers or books with relevant history. Sometimes, the progress starts after a good review paper or book has been published, thus unifying the terms and their definitions. All this must be studied case by case since there are only a few papers and books to list and classify the system theories. The most important ones include (von Bertalanffy 1971; Bahg 1990; Francois 1999; Ramage and Shipp 2020).

Circuit theory The terms *circuit* and *network* are sometimes synonymous and commonly used. However, according to an IRE standard (1960), a network or graph is an idealized model of a circuit of physical devices, and the network theory becomes a mathematical discipline (Belevitch 1962). Ohm's law by Georg Ohm (1827) and Kirchhoff's laws by Gustav Kirchhoff (1845) started the circuit theory. Charles P. Steinmetz (1894) used complex numbers to analyze alternating current (AC). George Campbell invented the electronic filter in 1910, first using the ladder structure, and Karl Willy Wagner made a similar invention independently but could not publish it during the war. Stephen Butterworth (1930) was the first to design a filter systematically according to specifications. Heinz E. Kallman (1940) discovered the tapped delay line filter using the term transversal filter. Such a nonrecursive filter is common in many estimators, now called as a finite impulse response filter in digital signal processing. Harold S. Black (1927) invented the feedback amplifier, and Harry Nyquist (1932) defined its stability conditions. The dating of the beginning of circuit theory in the 1920s is based on the paper (Belevitch 1962).

Linear system theory Circuit theory was a precursor of the more general linear system theory. Rene Descartes (1637) was one of the first to use the coordinate system in geometry. A first-order function can be drawn as a straight line in the coordinate system from which the term linearity comes. Hermann Grassman (1844) showed that the number of spatial dimensions is not bounded to three. Gustav R. Kirchhoff (1845) used a superposition theorem that now defines a linear system.

Table 6.5 Development of systems thinking

Year	Discoverer	Discovery
1735	C. von Linne	Taxonomies in biology
1776	A. Smith	Free-market economics
1859	C. Darwin	Theory of evolution
1869	M. Mendeleev	Periodic table of elements
1876	W. Gibbs	Thermodynamics
1890	H. Poincare	Deterministic chaos
1916	V. Pareto	Social cycle theory
1917	D. W. Thompson	Physics of morphogenesis
1920s	Many discoverers	Circuit theory
1925	A. J. Lotka	Open systems
1926	J. Smuts	Holism
1931	K. Gödel	Incompleteness theorems
1936	J. M. Keynes	Macroeconomics
1936	A. Turing	Theory of computation
1940s	Many discoverers	Network and graph theory
1940s	Many discoverers	Systems engineering
1944	J. von Neumann and O. Morgenstern	Game theory
1947	W. R. Ashby	Adaptive and self-organizing systems
1948	C. E. Shannon	Theory of information transmission
1948	N. Wiener	Cybernetics
1950	L. von Bertalanffy	General theory of systems
1950s	Many discoverers	Linear system theory
1950s	Many discoverers	Optimization and decision theory
1950s	Many discoverers	Detection and estimation theory
1953	H. Simon	Bounded rationality
1954	H. Simon	Feedback in a human agent
1955	I. Prigogine	Nonequilibrium thermodynamics
1956	K. E. Boulding	Hierarchy of systems
1956	J. McCarthy et al.	Artificial intelligence
1957	IBM	Modularity in computers
1958	J. Forrester	System dynamics
1960	D. Dantzig and P. Wolfe	Distributed optimization
1962	H. Simon	Hierarchy theory
1963	M. Maruyama	Positive feedback
1964	P. Baran	Degrees of centralization
1965	E. W. Dijkstra	Concurrent computing
1967	S. Milgram	Small-world networks

(continued)

Table 6.5 (continued)

Year	Discoverer	Discovery
1968	E. W. Dijkstra	Hierarchical programming
1969	E. W. Dijkstra	Structured programming
1970	M. D. Mesarovic	Hierarchical control
1970	D. Silverman	Actors approach
1970s	Many discoverers	Optimization decomposition
1971	S. Cook and L. Levin	Computational complexity
1971	H. Haken	Synergetics
1972	R. Thom	Catastrophe theory
1973	H. Simon	Loose coupling
1973	J. Maynard Smith and G. Price	Evolutionary game theory
1977	C. Hewitt	Distributed AI
1977	Many discoverers	Chaos theory
1978	J. G. Miller	Hierarchy of living and social systems
1980	H. R. Maturana and F. J. Varela	Autopoiesis
1981	H. von Förster	Second-order cybernetics
1984	Many discoverers	Complexity theory
1985	P. T. Lewis	Internet of Things
1987	M. R. Genesereth and N. J. Nilsson	AI as a theory of rational agents
1991	D. Christian	Big history
1991	M. Weiser	Ubiquitous computing
1995	L. R. Medsker	Hybrid intelligent systems
1997	R. K. Chellappa	Cloud computing (term)
1998	J. Mashey et al.	Big data
2000s	Many discoverers	Systems biology
2011	Many discoverers	Microservices
2012	Many discoverers	Deep learning breakthrough
2017	H. B. McMahan et al.	Federated learning
2017	Many discoverers	Large language models
2020	T. Suntola	Dynamic universe

Gabriel Cramer (1750) used determinants to solve simultaneous linear equations. Pierre-Simon Laplace (1812) developed the Laplace transform, making it easier to solve linear differential equations and analyze linear systems using the transfer function concept. The Laplace transform is now commonly used in circuit theory and control engineering. Joseph Fourier (1822) analyzed periodic signals using the Fourier series, which was generalized to nonperiodic signals using the Fourier transform. The Fourier series has also been generalized to other orthogonal series. Fourier series and transform are now used in signal theory, which is useful in communications engineering. Bello (1963) extended the transfer function concept to time-varying systems (Bello 1963).

James J. Sylvester (1850) started using matrices, essential for describing linear systems. Thomas Kailath was one of the first to extend the matrix expression to time-varying systems (Kailath 1960). During the 1920s, Karl Küpfmüller significantly developed the theory of linear systems using the systems thinking. He noticed that the rise time of a band-limited signal depends on the inverse of the bandwidth, thus seeing the significance of the time-bandwidth product, which Dennis Gabor (1946) later studied more rigorously. He also started to use the complex envelope concept as a model of bandpass signals and systems (Kailath 1966). David Hilbert (1905) discovered the Hilbert transform, needed to define the complex envelope. The popularity of linear system theory and the Laplace and Fourier transforms increased in the 1950s.

Probability theory started in 1654 when Pierre Fermat and Blaise Pascal wrote about probability in a gambling problem. In 1933, Andrei Kolmogorov's axiomatic framework started modern probability theory, and the theories of probability and stochastic processes became part of mathematics.

Game theory John Von Neumann and Oscar Morgenstern (1944) developed game theory in economics (Lasaulce and Tembine 2011; Bacci et al. 2016). The theory is based on the *minimax theorem* for two-player zero-sum games by von Neumann (1928), which states that we should choose a strategy that minimizes our maximum loss and maximizes our minimum gain. In zero-sum games, if one side wins, the other side loses. Most games in practice are nonzero-sum games (Hall 1962, p. 319). For example, in a war, both sides lose since many kinds of values are destroyed. Another example is systems engineering where both sides win since new wealth is created. This is called a win–win situation.

The game theory is now part of artificial intelligence (Russell and Norvig 2022). Heinrich von Stackelberg defined the Stackelberg game in 1934. John Nash (1950) introduced the Nash equilibrium for a noncooperative games and the Nash bargaining solution (NBS) for cooperative games. He received a Nobel Prize in economics in 1994. John Maynard Smith (1973) and others developed an evolutionary game theory that combines competition and cooperation (Nowak 2006).

Cybernetics Cybernetics was founded by Warren McCulloch, Norbert Wiener, Gregory Bateson, Margaret Mead, and W. Ross Ashby (Scott 2004). Norbert Wiener (1948) named the discipline cybernetics in his book *Cybernetics: Or Control and Communication in the Animal and the Machine*, thus combining control and communication (Wiener 1961). The word cybernetics comes from the Greek *kybernetes*, "steersman." One of the first theoretical results in control engineering was the PID control that Nicolas Minorsky (1922) discovered by studying how a ship's steersman worked (Bennett 1979a). He noticed that any automatic steering system must consider not just the angular deviation from the set course but also the rate of change of the angular deviation. His result was published in "Directional stability or automatically steered bodies." The ideas for cybernetics were discussed in Josiah Macy Foundation conferences between 1946 and 1953 (Scott 2004; Umpleby 2016). The original title of the conference was "Circular causal and feedback mechanisms in biological and social systems." Warren McCulloch, Gregory Bateson, and Margaret Mead were influential in them.

The feedback has an ancient origin. James Watt (1769) used feedback in his governor as part of his steam engine, and James Clerk Maxwell (1868) analyzed the stability of speed-controlled steam engines using differential equations. The generality of feedback was understood after Harry Nyquist (1932) and Henrik W. Bode (1945) published their stability analyses (Gao 2014). Earlier Maxwell's analysis was forgotten, but later, it was found by Norbert Wiener (1948) (Wiener 1961). Engineers preferred Nyquist and Bode's frequency response method. The term automation was widely used in 1948 (Online Etymology Dictionary 2024). The term automatic comes from Greek *automatos*, referring to persons "acting of one's own will." David Hartley (1748) used the same term for involuntary actions.

The term adapt comes from the Latin *adaptare*, "adjust, fit to" (Online Etymology Dictionary 2024). The modern meaning is "to undergo modification to fit new circumstances." The term adaptive was used by Charles Darwin (1859) and his predecessors. W. Ross Ashby (1940, 1947) coined the terms adaptive and self-organizing systems for technical systems, but they developed slowly (Ramage and Shipp 2020). His work is not well known outside of cybernetics (Umpleby 2009). The first technical adaptive system was his homeostat (1948), which simulated the brain (Mämmelä et al. 2018).

W. Ross Ashby (1952) introduced the concept of *ultrastability* based on *double feedback*; see Fig. 6.1. The inner loop operates relatively fast and makes minor corrections (Umpleby 2009). The outer loop operates relatively slowly and changes the system parameters and structure when the *essential variables* go outside the bounds required for survival. The system is thus self-organizing: changing its structure to improve stability when there are significant changes in the environment. In the OSI model of Table 4.8, the outer loop is in the network layer and the inner loop is in the data link and physical layers. The network layer corresponds to the structural level in the FBS model, and the data link and physical layers correspond to the behavioral level, see Table 5.9. The double-feedback principle is more general than Adam Smith's, Charles Darwin's, Karl Popper's, and Burrhus Frederic Skinner's theories. Using double feedback, Chris Argyris and Donald Schön (1978) developed the concepts of single- and *double-loop learning* where the outer loop changes the governing variables. Gregory Bateson (1972) coined deutero learning, which means learning to learn. In human organizations, process improvement is an example of double feedback. The outer loop now results in slow structural changes in the process.

A related concept to ultrastability is *self-stabilization* developed by Edsger W. Dijkstra (1974). It refers to a property of distributed computing systems that allows them to recover from any arbitrary state, including states that may result from faults or errors. This means that regardless of the initial conditions or any transient faults that may occur, a self-stabilizing system will eventually converge to a legitimate state and remain in that state, allowing systems to maintain functionality.

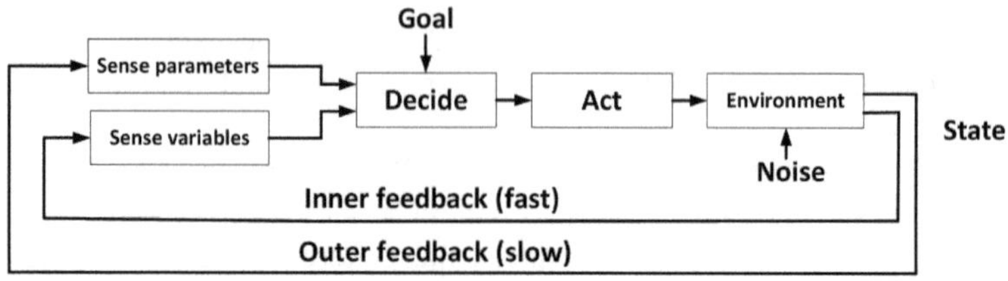

Fig. 6.1 Double feedback leading to self-organization and ultrastability

Peter D. Joseph and Julius T. Tou (1961) developed the separation theorem that separated estimation and control in analog systems. T. L. Gunckel, II, and Gene F. Franklin (1963) did the same in digital systems.

Karel Čapek (1920) used the term "robot" in his science fiction play "R.U.R." Rossum's Universal Robots to denote an automaton (Mämmelä et al. 2018). The word comes from Czech *robotnik*, "forced worker," essentially an enslaved person (Online Etymology Dictionary 2024). Nikola Tesla (1898) developed a remote control for a radio-controlled miniature boat. Willard V. Pollard (1938) studied a robotic arm. In a science fiction novel, Robert A. Heinlein (1942) proposed a primitive master–slave manipulator system. Raymond C. Goertz (1945) started his work on an electronically controlled telemanipulator using a remote control known as teleoperation at that time. R. C. Goertz and W. M. Thompson published the results in 1954. In 1966, William R. Ferrell (1966) published the first paper to consider a constraint in a control loop in contact force feedback. It was the first rudimentary kinesthetic feedback system, showing that a delay of 100 ms made the system unstable. Control Area Network (CAN) (1983–1986) was one of the first networked control systems (NCSs). Robert J. Anderson and Mark W. Spong (1989) studied the stability problem caused by the feedback delay. Ken Goldberg et al. (1995) started remote control over the Internet. Later, Imad Elhajj et al. (2001) and Gerhard P. Fettweis (2014) used haptic and tactile feedback over the Internet, respectively.

The results of control and computer engineering are combined in autonomous robots, which are agents at the same time (Mämmelä et al. 2018). W. Grey Walter (1948–1949) built the first autonomous mobile robots in the form of two tortoises. Nils J. Nilsson (1969) developed one of the first robot architectures in a robot called Shakey. Only one hierarchy level was used; such robots were slow and clumsy. Layer hierarchy is now the most common robot architecture. Rodney Brooks (1986) developed the reactive subsumption architecture, and it was the first significant improvement where the layers were directly connected to the sensors and actuators. Ronald C. Arkin (1986) developed an autonomous robot architecture. James S. Albus, Alexander M. Meystel, and George A. Bekey summarized several intelligent architectures in Albus and Meystel (2001) and Bekey (2005). Anthony J. Barbera et al. (1979) developed a Real-Time Control System (RCS), later used by Albus and Meystel. Robert J. Firby (1989) originated the modern proactive architectures where the lowest layer is responsible for the movement, the next layer chooses the current movement, and the uppermost layer makes plans for the long-term goals within the resource constraints.

The most advanced robots are social robots that can interact with each other (Bekey 2005, pp. 391–439). Maja Mataric (1992) developed one of the first multiple-robot architectures that used simple primitives, including collision avoidance, following, dispersion, aggregation, homing, and flocking. George A. Bekey summarized the results of five such architectures: communication between robots and cooperation without communication. Some robots use swarm intelligence to formation control.

System dynamics System dynamics is described as applying feedback concepts to social systems (Forrester 1968, 2007a, b). The founding father of system dynamics was Jay Forrester (1958), who counted the start of system dynamics from his first paper, "Industrial dynamics: a major breakthrough for decision makers," published in 1958. He published his first results in book form titled *Industrial Dynamics* in 1961. System dynamics is cybernetics of social systems, but the system dynamics follows the servomechanism thread. Simon (1954) was one of the first to model a human as a feedback loop (Richardson 1991). Norbert Wiener was cautious in applying cybernetics to social sciences because cybernetics is mechanistic and based on physics (Hayden 2006). According to him, social systems are too open, irregular, and dynamic for a mechanistic theory to apply. In cybernetics, we treat feedback as a "tool for controlling systems in the face of [external] disturbances." In contrast, in system dynamics, we see feedback loops "as an internal aspect of the structure of social systems" (Richardson 1991, p. 164; Ramage and Shipp 2020). However, system dynamics has been able to predict, for example, both the short-term business cycles and long-term Kondratiev cycles (Forrester 2007a). Analysis is not generally possible if there are many feedback loops or nonlinearity, as in many real systems. Using computer models, Forrester noticed that interaction delays created positive feedback loops, causing instability (Ramage and Shipp 2020).

The long-term forecasts in the reports by the Club of Rome were based on system dynamics. Results may be rough, but a better understanding of macrophenomena in our society may help us to prevent harmful effects so that we are not only extinguishing fires. According to Charles Francois, systems thinking has not been used much in economics (Francois 1999). However, this may be dangerous in cases like sustainability, including global management of energy flows, waste recycling, and short- and long-term stability. Governments can make the long-term instability more severe by encouraging over-building (Forrester 2007a).

Thermodynamics Herman Helmholtz (1847) formulated the first law of thermodynamics based on the earlier work by James Joule (1843) and others. Sadi Carnot (1824) showed a fundamental limit to how much energy could be extracted from a heat engine. Rudolf Clausius (1850) generalized the observation to the entropy law, which is the second law of thermodynamics. He used the term entropy to measure a system's disorder for the first time in 1865 (Corning 2002; Marcos and Arp 2013). The term entropy takes its analogy from the term energy and comes from Greek *entropia* that includes the Greek *trope* "a transformation" (Online Etymology Dictionary 2024). Clausius thus replaced his earlier expression "transformation content of the body" with the new word entropy. Thermodynamics was born after Willard Gibbs published his extensive paper in 1876–1878, and Helmholtz published his paper "Thermodynamik chemischer Vorgänge" in 1882. Under certain conditions, either the Clausius internal energy or Gibbs or Helmholtz free energy is minimized in a closed system. William Thomson or Lord Kelvin (1848) found the absolute zero temperature and defined the third law of thermodynamics (1854).

Nonequilibrium thermodynamics Nonequilibrium thermodynamics is the product of the work by Ilya Prigogine, started in 1947. The inspiration came from Henri Bergson's (1911) comment as to why, according to physical theories, systems either continue without change, as in Newtonian mechanics, or decline, as in the entropy law (Boulton et al. 2015). He published the book *Introduction to Thermodynamics of Irreversible Processes* in 1955. He received a Nobel Prize in chemistry in 1977 "for his contributions to nonequilibrium thermodynamics, particularly the theory of dissipative structures."

Nonequilibrium economics In his book *Entropy Law and the Economic Process* (Bahg 1990; Swilling 2020), Nicholas Georgescu-Roegen (1971) found various similarities between economy and entropic processes. Some authors think this result was the most important work in economics for several decades. Nonequilibrium or complexity economics has been a product of many economists (Arthur 2021). The most visible of them seems to be W. Brian Arthur.

Theory of information transmission Information theory by Claude E. Shannon is an extension of the earlier work by Harry Nyquist (1924) and Ralph Hartley (1928). Nyquist derived the maximum symbol rate that is equivalent to the minimum sampling frequency for band-limited signals, and Hartley approximated the channel capacity. Shannon presented a rigorous theory for both of them. Marcel J. E. Golay (1949) derived the Shannon limit using Shannon's capacity equation.

The sampling theorem is the basis for analog-to-digital conversion (ADC) (Kester 2015). If the sampling rate is larger than twice the signal bandwidth, the original signal can be reconstructed from the samples using a suitable low-pass filter. The low pass filter is a digital-to-analog converter (DAC), conceptually much more straightforward than the ADC. For digital signal processing, the samples are discretized in amplitude. Willard M. Miner (1903) patented a time-division multiplexing (TDM) method by sampling an analog signal before the Nyquist sampling theorem was known. Paul M. Rainey patented pulse-code modulation (PCM). The patent was filed in 1921 and issued in 1926. Alec H. Reeves (1937) invented PCM independently for digital speech transmission. PCM was the first practical method for analog-to-digital conversion. Harold S. Black and J. O. Edson (1947) developed the first successive approximation ADC.

Network theory Network or graph theory started when Leonhard Euler (1736) studied the seven bridges of Königsberg (Newman 2010). He proved that there was no solution to the problem: it was impossible to pass each bridge only once. Helen Hall Jennings and Jacob Moreno (1938) were the first to use the concept of random graphs, and P. Erdos and A. Renyi (1959) derived the random graph theory.

Milgram (1967) was the first to study the small-world network using the postal service (Milgram 1967; Buchanan 2002; Watts 2004). He sent 160 letters to randomly selected people in Nebraska and Kansas and asked them to forward the letter to a stockbroker in Boston without giving them the address. They were advised to send the letter to a friend who was socially closer to the stockbroker. Surprisingly, the number of mailings was typically only six or so. It takes only six handshakes to go between any two people in the world. The number was called "six degrees of separation," and the network thus observed was called the small-world network. Duncan Watts and Steven H. Strogatz (1998) started to analyze the small-world networks. They have been found in many unexpected and unrelated networks made by humans or evolution: global ecosystems, power lines, the Internet, living cells, the nervous system in a nematode worm, and the human brain.

Derek J. de Solla Price (1965) noticed by studying citation networks a property according to which they were later called *scale-free networks*. The phenomenon is referred to as preferential attachment: papers with many citations receive more citations since they are better known. The phenomenon means that "rich are getting richer" (Buchanan 2002). Albert-Laszlo Barabasi and Reka Albert (1999) made a test where preferential attachment was considered. All the networks they produced were small-world networks, but they were also scale-free or aristocratic. The networks were clustered to have a hub feature since some people acted as connectors in the networks. They have a power-law pattern: if we double the number of links, the number of persons with that many links to other persons falls off by about eight. The power-law pattern is the reason why they are called scale-free, a name coined by Barabasi and Albert. A similar phenomenon appears in groupthink, which was studied by Irving Janis (1972). A few people dominate the opinions of the others, and all tend to think similarly and do not consider alternative options.

General theory of systems Ludwig von Bertalanffy was the pioneer in the general theory of systems, publishing his first papers in English in 1950 (von Bertalanffy 1950a, b). He introduced the open system concept to biology in 1932 and summarized his work in the anthology (von Bertalanffy 1971). Since then, the theory has significantly progressed, and a more advanced theory is complexity theory.

Hierarchy theory The hierarchy theory is summarized in Wu (2013). Herbert Simon pioneered this theory (Simon 1962, 1973) and summarized it in the book (Simon 1996). Initially, he used the term near decomposability (Simon 1962) for loose coupling, and later, he developed the concepts of vertical and horizontal loose coupling (Simon 1973). However, in his book (Simon 1996), he again uses the term near decomposability. Kenneth E. Boulding developed a complexity hierarchy for natural systems (Boulding 1956, 1985). He also presented a physical, biological, social, economic, political, communication, and evaluative (decision-making) systems hierarchy. James G. Miller (1973) noticed that feedback is a core concept in various living and social systems. Thus, he could unify the biological and social sciences in a hierarchy.

Optimization and decision theory The origin of the utility theory is in the works by Blaise Pascal and Pierre de Fermat (1654). Utilitarianism is a product of Jeremy Bentham (1789) and John Stuart Mill (1863). Utilitarian means "one guided by the doctrine of the greatest happiness for the greatest number" (Online Etymology Dictionary 2024). The word utility comes from the Latin *utilitatem*, "usefulness." Bentham defined utility as "that property in any object whereby it tends to produce pleasure, good or happiness, or to prevent the happening of mischief, pain, evil or unhappiness to the party whose interest is considered" (Encyclopedia Britannica 2024).

The word heuristic means "serving to discover or find out," similar to the Greek *heuriskein*, "to find out, discover, devise, invent," and *heurema*, "an invention, a discovery; that which is found unexpectedly" (Online Etymology Dictionary 2024). The word eureka comes from the Greek *heureka*, "I have found (it)." The word was famously used by Archimedes after one of his discoveries.

The history of multiple criteria decision-making (MCDM) started in the 1700s with the works of Benjamin Franklin and Marquis de Condorcet (Köksalan et al. 2011). Francis Y. Edgeworth and Vilfredo Pareto developed the main concepts of MCDM. The jointly optimal system is sometimes called the Edgeworth-Pareto optimum since Edgeworth (1881) developed the idea of the Pareto optimum 25 years before Pareto (1906). Harry Markowitz (1952) defined the efficient frontier as one corresponding to the Pareto optima set.

Optimization and decision theory are parts of operations research, each with a long history (Bahg 1990; Gass and Assad 2005). Operations research started in the 1940s, and decision and optimization theory began in the 1950s. According to Gass and Assad (2005), the birth of operations research cannot be stated equivocally, but it started between 1936 and 1946, and there were many precursors since the 1500s and 1600s. The term operational research is the British natal name of the area. The first integrated text on operations research was *Introduction to Operations Research* by C. West Churchman et al. (1957).

The complexity of an optimization problem is usually exponential in terms of its size, and some heuristic methods are used (Talbi 2009, pp. 14, 22). Since the optimum is generally not unique, we must decide which optimum should be used.

Optimization decomposition has a rich history dating back to the 1950s, and it is closely related to different separation theorems, near decomposability, and loose coupling. The term decomposition has meant "act or process of separating the constituent elements of a compound body" since 1762 (Online Etymology Dictionary 2024). The term composition comes from the Latin *compositionem*, "a putting together, connecting, arranging." Shannon (1948) separated source and channel coding in a communication link (Chiang et al. 2007). Robert Price (1956) used the separation theorem in his estimator-correlator receiver. Peter D. Joseph and Julius T. Tou (1961) separated estimation and control in analog control systems. Similar separation theorems were derived for time-discrete systems. K. Watt and P. Craig (1988) presented their system separability principle, which states that system stability increases when the parts are loosely coupled.

Richard E. Bellman coined in 1952 the term *principle of optimality* and developed in 1953 dynamic programming as an optimization technique for multistage decision problems (Köksalan et al. 2011). His book (Bellman 1957) elaborated the idea, and the term curse of dimensionality also appears. Some other key contributions to optimization decomposition came from pioneers like George Dantzig and Philip Wolfe (1960) and J. F. Benders (1962), who started the area of *distributed optimization*. One of the most recent results is the application of network utility maximization to network optimization (Chiang et al. 2007). The hierarchical solution includes vertical decomposition into layers with protocol stacks and horizontal decomposition into distributed computation and control across geographically disparate network elements.

Detection and estimation theory Detection and estimation theories were products of the 1950s. Much earlier, Carl F. Gauss (1795) and Adrien-Marie Legendre (1805) discovered independently the least squares estimator (Haykin 2014), and Ronald A. Fisher (1920) developed the maximum likelihood estimator (Gass and Assad 2005; Kim and Shevlyakov 2008). Fisher realized the importance of distinguishing probability and likelihood. Dwight O. North (1943) and J. H. Van Vleck and David Middleton (1946) invented the matched filter, and P. M. Woodward and I. L. Davies (1952) used the maximum a posteriori probability (MAP) receiver, both in a known channel. Andrei N. Kolmogorov (1939), Mark G. Krein (1945), and Norbert Wiener (1949) invented the nonrecursive Wiener filter, and Peter Swerling (1958) and Rudolf E. Kalman (1960) the recursive Kalman filter, both for minimizing the mean-square error (Young 2011; Haykin 2014). Robert Price (1956) and Kailath (1960, 1969) developed the estimator-correlator receiver in an unknown linear or nonlinear channel having additive Gaussian noise. This idea is identical to the separation theorem later discovered in control engineering with similar assumptions. The receivers were later generalized to symbol sequence estimation, where the symbols have intersymbol interference (Proakis and Salehi 2008). Similarly, the receivers were generalized to many interfering users of a shared channel (Lucky 1973).

Artificial intelligence Many histories of artificial intelligence (AI) exist, including (McCorduck 2004; Nilsson 2010). The AI started at the "Summer Research Project on Artificial Intelligence" conference at Dartmouth College, Hanover, NH, in the summer of 1956. It was a workshop for six weeks, organized by John McCarthy, who in 1955 coined the term artificial intelligence (Nilsson 2010, pp. 52–56).

There were many contributors to the concept of an agent and the history remains somewhat vague. Norbert Wiener (1948) can be seen as the developer of the idea of the human agent as a "circular process", i.e., a feedback loop. However, he did not use the term agent (Wiener 1961, p. 8): "The central nervous system no longer appears as a self-contained organ, receiving inputs from the senses and discharging into the muscles. On the contrary, some of its most characteristic activities are explicable only as circular processes, emerging from the nervous system into the muscles, and re-entering the nervous system through the sense organs, whether they be proprioceptors or organs of the special senses." In various contexts, Simon (1954) asked how people solve problems and make decisions (Simon 1954; Richardson 1991, pp. 3, 145, 147–148, 272). He identified feedback as a primary mechanism of adaptive behavior and introduced the concept of bounded rationality. He suggested that the feedback concept is a basis for models for human behavior. The model is a human agent. He emphasized that the idea of a physiological system was not novel (probably referring to cybernetics), but the idea of a social system was relatively new. He did not develop the concept much further. His ideas became cornerstones in Jay Forrester's system dynamics on social systems.

The founders of AI were John McCarthy, Marvin Minsky, Allen Newell, and Herbert A. Simon. McCarthy selected the name so that AI would stand out from the theory of automata and cybernetics. The latter focused on analog feedback. AI is a combination of control, computing, and communication (Mämmelä et al. 2018). Other people attending the workshop included Arthur Samuel and Oliver Selfridge. Newell and Simon did not like the term AI and used the term complex information processing for many years, which looks like a precursor of complex adaptive systems. In 1955, Newell and Simon studied heuristic problem solving, which Simon called a thinking machine since he thought humans use similar methods.

Alan Kay stated that "the idea of an agent originated with John McCarthy in the mid-1950s, and the term was coined by Oliver G. Selfridge a few years later when they were both at the Massachusetts Institute of Technology" (Kay 1984). Furthermore, "the origins of the software agent concept are often traced back to the pioneers of artificial intelligence—John McCarthy, the creator of LISP programming language, and Carl Hewitt, the father of distributed artificial intelligence (DAI)" (Stanek et al. 2008). Hewitt acknowledges the conversations with Kay, McCarthy, and Newell (Hewitt 1977). The distributed AI is now called the multiagent systems (MAS). The meaning of the term agent has been since the fifteenth century "the one who acts," coming from the Latin *agentem*, "effective, powerful" (Online Etymology Dictionary 2024).

Arthur Samuel (1959) proposed the term machine learning, and James C. Bezdek (1994) the term computational intelligence (Mämmelä et al. 2018; Riekki and Mämmelä 2021). They are now included in AI. Many machine learning and computational intelligence systems and those used in data science are monitoring systems. Although the environment is often not controlled, they may apply feedback, for example, in reinforcement learning. Marvin Minsky (1954) discovered reinforcement learning and later published it in Minsky (1961), referring to B. F. Skinner's earlier work.

Carl Hewitt used the software agent concept in distributed AI in 1977 (Hewitt 1977; Decker 1987; Sen 1997; Sycara 1998). He often used the term "actor," which is a human agent in social sciences. The agents passed messages using distributed control. Reid Smith (1980) contributed to multiagent systems using contract nets. This new field of distributed AI was later divided into multiagent systems and distributed problem-solving. The idea of multiagent systems developed slowly in the 1980s and became popular only at the beginning of the 1990s. The theory of agents became a significant part of AI in about 1987 (Russell and Norvig 2022, p. 79), soon after Jeff Rosenschein and Michael Genesereth (1985) applied game theory in multiagent interactions in their paper "Deals among rational agents" (Nilsson 2010, p. 467). The first conference on multiagent systems was organized in San Francisco, CA, in June 1995. The agents are still very much alive in complexity theory.

Initially, the AI researchers focused on self-organizing systems and organized three conferences around 1960 (Umpleby 2009). The researchers were too optimistic and realized they had to select more narrow topics. A bottom-up approach was needed to understand high-level concepts. The complexity theory focuses on self-organizing systems called complex adaptive systems (CASs), and interacting agents were taken as the central concept (Holland and Miller 1991; Holland 1992, 1995; Benbya and McKelvey 2006; Mobus 2022). Thus, researchers have traveled a full circle since 1962. The concept of CASs has been significantly discussed in natural and social sciences, and it was later introduced to engineering sciences (McCarthy et al. 2006). The CAS is essentially a multiagent system. Physical sciences developed chaos theory: complex patterns or order can arise from the complexity through self-organization (Dooley 1997). In biological sciences, the CAS theory allows us to analyze the self-organizing system holistically.

A holonic multiagent system is one of the agent organizations (Horling and Lesser 2004; Calabrese et al. 2010; Dorri et al. 2018). Agent-oriented and holonic manufacturing paradigms have received much attention in industry and academia (Bussman 1998). Originally, holons were recursive structures as implied by the nested hierarchy, but this property is not characteristic of agents (Calabrese et al. 2010). Holons form holarchies generally represented as dynamic hierarchical structures, but agent architectures form horizontal and vertical organizations. The IEC 61499 standard "Function blocks for industrial process measurement and control systems" (2005) defined a holonic manufacturing system (HMS) (Strasser et al. 2011). The standard has also been applied in smart grids that use bidirectional communications with distributed intelligent devices (Strasser et al. 2015).

AI had many precursors. An important theory now included in AI is the optimization and decision theory. Some of the first papers on pattern recognition were published in 1954. Knowledge discovery and data mining started in about 1990. John Mashey (1998) suggested the term big data. Also, in 1998, the term appeared in the book *Predictive Data Mining: A Practical Guide* by Sholom M. Weiss and Nitin Indurkhya.

The *Internet of Things (IoT)* offers large amounts of data. Peter T. Lewis (1985) first proposed the concept and the term IoT (Jerabandi and Kodabagi 2017). Mark Weiser's 1991 paper "The computer of the twenty-first century" on ubiquitous or pervasive computing essentially offered a detailed description of the IoT and the smart world although the terms were not used in that paper (Riekki and Mämmelä 2021).

Edward Feigenbaum (1975) developed the first practical AI systems called expert systems (Mämmelä et al. 2018). According to Albus and Meystel (2001, p. 112), AI focuses on static systems, whereas dynamic systems belong to control engineering. For example, the book (Russell and Norvig 2022) never mentions the term self-organization which would imply dynamic operation. Still, in modern reviews of multiagent systems, self-organization is an important topic (Ye et al. 2017; Dorri et al. 2018). Now, complexity theory is very much interested in interacting agents in the theory of self-organization (Holland and Miller 1991; Dooley 1997).

In neural networks, Warren McCulloch and Walter Pitts (1943) published the artificial neuron forming a neural network, and Frank Rosenblatt (1958) the perceptron, which is a simple supervised learning algorithm for a single-layer neural network (Corchado et al. 2023). Different multilayer neural networks have been developed since 1965. The limitations of this network and the limited computing speed at that time led to reduced interest in artificial intelligence until David E. Rumelhart, Geoffrey E. Hinton, and Ronald J. Williams (1986) invented the backpropagation algorithm, which could train multilayer networks. John J. Hopfield (1982) invented the Hopfield network, which can store exponentially many patterns and retrieve the pattern with one update. Alex Krizhevsky, Ilya Sutskever, and Geoffrey E. Hinton (2012) introduced a convolutional neural network, thus starting a high interest in deep learning (LeCun et al. 2015; Zappone et al. 2019). Natural language processing (NLP) began in the 1950s by combining AI and linguistics. The idea for transformers is originally from Vaswani et al. (2017). In 2024, Hopfield and Hinton shared a Nobel Prize in physics "for foundational discoveries and inventions that enable machine learning with artificial neural networks."

Self-organizing systems Histories of self-organization are included in De Wolf and Holvoet (2005) and Tzafestas (2018), and a history of multiagent systems in Sen (1997). Surveys on self-organizing and multiagent systems are presented in Prehofer and Bettstetter (2005), Dressler (2008), Ye et al. (2017) and Dorri et al. (2018).

In biology, one of the greatest problems is morphogenesis, which corresponds to self-organization (von Bertalanffy 1971). The term morphogenesis has been used since 1863, meaning "the production of the form or shape of an organism" (Online Etymology Dictionary 2024). The term comes from Greek *morph-* "form or shape" and *genesis* "origin, creation, generation." Thompson (1917) and Turing (1952) described it scientifically (Briscoe and Kicheva 2017).

In physical sciences, biology, and engineering, the term self-organization is also used; in social sciences, a common term is *spontaneous order*. An alternative term for self-organization is *pattern formation*. W. Ross Ashby (1947) was the first to propose the concept of a self-organizing system in his paper "Principles of the self-organizing dynamic system" (Ramage and Shipp 2020). He studied the problem if a system can be "'self-organizing,' i.e., that it can be determinate and yet able to undergo spontaneous changes of internal organization."

Initially, the word *organ* meant "instrument" and later, "a body part" (Online Etymology Dictionary 2024). The broad meaning "that which performs some function" is from the 1540s. The word *organize* with the modern meaning "to form into a whole consisting of interdependent parts" is from the 1630s.

Two theoretical approaches have been proposed to the problem of self-organization, using either a combination of positive and negative feedback or second-order cybernetics (Francois 1999). These ideas have not been widely used in technical self-organizing systems, but positive feedback is used within a negative feedback loop (Ogata 2010). Maruyama (1963) was one of the first to notice that positive or deviation-amplifying feedback is an essential component in natural and social systems, in addition to negative or deviation-counteracting feedback (Maruyama 1963). Positive and negative feedback are used in morphogenesis. Another example is evolution, which includes positive feedback in several ways. Based on this idea, Maruyama suggested second cybernetics, which combines positive and negative feedback and is now used in system dynamics, which could be called second cybernetics. Another theory for self-organization is second-order cybernetics or observing systems (Scott 2004; Umpleby 2016; Ramage and Shipp 2020) that should not be mixed with second cybernetics (Francois 1999). Heinz Von Förster (1974) suggested second-order cybernetics.

Self-organizing networks Reviews on the history of self-organizing networks (SONs) are included in Robertazzi and Sarachik (1986), Ramanathan and Redi (2002), Di Marzo Serugendo et al. (2011) and Aliu et al. (2013). Initially, the AI researchers focused on self-organizing systems, and several books were published. The first major conference on self-organizing systems was organized in Chicago, IL, on 5–6 May 1959 (Ramage and Shipp 2020). The papers were published in the book *Self-Organizing Systems* (1960), edited by Marshall C. Yovits and S. Cameron. Soon afterward, two additional conferences were organized. For example, Marshall C. Yovits, George T. Jacobi, and Gordon D. Goldstein published the edited book *Self-Organizing Systems* in 1962 (Hoffman 1964; Cohen and Feigenbaum 1982; Mämmelä et al. 2023). Ashby's classic self-organization paper was published then (Ashby 1962). According to him, self-organization has two meanings: (1) a system that starts from an unorganized set of separate parts to an organized system or (2) a system that changes from a bad organization to a good one. In the preface of one of those conference proceedings (1962), there is the definition: "A self-organizing system is a system which changes its basic structure as a function of its experience and environment" (Hoffman 1964; Cohen and Feigenbaum 1982; Mämmelä et al. 2023). An example was a growing crystal. The topic was seen as interdisciplinary and exciting and involved mathematics, physics, biology, psychology, engineering, and neurophysiology. Two different kinds of self-organizing systems were identified. The first has a goal structure imposed externally, as in technical systems. The second one is much more complex and has an internally evolved goal-structure as in living systems.

The first self-organizing network was the Arpanet (1969), which was based on packet switching, invented by Leonard Kleinrock (1961), Baran (1964), and Donald W. Davies (1965) (Huurdeman 2003; Mämmelä et al. 2018; Riekki and Mämmelä 2021). Kleinrock published in 1964 his results in the book *Communication Nets*. Baran (1964) devised a distributed network to survive nuclear attacks (Baran 1964). It was Davies who introduced in 1967 the term message *packet*. Joseph C. R. Licklider, Leonard Kleinrock, and Laurence C. Roberts developed Arpanet independently of Baran's work. Arpanet eventually became the Internet (1983) as a distributed best-effort network (Wydrowski and Zukerman 2002). The performance can be improved using various techniques to make it look more like a dedicated Internet for a user.

Packet radio networks were the first ad hoc networks that were special cases of self-organizing networks. They have been developed for wireless communications since 1972 (Kahn et al. 1978). Distributed self-organizing networks were systematically studied in the 1980s (Robertazzi and Sarachik 1986). Ad hoc networks are their special form. The term "ad hoc network" was recommended by the IEEE 802.11 subcommittee in 1993 (Ramanathan and Redi 2002), but the term had been used earlier in the literature. Swarm intelligence is a form of evolutionary computing that is practical in ad hoc networks (Zhang et al. 2014; Mämmelä et al. 2023). Swarm intelligence is the collective intelligence of simple agents that form a distributed self-organizing system. Gerardo Beni and Jing Wang (1993) invented swarm intelligence using the concept of cellular automata.

Until about 2010, it was believed that self-organization would be based on distributed control (Prehofer and Bettstetter 2005; Dressler 2008; Roy 2008; Frampton et al. 2010) because biological organisms behave like that. Distributed control implies that the system does not need any goal. Biological organisms do not have any set-point value (Bekey 2005). For example, there is no target value for our body temperature, but it still stays close to the 36.5–37.5 °C range. We do not know how organisms work. Without a goal, a technical self-organizing system may have stability problems. Distributed self-organizing systems can become a primary source of failure since local optimization does not result in global optimization, and global behavior cannot be predicted from local behavior due to the emergence of nonlinear systems (Bongaerts et al. 2000; Cao et al. 2013; Silk et al. 2016). Therefore, a self-organizing network needs at least a weak centralized control offering a goal. In a society, the goal consists of the values, beliefs, and visions forming our culture (Boulding 1969; Guiso et al. 2006; Korkman 2022).

Chess et al. (1995) suggested mobile agents using the term itinerant agents for active networks (Chess et al. 1995; Breugst and Magedanz 1998). The networks are called active since the nodes can modify the packet contents. Mobile agents, as software agents, can roam between the nodes. However, roaming may increase energy consumption, network management becomes complex, and the agents in modern networks are not mobile. SDNs were networks where the data and control planes are separated (1998) (Feamster 2013; Nunes et al. 2014; Qiu 2016). Now, the more general term *network automation* is preferred since one can use application programming interfaces (APIs) (2008) in programmable networks. OpenFlow (2008) is an excellent example of this. The OSI model (1984) already included standardized horizontal interfaces or APIs for all its layers (Pautasso and Wilde 2009). Using agents in SONs was suggested in Bauer and Müller (2001) and Piraveenan et al. (2008).

Somers (1996) was among the first to discuss H-SONs in communications (Somers 1996). In 3GPP Rel. 8 (2008), the concepts of C-SON, D-SON, and H-SON were defined briefly without any details (Fourati et al. 2021). Soon after, the GANA architecture was proposed using the terminology developed for autonomic computing (Kephart and Chess 2003). The ETSI published a GANA white paper (2016), which later became an ETSI standard (ETSI 2018). The hybrid systems have been used in other disciplines with different names, including multilevel, multigoal systems in hierarchical control (Mesarovic et al. 1970) and holonic control architecture (Bongaerts et al. 2000). In social systems, subsidiarity is the closest to the hybrid systems.

Hybrid systems combine the beneficial properties of hierarchical, centrally controlled, and distributed systems and loose coupling (Strasser et al. 2011, 2015). The lower-level agents are almost autonomous (Bongaerts et al. 2000). In addition to hybrid systems, locality or local interaction is used in cellular automata and systolic arrays (Mämmelä et al. 2023). Systolic arrays were initially used in the Mark 2 Colossus computer (1944) for massively parallel computing and regular data flow, and Hsiang-Tsung Kung and Charles E. Leiserson (1979) elaborated on the idea (Kung 1984). Energy consumption and delays are minimized by using locality.

Autopoiesis John Von Neumann (1948) developed a cellular automaton to simulate self-replicating or self-producing systems (Sarkat 2000). The idea was published by Stanislav M. Ulam and John von Neumann (1950) and posthumously in a further developed form by von Neumann (1963). Nils A. Barricelli (1954) presented the idea of artificial life (Fogel 2006). His paper was also the first one on evolutionary simulation. Christopher Langton (1986) proposed the term artificial life, but the term is controversial since such things are not living but just self-organizing. Humberto R. Maturana (1974) proposed *autopoiesis* (Ramage and Shipp 2020). It is a theory of self-producing systems that maintain their boundary. Maturana and Francesco J. Varela (1980) developed the theory of autopoiesis in biology. As discussed in Cornish-Bowden and Luz Cardenas (2020), there are five major life theories and autopoiesis is among them.

Complexity theory Santa Fe Institute was founded in 1984 in Santa Fe, NM, after two two-day workshops. The original idea came from George Cowan, a chemist who had dreamed of it since the 1950s. His talk at the Aspen Institute in 1956 was ahead of time. He believed that the physical sciences could solve human problems. In the first board meeting, Cowan was selected as the first president, and the board's first chairman was Murray Gell-Mann. Soon afterward, David Pines, a physicist, became the chairman. Gell-Mann, Kenneth J. Arrow, and Philip W. Anderson were Nobelists involved in the new Santa Fe Institute.

A two-week workshop on complex adaptive systems was organized in 1986, and complex adaptive systems were selected as a unifying concept (Holland 1995, 1998). Originally, complexity theory started from chaos theory: how order emerges at the edge of order and chaos. It was an active field of study at that time.

Walter F. Buckley (1968) was probably the first to use the term complex adaptive systems in his book chapter "Society as a complex adaptive system," published in the book *Systems Research for Behavioral Science* edited by Buckley. John Holland, Murray Gell-Mann, and Stuart Kauffman were some of the significant figures to expand the idea of complexity theory (Holland 1995; Kauffman 1995; Ramage and Shipp 2020). Researchers at the Santa Fe Institute have published many important books, such as West (2017). Murray Gell-Mann received a Nobel Prize in physics in 1969 for his work on elementary particles. The CAS concept corresponds to the multiagent systems developed independently in artificial intelligence since the work in Hewitt (1977).

John Holland probably published the first scientific papers explicitly defining complex adaptive systems using interacting agents (Holland and Miller 1991; Holland 1992, 1995, 2006). Holland emphasizes that all CASs are formed, without exception, by those agents (Holland 1995). A CAS is a network of interacting agents so that each agent has other agents in its environment. The CAS has three properties: evolution, aggregate behavior, and anticipation. The agents evolve in Darwinian fashion. An agent is adaptive if it has a measure of goodness whose value the agent can increase. The measure of goodness may be, for example, utility, payoff, or fitness. The network shows dynamic aggregate behavior that emerges from the individual actions of the agents. The agents can anticipate the consequences of their actions. They are thus proactive, not only reactive.

Feedback was only implicit in early Holland's texts, but the term appeared in Holland (2006). He initially defined agents using stimulus–response rules with an if–then–else structure, which implicitly includes feedback. The "if" command refers to the sense operation, the "then" command refers to the act operation, and the "else" command is an alternative, and the structure implies decision-making. The if–then–else structure is a simple rule-based agent.

Dooley (1997) later discussed the definition further. Agents may exchange information and resources. They sense their environment and take action to adapt to the observation. Dooley thus included the idea of feedback in his definition, although he did not use the term explicitly.

Nonlinear dynamics and chaos theory The history of nonlinear dynamics in economics is presented in Perona (2005) and chaos theory in Diacu and Holmes (1996), where the authors' goal was also to go deeper into the mathematical foundations of the *n*-body problem in physics from where Henri Poincare (1890) had started. Poincare also opened the field of instability studies (Francois 1999). Edward Lorenz (1963) encountered the problem when he forecasted weather using simulations (Gleick 1987; Casti 1994). When he continued a simulation, he used rounded numbers and noticed that the results were sensitive to rounding operations. He also discovered the strange attractor whose shape led to the *butterfly effect*: a butterfly flapping its wings, for example, in Brazil, can cause a snowstorm in Alaska the next day. Chaos theory in the modern mathematical sense was first used in about 1977 when the New York Academy of Sciences organized the first symposium on chaos.

Catastrophe theory Catastrophe theory was developed by Rene Thom (1972), who studied catastrophes in morphogenesis (Casti 1994). Initially, the cells are of generic types and later differentiated to become, for example, liver, muscle, and brain cells. The problem is how the fate of each cell is decided through chemical interactions of neighboring cells. Morphogenesis had earlier been studied by D'Arcy W. Thompson, Alan Turing, and Conrad H. Waddington. Earlier results also included those of Hassler V. Whitney (1955), who studied singular transformations caused by twisting, folding, and bending a paper. The transformations are unstable points in catastrophe theory. There are only a limited number of catastrophic situations.

System archetypes

In Mämmelä et al. (2018, 2023), we studied the elements of system archetypes that included feedback, optimization, decision-making, hierarchy, and degree of centralization. All of them are covered next except the history of optimization and decision-making, which we covered among system theories.

Feedback Several authors have summarized the feedback history (Mayr 1970a, b; Bennett 1979a, b, 1996, Bennett 2002; Richardson 1991; Bernstein 2002). The concept is seen as an invisible thread in the history of technology. The term *feedback* was used for the first time in a paper titled "An inductive feed-back in relation to the secondary system generates local oscillations" in *Wireless Age* in 1920 (Bennett 1979a, p. 1). The feedback was, in this case, parasitic. Feedback means "the return of a fraction of an output signal to the input of an earlier stage" (Online Etymology Dictionary 2024). The concept of feedback has been reinvented many times with different terms (Table 6.6). Often, feedback is called a *loop*, as in the OODA loop, a *cycle*, as in the V-cycle, or a *wheel*, as in the Deming wheel.

The earliest known use of feedback was in Ktesibios's water clock in about 270 BCE (Mayr 1970a; Encyclopedia Britannica 2024). In modern times, Cornelis Dreppel (1624) invented a thermostat. Adam Smith (1776) used negative feedback in his law of supply and demand in economics (Richardson 1991). Thomas Malthus (1798) predicted exponential population growth with what we now would call positive feedback. Carl Ludwig and Elie de Cyon (1866) discovered the first example of the biological regulator in the human body, determining the heart's work (Neil 1962; Francois 1999).

Robert Goddard (1912) was the first to consciously apply feedback principles in electronics to a vacuum tube oscillator (Lee 2004). However, Robert A. Scholtz mentions in his spread-spectrum history that a patent on feedback control existed already in 1905 (Scholtz 1982) without specifying what patent it was.

Edwin H. Armstrong (1913) used positive feedback in his audion receiver to improve the gain of the amplifier (Bennett 1979a, p. 186). He noticed the possibility of instability if the gain was too large. At the same time, Charles S. Franklin was the first to describe the positive feedback in his regenerative amplifier clearly. Nicolas Minorsky (1922) studied a ship's steering and developed the PID control, also called three-term control (Bennett 1979a). He noticed that a good helmsman must consider not only the angular deviation but also the rate of change of that deviation, a form of anticipation. His result was one of the first theoretical analyses of controllers, but initially, it received little attention. Harold S. Black (1927) invented a negative feedback amplifier and filed a patent application. Still, it took many years before the application was approved since reviewers did not understand the principle when the dominant architecture was Armstrong's positive feedback. Black published the idea in 1934 (Black 1934, 1977). The generality of feedback was understood after Black's assistant Nyquist (1932) published his stability analysis (Nyquist 1932). Since 1948, feedback has formed the basis of automation (Online Etymology Dictionary 2024).

Harold L. Hazen (1934) analyzed servomechanism (Mayr 1970a, p. 132; Bennett 1979a, pp. 195, 202) and Norbert Wiener (1948) cybernetics. George P. Richardson

Table 6.6 Feedback concept in the history of science and technology

Year	Discoverer	Discovery
c. 270 BCE	Ktesibios	Feedback in a water clock
1624 CE	C. Drebbel	Thermostat
1769	J. Watt	Governor in a steam engine
1776	A. Smith	Supply and demand
1798	T. R. Malthus	Exponential population growth
1878	C. Bernard	Homeostasis and equilibrium
1910	J. Dewey	Reflective thinking and action
1911	F. Taylor	Plan-do (scientific management)
1913	E. H. Armstrong and C. S. Franklin	Positive feedback amplifier
1920	Many discoverers	Inductive feedback
1922	N. Minorsky	PID control
1927	H. S. Black	Negative feedback amplifier
1932	W. B. Cannon	Homeostasis
1934	H. L. Hazen	Servomechanism
1938	B. F. Skinner	Reinforcement learning
1940	W. R. Ashby	Positive and negative feedback
1943	A. Rosenblueth et al.	Purposeful behavior
1946	K. Lewin	Action research: planning-action-fact finding
1948	N. Wiener	Cybernetics
1948	W. R. Ashby	Homeostat
1950	R. F. Bales	Orientation-evaluation-control
1951	W. E. Deming	Plan-do-check-act (PDCA)
1952	W. R. Ashby	Double feedback and ultrastability
1954	H. Simon	Feedback in a human agent
1956	S. S. L. Chang	Decision and information feedback
1960	P. Eykhoff	Measurement-learning-decision-adjustment
1961	E. M. Glaser	Decision-directed receiver
1963	M. Maruyama	Positive feedback
1972	M. B. Rosenberg	Nonviolent communication
1974	H. von Förster	Second-order cybernetics
1976	J. Boyd	OODA loop
1978	C. Argyris and D. A. Schön	Double-loop learning
1984	D. Kolb	Experiential learning
1986	B. J. Zimmermann	Self-regulated learning

(continued)

Table 6.6 (continued)

Year	Discoverer	Discovery
1999	J. Mitola, III	Cognition cycle
2003	J. O. Kephart and D. M. Chess	MAPE-K loop

observed that this has led to two independent threads of thought in the social sciences: the servomechanisms thread and the cybernetics thread (Richardson 1991; Ramage and Shipp 2020). According to him, the feedback concept is "one of the most penetrating fundamentals in all social science," but the concept is not well understood there. Wiener used only negative feedback, but Maruyama (1963) noticed the importance of positive feedback.

The concept of artificial intelligence (AI) was developed in 1956 to separate it from cybernetics (Ramage and Shipp 2020). Therefore, since then, computing has been included in system theories in addition to control and communications in cybernetics.

Claude Bernard (1878) was the first to discuss *homeostasis* and *equilibrium* in physiology using the term internal environment ("internal milieu") (Cooper 2008; Bardin and Ferrari 2022). He thus made a clear difference between a system and its environment (Francois 1999). For example, our body temperature is kept almost constant, independently of the environment's temperature. Since 1926, homeostasis has meant a "tendency toward stability among interdependent elements" (Online Etymology Dictionary 2024). Later, Walter B. Cannon (1932) used the open system concept for organisms and elaborated on homeostasis (Cooper 2008). Higher organisms keep the physiological variables almost constant. That is why Cannon used the Greek *homeo* 'like, similar' instead of *homo* 'same, fixed.'

Cannon's student Arturo Rosenblueth collaborated with Norbert Wiener and formed the intellectual bridge between the physiological concept of homeostasis and the cybernetic concept of feedback. With Julian Bigelow, they defined purposeful behavior using negative feedback, and their paper "Behavior, purpose and teleology" (1943) is one of the most essential papers in the early history of cybernetics. Cybernetics was developed during Macy conferences that were organized between 1946 and 1953.

David Kolb (1984) developed the *learning loop* using earlier work by John Dewey, Kurt Lewin, and Jean Piaget, as Kolb himself emphasized. The idea eventually led to Kolb's *experiential learning* (Miettinen 2000). Dewey studied *reflective thinking* and *action* in his books from 1910 to 1938. Lewin (1946) developed *action research*, a circle of planning, action, and fact-finding about the result of the action. Lewin developed the idea after attending the first Macy conferences on cybernetics (Ramage and Shipp 2020). Action research is a form of experimental research based on a feedback loop. After Lewin, the feedback concept became commonly used in social sciences. Piaget studied the cognitive development of children. Education aims at life-long learning skills. Barry J. Zimmerman (1986) developed the concept of *self-regulated learning* so that students can learn independently (Zimmerman 2002). Self-regulated learners are aware of their strengths and limitations. They are proactive and guide themselves using the goals and methods they have set. They also monitor their success.

Kolb's learning loop includes four phases: (1) new concrete experience, (2) reflective observations of the experiences from many perspectives, (3) formation of concepts and generalizations into theories, and (4) use of the theories in active experiments to make decisions and solve problems. The loop corresponds to the research method presented in Fig. 1.6, using an experiment, hypothesis, deduction, and verification loop.

Bales (1950) developed an equilibrium model of group development using the phases (1) orientation (what the situation is), (2) evaluation (what attitudes should be taken towards the situation), and (3) control (what to do) (Bales 1950; Bales and Strodtbeck 1951). Simon (1954) suggested that feedback could be used as a model of human behavior (Richardson 1991, pp. 3, 145, 147). This idea, originally from Norbert Wiener, eventually led to the concept of a human actor or agent.

In quality control, feedback has a long history, starting from Francis Bacon's scientific method in the form of hypothesis-experiment-evaluation (Watson and DeYong 2010). Frederick Taylor (1911) developed principles of scientific management and made a distinction between "planning" and "doing" according to the division of labor. Walter A. Shewhart (1939) started from Bacon's model and used the terms (1) specification (i.e., making a hypothesis), (2) production (i.e., experimenting), and (3) inspection (i.e., testing the hypothesis). W. Edwards Deming (1951) called this iterative method the *Shewhart cycle*, but after he gave a talk, it has been called Deming wheel and plan-do-check-act (PDCA), although Deming referred to Shewhart and preferred the term plan-do-study-act (PDSA). Another name for the Shewart cycle in Japan is *kaizen* ("improvement" in Japanese), which is defined as "a continuous improvement process involving everyone, managers and workers alike" (Vinodh et al. 2021). It was seen as a key to Japan's competitive success. Mikel Harry (1985) compared a variety of corporate models, and by focusing on statistical aspects, the name was changed to define-measure-analyze-improve-control (DMAIC) (Watson and DeYong 2010).

Often, adaptive filtering does not name the feedback loop's different phases. Eykhoff (1960) used adaptive filtering to measure, reduce data or learn, make decisions, and adjust (Eykhoff 1960). This is very close to the idea that there should be sense (measurement), decision, and act (adjustment) blocks. Before the decision, some kind of data reduction and learning must be done.

Marshall B. Rosenberg (1972) developed and later refined a concept called nonviolent communication (Rosenberg 2015). It forms an observation, feelings, needs, and requests loop. Thus, a human is part of the loop since human feelings and needs are included in the decision phase. The parties approach each other with respect, ask about needs and feelings, and they reach a connection. Heinz von Förster (1974) called a human in the loop system second-order cybernetics.

Miller (1978) observed that feedback appears repeatedly at all levels of biological and social organizations (Richardson 1991). John Boyd (1976) used the term observe, orient, decide, and act (OODA) loop to describe the combat operations process (Osinga 2005). This term has become rather popular in different disciplines. Joseph Mitola III (1999) used the term cognition cycle, similar to the OODA loop. Haykin (2005) changed the term to cognitive cycle, making it more concrete for communications applications. Jeffrey O. Kephart and David M. Chess (2003) started to use the term monitor, analyze, plan, execute, and knowledge loop (MAPE-K) in autonomic computing (Kephart and Chess 2003). This is another popular term in addition to OODA.

In communications, feedback from the receiver to the transmitter was used initially in two forms: information feedback and decision feedback (Chang 1956; Harris and Morgan 1958). In *information feedback*, the receiver reports the received information back, in whole or in part, and the transmitter decides whether or not the receiver has adequately interpreted the message. In *decision feedback*, the receiver chooses whether the received message can be interpreted appropriately and then reports its decision to the transmitter. Some form of channel coding is used to detect the errors. The former method is now used for adaptive transmission, such as power or bit rate control (Love et al. 2008). It is also used in remote control based on networked control systems where a human acts as a decision-maker (Zhang et al. 2013). The latter method is now known as automatic repeat request (ARQ), whose modern form is hybrid ARQ (H-ARQ), where ARQ is combined with forward error correction (FEC), which corrects errors using redundant symbols in addition to detecting them (Lin et al. 1984).

Soon, it was observed that decision feedback can also be used *within* a receiver. Such a decision feedback receiver is often called *decision-directed*. Its history is somewhat vague. Spragins (1966) presented a decision-directed receiver and mentioned that his receiver is equivalent to that analyzed by E. M. Glaser (1961) (Spragins 1966). On the other hand, according to John G. Proakis the decision feedback became known from the work by Robert Price (1962) (Proakis and Salehi 2008), and since then, similar systems have been analyzed, for example, by Proakis (1964), Henry J. Scudder, III (1965), and William D. Gregg and John C. Hancock (1968). Glaser was among the first to use decision feedback within the receiver, although he used neither the term "decision feedback" nor "decision-directed."

Hierarchy and modularity The history of hierarchy is summarized in O'Neill et al. (1986), Verdier (2006) and Wu (2013), and the history of modularity in Russell (2012). The army has long used the concept of hierarchy (Mämmelä et al. 2023). The army of Alexander the Great and the Roman army were some of the first formal hierarchies. In the army, there are various military units, commanders, and leaders in the command hierarchy. The military units form a nested hierarchy, and the command hierarchy forms a nonnested hierarchy (Wu 2013). The term hierarchy has been used since the 1610s in the modern meaning "ranked organization of persons or things" (Online Etymology Dictionary 2024). The meaning was probably influenced by the word "higher." Frank E. Egler (1942) studied hierarchy in ecology, and Alex B. Novikoff (1945) studied it in biology (O'Neill et al. 1986).

The scientific research on hierarchies started with Herbert Simon's work (Wu 2013; Simon 1962, 1973). He described hierarchy and modularity, but he called modules subsystems. He suggested that a good hierarchy should be loosely coupled vertically and horizontally. Mesarovic et al. (1970) divided control hierarchies into stratified (nested), multilayer, and multiechelon (dominance) hierarchies (Mesarovic 1970; Mesarovic et al. 1970). The terms stratified and multiechelon hierarchy are now seldom used.

The OSI reference model (1984) uses the multilayer hierarchy (Tanenbaum and Wetherall 2011; Kurose and Ross 2013). Koestler (1967) (Koestler 1967) referred to (Simon 1962) and agreed that biological systems use a nested hierarchy whose modules he called holons. He called the corresponding architecture a holarchy. The holonic control architecture in manufacturing systems combines centralized and distributed control (Bongaerts et al. 2000). Some early papers on holonic manufacturing systems are mentioned in Bussman (1998) and Bongaerts et al. (2000). The first experiments with the holonic concept applied to manufacturing were already done in Japan in 1989. Many authors think the holonic architecture is nested or recursive (Horling and Lesser 2004; Calabrese et al. 2010; Dorri et al. 2018). However, in Bongaerts et al. (2000), the holonic architecture is based on a nonnested dominance hierarchy.

According to van der Hoek and Lopez (2011), modularity was used already in the early punch cards. Albert Farwell Bemis (1936) was the first to use the concept of modularity (Russell 2012). He used the term modular in architectural theories in modern terms, meaning "composed of interchangeable units" (Online Etymology Dictionary 2024). His four-inch cubical modules were a way to rationalize building methods. National Bureau of Standards (1949) started modular electronics design (Russell 2012). Later, IBM applied modularity in 1957 in its computers, which was a reason for the company's success in the computer business.

In software design, the ALGOL 60 programming language includes support for block structures (van der Hoek and Lopez 2011). J. C. Emery (1962) was one of the first to use "segmented" modularity instead of a "monolithic behemoth." Corrado Böhm and Giuseppe Jacopini (1966) presented a theorem that is now called the structured program theorem, but it was Edsger W. Dijkstra (1969) who first coined the term *structured programming* (Weiner 1978). In his opinion, jump instructions using goto commands were harmful. In 1968, he also proposed a hierarchical structure for a program (Parnas 1972). Harlan D. Mills (1971) emphasized the importance of top-down design in large systems. He insisted that only some basic control structures of structured programming (sequential, if–then–else, do–while, and case) should be used, and the code should be developed step-by-step.

Following a similar term used on software design, Rainer W. Hartenstein (1974) coined the term *structured hardware design* in integrated circuits using a modular methodology. Carver A. Mead and Lynn A. Conway (1980) used a structured design using rectangular macro blocks in VLSI circuits to minimize the area needed for wiring. A nested hierarchy is used in complicated designs.

In computing, Dijkstra (1974) developed the concept of *separation of concerns* supporting hierarchy and modularity. It is a design principle in computer science and software engineering that emphasizes the importance of isolating different aspects or responsibilities of a system. This concept allows developers to manage complexity by dividing a program into distinct sections, each addressing a specific concern without overlapping functionalities. Hierarchy and modularity became standard practice in software design after Parnas (1972) defined the necessary criteria (Parnas 1972). After this, the time was ready for loosely coupled systems (Mämmelä et al. 2023). Although closely related, modularity and loose coupling were originally different concepts and, therefore, had to be invented separately.

Degrees of centralization A history of centralized and decentralized information systems is presented in Hugoson (2009). The term centralization was first used in 1801, and soon after that, the term decentralization was introduced in 1839 (Online Etymology Dictionary 2024; Mämmelä et al. 2023). The term centralization is from Napoleon's France, meaning "concentration of administrative power in the central government at the expense of local self-government." Decentralization was later defined as the "act or principle of removing local or special functions of government from immediate control of central authority."

Theoretical research on different control topologies and degrees of centralization started in the 1960s in communications and distributed control and computing (Baran 1964; Sandell et al. 1978; Stankovic 1984; Coulouris et al. 2012; Cao et al. 2013). Paul Baran was among the first to define the degrees of centralization in communications (Baran 1964). In his opinion, a centralized network is a star network, a decentralized network is a hierarchical network with a central controller, and a distributed network is a mesh network. However, for Nils R. Sandell, Jr., the decentralized control is assumed to be completely decentralized without any central controller (Sandell et al. 1978). Mihajlo D. Mesarovic et al. presented a hybrid system in Mesarovic et al. (1970, Fig. 2.10).

According to Rajsbaum and Raynal (2020), the history of concurrent computing starts from multiprogramming in the Atlas computer in 1961. Edsger W. Dijkstra started the theory of concurrent computing systems in 1965 (Brinch Hansen 2002; Laplante et al. 2008; Rajsbaum and Raynal 2020). His first paper was "Cooperating sequential processes." In his opinion, software must be partitioned and structured, and he also introduced the idea of layered structures for operating systems. All the classic papers turned out to be written by Dijkstra, Brinch Hansen, and Charles Antony Richard (Tony) Hoare (Brinch Hansen 2002, pp. 4–7).

Loose coupling Simon (1962) was the first to study loosely coupled systems scientifically using the descriptive term *near decomposability* (Simon 1962). The term decomposition is used in mathematical optimization decomposition (Chiang et al. 2007). Since 1762, decomposition has meant the "act or process of separating the constituent elements of a compound body" (Online Etymology Dictionary 2024). Optimization decomposition became popular in the 1970s. Simon described the principle of near decomposability in physical, biological, and social systems. All multicell biological organisms use this principle because only such systems with their stable intermediate forms could succeed in evolving in the available time. They have survived since they have a fast adaptation rate (Simon 1962, 2002). Simon (1973) defined the vertical and horizontal loose coupling in Simon (1973). Still, he continued to use the term near decomposability, for example, in Simon (1996); thus, his book chapter (Simon 1973) is not well known.

Loose coupling in natural sciences In 1656, Christiaan Huygens invented the pendulum clock after Galileo had investigated it (Mämmelä et al. 2023). When there was a loose coupling between two clocks, Huygens observed the resonance (1665) (Francke et al. 2020). Only recently, Yoshiki Kuramoto (1975) was able to analyze this loose coupling (Hermoso de Mendoza et al. 2014). The Kuramoto model links physical concepts such as self-organization and emergence.

Leonor Michaelis and Maud Menten (1913) observed time-scale separation in biological systems (Gunawardena 2014). In meteorology, there is a time-scale separation between weather and climate. At about the same time as Simon (Simon 1973), Robert B. Glassman independently used the term loose coupling in biology (Glassman 1973). He used also the term tight coupling. A physical model of stable loose coupling exists since rotating parts can have flexible mechanical couplings. In celestial mechanics, such as our solar system, loose coupling can be formed using *mass hierarchy*. The system is highly stable if one of the bodies is much larger in mass than the others. The masses can be treated as point masses in analysis if the distances are much larger than the sizes of the bodies.

Loose coupling in social sciences Subsidiarity is based on loose centralized control. Subsidiarity has been used with different terms for centuries (Evans and Zimmermann 2014). Already, Aristotle (300s BCE) discussed subsidiarity. Althusius (1603) developed the concept of sovereignty, a form of federalism and subsidiarity. Subsidiarity and loose coupling were developed independently. According to Scheerens (2015), subsidiarity is a more prescriptive term than loose coupling. The subsidiarity concept was used when writing the constitutions of the USA (1787) and EU (1992). The term subsidiarity (*Subsidiarität*) was first used in German legal literature (1809) (Economides 2012). The term comes from the Latin verb *subsidio* (to help) and the noun *subsidium* (assistance). Subsidiarity has been one of the three basic principles of the Catholic Church since Pope Pius IX (1931). Warren S. McCulloch (1945) developed the concept of heterarchy (i.e. a distributed system) for cognitive sciences as the opposite of hierarchy (Crumley 2008). James D. Thompson (1967) was one of the first to mention loose coupling in organizations (Pautasso and Wilde 2009). George J. Klir (1969) defined loose coupling in general systems (Mämmelä et al. 2023). Weick (1976) used loose coupling in educational organizations (Weick 1976; Orton and Weick 1990).

E. Colin Cherry (1953) defined the cocktail party effect in social systems, a concept later introduced to communication networks as an example of tight coupling (Mämmelä et al. 2023). J. G. March and Herbert Simon (1958) discussed conflicts in human organizations. The idea finally led to self-coordination methods (2011) to avoid and resolve conflicts in self-organizing networks (Lateef 2015; Bayazeed et al. 2021).

Loose coupling in control systems In control engineering, loose coupling is often called weak coupling (Gajic et al. 2008). Milne (1965) analyzed weakly coupled feedback control loops (Milne 1965), and soon after that, Peter L. Falb and William A. Wolovich (1967) presented a method to decouple the loops (Mämmelä et al. 2023). Mesarovic et al. (1970) were probably the first to use the concept of time-scale separation or separation of time scales for fast and slow dynamics in control engineering. They used the term decision period, which was longer at higher than lower levels (Mesarovic et al. 1970). At the beginning of the 1970s, the term time-scale separation was introduced to control engineering (Sandell et al. 1978). Some essential references from the 1970s on time-scale separation are listed in Sandell et al. (1978).

Loose coupling in computer engineering After the concept of modularity was introduced in electronics and in computer hardware (Russell 2012) and software (van der Hoek and Lopez 2011), Chen (1972) used loose coupling in multiprocessor architectures (Chen 1972), further discussed in Gonzalez (1978). Independently of Edsger W. Dijkstra's (1969) idea on structured programming, Larry L. Constantine developed structured software design in the 1960s, and Wayne P. Stevens, Gleford J. Myers, and Edward Yourdon published the results with him (Stevens et al. 1974; Yourdon and Constantine 1978). Myers used the term composite design and published his results in 1975 in the book *Reliable software through composite design.* Using this background, since about 2000, it has become natural to use loose coupling in service-oriented architectures (Pautasso and Wilde 2009; Mämmelä et al. 2023). At about the same time, the concept of SaaS was introduced. Service-oriented architectures have since 2011 been implemented in the form of loosely coupled microservices (Dragoni et al. 2017).

Information can be exchanged in computing using message passing or shared memory (Decker 1987). Message passing was originally used in the mid-1960s in the design of operating systems (Walker 1995). The idea of message passing has been used for loose coupling in distributed computing since the late 1970s, leading finally to the standardized Message Passing Interface (1994). David W. Walker, one of the contributors to the standard, wrote: "The idea of communicating sequential processes as a model for parallel execution was developed by Hoare in the 1970s and is the basis of the message passing paradigm." In tight coupling, shared memory is used in information exchange as in the blackboard architecture (Nii 1986). IBM System/360 (1964) used one of the first shared memory architectures. Lee D. Ehrman et al. (1980) developed it between 1971 and 1976. These ideas were later used in cognitive radio systems using independently the terms control channel (message passing) and database (shared memory) (Haykin 2005). A modern example of tight coupling is federated learning in McMahan et al. (2017).

In software engineering, in addition to coupling, there is another attribute called *cohesion*, developed also by Constantine (Stevens et al. 1974; Yourdon and Constantine 1978). The basic rule for good software is loose coupling between software modules and high cohesion within software modules. High cohesion leads to understandability, reusability, testability, reliability, and robustness. If the cohesion is low, a module includes tasks which are not related to each other.

Loose coupling in communications In communication networks, introducing the terminology involving loose coupling has been surprisingly slow (Kawadia and Kumar 2005; Akyildiz and Wang 2008), although the terminology has been known in control and computer engineering (Milne 1965; Stevens et al. 1974; Yourdon and Constantine 1978) for many decades. Some of the most popular textbooks on computer networks do not mention the loose coupling concept (Tanenbaum and Wetherall 2011; Kurose and Ross 2013). Leonard Kleinrock (1961) invented packet switching, which was introduced to the Arpanet (1969). The hierarchical OSI model (1984) (Day and Zimmermann 1983) is based on vertical loose coupling and thus uses time-scale separation. However, the authors in Day and Zimmermann (1983) only briefly refer to the principles used in structured software design without any reference. The TCP/IP model was defined in 1974, and Arpanet adopted it in 1983 and became the Internet (Alani 2014). The TCP/IP model took its name from two existing protocols, whereas the OSI model was more comprehensive. However, the TCP/IP model was widely adopted because of its use in the Arpanet and the Internet. Still, the OSI model provides educational insight into the operation of networks.

Loose coupling is used in network roaming in interworking architectures (Salkintzis et al. 2002). The authors use the terms tight and loose coupling. The authors' original reference is an ETSI Technical Report (2001) discussing a version of the High Performance Local Area Network (HIPERLAN) standard. Vikas Kawadia and Panganamala R. Kumar were the first to suggest time-scale separation in cross-layer design to improve the stability of the network. Loose coupling is mentioned briefly in Lin et al. (2006), Johansson et al. (2006) and Chiang et al. (2007). The terminology was finally clearly summarized in Akyildiz and Wang (2008). Table 6.7 summarizes the history of self-organization described in various parts of this book.

Fundamental limits The authors of Barrow (1998), Lundheim (2002), Dewdney (2004), Cockshott et al. (2012) and Markov (2014) summarize open questions and fundamental limits in different disciplines. Emil du Bois-Reymond (1880s) started the general discussion on open questions of science (Barrow 1998). There are everlasting open questions that are extremely difficult to solve and form limitations on human knowledge. The most difficult are related to the beginning of everything, life, and consciousness. We have no idea about them, although some people believe we can solve everything using big data and no theories are needed (West 2017; Larson 2021). Lars Lundheim noticed that most practical and fundamental limits were discovered roughly in 1850–1950 (Lundheim 2002).

Table 6.7 Self-organization in the history of science and technology

Year	Discoverer	Discovery
250 BCE	Zhuangzi	Spontaneous order (concept)
1863	Many discoverers	Morphogenesis (term)
1917	D. W. Thompson	Physics of morphogenesis
1938	H. H. Jennings and J. Moreno	Random graph
1941	M. Polanyi	Spontaneous order (term)
1947	W. R. Ashby	Adaptive and self-organizing systems
1948	J. von Neumann	Cellular automaton
1948	W. R. Ashby	Homeostat, the first adaptive system
1950s	Many discoverers	Pattern recognition
1952	A. Turing	Chemistry of morphogenesis
1952	W. R. Ashby	Double feedback and ultrastability
1954	N. A. Barricelli	Artificial life, evolutionary simulation
1955	I. Prigogine	Nonequilibrium thermodynamics
1959	B. Belousov and A. Zhabotinsky	BZ reaction
1960	H. von Foerster	Order from noise
1961	L. Kleinrock	Packet switching
1964	IBM	Shared memory
1965	D. de Solla Price	Scale-free networks (concept)
1967	S. Milgram	Small-world networks
1968	R. W. Dijkstra	Hierarchical programming
1970s	Many discoverers	Pattern formation
1971	N. Georgescu-Roegen	Thermodynamics in economics
1971	M. Eigen	Hypercycle
1972	R. E. Kahn	Packet radios
1973	H. R. Maturana and F. J. Varela	Autopoiesis
1974	E. Dijkstra	Self-stabilization
1977	H. Haken	Synergetics
1977	C. Hewitt	Distributed artificial intelligence
1978	C. A. R. Hoare	Message passing
1981	D. J. Baker and A. Ephremides	Distributed self-organizing network
1984	Many discoverers	Complexity theory
1990	P. Senge	System archetypes
1993	G. Beni and J. Wang	Swarm intelligence
1993	IEEE	Ad hoc network
2008	Many discoverers	Guided self-organization
2010	W. B. Arthur	Complexity economics

6.4.5 *Vision of the Future*

If we assume almost deterministic changes, we can sometimes make a long-term forecast for up to one hundred years. Often the forecasts include a random component. Examples of long-term forecasts include Nikolai Kondratiev's cycles for macroeconomics (Wilenius 2014), Dennis Gabor's and Isaac Asimov's 50 years forecasts from 1964 to 2014 (Asimov 1964), the 100 years forecasts of the Club of Rome from 1972 to 2072 (Meadows and Wright 2008), and Moore's law for the development of integrated circuits. The law was roughly valid for over 60 years until saturation, from 1959 to about 2021 (Mämmelä and Anttonen 2017; Theis and Wong 2017). Still, there have been energy efficiency problems since 2004, and not all transistors on a chip could be used simultaneously. Usually, only a ten-year vision can be made reasonably accurately (Albus and Meystel 2001; Schoemaker 2020).

We expect that the list of system theories and archetypes will be improved and widely used since they have survived the test of time. Most of the time, we could do with 10–20 archetypes (Forrester 2007b). We are primarily interested in electronics, control, communication, and computing topologies, but the theories and archetypes have counterparts in other disciplines. Complex adaptive systems comprise interacting agents that form a self-organizing system. Even our society can be modeled with such a system when we interpret the agents as human actors. A complex adaptive system cannot be only a distributed system; it must have some hierarchical and modular structure that uses a goal given by a human actor. Hierarchy, modularity, and loose coupling are standard tools to improve stability, scalability, and performance of a system.

The essential archetypes so far identified include small-world networks, open-loop and feedback control, hierarchy, optimization and decision-making, and the various degrees of centralization. We also use different degrees of coupling, sequential and concurrent computing, energy minimization for closed systems, and nonequilibrium thermodynamics for open systems. Information is exchanged using shared memory or message passing. The tragedy of the commons is an essential problem caused by the social dilemma in using common and scarce resources. The tragedy can be solved by education, privatization, and regulation. Hybrid control topology, called subsidiarity in social sciences, combines centralized and distributed control and will become common to avoid harmful emergence until we have a good theory for it. Social systems may encourage creativity that is not a product of a rigid hierarchy but comes from the bottom up. Complexity engineering, also called emergent engineering, may be developed for practical applications using biology as an example, thus offering simplicity and low energy consumption. Loose coupling is an intermediate solution for effective engineering design to avoid emergence until we understand emergence phenomenon better.

It is an open problem whether artificial intelligence can work reliably in uncertain dynamical environments (Roberts 2020). One significant limitation is that AI uses deductive, inductive, and statistical methods, whereas humans are more creative and can use abduction to solve problems (Larson 2021). A significant challenge is that we need a theory for life and consciousness that has developed so far only using organic materials through evolution, which is a prolonged process.

In addition to physics and chemistry, we now need knowledge of biology and social sciences to solve engineering problems efficiently. Efficiency maximization is a multiobjective optimization problem between incommensurate resources. Prices are formed using the law of supply and demand, thus creating the common currency. Instead of optimization, a solution to complex problems is the satisficing principle since there is no alternative (Simon 1996). Analytic hierarchy process (Saaty 2008) and other rank-based strategies (Walasek and Brown 2023) seem to be examples of the satisficing principle.

There has been a long-standing debate about whether an organism is a mechanism and whether it can be described with algorithms, i.e., whether it is computable (Rosen 1996; Penrose 1999). Jacques Monod claimed that all material systems are mechanisms, i.e., simple or complicated and computable, not complex (Rosen 1996). An equivalent discussion is going on about artificial general intelligence (AGI). A challenge is the phenomenon of emergence closely related to the curse of dimensionality. Complex systems include emergence that comes from nonlinearity and feedback, thus making the system mathematically intractable (Camazine et al. 2001). The problem is that we need to learn how life and consciousness emerge from nonliving matter. Different approaches have been proposed to implement AGI. The earliest idea was to simulate the brain with a good enough model called "a net of neurons" (Corchado et al. 2023).

Rene Descartes was one of the first to use the machine metaphor for a human (Mikulecky 2000). Alan Turing (1950) asked whether computers have intelligence at the human level (Poundstone 1988). He says this can be tested using an imitation game where a human communicates via a computer terminal. If a computer can communicate so that humans cannot tell whether the computer is a human or a machine, it has passed the *Turing test*.

If the AI could develop its consciousness and have free will, it could define its own goals, which may conflict with the goals of humans. Stephen Hawking suggests that the computers should have a switch to turn the power off (Hawking 2018). John von Neumann was one of the first to use the *singularity* concept in technology. Irving Good (1965) predicted that computers could start to develop themselves, which, according to Vernor Vinge (1993), may lead to a superintelligence and technological singularity where the intelligence improves without any limits (Kurzweil 1999). However, this is not certain since the miniaturization of electronics will not continue (Waldrop 2016). High computing speed is different from intelligence. Supercomputers have a higher computing speed than the human brain but with several orders of magnitude higher energy consumption (Mämmelä and Anttonen 2017). No consciousness has emerged.

Expert systems in the form of rule-based systems were the first successful AI applications, imitating the decision-making process of human experts (Lenat 2022). Douglas Lenat initially proposed that intelligence could be implemented using ten million rules, but such intelligence has not materialized. A recent trend is to use a large memory and statistical processing of big data with feedback for improved performance. However, human intelligence is something different. Recently, deep learning for neural networks was developed (LeCun et al. 2015). A more advanced concept is a transformer based on statistical analysis of big data (Vaswani et al. 2017). This idea can also be used to generate pictures and videos. A new alternative is to implement AGI-native networks and thus extend the AI's capabilities using distributed computing (Saad 2024). These are all good complementary approaches towards the idea that the whole universe is used for computing. The proposals produce mechanisms, but the existing intelligence is based on organisms thus forming biological intelligence.

So far, the only working approach to human-level intelligence is natural selection based on evolution using organic matter from where life, consciousness, and intelligence emerge. We may need unknown physical laws of organic matter (Elsasser 1966; Morowitz 2002; Gatherer 2008; Kauffman 1995). Erwin Schrödinger (1944) already anticipated that there are physical laws that are unknown to us (Stonier 1997). Walter Elsasser (1958) called the unknown laws *biotonic laws*.

Life and consciousness are open problems in science. Many experts have offered a negative answer to the possibility of artificial general intelligence at the human level (Poundstone 1988). The suggestion implies that an organism is not a mechanism. Hubert L. Dreyfus (1972) claimed that intelligence cannot be based on symbol manipulation and deduction as in computers (Dreyfus 1992). Robert Rosen also presented similar ideas, stating that organisms are not machines and, therefore, are not computable (Rosen 1991, 1996; Mikulecky 2000). He claimed that the metabolism-repair (M-R) systems cannot be presented as a mechanism. An organism is continuously repairing itself.

According to Roger Penrose, consciousness is a requisite for true intelligence (Penrose 1999, pp. 64, 526, 539, 558). Algorithms cannot simulate our intelligence and consciousness; therefore, our mind is not a computer. Even if the future were deterministic, it is not necessarily computable. Penrose linked quantum theory and the human mind (Penrose 1999).

In John Searle's (1980) Chinese room example, a human who does not know Chinese is in a locked room, and he or she has a book that explains what to do (Poundstone 1988). The person outside the room gives a sheet of paper with Chinese writing. The person in the room uses the instructions in the book and reacts accordingly. The answers cannot be distinguished from those that a native Chinese speaker would give. Now, the question is whether the person inside the room understands Chinese. Searle concluded that consciousness is not an algorithm. Searle observed that a simulation of photosynthesis cannot produce real sugar as living plants do. Therefore, a computer made of wires and integrated circuits without using organic matter cannot have consciousness, although it would pass the Turing test (Poundstone 1988, pp. 229–230).

There is a tremendous conceptual difference between mechanistic and organismic (biological) intelligence (Bohm and Peat 2000). In biology, there is intelligence at different levels, from the rudimentary intelligence in plants and more advanced intelligence in insects to human intelligence. David Bohm proposed that the static mechanistic part of our mind should be called intellect, and intelligence is the dynamic and creative part (Bohm and Peat 2000). He said that artificial intelligence should be more appropriately called *artificial intellect*. According to Erik J. Larson, human and machine intelligence are entirely different (Larson 2021, pp. 1, 113, 189). Human intelligence is based on abductive inference, for which we have no theory, which a machine cannot achieve, and which machines do not understand. Artificial intelligence is developing rapidly. EU AI Act is the world's first comprehensive law on artificial intelligence.

There is no method to predict the structure of an organic molecule, although we know all the atoms (Rosen 1991; Wilson 1998). There are too many forces involved, even for a supercomputer. The organic molecule is a basic example of emergence that appears in an unknown way when we move upwards in a hierarchy. The curse of dimensionality is valid here: not even all the atoms in the universe and the total age of the universe are probably enough to solve the general problem of emergence (Bellman 1957). Thus, all the mechanistic approaches may fail. However, there is nothing mystical about emergence; organisms follow known and unknown physical laws (Camazine et al. 2001). A recent form of biocomputing called *organoid intelligence* is presented in Smirnova et al. (2023). The hardware is made of brain organoids or neural structures connected to sensors and output devices and trained by machine learning, big data, and other techniques. Complexity engineering may appear valid, especially in some simple cases. We already know that our brain uses some exciting principles: small-world networks (Liao et al. 2017), energy minimization (Friston et al. 2006; Friston 2010), reinforcement learning (Friston 2010; Dabney et al. 2020), and hierarchy and time-scale separation (Kiebel et al. 2008).

We need a common vocabulary with clear definitions to develop systems thinking further. A good starting point is SE VOCAB (2024), but we must continuously update and unify it, usually through the efforts of ISO, IEC, ITU, and IEEE. Now, ITU is missing from SE VOCAB. A typical problem in standardization is that the terms and definitions are not unified between different standards. Not all can be unified, and some terms have their place in specific disciplines. An excellent example of unification is the VIM standard in metrology (JCGM 2012).

6.5 Chapter Summary and Recommended Reading

Knowledge of history belongs to the general knowledge (*Bildung*) of all researchers and is, therefore, essential for understanding the present and envisioning the future. Imagination is also needed. Information retrieval is made efficient using a hierarchical approach and the focus is initially on books and review papers. We also now use various databases where citations are given to find the newest information. Technology has improved the writing process. The peer review process keeps the quality of scientific papers high, and it was invented in the middle of the 1700s. Still, it was only in the 1950s that it became a common practice when suitable technology, such as photocopiers, was widely available. Scientific societies have an essential role in the publishing process. Many books and papers are published as open access, but not all publishers are reliable enough, and we must focus on prominent publishers. Writing is made systematic by using the IMRDC structure and the various moves within it. Louis Pasteur developed the basic structure at the end of the 1800s.

The Egyptian and Babylonian science was based on numerical examples ("practice," no "theory"). Still, Greek science developed idealization and generalization, emphasized rationalism, and was based on axiomatic methods and deduction ("theory") but undervalued experimental method (no "practice"). Arabic culture saved the Greek tradition until Europe became interested in scientific thought again. Many modern concepts were invented before the scientific revolution, but their significance was not widely understood. For example, Alhazen invented the analytical and experimental method almost 600 years before Galileo.

The modern analytical thinking was developed in the 1600s by Galileo, Francis Bacon, Rene Descartes, and Isaac Newton and is based on the combination of rationalism and empiricism ("theory and practice"). The first theories were axiomatic theories, and theories based on models are a rather recent discovery. Simulations were possible after the invention of the digital computer.

The newest idea is the system concept of the last century by Ludwig von Bertalanffy, Norbert Wiener, Kenneth E. Boulding, and many others since about 1950. Core ideas include open systems, emergence, and self-organization. Our book is in the cybernetics tradition, followed by artificial intelligence, system dynamics, and complexity theory. Complicated systems are developed using system archetypes, a concrete example of unifying systems. The most crucial system archetypes use hierarchy, modularity, and loose coupling. We presently try to avoid emergence, but it is possible that complexity engineering will be developed to the point that emergence can be used for our benefit at least in some simple cases.

Stephen F. Mason's book includes many historical notes on scientific societies and writing (Mason 1962). John Losee presents a history of philosophy of science and analytical thinking (Losee 2001). Peter Checkland includes a history of systems thinking (Checkland 1999). The bibliography of our book includes additional references on the details of the history and philosophy of different core disciplines of our interest.

The feedback concept has an ancient origin, but only after Harry Nyquist (1932) defined the stability conditions did we finally understand the generality of feedback, and we saw this as the starting point of modern control engineering. R. Ross Ashby (1947) clarified the terminology and separated adaptive and self-organizing systems. Norbert Wiener (1948) combined control and communication and started a new discipline called cybernetics. At the same time, Claude E. Shannon (1948) defined statistical information theory, which we see as the start of modern digital communications without including the semantics of information. Alan Turing (1938) and John von Neuman (1946) were some of the key figures who developed the concept of modern digital computers.

John McCarthy and others (1956) combined cybernetics and computing and named the new discipline artificial intelligence. There was a long history in the agent concept that later became the core component of AI in the form of multiagent systems by Carl Hewitt (1977). Later, John Holland and others (1992) defined complexity theory as a theory of complex adaptive systems, which are multiagent systems. Complexity theory became a theory of self-organization, especially in biology and social sciences. Still, self-organizing networks had been independently an active topic much earlier, especially in the form of packet switching (1961), packet radio networks (1972), distributed self-organizing networks (1981), ad hoc networks (1993), active networks (1995), separation of control and data planes (1998), application programming interfaces (2008), and hybrid self-organizing networks (2008).

Discussion Questions

1. How were the research methods developed? Why should we combine analytical and systems thinking and why this is not often done?
2. How did the concepts of hierarchy, modularity, and loose coupling develop?
3. What are the most important system theories and their relationships?
4. What are the most important system archetypes in engineering?
5. What is the difference, if any, between artificial and biological intelligence?

References

Aaltonen M (2007) The return to multi-causality. J Futures Stud 12(1):81–86
Ackoff R, Gharajedaghi J (1996) Reflections on systems and their models. Syst Res 13(1):13–23
Acosta G et al (2020) Need for a careful comparison between hypotheses: case study of epicycles. In: Acosta G et al (eds) Towards analytical techniques for systems engineering applications. Springer, Cham, Switzerland, pp 61–64
Adamatzky A (ed) (2017) Advances in unconventional computing: volume 1: theory. Springer Nature, Cham, Switzerland
Agnoli P, D'Agostini G (2005) Why does the meter beat the second? Preprint at arXiv:physics/0412078v2
Akers W et al (2015) The nature and behaviour of complex system archetypes. Int J Syst Syst Eng 6(4):302–326
Akyildiz IF, Wang X (2008) Cross-layer design in wireless mesh networks. IEEE Trans Veh Technol 57(2):1061–1076
Alani MM (2014) Guide to OSI and TCP/IP models. Springer, Cham, Switzerland
Albus JS, Meystel AM (2001) Engineering of mind: an introduction to the science of intelligent systems. Wiley, New York
Alcott B (2005) Jevons' paradox. Ecol Econ 54(1):9–21
Ali SM, Zimmer RM (1998) Emergence: a review of the foundations. Syst Res Inf Syst 8(1):1–24
Aliu OG et al (2013) A survey of self organisation in future cellular networks. IEEE Commun Surv Tutor 15(1):336–361
Alon U (2020) An introduction to systems biology: design principles of biological circuits, 2nd edn. Chapman & Hall/CRC, Boca Raton, FL

ANSI (1977) American national standard for writing abstracts. IEEE Trans Prof Commun 20(4):252–254

ANSI (1979) American national standard for the preparation of scientific papers for written and oral presentation, Z.39.16-1979

ANSI/NISO (2010) Guidelines for abstracts, Z39.14-1997 (R2009)

Arbnor I, Bjerke B (1997) Methodology for creating business knowledge, 2nd edn. Sage, London

Arthur WB (2021) Foundations of complexity economics. Nat Rev Phys 3:136–145. https://doi.org/10.1038/s42254-020-00273-3

Ashby WR (1962) Principles of the self-organizing system. In: Von Foerster H, Zopf GW Jr (eds) Principles of self-organization: transactions of the University of Illinois symposium. Pergamon Press, London, pp 255–278

Asimov I (1960) Realm of measure. Houghton Mifflin Company, Boston, MA

Asimov I (1964) Visit to the world's fair of 2014. The New York Times, 16 Aug. https://archive.nytimes.com/. Accessed 6 Sept 2022

Asimov I (1982) Asimov's biographical encyclopedia of science & technology: the lives & achievements of 1510 great scientists from ancient times to the present, 2nd rev edn. Doubleday & Company, Garden City, NY

Asimov I (1984) The history of physics, rev. Walker and Company, New York

Asimov I (1987) Asimov's new guide to science, 4th edn. Penguin Books, Middlesex, England

Asimov I (1994) Asimov's chronology of science & discovery, Updated and illustrated. Harper & Row, New York

Bacci G et al (2016) Game theory for networks: a tutorial on game-theoretic tools for emerging signal processing applications. IEEE Signal Process Mag 33(1):94–119

Bahg CG (1990) Major system theories throughout the world. Behav Sci 35(2):79–207

Bailer-Jones DM (2009) Scientific models in philosophy of science. University of Pittsburgh Press, Pittsburgh, PA

Bales RF (1950) A set of categories for the analysis of small group interaction. Am Sociol Rev 15(2):257–263

Bales RF, Strodtbeck FL (1951) Phases in group problem-solving. Psychol Sci Public Interest 46(4):485–495

Baran P (1964) On distributed communications networks. IEEE Trans Commun Syst 12(1):1–9

Barbour IG (1997) Religion and science: historical and contemporary issues. HarperCollins, New York

Bardin A, Ferrari M (2022) Governing progress: from cybernetic homeostasis to Simondon's politics of metastability. Sociol Rev Monogr 70(2):248–263

Barlow RE, Proschan F (1976) Some current academic research in system reliability theory. IEEE Trans Reliab 25(3):198–202

Barnett J (2001) Adapting to climate change in Pacific Island countries: the problem of uncertainty. World Dev 29(6):977–993

Barrow JD (1998) Impossibility: the limits of science and the science of limits. Oxford University Press, New York

Bauer N, Müller J (2001) Software agents in mobile telecommunication services. Softw Focus 2(2):37–43

Bayazeed A et al (2021) A survey of self-coordination in self-organizing network. Comput Netw 196:1–32. https://doi.org/10.1016/j.comnet.2021.108222

Bekey GA (2005) Autonomous robots: from biological inspiration to implementation and control. MIT Press, Cambridge, MA

Belevitch V (1962) Summary of the history of circuit theory. Proc IRE 50(5):848–855

Bell ET (1986) Men of mathematics. Simon & Schuster, New York

Bellman R (1957) Dynamic programming. Princeton University Press, Princeton, NJ

Bello PA (1963) Characterization of randomly time-variant linear channels. IEEE Trans Commun Syst 11(4):360–393

Benbya H, McKelvey B (2006) Toward a complexity theory of information systems development. Inf Technol People 19(1):12–34
Bennett S (1979a) A history of control engineering, 1800–1930. Peter Peregrinus, Stevenage, UK
Bennett S (1979b) A history of control engineering, 1930–1955. Peter Peregrinus, Stevenage, UK
Bennett S (1996) A brief history of automatic control. IEEE Control Syst 16(3):17–25
Bennett S (2002) Otto Mayr: contributions to the history of feedback control. IEEE Control Syst Mag 22(2):29–33
Bernstein DS (1999) A student's guide to research. IEEE Control Syst Mag 19(1):102–108
Bernstein DS (2002) Feedback control: an invisible thread in the history of technology. IEEE Control Syst Mag 22(2):53–68
Bjerregaard T, Mahadevan S (2006) A survey of research and practices of network-on-chip. ACM Comput Surv 38(1):1–51
Black HS (1934) Stabilized feedback amplifiers. Bell Syst Techn J 13(1):1–18
Black H (1977) Inventing the negative feedback amplifier. IEEE Spectr 14(12):55–60
Bohm D, Peat FD (2000) Science, order, and creativity, 2nd edn. Routledge, London
Bolin RL (1999) The 'lost' U.S. technical reports: obtaining reports from the 1940s and '50s. J Gov Inf 26(5):501–508
Bongaerts L et al (2000) Hierarchy in distributed shop floor control. Comput Ind 43(2):123–137
Bookstein FL (2009) How quantification persuades when it persuades. Biol Theory 4(2):132–147
Bossel H (2007) Systems and models: complexity, dynamics, evolution, sustainability. Books on Demand, Norderstedt, Germany
Boulding KE (1956) General systems theory. Manage Sci 2(3):197–208
Boulding KE (1969) Economics and a moral science. Am Econ Rev 59(1):1–12
Boulding KE (1985) The world as a total system. Sage, Beverly Hills, CA
Boulton JG et al (2015) Embracing complexity: strategic perspectives for an age of turbulence. Oxford University Press, Oxford, UK
Boyer CB, Merzbach UC (1991) A history of mathematics, 2nd rev. Wiley, New York
Brauckmann S (2000) The organism and the open system: Ervin Bauer and Ludwig von Bertalanffy. Ann N Y Acad Sci 901(1):291–300
Bregman B (2020) Humankind: a hopeful history. Little, Brown and Company, New York
Breugst M, Magedantz T (1998) Mobile agents—enabling technology for active intelligent network implementation. IEEE Netw 12(3):53–60
Brinch Hansen P (ed) (2002) The origin of concurrent programming: from semaphores to remote procedure calls. Springer-Verlag, New York
Briscoe J, Kicheva A (2017) The physics of development 100 years after D'Arcy Thompson's "on growth and form." Mech Dev 145:26–31. https://doi.org/10.1016/j.mod.2017.03.005
Brittain JE (1996) The evolution of electrical and electronics engineering and the proceedings of the IRE: 1913–1937. Proc IEEE 84(12):1747–1772
Buchanan M (2002) Small world: uncovering nature's hidden networks. W. W. Norton and Company, New York
Buenstorf G (2000) Self-organization and sustainability: energetics of evolution and implications for ecological economics. Ecol Econ 33(1):119–134
Burnham JF (2006) Scopus database: a review. Biomed Digit Libr 3(1):1–8. http://www.bio-diglib.com/content/3/1/1
Bussman S (1998) An agent-oriented architecture for holonic manufacturing control. In: Proceedings of the first open workshop IMS Europe, Lausanne, Switzerland, pp 1–12
Calabrese M et al (2010) Hierarchical-granularity holonic modelling. J Ambient Intell Humaniz Comput 1:199–209. https://doi.org/10.1007/s12652-010-0013-3
Calude CS (2017) Unconventional computing: a brief subjective history. In: Adamatzky A (ed) Advances in unconventional computing: volume 1: theory. Springer International Publishing, Switzerland, pp 855–864
Camazine S et al (2001) Self-organization in biological systems. Princeton University Press, Princeton, NJ

Cao Y et al (2013) An overview of recent progress in the study of distributed multi-agent coordination. IEEE Trans Ind Inf 9(1):427–438
Caradonna JL (2014) Sustainability: a history. Oxford University Press, New York
Carlisle R (2004) Scientific American inventions and discoveries: all the milestones in ingenuity-from the discovery of fire to the invention of the microwave oven. Wiley, Hoboken, NJ
Casti JL (1994) Complexification: explaining paradoxical world through the science of surprise. Abacus, London
Chang S (1956) Theory of information feedback systems. IRE Trans Inf Theory 2(3):29–40
Checkland P (1999) Systems thinking, systems practice: includes a 30-year retrospective, rev. Wiley, Chichester, UK
Chen TC (1972) Distributed intelligence for user-oriented computing. In: Proceedings of the fall joint computing conference (AFIPS'72), Anaheim, CA, pp 1049–1056
Chernin E (1988) The "Harvard system": a mystery dispelled. BMJ 297(6655):1062–1063
Chess D et al (1995) Itinerant agents for mobile computing. IEEE Pers Commun 2(5):34–49
Chiang M et al (2007) Layering as optimization decomposition: a mathematical theory of network architectures. Proc IEEE 95(1):255–312
Cockshott P et al (2012) Computation and its limits. Oxford University Press, Oxford, UK
Coelho RL (2009) On the concept of energy: how understanding its history can improve physics teaching. Sci Educ 18:961–983. https://doi.org/10.1007/s11191-007-9128-0
Cohen R, Feigenbaum EA (1982) The handbook of artificial intelligence, vol 3. HeurisTech Press, Stanford, CA
Cook SA (1983) An overview of computational complexity. Commun ACM 26:401–408
Cooper SJ (2008) From Claude Bernard to Walter Cannon: emergence of the concept of homeostasis. Appetite 51(3):419–427
Corchado JM et al (2023) Generative artificial intelligence: fundamentals. ADCAIJ Adv Distrib Comput Artif Intell J 12(1):1–43. https://doi.org/10.14201/adcaij.31704
Corning PA (2002) Thermoeconomics: beyond the second law. J Bioecon 4:57–88. https://doi.org/10.1023/A:1020633317271
Cornish-Bowden A, Luz Cardenas M (2020) Contrasting theories of life: historical context, current theories. In search of an ideal theory. Biosystems 188:1–50. https://doi.org/10.1016/j.biosystems.2019.104063
Coulouris G et al (2012) Distributed systems: concepts and design, 5th edn. Addison-Wesley, Boston, MA
Courtland R (2016) Transistors could stop shrinking in 2021. IEEE Spectr 53(9):9–11
Crumley CL (2008) Heterarchy and the analysis of complex societies. Archaeol Pap Am Anthropol Assoc 6(1):1–5
Cuddington K et al (eds) (2007) Ecosystem engineers: plants to protists. Academic Press, Burlington, MA
Dabney W et al (2020) A distributional code for value in dopamine-based reinforcement learning. Nature 577:671–675. https://doi.org/10.1038/s41586-019-1924-6
Day RA (1989) Origins of the scientific paper: the IMRAD format. AMWA J 4(2):16–18
Day JD, Zimmermann H (1983) The OSI reference model. Proc IEEE 71(12):1334–1340
de Botton A (2000) Consolations of philosophy. Vintage Books, New York
de Haen P (1968) Modernizing the structure of reports on drugs. Clin Pharmacol Ther 9(5):547–549
De Wolf T, Holvoet T (2005) Emergence versus self-organisation: different concepts but promising when combined. In: Brueckner S et al (eds) Engineering self-organizing systems, methods, and applications. Springer-Verlag, Berlin, pp 1–15
Decker KS (1987) Distributed problem-solving techniques: a survey. IEEE Trans Syst Man Cybern 17(5):729–740
Dewdney AK (2004) Beyond reason: eight great problems that reveal the limits of science. Wiley, Hoboken, NJ
Di Marzo SG et al (eds) (2011) Self-organising software: from natural to artificial adaptation. Springer-Verlag, Berlin

Diacu F, Holmes P (1996) Celestial encounters: the origins of chaos and stability. Princeton University Press, Princeton, NJ

Diez JA (1997a) A hundred years of numbers. An historical introduction to measurement theory 1887–1990. Part I: the formation period. Two lines of research: axiomatics and real morphisms, scales and invariance. Stud Hist Philos Sci 28(1):167–185

Diez JA (1997b) A hundred years of numbers. An historical introduction to measurement theory 1887–1990. Part II: suppes and the mature theory. Representation and uniqueness. Stud Hist Philos Sci 28(2):237–265

Dilley J et al (2002) Globally distributed content delivery. IEEE Internet Comput 6(5):2–10

Dooley KJ (1997) A complex adaptive systems model of organization change. Nonlinear Dyn Psychol Life Sci 1(1):69–97

Dori D et al (2020) System definition, system worldviews, and systemness characteristics. IEEE Syst J 14(2):1538–1548

Dorri A et al (2018) Multi-agent systems: a survey. IEEE Access 6:28573–28593

Drack M (2009) Ludwig von Bertalanffy's early system approach. Syst Res Behav Sci 26(5):563–572

Dragoni N et al (2017) Microservices: yesterday, today, and tomorrow. In: Mazzara M, Meyer B (eds) Present and ulterior software engineering. Springer, Cham, Switzerland, pp 195–216

Dressler F (2008) A study of self-organization mechanisms in ad hoc and sensor networks. Comput Commun 31(13):3018–3029

Dreyfus H (1992) What computers still can't do: a critique of artificial reason. MIT Press, Cambridge, MA

du Plessis C (2022) The city sustainable, resilient, regenerative—a rose by any other name? In: Roggema R (ed) Design for regenerative cities and landscapes: rebalancing human impact and natural environment. Springer Nature, Cham, Switzerland

Dudley P (1996) Back to basics? Tektology and general system theory (GST). Syst Pract 9:273–284. https://doi.org/10.1007/BF02169018

Dummer GWA (1997) Electronic inventions and discoveries: electronics from its earliest beginnings to the present day, 4th edn. Institute of Physics Publishing, Philadelphia, PA

Economides K (2012) Centre-periphery tensions in legal theory and practice: can law and lawyers resist urban imperialism? Int J Rural Law Policy 2:1–8

E. J. H. (1967) Ingelfinger and IMRAD. Ann Intern Med 67(5):1117. https://doi.org/10.7326/0003-4819-67-5-1117

Elsasser W (1966) Atom and organism. Princeton University Press, Princeton NJ

Elsasser WM (1987) Reflections on a theory of organisms: holism in biology. The Johns Hopkins University Press, Baltimore, MD

Encyclopedia Britannica (2024). https://www.britannica.com. Accessed 5 Nov 2024

ETSI (2018) Autonomic network engineering for the self-managing future internet (AFI); generic autonomic network architecture; part 2: an architectural reference model for autonomic networking, cognitive networking and self-management. ETSI TS 103 195-2 V1.1.1

Evans M, Zimmermann A (eds) (2014) Global perspectives on subsidiarity. Springer, Dordrecht, The Netherlands

Eykhoff P (1960) Adaptive and optimalizing control systems. IEEE Trans Autom Control 5(2):148–151

Feamster N (2013) The road to SDN: an intellectual history of programmable networks. ACM Queue 11(12):1–21

Feeny D et al (1990) The tragedy of the commons: twenty-two years later. Hum Ecol 18(1):1–9

Fernandez-Cano A et al (2004) Reconsidering Price's model of scientific growth: an overview. Scientometrics 61(3):301–321

Fogel DB (2006) Nils Barricelli—artificial life, coevolution, self-adaptation. IEEE Comput Intell Mag 1(1):41–45

Forrester JW (1968) Industrial dynamics—after the first decade. Manage Sci 14(7):398–415

Forrester JW (2007a) System dynamics—a personal view of the first fifty years. Syst Dyn Rev 23(2/3):345–358
Forrester JW (2007b) System dynamics—the next fifty years. Syst Dyn Rev 23(2/3):359–370
Fortnow L, Homer S (2014) Computational complexity. In: Handbook of the history of logic, vol 9, pp 495–529. https://doi.org/10.1016/B978-0-444-51624-4.50011-3
Fourati H et al (2021) Comprehensive survey on self-organizing cellular network approaches applied to 5G networks. Comput Netw 199:1–24. https://doi.org/10.1016/j.comnet.2021.108435
Frampton KD et al (2010) A comparison of decentralized, distributed, and centralized vibro-acoustic control. J Acoust Soc Am 128:2798–2806. https://doi.org/10.1121/1.3183369
Francke M et al (2020) Huygens' clocks: 'sympathy' and resonance. Int J Control 93(2):274–281
Francois C (1999) Systemics and cybernetics in a historical perspective. Syst Res Behav Sci 16(3):203–219
Friston K (2010) The free-energy principle: a unified brain theory? Nat Rev Neurosci 11:127–138. https://doi.org/10.1038/nrn2787
Friston K et al (2006) A free energy principle for the brain. J Physiol Paris 100(1–3):70–87
Fukuyama F (2011) The origins of political order: from prehuman times to the French revolution. Farrar, Straus and Giroux, New York
Gajic Z et al (2008) Optimal control: weakly coupled systems and applications. CRC Press, Boca Raton, FL
Gao Z (2014) Engineering cybernetics: 60 years in the making. Control Theory Technol 12(2):97–109
Garfield E (1985) The life and career of George Sarton: the father of the history of science. J Hist Behav Sci 21(2):107–117
Garfield E (2006) The history and meaning of the journal impact factor. JAMA 295(1):90–93
Garfield E (2007) The evolution of the science citation index. Int Microbiol 10(1):65–69
Gass SI, Assad AA (2005) An annotated timeline of operations research: an informal history. Springer Science + Business Media, New York
Gastel B, Day RA (2016) How to write and publish a scientific paper, 8th edn. Greenwood, Santa Barbara, CA
Gatherer D (2008) Finite universe of discourse: the systems biology of Walter Elsasser (1904–1991). Open Biol J 1:9–20. https://doi.org/10.2174/1874196700801010009
Gitt W (1989) Information: the third fundamental quantity. Siemens Rev 56(6):2–7
Glassman RB (1973) Persistence and loose coupling in living systems. Behav Sci 18(2):83–98
Glavic P (2021) Review of the international systems of quantities and units usage. Standards 1(1):2–16
Gleick J (1987) Chaos: making a new science. Penguin Books, New York
Goldstein J (1999) Emergence as a construct: history and issues. Emergence 1(1):49–72
Gonzalez MJ Jr (1978) Workshop report: future directions in computer architecture. Computer 11(3):54–62
Goodsett M (2014) Discovery search tools: a comparative study. Ref Rev 28(6):2–8
Gorini R (2003) Al-Haytham the man of experience: the first steps in the science of vision. J Int Soc Hist Islam Med 2(4):53–55
Gribbin J (2003) The scientists: a history of science told through the lives of its greatest inventors. Random House, New York
Guiso L et al (2006) Does culture affect economic outcomes? J Econ Perspect 20(2):23–48
Gunawardena J (2014) Time-scale separation—Michaelis and Menten's old idea, still bearing fruit. FEBS J 281(2):473–488
Hall AD (1962) A methodology for systems engineering. D. Van Nostrand Company, Princeton, NJ
Hammond D (2003) The science of synthesis: exploring the social implications of general systems theory. University Press of Colorado, Boulder, CO
Hardin G (1968) The tragedy of the commons: the population problem has no technical solution; it requires a fundamental extension in morality. Science 162(3859):1234–1248

Hardin G (1974) Living on a lifeboat. Bioscience 24(10):561–568
Harmon JE (1989) The structure of scientific and engineering papers: a historical perspective. IEEE Trans Prof Commun 32(3):132–138
Harmon JE (1992) Evolution of the scientific paper. In: Proceedings of the IEEE international professional communications conference (IPCC'92), Santa Fe, NM, pp 468–475
Harre R (1981) Great scientific experiments: twenty experiments that changed our view of the world. Phaidon Press, Toronto, Canada
Harris JR (1952) A transistor shift register and serial adder. Proc IRE 40(11):1597–1602
Harris B, Morgan KC (1958) Binary symmetric decision feedback systems. Trans Am Inst Electr Eng Part I Commun Electron 77(4):436–443
Hartley J (1999) From structured abstracts to structured articles: a modest proposal. J Tech Writ Commun 29(3):255–270
Hawking S (2018) Brief answers to the big questions. John Murray, London
Hayden FG (2006) The inadequacy of Forrester system dynamics computer programs for institutional principles of hierarchy, feedback, and openness. J Econ Issues 40(2):527–535
Haykin S (2005) Cognitive radio: brain-empowered wireless communications. IEEE J Sel Areas Commun 23(2):201–220
Haykin S (2014) Adaptive filter theory, 5th edn. Prentice Hall, Upper Saddle River, NJ
Henderson LJ (1913) The fitness of the environment: an inquiry into the biological significance of the properties of matter. Am Nat 47(554):105–115
Hermoso de Mendoza I et al (2014) Synchronization in a semiclassical Kuramoto model. Phys Rev E 90(5). https://doi.org/10.1103/PhysRevE.90.052904
Hewitt K (1977) Viewing control structures as patterns of passing messages. Artif Intell 8(3):323–364
Higham NJ (1998) Handbook of writing for the mathematical sciences, 2nd edn. Society for Industrial and Applied Mathematics, Philadelphia, PA
Hoffman JG (1964) Self-organizing systems 1962. Phys Today 17(5):85–86
Holford J (2014) The lost honour of the social dimension: Bologna, exports and the idea of the university. Int J Lifelong Educ 33(1):7–25
Holland JH (1992) Complex adaptive systems. Daedalus 121(1):17–30
Holland JH (1995) Hidden order: how adaptation builds complexity. Perseus Books, Reading, MA
Holland JH (1998) Emergence: from chaos to order. Oxford University Press, Oxford, UK
Holland JH (2006) Studying complex adaptive systems. J Syst Sci Complexity 19:1–8. https://doi.org/10.1007/s11424-006-0001-z
Holland JH, Miller JH (1991) Artificial adaptive agents in economic theory. Am Econ Rev 81(2):365–370
Honderich T (ed) (2005) Oxford companion to philosophy, 2nd edn. Oxford University Press, Oxford, UK
Horling B, Lesser V (2004) A survey of multi-agent organizational paradigms. Knowl Eng Rev 19(4):281–316
Hosticka BJ (1985) Performance comparison of analog and digital circuits. Proc IEEE 73(1):25–29
Houghton B (1975) Scientific periodicals: their historical development, characteristics, and control. Shoe String Press, Hamden, CT
Houle D et al (2011) Measurement and meaning in biology. Q Rev Biol 86(1):3–34
Hugoson MÅ (2009) Centralized versus decentralized information systems: a historical flashback. In: Impagliazzo J et al (eds) History of Nordic computing 2 (HiNC 2007). IFIP advances in information and communication technology, vol 303. Springer, Berlin, pp 106–115
Huurdeman A (2003) The worldwide history of telecommunications. Wiley, Hoboken, NJ
IEEE (2012) How to write for technical periodicals & conferences. IEEE, Piscataway, NJ
IEEE Spectrum (1965) Information for IEEE authors. IEEE Spectr 2(8):111–115
IEEE Spectrum (1966) A supplement to "information to IEEE authors". IEEE Spectr 3(5):91
Jacobides MG et al (2018) Towards a theory of ecosystems. Strateg Manag J 39:2255–2276. https://doi.org/10.1002/smj.2904

JCGM (2012) International vocabulary of metrology—basic and general concepts and associated terms (VIM), 3rd edn. Joint Committee for Guides in Metrology (JCGM)
Jerabandi M, Kodabagi MM (2017) A review on home automation system. In: Proceedings of the 2017 international conference on smart technologies for smart nation (SmartTechCon'17), Bengaluru, India, pp 1411–1415
Jess JAG (2000) Designing electronic engines with electronic engines: 40 years of bootstrapping of a technology upon itself. IEEE Trans Comput Aided Des Integr Circuits Syst 19(12):1404–1427
Johansson B et al (2006) Mathematical decomposition techniques for distributed cross-layer optimization of data networks. IEEE J Sel Areas Commun 24(8):1535–1547
Juran JM, Godfrey AB (1999) Juran's quality handbook, 5th edn. McGraw-Hill, New York
Kahn RE et al (1978) Advances in packet radio technology. Proc IEEE 66(11):1468–1496
Kailath T (1960) Correlation detection of signals perturbed by a random channel. IRE Trans Inf Theory 6(3):361–366
Kailath T (1966) The complex envelope of white noise. IEEE Trans Inf Theory 12(3):397–398
Kauffman S (1995) At home in the universe: the search for laws of self-organization and complexity. Oxford University Press, Oxford, UK
Kauppinen-Räisänen H, Jauffret MN (2018) Using colour semiotics to explore colour meanings. J Cetacean Res Manag 21(1):101–117
Kawadia V, Kumar PR (2005) A cautionary perspective on cross-layer design. IEEE Wirel Commun 12(1):3–11
Kay A (1984) Computer software. Sci Am 251(3):53–59
Kearsey BN, Jones WT (1985) International standardisation in telecommunications and information processing. Electronics and power 31(9): 643-651
Kennefick D (2005) Einstein's papers were never peer reviewed (except for once when it failed). Phys Today 58(9):43–48
Kephart JO, Chess DM (2003) The vision of autonomic computing. Computer 36(1):41–50
Kester A (2015) A brief history of data conversion: a tale of nozzles, relays, tubes, transistors, and CMOS. IEEE Solid-State Circuits Mag 6(3):16–37
Keyes RW (1981) Fundamental limits in digital information processing. Proc IEEE 69(2):267–278
Kiebel SJ et al (2008) A hierarchy of time-scales and the brain. PLoS Comput Biol 4(11):1–12
Kim KD, Kumar PR (2012) Cyber-physical systems: a perspective at the centennial. Proceedings of the IEEE 100 (special centennial issue), pp 1287–1308
Kim K, Shevlyakov G (2008) Why Gaussianity? [An attempt to explain this phenomenon]. IEEE Signal Process Mag 25(2):102–113
Klein HA (1988) The science of measurement: a historical survey. Dover Publications, Mineola, NY
Klein JT (1990) Interdisciplinarity: history, theory, and practice. Wayne State University Press, Detroit, MI
Kline SJ (1995) Conceptual foundations of multidisciplinary thinking. Stanford University Press, Stanford, CA
Koestler A (1967) The ghost in the machine. Hutchinson & Co, London
Köksalan M et al (2011) Multiple criteria decision making. World Scientific Publishing, Singapore
Korkman S (2022) Talous ja humanismi. Otava, Helsinki, Finland
Krantz SG (2017) A primer of mathematical writing: being a disquisition on having your ideas recorded, typeset, published, read, and appreciated, 2nd edn. American Mathematical Society, Providence, RI
Krantz DH et al (1971) Foundations of measurement. Academic Press, New York
Kronick D (1976) A history of scientific and technical periodicals: the origins and development of the scientific and technical press 1665–1790, 2nd edn. Scarecrow, Metuchen, NJ
Kung SY (1984) On supercomputing with systolic/wavefront array processors. Proc IEEE 72(7):867–884
Kurose JF, Ross KD (2013) Computer networking: a top-down approach featuring the Internet, 6th edn. Addison-Wesley, Boston, MA

Kurzweil R (1999) The age of spiritual machines: when computers exceed human intelligence. Penguin Group, New York
Lakatos I (1970) Falsification and the methodology of scientific research programmes. In: Lakatos I, Musgrave A (eds) Criticism and the growth of knowledge. Cambridge University Press, Cambridge, pp 91–195
Lapaine M (2017) Modelling the world. In: Kent AJ, Vujakovic P (eds) The Routledge handbook of mapping and cartography. Routledge, New York, pp 187–201
Laplante PA et al (2008) What's in a name? Distinguishing between SaaS and SOA. IT Prof 10(3):46–50
Larson EJ (2021) The myth of artificial intelligence: why computers can't think the way we do. Belknap Press, Cambridge, MA
Lasaulce S, Tembine H (2011) Game theory and learning for wireless networks: fundamentals and applications. Academic Press, Oxford, UK
Lateef HY (2015) LTE-advanced self-organizing network conflicts and coordination algorithms. IEEE Wirel Commun 22(3):108–117
LeCun Y et al (2015) Deep learning. Nature 521:436–444. https://doi.org/10.1038/nature14539
Lee TH (2004) The design of CMOS radio-frequency integrated circuits, 2nd edn. Cambridge University Press, Cambridge, UK
Lenat D (2022) Creating a 30-million-rule system: MCC and Cycorp. IEEE Ann Hist Comput 44(1):44–56
Leon JC (1999) Science and philosophy in the west. Prentice Hall, Upper Saddle River, NJ
Liao X et al (2017) Small-world human brain networks: perspectives and challenges. Neurosci Biobehav Rev 77:286–300. https://doi.org/10.1016/j.neubiorev.2017.03.018
Lin S et al (1984) Automatic-repeat-request error-control schemes. IEEE Commun Mag 22(12):5–17
Lin X et al (2006) A tutorial on cross-layer optimization in wireless networks. IEEE J Sel Areas Commun 24(8):1452–1463
Liu M, Wong HSP (2024) The path to a 1-trillion-transistor GPU: AI's boom demands new chip technology. IEEE Spectr 61(7):22–27
Losee J (2001) A historical introduction to the philosophy of science, 4th edn. Oxford University Press, Oxford, UK
Love DJ et al (2008) An overview of limited feedback in wireless communication systems. IEEE J Sel Areas Commun 26(8):1341–1365
Lucky RW (1973) A survey of the communication theory literature: 1968–1973. IEEE Trans Inf Theory 19(6):725–739
Lundheim L (2002) On Shannon and 'Shannon's formula.' Telektronikk 98(1):20–29
Mämmelä A, Anttonen A (2017) Why will computing power need particular attention in future wireless devices? IEEE Circuits Syst Mag 17(1):12–26
Mämmelä A et al (2018) Multidisciplinary and historical perspectives for developing intelligent and resource-efficient systems. IEEE Access 6:17464–17499
Mämmelä A et al (2023) Loose coupling: an invisible thread in the history of technology. IEEE Access 11:59456–59482
Marcos A, Arp R (2013) Information in the biological sciences. In: Kampourakis K (ed) The philosophy of biology: a companion to educators. Dordrecht, Springer Science + Business Media, The Netherlands, pp 511–547
Markov IL (2014) Limits on fundamental limits to computation. Nature 512:147–154. https://doi.org/10.1038/nature13570
Martinelli D (2001) Systems hierarchies and management. Syst Res 18(1):69–82
Maruyama M (1963) The second cybernetics: deviation-amplifying mutual causal processes. Am Sci 5(2):164–179
Mason S (1962) A history of the sciences. Macmillan, New York
Matricciani E (1991) The probability distribution of the age of references in engineering papers. IEEE Trans Prof Commun 34(1):7–12

Mayr O (1970a) The origins of feedback control. MIT Press, Cambridge, MA

Mayr O (1970b) The origins of feedback control. Sci Am 223(4):110–119

Mayr FE (1982) The growth of biological thought: diversity, evolution, and inheritance. The Belknap Press of Harvard University Press, Cambridge, MA

McCarthy IP et al (2006) New product development as a complex adaptive system of decisions. J Prod Innov Manag 23(5):437–456

McCorduck P (2004) Machines who think. A K Peters, Natick, MA

McMahan HB et al (2017) Communication-efficient learning of deep networks from decentralized data. In: Proceedings of the international conference on artificial intelligence and statistics (AISTATS'17), Ft. Lauderdale, FL, pp 1273–1282

Meadows AJ (1985) The scientific paper as an archaeological artefact. J Inf Sci 11(1):27–30

Meadows DH, Wright D (eds) (2008) Thinking in systems: a primer. Chelsea Green Publishing, White River Junction, VT

Mendel JM, Fu KS (eds) (1970) Adaptive, learning, and pattern recognition systems: theory and applications. Academic Press, New York

Merriam-Webster (2024). https://www.merriam-webster.com. Accessed 5 Nov 2024

Mesarovic MD (1970) Multilevel systems and concepts in process control. Proc IEEE 58(1):111–125

Mesarovic MD et al (1970) Theory of hierarchical, multilevel systems. Academic Press, New York

Miettinen R (2000) The concept of experiential learning and John Dewey's theory of reflective thought and action. Int J Lifelong Educ 19(1):54–72

Mikulecky DC (2000) Robert Rosen: the well-posed question and its answer: why are organisms different from machines? Syst Res Behav Sci 17(5):419–432

Milgram S (1967) The small-world problem. Psychol Today 1(1):61–67

Miller JG (1978) Living systems. McGraw-Hill, New York

Milne RD (1965) The analysis of weakly coupled dynamical systems. Int J Control 2:171–199. https://doi.org/10.1080/00207176508905535

Minsky M (1961) Steps towards artificial intelligence. Proc IRE 49(1):8–30

Misra S et al (2012) Agile software development practices: evolution, principles, and criticisms. Int J Qual Reliab Manag 29(9):972–980

Mobus GE (2022) Systems science: theory, analysis, modeling, and design. Springer Nature, Cham, Switzerland

Morowitz HJ (2002) The emergence of everything: how the world became complex. Oxford University Press, New York

Morris CW (1938) Foundations of the theory of signs. In: Neurath O, Carnap R, Morris CW (eds) International encyclopedia of unified science, vol I, no 2. University of Chicago Press, Chicago, IL, pp 1–59

Narens L, Luce RD (1986) Measurement: the theory of numerical assignments. Psychol Bull 99(2):166–185

Neil E (1962) Neural factors responsible for cardiovascular regulation. Circ Res 11(1):137–143

Netherwood DB (1958) Logical machine design: a selected bibliography. IRE Trans Electron Comput 7(2):155–178

Neufeld ML, Cornog M (1986) Database history: from dinosaurs to compact discs. J Am Soc Inf Sci 37(4):183–190

Newman MEJ (2010) Networks: an introduction. Oxford University Press, New York

Nichols T (2017) The death of expertise: the campaign against established knowledge and why it matters. Oxford University Press, New York

Nii HP (1986) The blackboard model of problem solving and the evolution of blackboard architectures, part 1. AI Mag 7(2):38–53

Nilsson NJ (2010) The quest for artificial intelligence. Cambridge University Press, New York

Nola R, Sankey H (2007) Theories of scientific method. Acumen, Stocksfield, UK

Nowak M (2006) Evolutionary dynamics: Exploring the equations of life. The Belknap Press, Cambridge, MA

Nunes BAA et al (2014) A survey of software-defined networking: past, present, and future of programmable networks. IEEE Commun Surv Tutor 16(3):1617–1634
Nwogu KN (1997) The medical research paper: structure and functions. Engl Specif Purp 16(2):119–138
Nyquist H (1932) Regeneration theory. Bell Syst Tech J 11(1):126–147
Ogata K (2010) Modern control engineering, 5th edn. Prentice Hall, Boston, MA
Ogras UY, Marculescu R (2006) "It's a small world after all": NoC performance optimization via long-range link insertion. IEEE Trans Very Large Scale Integr (VLSI) Syst 14(7):693–706
O'Neill RV et al (1986) A hierarchical concept of ecosystems. Princeton University Press, Princeton, NJ
Online Etymology Dictionary (2024). https://www.etymonline.com. Accessed 5 Nov 2024
Orton JD, Weick KE (1990) Loosely coupled systems: a reconceptualization. Acad Manag Rev 15(2):203–223
Osinga F (2005) Science, strategy and war: the strategic theory of John Boyd. Eburon Academic Publishers, Delft, The Netherlands
Parnas DL (1972) On the criteria to be used in decomposing systems into modules. Commun ACM 15(12):1053–1058
Pautasso C, Wilde E (2009) Why is the web loosely coupled? A multi-faceted metric for service design. In: Proceedings of the 18th international conference on world wide web (WWW'09), Madrid, pp 911–920
Penrose P (1999) The emperor's new mind: concerning computers, minds and the laws of physics, new. Oxford University Press, Oxford, UK
Perkin H (2006) History of universities. In: Forest JF, Altbach PG (eds) International handbook of higher education. Springer, Dordrecht, The Netherlands, pp 159–205
Perona E (2005) Birth and early history of nonlinear dynamics in economics. Rev Econ Estadist 43(2):29–60
Pinker S (2018) Enlightenment now: the case for reason, science, humanism, and progress. Viking, New York
Piraveenan M et al (2008) Decentralized multi-agent clustering in scale-free sensor networks. In: Fulcher J, Jain LC (eds) Computational intelligence: a compendium. Springer-Verlag, Berlin, pp 485–515
Platt JR (1964) Strong inference: certain systematic methods of scientific thinking may produce much more rapid progress than others. Science 146(3642):347–353
Poundstone W (1988) Labyrinths of reason: paradox, puzzles and the frailty of knowledge. Penguin Books, London
Pouvreau D, Drack M (2007) On the history of Ludwig von Bertalanffy's "general systemology", and on its relationship to cybernetics. Part I: elements on the origins and genesis of Ludwig von Bertalanffy's "general systemology". Int J Gen Syst 36(3):281–337
Prehofer C, Bettstetter C (2005) Self-organization in communication networks: principles and design paradigms. IEEE Commun Mag 43(7):78–85
Proakis JG, Salehi M (2008) Digital communications, 5th edn. McGraw-Hill, New York
Proceedings of the IRE (1954) Information for proceedings authors. Proc IRE 42(11):1604–1605
Proceedings of the IRE (1960) Information for IRE authors. Proc IRE 48(9):1536–1539
Qin Z et al (2023) A generalized semantic communication system: from sources to channels. IEEE Wirel Commun 30(3):18–26
Qiu Y (2016) The openness of open application programming interfaces. Inf Commun Soc 20(11):1–17. https://doi.org/10.1080/1369118X.2016.1254268
Rajsbaum S, Raynal M (2020) 60 years of mastering concurrent computing through sequential thinking. ACM SIGACT News 51(2):59–88
Ramage M, Shipp K (2020) Systems thinkers, 2nd edn. Springer, London
Ramanathan R, Redi J (2002) A brief overview of ad hoc networks: challenges and directions. IEEE Commun Mag 40(5):20–22
Random House Webster's College Dictionary (1999) Random House, New York

Ray PP (2018) An introduction to dew computing: definition, concept and implications. IEEE Access 6:723–737
Richardson GP (1991) Feedback thought in social science and system theory. University of Pennsylvania Press, Philadelphia, PA
Riekki J, Mämmelä A (2021) Research and education towards smart and sustainable world. IEEE Access 9:53156–53177
Robertazzi T, Sarachik P (1986) Self-organizing communication networks. IEEE Commun Mag 24(1):28–33
Roberts S (2020) The power of not thinking: how our bodies learn and why we should trust them. Blink Publishing, London
Rosen R (1991) Life itself: a comprehensive inquiry into the nature, origin, and fabrication of life. Columbia University Press, New York
Rosen R (1996) On the limitation of scientific knowledge. In: Casti JL, Karlqvist A (eds) Boundaries and barriers on the limits of scientific knowledge. Perseus Books, Reading, MA, pp 199–214
Rosenberg MB (2015) Nonviolent communication, 3rd edn. PuddleDancer Press, Encinitas, CA
Rosenberg A, McIntyre L (2020) Philosophy of science: a contemporary introduction, 4th edn. Routledge, New York
Rothman T (2003) Everything's relative and other fables from science and technology. Wiley, Hoboken, NJ
Roy S (2008) Minimalist self-organization in wireless networks. In: Proceedings of the international conference on advanced technologies for communications 2008, Phoenix Park, Korea, pp 451–456
Ruparelia NB (2010) Software development lifecycle models. ACM SIGSOFT Softw Eng Notes 35(3):8–13
Russell AL (2012) Modularity: an interdisciplinary history of an ordering concept. Inf Cult 47(3):257–287
Russell S, Norvig P (2022) Artificial intelligence: a modern approach, 3rd edn. Pearson Education, Harlow, UK
Ryan A (2012) On politics: a history of political thought from Herodotus to the present. W. W. Norton, New York
Ryerson CM (1962) The reliability and quality control field from its inception to the present. Proc IRE 50(5):1323–1338
Saad W (2024) Artificial general intelligence (AGI)-native wireless systems: a journey beyond 6G. Preprint arXiv:2405.02336 [cs.AI]
Saaty TL (2008) Decision making with the analytic hierarchy process. International Journal of Services Sciences 1(1): 83-98
Saleh LH, Marais K (2006) Highlights from the early (and pre-) history of reliability engineering. Reliab Eng Syst Saf 91(2):249–256
Salkintzis AK et al (2002) WLAN-GPRS integration for next-generation mobile data networks. IEEE Wirel Commun 9(5):112–124
Sandell N Jr et al (1978) Survey of decentralized control methods for large scale systems. IEEE Trans Autom Control 23(2):108–128
Sarkat P (2000) A brief history of cellular automata. ACM Comput Surv 32(1):80–107
Scheerens J (2015) Theories on educational effectiveness and ineffectiveness. Sch Eff Sch Improv 26(1):10–31
Schoemaker PJH (2020) How historical analysis can enrich scenario planning. Futures Foresight Sci 2(3–4):1–13
Scholtz RA (1982) The origins of spread-spectrum communications. IEEE Trans Commun 30(5):822–854
Schulz KF et al (2010) CONSORT 2010 statement: updated guidelines for report parallel group randomised trials. J Pharmacol Pharmacother 1(2):73–130
Schwartz M et al (1966) Communication systems and techniques. McGraw-Hill, New York

Scott B (2004) Second-order cybernetics: an historical introduction. Kybernetes 33(9/10):1365–1378
SE VOCAB (2024) Software and systems engineering vocabulary. IEEE Computer Society and ISO/IEC JTC 1/SC7. https://pascal.computer.org. Accessed 6 Nov 2024
Sen S (1997) Multi-agent systems: milestones and new horizons. Trends Cogn Sci 1(9):334–340
Senge P (2006) The fifth discipline: the art and practice of the learning organization, rev. Doubleday, New York
Shannon CE (1948) A mathematical theory of communication. Bell Syst Tech J 27(3):349–423
Shannon CE, Weaver W (1998) The mathematical theory of communication. University of Illinois Press, Chicago, IL
Shapiro AE (1989) Huygens' Traité le la Lumière and Newton's opticks: pursuing and eschewing hypotheses. Notes Rec R Soc J Hist Sci 43(2):223–247
Shapiro FR (1992) Origins of bibliometrics, citation indexing, and citation analysis: the neglected legal literature. J Am Soc Inf Sci 43(5):337–339
Silk H et al (2016) Design of self-organizing networks: creating specified degree distributions. IEEE Trans Netw Sci Eng 3(3):147–158
Simmons JG (1996) The scientific 100: a ranking of the most influential scientists, past and present. Kensington Publishing, New York
Simon H (1954) Some strategic considerations in the construction of social science models. In: Lazarsfeld P (ed) Mathematical thinking in the social sciences. Free Press, Glencoe, IL, pp 388–438
Simon HA (1962) The architecture of complexity. Proc Am Philos Soc 106(6):467–482
Simon HA (1973) The organization of complex systems. In: Pattee HH (ed) Hierarchy theory: the challenge of complex systems. George Braziller, pp 1–27
Simon HA (1996) The sciences of the artificial, 3rd edn. MIT Press, Cambridge, MA
Simon HA (2002) Near decomposability and the speed of evolution. Ind Corp Change 11(3):587–599
Sipilä H (2014) The zero-energy principle as a fundamental law of nature. La Nuova Crit Spec Issue 63–64:29–33
Skelton J (1994) Analysis of the structure of original research papers: an aid to writing original papers for publication. Br J Gen Pract 44(387):455–459
Skolnik H (1979) Historical aspects of patent systems. IEEE Trans Prof Commun 22(2):59–63
Skyttner L (2005) General systems theory: problems, perspectives, practice, 2nd edn. World Scientific Publishing, Singapore
Smirnova L et al (2023) Organoid intelligence (OI): the new frontier in biocomputing and intelligence-in-a-dish. Front Sci 1:1–23. https://doi.org/10.3389/fsci.2023.1017235
Soffer A, Weinberg SL (1975) Flexibility in medical writing. Chest 67(1):5–7
Sollaci LB, Pereira MG (2004) The introduction, methods, results, and discussion (IMRAD) structure: a fifty-year survey. J Med Libr Assoc 92(3):364–367
Somers F (1996) Hybrid: unifying centralized and distributed network management using intelligent agents. In: Proceedings of the IEEE network operations and management symposium (NOMS'96), Kyoto, Japan, pp 34–43
Spier R (2002) The history of the peer-review process. Trends Biotechnol 20(8):357–358
Spragins M (1966) Learning without a teacher. IEEE Trans Inf Theory 12(2):223–230
Stanek S et al (2008) Software agents. In: Adam F, Humhreys P (eds) Encyclopedia of decision making and decision support technologies. Information Science Reference, New York, pp 798–806
Stankovic JA (1984) A perspective on distributed computing systems. IEEE Trans Comput 33(12):1102–1115
Stevens SS (1946) On the theory of scales of measurement. Science 103(2684):677–680
Stevens SS (1957) On the psychophysical law. Psychol Rev 64(3):153–181
Stevens WP et al (1974) Structured design. IBM Syst J 13(2):115–139
Stonier T (1992) Beyond information: the natural history of intelligence. Springer, Berlin

Stonier T (1997) Information and meaning: an evolutionary perspective. Springer, Berlin
Strasser T et al (2011) Design and execution issues in IEC 61499 distributed automation and control systems. IEEE Trans Syst Man Cybern Part C Appl Rev 41(1):41–51
Strasser T et al (2015) A review of architectures and concepts for intelligence in future electric energy systems. IEEE Trans Ind Electron 62(4):2424–2438
Strogatz SH (2014) Nonlinear dynamics and chaos: with applications to physics, biology, chemistry, and engineering, 2nd edn. CRC Press, Boca Raton, FL
Suntola T (2018) The short history of science—or the long path to the union of metaphysics and empiricism, 3rd edn. Physics Foundations Society and The Finnish Society for Natural Philosophy. https://physicsfoundations.org
Surbiryala J, Rong C (2019) Cloud computing: history and overview. In: Proceedings of the 2019 IEEE cloud summit, Washington, DC, pp 1–8
Swilling M (2020) The age of sustainability: just transitions in a complex world. Routledge, New York
Sycara KP (1998) Multi-agent systems. AI Mag 19(2):79–92
Talbi EG (2009) Metaheuristics: from design to implementation. Wiley, Hoboken, NJ
Tanenbaum AS, Wetherall DJ (2011) Computer networks, 5th edn. Prentice Hall, Englewood Cliffs, NJ
Theis TN, Wong HSP (2017) The end of Moore's law: a new beginning for information technology. Comput Sci Eng 19(2):41–50
Thompson JD (2017) Organizations in action: social science bases of administrative theory. Routledge, New York
Tillman FA et al (1982) Bayesian reliability & availability—a review. IEEE Trans Reliab 31(4):362–372
Treptow RS (1986) Conservation of mass: fact or fiction? J Chem Educ 63(2):103–105
Treptow RS (2005) $E = mc^2$ for the chemist: when is mass conserved? J Chem Educ 82(11):1636–1641
Tsypkin YZ (1972) Adaptation and learning in automatic systems. Academic, New York
Tzafestas SG (2018) Energy, feedback, adaptation, and self-organization: the fundamental elements of life and society. Springer International Publishing, Cham, Switzerland
Umpleby SA (2009) Ross Ashby's general theory of adaptive systems. Int J Gen Syst 38(2):231–238
Umpleby SA (2016) Second-order cybernetics as a fundamental revolution in science. Construct Found 11(3):455–465
van der Hoek A, Lopez N (2011) A design perspective on modularity. In: Proceedings of the aspect-oriented software development (AOSD'11), Pernambuco, Brazil, pp 265–280
Vaswani A et al (2017) Attention is all you need. In: Proceedings of the neural information processing systems (NIPS'17), Long Beach, CA
Verdier N (2006) Hierarchy: a short history of a word in western thought. In: Pumain D (ed) Hierarchy in natural and social sciences. Springer, Dordrecht, The Netherlands, pp 13–37
Vinodh S et al (2021) Integration of continuous improvement strategies with Industry 4.0: a systematic review and agenda for further research. TQM J 33(2):441–472
von Bertalanffy L (1932) Theoretische Biologie. Erster Band: Allgemeine Theorie, Physikochemie, Aufbau und Entwicklung des Organismus. Verlag von Gabrüder Borntraeger, Berlin
von Bertalanffy L (1950a) The theory of open systems in physics and biology. Nature 111(2872):23–29
von Bertalanffy L (1950b) An outline of general system theory. Br J Philos Sci 1(2):134–165
von Bertalanffy L (1971) General system theory: foundations, development, applications, rev. George Braziller, New York
Wagner-Döbler R (2001) Rescher's principle of decreasing marginal returns of scientific research. Scientometrics 50(3):419–436
Walasek L, Brown GDA (2023) Incomparability and incommensurability in choice: No common currency of value? Perspectives on Psychological Science. https://doi.org/10.1177/17456916231192828

Waldrop MM (2016) More than Moore. Nature 530(7589):145–147

Walker DW (1995) An introduction to message passing paradigms. In: Proceedings of the CERN School of Computing, Arles, France, pp. 165-184

Wang Y, Blei DM (2019) The blessings of multiple causes. J Am Stat Assoc 114(528):1574–1596

Watson GH, DeYong CF (2010) Design for six sigma: caveat emptor. Int J Lean Six Sigma 1(1):66–84

Watts DJ (2004) Six degrees: the science of a connected age. W. W. Norton & Company, New York

Weick KE (1976) Educational organizations as loosely coupled systems. Adm Sci Q 21(1):1–19

Weiner LH (1978) The roots of structured programming. ACM SIGCSE Bull 10(1):243–253

West G (2017) Scale: the universal laws of life and death in organisms, cities and companies. Penguin Books, New York

Westerhoff HV et al (2009) Systems biology: the elements and principles of life. FEBS Lett 573(24):3882–3890

Whitaker RD (1975) An historical note on the conservation of mass. J Chem Educ 52(10):658–659

Widrow B, Stearns AD (1985) Adaptive signal processing. Prentice Hall, Englewood Cliffs, MA

Widrow B, Walach E (1984) On the statistical efficiency of the LMS algorithm with nonstationary inputs. IEEE Trans Inf Theory 30(2):211–221

Wiener N (1961) Cybernetics: or control and communication in the animal and the machine, 2nd edn. MIT Press, Cambridge, MA

Wilenius M (2014) Leadership in the sixth wave—excursions into the new paradigm of the Kondratieff cycle 2010–2050. Eur J Futures Res 2:1–11. https://doi.org/10.1007/s40309-014-0036-7

Wilson EB (1990) An introduction to scientific research. Dover, Mineola, NY

Wilson EO (1998) Consilience: the unity of knowledge. Vintage Books, New York

Witty FJ (1973) The beginnings of indexing and abstracting: some notes towards a history of indexing and abstracting in antiquity and the middle ages. The Indexer 8(4):193–198

Wu J (2011) Improving the writing of research papers: IMRAD and beyond. Landscape Ecol 26:1345–1349. https://doi.org/10.1007/s10980-011-9674-3

Wu J (2013) Hierarchy theory. In: Rozzi R et al (eds) Linking ecology and ethics for a changing world: values, philosophy, and action. Springer Science + Business Media Dordrecht, The Netherlands, pp 281–302.

Wydrowski B, Zukerman M (2002) QoS in best-effort networks. IEEE Commun Mag 40(12):44–49

Yan Z et al (2013) A survey and analysis of multi-robot coordination. Int J Adv Rob Syst 10(12):399–416

Yang S, Hanzo L (2015) Fifty years of MIMO detection: the road to large-scale MIMOs. IEEE Commun Surv Tutor 17(4):1941–1988

Ye D et al (2017) A survey of self-organization mechanisms in multiagent systems. IEEE Trans Syst Man Cybern Syst 47(3):441–461

Young PC (2011) Gauss, Kalman and advances in recursive parameter estimation. J Forecast 30:104–146. https://doi.org/10.1002/for.1187

Yourdon E, Constantine LL (1978) Structured design: fundamentals of a discipline of computer programs and systems design, 2nd edn. Yourdon Press, New York

Zappone A et al (2019) Wireless networks design in the era of deep learning: model-based, AI-based, or both? IEEE Trans Commun 67(10):7331–7376

Zhang L et al (2013) Network-induced constraints in networked control systems—a survey. IEEE Trans Ind Inf 9(1):403–416

Zhang Z et al (2014) On swarm intelligence inspired self-organized networking: its bionic mechanisms, designing principles and optimization approaches. IEEE Commun Surv Tutor 16(1):513–537

Zimmerman BJ (2002) Becoming a self-regulated learner: an overview. Theory Pract 41(2):64–70

Chapter 7
Summary

In the absence of purpose, life becomes an endless journey to nowhere. Seneca (4 BCE–65)
What we know is a drop, what we don't know is an ocean. Isaac Newton (1642–1727)
Nowadays people know the price of everything and the value of nothing. Oscar Wilde (1854–1900)
When all else fails, tell the truth. Donald T. Regan (1918–2003)
You can't connect the dots looking forward; you can only connect them looking backwards. So you have to trust that the dots will somehow connect in your future. Steve Jobs (1955–2011)

Abstract Research is an advanced learning process described in David Kolb's experiential learning cycle. The research process follows the same cycle but uses a somewhat different terminology. Research differs from learning because the solution is not initially known. All technical systems are causal, but complex systems include emergent properties. Systems thinking is inter- and transdisciplinary, aiming at a unified understanding of the world. The most important results of systems thinking are system theories and archetypes. Future systems will be highly dynamic and able to adapt to environmental changes. We are in the age sustainability, where we should follow the principles of fairness between generations.

Analytical and systems thinking in research are complementary and not mutually exclusive. They both benefit from each other. Research starts with an idea and a problem statement. We must define the scope of the study relatively early in the research since the amount of literature is vast and exponentially growing. The conceptual analysis must complement the definition of the scope. In the analytical thinking, we must follow reduction and a bottom-up or inside-out approach, generalizing from simple to complex. After the initial data collection, we formulate a hypothesis using the experimental-abductive method. Then, we refine and verify or falsify the theory using the hypothetico-deductive method. In systems thinking we use the complementary top-down or outside-in approach. It corresponds to deduction in simple linear problems.

A. Mämmelä, *Unifying Systems*, https://doi.org/10.1007/978-3-031-85012-7_7

Intelligence, rationality, creativity, wisdom, and ethical principles Intelligence and rationality were synonymous terms in the older literature. In modern psychology, intelligence refers to an ability to reasoning using the rules of logic in the algorithmic mind whereas rationality is a higher-level concept that means that intelligent persons can also use reflections and reach their goals efficiently with the available resources in an uncertain environment. Rational behavior means building the society that we see as the purpose of life. Not all intelligent people are creative or practical or even rational. Creativity is in individuals working freely in a democratic society. Some kind of chaos generates new ideas, but only if there is a solid and safe basis for building them. Wisdom refers to successful management of conflicts in social situations. Science must follow strict ethical principles. In a society, the most important value is trust, which requires respect and fairness and leads to cooperation and safety. Respect means that we want good for other people, even for those who do not understand our viewpoint.

Learning David Kolb's experiential learning cycle corresponds to the cycle we use in research. We learn best from the bottom up and from inside out, but we can improve our understanding from the top down and from outside in. After concrete experiments, we use reflections to find an explanation. Before we can start learning, we must focus our attention to a small part of the world, otherwise we are confused. This is called reduction. That is why we have different subjects and school classes, and we proceed from the bottom up. Integrative learning is top-down learning which is only possible when there is something to integrate. Part of any learning is conceptual analysis where we show the hierarchical relationships between the concepts.

Our knowledge is restricted in various ways. There are emergent properties that are mathematically intractable. Mathematics is known to be incomplete with a finite set of axioms. An axiomatic system cannot be complete and consistent at the same time. The halting problem and the existence of strange attractors demonstrate the incompleteness of mathematics. Emergence leads to problems that still need to be solved, such as the origin of matter and energy, life, consciousness, and free will within consciousness. Additional limitations come from the limited computing capacity and energy and space used. Many problems have exponential complexity. There are also physical fundamental limits that no physical system can surpass. Some paradoxes still wait for an explanation. Science is divided into many disciplines because of emergence and our bounded rationality and memory. Paradoxes represent dilemmas or conflicts, which cannot be easily solved, for example the social dilemma, which is a tension between individual and collective rationality and not solved in market economy unless mixed or hybrid economy is used. Systems must be dynamic and make trade-offs using ambidexterity.

Information retrieval We must use efficient methods to manage the existing knowledge. Knowing the history is an integral part of our expertise. We must approach information retrieval hierarchically, from more general to more specific. We start with books and proceed to reviews, tutorial papers, original journal papers, and finally, the newest conference papers. If we know a recent exciting paper, we can find other papers using the list of references and citations collected in databases. An efficient way is to use bibliographies, often in the introductions of original papers. A problem is the terminology that frequently depends on the discipline. Interdisciplinary topics can be studied using Google Scholar or large databases such as Scopus and Web of Science. It is best to rely on famous publishers. The amount of literature is increasing exponentially, but eventually, the growth will be saturated. The state of the art only accumulates some of the history since new paradigms are often accepted only after many decades. There may be Sleeping Beauties whose value is understood only afterwards. We could cover the most relevant papers if we study the last 50–100 years for a review paper, but for an original paper with a focused topic, the previous ten years may be enough. It is best to find out the origin of each relevant idea. One benefit regarding learning is that the theories are in their simplest form in the beginning.

Writing In the beginning, we write a literature review, and in the end, we write a publication. Writing a scientific publication improves the quality of research. A standard approach uses the IMRDC structure where we have the introduction, materials and methods, results and discussion, and conclusion. The structure supports the top-down approach we must follow when writing to experts. For each section, we have several moves which give guidelines for writing. The novelty claim is the most essential part of the introduction. Even books and review papers must have some novelty. Anonymous peer reviewers evaluate the quality of the manuscript. The opinion of authorities is not a criterion for the reliability of knowledge since sometimes we must abandon old paradigms. Paradigms establish the status of scientific knowledge, but they may also slow down development if they change to dogmas that we cannot suspect or criticize.

Analytical thinking Research is a demanding learning process where people initially need to discover the solution; otherwise, it would not be novel. Theories may be axiomatic systems or model-based theories. They have a similar structure consisting of undefined primitive terms, definitions, assumptions, deduction, and conclusions. The research consists of conceptual analysis and the formation of theories. In conceptual analysis, we use clear hierarchical definitions of the concepts and terms as a basis for communication. In our diagrams, the real world is always at the bottom, and a theory is at the top; the higher, the more comprehensive a theory is. In research, reflections in David Kolb's learning cycle correspond to abduction, which is inference to the best solution. To support reflections, we use methodological reduction and experimental-abductive methods. We use several competing hypotheses to select the best in strong inference, thus simulating reflection and abduction.

Ultimately, the hypothesis is verified or falsified using the hypothetico-deductive method. The experimental-abductive and hypothetico-deductive methods complement each other. In engineering, we verify the system in a laboratory environment so that we see that it fulfills the requirements. In addition to verification, we validate the system in a real environment or in the field. In validation, we verify that the requirements really correspond to user needs.

Philosophically, truth theories include coherence, correspondence with reality, and pragmatism. We consider such theories true that work in practice. However, we see the truth as unattainable. Typical quality criteria for science are simplicity, coherence, correspondence, generality, and fertility. Criteria for papers include originality, significance, correctness, readability, and suitability for the planned audience. The paper should be outlined from the beginning since there will never be "more time."

Systems A system is defined to be a set of parts and their relationships. Complex systems consist of interacting agents, which are sense-decide-act feedback loops. We implement systems using the basic resources offered by nature, including materials, energy, information, time, frequency, and space. Conservation of energy is an essential law since energy does not disappear anywhere but only changes its form, eventually becoming heat, according to the entropy law.

Systems are divided into isolated, closed, and open systems. Closed systems exchange energy with the environment but no matter. Open systems exchange both matter and energy. Practical systems are open or closed but usually not isolated. Entropy law is valid only in isolated systems. In closed systems, energy minimization principle is an approach to self-organization. In open systems, we have nonequilibrium systems when there is a continuous flux of matter and energy to be used in dissipative systems. This is an alternative approach in nature to self-organization. Either matter or energy carries information. Depending on the maturity level, there are several forms of information, including data, information, knowledge, and wisdom.

Desirable properties of systems include stability, scalability, efficiency, reliability, and agility. Stability may be a problem in systems consisting of feedback loops. In general, hierarchical systems should be vertically and horizontally loosely coupled. Vertical loose coupling means time-scale separation. Horizontal loose coupling refers to weak coupling between modules.

Emergence and causality Many hierarchical nonlinear feedback systems have emergent properties. Such systems are called complex, implying that they are analytically intractable. Emergence means that a hierarchical system may have properties and behavior that we cannot predict from the properties and behavior of the lower levels. Intractability usually comes from nonlinear feedback loops perhaps using multicausality, often changing the structure of a dynamic system in self-organization. An example of an intractable problem is the multibody problem is physics. A similar problem in chemistry is the prediction of the structure of a complex organic molecule. Complexity engineering aims to use emergence for practical purposes, but so far it is not well developed. Possible explanations for new events include causality, chance, and free will. Causal systems are deterministic (i.e., nonrandom) and either discrete or continuous, and a cause always precedes or coincides with an effect, forming a causality chain. For chance and free will, the earlier effects are either unknown or neglected. In a hierarchical system, causality may be same-level, downward, or upward causality. There may be multiple causes in multicausality. In hierarchical control systems, sensing signals proceed from the bottom up and control or act signals from the top down.

Systems thinking Inter- and transdisciplinary systems thinking represents the final goal of any science, producing an integrated view of the world. Systems thinking may improve our learning and creativity. The synthesis part is supported by using generic structures called system archetypes that have survived the test of time. We can best manage history by focusing on system theories and archetypes, but it has been challenging to locate them because fragmented disciplinary work dominates. There is a limited number of system archetypes. We have bounded rationality and memory, and therefore, hierarchy is needed when the complexity of the problem is exponential. This same problem exists in organisms (i.e., humans) and mechanisms (for example, computers). Intractable problems show that also computers have bounded rationality, and we must find satisfactory solutions such as approximations and heuristics. In teaching, it may be reasonable to focus on the history of system theories and system archetypes when the time is limited. We also use Kolb's learning cycle in systems thinking, but now we support abduction by using system archetypes. We complement the analysis with computer simulations.

We can present systems in a hierarchy of complexity, which is different in natural and technical systems. In natural systems, we have static and simple dynamic systems, homeostasis, morphogenesis, and reproductive, conscious, and social systems. In technical systems, we have static and simple dynamic systems and control, adaptive, learning, and self-organizing systems that humans must supervise. Technical systems can simulate rudimentary social systems without consciousness. A machine does not have free will, and thus it cannot set its own goals. Humans can also make mistakes, but we can minimize them when there are many sophisticated decision-makers.

We need a broad understanding of core sciences. In physics and chemistry, the interest is in mechanisms. In biology, the interest is in living organisms whose origin is not yet understood entirely. Similarly, psychology is different from biology since it covers consciousness. More generally, social sciences study collective consciousness and are divided into disciplines that consider different forms of relationships between humans. Sociology was initially a form of social physics, but such a discipline cannot be complete because the "parts" of a society are conscious human agents with different goals. In economics, we are interested in exchange; in political science, the objects of research are political relationships that include trust and threat.

System theories Because the analytical method is limited regarding intractable problems, leading to emergent properties, there are many system theories for different aspects. The system theories include linear system theory and circuit theory; nonlinear system theory and chaos and catastrophe theory; theory of evolution and theory of living systems; thermodynamics and nonequilibrium thermodynamics; optimization and decision theory, game theory, and detection and estimation theory; cybernetics, artificial intelligence, and system dynamics; theory of information transmission and network and hierarchy theory; theory of computing and computational complexity theory; and general theory of systems and complexity theory. The theory of information transmission is usually called information theory. Multiagent systems within artificial intelligence, system dynamics, and complexity theory are closely related theories for self-organizing systems using interacting agents. The three theories have a common origin in cybernetics, but for some reason they have wanted to downplay their cybernetic background and therefore the overall picture is blurred.

They are modern forms of general theory of systems. In system dynamics the agents simulate humans having bounded rationality and using satisficing principle instead of optimization. A solution is satisfactory if satisfaction is positive in all, usually incommensurate, objectives. In addition to finding an equilibrium in energy minimization and nonequilibrium systems, other principles of self-organization include synergetics, optimizing algorithms, swarm intelligence, cellular automata, evolutionary computation, random graphs, small-world networks, scale-free networks, and the related concepts of double feedback, ultrastability, and self-stabilization. There are also five major theories of life, including metabolism-repair systems, hypercycle, chemoton, autopoiesis, and autocatalytic sets. In technical systems, because of its immaturity, self-organization may be a major source of failure.

System archetypes There are some 20 system archetypes with which we can manage over 90% of situations. Information technology includes electronics and control, computer, and communications engineering. We use electronics to implement control, computer, and communication systems. For information transmission, they use a network consisting of interacting agents. In artificial intelligence, we use the term multiagent systems; in complexity theory, we use the term complex adaptive systems. They are synonymous terms. In a network, we transfer communication and control signals, and we control the network so that it is self-organizing and able to adapt to environmental changes.

System theories and archetypes overlap. Examples of archetypes include small-world networks, open-loop and closed-loop feedback control, optimization and decision-making, hierarchy and modularity, degrees of centralization, degrees of coupling, multiagent systems or complex adaptive systems, sequential and concurrent computing, message passing and shared memory for information exchange, hierarchy of systems, and principles of self-organization. Not all problems can be solved using ordinary sequential computing.

Small-world networks are both locally and globally optimal for communications. Such networks are between random and ordered networks and include shortcuts. A small-world network implies that we use recursion in a hierarchy; therefore, we can reach a distant agent with a small number of hops since the number contacts increases exponentially. Feedback may be positive or negative, and we usually prefer the latter because of its stability. Feedback control is more accurate than open-loop control and can track slow environmental changes. A hierarchy may be nested or nonnested; the nonnested hierarchy may be a dominance or layer hierarchy. Concurrent computing includes parallel and distributed computing.

We divide a network of agents into centralized, decentralized, distributed, and hybrid systems. In general, global behavior cannot be predicted from local behavior and global optimum cannot be found using local optimization in decentralized systems. Centralized systems can find a global optimum. In decentralized systems, the agents do not cooperate at all. In distributed systems, the agents exchange information at least with the nearest neighbors. A good starting point for the degree of centralization is a hierarchical hybrid system combining centralized and distributed control. This system can be optimal locally and globally, as in small-world networks for information exchange. Hybrid systems offer the beneficial properties of centralized and distributed systems. There is vertical and horizontal loose coupling between hierarchy levels and modules, respectively. We have a solid basis for this kind of model from the optimization decomposition theory. The hybrid system is highly flexible as its special cases include centralized, decentralized, and distributed systems. The degree of coupling depends on the situation and often the environment is dynamic and therefore the degree of coupling must also be dynamic. Natural systems are often distributed, but the principles are not well understood. Distributed control is also popular in social sciences in the form of subsidiarity. Still, it has problems with stability, especially if there is no common goal and different feedback loops are interacting, or there are delays in feedback loops.

Importance of a goal In any feedback system, a goal is essential to improve stability. We classify feedback systems into goal-directed, goal-seeking, and goal-achieving. Goal-directed systems have an explicit goal usually given externally. Goal-seeking systems move towards an equilibrium such as minimum energy or they can be dynamic and far from equilibrium as in nonequilibrium systems. Goal-achieving systems rely on serendipity and use random search methods. We need free will to define an explicit goal; a machine cannot do that. A social or technical system needs a goal to have stable operation. An example is a flock of birds that should have a leader, as in a wedge of cranes, since otherwise, the flock does not move anywhere. It may still rapidly react to raptors. Natural systems seem to be either goal-achieving or goal-seeking, not goal-directed unless there is some form of consciousness involved. In technical systems, a human must define the goal or utility and supervise the machine since otherwise the machine can make stupid mistakes since it does not have any understanding of semantics.

Optimization and satisficing Before decision-making, we usually do optimization, which is fundamentally the survival of the fittest, and the corresponding optimization criterion is fitness. It is an implicit optimization criterion in biological systems, and we can extend it to social and technical systems where the law of supply and demand is valid. Instead of optimizing in complex problems, we try to find a satisfactory, robust solution. We may need heuristics or rules of thumb and approximations. Optimal systems are not necessarily robust since they minimize redundancy.

Evolution is nature's pruning algorithm offering emergent properties. The environment is a selecting agent that changes over time and from one region to another. In addition to biology, fitness is also helpful in social sciences and engineering in the form of the law of supply and demand. Optimization problems have, in general, exponential complexity. We can decompose a large loosely coupled problem into smaller tightly coupled problems that we solve using conventional optimization methods. Decomposition may be vertical or horizontal. We classify optimization methods based on parametric models, neural networks, and evolutionary processes. Our brain uses small-world networks, energy minimization, reinforcement learning, hierarchy, and time-scale separation, which makes these principles particularly interesting.

Pareto optimal systems are neither unique nor fair but show the trade-offs in the Pareto frontier showing the effect of the social dilemma. Fairness is an ethical choice.

Since the requirements are mutually conflicting, we may use a noncooperative game that leads to a Nash equilibrium, which is generally not Pareto optimal, unique, or fair. However, a cooperative game leads to a distributed Nash bargaining solution that is unique, optimal, and fair. In optimization, we make a trade-off in the use of incommensurable basic resources. Although the Nash bargaining solution may be complicated to attain, especially in geographically distributed systems where everybody is unwilling to cooperate, it forms a basis for comparing less optimal systems. We can approximate it using a leader-follower structure in the Stackelberg game. Nonequilibrium systems are dynamic and create a different optimization approach far from any equilibrium. Most optimization problems in practice are NP-hard and require exponential time to be solved and therefore often a satisfactory solution is accepted.

Complex problems must be solved using a satisficing principle. We abandon the common-currency assumption and use strategies that radically differ from conventional utility-based approaches. We can use analytic hierarchy process and other rank-based strategies. The heuristic strategies lead to inconsistencies in decision-making, such as preference reversals, also observed in experimental studies. It appears that it will never be possible to develop consistent single-quantity-maximizing models for decision-making.

Sustainability We are now in the age of sustainability, and we must consider the needs of future generations. We cannot be happy if our grandchildren and their children suffer from our decisions. Overpopulation, overuse of resources, pollution, and climate change result from the tragedy of the commons. Education, privatization, and regulation can solve this tragedy. We approach the fundamental limits of nature, and a major problem will be complexity. We use interdisciplinary systems thinking to find consolidated solutions to complex problems.

History We must understand the history to be able to see the future. The last 500–1000 years have shown that a country cannot exist without military strength. In addition to military history, we must know the cultural history. Systematic research started in ancient Greece. The Greeks developed the axiomatic system. They discovered many modern ideas early, but they were not appreciated. In Europe, the interest in science decreased for hundreds of years. At the beginning of the second millennium, the interest in rational thinking started again in Europe, first in the form of Scholasticism and later in the Renaissance. In the 1600s, the scientific revolution started because of the invention of the modern research method based on reductionism, leading to the success of Western culture. The method was invented in Europe and then spread across the world. Superstition still prevailed until the Enlightenment of the 1700s, when we started to appreciate reason, science, humanism, and progress.

Enlightenment resulted in the triumphal march of representative liberal democracy that offered efficiency, innovations, and progress possibilities. Liberal democracy is a narrow corridor between anarchy and an authoritarian regime. We are always in a democracy crisis. Liberal democracy is a solution to the social dilemma through ambidexterity. Trust binds people to each other. To keep democracy and stability, we need to understand that we need a common goal in the form of overall satisfaction and happiness. Systems thinking does not mean centralized but hybrid control combining loose centralized control and distributed control as in subsidiarity. The main reason for our conclusion is the bounded rationality of any individual; we cannot solve complex problems otherwise. We must use the wisdom of the crowds among educated people. Our culture is based on shared ethical values, beliefs, and common visions, which can only come from the education of people since otherwise, we are doomed to stagnation where people are unequal and neither safe nor creative. The values are our axioms or assumptions, and the visions are our goals.

Vision Research needs visions, roadmaps, problems, and hypotheses based on system archetypes. Without a goal or vision, we act like driftwood, controlled by the environment. With a vision, we behave like adults and control the environment with respect. In engineering, part of the vision is scenarios and use cases, making defining system requirements easier. We prepare visions typically for the next ten years and update them regularly. The future is always uncertain and surprising, but we must make visions with knowledge of history. In addition to knowing history, imagination is needed to anticipate turning points. We must understand the megatrends and the weak signals and imagine alternative futures, thus forming a basis for a roadmap.

The requirements translate the user needs to a quantitative form. The requirements usually lead to an optimization problem corresponding to a demanding multiobjective optimization, but often, a satisfactory solution is enough and perhaps the only possibility. All information technologies, including control, computer, communications engineering, and electronics, will work together. There will be a more comprehensive list of system archetypes. A core component in complex systems is a multiagent system, also called a complex adaptive system. We must unify the terminology for systems thinking across all disciplines. Sometimes, we cannot find a complete correspondence; for example, morphogenesis in biology is more general and advanced than self-organization and a feedback loop.

Nonequilibrium thermodynamics may become a basis for future system theories because of its generality, dynamic nature, and usefulness in physical, chemical, biological, and economic systems. We have only achieved human-level intelligence by natural methods using organic carbon-based materials. Artificial intelligence will make specific human work more efficient but does not replace humans. So far, AI agents do not understand anything because they are mechanisms, not organisms. Consciousness is a requirement for actual intelligence. Only biological intelligence can understand the semantic meaning of information. Complexity engineering may become an important new research field after we know how emergence appears in simple cases, for example in relatively small organic molecules. We follow here Descartes' advice to proceed from simple to complex.

This book is not perfect; there are many repetitions, gaps in reasoning, and even conflicting claims. I comfort myself with the words of Kari Suomalainen (1920–1999), a Finnish caricaturist, who said: "A perfect drawing irritates people since they cannot criticize anything."

I challenge all the readers to protect our liberal democracy and solve our most significant problems regarding sustainability. Nature does not need us, but we need nature to survive. Population explosion, limited resources, environmental contamination, and climate change are our common enemies, and we should join our forces. We should respect different people to improve our creativity that is in individuals, not in any administration. We should strengthen our historical knowledge to be able to understand the state of the art, forecast the future, form common goals, and finally respect interdisciplinarity since although disciplinary work is efficient, interdisciplinary collaborative work is effective. We cannot all be generalists, but we should be able to communicate using common vocabulary and system theories and archetypes. Sustainability solutions can only be found in strong democratic countries working together, respecting each other, and consisting of enlightened citizens using interdisciplinary systems thinking.

> Be that as it may
> I've skied a trail for singers
> skied a trail, snapped a treetop
> lopped off boughs and shown the way:
> that is where the way goes now
> where a new track leads
> for more versatile singers
> more abundant bards
> among the youngsters rising
> among the people growing.[1]

[1] Vaan kuitenki kaikitenki, la'un hiihin laulajoille, la'un hiihin, latvan taitoin, oksat karsin, tien osoitin. Siitäpä nyt tie menevi, ura uusi urkenevi, laajemmille laulajoille, runsahammille runoille, nuorisossa nousevassa, kansassa kasuavassa. Kalevala (1849), a Finnish epic, compiled by Elias Lönnrot, English translation by Keith Bosley (1989).

Glossary[1]

Abduction (philosophy of science) inference to the best explanation, opposite to deduction, simulated with strong inference

Abstraction (philosophy of science) idealization, undermodeling where the nonessentials are stripped off

Accuracy (metrology) a property of a measurement result that describes qualitatively the total measurement error, including trueness and precision

Action research (social sciences) a research method where problems of a society are solved iteratively by influencing the society, evaluating the consequences, and determining new ways of influencing

Actor (social sciences) a human agent with a role in a society as a research object

Actors approach (social sciences) a form of systems approach that includes a society consisting of human agents as part of the research

Adaptive system (signal processing) an automatic system that improves its performance in a slowly varying environment by using a performance criterion and an algorithm to eliminate the effect of variable disturbances on the performance, often based on a feedback loop

Agent (computer engineering, complexity theory) intelligent agent, rational agent, an active element in a complex adaptive system consisting of a sense-decide-act feedback loop; also an open-loop control without any sensing is called an agent

Algorithm (computer engineering) a sequence of operations for solving a problem; we divide algorithms into batch and sequential algorithms, and we divide sequential algorithms into recursive and iterative algorithms

Analysis (philosophy of science) separation of a whole into its parts; (mathematics) proof using deduction or derivation of results using statistical methods

[1] The glossary includes definitions of concepts related to analytical and systems thinking and their areas of use. You can find more detailed and alternative definitions from *Merriam-Webster Dictionary* and the etymology from *Online Etymology Dictionary*. The references can be found from other parts of this book.

A. Mämmelä, *Unifying Systems*, https://doi.org/10.1007/978-3-031-85012-7

Analytical thinking (philosophy of science) thinking using an analytical or reductive approach, a research method where a system is studied from the bottom and from inside out, and a problem is divided into parts so that it is easier to solve

Apobetics (semiotics) a level of information where the purpose of symbols or signs is studied

Architecture (systems engineering) structure of a system in terms of components, connections, and constraints

Assumption (mathematics) a starting point of logical reasoning, for example an axiom

Automatic system (control engineering) a system working without human intervention but that may need human supervision and some external control signals during operation in the form of set-point value, reference signal, or reference trajectory

Autonomic system (biology) a system such as a nervous system acting involuntarily; (computer engineering) self-managing system, an autonomous or self-organizing system based on self-management that includes self-configuration, self-optimization, self-healing, and self-protection

Autonomous system (control engineering) a self-governing system, an automatic learning system that may need human supervision but achieves an externally given goal using sensing signals but without any other external control signals during operation

Axiology (philosophy) value theory, a part of philosophy that studies values, including ethics and aesthetics

Behavior (systems thinking) a set of successive states of a system; in technical systems, the behavior is described with algorithms

Behavioral level (systems thinking, computer engineering) a description level between functional and structural levels in the FBS model describing the internal behavior of or the used algorithms at the functional level using a theoretical model

Benchmark (systems engineering, computer engineering) a commonly agreed standard test to measure the performance of a system

Boundary (systems thinking) a dividing line between a system and its environment, defined by an observer

Boundary condition (philosophy of science) a condition in which the defined theories are assumed to be valid

Bounded rationality (systems thinking, system dynamics) our rationality is bounded and therefore we cannot find optimal solutions to complex problems, but we must use the principle of satisficing; mathematically intractable problems show that also computers have bounded rationality

Brainstorming (philosophy of science) a working method where a small group has a problem, and the group offers solutions without immediate criticism, thus simulating collective intelligence

Case study (social sciences) a research method in social sciences where general principles are formulated by analyzing particular cases, essentially an experimental-abductive method, complementary to action research

Causality (philosophy of science) causation, a relationship between a cause and its effect

Cause (philosophy of science) efficient cause, a reason for an effect, resulting in a relation between two events so that the cause always precedes or coincides the effect, and thus causality proceeds forward in time, opposite to the assumed final cause

Centralized system (control, computer, and communications engineering) a hierarchical control system consisting of a central agent, also called an arbitrator or leader, that controls lower-level agents that act as followers

Closed-loop control (control engineering) control based on a sense-decide-act feedback loop, usually having an externally given goal

Closed system (thermodynamics, system theory) a system that exchanges energy with the environment but no matter; in natural closed systems energy minimization principle is valid

Coherence (philosophy of science) unity of knowledge, consistency, or consilience, one of the theories of truth, ideally guaranteed using deduction; (mathematics) a statement is coherent with other statements if we can derive it from the other true statements by mathematical deduction, otherwise it is false

Complex adaptive system (complexity theory) a multiagent system

Concept (philosophy of science) an idea of an object that we describe with a definition and which we represent by a term in a semiotic triangle

Conceptual analysis (philosophy of science) a clarification of the meaning of the used concepts and terms and their relationships

Concurrent computing (computer engineering) parallel or distributed computing, complementary to sequential computing

Conjecture (mathematics) a hypothesis of a theorem that we must prove

Consciousness (social sciences) the state of being aware of something within oneself, including sensing, emotions, free will, and thoughts

Constraint (mathematics) a limitation of freedom in optimization

Constructive research (systems engineering) a research method where we implement the solution as a prototype, leading to a proof of concept, complementary to nomothetic research

Control system (control engineering) an automatic system acting upon controlled variables to eliminate the effect of disturbances; a control system can be either open-loop control or closed-loop feedback control and includes a controller

Controller (control engineering) a decision-making device in a feedback loop producing control signals from sensing signals using a goal or reference input to change the state or performance of the environment called a plant or process

Correlation (mathematics) interdependence between random variables shown by statistical means

Correspondence (philosophy of science) agreement with reality as one of the theories of truth, verified with a hypothetico-deductive method

Coverage interval (metrology) an interval used to describe the uncertainty of a measurement result; the interval includes the true value of a measurement quantity with a given coverage probability; (mathematics) confidence interval

Coverage probability (metrology) the probability with which the measurement result is in a coverage interval; (mathematics) level of confidence

Criterion (mathematics) performance criterion, objective, a metric proposed for optimization

Decentralized system (control, computer, and communications engineering) a control system consisting of autonomous agents without any hierarchy

Decision-making (decision theory) selection of one of the optima in multiobjective optimization, using, for example, fairness as an additional criterion

Deduction (mathematics, philosophy of science) a method of inference that preserves the truth, a form of analysis: if the premises are true, the conclusions must be true, a particular conclusion made from general truths, opposite of abduction

Definition (philosophy of science) explanation of the meaning of a term; we classify definitions into ostensive, dictionary, and stipulative definitions

Degree of centralization (control and communications engineering) a qualitative measure of how centralized a system is; degrees of centralization include centralized, decentralized, distributed, and hybrid, where centralized and decentralized are the two extremes and hybrid is a combination of centralized and distributed control

Development (systems engineering) systematic use of existing knowledge to produce useful materials, systems, and methods

Dimension (systems thinking) number of parts in a system

Dissipative structure (biology) a system that dissipates a flux of matter and energy, especially in the form of a whirlpool in nonequilibrium thermodynamics

Distributed computing (computer engineering) a form of concurrent computing that uses a distributed memory using message passing, local clocks, and loose coupling between computing units

Distributed system (control, computer, and communications engineering) an intermediate form of control between centralized and decentralized control consisting of almost autonomous agents that exchange sensing information at least with their nearest neighbors without any hierarchy

Dominance hierarchy (systems thinking) organizational hierarchy, multiechelon hierarchy, a nonnested control hierarchy where each level dominates or controls the lower levels

Dynamic system (physics) a moving or changing system; (control engineering) a system having memory, opposite to a static system

Effectiveness (systems thinking) doing the right things

Efficiency (systems thinking) doing things right, performance that we measure as the ratio of benefits and expenditures where the benefits are for example the number of transmitted bits or implemented operations and expenditures are basic resources such as energy, time, or bandwidth

Emergence (philosophy of science) an unexpected property or behavior that is produced when moving from a lower hierarchy level to an upper level and which cannot be explained by the properties or behavior of the lower level, a mathematically intractable phenomenon coming from the nonlinear feedbacks in a hierarchical system

Empiricism (philosophy of science) empirism, a view emphasizing the significance of experiments and observations in the discovery of knowledge, opposite to rationalism

Entropy (physics) disorder that is kept constant or increasing in an isolated system

Environment (systems thinking) the space outside the boundary of a system; in control engineering, the plant or the process to be controlled; regarding the environment, we usually have limited observability and controllability

Epistemology (philosophy) a part of philosophy that studies the origin, nature, methods, and limitations of human knowledge

Error (metrology) the difference between the measured value and a reference value

Error signal (control engineering, signal processing) reference signal minus estimated or sensed signal used in the feedback to adjust a control system or an adaptive filter

Estimation (signal processing) assessment of the parameters of a known model in the presence of noise, usually done in some optimal way, complementary to identification

Evolution (biology) changes in the descent of species resulting in natural selection where intergenerational survival depends on the fitness to the environment

Experimental-abductive method (philosophy of science) a research method where we make experiments and observations and we find generalizations abductively to provide a theory that explains the experimental results, often replaced by the more limited experimental-inductive method, complements the hypothetico-deductive method

Falsification (philosophy of science) refutation, demonstration that a theory is wrong, opposite to verification

Feedback (control engineering) cycle, loop, transmission of information about the performance of a system to an earlier stage to modify its operation, an operation that in negative feedback tends to reduce the difference between the output of the system environment and some reference input, usually formed as a sense-decide-act closed-loop control

Field study (social sciences, systems engineering) a study made in the actual environment, not only with simulations or in a laboratory, eventually leading to the validation of the results

Final cause (philosophy of science) an assumed teleological cause that proceeds backward in time from a purpose to an effect, rejected in modern philosophy of science, opposite to efficient cause

Formal science (philosophy of science) a science such as mathematics based on axiomatic deductive systems and not on experiments or observations, thus ignoring the correspondence with the reality and emphasizing coherence

Function (mathematics) input–output transformation of a system that may be nonlinear and time-variant

Functional level (systems and computer engineering) the uppermost description level above the behavioral level in the FBS model using a mathematical black box model where we describe a system by a function representing the needed transformation; at this level, we are interested in what the design does, but not in how it is built

Fundamental limit (physics) physical limit in nature

Generalization (philosophy of science) inductively of abductively derived general solutions for classes of problems

Generative order (philosophy of science) an overall, stepwise progressing order that produces a whole from its parts creatively and whose phases have complicated mutual relationships, complementary to sequential order

Goal (control engineering) a reference input, a reference trajectory, or a utility, a desired state of or a target for performance, given by evolution or design as a set-point value, if in a technical system there is no goal or no leader, the feedback system is in an aimless drift; (systems thinking) a hypothesis, a tentative solution to a problem, an complementary to an objective

Groupthink (philosophy of science) a noncritical way of thinking in a group

Heuristics (psychology) a form of intuition, often based on unexpected discoveries, using, for example, trial and error, feedback, rules of thumb, guesses, and stereotypes

Hierarchy (systems thinking) a system whose subsystems are organized into different levels of importance; a hierarchy may be nested or nonnested, and nonnested hierarchies include dominance and layer hierarchies

Holarchy (biology) a hierarchical, usually nested architecture based on holons

Holism (social sciences) systems view in social sciences

Holon (biology) a subsystem or module in a holarchy

Homeostasis (biology) a self-regulating process by which biological systems tend to maintain stability while adjusting to conditions that are optimal for survival, a tendency toward an equilibrium in an organism or group based on feedback

Hybrid system (communications) a system that is a combination of hierarchical centralized control and distributed control, (control engineering) a combination is analog and digital control

Hypothesis (philosophy of science) an tentative solution to a problem in the form of theory or model, in empirical sciences usually a causal relationship; a weaker hypothesis is correlation, which does not necessarily imply causality

Hypothetico-deductive method (philosophy of science) hypothesis testing, a research method where a hypothesis is verified indirectly by deriving deductively numerical results from it and by comparing them with the measurement results, complements the experimental-abductive method

Idiographic research (philosophy of science) research concerning particular cases, especially in history, opposite to nomothetic research

Impact factor (bibliometrics) journal impact factor, the average number of citations per year to papers published in a journal during the last two or five years, not to be confused with the average number of citations per paper

Incommensurability (systems thinking) a property of resources which do not have a common price since we do not have a common currency, but the price must usually be found using the law of supply and demand

Incompleteness theorem (mathematics) a theorem according to which a finite axiomatic system cannot be made complete, i.e., not all true conjectures can be proved with a finite set of axioms, a finite formal system cannot be simultaneously complete and consistent (i.e., coherent)

Induction (philosophy of science) generalization, inference of a general truth from particular cases, inference to some explanation, weaker than abduction, a form of synthesis

Inductive-statistical model (philosophy of science) a model of explanation for statistical generalizations instead of deterministic laws, complementary to the deductive-nomological model of explanation

Information (philosophy of science) an ordered pattern that we can communicate; information is communicated when another system responds selectively, and the meaning of the information depends on the wider context where it is interpreted; information can be transfered using matter (materials) or energy; in semiotics, we classify information into statistical, syntactic, semantic, pragmatic, and apobetic information; information is also in the data, information, knowledge, and wisdom hierarchy

Initial condition (philosophy of science) a state where a system is at the beginning of the observation period

Intelligence (psychology, computer engineering) an algorithmic ability based on logical reasoning, part of rationality

Interface (systems thinking) the dividing line between two levels in a hierarchy

Intractability (mathematics) a property of a complex problem that does not allow mathematical analysis because of emergence

Intuition (psychology) a product of the unconscious mind and a source of creativity resulting from instincts and experience, complementary to rational reasoning, which is much slower; intuition is useful when there is either too little or too much information or the problem is nonlinear or multidimensional, the results of intuition must be verified because of possible distortions of intuition

Isolated system (thermodynamics, system theory) a system that exchanges neither materials nor energy with the environment; in an isolated system the entropy law is valid

Iterative algorithm (signal processing) an algorithm based on repetitive steps to find a solution, often having overshoots or undershoots and may not converge if stability conditions and not met, complementary to a recursive algorithm

Knowledge (philosophy of science) opposite of ignorance, a justified true belief, structured and established information verified scientifically

Layer a level in a layer hierarchy

Layer hierarchy (control and communications engineering) multilayer hierarchy, a special case of dominance hierarchy where the number of subsystems is one at each level; in communication networks, dominance hierarchy is often called a layer hierarchy

Learning system (psychology, communications engineering) a cognitive system, an adaptive system that can change its behavior based on past experience that is stored in a memory so that the performance is improved during learning; learning may be unsupervised, supervised, reinforcement, or evolutionary learning

Legitimacy (systems thinking) a property to fulfill a purpose at the service of a larger whole

Level (control engineering, systems thinking) a vertical position is a hierarchy that may be either a stratum, echelon, or layer

Linear system (system theory) a system that has the properties of homogeneity and additivity, thus following the superposition theorem, an opposite is a nonlinear system

Loose coupling (systems thinking) weak coupling, near decomposability, loose interactions in a hierarchical and modular system between hierarchy levels (vertical loose coupling) and modules at the same hierarchy level (horizontal loose coupling); (social sciences) subsidiarity

Machine (engineering) a system consisting of mechanisms whose internal state and the state of its environment called input define uniquely the next state

Mechanism (physics) a system whose operation is determined by the laws of physics and chemistry, an opposite is organism

Method (philosophy of science) scientific method, a concrete principle by which new knowledge is produced in practice

Metric (mathematics) criterion or objective used in optimization

Model (philosophy of science) system model, a simplified description of regularities in a system; models are divided into scale models, analog models, mathematical models, and theoretical models

Module (engineering) a subsystem that is only loosely coupled with other modules at the same hierarchy level and with other hierarchy levels; (biology) a holon

Monitoring system (control and communications engineering) a sensing system that collects performance data about the environment, such as computer or network without controlling the environment, and if control is needed, it is done manually

Morphogenesis (biology) emergence of form, pattern formation, self-organization in biology

Multiagent system (computer engineering) a set of interacting agents

Multicausality (systems thinking) a phenomenon with multiple causes

Nash bargaining solution (game theory) a fair, unique, and Pareto optimal distributed solution in a cooperative game obtained by negotiations between all players

Nash equilibrium (game theory) a situation in a noncooperative game where players cannot gain anything by unilaterally changing their strategy, in general not fair, unique, nor Pareto optimal

Near decomposability (biology) vertical and horizontal loose coupling

Negative feedback (control engineering, system dynamics) balancing, correcting, or goal-directed feedback, feedback that corrects any deviations from a goal, a goal-directed system that generates actions to minimize the difference between the desired state and the actual state or to maximize its performance and moving towards a steady state in a time-invariant environment if it is stable

Nested hierarchy (biology, control engineering) stratified hierarchy, a hierarchy where the lower-level systems are inside the higher-level system, the opposite to nonnested hierarchy

Neural network (computer engineering) artificial neural network, a computer architecture that resembles neurons and their interconnections in a human brain

Nomothetic research (philosophy of science) a nomological research method providing theories from experiments and observations to the deductive-nomological model of explanation, opposite to idiographic research and complementary to constructive research

Nonequilibrium thermodynamics (biology) a theory according to which organisms can resist the entropy law by accessing external resources of matter and energy, and they operate as dissipative structures far from equilibrium

Norm (philosophy) a rule of behavior to protect a value

NP-complete problem (computing) an NP problem that we cannot solve in polynomial time as far as is known

NP-hard problem (computing) a problem that we cannot always verify in polynomial time

NP problem (computing) a nondeterministic polynomial problem that we can verify in polynomial time; the problem is easy to verify but cannot always be solved in polynomial time

Objective (mathematics) metric or criterion; (systems engineering) refined problem statement, complementary to a goal

Ockham's razor (philosophy of science) Occam's razor, principle of parsimony, according to which we select the simpler from two competing theories explaining the observations; not necessarily valid in biological systems

Ontology (philosophy) a part of metaphysics that studies the basic essence of things; (computer engineering) a study of categories of things

Open-loop control (control engineering) a rough control method that works without any sensing information and where the control is based on earlier experience, for example, using a predetermined time

Open system (thermodynamics, system theory) a system that exchanges materials and energy with the environment; open systems are dissipative systems if there is a continuous flux of materials and energy and nonequilibrium thermodynamics is valid

Optimization (mathematics) a process of making something as efficient as possible

Order (mathematics) the highest order of the derivative of the unknown variable in a differential equation representing a linear system; (control engineering) the degree of the denominator polynomial of a transfer function; the number of independent energy storage elements like capacitors or inductors in a system

Organism (biology) a living being for which no mechanistic explanation is known

Ostensive definition (philosophy of science) a pseudodefinition that only describes the object or presents examples of it

Paradigm (philosophy of science) a world view, a general model of thinking among scientists, a scientific dogma that is not questioned, although it can sometimes be erroneous

Paradox (philosophy of science) a statement that looks contradictory or opposed to common sense and yet may be true, often in the forms of dilemmas and conflicts between opposites, for example the social conflict, resulting in the need for ambidexterity

Parameter (mathematics, signal processing) a quantity that is usually assumed to be a constant during observation but may obtain different values in different observations as a and b in the function $f(x) = ax + b$ where x is a variable; (software design) a constant passed from a main program to a subprogram; (systems thinking) a quantity that describes an interaction between two parts of a system, complementary to a variable

Parameter estimation (signal processing) determination of the parameter values of a system, assuming the structure is known, complementary to system identification

Parallel computing (computer engineering) a form of local concurrent computing using a shared memory, a global clock, and tight coupling between computing units

Pareto optimum (mathematics) a solution to a cooperative game is Pareto optimal if no improvement in any criterion can be made without worsening some other criterion

Pattern formation (biology) formation of a higher organism out of a single cell; (computer engineering) the formation of patterns or structures that can survive in a given environment, opposite of pattern recognition

Pattern recognition (computer engineering) the ability of a computer to recognize patterns or structures in data containing some information

Performance efficiency with which something fulfills its intended purpose

Philosophy of science (philosophy of science) theory of science, a part of epistemology that studies general principles of science such as research methods

Physical level (systems thinking, computer engineering) a description level below the structural level of the FBS model describing the physical implementation of a system; the physical level neglects what the design is supposed to do and binds its structure in space

Planning (systems thinking) imagining the future and selecting the best course of action to achieve a goal

Plant (control engineering) a system or process to be controlled

Positive feedback (system dynamics, biology) reinforcing feedback, a feedback system that enhances or amplifies the direction of any change, thus potentially causing instability in the form of exponential growth

Pragmatics (semiotics) a level of information where the intention of signs or symbols leading to practical action is studied

Pragmatism (philosophy of science) a view according to which the value of scientific knowledge is measured by its practical consequences, thus representing one of the theories of truth

Precision (metrology) a property of a measurement result that describes qualitatively the random part of the measurement error

Primitive term (philosophy of science) a term that is not defined or defined only using an ostensive definition

Problem (philosophy of science) a question, the starting point of any research

Process (control engineering) a series of actions or operations leading to an end; a system to be controlled

Proof (mathematics) derivation of a theorem deductively from axioms, not to be confused with verification

Proof of concept (systems engineering) proof of principle, realization of an idea to demonstrate or verify its feasibility in practice, not a mathematical proof

Property (systems thinking) numerical value describing a system and defining the state of the system, the properties may be the values of system variables and parameters

Prototype (systems engineering) the first design of a system from which other designs are developed

Purpose (systems thinking, philosophy) a goal of a system defined by a human

Range (metrology, control engineering) scope, span, interval, the limits between which amplitude, time, frequency, or space vary using some resolution

Rational reasoning (psychology) reasoning in the conscious mind, based for example, on computations, deductive logic, and causation, including intelligence and reflections; opposite to intuitive reasoning

Rationalism a view emphasizing the significance of rational reasoning and deduction in the discovery of knowledge, opposite to empirism

Rationality (psychology) the ability to reach goals efficiently with the available resources in an uncertain environment, complementary to intuition; a rational person is assumed to be coherent, responsive, and self-critical

Realism (philosophy of science) classical realism, a view according to which scientific models and theories represent the world as it is, independently of the observer

Recursive algorithm (signal processing) a sequential algorithm complementary to an iterative algorithm, a recursive algorithm finds an exact solution, which is obtained in stages and leads to the same solution as the corresponding batch algorithm; it may be time-recursive or order-recursive

Recursive function (computer engineering) a function to call itself in a nested fashion

Reduction (philosophy of science) process of reducing, orientation, definition of scope; we classify reduction into (1) methodological reduction, that refers to the analytical thinking where we use ontological and epistemological reduction to study the behavior of complex wholes by analyzing their parts and properties, respectively, (2) epistemological reduction which expresses a relation between theories so that the most general theory is at the top and the most primitive theory is at the bottom just above observations, and (3) ontological reduction where we claim that the reality consists of simple parts organized hierarchically; the concept of reducibility is also called separability, and the idea is used in optimization decomposition

Reference signal (control engineering, signal processing) reference input, a signal used to form the error signal between the reference signal and the measured or sensed signal; the reference signal can also be a constant set-point value or a reference trajectory, which are examples of goals

Reference value (metrology) the true value or the agreed conventional value of a quantity with a small error, used to measure the error between the measured value and the reference value

Reflection (psychology) a part of rationality, careful thought about something

Regeneration a process where the system is formed or created again

Relationship (systems thinking) interaction between different parts of a system; in technical systems, the relationships are always causal; relationships may be logical, temporal, or spatial; an important relationship is coupling through materials, energy, and information, for example, using the gravitation force between masses; a mathematical function is a deterministic relationship or transformation

Repeatability (metrology) a property of a measurement result that can be repeated precisely enough in the same laboratory

Reproducibility (metrology) repeatability of a measurement result in independent laboratories

Requirement (systems engineering) functional and nonfunctional specification of user needs

Research (philosophy of science) systematic discovery of new knowledge and concepts in science and engineering, complementary to development

Resilience (systems thinking) a property how a system recovers its operational condition quickly after a failure

Resolution (metrology, control engineering) the smallest resolved change within a certain range in a quantity being measured; the corresponding interval is called a resolution cell or resolution bin or pixel (in imaging), the resolution is high if the resolution cell is narrow or small, otherwise it is low

Resource (systems thinking) a source of wealth used as an input in systems; the basic resources include materials, energy, information, time, frequency, and space

Roadmap (systems thinking) a plan, the steps needed to approach the vision

Satisficing (systems thinking) a principle where, we accept a satisfactory result with our bounded rationality since there is no choice in complex problems; the result is not necessarily optimal

Science (philosophy of science) systematic knowledge obtained through observation and experimentation

Scope (philosophy of science) problem framing, orientation, reduction

Self-organizing system (physical sciences, biology, engineering) an autonomous system that changes its structure as a function of its experience and environment; (social sciences) a system producing order spontaneously

Self-reproductive system (biology) self-replicating system, a self-organizing system able to replicate itself and eventually evolve

Self-stabilization (computer engineering, systems thinking) a property of systems related to ultrastability allowing systems to recover from any arbitrary state, including states that may result from faults or errors meaning that regardless of the initial conditions or any transient faults, a self-stabilizing system will eventually converge to a legitimate state and remain in that state, allowing systems to maintain functionality

Semantics (semiotics) a level of information where the meaning, i.e., the relationship with reality, of symbols or signs is studied

Semiotics (semiotics) study of signs and symbols in languages, originally consisting of syntactics, semantics, and pragmatics as the three levels of information

Semiotic triangle (semiotics) a triangle whose corners correspond to an object, concept, and term that are different but closely related to each other

Sensitivity (communications) ability to detect weak signals in noise; (metrology) the ratio of the change in an indication of a measuring system and the corresponding change in a measured value

Sequential order (philosophy of science) a temporal order, complementary to generative order

Sequential computing (computer engineering) computing where the steps are sequential or in serial form and computers execute one instruction at a time, complementary to parallel or distributed computing

Signal (signal processing, communications engineering) a function of time, frequency, or space that conveys information

Simulation (signal processing) imitation of a real system with a computer by using a mathematical or theoretical model

Social dilemma (social sciences) a tension between individual and collective rationality, such as in the tragedy of the commons

Social system (social sciences) a group of human actors and their relationships

Specification (systems engineering) definition of requirements or a model of a system

Spiral model (systems thinking) a design method based on repetitions of the V-model

Stability (control engineering) a property of a feedback system that has a bounded output to a bounded input called BIBO stability; stable behavior usually implies that the system moves toward an equilibrium after being disturbed or remains within specified limits; unstable behavior leads to exponential growth, collapse, or oscillation; also many other stability criteria exist especially for nonlinear systems

State (control engineering, signal processing, systems thinking) numerical values of all properties of a system at a given time using variables and parameters; the final value of the state is called the steady state after the transient of the response has faded

Static system (physics) a system that shows little change, a nonmoving system, (control engineering) a system without memory, opposite to a dynamic system

Statistics (semiotics) a level of information where the statistical relationships of symbols or signs are studied

Strong inference (philosophy of science) method of multiple working hypotheses, inference using several competing hypotheses and choosing the best one, thus simulating abduction

Structural level (systems thinking, computer engineering) a description level between the behavioral and physical levels in the FBS model describing the relationship of the parts in a system; it is a mapping of the behavioral level onto a set of components and connections under constraints such as cost, area, and time

Structure (systems thinking) organization, topology, a set of parts coupled to form a whole, a set of parts and their relationships connecting the parts and the environment in a system

Subsidiarity (social sciences) a form of vertical loose coupling in a society

Sustainability a condition where we fulfill the needs of the present generation without compromising the ability of future generations to meet their own needs

Symbol (communications) information entity that corresponds to one or more bits in digital communications, usually transmitted serially and modulated on a carrier or transmitted through a cable using a line code in the baseband at low frequencies

Syntactics (semiotics) a level of information where the structural relationships of signs or symbols are studied

Synthesis combination of parts so as to form a whole, opposite to analysis

System (systems thinking) a whole consisting of a set of parts with certain relationships between the parts and the environment; a technical system has a purpose, structure, boundary, environment, input, output, properties such as stability, state, and behavior, a system may be linear or nonlinear; static or dynamic; time-invariant or time-varying; continuous-time or discrete-time; continuous state, discrete state, or finite state; deterministic (nonrandom) or random; differential or nondifferential; simple, complicated, or complex; and isolated, closed, or open

System archetype (system dynamics) a generic structure that produces desirable behavior and has survived the test of time, and used in systems thinking to support synthesis, which is a creative process

System identification (signal processing) determination of the structure or topology of a system, complementary to parameter estimation

System model a model used to define the function, behavior, or structure of a system

Systems thinking (philosophy of science) holistic approach, a research method where a system is studied from top down or from outside in

Technology application of knowledge to practical ends by using the results of mathematics, natural sciences, and engineering; all methods with which a society produces its products and services

Term a word that corresponds to a particular concept and object in the semiotic triangle

Theorem a proved conjecture in an axiomatic system

Theory (philosophy of science) an explanation based on observation and reasoning, a generalization made from observations and experiments, a compressed description of reality

Theory of truth (philosophy of science) a theory on a relation between a belief and reality; major theories of truth include coherence, correspondence, and pragmatism; the truth is philosophically a controversial concept and in practice, because of the problem of induction, we can only verify or falsify statements using the hypothetico-deductive method

Trueness (metrology) a property of a measurement result that describes qualitatively the systematic error between the average of measurements and a reference value, complementary to precision

Ultrastability (systems thinking) a form of self-stabilization in self-organizing systems based on double feedback where the inner loop operates fast and makes minor corrections and the outer loop operates slowly and changes system parameters and structure when there are significant changes in the environment

Uncertainty (metrology) a parameter characterizing the dispersion of a measurement result, described by a coverage range and further quantified by a coverage probability

Utility function (optimization theory) a possibly nonlinear function used for weighted aggregation of different metrics to express the total utility

Validation (systems engineering) verification done in the field to confirm that the specified requirements are suitable for the intended purpose and correspond to user needs

Variable (mathematics) a quantity that is assumed to change as x in the function $f(x) = ax + b$ where a and b are constant parameters, (systems thinking) a quantity that describes the state of a certain part in a system, complementary to a parameter

Verification (philosophy of science, systems engineering) confirmation of a theory by using the hypothetico-deductive method, opposite to falsification or refutation; (engineering) confirmation that an object fulfills the specified requirements

Vision (systems thinking) an imagined state of the world in the future, needed in planning to make decisions and to define research problems

Wisdom (psychology) the highest form of rationality, a property where a person has broad view and good social abilities to be able to understand the points of view of other people

Bibliography[2]

History of Different Sciences: Mathematics

Boyer CB, Merzbach UC (1991) A history of mathematics, 2nd rev. Wiley, New York
Gorroochurn P (2016) Classic topics on the history of modern mathematical statistics: from Laplace to more recent times. Wiley, Hoboken, NJ
Stigler SM (1986) The history of statistics: the measurement of uncertainty before 1900. Harvard University Press, Cambridge, MA

History of Different Sciences: Physics

Holton GJ, Brush SG (2001) Physics, the human adventure: from Copernicus to Einstein and beyond, 3rd edn. Rutgers University Press, Piscataway, NJ
Kragh H (1999) Quantum generations: a history of physics in the twentieth century. Princeton University Press, Princeton, NJ
Pyenson L, Sheets-Pyenson S (1999) Servants of nature: history of scientific institutions, enterprises, and sensibilities. W. W. Norton & Company, New York
Simonyi K (2012) A cultural history of physics. CRC Press, Boca Raton, FL

History of Different Sciences: Chemistry

Brock WH (2000) The chemical tree: a history of chemistry, reprint edn. W. W. Norton & Company

[2] This bibliography includes some of the best books on analytical and systems thinking; it is divided according to the subjects. It covers the core disciplines described in the book. I collected the books with the idea that the philosophy and history of each discipline give the best overview of the theoretical content and development of the disciplines. You can find more information in recent books and review papers. Sometimes, there are many similar excellent books, and I made the selection based on popularity, the year of publication, readability, reliability, broad scope, and an exceptional approach to the topic. Best books cover the history from ancient times. The choices cannot be exhaustive or completely objective.

A. Mämmelä, *Unifying Systems*, https://doi.org/10.1007/978-3-031-85012-7

Brock WH (2016) A history of chemistry: a very short introduction. Oxford University Press, Oxford, UK

History of Different Sciences: Biology

Bowler PJ (2009) Evolution: the history of an idea, 25th anniversary. University of California Press, Berkeley, CA
Mayr FE (1982) The growth of biological thought: diversity, evolution, and inheritance. The Belknap Press of Harvard University Press, Cambridge, MA
Morris D (1967) The naked ape: a zoologist's study of the human animal. Random House, New York
Sapp J (2003) Genesis: the evolution of biology. Oxford University Press, New York
Wickens P (2015) A history of the brain: from stone age surgery to modern neuroscience. Psychology Press, London

History of Different Sciences: Psychology

Henley T (2023) Hergenhahn's: an introduction to the history of psychology, 9th edn. Cengage, Boston, MA
Leahey TH (2018) A history of psychology: from antiquity to modernity, 8th edn. Routledge, New York, p 2018
Schulz DP, Schultz SE (2017) Theories of personality, 11th edn. Cengage Learning, Boston, MA

History of Different Sciences: Sociology

Gordon HS (1991) The history and philosophy of social science. Routledge, London
Levine DN (1995) Visions of the sociological tradition. University of Chicago Press, Chicago, IL
Seidman S (2017) Contested knowledge: social theory today, 6th edn. Wiley, Hoboken, NJ

History of Different Sciences: Economics

Backhouse R (2023) The ordinary business of life: a history of economics from the ancient world to the twenty-first century, 2nd edn. Princeton University Press, Princeton, NJ

History of Different Sciences: Political Science

Arrighi G (2010) The long twentieth century: money, power and the origins of our times, new. Verso, New York
Ryan A (2012) On politics: a history of political thought from herodotus to the present. W. W. Norton, New York

Stasavage D (2020) The decline and rise of democracy: a global history from antiquity to today. Princeton University Press, Princeton, NJ
Tilly C (1992) Coercion, capital, and European states, AD 990–1990, rev. Wiley-Blackwell, Oxford, UK

History of Different Sciences: History

Christian D (2004) Maps of time: an introduction to big history. University of California Press, Berkeley, CA
Diamond J (1997) Guns, germs, and steel: the fates of human societies. W. W. Norton, New York
Harari YN (2014) Sapiens: a brief history of humankind. Random House, New York
Kennedy P (1988) The rise and fall of the great powers: economic change and military conflict from 1500 to 2000. Unwin Hyman, London
McNeill WH (1991) The rise of the west: history of the human community with a retrospective essay, rev. University of Chicago Press, Chicago, IL
McNeill JR, McNeill WH (2003) The human web: a bird's-eye view of world history. W. W. Norton & Company, New York

History of Different Sciences: Philosophy

Grayling AC (2019) The history of philosophy. Penguin Books, London
Kenny A (2019) An illustrated brief history of western philosophy, 20th anniversary. Wiley, Hoboken, NJ
Russell B (1945) A history of western philosophy and its connection with political and social circumstances from the earliest times to the present day. Simon & Schuster, New York

Philosophy and Systems View of Different Sciences: Mathematics

Lakoff G, Nunez RE (2001) Where mathematics comes from: how the embodied mind brings mathematics into being. Basic Books, New York
Shapiro S (2000) Thinking about mathematics: the philosophy of mathematics. Oxford University Press, New York

Philosophy and Systems View of Different Sciences: Physics

Lange M (2002) An introduction to the philosophy of physics: locality, fields, energy, and mass. Blackwell Publishing, Malden, MA
Mihailovic DT et al (2024) Physics of complex systems: discovery in the age of Gödel. CRC Press, Boca Raton, FL
Penrose R (1999) The emperor's new mind: concerning computers, minds and the laws of physics, new. Oxford University Press, Oxford, UK

Rosenberg A, McIntyre L (2020) The philosophy of science: a contemporary introduction, 4th edn. Routledge, New York

Philosophy and Systems View of Different Sciences: Chemistry

van Brakel J (2000) Philosophy of chemistry: between the manifest and the scientific image. Leuven University Press, Leuven, Belgium

Philosophy and Systems View of Different Sciences: Biology

Camazine S et al. Self-organization in biological systems. Princeton University Press, Princeton, NJ
Capra F, Luisi PL (2014) The systems view of life: a unifying vision. Cambridge University Press, Cambridge, UK
Haier RJ (2023) The neuroscience of intelligence, 2nd edn. Cambridge University Press, New York
Kasting JF et al (2020) The Earth system, 4th edn. Kendall Hunt Publishing, Dubuque, IA
Kauffman S (1995) At home in the universe: the search for laws of self-organization and complexity. Oxford University Press, Oxford, UK
Rosenbaum DA (2010) Human motor control, 2nd edn. Elsevier, London
Rosenberg A, McShea DW (2008) Philosophy of biology: a contemporary introduction. Routledge, New York

Philosophy and Systems View of Different Sciences: Psychology

Botterill G, Carruthers P (1999) The philosophy of psychology. Cambridge University Press, Cambridge, UK
Brennan JF, Houde KA (2023) History and systems of psychology, 8th edn. Cambridge University Press, Cambridge, UK

Philosophy and Systems View of Different Sciences: Sociology

Risjord M (2023) Philosophy of social science: a contemporary introduction, 2nd edn. Routledge, New York
Rosenberg A (2018) Philosophy of social science, 5th edn. Routledge, New York

Philosophy and Systems View of Different Sciences: Economics

Arbnor I, Bjerke B (2009) Methodology for creating business knowledge, 3rd edn. Sage, London

Ayres R (2016) Energy, complexity and wealth maximization. Springer International Publishing, Switzerland
Reiss J (2013) Philosophy of economics: a contemporary introduction. Routledge, New York

Philosophy and Systems View of Different Sciences: Political Science

Dowding K (2016) The philosophy and methods of political science. Palgrave, London

Philosophy and Systems View of Different Sciences: History

Kragh HS (1987) An introduction to the historiography of science. Cambridge University Press, Cambridge, UK
Little D (2010) New contributions to the philosophy of history. Springer, Dordrecht, The Netherlands

Philosophy and Systems View of Different Sciences: Philosophy

Honderich T (ed) Oxford companion to philosophy, 2nd edn. Oxford University Press, Oxford, UK
Laszlo E (1972) Introduction to systems philosophy: toward a new paradigm of contemporary thought. Gordon & Breach, New York
Losee J (2001) A historical introduction to the philosophy of science, 4th edn. Oxford University Press, Oxford, UK
Williamson T (2022) The philosophy of philosophy, 2nd edn. Wiley, Hoboken, NJ

History and Theories of Information Technology: General

Asimov I (1994) Asimov's chronology of science & discovery, Updated and illustrated. Harper & Row, New York
Carlisle R (2004) Scientific American inventions and discoveries: all the milestones in ingenuity—from the discovery of fire to the invention of the microwave oven. Wiley, Hoboken, NJ
Klein HA (1988) The science of measurement: a historical survey, corrected. Dover Publications, New York
McClellan JE III, Dorn H (2015) Science and technology in world history: an introduction, 3rd edn. John Hopkins University Press, Baltimore, MD
Pacey A, Bray F (2021) Technology in world civilization: a thousand-year history, rev. MIT Press, Cambridge, MA
Treese SA (2018) History and measurement of the base and derived units. Springer International Publishing, Cham, Switzerland

History and Theories of Information Technology: Engineering Research

Bock P (2020) Getting it right: R&D methods for science and engineering, 2nd edn. Academic Press, San Diego, CA
Morawski RZ (2024) Technoscientific research: methodological and ethical aspects, 2nd edn. Walter de Gruyter, Berlin
Thiel DV (2014) Research methods for engineers. Cambridge University Press, Cambridge, UK

History and Theories of Information Technology: Electronics

Berger LI (1997) Semiconductor materials. CRC Press, Boca Raton, FL
Braun E, MacDonald S (1982) Revolution in miniature: the history and impact of semiconductor electronics, 2nd edn. Cambridge University Press, Cambridge, UK
Lee TH (2004) The design of CMOS radio-frequency integrated circuits, 2nd edn. Cambridge University Press, Cambridge, UK
Lojek B (2007) History of semiconductor engineering. Springer, Berlin
Maloberti F, Davies AC (eds) (2024) A short history of circuits and systems, 2nd edn. River Publishers, Gistrup, Denmark
Sedra A et al (2020) Microelectronic circuits, 8th edn. Oxford University Press, New York
Storey N (2017) Electronics: a systems approach, 6th edn. Pearson Education, Harlow, UK

History and Theories of Information Technology: Control Engineering

Albus JS, Meystel AM (2001) Engineering of mind: an introduction to the science of intelligent systems. Wiley, New York
Bennett S (1979a) A history of control engineering, 1800–1930. Peter Peregrinus, Stevenage, UK
Bennett S (1979b) A history of control engineering, 1930–1955. Peter Peregrinus, Stevenage, UK
Dorf RC, Bishop RH (2021) Modern control systems, 14th edn. Pearson, New York
Mayr O (1970) The origins of feedback control. MIT Press, Cambridge, MA
Ogata K (2010) Modern control engineering, 5th edn. Prentice Hall, Boston, MA

History and Theories of Information Technology: Computer Engineering

Coulouris G et al (2012) Distributed systems: concepts and design, 5th edn. Addison-Wesley, Boston, MA
Haig T, Ceruzzi PE (2021) A new history of modern computing. MIT Press, Cambridge, MA
Hennessy JL, Patterson DA (2017) Computer architecture: a quantitative approach, 6th edn. Morgan Kauffman, Waltham, MA
Nilsson NJ (2010) The quest for artificial intelligence. Cambridge University Press, New York, NY

History and Theories of Information Technology: Communications

Haykin S, Moher M (2009) Communication systems, 5th edn. Wiley, Hoboken, NJ
Huurdeman A (2003) The worldwide history of telecommunications. Wiley, Hoboken, NJ
Peterson LL, Davie BS (2022) Computer networks: a systems approach, 6th edn. Morgan Kaufmann, Cambridge, MA
Proakis JG, Salehi M (2008) Digital communications, 5th edn. McGraw-Hill, New York
Sklar B, Harris F (2021) Digital communications: fundamentals and applications, 3rd edn. Pearson Education, London
Tanenbaum AS et al (2021) Computer networks, 6th edn. Pearson, Harlow, UK
Ziemer RE, Tranter WH (2014) Principles of communications: systems, modulation, and noise, 7th edn. Wiley, Hoboken, NJ

History and Theories of Information Technology: Interdisciplinary, Transdisciplinary, and Systems Thinking

Boulding KE (1985) The world as a total system. Sage, Beverly Hills, CA
Checkland P (1999) Systems thinking, systems practice, rev. Wiley, Chichester, UK
Epstein D (2019) Range: why generalists triumph in a specialized world. Macmillan, London
Hall AD (1962) A methodology for systems engineering. D. Van Nostrand Company, Princeton, NJ
Hubka V, Eder WE (1988) Theory of technical systems: a total concept theory for engineering design. Springer-Verlag, Berlin
Jackson MC (2019) Critical systems thinking and the management of complexity. Wiley, Hoboken, NJ
Klein JT (1990) Interdisciplinarity: history, theory, and practice. Wayne State University Press, Detroit, MI
Kline SJ (1995) Conceptual foundations of multidisciplinary thinking. Stanford University Press, Stanford, CA
Kossiakoff A et al (2020) Systems engineering: principles and practice, 3rd edn. Wiley, Hoboken, NJ
Maier MW, Rechtin E (2009) The art of systems architecting, 3rd edn. CRC Press, Boca Raton, FL
Meadows DH, Wright D (eds) Thinking in systems: a primer. Chelsea Green Publishing, White River Junction, VT
Ramage M, Shipp H (2020) Systems thinkers, 2nd edn. Springer, London
Repko F, Szostak R (2020) Interdisciplinary research: process and theory, 4th edn. Sage, Thousand Oaks, CA
Richardson GP (1991) Feedback thought in social science and system theory. University of Pennsylvania Press, Philadelphia, PA
Senge P (2006) The fifth discipline: the art and practice of the learning organization, rev. Doubleday, New York
Skyttner L (2005) General systems theory: problems, perspectives, practice, 2nd edn. World Scientific Publishing, Singapore
Sterman JD (2000) Business dynamics: systems thinking and modeling for a complex world. McGraw-Hill, Boston, MA
Stonier T (1992) Beyond information: the natural history of intelligence. Springer, Berlin
Stonier T (1997) Information and meaning: an evolutionary perspective. Springer, Berlin
von Bertalanffy L (1971) General system theory: foundations, development, applications, rev. George Braziller, New York

Wilson EO (1998) Consilience: the unity of knowledge. Vintage Books, New York

History and Theories of Information Technology: Complexity Theory, Self-organizing Systems, and Emergence

Boulton JG et al (2015) Embracing complexity: strategic perspectives for an age of turbulence. Oxford University Press, Oxford, UK
Holland JH (1995) Hidden order: how adaptation builds complexity. Basic Books, New York
Holland JH (1998) Emergence: from chaos to order. Basic Books, New York
Humphreys P (2016) Emergence: a philosophical account. Oxford University Press, New York
Kjelstrup S et al (2017) Non-equilibrium thermodynamics for engineers, 2nd edn. World Scientific Publishing, Singapore
Lebon G et al (2008) Understanding non-equilibrium thermodynamics: foundations, applications, frontiers. Springer-Verlag, Berlin
Miller JH, Page S (2007) Complex adaptive systems: an introduction to computational models of social life. Princeton University Press, Princeton, NJ
Mobus GE (2022) Systems science: theory, analysis, modeling, and design. Springer Nature, Cham, Switzerland
Morowitz HJ (2002) The emergence of everything: how the world became complex. Oxford University Press, New York
Page SE (2011) Diversity and complexity. Princeton University Press, Princeton, NJ
Prigogine I (1996) The end of certainty: time, chaos, and new laws of nature. Free Press, New York
Strogatz S (2003) Sync: the emerging science of spontaneous order. Hyperion, New York
Strogatz SH (2014) Nonlinear dynamics and chaos: with applications to physics, biology, chemistry, and engineering, 2nd edn. CRC Press, Boca Raton, FL
Thurner et al (2018) Introduction to the theory of complex systems. Oxford University Press, Oxford, UK

History and Theories of Information Technology: Hierarchy

Ahl V, Allen TFH (1996) Hierarchy theory: a vision, vocabulary, and epistemology. Columbia University Press, New York
Mesarovic M et al (1970) Theory of hierarchical, multilevel systems. Academic Press, New York
Pumain D (ed) (2006) Hierarchy in natural and social sciences. Springer, Dordrecht, The Netherlands

History and Theories of Information Technology: Intelligence and Creativity

Bennis W, Biederman PW (1997) Organizing genius: the secrets of creative collaboration. Addison-Wesley, Reading, MA
Bohm D, Peat FD (2000) Science, order, and creativity, 2nd edn. Routledge, New York
de Bono E (1990) Lateral thinking: a textbook of creativity. Penguin, New York
Stanovich KE et al (2016) The rationality quotient: toward a test of rational thinking. MIT Press, Cambridge, MA

Sternberg RJ, Lubart TI (1995) Defying the crowd: cultivating creativity in a culture of conformity. Free Press, New York

History and Theories of Information Technology: Modeling and Simulation of Systems

Bailer-Jones DM (2009) Scientific models in philosophy of science. University of Pittsburgh Press, Pittsburgh, PA
Casti JL (1996) Would-be worlds: how simulation is changing the frontiers of science. Wiley, New York
Gardner FM, Baker JD (1996) Simulation techniques: models of communication signals and processes. Wiley, New York
Gershenfeld N (1999) The nature of mathematical modeling. Cambridge University Press, Cambridge, UK
Giordano FR et al (2013) A first course in mathematical modeling, 5th edn. Brooks/Cole Publishing Company, Monterey, CA
Ingalls BP (2013) Mathematical modeling in systems biology: an introduction. MIT Press, Cambridge, MA
Jeruchim MC et al (2000) Simulation of communication systems: modeling, methodology and techniques, 2nd edn. Kluwer Academic Publishers, New York
Sayama H (2015) Introduction to the modeling and analysis of complex systems. Open Suny Textbooks, Geneseo

History and Theories of Information Technology: Paradoxes and Limits of Science

Barrow JD (1998) Impossibility: the limits of science and the science of limits. Oxford University Press, New York
Casti JL (1994) Complexification: explaining paradoxical world through the science of surprise. Abacus, London
Cockshott P et al (2015) Computation and its limits. Oxford University Press, Oxford, UK
Yanofsky NS (2013) The outer limits of reason: what science, mathematics, and logic cannot tell us. MIT Press, Cambridge, MA

History and Theories of Information Technology: Digital Signal Processing, Estimation Theory, and Adaptive and Learning Systems

Bekey GA (2005) Autonomous robots: from biological inspiration to implementation and control. MIT Press, Cambridge, MA
Bishop CM (2006) Pattern recognition and machine learning. Springer, Singapore
Haykin S (2014) Adaptive filter theory, 5th edn. Pearson Education, Harlow, UK
Kay SM (1988) Modern spectral estimation: theory and application. Prentice-Hall, Englewood Cliffs, NJ

Kay SM (1993) Fundamentals of statistical signal processing, vol. I: estimation theory. Prentice Hall, Englewood Cliffs, NJ
Marple SL Jr (2019) Digital spectral analysis, 2nd edn. Dover Publications, Mineola, NY
Marsland S (2015) Machine learning: an algorithmic perspective, 2nd edn. Chapman & Hall/CRC, New York
Mendel JM (1995) Lessons in estimation theory for signal processing, communications, and control. Prentice Hall, Englewood Cliffs, NJ
Oppenheim AV, Schafer RW (2009) Discrete-time signal processing, 3rd edn. Prentice Hall, Upper Saddle River, NJ
Proakis JG, Manolakis DG (2007) Digital signal processing: principles, algorithms, and applications, 4rd edn. Pearson Education, Upper Saddle River, NJ
Russell S, Norvig P (2022) Artificial intelligence: a modern approach, 4th edn. Pearson Education, Harlow, UK
Widrow B, Stearns AD (1985) Adaptive signal processing. Prentice Hall, Englewood Cliffs, MA

History and Theories of Information Technology: Optimization, Decision Making, and Computational Complexity

Arora S, Barak B (2009) Computational complexity: a modern approach. Cambridge University Press, Cambridge, UK
Gass SI, Assad AA (2005) An annotated timeline of operations research: an informal history. Springer, Berlin
Köksalan MM et al (2011) Multiple criteria decision making: from early history to the 21st century. World Scientific Publishing, Singapore
Lasaulce S, Tembine H (2011) Game theory and learning for wireless networks: fundamentals and applications. Academic Press, Oxford, UK
Michalewicz Z, Fogel DB (2004) How to solve it: modern heuristics, 2nd edn. Springer, Berlin
Sipser M (2006) Introduction to the theory of computation, 2nd edn. Thomson Course Technology, Boston, MA
Talbi EG (2009) Metaheuristics: from design to implementation. Wiley, Hoboken, NJ

Index

A

Abduction, 14, 15, 18, 25, 29, 69, 97, 104–106, 116, 119, 173, 301, 354, 358–360, 408, 431, 433
Abstract database, 51
Abstraction, 7, 17, 71, 96, 97, 356
Accuracy, 54, 121, 123, 147, 159, 162, 235, 237, 249, 269, 376
ACM Digital Library, 42, 59, 343, 347
Action research, 84, 398, 399
Actor (human agent), 12, 84, 157, 171, 197, 380, 389, 390, 398, 400, 408, 433
Adaptation system, 263
Adaptive system, 272–278, 299, 312, 313, 383, 407
Agility, 142, 163, 242, 257, 316, 432
Altruism, 167, 193
Ambidexterity, 195, 196, 201, 253, 430, 436
Analogy, 7, 15, 17, 98, 99, 110, 111, 119, 259, 359
Analytical thinking, 1, 16, 81–84, 95, 97, 115, 124, 125, 137, 138, 212, 213, 341, 353, 357, 412, 429, 431
Anarchy, 193, 194, 196, 199, 283, 320, 436
Annotation, 32, 33, 36, 51, 351
Anomaly, 264, 301
Apobetics, 236, 237
Aristotle, 114, 173, 181, 188, 199, 204, 355–360, 373, 379, 404
Artificial intelligence, 4, 7, 8, 12, 17, 39, 44, 102, 152, 175, 176, 205, 210, 227, 280, 281, 297, 300–302, 310, 311, 320, 361, 364, 368, 380, 382, 389, 390, 392, 396, 399, 407, 408, 411–413, 433, 434, 437
Ashby, W. R., 43, 205, 272, 277, 288, 311, 373, 382, 383, 392, 393, 398, 407, 412
Association for Computing Machinery (ACM), 39, 42, 51, 343
Association for Interdisciplinary Studies (AIS), 8, 38, 210, 300, 364, 381, 389–391
Attractor, 252, 254, 283, 287, 309, 396, 430
Authoritarian regime, 186, 196, 197, 199, 320, 436
Automatic system, 207, 269, 272–274, 301
Autonomic system, 276
Autonomous system, 147, 269, 273–275
Autopoiesis, 166, 381, 395, 407, 434
Auxiliary hypothesis, 109, 110, 161, 248
Availability, 53, 169, 190, 232, 245, 258, 368
Axiology, 204, 205
Axiomatic system, 108–110, 120, 251, 259, 355, 356, 359, 430, 431, 436

B

Bacon, F., 25, 105, 204, 341, 344, 357, 358, 374, 400, 412
Bandwidth, 212, 231, 232, 238, 240, 241, 244, 245, 249, 250, 254, 258, 261, 268, 269, 298, 317, 365, 382, 386
Basic resource, 56, 90, 148, 154, 210, 213, 227, 230–233, 235, 241, 242, 258, 320, 374, 432, 436
Behavioral level, 265, 266, 383
Benchmark, 257
Bertalanffy, L. von., 7, 8, 83, 99, 150, 168, 230, 252, 280, 289, 309, 341, 363, 373, 378–380, 387, 392, 412

A. Mämmelä, *Unifying Systems*, https://doi.org/10.1007/978-3-031-85012-7

Bibliography, 6, 18, 23, 32, 33, 35, 36, 42, 45, 46, 63, 66, 72, 157, 206, 342, 366, 412, 431
Bildung system, 362
Biography, 17, 48, 57, 213, 353
Biological evolution, 167, 184, 187, 189, 283
Biology, 4, 7, 99, 104, 106, 108, 118, 146, 150, 151, 156–159, 162–164, 166, 168, 171–173, 203, 207, 209, 212, 213, 242, 243, 258, 259, 263, 271, 281, 283, 284, 288, 289, 344, 349, 360, 363, 368, 378, 380, 381, 387, 392, 393, 395, 402, 404, 408–410, 413, 433, 435, 437
Bologna declaration, 362
Boulding, K. E., 6, 8, 99, 100, 118, 151, 155, 156, 159, 164, 165, 167–169, 181, 182, 184, 189, 193, 196, 198, 199, 205, 228, 231, 232, 271, 274, 275, 279, 283, 290, 291, 296, 297, 305, 319, 341, 363, 372, 374, 380, 387, 394, 412
Boundary condition, 9
Bounded memory, 177, 289
Bounded rationality, 99, 147, 177, 186, 189, 279, 288–290, 294, 306, 321, 380, 390, 430, 433, 434, 437
Brain, 12, 114, 115, 142, 145, 165, 167, 169–172, 174, 176, 177, 183, 184, 186, 203, 209, 210, 263, 281, 305, 316, 350, 383, 387, 396, 409, 411, 435
Brainstorming, 96, 98

C
Capitalism, 190, 191
Carbon cycle, 167
Case study, 14, 84
Catastrophe theory, 199, 254, 281–283, 381, 396, 433
Causality, 82, 84, 85, 113–115, 160, 161, 173, 204, 238, 248, 280, 355, 359, 432
Cause and effect, 114, 171, 248
Centralized system, 279, 318, 319, 434
Certification, 121, 146
Chaos theory, 100, 107, 139, 154, 252, 254, 255, 281–283, 287, 309, 381, 391, 395, 396
Chemistry, 2, 118, 141, 155–159, 162, 163, 168, 212, 281, 289, 345, 350, 374, 386, 407, 409, 432, 433
Church–Turing thesis, 149, 210, 247, 369
Circuit theory, 281, 379–381, 433
Citation, 23, 28, 32, 36, 40–47, 50, 57, 58, 60, 64–66, 72, 309, 343–346, 352, 387, 411, 430
Citation database, 35, 40, 41, 346
Climate change, 6, 141, 167, 188, 191, 201, 229, 372, 436, 438
Closed-loop control, 12, 208, 260, 262, 263
Closed system, 148, 162, 163, 229, 285, 286, 312, 313, 372, 377, 378, 386, 408, 432
Coherence, 24, 81, 107, 121, 251, 360, 431, 432
Collective intelligence, 96, 120, 147, 184–186, 189, 350, 394
Communications engineering, 3, 205, 206, 210, 281, 364, 370, 374, 434, 437
Commutability, 282
Complex adaptive system, 12, 16, 102, 137, 212, 265, 267, 274, 302, 310, 312, 364, 390, 391, 395, 396, 408, 413, 434, 437
Complex envelope, 46, 126, 382
Complexity, 88, 103, 145, 149, 156, 163, 167, 168, 183, 193, 199, 203, 206, 209, 210, 212, 234, 241, 242, 249, 250, 253, 268, 269, 275–278, 290, 294, 301–307, 309, 370, 381, 386–388, 391, 403, 407, 430, 433, 435, 436
Complexity engineering, 150, 408, 411, 412, 432, 437
Complexity theory, 7, 12, 17, 102, 145, 150, 158, 204–206, 209, 227, 267, 275, 280–282, 286, 301, 309, 310, 320, 321, 364, 381, 387, 391, 392, 395, 407, 412, 413, 433, 434
Complex system, 38, 84, 96, 104, 137, 144, 149, 151, 158, 180, 213, 234, 252, 254, 259, 260, 266, 267, 273, 276, 279, 282, 288, 305, 359, 409, 429, 432, 437
Complicated system, 6, 104, 110, 139, 146, 255, 316, 321, 412
Computational complexity theory, 209, 281, 283, 305, 308, 370, 433
Computational intelligence, 300, 390
Computing, 7, 8, 39, 42, 142, 143, 153, 205, 207–210, 231, 232, 240, 243, 250, 254, 257, 276, 281, 300, 305, 311, 312, 317, 319, 364, 367, 369–371,

381, 390–392, 394, 399, 401, 403, 405, 408–410, 413, 430, 433
Computing problems, 305–307
Conceptual analysis, 4, 5, 29, 46, 81, 102, 125, 277, 361, 429–431
Conceptual thread, 43, 44
Concurrent computing, 209, 310, 312, 380, 403, 408, 434
Conference proceedings, 36, 38, 49, 70, 342, 345, 393
Conjecture, 28, 108, 109, 149
Consciousness, 84, 115, 145, 150, 156, 173, 184, 275, 276, 302, 314, 406, 409, 410, 430, 433, 435, 437
Conservation laws, 107, 161, 251, 273, 358, 374
Conservation of energy, 116, 161, 247, 251, 285, 374, 432
Constraint, 143, 168, 245, 246, 270, 275, 278, 279, 290–294, 308, 385
Constructive research, 85, 89, 259
Control engineering, 7, 12, 43, 44, 114, 126, 205–208, 212, 238, 287, 294, 295, 300, 301, 311, 317, 364, 368, 381, 382, 389, 391, 405, 412
Controller, 12, 43, 143, 207, 269, 274, 276, 277, 294, 314, 397, 403
Control system, 99, 110, 114, 143, 144, 196, 207, 208, 260, 261, 269, 272–274, 287, 300, 311, 314, 368, 384, 388, 401, 405
Copy editor, 49, 71
Copyright, 41, 58, 60, 71, 73, 342, 347, 348
Coupling, 8, 9, 144, 198, 209, 260, 268, 269, 294, 305, 310, 312, 316, 317, 321, 404, 405, 408, 432, 434
Coverage interval, 52, 53, 152
Coverage probability, 52–54
Creativity, 4, 7, 32, 81, 92–95, 97–99, 102, 110, 119, 125, 139, 154, 176, 301, 361, 373, 430, 433, 438
Criterion, 5, 24, 30, 54, 55, 67, 99, 108, 112, 122, 123, 143, 164, 170, 175, 230, 241, 242, 253, 274, 289–291, 294–296, 303, 315, 388, 403, 431, 432
Cultural evolution, 90, 159, 165, 184, 185, 187, 189, 200, 281, 283
Curse of dimensionality, 294, 309, 389, 409, 411
Cybernetics, 7, 17, 35, 43, 44, 205, 227, 235, 236, 255, 272, 280, 281, 287, 288, 300, 301, 310, 320, 363, 364, 368, 373, 380–383, 385, 390, 392, 393, 397–400, 412, 413, 433

D

Darwin, C., 68, 137, 160, 164, 166, 168, 278, 283, 284, 380, 383
Decentralized system, 269, 279, 297, 317, 319, 434
Decision-making, 4, 8, 9, 12, 13, 99, 142, 143, 151, 156, 171, 190, 194, 210, 227, 228, 260, 275, 289, 291, 293, 298, 310, 312, 318, 320, 387, 396, 397, 408, 409, 434–436
Decision problems, 209, 275, 306, 389
Decision theory, 8, 205, 281, 289, 298, 300, 380, 388, 391, 433
Deduction, 14, 15, 18, 25, 29, 55, 83, 97, 104–108, 110, 113, 116, 120, 121, 137, 158, 173, 176, 210, 213, 251, 259, 301, 354–356, 400, 410, 412, 429, 431
Degree of centralization, 9, 208, 227, 260, 318, 320, 397, 434
Degree of coupling, 268, 305, 316, 317, 435
Descartes, R., 28, 88, 120, 204, 341, 352, 357–359, 373, 379, 409, 412, 437
Detection theory, 281, 289, 298, 299
Determinism, 85, 114, 115, 252, 255
Dialogue, 32, 92, 96, 102, 120, 154, 194
Digital library, 35, 40, 42, 59, 343, 346, 347
Dimensions of culture, 185
Directory of Open Access Journal (DOAJ), 40
Disciplinary work, 3, 4, 140, 433, 438
Discovery tool, 35, 40–42, 343, 347
Disinformation, 34, 125
Dissemination, 30
Dissipative structure, 280, 287, 312, 386
Distributed computing, 209, 305, 311, 312, 369, 383, 405, 410, 434
Distributed control, 280
Distributed optimization, 380, 389
Distributed system, 7, 8, 165, 193, 211, 228, 264, 278, 279, 295, 312, 318–320, 365, 395, 404, 408, 434–436
Divide and conquer, 119, 292, 293
Doctor, 28, 93, 253, 362
Doctoral thesis, 35, 37, 67
Dogma, 109
Dominance hierarchy, 263, 264, 402
Double-anonymized review, 67, 353
Double feedback, 288, 383, 384, 398, 407, 434

Double-loop learning, 383, 398
Dunbar's number, 186
Dunning–Kruger effect, 147
Dynamic programming, 292, 293, 312, 389
Dynamic system, 8, 143, 207, 208, 251, 272–274, 391, 392, 432, 433
Dynamic universe, 100, 118, 160, 248, 256, 381

E

Economic conflict, 195, 196, 201, 254
Ecosystem, 99, 154, 155, 164, 165, 187, 230, 270, 271, 287, 320, 372, 373, 387
Effectiveness, 6, 94, 141, 142, 237, 242, 258, 320, 368, 375
Efficiency, 3, 6, 56, 140, 142, 153, 164, 168, 187, 188, 190, 192, 206, 212, 228, 231, 234, 242–244, 246, 251, 254, 257, 258, 278, 279, 289, 294, 304, 305, 316, 319, 320, 366, 367, 373, 408, 409, 432, 436
Efficient cause, 113, 114, 166, 358, 359
Einstein, A., 4, 5, 27, 92, 97, 100, 110, 113–116, 118, 123, 160, 247, 248, 256, 352, 360, 374
Electronics, 3, 7, 8, 38, 39, 42, 55, 111, 153, 205, 206, 209, 232–234, 239–241, 257, 258, 265, 266, 285, 312, 342–346, 349, 361, 364, 365, 367, 368, 370, 379, 397, 402, 405, 408, 409, 434, 437
Embargo period, 71
Empiricism, 107, 341, 355, 359, 360, 412
Encyclopedia, 4, 17, 27, 32, 34, 35, 59, 125, 140, 349, 350
Encyclopedia Britannica, 34, 37, 59, 157, 165–168, 197, 232–234, 259, 270, 320, 343, 347, 349, 350, 359, 388, 397
Energy minimization, 162, 286, 312, 408, 411, 432, 434, 435
Engineering Village, 40–42, 59, 343, 346
Enlightenment, 90, 174, 182, 184, 193–197, 199, 202, 203, 237, 284, 353, 358, 436
Entropy, 99, 162, 167, 168, 247, 252, 254, 256, 269, 280, 285–287, 294, 302, 303, 378, 385, 386
Entropy law, 168, 203, 247, 251, 252, 254–256, 286, 358, 378, 385, 386, 432
Environmental chamber, 56
Epistemology, 5, 204, 205, 355
Equilibrium, 162, 163, 278, 280, 281, 285–287, 313, 363, 378, 398–400, 434–436
Estimation theory, 249, 281, 294, 298, 299, 380, 389, 433
Ethical principles, 82, 183, 430
Evolution, 25, 26, 32, 58, 90, 95, 114, 118, 144, 145, 159, 162–168, 171, 173, 184, 191, 199, 203, 228, 258, 259, 273, 275, 276, 283, 284, 286, 288, 297, 298, 301, 302, 314, 360, 364, 387, 393, 396, 409, 410, 435
Evolutionary dynamics, 284, 298
Evolutionary game theory, 94, 190, 284, 298, 381, 382
Evolutionary learning, 274, 301
Evolutionary model, 144, 145
Executive summary, 52
Experimental-abductive method, 14–16, 25, 119, 359, 429, 431
Experimental-inductive method, 14, 105, 358, 359
Extended abstract, 51, 52

F

Fabrication, 101
Fairness, 82, 100–102, 172, 178–182, 191, 192, 194, 200–202, 228, 289, 295, 297, 316, 429, 430, 435
Field study, 33
Final cause, 114, 125, 259
Fitness (to the environment), 145, 164, 168, 171, 188, 203, 242, 243, 251, 276, 278, 284, 285, 291, 294, 298, 396, 435
Forecasting, 142, 228
Formal science, 108–110, 155, 157, 213
Formation of hypotheses, 16, 106
Forrester, J., 7, 44, 190, 279, 309, 364, 380, 385, 390, 408
Free will, 84, 114, 115, 168, 173, 189, 207, 254, 259, 261, 275, 314, 409, 430, 432, 433, 435
Functional, Behavioral, and Structural (FBS) model, 143, 146
Functionality, 56, 142, 152, 242, 243, 257, 383, 403
Functional level, 265, 266
Fundamental limit, 90, 137, 152–154, 171, 209, 234, 246, 251, 257, 294, 362, 367, 368, 385, 406, 430, 436
Fundamental principle, 91, 168, 247, 251

G

Galileo, 85, 88, 116, 117, 120, 122, 158, 341, 349, 356–359, 361, 376, 404, 412
Game theory, 94, 181, 183, 189, 190, 278, 281, 284, 289, 293, 295, 297, 300, 380, 382, 390, 433
Generalist, 5, 17, 125, 141, 142, 438
Generalization, 13, 14, 23–25, 56, 84–86, 105, 106, 110, 154, 157, 158, 240, 356, 400, 412
General knowledge, 341, 362, 411
General theory of systems (general system theory), 8, 17, 38, 205, 227, 252, 281, 309, 310, 320, 363, 373, 380, 387, 433, 434
Ghost author, 50
Global Alliance for Inter- and Transdisciplinarity (ITD Alliance), 38
Global optimization, 84, 187, 213, 257, 278, 289, 319, 394
Goal-achieving system, 275, 278, 313, 314, 435
Goal-directed system, 11, 278, 313, 314, 435
Goal-seeking system, 278, 313, 435
Google Scholar, 42, 59, 65, 343, 344, 347, 431
Groupthink, 92, 95, 99, 142, 187, 387

H

Halting problem, 251, 307, 309, 430
Happiness, 101, 173, 180–182, 186, 196, 199–201, 291, 388, 437
Heuristics, 144, 174, 275, 290, 291, 296, 302, 308, 388, 390, 433, 435, 436
Hierarchical control, 269, 381, 395, 432
Hierarchy level, 33, 139, 146, 163, 168, 169, 171, 237, 266, 268–272, 274, 280, 285, 311, 312, 316, 384, 435
Hierarchy of complexity, 144, 271, 272, 433
Hierarchy of everything, 270, 271
Hierarchy of natural systems, 363
Hierarchy of technical systems, 227, 272, 274, 312, 320
Hierarchy theory, 281, 305, 380, 387, 433
Historicism, 85, 199, 203
Holism, 98, 204, 364, 380
Holland, J., 7, 12, 102, 112, 205, 267, 281, 284, 296, 300, 310, 364, 373, 391, 392, 395, 396, 413
Homeostasis, 157, 167, 168, 171, 228, 272, 275, 288, 398, 399, 433
Honorary author, 50, 65
Horizontal integration, 125
Human in the loop, 12, 261, 288, 400
Humanism, 202, 353, 360, 436
Humanities, 47, 97, 154–156, 172, 176, 178, 181, 201, 202, 360
Hume's law, 172
Hybrid control, 192, 198, 279, 408, 437
Hybrid system, 279, 319, 394, 395, 403, 434, 435
Hype cycle, 44, 45, 207
Hypothetico-deductive method, 14–16, 24, 25, 81, 107, 108, 120, 121, 123, 350, 358, 359, 429, 431

I

Idiographic research, 84, 85
IEEE Xplore, 38, 42, 59, 104, 343, 345, 346, 349
Immense number, 308
Impact factor, 40, 64, 346
IMRDC structure, 48, 49, 52, 71, 72, 87, 110, 111, 350, 351, 412, 431
Incommensurability, 192, 291, 298
Incompleteness theorems, 158, 247, 251, 283, 309, 356, 380
Inductive-statistical model, 84
Information and communication technologies, 7, 102, 206
Information feedback, 235, 262, 398, 401
Information retrieval, 18, 23, 32, 40–42, 72, 308, 341–343, 346, 411, 430
Information technology, 7, 8, 16, 66, 137, 142, 206, 208, 211, 265, 364, 365, 434, 437
Information theory, 85, 99, 102, 159, 210, 235, 237, 249, 252, 281, 302, 303, 364, 370, 371, 386, 412, 433
Initial condition, 85, 107, 139, 147, 252, 280, 282, 383
Innovation, 38, 39, 66, 81, 90, 125, 152, 165, 185, 186, 190, 191, 198, 353, 374, 436
Institute of Electrical and Electronics Engineering (IEEE), 8, 34, 36–39, 48–50, 52, 56–59, 61, 66, 71, 73, 74, 104, 154, 343–346, 349–352, 367, 368, 394, 407, 411
Institutionalism, 200
Integrative learning, 87, 430

Intelligence, 93, 94, 144, 145, 154, 165, 167, 170, 171, 174–177, 179, 183, 186, 203, 206, 210, 231, 278, 284, 287, 291, 300, 301, 310, 350, 354, 365, 385, 394, 407, 409–411, 413, 430, 434, 437
Interdisciplinarity, 3, 4, 7, 140, 141, 438
Interface, 211, 264, 311, 369, 394, 413
International Council on Systems Engineering (INCOSE), 34, 38, 364
International Electrotechnical Commission (IEC), 37, 59, 104, 211, 343, 344, 349, 377, 391, 411
International Organization for Standardization (ISO), 37, 59, 62, 73, 104, 121, 211, 343, 344, 349, 351, 377, 411
International Society for the Systems Sciences (ISSS), 7, 38, 363, 364
International Telecommunications Union (ITU), 37, 104, 189, 239, 245, 342, 348, 349, 411
Internet of Things, 209, 381, 391
Intractability, 138, 282, 303, 432
Intractable problem, 158, 210, 247, 290, 306, 307, 432, 433
Intuition, 15, 94, 95, 113, 120, 125, 173, 174, 176, 254, 255, 283
Invention, 14, 25, 37, 39, 67–69, 90, 153, 184, 190, 197, 202, 206, 353, 356, 359–361, 365–367, 370, 376, 378, 379, 388, 392, 412, 436
Invisible college, 42, 43, 344
Invisible hand, 191
Irrationality, 94
Isolated system, 117, 147, 148, 161, 251, 252, 255, 285, 286, 377, 432
Iterative algorithm, 292, 299
Iterative improvement, 119, 120

J

Jevons paradox, 188, 228, 253, 254, 377

K

Kuhn, T., 204, 360, 361

L

Lakatos, I., 17, 360
Large language models, 302, 361, 381
Lateral thinking, 97
Layer hierarchy, 208, 264, 384, 434
Learning loop, 13, 87, 399, 400
Learning system, 17, 272–275, 281
Legitimacy, 194, 242, 258, 320
Lewin, K., 399
Liberal democracy, 124, 157, 172, 180, 187, 190, 193–201, 203, 320, 353, 436, 437
Liberal education, 362
Life, 64, 100, 145, 150, 151, 156, 159, 161–163, 165–168, 171–173, 177–182, 188, 200, 203, 229, 252, 255, 281, 287, 350, 373, 395, 406, 407, 409, 410, 430, 434
Linear system, 119, 122, 125–128, 143, 238, 265, 282, 292, 379, 381, 382
Linear system theory, 125, 127, 281, 379, 380, 382, 433
Literature review, 23, 28, 31–33, 35, 37, 46, 47, 49, 52, 54, 57, 63, 66, 72, 98, 138, 212, 431
Local computing, 209
Local optimization, 187, 213, 276, 278, 291, 319, 394, 434
Logic, 5, 107, 108, 145, 157, 158, 204–206, 241, 251, 255, 266, 300, 310, 312, 351, 355, 360, 366, 367, 430
Loose coupling, 31, 139, 145, 161, 165, 168, 201, 209, 267–269, 279, 282, 303, 305, 312, 316, 317, 321, 371, 381, 387, 388, 395, 403–406, 408, 412, 413, 432, 435

M

Machine, 84, 115, 145, 148, 149, 153, 159, 176, 205, 210, 233, 237, 254, 257, 262, 263, 266, 274–276, 287–289, 300–302, 310, 312, 314, 353, 363, 366, 369, 382, 390, 392, 409–411, 433, 435
Market economy, 190, 194, 296, 372, 430
Mathematics, 47, 59, 73, 96, 126, 155, 157, 158, 213, 251, 259, 281, 354, 356, 366, 382, 393, 430
Measurement scales, 243, 244
Measurement units, 232, 244, 376
Mechanism, 163, 194, 409, 410
Megatrend, 151, 437
Merriam-Webster dictionary, 59
Metabolism, 163, 166, 167, 287, 377, 410, 434
Metadata, 41, 42, 44–46
Methodology, 6, 66, 97, 281, 289, 351, 402

Metric, 26, 66, 143, 161, 208, 244, 245, 258, 289–291, 294, 295, 317, 319, 376
Mind, 89, 115, 121, 156–158, 172–176, 183, 202, 209, 410, 411, 430
Misinformation, 34, 124
Mixed economy, 191, 193
Mixed strategy (in game theory), 298, 320
Module, 146, 168, 253, 263, 269, 312, 316, 317, 367, 402, 406, 432, 435
Monitoring system, 208, 260, 261, 263, 300, 390
Monograph, 32, 34, 35, 125
Monopoly, 37, 95, 191, 284, 295
Moore's law, 153, 206, 212, 257, 367–369, 408
Moral development, 182, 183
Morphogenesis, 157, 168, 171, 275, 288, 349, 380, 392, 393, 396, 407, 433, 437
Multiagent system, 12, 44, 102, 279, 297, 300, 310–312, 317, 318, 364, 365, 390–392, 396, 413, 433, 434, 437
Multicausality, 113–115, 125, 158, 277, 359, 432
Multidisciplinarity, 140
Multiobjective optimization, 164, 242, 289, 291, 294, 409, 437
Multiple criteria decision making, 289, 388

N

Nash bargaining solution, 278, 279, 289, 295, 297, 312, 319, 321, 382, 436
Nash equilibrium, 279, 297, 321, 382, 436
Natural science, 4, 90, 107, 155–158, 160, 189, 202, 204, 288, 404
Near decomposability, 7, 139, 168, 387, 388, 403, 404
Needs, 3, 16, 26, 71, 90, 93, 95, 101, 121, 123, 124, 138, 139, 141, 142, 144, 146, 152, 154, 163, 167, 170–174, 179–183, 187, 189–191, 193, 196, 198–200, 204–208, 210, 212, 213, 227, 228, 232, 241, 246, 257, 258, 314, 400, 431, 437
Negative feedback, 10–12, 16, 68, 69, 93, 114, 189, 191, 207, 260, 261, 272, 282, 288, 301, 310–312, 314–316, 321, 363, 392, 393, 397–399
Nested hierarchy, 163, 164, 168, 264, 312, 319, 391, 401, 402
Network information theory, 252, 303
Network theory, 281, 304, 305, 316, 379, 386
Network utility maximization, 253, 305, 389
Neumann, J. von, 190, 208, 250, 302, 312, 369, 370, 380, 382, 395, 407, 409
Neural network, 144, 145, 169–172, 300, 302, 310, 312, 316, 369, 392, 410, 435
Newton, I., 108, 109, 112, 116, 117, 122, 159, 160, 247, 248, 256, 341, 357–361, 374, 376, 377, 412
Nitrogen cycle, 167
Noise, 13, 55, 56, 96, 115, 139, 146, 153, 187, 208, 232, 234, 240, 241, 249, 250, 252, 261, 264, 282, 288, 289, 294, 295, 298–300, 303, 314, 315, 370, 389, 407
Nomothetic research, 84
Nonalgorithmic phenomena, 287
Nonequilibrium thermodynamics, 150, 160, 168, 171, 193, 280, 281, 286, 287, 310, 363, 378, 380, 386, 407, 408, 433, 437
Nonlinear dynamics, 147, 150, 255, 282, 283, 396
Nonlinearity, 1, 16, 65, 144, 150, 158, 243, 245, 252, 254, 274, 278, 280, 282, 288, 385, 409
Nonnested hierarchy, 208, 263, 264, 401, 434
Norm, 101, 181, 182, 201
Not Invented Here (NIH) syndrome, 95
NP-complete problem, 306–309, 370
NP-hard problem, 307–309
NP-intermediate problem, 307, 309
NP problem, 306–309
Numerical method, 112, 361
Nyquist, H., 7, 69, 126, 207, 246, 249, 287, 315, 364, 370, 379, 383, 386, 397, 412

O

Ockham's razor, 106, 355, 357
Ontology, 102, 205
OODA loop, 42, 397, 398, 401
Open access, 40, 343, 412
Open-loop control, 12, 208, 260, 262, 263, 287, 310, 312, 368, 434
Open problems, 36, 91, 97, 246, 252, 301, 378, 408, 410
Open Researcher and Contributor Identification (ORCID), 51

Open system, 1, 9, 10, 16, 18, 147–149, 161, 168, 171, 210, 211, 230, 231, 252, 255, 259, 265, 285–287, 312, 363, 377, 378, 380, 387, 399, 408, 412, 432
Optimal system, 55, 289, 388, 435, 436
Optimization criteria, 55, 123, 164, 187, 288, 291, 294, 313, 314, 435
Optimization decomposition, 210, 292, 293, 305, 312, 371, 381, 388, 389, 403, 435
Optimization problems, 123, 278, 289, 292–297, 306, 307, 309, 388, 435–437
Optimization theory, 289, 304, 388
Organism, 99, 151, 162–167, 169, 257, 258, 263, 270, 271, 378, 392, 409, 410
Originality, 30, 33, 49, 52, 58, 94, 432
Orthogonality, 317
Oxford English Dictionary, 59, 73, 177, 343, 350

P

Paradigm, 27, 68, 89, 99, 100, 105, 152, 161, 172, 180, 183, 204, 209, 267, 276, 300, 317, 354, 360–362, 391, 431
Paradox, 90, 166, 187, 195, 210, 238, 248, 252–257, 283, 285, 430
Parallel computing, 209, 246, 312, 367, 395
Parameter, 9, 13, 54, 56, 62, 85, 105, 112, 122, 123, 143–145, 147, 162, 176, 207, 208, 261, 262, 265–267, 280, 289, 293, 298, 299, 302, 308, 314, 317, 321, 368, 372, 383
Parameter estimation, 13, 144
Parametric model, 144, 145, 312, 435
Pareto optimum, 192, 295, 297, 312, 388
Patent, 27, 35, 37, 60, 67, 69, 90, 97, 342, 348, 397
Pattern formation, 145, 235, 392, 407
Pattern recognition, 39, 98, 145, 235, 263, 274, 301, 371, 391, 407
Peer review, 31, 34, 36, 37, 66, 67, 70, 74, 342, 352, 411
Performance, 11, 12, 26, 54–56, 90, 112, 123, 142, 143, 176, 235, 242, 245, 249, 253, 257, 258, 260, 261, 264, 266, 274, 275, 279, 289, 290, 293, 294, 299, 302, 312, 314, 318, 319, 393, 408, 410
Personality, 92, 98, 176–178, 183
Philosophy, 6, 35, 102, 107, 108, 118, 125, 155–157, 172, 178, 197, 202, 204, 213, 251, 281, 283, 305, 353, 355, 359, 360, 362, 366, 373, 412
Philosophy of science, 16, 101, 119, 125, 204, 205, 259, 353, 358, 360, 361, 412
Photosynthesis, 163, 167, 229, 234, 287, 410
Physical level, 265, 266, 275
Physics, 4, 42, 47, 53, 88, 100, 114, 118, 138, 139, 147, 150, 156–162, 168, 183, 189, 204, 212, 213, 243, 251, 252, 254–256, 266, 270, 281, 283, 286, 287, 289, 305, 351, 352, 357, 359, 376, 380, 385, 392, 393, 395, 396, 407, 409, 432, 433
Plagiarism, 58, 60, 101
Plausibility, 30, 36, 122, 358, 360
Political conflict, 195, 196, 199, 201, 253, 254
Popper, K., 15, 85, 101, 109, 199, 203, 360, 383
Positive feedback, 11, 67, 70, 169, 189, 207, 229, 260, 272, 277, 288, 311, 315, 321, 363, 380, 385, 392, 393, 397–399
Positivism, 107, 184, 358, 360
Power consumption, 170, 209, 241, 367
P problems, 307, 308
Pragmatics, 236, 237, 375
Pragmatism, 107, 431
Precision, 54
Prigogine, I., 168, 252, 255, 277, 280, 286, 287, 363, 378, 380, 386, 407
Primitive term, 431
Priority disputes, 67
Prisoner's dilemma, 187, 284, 285, 298
Problem of induction, 15, 105, 107, 122, 358–360
Proof, 33, 106, 122, 303, 351, 371
Proof of concept, 122
Prototype, 27, 28, 85, 89, 107, 111, 121, 259, 361, 365, 376
Pruning, 168, 284, 435
Psychology, 4, 5, 118, 150, 151, 155–157, 169, 172, 173, 176, 181, 183–186, 194, 212, 281, 288, 290, 291, 310, 360, 393, 430, 433
Publisher, 31, 34, 35, 37, 39–42, 49, 51, 57, 58, 60, 63, 64, 66, 71, 73, 342, 344, 346, 350, 412, 431

Q
Quality control, 54, 368, 400
Quantum computer, 149, 206, 256, 309
Quantum decoherence, 159, 255, 256
Quantum mechanics, 85, 107, 118, 146, 159, 160, 162, 168, 255

R
Random process, 128, 282
Random variable, 82, 108, 128, 157, 243, 245
Range, 27, 169, 175, 177, 267, 268
Rational agent, 175, 183, 205, 210, 278, 284, 300, 302, 312, 318, 381, 391
Rationalism, 107, 190, 341, 353, 355, 356, 359, 360, 412
Rationality, 93, 94, 98, 174–177, 183, 187, 253, 254, 284, 289, 290, 298, 301, 310, 430
Realism, 107, 108
Real science, 155–157
Real world, 1, 13–16, 24–26, 84, 108, 110, 112, 121, 124, 125, 237, 256, 260, 303, 431
Recursive algorithm, 263, 292, 299
Recursive function, 292
Reduction, 13–16, 18, 29, 84, 88, 96, 115–119, 137, 156, 213, 301, 354, 359, 360, 400, 429–431
Reductionism, 120, 123, 149, 204, 357–359, 373, 436
Reference signal, 10, 12, 16, 274, 276, 301, 313, 314
Reference trajectory, 10, 16, 275, 313–315
Reference value, 53, 54, 314
Reflection, 14, 89, 174, 248, 264, 355, 360, 430, 431
Regeneration, 67, 228, 372
Regulation, 163, 169, 171, 179, 188, 189, 191, 193, 272, 288, 315, 408, 436
Reinforcement learning, 171, 173, 273, 274, 292, 301, 390, 398, 411, 435
Reliability, 5, 31, 33, 42, 53, 101, 142, 171, 242, 245, 246, 257–259, 316, 319, 368, 370, 406, 431, 432
Renaissance, 4, 5, 199, 353, 358, 436
Repeatability (in measurements), 52, 349
Reproducibility (in measurements), 5, 6, 24, 52, 56, 101, 175, 179
Reproductive system, 271–273
Research culture, 28, 91
Research method, 5, 13, 14, 16, 17, 25, 49, 51, 55, 72, 82, 84, 92, 100, 357–359, 400, 413, 436
Research problem, 7, 27, 28, 49, 51, 81, 91, 101, 123, 137, 151, 154, 157, 212
Resilience, 165, 167, 198, 228, 275, 278, 280, 372
Resolution, 112, 172, 247, 256, 267, 268
Resource, 6, 93, 123, 153, 154, 164, 174, 175, 186–191, 193, 201, 209, 212, 228–233, 235, 242, 243, 257, 269, 284, 287, 294–298, 310, 347, 362, 372, 385, 396, 408, 409, 430, 436, 438
Review paper, 6, 31, 32, 35, 36, 44, 45, 48, 57, 58, 66, 92, 104, 212, 350, 431
Roadmap, 33, 91, 137, 151, 152, 212, 213, 258, 367, 368, 437
Robotics, 8, 205, 206, 269, 369, 384
Robustness, 164, 171, 278–280, 290, 319, 406

S
Santa Fe Institute, 310, 395
Satisfaction, 101, 141, 180–182, 186, 194, 199, 200, 290, 291, 296, 314, 368, 434, 436
Satisficing, 289–291, 294, 306, 321, 409, 434–436
Scalability, 142, 143, 257, 316, 319, 408, 432
Scenario, 26, 27, 30, 152, 164, 177, 230, 235, 258, 437
Scholasticism, 199, 353, 358, 436
Scientific method, 6, 17, 81, 101, 107, 254, 355–358, 360, 400
Scientific revolution, 105, 204, 341, 357, 358, 360, 412, 436
Scientific societies, 37–40, 44, 51, 57, 65, 66, 342, 344, 347, 349, 357, 412
Scientometry, 347
Scopus, 40, 41, 59, 64, 65, 343, 346, 431
Search problems, 305, 306
Self-citation, 50, 65
Self-organizing network, 103, 198, 311, 318, 393, 394, 404, 407, 413
Self-organizing system, 11, 137, 145, 147, 150, 212, 227, 267, 269, 272, 273, 275–278, 280, 282, 287, 312, 320, 380, 383, 391–394, 407, 408, 412, 433
Self-regulated learning, 398, 400

Self-stabilization, 383, 407, 434
Semantics, 109, 210, 236, 237, 252, 302, 303, 375, 378, 412, 435, 437
Seminar, 37, 71, 89, 92, 96, 120
Semiotics, 236, 375
Semiotic triangle, 103, 375
Sense-decide-act loop, 260, 287, 311, 313
Separation theorem, 43, 208, 212, 300, 384, 388, 389
Sequential algorithm, 299
Sequential computing, 209, 434
Set-point value, 10, 12, 16, 273, 274, 301, 313, 314, 394
Shannon, C. E., 69, 212, 237, 240, 246, 249, 250, 302, 303, 366, 370, 375, 378, 380, 386, 388, 412
Simon, H. A., 4, 7, 108, 139, 142, 146, 149, 151, 168, 175, 177, 198, 199, 267–269, 277, 279, 281, 283, 288–291, 293, 294, 303, 305, 306, 363, 378, 380, 381, 385, 387, 389, 390, 398, 400, 402–404, 409
Simulation, 28, 36, 55, 56, 71, 84, 98, 110, 112, 113, 120, 146, 147, 154, 157, 235, 246, 258, 259, 321, 361, 369, 395, 396, 407, 410, 412, 433
Single-objective optimization, 294
Singularity, 409
Sleeping Beauty, 66, 152, 431
Small-world network, 171, 295, 304, 305, 312, 320, 387, 408, 411, 434, 435
Smith, A., 51, 57, 97, 118, 155, 156, 172, 179, 181, 183, 187, 189–191, 193, 194, 200, 202, 298, 372, 380, 383, 397, 398
Social contract, 157, 179, 180, 183, 188, 193, 198, 200, 201, 203
Social Darwinism, 283
Social dilemma, 156, 187–191, 195, 196, 201, 253, 254, 278, 279, 295, 298, 408, 430, 435, 436
Social science, 3, 7, 14, 17, 18, 38, 42, 43, 84, 85, 97, 108, 110, 151, 154–158, 163, 172, 183, 189, 202, 213, 261, 281, 283, 285, 288, 316, 320, 344, 357, 364, 385, 387, 390–392, 399, 404, 408, 409, 413, 433, 435
Social system, 107, 111, 139, 151, 184, 189, 198, 202, 212, 272, 275, 276, 279, 283, 285, 288, 291, 297, 319, 378, 381, 383, 385, 387, 390, 393, 395, 403, 404, 408, 433
Sociology, 4, 88, 118, 156, 157, 172, 183, 184, 186, 189, 212, 288, 433
Sociotechnical system, 154, 155
Software-defined network, 103, 211, 311
Speed of light, 118, 123, 160, 161, 240, 248, 285
Spiral model, 146, 373
Spontaneous order, 206, 278, 392, 407
Stackelberg game, 279, 295, 298, 382, 436
State of nature, 180–182, 193, 198, 203, 320
State of the art, 27, 31, 33, 36, 52, 72, 91, 92, 152, 348, 431, 438
State space, 9, 139, 283
Static system, 143, 157, 272–274, 310, 391
Statistics, 52, 55, 64, 108, 138, 157, 237, 248, 259, 299, 368
Strong inference, 15, 85, 97, 98, 106, 360, 431
Structural level, 265, 266, 275, 383
Structured hardware design, 367, 402
Structured programming, 381, 402, 405
Suboptimal system, 55
Subsidiarity, 7, 31, 139, 196, 198, 201, 373, 395, 404, 408, 435, 437
Supercomputer, 206, 210, 369, 409, 411
Supervised learning, 273, 274, 301, 392
Survey paper, 35, 36
Survivability, 26, 99, 164, 171, 175, 179, 187, 242, 243, 273, 284, 294, 301
Sustainability, 6, 141, 181, 228–231, 233, 362, 372, 385, 429, 436–438
Synergetics, 150, 281, 287, 381, 407, 434
Synergy, 150
Syntactics, 236, 237, 375
System archetypes, 1, 4, 7, 16, 227, 258, 260, 309, 311, 312, 320, 321, 374, 397, 407, 412, 413, 433, 434, 437
System dynamics, 7, 17, 227, 229, 280, 281, 287, 288, 309, 310, 320, 364, 374, 380, 385, 390, 393, 412, 433, 434
System identification, 11, 12, 123, 124, 144
System models, 1, 7, 12, 16, 28, 30, 33, 47, 49, 52, 54, 56, 58, 93, 107, 110, 121, 126, 128, 138, 145, 146, 151, 154, 258, 311, 321
System of systems, 143
Systems architecting, ix
Systems engineering, 15, 17, 34, 38, 59, 74, 104, 155, 281, 344, 364, 380, 382
Systems thinking, 1–4, 6, 7, 9, 12, 13, 16–18, 27, 38, 82–84, 88, 91, 94, 96–98, 100, 125, 138–141, 147, 149,

150, 153, 154, 193, 204, 212, 213, 228, 278, 281, 341, 344, 349, 361, 363, 374, 380, 382, 385, 411–413, 429, 432, 433, 436–438
System theories, 4, 6, 7, 16, 17, 73, 202, 205, 213, 227, 254, 280–282, 320, 321, 363, 364, 379, 397, 399, 408, 413, 429, 433, 434, 437, 438
Szilard (Landauer) limit, 234, 250, 367

T
Tacit knowledge, 89, 379
Taxonomy, 23, 46, 72, 73, 104, 119, 146, 157, 163, 243, 281, 380
Temperament, 177
Theoretical world, 13, 25, 108, 109, 256
Theory of evolution, 68, 160, 164, 166, 171, 281, 283, 284, 380, 433
Theory of truth, 105
Thermodynamics, 85, 99, 116, 148, 150, 151, 159–162, 168, 193, 233, 251, 256, 280, 281, 285, 286, 302, 303, 313, 373, 374, 377, 380, 385, 386, 407, 433
Tractable problem, 306
Trademark, 60, 348
Trade-off, 142, 153, 164, 193, 204, 212, 230, 232, 253, 295, 430, 435
Tragedy of the commons, 188, 190–192, 229, 298, 372, 408, 436
Trajectory (in a state space), 9, 126, 139, 145, 258, 275, 283, 293, 356
Transdisciplinarity, 3, 38, 140, 141, 362
Transitivity, 94
Triple hierarchy, 99
Trueness, 54
Turing, A., 69, 149, 158, 175, 176, 208, 247, 369, 380, 392, 396, 407, 409, 410, 412
Turing machine, 149, 208, 369
Turing test, 409, 410
Tutorial paper, 35, 36, 57, 430
Types of coupling, 317

U
Ultrastability, 383, 384, 398, 407, 434
Unconventional computing, 369
Underdetermination, 105
University education, 7, 362
Unsolvable problems, 306, 307
Unsupervised learning, 273, 274, 301
Use case, 30, 152, 235, 258, 437
Utility function, 94, 245, 278, 291, 292, 295, 296, 305

V
Validation, 49, 55, 121, 124, 125, 146, 258, 259, 431
Variable, 9, 54, 62, 73, 85, 122, 127, 145, 245, 262, 266, 267, 274, 292, 294, 317, 372, 383, 399
Verification, 5, 16, 24, 25, 28–30, 49, 55, 81, 101, 104, 107, 109, 119, 121–125, 146, 157, 258, 259, 306–308, 359, 400, 431
Vertical integration, 87
Vertical thinking, 97
Vision, 6, 7, 27, 31, 33, 36, 66, 72, 91, 98, 137, 138, 141, 151, 152, 154, 181, 196, 212, 213, 258, 341, 361, 368, 394, 408, 437
V-model, 15, 146, 147, 373

W
Water cycle, 167, 287
Waterfall model, 146, 373
Weak signal, 121, 151, 437
Web of Science, 41, 42, 59, 64, 65, 343, 346, 431
Welfare economics, 192, 298, 318
Wiener, N., 7, 8, 43, 175, 205, 280, 288, 341, 363, 364, 373, 378, 380, 382, 383, 385, 389, 397–400, 412
Wikipedia, 34, 59, 343, 350
Wisdom of the crowds, 142, 147, 186, 187, 189, 437

Z
Zeeman's geometrical model of ideologies, 195

MIX
Papier aus verantwortungsvollen Quellen
Paper from responsible sources
FSC® C105338

If you have any concerns about our products,
you can contact us on
ProductSafety@springernature.com

In case Publisher is established outside the EU,
the EU authorized representative is:
Springer Nature Customer Service Center GmbH
Europaplatz 3, 69115 Heidelberg, Germany

Printed by Libri Plureos GmbH
in Hamburg, Germany